Introductory
Psychology

D. C. Heath and Company

Lexington, Massachusetts   Toronto

Introductory Psychology

Morris K. Holland
University of California, Los Angeles

Photo Credits:

Cover: © Frank Siteman, 1980

Chapter-opening photos:

1 David Powers/Stock, Boston
2 Richard Chase
3 Julie O'Neil/Stock, Boston
4 © Frank Siteman/The Picture Cube
5 Frank Siteman/The Picture Cube
6 © Margaret Thompson 1980
7 George Bellerose/Stock, Boston
8 Michael Weisbrot and Family
9 George N. Peet/The Picture Cube
10 © Erika Stone 1977/Photo Researchers, Inc.
11 Oliver R. Pierce/Stock, Boston
12 Paul S. Conklin
13 © Ken Robert Buck
14 Richard Chase
15 Rudolph R. Robinson
16 Michael Weisbrot and Family
17 Dennis Stock/© 1967 Magnum Photos, Inc.
18 Eve Arnold/Magnum Photos, Inc.
19 © Jean-Claude Lejeune
20 © Joel Gordon 1978
21 Karen R. Preuss/Jeroboam Inc.
22 © 1977 George E. Jones III/Photo Researchers, Inc.
23 Charles Harbutt/© Magnum Photos, Inc.
24 © Rohn Engh/Photo Researchers, Inc.
25 © Joel Gordon 1980
26 © Joel Gordon 1978

Preface

My purpose in writing *Introductory Psychology* was to create a highly effective teaching text, a book that supports the efforts of instructors to help their students master the rapidly expanding field of psychology. As a teacher of introductory psychology for many years, and as an educational psychologist concerned about the learning skills of college students, I recognize the importance of textbooks as teaching tools. Even the most experienced teachers need the support of effective textbooks, for college teaching is more challenging today than ever before. I have thus worked hard to write a book that would achieve breadth and depth of coverage, that would be clear and highly readable, and that would stimulate student interest.

An effective teaching text must offer comprehensive, detailed, and accurate coverage. *Introductory Psychology* covers the full range of important topics—from motivation and emotion to attribution theory, from the superego to the brain chemical called endorphin, and from classical conditioning to cognitive restructuring. Each major academic area is surveyed in depth, and important theories and recent findings are discussed.

An effective teaching text must not only cover essential material but also promote mastery of that material. This book was written to help students at all levels master the important facts, concepts, and theories of psychology. It was designed to be easy to read, with clear definitions, explanations, and examples. Chapter glossaries, chapter summaries, and interim summaries aid student learning. Finally, a unique chapter on academic learning and retention helps students identify their study problems and teaches them how to apply basic psychological principles, in order to become more efficient and independent learners.

An effective teaching text must stimulate the natural interest of students in human behavior, so that they will want to read about it on their own. I believe students will find this book meaningful because of its discussion of research and principles on topics of great personal and social significance—for example, career choice, consumer psychology, crime, sex, and the psychology of energy conservation. In addition, checklists and inventories are placed throughout the book to help students connect the textual material to their own lives.

Introductory Psychology is intended for use in courses in introductory or general psychology and for students who are psychology majors as well as for students who will never take another psychology course. It was designed to be a flexible text, one that can fit a variety of courses and course organizations. The order of chapter assignments can be altered to fit an instructor's own preferred sequence of topics. For those instructors who teach courses with an experimental emphasis, research methods and statistics are presented in the Appendix.

No book stands alone, unrelated to previous works. This book has benefited from my earlier text, the second edition of *Psychology: An Introduction to Human Behavior;* some of the chapters of the current book are based on chapters of the earlier one. However, the present book is distinctly different and has an identity of its own. *Introductory Psychology* has much

v

more depth and breadth of coverage, a much stronger research base, and a more traditional organization.

Many people were involved in helping me write this book. I am particularly indebted to my wife, Becky Holland, who assisted me in all stages of the development of this book, and whose suggestions and encouragement enabled me to overcome many obstacles along the way. I also appreciate the efforts of the following talented psychologists who reviewed portions of the manuscript and whose observations and analyses significantly improved the book:

Robert Abdo
North Country Community College

W. Eastwood Atwater, Jr.
Montgomery County Community College

Larry J. Bloom
Colorado State University

Ruth Cline
Los Angeles Valley College

Jane Crolley
Horry-Georgetown Technical College

Gene V. Elliott
Glassboro State College

Dennis Farrell
Luzerne County Community College

Jackie Goldstein
Community College of Allegheny County

Edward J. Gunderson
Milwaukee Area Technical College

Joseph A. Gutenson
Thornton Community College

Arthur J. Hannan
Greenfield Community College

Thomas T. Hewett
Drexel University

Edward Kobesky
Luzerne County Community College

John W. Lelak, Jr.
Sinclair Community College

Kenneth B. LeSure
Plymouth State College

Ken Murdoff
Lane Community College

Gary K. Scott
Lincoln University

Ada M. Smith
Richland College

Joyce M. Smith
Central YMCA Community College

Anthony T. Soares
University of Bridgeport

Thomas F. Staton
Huntingdon College

James L. Tichenor
Northeast Missouri State University

William R. Woodward
University of New Hampshire

Rudolph L. Zlody
College of the Holy Cross

Morris K. Holland

Brief Table of Contents

Contents

Part I

Introduction

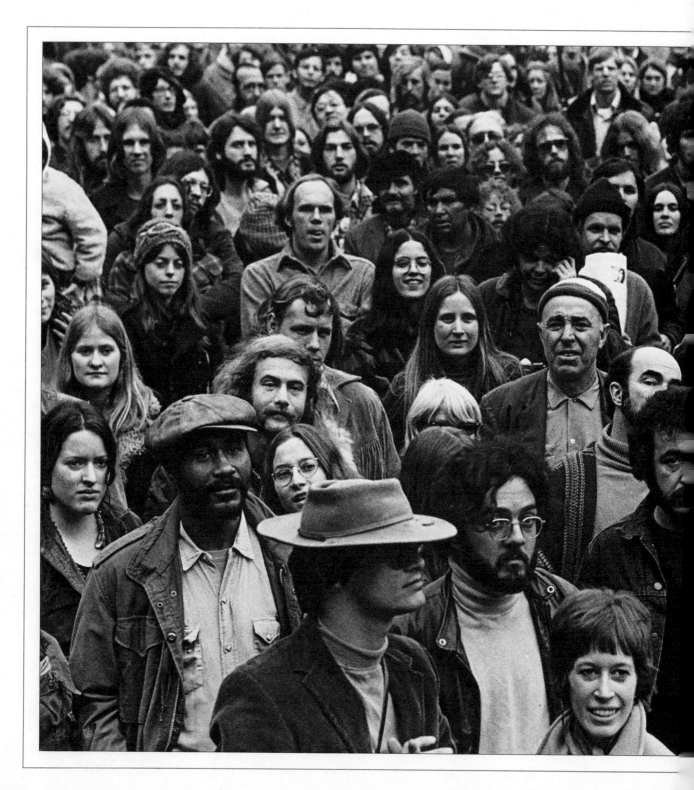

Chapter 1

The Nature of Psychology

Key Questions   1. What is psychology?
                 2. What are the goals of psychology?
                 3. What is the history of psychology?
                 4. What do psychologists do?

Psychology is concerned with the scientific study of behavior. It is a science with real applications to human problems. Inflation, crime, the energy crisis, loneliness, anxiety, depression—all can be understood only by studying and understanding human behavior.

You spend a lot of time studying people and trying to understand them. What could possibly be more interesting than people? You find them amusing, delightful, fascinating, and sometimes appalling or terribly annoying. And you wonder. Why do they do what they do? What are they thinking? Why do they act that way?

Each day the newspaper reports unusual accounts of human behavior. A recent article reported that fourteen students from a high school in Arlington Heights, Illinois, leapfrogged for twelve hours, traveling 56 miles, and beating the 1973 record by 6 miles.[1] The same day another story reported that a California artist bought ten tons of clay and molded 5,000 giant shark teeth; he then arranged them on a dry lake bed in the desert.[2] A third newspaper story reported that a seventeen-year-old boy hanged himself from a persimmon tree.[3] At the foot of the tree a jar was found with a note inside addressed to "Mom and Dad." The note said, "When you stop growing you are dead. I stopped growing long ago."

When you read stories like the last one, you wonder: Why did he do it? In his circumstances, would I have done it? You wonder about yourself, your life, your growth. You wonder how you came to think, feel, and act the way you do. You review your memories and study your behavior to seek an understanding of yourself.

You are a student of human behavior and you already know a lot about psychology. The purpose of this book is to deepen that understanding.

What Is Psychology?

You are at a noisy party; a friend walks up to talk, but you can hear only part of what she says: "Hello! How are . . . ? Where have you been? I haven't seen you in a long . . ." Can you supply the missing words? You understand what is being said even when you can't hear all the words. That is because you can predict what the missing words should be, and can fill them in yourself. You know the missing words are "you" and "time." You have learned to predict what other people will do.

You are out shopping; when the light turns red, you cross a busy downtown street, hardly glancing at the cars speeding toward you. You are predicting that they will stop, and you are betting your life on that prediction. A lot of the time you know what people are going to do before they do it. You understand other people fairly well.

Understanding other people is possible because, to a certain extent, they act consistently. There are two kinds of consistency that are important in the understanding of other people. First, a person is relatively consistent from day to day; if you know what the person did in the past, you can predict (with some accuracy) what the person is going to do in the future. Your shy, soft-spoken little sister is not likely to suddenly start shouting and fighting; although everybody changes, large and sudden changes are rare.   Second, there is consistency among different people; your behavior is similar to the behavior of other people in similar circumstances.   Because you are similar to other people, I can, for example, predict that you are reading this book right-side-up, not upside-down.   Everybody is unique, but we are also all alike in some ways.

Because of these two kinds of consistency in people, a science of behavior is possible.   Psychology is that science.

The Definition of Psychology

Psychology is the science of behavior.   It is the study of individual people and what they do.   It is a *science* because it is a systematic study, involving observation, description, and explanation.   Psychology is a science of *behavior;* the term **behavior** refers to activities, things that you do.   Psychology studies the activities of the mind (mental activities such as thinking and experiencing) as well as the activities of the body (motor activities such as moving and talking).   All of the things that you do are types of behavior that are studied by psychology.

For example, one type of behavior that psychology studies is aggression.   Why do you think people fight, kill, and make war?   Some have argued that people have "killer instincts," but there is little evidence to support this claim.   Do children grow up to be aggressive adults because of their continual exposure to television violence?   These questions have been examined in hundreds of psychological studies.

An example of a different type of behavior is dreaming.   In a recent study of dreaming, sixteen college students slept in a laboratory for three nights.[4]   On one of these nights a stressful film, showing a terrible accident, was shown just before the students went to sleep.   Later, the students reported dreaming about parts of the film.   This study and other similar studies show that dreams often incorporate aspects of waking experience.

People can be understood because, to some degree, they behave consistently from day to day.   A shy child is not likely to change suddenly into an outspoken child.   For this reason, human behavior is partially predictable. (B. A. King)

Another example of behavior is language.   Psychologists are very interested in studying how children's use of language begins and how it grows.   Typically this research involves observing infants, but a recent case was dramatically different.   Genie, a girl of thirteen years, nine months, was taken into protective custody by the police; her parents had kept her isolated in a small closed room, tied to a chair, for her entire life.[5]   Genie was extremely thin and unable to stand erect.   She did not speak and did not seem to understand language.   Within a few weeks, however, she began to imitate words, and was using sentences within a year after she was discovered.   Studies of

Genie's language development showed that she progressed through the same stages of growth that an infant displays in learning language.

Behavior Checklist

Which of the following are examples of behavior studied by psychologists?*

☐ Problem solving   ☐ Reading
☐ Blinking   ☐ Sex
☐ Remembering   ☐ Hypnosis
☐ Forgetting   ☐ Eating
☐ Tasting   ☐ Smiling
☐ Imagining   ☐ Electrical activity of the brain
☐ Learning   ☐ Muscle tension
☐ Heart rate   ☐ Intelligence
☐ Fighting   ☐ Crime
☐ Liking   ☐ Drug addiction
☐ Salivating   ☐ Hormone secretion
☐ Talking   ☐ Attitudes
☐ Headache   ☐ Anxiety

The Special Language of Psychology

Psychologists have developed a special vocabulary for discussing behavior. The term **response** refers to behavior and is used in a fairly general sense. For example, a psychologist might write, "Aggressive responses were found to increase following exposure to television violence." This sentence means that after people watched violent television programs, they became more aggressive. Another general word referring to behavior is **tendency.** For example, a psychologist might write, "The new drug reduces aggressive tendencies." This sentence means that people who take this drug act, on the average, less aggressively. A more complex behavioral word is the term **trait,** which refers to a relatively enduring personal characteristic or way of behaving. For example, a psychologist might write, "The trait of aggressiveness

* All of them, plus thousands of others!

is not universally evident among human beings." This sentence means that not all peoples in the world have an aggressive way of behaving. The term **state** refers to a temporary condition, a way of reacting or behaving that does not endure. For example, a psychologist might write, "Pain sometimes produces an immediate state aggressiveness." This sentence means that a temporary condition of aggressiveness is sometimes caused by pain. The terms "response," "tendency," "trait," and "state" are used to refer to a wide variety of behavior.

The term **stimulus** refers to anything that is sensed or that produces a reaction. (The plural form of this word is **stimuli.**) At a simple level, a stimulus can be a light or a sound that is sensed and that elicits some response. At a more complex level, a stimulus can be a textbook, a school, or some other highly complicated event or environment. The relationship between different types of stimuli and different types of responses has been of special interest to psychologists for many years.

Since a stimulus stimulates or provokes a response, the stimulus must come before the response or must occur concurrently with it. Psychologists also have terms for events that come after responses. One such event is a **reinforcer,** something that strengthens the response by making it more likely to occur in the future. Just as a wall can be reinforced and made stronger, a response can also be reinforced. An example of a reinforcer is food when you are hungry. When you were young, your mother may have reinforced you for making a good grade on a test by giving you a piece of candy.

When psychologists try to understand behavior, they are concerned with identifying the conditions that influence the behavior. For example, one of the conditions that influences the behavior of dreaming is age; studies show that as you grow older, you spend less and less time dreaming. One of the conditions that influences the formation of friendships is the degree of similarity of values and beliefs. One of the conditions that influences aggression in a child is the type of discipline used in the home. These and other "conditions" that influence behavior are called **variables.** The aspects of behavior that are influenced by these conditions—amount of dreaming, number of friendships, or degree of aggressiveness—are also called variables. Psychologists use the term *variable* to refer to anything that varies in value or degree.

Checklist for Psychological Concepts

Each of the following is generally considered either a stimulus, a response, or a trait. Indicate the nature of each by writing S (stimulus), R (response), or T (trait) in the blanks by each item.*

1 ____ talking	9 ____ a city park
2 ____ studying psychology	10 ____ increase in blood pressure
3 ____ aggressiveness	11 ____ generosity
4 ____ green light	12 ____ seeing
5 ____ depression	13 ____ sound of a siren
6 ____ thinking	14 ____ shyness
7 ____ hostility	15 ____ walking
8 ____ a sour taste	16 ____ a psychology textbook

As you read this text, you will encounter hundreds of terms that will either be completely new to you or—more often—will be used in a special sense unique to psychology. The terms printed in boldface type in the text are listed in the Key Concepts section at the end of each chapter. In order to understand psychology, you must take special care to master this vocabulary of terms. To go beyond a surface understanding of psychology, however, you must not only understand the words psychologists use but also understand what psychologists do and how psychologists think about human behavior.

The Goals of Psychology

Psychology is the science that seeks to understand behavior of all kinds. As a science, it has the goals of

*Stimulus: 4, 8, 9, 13, 16; Response: 1, 2, 6, 10, 12, 15; Traits: 3, 5, 7, 11, 14.

description, prediction, explanation, and *control.* Psychologists seek to describe a particular behavior so that we can understand what it is. We seek to predict it so that we can understand who will behave in that manner and when and where they will do so. We seek to explain a behavior so that we can understand why it occurs. We seek to control a behavior so that we can manage our lives better and help others manage theirs. These goals of psychology can be demonstrated by considering the problem of anxiety.

Description • Anxiety is a feeling of worry, tension, dread, or foreboding. It is a feeling that something terrible is about to happen, a feeling of despair and of hopelessness. Everyone has felt anxiety at one time or another; in fact, we live with mild anxiety every day. Extreme anxiety can be an unpleasant problem for some people.

Anxiety and fear are so closely related that there is no clear dividing line between the two concepts. The term **fear** is used to describe a person's reaction to a specific threatening object (you may fear a snarling

Anxiety—a vague feeling of worry, tension, or despair—is a common human experience in our stressful world. Psychologists study anxiety in an effort to help people feel better and often succeed in explaining and controlling it. (Marion Bernstein)

dog or a loaded gun pointed at you).   The term **anxiety** is used to describe a vague worry or apprehension that has no specific cause (you may feel anxiety when in crowds or when talking to strangers).   Anxiety may be acute or chronic.   **Acute anxiety** is a reaction of anxiety that happens suddenly and does not last for long.   **Chronic anxiety** is anxiety that is continual; it does not come and go.   In the description below, a young woman explains her acute anxiety to her roommate:

I'm on edge tonight.   I feel worried, but I don't know what it's about.   My heart is pounding, and I'm perspiring more than usual.   It's almost like I was waiting for something to happen. . . .   I feel frightened and fearful, but I don't really know why I feel this way. . . .   Things seem to be going well, and I shouldn't have any reason to be so uneasy.[6]

Prediction •   Whom, where, and when will anxiety strike?   Psychologists have been able to make certain predictions.   By studying what happens just before people feel anxious, we have found certain regularities.   Anxiety often follows some kind of *threat,* either real or imagined, and either physical or psychological.   Anxiety is aroused by the stress of failure, by the anticipation of being evaluated, by the loss of a loved one, by punishment, and by uncertainty.   We can predict that almost everyone in these **aversive** (unpleasant) circumstances will feel anxious, and our predictions will be confirmed.   There are also individual reactions of anxiety, ones not shared by the majority.   For example, some people are made anxious by open spaces, cats, clocks, or closets.

One of the ways psychologists can predict anxiety is to study individual differences in anxiety.   Some people are frequently anxious and some are not; in a particular situation, some people will be extremely anxious while other people will not be anxious at all.   Psychologists can predict who will and who will not be anxious by asking people to report their reactions.   This is typically done with a questionnaire.   For example, the following items come from a questionnaire

concerned with **test anxiety,** the anxiety aroused by tests and exams.   How anxious are you during tests?

	Generally	Rarely or Never
While taking a test, I feel nervous, tense, or upset.	☐	☐
While taking a test, I perspire a lot.	☐	☐
While taking a test, my hands shake or tremble.	☐	☐
While taking a test, my heart "pounds."	☐	☐
While taking a test, I experience an upset stomach.	☐	☐
While taking a test, I experience a shortness of breath.	☐	☐
While taking a test, I experience an ache in the back of my neck.	☐	☐

Each of these items is a **symptom** of anxiety; that is, each of the above is characteristic of, or indicates the presence of, anxiety.   Answers to questionnaires like this one can be used to predict how people will react to taking tests.

Explanation •   Psychology has studied the **physiology** of anxiety (the bodily processes involved in the experience of anxiety).   It is now known that certain brain structures are activated in the anxious person and that this leads to the secretion of chemicals called **hormones** into the bloodstream.   The body reacts with trembling, sweaty palms, muscular tension, an increased heart rate, and a dry mouth.

Sigmund Freud, the founder of psychoanalysis, believed that anxiety was due to **unconscious conflicts,** internal "tugs-of-war" between biological impulses for sex or violence on the one hand and moral standards of conduct on the other.   More recently psychologists have stressed other sources of internal conflicts, such as dependence versus independence or trust versus mistrust.

Is anxiety a result of the activity of the brain or is it a result of conflicts in the unconscious mind? The answer is both, and more besides. The effect of significant conflicts in your life may be to arouse certain brain structures, causing the bodily signs of anxiety. However, the causes of anxiety are not as well understood as this explanation implies. Many psychologists reject Freud's theory of the unconscious, proposing instead a variety of other ideas. The facts are not certain, and the issue is not yet settled.

Many questions about anxiety have not been answered. For the time being, psychology is proceeding in several directions at once in its effort to understand this problem. Single explanations are often inadequate. Most behavior can be understood in more than one way.

Psychologists study and attempt to explain many human problems and experiences. For some of these problems, they have developed multiple explanations, each adding to our understanding.

Control • Anxiety can be controlled in a variety of ways. One way is through the use of tranquilizing drugs. Another way is through training in muscle relaxation. The experience of anxiety is associated with muscle tension; by learning to control muscle tension, people can control anxiety. This case shows how a student with test anxiety learned to control it:

Susan, an 18-year-old freshman, came for help with extreme nervousness over taking tests. . . . Susan stated that, while she studied 25–30 hours each week on her coursework, she had received only D's and F's on her exams and quizzes. She felt that in each case she knew the material prior to the exam, but was "unable to put it down on paper." Discussion revealed that Susan came from a small rural high school where exams were rarely given.[7]

Susan came to the counseling center at her college and was taught a special type of deep muscle relaxation; she was taught how to relax when she needed to do so. Her performance on examinations improved dramatically, and she finished the term with a B average.

Many studies have shown that anxiety **impairs** (inteferes with) academic achievement, while relaxation **facilitates** it (makes it easier).

Its Relation to Other Sciences

Psychology is not a narrowly defined field of study; instead—like the object of its study, human beings—it is broad in scope, deep, and very complex. It involves *biology,* because behavior and experience depend upon the structure and function of the body, particularly the nervous system. Psychologists with a special interest in biology, for example, may study the electrical activity of individual cells in the brain. Psychology involves *chemistry,* because the chemistry of the body— particularly of the brain—is important in understanding behavior. Psychologists with special training in chemistry, for example, may study the effects of various drugs on chemical changes in the brain.

Psychology involves *sociology* (the study of social groups), because individual behavior always occurs within the context of a social system. Psychologists with special interests in social processes, for example, may study how an individual's attitudes and values are affected by other people. Psychology involves *anthropology* (the comparative study of culture), because most behavior is relative to its culture. A psychologist with an anthropological orientation, for example, may study the cross-cultural differences in child-rearing practices in Asia and Africa. Psychology involves *mathematics,* because the tools of mathematics are needed to draw conclusions from complex data concerning human behavior. These and other sciences are used by psychologists and, in turn, many of these sciences draw upon the knowledge of psychology.

What then is the difference between psychology and biology? Where is the line between psychology and sociology? There is no clear line, but there is a general rule: common to the variety of ways of studying psychology is the goal of understanding *individual behavior.* When psychology uses other sciences, it is always in pursuit of this goal.

Interim Summary   Psychology is the science of behavior.   The term *behavior* refers to such varied activities as talking, moving, thinking, perceiving, and feeling.   The goals of psychology are the description, prediction, explanation, and control of behavior.   Psychology uses and is related to many other sciences but is unique in its emphasis on understanding individual behavior.

The History of Psychology

How are we to understand ourselves?   People have wondered about their own behavior and have invented theories to explain it for thousands of years.   Two early influential psychologists were the Greek philosophers Plato and Aristotle.

Plato (about 400 B.C.) believed that the world known by the senses—the perceptual world—is but a faint copy of the perfect world of ideas.   This world of ideas, Plato believed, exists quite separately from human beings and is permanent and unchangeable. We are born, according to Plato, with knowledge of this world of ideas; that is, we have **innate ideas** (inborn ideas).   Although knowledge of this perfect world of ideas is inborn, awareness of the ideas requires meditation and rational thought.

Plato's student Aristotle held a different view; he believed that all knowledge comes from experience. According to Aristotle, there are no innate ideas.   The mind at birth is quite empty, like a "blank tablet," or **tabula rasa.**   Aristotle was a careful student of human behavior and wrote about the human personality, the senses, memory, and thinking.   Both Plato's conception of innate ideas and Aristotle's emphasis on the role of experience have strongly influenced the past two thousand years of psychological thought.

The Origins of Scientific Psychology

Modern scientific psychology is believed to have started in about 1879 with a German named Wilhelm Wundt.   Wundt defined psychology as the science of

consciousness (awareness); he believed that the task of psychology was to analyze and classify experience into elementary sensations and feelings.

Wundt's method of investigation was **trained introspection,** or self-observation.   We are all occasionally introspective; we pay attention to our inner feelings and experiences.   But Wundt's approach was more systematic.   In his laboratory people were trained to be careful and reliable observers of their experiences.   Furthermore, Wundt was not interested in experiences that were random or accidental; he controlled the experiences by controlling the stimuli— tones, lights, odors, or other events that stimulated reactions.   Wundt believed that people could be un-

Wilhelm Wundt

derstood by studying conscious experience produced by simple stimuli.

As a child in Germany, Wundt did so poorly in school that he was held back a year, but he was a determined student and eventually earned a degree in medicine. After years of teaching physiology in the university, he established in 1879 the world's first laboratory for the scientific study of psychology. Wundt was a methodical and humorless man who had little tolerance for any views except his own. He was a popular lecturer in the university but had a rather stiff classroom manner. Try to imagine yourself sitting in his class in 1880:

Wundt would appear at exactly the right minute—punctuality was essential—dressed all in black and carrying a small sheaf of lecture notes. He clattered up the side aisle to the platform with an awkward shuffle and a sound as if his soles were made of wood. . . . His voice was weak at first, then gained in strength and emphasis. . . . He seldom referred to the few jotted notes. As the clock struck the end of the hour he stopped and, stooping a little, clattered out as he had clattered in.[8]

Wundt's approach to studying psychology by analyzing conscious experience was later attacked as unscientific. The mind, it was argued, cannot be reliably observed, and therefore cannot be objectively studied. After a lapse of about sixty or seventy years, psychology is once again studying consciousness with great interest, this time with modern objective methods.

Contrasting Approaches

The history of psychology is a history of our conception of our own nature. Over the years psychologists have offered a variety of views to explain human nature. What are your views on human nature?

Freud, Watson, and Maslow represent three views that still influence modern psychology. The ideas of each of these men all stem from their different opinions on one central issue: What is human nature? How can we understand ourselves?

Freud and Psychoanalysis • Sigmund Freud believed that people can be understood only by understanding the contents of their unconscious minds. Like other animals, Freud believed, we have biological impulses and drives that compel us to irrational violence or sexual gratification. These impulses are unconscious, below the surface of awareness, in the dark unconscious mind.

Freud grew up and spent his life in Vienna, Austria. A small, lively man who wore a moustache and a pointed beard, Freud developed a theory of personality that has influenced Western thought more than that of any other psychologist.

Freud's theory of personality development was very controversial because he stated that infants have sexual impulses and seek sexual gratification. Adult personality, according to Freud, is highly influenced by experiences that occur before the age of three, particularly by experiences arising from the infant's sexual desires. Freud's ideas about sex are discussed in Chapter 14.

Freud emphasized the importance of **unconscious motivation**: people are often unconscious (un-

Sigmund Freud

aware) of their motives (why they do what they do). Personality, Freud wrote, consists of three basic processes: the **id** (storehouse of unconscious impulses, often sexual or aggressive in nature); the **superego** (conscience, the guardian of right and wrong); and the **ego** (the rational self which attempts to satisfy the demands both of the id and of the superego).   Freud's method of treating personality disorders is called **psychoanalysis.**   The goal of psychoanalysis is to make conscious what is presently unconscious, to bring unconscious memories and impulses to the light of day. Psychoanalysis is discussed in more detail in Chapter 21.

What was Freud like?   Freud had an unorthodox and brilliant mind, capable of intense concentration in the search for truth.   Even the smallest detail would capture his attention, for he was convinced that everything a person did was meaningful, even small "slips of the tongue" (now called Freudian slips).   As one person described him:

The half-peering and half-piercing gaze beneath the heavy brows showed a power to see beneath the surface and beyond the boundaries of ordinary perceptions.   But it also expressed capacity for patient, careful scrutiny and for suspended judgment so rare as to be unrecognizable by many; his cool skepticism has even been misread as cynicism or pessimism.   There was in him a conjunction of the hunter on an endless trail and the persistent immovable watcher who checks and revises; it was from this conjunction that his power of discovering and understanding the sources of the feelings and behavior of men and women sprang.[9]

Freud lived a long and full life.   For most of his adult years he was a heavy cigar smoker, often smoking as many as twenty cigars a day.   This habit may have contributed to his dying of cancer of the mouth.

Watson and Behaviorism • John Watson, an American psychologist, disagreed with both Wundt and Freud.   People are to be understood, Watson believed, only by understanding their observable behavior.   Psychology should be the science of publicly observable behavior, not the science of the conscious or unconscious mind.   Behavior, Watson argued, is controlled by the **environment,** the physical and psychological context of behavior; people are like machines run by external forces and can be understood by studying the ways the environment controls their observable behavior.

John Watson was born near Greenville, South Carolina, in 1878, and as a child attended a one-room rural schoolhouse.   His teachers reported that he was a poor student and was lazy and argumentative.   He went to the University of Chicago for graduate study in psychology, working his way through school as a waiter and janitor.   His Ph.D. thesis involved a study of how rats learn to run through a maze after they have been made blind or deaf.

Watson became a professor at Johns Hopkins University in Baltimore and published a paper in 1913 that launched a radical new movement in psychology, **behaviorism.**   Watson called for a purely objective approach to psychology, defining the task of the science as the prediction and control of observable behavior.   Thinking, feeling, and dreaming could not be publicly observed and so, according to Watson, could not be studied scientifically unless they could be translated into body movements or glandular secretions.

John Watson

Watson later claimed that thinking consisted of "subvocal speech," and could be studied by measuring small movements of the vocal cords and tongue.

Watson believed that adult intelligence and personality could be attributed to **conditioned reflexes,** involuntary reactions acquired through an elementary form of learning. According to Watson, these reactions developed through the years by the interaction of a child with the environment. He made the startling claim that he could take any baby at random and make it into a lawyer, thief, or Indian chief by properly conditioning its feelings and actions.

Maslow and Humanistic Psychology • Abraham Maslow believed that Wundt, Freud, and Watson were wrong. According to Maslow, people cannot be understood by analyzing their elementary sensations; they cannot be understood as controlled by animalistic impulses or by external forces. Instead, human beings are conscious, creative, and unique among other creatures, Maslow wrote. They are not bound to their environment; they are free agents, not robots.

Maslow objected to psychology's focus on rats, mental illness, involuntary reactions, and the negative side of people's nature. He advocated the study of the normal, healthy, and creative person. According to Maslow, people are born inherently good, with an inner motivation toward fulfilling their potential. They become bad, abnormal, or destructive only when the environment blocks or frustrates this inner nature.

Fulfilling your potential is termed **self-actualization.** Maslow wrote:

All the evidence that we have . . . indicates that it is reasonable to assume in practically every human being, and certainly in almost every newborn baby, that there is an active will towards health, an impulse towards growth, or towards the actualization of human potentialities.[10]

Maslow studied the lives of a few unusual individuals who, he believed, had fulfilled their potential; he called these rare persons self-actualized. He found that these self-actualized people experienced more moments of intense happiness, awe, or wonder than most other people. During these "peak" experiences, the individuals tended to become less conscious of themselves and to feel more spontaneous and in touch with the world. While these moments occur only rarely for most people, self-actualized persons experienced them more often. Maslow's theories are discussed in more detail in Chapter 18.

Maslow's research and theories have stimulated the development of an important new direction in psychology—**humanistic psychology.** Maslow called humanistic psychology the "third force" in psychology, the first two forces being psychoanalysis and behaviorism. Humanistic psychology is more concerned with human potential than with personality disorders; it seeks ways to promote self-development and growth.

Psychology Today

Modern psychology is enormous in its scope. It includes Freud's psychoanalysis, Watson's behaviorism, and Maslow's humanism in various modified and modernized versions. Modern views of the human personality and neurotic and psychotic disorders have

Abraham Maslow

been strongly influenced by Freud. Although many different types of psychotherapy have been developed since Freud, most are still variations of the "talking cure" that he used, psychoanalysis. The influence of Watson's behaviorism can be seen in most areas of modern psychology today. The study of conditioning and conditioned reflexes, which Watson popularized, has been a consistent interest in psycholgy ever since. Many psychologists still believe that human beings are controlled by their environments. Maslow's humanism—the "third force" in psychology—has formed the basis for the development of the recent emphasis on human potential. The concepts of self-actualization and personality growth have inspired many best-selling self-improvement books.

The study of the conscious mind—systematically begun by Wundt, but long out of favor—has recently been a major focus in modern psychology. The study of the conscious mind involves studying perception, imagery, thinking, and memory and is now referred to as **cognitive psychology.** Cognitive psychologists today are interested in how people perceive their worlds, how they acquire and retain knowledge, and how they solve problems.

Interim Summary   Modern scientific psychology began with Wilhelm Wundt, a German who established the world's first laboratory for the scientific study of psychology. Wundt was interested in studying conscious experience, an area of study that is currently popular called cognitive psychology. Sigmund Freud, the founder of psychoanalysis, emphasized the importance of the unconscious mind in influencing behavior; he developed a theory of personality based on three processes: the id, ego, and superego. John Watson denied that psychology should study either the conscious or the unconscious mind; instead, he stated, psychology should be the science of publicly observable behavior. Abraham Maslow emphasized the uniqueness of human beings and their natural drive for growth; people are not like machines or lower animals, he argued, but are conscious and creative free agents.

Careers in Psychology

Many different kinds of people become psychologists. Psychologists are teachers, scientists, counselors, and therapists. Psychologists teach psychology in high schools and colleges as an academic discipline; they do research in psychology to advance scientific knowledge of human behavior; and, as professionals, they apply psychological principles to help individuals, schools, businesses, and communities. Many psychologists work in more than one area; they combine the roles of teacher and researcher, or the roles of researcher and professional, or the roles of teacher and professional.

Teaching Psychology

The teaching of psychology occupies a large number of psychologists every year. Throughout the country interest in psychology is growing as people begin to see the task of understanding each other as a greater challenge than the task of conquering nature. Psychology is chosen by many students as a college major, and dedicated people are needed to teach the science of human behavior.

Why do people become teachers of psychology? One prominent teacher of psychology is Bill McKeachie, a professor at the University of Michigan who has taught psychology and studied the psychology of teaching for many years. McKeachie described his initial exposure to the field of psychology as follows:

In 1935 I was fourteen years old, an ardent baseball player, a dedicated Presbyterian, and secretary-treasurer of the Sunday school of the small rural church near my home in White Lake Township, Oakland County, Michigan. Each Sunday afternoon I counted the collection (average per Sunday, 77 cents), checked the date on each penny for my penny collection, and read the Sunday school paper, Young People. *It was on a Sunday afternoon that I read the half-page article on psychology as a vocation, and from that day to this, psychology has seemed to me the most fascinating field in which one could work.*[11]

Research in Psychology

The scientific investigation of human behavior is the full- or part-time work of thousands of psychologists. Many researchers conduct their studies at colleges and universities. In addition to their research in psychology they may also teach.

Researchers in psychology are motivated by a driving curiosity to understand behavior. They have many questions about people that they want to answer, and they find their answers by systematically observing behavior. Recently researchers have asked, "What is the effect on the minds of children of observing violence on television?" (Their conclusions are reported later in this book.) Researchers have asked, "How can memory be improved?", "How often do people dream?", and "What causes mental disorders?" The results of their studies are discussed in later chapters.

Scientific psychology is both a method of investi-

Researchers in psychology try to answer basic questions about human behavior through careful and systematic observation and study. Most psychological research is conducted in laboratories, such as the one shown above, because of the greater opportunity for measurement and control. (Judy Sedwick)

gation and a body of accumulated knowledge. Researchers in psychology use this method to discover facts and principles that can be added to this body of knowledge about human behavior. This method will be discussed in greater detail in the next chapter.

Professional Psychological Services

Psychology is a helping profession; psychologists provide their professional services to individuals and groups who seek help. Over the hundred years or so during which psychology has flourished as a science, many theories and principles have been developed that can be applied to specific psychological problems. These principles are applied by professional psycholo-

Clinical psychologists such as the one shown above, offer help to people who are depressed, anxious, or facing crises in their lives. In addition, clinical psychologists help people examine their values, become more aware of their feelings, and grow toward improved psychological health. (Frank Siteman/The Picture Cube)

gists who are actively engaged in practical problem solving.

Clinical and Counseling Psychology • Clinical and counseling psychologists advise and help people who have personal problems. A **counselor** may offer advice and guidance on educational and vocational decisions and may provide assistance in solving personal and marital problems. A **clinical psychologist** does similar work but typically concentrates on such tasks as diagnosing and treating personality disorders and providing therapy for individuals facing crises in their lives or for those who wish to promote their personal growth and development. A clinical psychologist typically has a Ph.D. in psychology with training in testing and research. **Psychiatrists** differ from clincial psychologists in that (1) psychiatrists are medical doctors and are licensed to prescribe drugs, and (2) clinical psychologists receive extensive training in research while psychiatrists do not.

The work of a counseling psychologist in a uni-

versity counseling center has been described as follows:

Robert Franklin, Ph.D., counseling psychologist . . . interviews and tests students to assess ability, motivation, and interests, . . . works intensively with students who are having serious difficulty adjusting to college or are experiencing emotional problems which hamper their college work, . . . conducts group meetings in reading and study skills, . . . supervises three interns enrolled in the university's doctoral program in counseling psychology, . . . teaches undergraduate courses in child psychology, psychology of personality, and tests and measurements, . . . is faculty adviser to a group of student volunteers in mental hospitals.[12]

School and Industry • Counselors and clinical psychologists sometimes work in the public school system where they provide help to students and teachers with personal or educational difficulties and collect psychological information on students for purposes of guidance. **School psychologists** give psychological tests to students in order to learn how best to advise them. One such test is the standard IQ test of intelligence; another is a vocational aptitude test, which attempts to identify suitable career choices. Psycholo-

School psychologists give psychological tests to children in order to identify their problems and potential. Such tests are given under standard conditions so that the resulting scores can be meaningfully compared. (Cary Wolinsky/Stock, Boston)

gists in industry also use tests; with the data gathered they help to select qualified personnel for various tasks. In addition, they study ways of improving working conditions and employee motivation.

Criminology • Psychologists working in prisons provide diagnosis and treatment for psychological problems of prisoners, and they participate in the selection of prisoners to be paroled. Psychologists also work in special treatment programs for drug addicts, sexual offenders, and juvenile delinquents. Increasing attention is being given to crime prevention, through the early identification and treatment of potential criminals and through efforts to modify harmful environments; psychologists study ways of changing neighborhoods and schools to make them less likely to produce juvenile delinquents.

Interim Summary   Psychologists work in many different capacities. Teaching psychology is a popular and demanding career. Conducting research in psychology to answer questions about human behavior is another full- or part-time career. Finally, psychologists provide services to people asking for help. For example, a clinical psychologist provides therapy for people facing crises in their lives.

How Much Do You Know About Psychology?

You have been struggling to understand yourself and others for many years, and you have learned a lot in the process. You have already learned many things about psychology by observing yourself and other people. For example, you probably know that these are true statements:

- Rewards and punishments change behavior.
- People learn to behave differently in different cultures.
- Sometimes people may be doing or feeling something that they are not aware of at the time.
- Some people learn quickly, others slowly.
- When some people are frustrated, they become aggressive.
- Your brain is the "master control organ" for your behavior.

This book is about these important things that you already know, plus many others that you may not yet know. Following is a list of thirty-four state-ments, some of which are true and some false. How much do you know about psychology? Test yourself by marking each one true or false, then continue reading to check your answers.

True or False?

_____ 1. Psychology is primarily concerned with understanding the private experiences of particularly interesting individuals.

_____ 2. A psychologist is not the same as a psychiatrist.

_____ 3. The fact that students with high grades have more positive attitudes toward school proves that improving school attitudes will improve grades.

_____ 4. Pigeons can be taught to play Ping-Pong.

_____ 5. Most of your fears consist of inborn reactions.

_____ 6. It doesn't matter whether you learn something a little at a time or all at once.

_____ 7. Studying by rote repetition is one of the best ways to ensure long-term retention of important facts.

_____ 8. Each memory that you have is physically located in a particular part of your brain.

_____ 9. When you have trouble concentrating on studying, you should stop for a while instead of trying to continue.

——— 10. What you see is influenced by what you expect to see.

——— 11. Of all the different drugs in the news recently, only alcohol seems relatively harmless.

——— 12. You can learn to control your own blood pressure and heart rate.

——— 13. Everybody dreams several times each night.

——— 14. You can tell when people are dreaming by watching their eyelids.

——— 15. Eye color, but not intelligence, may be inherited.

——— 16. Your personality is completely determined by the age of three.

——— 17. For the first week after birth, most babies are unable to see or hear.

——— 18. Parental attention and love can increase a child's IQ.

——— 19. Babies need loving in order to grow up to be healthy adults.

——— 20. In the formation of relationships, the rule is that opposites attract.

——— 21. A person who has homosexual experiences as a child will likely turn out to be a homosexual adult.

——— 22. Masturbation can cause mental illness.

——— 23. What it means to be psychologically normal depends upon who you are and where you live.

——— 24. People who go to psychologists or psychiatrists for help are generally crazy.

——— 25. Highly creative people are frequently mentally disturbed.

——— 26. Psychoanalysis is the most common form of psychotherapy.

——— 27. Muscle relaxation reduces nervousness.

——— 28. People who are mentally disturbed are clearly different from people who are not.

——— 29. Most people who are confined to mental hospitals are dangerous.

——— 30. It is possible to become blind or deaf with no physical injury.

——— 31. Animals and people behave in more socially acceptable ways when they are crowded.

——— 32. Most people would not obey an order to injure someone else.

——— 33. Prejudiced persons tend to have different personalities than nonprejudiced persons.

——— 34. In getting people to buy a product, conserve energy, or protect the environment, telling them explicitly what to do is a highly effective approach.

(*Answers given at the bottom of this column.*)

These statements concern some of the many issues that will be discussed in the chapters to come. They follow the general outline of the book; the first few come from the first Part and the last few come from the later Parts. How well did you do in picking out the true and false statements on the preceding test? Take a few minutes right now and check your answers to see how much you already know about psychology. How many did you get right? A score of 22 or more correct indicates a significant level of knowledge about psychology.

Answers to the true-false test: 1. F   2. T   3. F   4. T   5. F 6. F   7. F   8. F   9. T   10. T   11. F   12. T   13. T   14. T 15. F   16. F   17. F   18. T   19. T   20. F   21. F   22. F 23. T   24. F   25. F   26. F   27. T   28. F   29. F   30. T 31. F   32. F   33. T   34. F

Preview of the Book

This book is an introduction to the science of psychology, the problems psychologists study, the methods used in psychological inquiry, and the ways in which psychological knowledge has been applied. Chapters are organized into clusters, or Parts, according to the major problems they discuss. These nine Parts of the book are summarized below.

Part I, entitled "Introduction," explores the history of psychology, the present status of the discipline, and the methods by which psychologists study human behavior in order to expand the body of psychological knowledge. This section explains what psychologists do and how they think about human problems.

Part II, "Learning and Memory," deals with the effects of your experience on feelings, actions, and understanding. Most of your behavior, attitudes, and emotional reactions are learned. Your ability to profit from past experience depends upon your memory. The psychology of learning and memory is explained in this section, and the principles involved are applied to the problem of academic learning and retention.

Part III, "Mind and Body," shows how your consciousness is related to the brain and nervous system and how consciousness is altered through hypnosis or drugs. It discusses how people experience the sensory world and the inner world of dreams. This section also discusses the way in which you perceive the world and the conditions that influence your perceptions.

Part IV, "Life Cycle Development," will give you a clearer view of how you came to be who you are and how you will progress through stages of development in adult life. This section discusses your physical, mental, moral, and personality development and explores the significance of the family in personality growth.

Part V, "Interpersonal Relationships," provides an overview of the nature and formation of the ties that bind us together. What is the basis of your friendships and romantic interests? What are the origins of sexual identity? This section discusses friendship, interpersonal attraction, and forms of sexual expression.

Part VI, "Personality and Growth," is about the normal personality and your potential for personal growth. People have very different personalities. How can these differences be understood? People change and grow, becoming more competent and more effective. How can these changes be explained? This section discusses personality, motivation, and human potential.

Part VII, "Conflict and Disorder," deals with the feelings of anxiety, the disabling consequences of neurosis, and the severe psychological disturbance called insanity or psychosis. This section discusses these psychological problems in terms of their symptoms and possible causes, and then reviews major approaches to psychotherapy.

Part VIII, "Social Psychology," is about how individual behavior is influenced by others. Most of your behavior is social. You are influenced by your interactions with other people and, in turn, you strive to influence them. This section also discusses the special problems of prejudice, crime, and aggression.

Part IX, "Applied Psychology," the final section, explores ways in which psychology is being applied in two special problem areas in modern society. The first is understanding consumers and their consumption. The twin problems of inflation and the energy crisis arise in part from consumer behavior and must be solved in part by changing that behavior. The second problem is understanding work and production. Solving problems associated with work, unemployment, and productivity is especially important in today's economy. Psychology can bring special insights to these problems.

Summary

1. Psychology is the science of behavior. The concept of behavior refers to all sorts of human activities, including thinking, dreaming, experiencing, and moving. As a science, psychology is concerned with systematic study and observation.

2. Psychologists describe behavior by using such terms as *response, trait, state, stimulus, reinforcer,* and *variable.* In beginning the study of psychology, mastering the special language of psychology is important.

3. The goals of psychology are to describe, predict, explain, and control behavior.

4. Psychology uses and is related to many other sciences but is unique in its emphasis on understanding individual behavior.

5. Psychology is an ancient discipline.   Two early Greek philosophers who discussed psychological topics were Plato, who believed that we are born with innate ideas, and Aristotle, who believed that the mind at birth is a *tabula rasa* (blank tablet).

6. Modern scientific psychology began with Wilhelm Wundt, a German who established the world's first laboratory for the scientific study of psychology.   Wundt's method of study was based on trained introspection, an approach that was later attacked as unscientific.

7. Sigmund Freud, the founder of psychoanalysis, emphasized the importance of the unconscious mind in influencing behavior, a process called unconscious motivation.   Freud developed a theory of personality based on three processes: the id (a storehouse of unconscious impulses), the superego (the conscience), and the ego (the rational self).   Freud's method of treating personality disorders is called psychoanalysis.

8. John Watson, the founder of behaviorism, argued that behavior is controlled by the environment—the physical and psychological context in which it occurs.   Watson called for a purely objective science of psychology based on the study of publicly observable behavior.

9. Abraham Maslow, the founder of humanistic psychology, argued that human beings are not controlled by their environment and are conscious and creative free agents.   Maslow believed that people were born inherently good and had a drive to become self-actualized.

10. Psychologists work in many different roles in society.   Psychologists are teachers, researchers, counselors, and therapists.   Some psychologists provide psychological services to individuals or groups seeking help.   For example, a clinical psychologist is concerned with diagnosing and treating personality disorders and providing assistance for individuals who wish to promote their own growth and development.   Psychiatrists differ from clinical psychologists in that psychiatrists are licensed to prescribe drugs and clinical psychologists are not.

Key Concepts

psychology   The science of behavior.

behavior   Activities; things that are done; includes actions, thoughts, attitudes, memories, perceptions, language, feelings, etc.

response   Any kind of behavior or reaction.

tendency   How people are inclined or prone to behave; an "aggressive tendency" refers to behavior that is, on the average, somewhat aggressive.

trait   A relatively enduring characteristic; a way of reacting or feeling that is lasting; for example, "She displays the trait of dominance."

state   A relatively temporary characteristic or way of behaving; for example, "Following her accident, she was in a highly anxious state."

stimulus (singular), stimuli (plural)   Anything that is sensed or that produces a reaction; at the simple level, these can be lights, tones, or odors; at a more complex level, they can be events, people, situations, words, or even books.

reinforcer   A favorable consequence; for example, a reward.

variable   A concept having different values;

"intelligence" is a variable, having many different values.

fear   The reaction of dread or apprehension to a specific threatening object; a person may feel fear when confronted with a loaded gun.

anxiety   The vague worry or apprehension that has no specific known cause; a person may feel anxiety in crowds but not know the reason for this feeling.

acute anxiety   A reaction of anxiety that happens suddenly and does not last for long.

chronic anxiety   Anxiety that is continual.

aversive   Unpleasant or punishing; for example, pain and nausea are aversive.

test anxiety   Anxiety over examinations.

symptom   Something that is a characteristic of, or an indication of, a problem.

physiology   The functions and processes of the body.

hormone   A chemical produced by a gland and deposited into the bloodstream.

unconscious conflict   An internal conflict of which a person is unaware; an example might be the conflict between moral standards and sexual desire.

impair   To interfere with or reduce in effectiveness; for example, "The damage to his eye impaired his vision."

facilitate   To make easier.

innate ideas   Ideas, concepts, or ways of perceiving the world that are inborn or present at birth.

tabula rasa   A "blank slate," or empty mind; according to Aristotle, the state of mind before any outside impressions.

consciousness   Mental life; the private awareness of thoughts, feelings, and perceptions.

trained introspection   A method of studying experience through self-observation under controlled conditions.

unconscious motivation   Needs and impulses that have been repressed so that a person is unaware of them.

id   According to Freud, that part of the personality that is the unconscious storehouse of basic biological drives.

superego   According to Freud, that part of the personality that is the internalized moral code or conscience.

ego   According to Freud, that part of the personality that deals with reality and is responsible for voluntary processes of thinking, perceiving, and remembering.

psychoanalysis   The method of psychotherapy developed by Freud; its major aim is to make unconscious material conscious.

environment   The physical and psychological context of behavior; trees, storms, your mother, school, and this book all form part of the context of your behavior.

behaviorism   A system of psychology started by John Watson; according to this system, psychology is limited to the study of publicly observable behavior.

conditioned reflexes   Involuntary reactions acquired through an elementary form of learning; for example, when your mouth waters in reaction to a picture of food.

self-actualization   An individual fullfilling his or her potential.

humanistic psychology   The "third force" in psychology; emphasizes personal growth and creativity.

cognitive psychology   The study of mental activities such as thinking, knowing, perceiving, and remembering.

counselor   A psychologist who specializes in offering advice and guidance.

clinical psychologist   A psychologist who specializes in treating personality disorders and providing therapy; typically has a Ph.D. degree with training in testing and research.

psychiatrist   A medical doctor trained in the treatment of personality disorders and licensed to prescribe drugs; has MD degree.

school psychologist   A psychologist who works in the schools, counseling and testing students.

Chapter 2

The Art and Science of Psychology

Key Questions

1. How are science and art both involved in the study and understanding of human behavior?
2. What are some of the ways in which observations can be biased?
3. What is the special perspective on behavior taken by psychologists?
4. What are the rules of science, and how are they applied?

You begin the study of psychology with an advantage. You have been using psychology all your life and already know a great deal about it. Whenever you carefully observe yourself and others, you are studying psychology. When you spend time trying to understand and predict the behavior of other people, you are studying psychology.

Most of what you have learned about human behavior you have learned by direct experience, by observing yourself and others. This kind of psychological knowledge is important and forms the basis for the *art* in psychology—for your special ability in understanding other people, in knowing how they feel, and in being sensitive to their changing moods. But there is another kind of knowledge about people—a

knowledge based on *science*. Scientific knowledge is concerned with verifiable principles that can be repeatedly tested and confirmed. The science of psychology is concerned with those facts that can be demonstrated to be true in describing people in general.

In its understanding of people, psychology depends on both science and art. Psychologists draw upon their own private experiences and intuition to find likely ideas to test scientifically. The art of psychology is involved when the psychologist has a hunch, a guess, or intuition that leads to a testable idea about human behavior. The science of psychology is involved when the psychologist tests this idea using the scientific method. In this way, psychology combines both art and science.

Observing Behavior

Both the art and the science of psychology are based on the careful observation of behavior. Many false conclusions about human behavior have resulted from hasty and incomplete observation, from deep prejudices based on appearance, and from social pressure.

Drawing conclusions about human behavior is hazardous. It is very easy to be misled and to make mistakes. As we listen to the views of our peers and parents, it is easy to believe that redheads are temperamental, that overweight people are jolly, that men are more aggressive than women, that some people never

dream, and that "sparing the rod will spoil the child." Yet these results of casual observation have been challenged by research psychologists who argue that you can't always believe what you hear and sometimes you can't even believe what you *see*.

Perhaps you have heard someone say, "Seeing is believing." But can you believe your eyes? Sometimes different people see different things. What you see is sometimes ambiguous or unclear. To most people, the figure on page 25 looks like a three-dimensional glass box. But which corner of the box is closest to you, corner A or B? Look again, and you may change your mind.

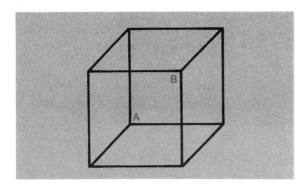

Distortions and the Halo Effect

Observations are sometimes distorted or biased. We have a tendency to oversimplify people, to see them as stereotypes. It is as if we put an imaginary "halo" over some people's heads—from our perspective, they can do no wrong. This kind of bias is called the **halo effect**—the tendency of people who have been judged positively in one respect to be judged positively in other respects.

Physical appearance biases our judgment and creates a kind of halo effect. In one study students were shown photographs of strangers and asked to rate their personalities.[1] The photographs had been previously separated by judges into categories of high, medium, or low attractiveness. The students rated the pictures of highly attractive people as more confident, happy, active, serious, perceptive, and flexible. Even though the pictures were of complete strangers, the students rated the attractive ones as positive and the unattractive ones as negative on a wide variety of personality traits.

The Prejudiced Eye

On the basis of physical appearance, people make all kinds of snap judgments about character, intelligence, honesty, sexuality, and personality. Since these psychological characteristics are rarely revealed in appearance, snap judgments are more often wrong than right.

People are judged on the basis of their hair color. According to surveys among Caucasians, blond men are seen as kind, and dark-haired men are seen as strong and intelligent.[2,3] Blond women are seen as social and brunettes as intelligent and dependable.[2] Men with beards are seen as more masculine, mature, dominant, and self-confident than clean-shaven men.[4]

People are also judged by the shapes of their bodies. Overweight people are viewed as lazy, weak, good-natured, and sympathetic; muscular people are viewed as adventurous, self-reliant, energetic, and competitive; thin people are viewed as tense, pessimistic, inhibited, and suspicious.[5]

What kind of snap judgments do you make about people? Imagine meeting a tall, thin woman with glasses. What kind of assumptions would you make about her personality? Imagine meeting a short, overweight man with a high voice. What would be your first impressions of his personality?

In the famous shell game, a magician asks which of three shells is covering a pea. You will invariably be wrong, for in this case, the hand is faster than the eye. Psychologists protect themselves against errors by insisting on careful, controlled, and repeated observations. (Robert Foothorap/Jeroboam Inc.)

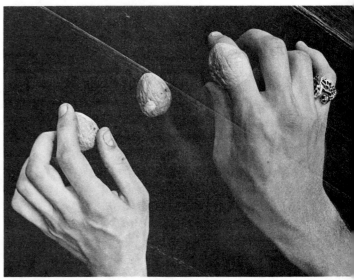

Do you make snap judgments about people on the basis of their size? What kind of assumptions do you make about the personality of a small man or a large woman? Such snap judgments are more often wrong than right. (Ken Robert Buck)

What are your snap judgments—your prejudices—about people with the following characteristics?

☐ men with full beards   ☐ overweight women
☐ tall women   ☐ men with heavy eyebrows
☐ blond women   ☐ short men
☐ red-haired men   ☐ women with large noses
☐ women with short hair   ☐ men with high voices

Expectancy and Bias

Expectations can bias observations. You may have heard, "What you expect is what you get." There is some truth in that. Expectations have a way of coming true. It is widely believed that a lion tamer who expects to be bitten has a greater chance of being

attacked. Many experiments in the psychology of perception have shown that, to some extent, you see what you expect to see. For example, what do you see at the center of the figure following?

12
A B C
14

Whether you see it as a "B" or as a "13" depends upon whether you are reading across or reading down—expecting a letter or a number; exactly the same figure can be seen as two different things. The results of psychology experiments can sometimes be influenced by the expectations of the experimenter, and the performance of a child can be influenced by the expectations of the teacher.[6] The tendency for your expectations to come true is called a **self-fulfilling prophecy.**

Selectivity and Bias

As far as your senses are concerned, the world has a great excess of information. How can you cope with all of the sounds and sights that demand your attention? You cannot pay attention to everything at once; you notice some things and ignore others. According to the **principle of selective attention,** you are able to attend to and perceive only a small portion of the information available in the world.

Magicians would be out of work were it not for this principle. Most magic tricks are based on your tendency to pay attention only to part of what is going on. Magicians learn how to divert your attention so that their hands are faster than your eyes. Early in this century a psychologist demonstrated this effect in front of his class:

I stood on the platform behind a low desk and begged the [psychology class] to watch and to describe everything which I was going to do from one given signal to another.   As soon as the signal was given, I lifted with my right hand a little revolving wheel with a color-disk and made it run and change its color, and all the time, while I kept the little instrument at the height of head, I turned my eyes eagerly toward it.   While this was going on, up to the closing signal, I took with my left hand, at first, a pencil from my vest pocket and wrote something at the desk; then I took my watch out and laid it on the table; then I took a silver cigarette box from my pocket, opened it, took a cigarette out of it, closed it with a loud click, and returned it to my pocket; and then came the ending signal.[7]

The observers then wrote down everything they observed.   The results showed that 18 out of the 100 students failed to observe *anything* that he did with his left hand.

The Psychological Perspective

Before you travel through a foreign country, you should familiarize yourself with the attitudes, interests, ways of thinking, and language of its people. You want to get into the right frame of mind, so that you can understand and appreciate what you are about to see.

Learning about psychology is like learning about a foreign country.   You need to begin by learning the language and special way of thinking that is unique to psychology.   This section will be your guidebook as you begin your study of psychology.

The Focus on Behavior

Psychology is the science of behavior.   The term **behavior** is used in a very broad sense to include such activities as running, crying, thinking, seeing, learning, dreaming, and talking.   In all cases, however, the object of study by psychologists is what people (or other organisms) do.

People behave in many ways that can be simply and directly observed.   For example, running, crying, and talking can all be observed in a public way.   With the proper instruments, one could even obtain a permanent record of how fast and far you ran, how loudly you cried, and what you said when you talked.   These records could then be analyzed to learn more about your behavior.

By contrast, many kinds of behavior cannot be directly observed.   You cannot determine what I am thinking by watching me, and you cannot tell when I begin to daydream and enter into the world of imagination.   These are private activities that cannot be publicly observed or recorded.

Psychologists, however, are interested in studying both public and private behavior.   But how can private behavior be studied if it cannot be seen directly?   The answer is that there are many indirect ways of studying private behavior.   The inner world of the mind is not completely hidden from view.   For example, a psychologist can study how people think by giving them problems to solve and measuring their errors and their speed in reaching a solution.   By changing the type of problem and observing the errors that are made, psychologists can learn something about how the mind works.   There are other ways of indirectly observing the inner world.   For example, psychologists have learned that when people begin to dream, their eyes flutter and the electrical activity of the brain changes in a systematic way. Therefore, it is possible to detect when dreaming occurs by using certain special measuring devices.

When psychologists study people, they are concerned with understanding their behavior. This is why, when you read a psychology text, the word *behavior* appears so often. You see references to "social behavior," "sexual behavior," "aggressive behavior," or "neurotic behavior." All of these terms refer to different aspects of what people do.

Analysis, Precision, and Measurement

How do psychologists think about behavior? They begin with a curiosity, a questioning, an urge to know, that is probably not much different from yours. Their desire to understand people is similar to your desire. However, what they do with this desire, this urge, is different.

When psychologists think about behavior, study individuals, or try to solve people's problems, their approach is highly analytic. **Analysis** consists of separating something into its component parts; it involves

Psychologists study mental activities by examining the electrical activities of the brain. The patterns of electrical activity change as the mind works and responds to problems. (*Judy Sedwick*)

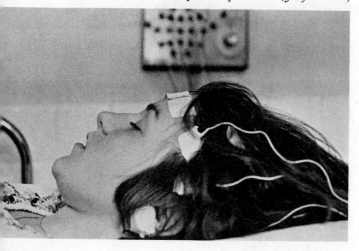

categorizing and clarifying these parts, and studying their relations to each other. Psychological thinking is also characterized by precision. **Precision** involves being exact and specific; psychologists dislike being vague and general and want instead to be precise and detailed. This need for precision is often served by measuring behavior. **Measurement** involves assigning a number to behavior; for example, rather than saying a child is very intelligent, a psychologist might say that the child has an IQ of 130. The concepts of analysis, precision, and measurement describe how psychologists approach the study of behavior.

How would you study personality? Your curiosity about people has led you to notice the many differences among individuals in their personalities. Some people tend to behave fairly consistently in one way, while other people behave in other ways. Psychologists in their study of personality take a somewhat different approach. Their interest in analysis leads psychologists to divide up the concept of personality into many different aspects or traits. Their interest in precision leads psychologists to define these traits as exactly as possible. Their interest in measurement leads psychologists to develop personality tests, ways of measuring personality traits so that individual differences can be precisely described.

Asking Psychological Questions

Are you the sort of person who often wonders, "What would happen if . . .," "Why do people do . . .," or "What causes . . ."?

The first step in research occurs when one person wonders about something. Research psychologists wonder about a lot of things, and then they take the next step and try to find the answers to their questions. Scientific research is a way of asking and answering questions, so research begins with questioning.

Asking questions is not as easy as you might think. Some scientists say that asking exactly the right question is nine-tenths of the work in research.

For scientific purposes, some questions are much better than others; some lead directly to important research while others are useless for research. How can you tell the difference?

To be valuable for scientific research, questions should satisfy two rules: (1) they must be significant (meaningful), and (2) they must be answerable.

There is no simple way to tell when your question is significant and when it is not; many scientists ask questions that later prove to be insignificant; and a question that is insignificant today may be significant tomorrow. Some questions are significant because they concern practical problems and their solutions: Is psychoanalysis an effective treatment for irrational fears? Some questions are significant because they concern basic psychological processes: What is the effect of anxiety on learning? Some questions are significant because they are related to an important theory in psychology: Are dreams of sex, as Freud would have predicted, more common during sexual abstinence?

The second criterion that scientific questions should satisfy is that they should be answerable by the methods of science. These methods answer questions by seeking the facts, by observing what *is,* by referring to experience. Popular opinion, fond wishes, expert judgment, and the dreams of gurus do not count. The term **fact** refers to information based on observation. Science accepts as fact only the results of careful observation. Some questions are not answerable by the scientific method. The question "Is murder evil?" is not answerable by carefully observing the world. The answer to this question rests on human values and moral beliefs.

An **empirical question** is a question that can be answered by observation or by referring to experience. An example of an empirical question is the following: What is the effect of alcohol on behavior? This is an empirical question because it can be answered by carefully observing the behavior of people who are intoxicated. The results of your observations are *facts*—not just opinions—and these facts can then be used to answer the original question. The scientific method answers empirical questions by seeking facts through careful observation.

A **value question** is different from an empirical question. Value questions cannot be answered by observation but instead must be answered by preference, opinion, or belief. An example of a value question is the following: Should people drink alcohol? This is a value question because it asks for a judgment of good and bad, a moral conclusion. To answer a value question, you must refer to your beliefs or values; the result will be a **value judgment,** not a fact. A value judgment is a conclusion based on values or beliefs. The scientific method cannot answer value questions.

A Test to Take

Here are twenty questions; some can be answered by the scientific method and some cannnot. Can you tell the difference? Check the questions you think are answerable scientifically.

- ☐ 1. Should mothers work or stay home with their children?
- ☐ 2. What are the psychological differences between the children of working and nonworking mothers?
- ☐ 3. Is premarital sexual intercourse wrong?
- ☐ 4. What is the relation between premarital intercourse and later marital sexual adjustment?
- ☐ 5. Is it bad for teachers to spank their students?
- ☐ 6. What proportion of teachers use physical punishment in classes?
- ☐ 7. Should people who are mentally disturbed be confined in mental hospitals even if they do not agree to it?
- ☐ 8. What is the effect of hospitalization on the severity of psychotic symptoms?
- ☐ 9. Should drug addicts be forced to accept psychotherapy?
- ☐ 10. What proportion of drug addicts remain drug-free five years after psychotherapy?
- ☐ 11. Is it better to be a conformist or a nonconformist?
- ☐ 12. What are the family backgrounds of conformists and nonconformists?
- ☐ 13. Is smoking marijuana wrong?
- ☐ 14. What is the effect of marijuana on thinking and memory?
- ☐ 15. Should homosexuality be a crime?
- ☐ 16. What are the causes of homosexuality?

☐ 17. Which is a better place to live—the country or the city?

☐ 18. What are the psychological effects of rural and urban environments?

☐ 19. Should all mothers love their babies?

☐ 20. What is the effect of inadequate love during infancy?

In this list only the even-numbered questions can be answered by the scientific method. The odd-numbered questions are *value questions,* employing such terms as "should," "right," "wrong," "good," and "bad." The even-numbered questions are *empirical questions,* asking about the facts as they are in the world. Psychology uses the scientific method to find answers to empirical questions; however, there are many questions about human behavior that cannot be answered by psychology because they involve values, moral and religious beliefs, or the laws of society.

Interim Summary   Both the art and science of psychology are based on careful observation of behavior—but sometimes different people see different things. The halo effect, self-fulfilling prophecy, and selective attention are three causes of possible distortion in observations. The unique psychological approach to the study of behavior is characterized by analysis, precision, and measurement. Psychologists are concerned with asking and answering questions about human behavior, but not all questions are valuable. A good scientific question is one that is both significant (meaningful) and empirical (answerable by the scientific method).

The Art of Psychology

Experienced counselors, therapists, and teachers frequently acquire an immense sensitivity and personal understanding of the feelings and problems of other people. From years of careful observation and study, those whose profession it is to work closely with people are sometimes able to understand how others feel without being told. It is not that they are able to read minds in some psychic way, but rather that they can read subtle clues in posture, facial expression, and speech. For example, an experienced counselor can tell from intonation and posture when a person is upset and anxious. From years of experience in working with people, a counselor is often able to find recurring patterns in how people have felt and reacted in specific circumstances. These patterns can be used to predict how other people will react in similar circumstances. Thus, direct experience in observing people can form the basis for a sensitive understanding of how they feel and react. This sensitive understanding is the source of the art of psychology.

Case Studies

One of the ways in which the art of psychology can be seen is through a **case study.** A case study is the result of an intensive study of one person. A clinical psychologist may work with an individual experiencing a problem and produce a case study at the conclusion of the therapy. Such a study would provide an in-depth understanding of that individual and would be based in part on the acquired sensitivity of the clinical psychologist. As such, it would be an example of the art of psychology. Great novels are, in a way, fictionalized case studies. Many of them are in-depth explorations of a single character.

A case study is an intensive and comprehensive study of one person. One famous case study is an in-depth study of a woman named Eve White. She displayed three separate personalities and would suddenly switch from one to the other. The above photo is from the movie that was based on her life. (Museum of Modern Art Film Stills Library. Coutesy of Twentieth-Century-Fox)

Each person is unique and has unique talents and problems. Understanding uniqueness is the special contribution of the case-study method. Case studies are careful descriptions of individuals, and as such they preserve the facts about cases for others to study. For example, a famous case study is the book *The Three Faces of Eve*. This book is a study of a young woman named Eve White who displayed three separate personalities. She was one of the rare cases of multiple personality, and her history is preserved in this popular book. Eve White was a shy and gentle woman who was seeing a therapist because of her severe headaches and blackouts. Nothing unusual occurred until one day when she suddenly switched personalities:

As if seized by sudden pain, she put both hands to her head. After a tense moment of silence, both hands dropped. There was a quick, reckless smile, and, in a bright voice that sparkled, she said "Hi there, doc!" ... This new and apparently carefree girl spoke casually of Eve

White and her problems, always using she *or* her *in every reference, always respecting the strict bounds of separate identity. . . . When asked her name, she immediately replied "Oh, I'm Eve Black."* [8]

Like other case histories, the case of Eve White reveals a great depth of understanding on the part of the researcher. How is this understanding achieved?

Information about the nature and source of psychological problems might come from a variety of sources. One source is the interview. By asking questions and listening carefully, the researcher can learn a great deal about what the person thinks, feels, and wants, about the early home life, and about other significant people who may be involved. A second source of information is psychological tests, which are useful in assessing personality and intelligence. Most tests yield scores that permit an individual to be compared with others on a variety of traits. A third source of information for case studies is existing records; an individual's life history is sometimes available from public legal records or medical records.

On the basis of interviews, tests, and other information, the psychologist puts together a picture of the individual as a whole. Often the facts lead the psychologist to a conclusion or inference about the nature of the problem. For example, on the basis of information from interviews and from certain psychological tests, a psychologist may infer that a psychotic person has a brain disorder and may recommend treatment accordingly. Such an inference, although supported by empirical evidence, is more in the nature of an informed guess than a definite fact. The psychologist cannot see the actual condition of the person's brain. The clinician must often rely on intuition when drawing a conclusion from insufficient evidence.

The Case of Michael Boland

The following case study shows how information is gathered and conclusions are reached in intensive studies of single individuals. It reports the case history of a young man named Michael Boland, who came to a clinic for help.

Michael Boland was 21 years old when he phoned for an appointment at a local guidance clinic. His problem, as he stated it on the phone, was that he tended to attract and be attracted to members of his own sex. He also felt that he was too shy and anxious.

Michael looked younger than 21 years of age. His tall, slim appearance, with wavy hair, long lashes, and even features, gave him an air of prettiness. Michael wore conspicuously stylish clothes and jewelry, with every article carefully matched.

Michael described his mother as a sweet, kind, and sensitive person, and said that he had been very close to her. He said that his mother had always been very protective in her relationship with him, and he missed not having guidance and concern that his mother had continuously provided.

Whenever Michael went out in the evening, his mother stayed awake until he got home and she expressed relief that he had returned without any mishaps befalling him. Michael would then feel extremely guilty because his mother was ill, and she had been kept awake because of worry and apprehension about his welfare.

Michael characterized his relationship with his father as one of coolness and distance, rather than open conflict. He said that he had never felt a deep emotional bond with his father, and they rarely had any extended conversations.

[After graduation from high school] Michael began to frequent homosexual bars at irregular intervals, but his mother did not allow him to spend every evening out of the house. He stated that many of the men he met at the bars were physically attracted to him, and this was a very enjoyable experience. Michael also said that he derived a great deal of physical pleasure from homosexual activity.

Michael reported that he often felt greatly troubled by the rights and wrongs of his sexual behavior and thought he was committing a sin.

Michael was seen by a female psychologist, Dr. T. The client appeared to be quite anxious during the first interview, and he tended to speak in a quavering and barely audible tone of voice. He found it difficult to maintain eye contact with the examiner, and often looked to one side or down at his hands.

The client completed a general personality inventory, the MMPI. He was asked to give stories to a number of cards from the Thematic Apperception Test (TAT), in order to gain more information about social relationships and interaction patterns.

There was evidence on the test material of anxiety, depression, and repetitive and bothersome thoughts. The client, however, was not overwhelmed by his personal difficulties.

The client's responses to the test material suggested an uncertainty about sexual identification. Some of the figures on the TAT cards were initially labeled as female, and then as male. He tended to view females his own age as physically unattractive and artificial. The client responded in a very negative manner to concepts about his own body. He also indicated that he sometimes wished that he were a girl.

In general, the test results confirmed the information about the client that had been gained from the interview.

Therapy was recommended in order to help Michael deal with his inner turmoil and guilt feelings about his sexual orientations, and to aid him in modifying his shy and dependent behavior. The goal of therapy was to enable the client to make future decisions, including the selection of a sexual partner, on the basis of a more open choice, rather than because of poor interpersonal skills.[9]

The preceding passage illustrates some of the techniques used in a case study to help the clinician and the client get a better understanding of the problem at hand. The client was asked to complete a series of tests solely for this purpose. One of these tests was the **Thematic Apperception Test (TAT)**, for which the client was shown a series of pictures and asked to make up stories about them. Then the clinician could evaluate the stories in terms of the problem being considered. Another test that was given was the **Minnesota Multiphasic Personality Inventory (MMPI)**. The MMPI is a general personality test, consisting of around 600 questions, each of which is answered "yes" or "no." It is designed to detect abnormal personality traits.

Clinical Intuition

As you have seen from the case study just presented, individuals reveal much information in clinical interviews. Some of this information is explicit and verbal, and some of it is implicit and nonverbal. Gestures, facial expressions, and intonations of the voice are often cues that an experienced clinician is able to use in coming to a conclusion about the person being interviewed.

The ability to come to a conclusion without having direct evidence is called **intuition.** Psychologists who spend a lot of time interviewing people often develop a highly refined clinical intuition. In a book called *Listening with the Third Ear,* Theodore Reik, a well-known therapist, described an instance of his clinical intuition during a therapy session with one of his patients:

One session at this time took the following course. After a few sentences about the uneventful day, the patient fell into a long silence. She assured me that nothing was in her thoughts. Silence from me. After many minutes she complained about a toothache. She told me that she had been to the dentist yesterday. He had given her an injection and then had pulled a wisdom tooth. The spot was hurting again. New and longer silence. She pointed to my bookcase in the corner and said, "There's a book standing on its head." Without the slightest hesitation and in a reproachful voice I said, "But why did you not tell me that you had had an abortion?" [10]

How was Reik able to reach this remarkable (and correct) conclusion? From Reik's point of view, the patient's silence during the interview indicated that she was resisting making her thoughts known and therefore something significant was on her mind. Reik regarded the idea of tooth extraction as a symbol of birth, and the remark about the upside-down book gave Reik an image of a fetus in the womb. Thus Reik came to the concept of an abortion on the basis of a number of cues evident during the course of the interview. While this intuition was correct in this case, not all clinical intuition hits the mark so accurately; intuition is often wrong.

Interim Summary   A sensitive understanding of people, based on long experience and careful observation, forms the basis of the art of psychology. The art of psychology is expressed in many different ways. One of these ways is the case study, an intensive study of a single individual based on information from interviews, tests, and other sources. The TAT and MMPI are commonly used psychological tests.

The Science of Psychology

Why do you dream?

This is a question that people have tried to answer for thousands of years, and many answers have been proposed. How can you determine which are true and which are false?

There are many possible ways for deciding what to call true and what to call false. You can decide on the basis of your intuitions or hunches ("My guess is that dreams are our contact with the spirit world"); you can decide on the basis of a popularity poll ("Everybody who believes that dreams are the work of the devil, raise your hand"); or you can decide on the basis of the opinion of some authority ("Just ask Holland"). Finally, you can decide on the basis of systematic study of dreams and people who dream; this is the way of science.

The Rules of Science

Science is a method of acquiring knowledge and also the body of knowlege acquired by that method. Chemistry is a science because it uses this method and has accumulated such a body of knowledge. Psychology is a science, too, though it rarely uses test tubes.

The method used in science—the **scientific method**—is a method for deciding what is probably true and what is probably false. The method consists of a set of rules for testing and observing the world. People who "play the game" of science agree to follow these rules. This minimizes disagreements. There are, of course, still quarrels among scientists about what is true and what is false. But there are fewer disagreements among scientists than among, say, politicians.

What are the rules of science? One rule is the **principle of empirical verification.** According to this principle, a scientific claim should be regarded as true only if it agrees with experience. To discover whether a statement is true, you must test it against your observation of the world. According to this principle, the opinion of an expert does not count; you must rely on experience, not opinion.

A second rule of science is the **principle of reliable evidence.** According to this principle, no claim should be accepted without evidence that is reliable. *Reliable evidence* is evidence that can be repeatedly observed. Reliable evidence is consistent evidence, evidence confirmed by different studies all finding the same result. When the results of studies do not agree, the evidence is unreliable. If something happens only once, it cannot be checked, and—according to this principle—should not be given much weight.

A third rule of science is the **principle of public evidence.** *Public evidence* is accessible to many people; your observations can be checked against theirs. Private evidence is accessible only to one person and therefore cannot be checked. If you were to claim that you thought of your dead grandmother every time you saw a white-haired woman, your claim could not be checked. The experience would be completely private, but sound evidence must be public. It must be available to others so that they can check it. Evidence that is empirical, reliable, and public is regarded as sound evidence and is scientifically acceptable.

The Scientific Method

The scientific method is a method of acquiring knowledge based on the rules of science. The method consists of classifying the events of the world ("This is a a dream, this is a cow, this is a book"); of observing the various relations between events ("After reading this book, I dreamed of a cow"); and of developing theories that attempt to make sense of those relations ("Dreams are fragments of memories, and the book in question was about cows").

When you classify things and observe relations among them, you are collecting facts, or data. There are many different ways psychologists collect facts: surveys, tests, interviews, experiments. Suppose, for example, you wanted to know the relation between dreaming and taking drugs. Do drugs increase or decrease dreaming? After taking drugs, a person might be more likely or less likely to dream. How could you collect the facts that would help you to answer the question?

In applying the principle of empirical verification, you would seek evidence based on experience, not just on someone's opinion. You would try to answer the question by systematically observing the facts of dreaming under drug use. Applying the principle of reliable evidence, you would not be satisfied with a single observation but would confirm your facts through repeated studies. Applying the principle of public evidence, you would not be satisfied with your private and subjective thoughts, but would seek objective evidence that could be publicly checked and confirmed.   But how could such a study be designed?

Surveys and Experiments

One possibility would be to conduct a survey of college students and to ask each student two questions: (1) During the past ten days have you used marijuana? and (2) During the past ten days, how many dreams do you recall having? One problem with conducting such a study is that some students might not tell the truth about their drug use.   Another problem is that the survey measures only the degree to which students *remember* their dreams, not the degree to which the dreams actually occurred.

But aside from these problems, even if a survey could find evidence of an association between drug use and dreaming, it would not be possible to conclude from that evidence that taking drugs *causes* people to dream more or to dream less. If it were found that students who use drugs dream less often, there would be several possible explanations for this result.   One possibility would be that drug usage reduces dreaming; a second possibility would be that the failure to dream incites people to take drugs; and a third possibility is that people who take drugs tend to be the sort of people who do not dream very much, and that drugs and dreaming are not related in terms of **causation**—that is, neither one causes the other or produces changes in the other.

A second possible way to collect facts relevant to the relation between drugs and dreaming would be to conduct an experiment.   In an **experiment,** the scientist not only observes what happens but also partially controls what happens.   The experiment is a scientific method aimed at testing how one variable influences a second variable.   An experiment on drugs and dreaming would be designed to test how the variable of *drug usage* influences the variable of *frequency of dreaming.*

It so happens that "frequency of dreaming" cannot be reliably determined just from asking people to recall their dreams.   The best, though still imperfect,

measure of dream frequency comes from observing the dreamer's pattern of brain waves and eye movements. The electrical activity of the brain and the movements of the eyes both change in a characteristic way when people dream.

A psychologist might conduct an experiment on drugs and dreaming by obtaining a number of volunteers who had not recently used drugs, and then randomly dividing them into two groups.   In an experiment, one group (the **experimental group**) is given a special treatment and a second group (the **control group**) is not.   Then, the behavior of the experimental group is later compared to the behavior of the control group in order to determine whether the special treatment had any effect (see Figure 2-1).   In the experiment on drugs and dreaming, members of the experimental group might be given pills containing a drug, while members of the control group would be given pills containing only sugar or an inactive sub-

Figure 2-1 Designing an Experiment on Drugs and Dreaming. *To test the effect of drugs on the frequency of dreaming, researchers randomly divide college students into an experimental group and a control group. Only the experimental group is given a real drug, however; in every other way, the two groups are treated exactly alike. A comparison of the data for the two groups reveals the effect of the drug on dream frequency.*

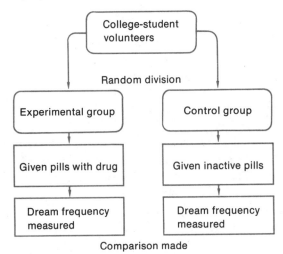

stance.   Then the frequency of dreaming in the two groups would be measured and compared, in order to determine whether taking the drugs reduced dream frequency.   As a matter of fact, experiments of this sort have shown that many drugs do have the effect of reducing dreaming.   Additional information on research methods in psychology can be found in the Appendix.

Interim Summary	Science is both a particular method for acquiring knowledge and the body of knowledge acquired by that method. The method is the scientific method, a set of rules for observing and testing the world in order to decide what is probably true. One such rule is the principle of empirical verification, the idea that you must rely on experience, not opinion, to decide what is true. A second rule of science is the principle of reliable evidence, the idea that evidence must be consistently found in repeated studies in order to be confirmed. A third rule of science is the principle of public evidence, the idea that evidence must be accessible to other people so that it can be checked. Sound scientific evidence conforms to these three rules. One way to obtain sound evidence is to conduct an experiment, a type of controlled observation in which the researcher manipulates one thing and then observes the consequences.

Research in Psychology

The scientific method has been applied to the study of human behavior for about a hundred years.   Many facts, principles, and theories about behavior have developed from research in psychology.   The kind of research that is done is classified into one of several different areas, depending upon both the method used in the research and the subject being studied.

Developmental Psychology

The study of the changes in behavior and ability that occur as people age is called **developmental psychology.**   Theorists have attempted to identify the important stages of development of the child, from birth to adulthood.   A **stage** is a period of growth, a step toward greater maturity.   The development of language, thinking abilities, motor coordination, moral beliefs, and sexual identity has been an important research area in developmental psychology.   In this book, some general principles of developmental psychology are presented in Part IV.

Jerome Kagan, a researcher in developmental psychology at Harvard University, has studied the perception and attention of infants; he has shown that important changes occur in the mind of a child between the ages of nine and twelve months.   Kagan's dedication to scientific research was highly influenced by his mother:

My mother viewed knowledge as a sacrament and must have reminded me hundreds of times that her father, whom I had never known and to whom she felt strong affection, died quietly in a stuffed living-room chair with an open book on his chest.   This image, which never had the opportunity to become tarnished, exerted its strong influence years later when I began to brood about a vocation.[11]

Kagan eventually decided to study psychology and to specialize in the study of children.

Personality and Clinical Psychology

Your **personality** is your typical way of behaving and relating to others. Research on personality attempts to identify the important ways in which people are psychologically different and to relate these differences to significant aspects of behavior and experience. For example, how can personality best be described—in terms of different types of people, different ways in which people differ, or different interactions between people and situations in the world? Research in **clinical psychology** examines the causes of personality disorders and the relative effectiveness of various types of treatment, or **therapy,** for these disorders. Clinical research also attempts to discover ways to promote self-development and personal growth.

A prominent modern researcher in clinical psychology is Carl Rogers. Rogers is a practicing therapist, a theorist, and an investigator in the techniques of psychotherapy. He originated a method of psychotherapy called nondirective or **client-centered therapy.** This is a form of therapy in which the therapist establishes a close and open relationship in which the clients can explore their own feelings safely. Rogers explains some of the things he has learned in the course of his study:

I would like to take you inside, to tell you some of the things I have learned from the thousands of hours spent working intimately with individuals in personal distress.

In my relationship with persons I have found that it does not help, in the long run, to act as though I were something that I am not.

I have found it highly rewarding when I can accept another person.

The more I am open to the realities in me and in the other person, the less do I find myself wishing to rush in to "fix" things.[12]

Rogers's approach to personality and psychotherapy will also be discussed in Chapter 21 of this book.

Social Psychology

Research in **social psychology** investigates how individual behavior is influenced by the groups to which individuals belong. The effects of group pressure on an individual's beliefs and actions, the way social attitudes are formed and changed, the basis for interpersonal liking or attraction, the effects of different types of leadership on small groups, and the causes and cures of intergroup prejudice—these are some of the important research problems investigated by social psychologists. Many of these topics are discussed in Part VIII of this book.

Stanley Milgram is a social psychologist who has studied the psychological basis for obedience to authority. At first Milgram believed that the people who blindly obeyed the Nazi authorities during Hitler's control of Germany were different from other people. To find out for sure, he devised a study in which participants were instructed to press a lever which, they believed, would cause a dangerous electric shock to be delivered to another person. Most participants obeyed. The details of this experiment are discussed in Chapter 22.

Educational Psychology

Research on the psychology of classroom teaching and learning is called **educational psychology.** Types of teaching, methods of organizing and presenting material, ways of improving special skills such as reading, and methods for evaluating the results of instruction have been important research areas. Educational psychologists ask questions: Is television instruction as effective as traditional "live" teaching? Are discussion groups superior to large lecture classes? Are rewards and punishments effective in the classroom? What is the most effective way to teach a retarded child to read?

A psychologist who is a theorist and researcher in educational psychology (in addition to other areas) is Jerome Bruner. Bruner's studies of the development of children's minds led him to propose an approach to teaching that is called the **discovery method**. Children who are taught by the discovery method of teaching are led to discover important principles themselves rather than to receive them passively from the teacher. Chapter 5 applies principles of educational psychology to academic learning.

Experimental Psychology

Experimental psychology is a broad area of research that is defined by its unique method of investigation,

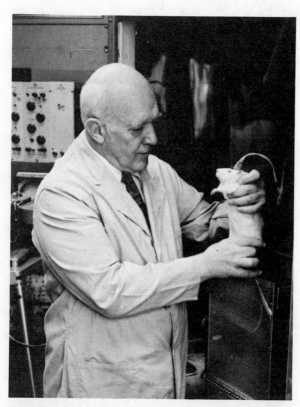

Experimental psychologists, like Neal Miller in the photo above, conduct experiments in order to expand the body of knowledge that is the science of psychology. Some of Miller's experiments have involved investigating how rats can be taught to control such "involuntary" bodily processes as heart rate. (Ingbert Grüttner for Rockefeller University Press)

the experiment. In an experiment researchers manipulate what they are studying and then observe the effects of their manipulation. Experimental psychologists studying perception may place participants in a specially constructed soundproof room and then, in different trials, present very quiet tones to them in order to determine the lower limits of human hearing. The experimenter is controlling the physical environment of the participant and is observing the effects. Experimental psychologists studying learning may vary the time allowed for rehearsal of a passage to be learned; they then measure the amount of learning that takes place. Perception and learning are discussed in Part II and in Chapter 7. The psychology experiment is discussed in detail in the Appendix.

Neal Miller is an experimental psychologist who has studied learning for many years. While most of Miller's work involves studies of the rat, he believes that the same learning principles that apply to rats also apply to human beings. In his recent experiments he has studied how rats can be taught to control their heart rate, blood pressure, and other supposedly involuntary bodily reactions. Some progress has been made in applying his discoveries to human problems of high blood pressure and heart irregularities.

Physiological Psychology

Physiological psychology is the study of how bodily processes relate to behavior. Some of the most important contributions to scientific knowledge made by psychologists in recent years have been made by researchers studying the brain and its direction and control of behavior. It is known that body chemistry affects behavior (consider what happens when drugs change body chemistry) and that brain structures affect behavior (consider what happens to behavior when the brain is damaged). Studies of these effects now form an important body of knowledge in psychology. Physiological psychology is discussed in Chapter 6.

Interim Summary

Research in psychology is conducted in many areas of study. Developmental psychology involves the study of changes in behavior and ability that occur with increasing age. Research in personality and clinical psychology involves studying individual differences in behavior and experience and ways to promote personal growth. Social psychology is concerned with how individual behavior is influenced by groups. Educational psychology involves studying classroom learning and teaching. Experimental psychology involves studying behavior by means of the psychology experiment. Physiological psychology involves studying how bodily processes relate to behavior.

Summary

1. The art of psychology is involved when a psychologist has an intuition that leads to a testable idea about human behavior. The science of psychology is involved when the psychologist tests this idea using the scientific method.

2. One source of bias in observations is the halo effect, the tendency to judge people positively in all respects because you judge them positively in one respect.

3. A second source of bias in observations is expectancy. Because to some degree you see what you expect to see, your prior prejudices affect your observations. The tendency for your expectations to come true is called the self-fulfilling prophecy.

4. A third source of bias in observations is selective attention, the fact that you can attend to and perceive only a small part of the world around you.

5. One aspect of the special psychological perspective is its focus on behavior. Another aspect of this perspective is the psychological way of thinking that involves analysis, precision, and measurement in the study and understanding of behavior.

6. Questions that are of value to science must be both significant and answerable. Only empirical questions are answerable by the scientific method. Value questions must be answered by reference to a value judgment based on beliefs or opinions.

7. A sensitive understanding, based on long experience and careful observation, forms the basis of the art of psychology. Case studies require a great deal of this sensitivity.

8. The scientific method consists of a set of rules for testing and observing the world and deciding what is probably true and what is probably false.

9. One rule of science is the principle of empirical verification, the idea that scientific claims should be regarded as true only if they conform to the facts of experience. A second rule of science is the principle of reliable evidence, the idea that confidence should be placed only in evidence that has been repeatedly observed and that has been confirmed by different studies, all finding about the same result. A third rule of science is the principle of public evidence, the idea that evidence must be available to others so that they can check it.

10. The experiment is a scientific method aimed at testing whether one variable influences a second variable; in an experiment, scientists not only observe what happens but also partially control what happens.

11. In an experiment, members of one group (the experimental group) are given some special treatment causing them to experience an experimental condition. A second group (the control group) does not receive this special treatment. Later, the behavior of the two groups is compared in order to determine whether the special treatment caused a behavior change.

12. Developmental psychology, personality and clinical psychology, social psychology, educational psychology, experimental psychology, and physiological psychology are common areas of research in psychology.

Key Concepts

halo effect   The tendency of people who have been judged positively in one respect to be judged positively in other respects; for example, the tendency for attractive people to be judged as honest.

self-fulfilling prophecy   The tendency for your expectations to come true.

principle of selective attention   The rule that you are able to attend to only a small portion of the information available in the world.

behavior   Activities; things that are done, including actions, memories, thoughts, attitudes, perceptions, language, feelings, and so on.

analysis   The act of separating something into its component parts.

precision   Accuracy; being exact and specific.

measurement   Assigning a number to behavior on the basis of a rule (for example, by using an IQ test).

fact   Information based on observation; a statement based on careful observation or experience.

empirical question   A question that can be answered by observation.

value question   A question that must be answered by preference, opinion, or belief; it cannot be answered by observation.

value judgment   A conclusion based on values or beliefs.

case study   An intensive study of one person.

Thematic Apperception Test (TAT)   A personality test that involves making up stories about pictures.

Minnesota Multiphasic Personality Inventory (MMPI)   A general personality inventory consisting of hundreds of questions; it is designed to test for a variety of abnormal personality traits.

intuition   The ability to come to a conclusion without having direct evidence.

science   A method of acquiring knowledge; also, the body of knowledge acquired by that method.

scientific method   A method for acquiring knowledge based on the rules of science; questions are answered by seeking facts from observations.

principle of empirical verification   The rule of science that a scientific claim should be regarded as true only if it agrees with experience or observation.

principle of reliable evidence   The rule of science that no claim should be accepted as true without consistent evidence, evidence that is repeatable.

principle of public evidence   The rule of science that no claim should be accepted as true without evidence that is accessible to many people and thus can be checked by more than one person.

causation   The degree to which one variable produces, influences, or modifies the other; a cause-and-effect relationship.

experiment   A form of controlled observation in which the researcher manipulates one thing and then observes the consequence.

experimental group   In an experiment, the group receiving the special treatment.

control group   In an experiment, the group receiving no special treatment; the comparison group.

developmental psychology   The study of the changes in behavior and ability that occur as people age.

stage   A period of growth in which behavior can be distinguished from that of other periods.

personality   An individual's typical way of relating to people and reacting to the world.

clinical psychology   The study of the causes of personality disorders and the effectiveness of different types of treatment.

therapy   The treatment of psychological problems and disorders.

client-centered therapy   A form of therapy based on close and open relationships between therapist and client; developed by Carl Rogers.

social psychology   The study of how individual behavior is affected by groups.

educational psychology   The study of teaching and school learning.

discovery method   A method of teaching that encourages students to discover important principles on their own.

experimental psychology   The study of behavior through the use of experiments.

physiological psychology   The study of how bodily processes, such as the activity of the brain, relate to behavior.

Part II

Learning and Memory

Chapter 3

Conditioning and Learning

Key Questions
1. What is the difference between learned and unlearned behavior?
2. How can learning a skill or learning from a book be made easier?
3. What is classical conditioning?
4. What is operant conditioning?
5. How can conditioning be used to manage a person's behavior?

You are learning as you read this book. And reading this book is something you learned how to do. Most of what you do, or could do, are things you learned how to do; but some things are *innate*—you could do them from birth or as soon after as your body was able. You did not know how to read when you were born—you had to learn how to read. But you have always known how to sneeze because your ability to sneeze is innate, not learned. This chapter will discuss what psychologists mean by the word *learning*.

What Is Learning?

Most of your intellectual abilities, your feelings about things, and your skills have been learned. You learned how to read; you learned to fear spiders; and you learned how to ride a bike. Learning is necessary for all these activities. What is learning? Psychologists define **learning** as a change in behavior or behavior potential as a result of experience.

Unlearned Behavior

The word *change* is important in the definition of learning. Some of human behavior, and much of animal behavior, does not change with time and experience; it is therefore not learned behavior. For example, certain complex behaviors called **instincts** are present at birth in some animals. The songs and nest-building of many birds are the result not of learning but of inborn instinctual behavior patterns.

Simpler, more specific inborn reactions are called **reflexes.** Reflexes are involuntary reactions to specific stimulation. If you tickle a dog on the right spot on its side, its back legs will move in a scratching mo-

tion. This is a reflex. You can demonstrate one of your own reflexes. Remain seated in your chair and cross your legs so that your right leg rests on top of your left leg and can swing freely. With the edge of your hand tap your right leg directly below your knee-cap. If you miss the right spot, nothing will happen; but if you hit your leg just right, the result will be a reflex knee jerk.

You have a variety of other highly specific built-in reactions. The hair on your forearm stands up when you are chilled ("goosebumps"); your eye blinks when an object comes too close or a loud noise occurs; your hand pulls back rapidly when it is burned; you sneeze when you have dust or pepper in your nose; you salivate when you put food in your mouth. You do not have to think about these reactions—they are involuntary. Anything that is sensed or that produces a reaction is called a **stimulus.** Any kind of behavior or reaction that results from a stimulus is called a **response.** In the case of a reflex, the event producing the reflex is called the *stimulus* (e.g., pepper), and the reaction is called the *response* (for example, a sneeze). Reflexes are inborn; they do not develop as a result of experience and are therefore not learned. You do not have to learn how to sneeze.

Learning is a change in behavior as a result of experience.   Many kinds of behaviors are not considered learned.   For example, re-flexes—such as the sneezing reaction to pepper or, as in the picture above, the response to a sour pickle—are involuntary inborn reac-tions.   (Margaret Thompson)

In order for learning to occur, behavior must change *as a result of experience.*   Certain kinds of be-haviors change, not as a result of experience in the world, but for other reasons.   For example, drugs and disease change behavior; but these changes are not termed "learning," because the changes are not caused by experience.   Another important type of behavior change occurs as a result of **maturation,** the physical growth and development of the body.   As your body develops and matures, you are able to do more and more things.   Changes due to maturation are not called "learning," because these changes are not caused by experience.

Most infants are able to sit without support by eight months but not by four months; most are able to crawl by ten months but not by five months; most are able to walk alone by fifteen months but not by ten months.[1,2]   These changes in behavior are made pos-sible by the development and increasing maturation of muscles, bones, and nerves in the infant's body.   The rate of this development and maturation seems little affected by experience.   Babies do not learn how to walk and do not need to practice in order to walk well.   In some cultures, infants spend most of their early life completely restricted, yet this does not slow down their motor development.   They are able to walk at the same age as other children.[3,4]   The ability to walk depends upon the maturation of muscles and nerves, not upon learning.

Learning and Experience

Learning is a change in behavior or behavior potential that results from *experience.*   Simple reflexes and in-stincts are not learned behavior, and changes due to maturation and development are not considered learn-ing.   Learning results from experience.   Reading this book is a kind of experience, and from it you are learning about psychology.   Your knowledge of the English language was learned from experience.   Your habits and skills were learned from experience.   From the pattern of experiences in your life, you have learned your beliefs, attitudes, and to some extent your personality.   You have learned to be human.

The behavior that is learned from experience can be simple or complex; you can learn to do something, or you can learn not to do something.   Sometimes what is learned is demonstrated right away in behav-ior, and sometimes it is stored away but never used.   In any case, if changes in behavior are the consequence of experience, then learning has occurred.

When learning occurs, what is it that is learned?   Some learning involves learning simple reactions. For example, your mouth learns to anticipate the candy with the flow of saliva juices. This kind of learning by association is seen in primitive animals as well as humans. Some learning consists of learning the consequences of different actions. Both animals and humans learn which actions are followed by favorable consequences and which by unfavorable consequences. These two types of simple learning are called **conditioning**. Studies of conditioning are concerned with how simple habits and emotional reac-

tions are acquired and modified. Some psychologists believe that these two types of simple learning—by association and by consequences—are the only kinds of learning possible. Most psychologists, however, believe that human learning is generally more complex and consists primarily of knowledge about ourselves, other people, and the world. This kind of learning cannot be reduced to simple behavioral reactions. The next section will discuss various types of human learning.

Interim Summary Instincts and reflexes are inborn reactions, do not develop from experience, and are therefore not learned. Changes in behavior due to the physical maturation of the body are also not a result of learning. Learning is a change in behavior as a result of experience. Learning can be simple or complex; your habits, emotional reactions, and knowledge are the result of learning.

Learning as Knowing

You know many things about yourself and the world. Some of this learning came from school and books, some from your parents and friends, and some from your other life experiences. Much of what you initially learned you have since forgotten; and, perhaps, some of what you now know you would like to forget. Sometimes you learned by rote, memorizing lists of words or numbers that made little sense at the time. For example, your initial learning of the multiplication table was rote learning. Most learning, however, involves meaningful relationships; it is organized or structured. Meaningful learning involves acquiring sets of organized ideas, plans, facts, and skills.

Learning an organized or structured set of ideas is far easier than learning an unrelated list of ideas. In addition, unrelated details are easily forgotten, while those that are part of a structure of ideas are more likely to be remembered.

Book Learning

Books are not lists of random words; they are organized or structured. Much of human learning involves written or spoken words, but in the animal world few species have any ability to understand symbolic language. Chimpanzees have recently been taught a form of human sign language used by the deaf,[5] but the tremendous efficiency of learning information from books remains beyond the capacity of any organisms but ourselves.

Learning verbal material is affected by other material learned either before or after the material in question. Your ability to remember a particular passage, for example this one, may be blocked by material read on the preceding page and on the following page. Learning verbal material is also affected by the meaningfulness of the material. In general, the more meaningful the material, the better it is learned. In order for an idea to be meaningful, it must be easily related to what you already know. How verbal material is organized also affects the learning process. Apparently human memory is best suited to remember material that is organized or structured into meaningful clusters, rather than material that is relatively unrelated. Thus, learning material from books is made easier when the material is meaningful and organized, and is hindered by interference from other learned material.

Social Learning

How did you learn to dance and to sing? Chances are, you learned how to do these things from social learning, by carefully observing and listening to other people. A person who is observed and copied is a **model.**

Much of human behavior is learned socially, through observing and imitating models. There are three types of models: real-life, symbolic, and representational. *Real-life models* are parents and teachers, for example, whose behavior is copied by children. Mod-

Observing and imitating models is an important part of human learning. Three types of models are the real-life model, such as the adult imitated by the child; the symbolic model, such as the person described in a book; and the representational model, such as the television personality "Captain Kangaroo." (Alice Kandell/ Photo Researchers, Inc.; Arthur Furst; and Wide World Photos)

els presented to us through symbolic language, such as the heroes of novels, are classified as *symbolic models.* Models presented through television and films are classified as *representational models.*[6] Observing and imitating models can teach not only what to do but also what not to do. A child who sees an adult receive a painful shock from touching an electric wire will learn not to touch the wire. Observing models can also teach when to do something, that is, the appropriate time for behaving in a particular manner. A boy may learn to yell at football games but not at weddings by observing and imitating his father.

Social learning occurs in all cultures. Among the Canadian Ojibwa Indians, a young boy may follow his father as he traps, hunts, and fishes. The earliest learning is solely by observation, not by teaching or explanation. The boy's father is a real-life model that the child watches and imitates.

Skill Learning

An important consideration involved in learning a skill is the method of practice. For example, should you practice the whole act every time, or should you practice a part of the act until you achieve competency with it, then practice another part? This question has been identified as the **whole-part issue,** and the answer depends upon the structure of the skill to be learned.

The method of practice (whole or part) should reflect whether the skill is organized as a whole or as separate parts. Research on this issue shows that when a skilled act is made up of a group of relatively independent parts, then practicing the several parts of the skill separately works better; but when the skilled act involves a highly integrated group of parts, ones that are highly interdependent, then it is better to practice the whole act. For example, the serve in the game of tennis is relatively independent from the other parts of the game and can effectively be practiced separately (part-practice); but the various movements that make up the serve are highly interdependent—

they form an integrated act—and should be practiced together (whole-practice).

Another important issue in learning a skill is the question of when practice should occur. Should your practice occur all together in one long session (cramming or *massed practice*), or should your practice periods be interrupted by rest periods (*spaced practice*)? The evidence on this question —the **massed-spaced issue**—shows that concentrated or massed practice does not work as well as spaced practice for most skills.

Recent studies show that certain skills can be practiced effectively just by thinking about them; mental or imaginary practice improves performance. Studies show dramatic improvement following the imaginary practice of perceptual-motor skills.[7] Can you imagine yourself shooting baskets in a game of basketball, or serving a ball in tennis, or throwing a dart? Once you know what to do and have tried it a few times, you can practice in your imagination and get better and better.

Learning to Learn

Most human learning is not the result of a single learning situation; a typical learning problem has been preceded by many other similar problems. Because problems are similar, there is usually some transfer of learning from one learning problem to another. If you know two foreign languages, you may find that learning your third foreign language is easier than learning your first or second; you may have learned *how to learn* a foreign language. If you learn several new dance steps, you may find that learning the fifth dance is easier than learning the first; you may have learned *how to learn* dancing. Learning how to learn a particular kind of problem provides you with a **learning set.**[8]

If you didn't develop learning sets, you would approach each new problem as if it were entirely new and unrelated to other problems you have successfully solved in the past. Your ability to develop learning sets means that you can adjust to new situations rapidly by taking advantage of similar situations in the past. You gain learning efficiency by taking advantage of the transfer of learning from one situation to the next. You develop general learning strategies.

The development of transfer and learning sets is more likely when the material to be learned is organized and structured. As the psychologist Jerome Bruner wrote,

The teaching and learning of structure, rather than simply the mystery of facts and techniques, is at the center of the classic problem of transfer. . . . If earlier learning is to render later learning easier, it must do so by providing a general picture in terms of which the relations between things encountered earlier and later are made as clear as possible.[9]

Psychologists have shown that learning sets are not unique to human beings. Other animals can also learn how to learn. Learning sets have been demonstrated in persons of all ages,[10] in monkeys,[8] in cats,[11] and even in rats.[12] We will discuss some examples of these in the remainder of this chapter.

Interim Summary	Meaningful human learning involves acquiring or modifying sets of organized ideas and skills. Learning is made easier when the material to be learned is organized or structured. Social learning occurs by observing models (other people) and imitating them. The best method of learning a skill involves a method of practice that reflects whether the skill is organized as a whole or as separate parts. There is usually some transfer of learning from one situation to another; with experience, you develop learning sets that make future learning easier.

Classical Conditioning

Virginia was involved in a serious accident—in a compact car—but fortunately escaped with only minor injuries. For several weeks thereafter, however, she found herself unable to ride in any car. Whenever she got into a car, she would feel extremely anxious; her limbs would tremble and her heart would race. The stimulus of cars and the response of fear had become associated through *conditioning,* so that the sight of a car gained the power to produce fear.

Steven, an alcoholic, was treated with a drug called Antabuse, which has a highly specific effect: any alcohol, even a small drink, causes severe nausea and vomiting. After several experiences of drinking and vomiting, Steven found that even thinking about taking a drink would make him slightly ill. When he went off the drug and tried to take a drink of whiskey, he became nauseated and vomited. The stimulus of whiskey and the response of nausea had become associated through *conditioning,* so that whiskey gained the power to cause nausea.

Ivan Pavlov

Ivan Pavlov, a Russian psychologist born in 1849, was the first to investigate conditioning by association, or **classical conditioning.** Pavlov, the son of a Russian priest, spent his entire life studying the physiology and psychology of the digestive system. He was fanatically dedicated to pure science and in 1904 won the Nobel Prize for his physiological discoveries.

Pavlov's Laboratory • What kind of a man was Pavlov? He was so dedicated to his work that there

Ivan Pavlov

was little room in his life for anything else. Only one thing really mattered—his research.

After one taste of research all the practical issues—his position, salary, living conditions, even the clothes he wore—became little more than unavoidable annoyances intruding upon the only part of life that really mattered. . . . Only unwavering faith enabled his wife and friends to put up with him. His complete inability to manage his financial affairs was not his only peculiarity: he was equally difficult in other matters. For example, he liked to take long walks with his wife, but he set such a strenuous pace that she often had to run to keep up. . . . During the [Russian] revolution he scolded one of his assistants for arriving ten minutes late for an experiment; shooting and fighting in the streets should not interfere when there was work to be done in the laboratory.[13]

Pavlov was concerned only with the physiology of the body and with observable behavior. There was no room in Pavlov's laboratory for such expressions as "consciousness" or "mind." If Pavlov's assistants mistakenly used one of these expressions, they were promptly fined. The "errors" added up to a comfortable petty-cash fund.

Pavlov and His Dogs • Pavlov's interest in digestion led him to study the salivary response in dogs—that is, how a dog's mouth waters when the dog eats food. One day, when studying how a dog salivates, Pavlov made an important psychological discovery, and he spent the next thirty years investigating it. Pavlov noticed that the dog began to salivate *before* it was fed, whenever it heard someone approaching with food.[14]

Just as your mouth begins to water before you bite into an apple, dogs learn to salivate in anticipation of food. This kind of automatic involuntary reaction Pavlov called a *reflex*. Salivating to the sound of footsteps signaling that food is coming is a *learned*, or *conditioned*, reflex. If a bell repeatedly accompanies a dog's feeding, the dog will salivate whenever it hears the bell. Pavlov established a new response in his dogs by pairing a bell with the presentation of meat powder. The bell and the presentation of meat powder in the mouth occurred at the same time. Following repeated pairings of meat powder and bell, the bell eventually acquired the power to produce salivation by itself. Thus, a new response—salivating to a bell—was learned. Whenever Pavlov rang a bell, his dogs began to salivate. (See Figure 3-1.)

The Law of Contiguity

In classical conditioning a connection is established between a stimulus and a response, in which the stimulus acquires the power to produce the response. In order for this stimulus-response connection to be made, they must occur at nearly the same time; that is, they must be *contiguous* (close together) in time. Classical conditioning is based on the **Law of Contiguity**: under certain circumstances, a stimulus that occurs at about the same time as a response will acquire the power to produce that response.

This law can be applied to the following everyday example of classical conditioning. Your saliva juices may flow when you see pictures of certain kinds

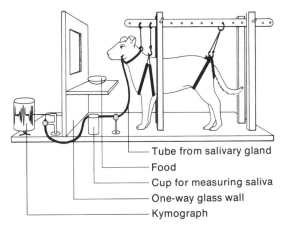

- Tube from salivary gland
- Food
- Cup for measuring saliva
- One-way glass wall
- Kymograph

Figure 3-1 Pavlov's Study of Classical Conditioning.
In this famous pioneering experiment, a dog was restrained in a harness. The dog's salivary response was measured by running a tube from the salivary gland to a cup and a kymograph, a recording device. On a number of trials, a bell was rung and food presented. Eventually, the dog was conditioned to salivate when it heard the bell.

of food, such as a slice of orange or lemon. In the past on many occasions, the sight of an orange slice has been closely followed by the experience of putting the orange into your mouth and chewing it. The presence of food in your mouth is a stimulus that elicits an automatic-reflex response of salivation. Thus, the sight of an orange slice (stimulus) and salivation (response) have occurred together repeatedly in the past. Because of the Law of Contiguity, the response of salivating has become classically conditioned to the sight of oranges so that now the sight alone is sufficient to produce salivation.

In this example, salivating to food in the mouth is an automatic reflex and is termed the **unconditioned response (UCR)**. Salivating at the sight of food is a learned response and is termed the **conditioned response (CR)**. The food in the mouth that causes the reflex response of salivation is termed the **unconditioned stimulus (UCS)**. The sight of food, which—after learning—acquires the power to produce salivation, is termed the **conditioned stimulus (CS)**. The procedure of classical conditioning con-

sists of pairing the CS (the sight of food) with the UCS (food in the mouth) so that they both occur at about the same time and both slightly precede the UCR (the response of salivating to the food in the mouth). With this procedure a connection is established, and the CS (the sight of food) eventually produces the CR (salivation).

The Components and the Procedure

The unconditioned stimulus (UCS) is something that consistently elicits a response before conditioning takes place. In Pavlov's famous experiments with his dogs, the unconditioned stimulus was meat powder in the mouth. The meat powder consistently caused the dogs to salivate, an inborn reaction requiring no prior learning. The unconditioned response (UCR) in classical conditioning is the reaction to the unconditioned stimulus. In Pavlov's experiments, the unconditioned response was the salivation to the meat powder. Other examples of unconditioned stimuli and their associated unconditioned responses are:

Unconditioned Stimulus	Unconditioned Response
1. lemon juice or other sour liquid	salivation
2. air puff to the eye	eye blink
3. tap below kneecap	knee jerk
4. sudden loud noise	startle reaction
5. electric shock	pain and emotional reactions

The conditioned stimulus (CS) is a neutral stimulus that, before conditioning, does not elicit a consistent response. Essentially anything can serve as a conditioned stimulus in the classical conditioning procedure. In one of Pavlov's experiments, the conditioned stimulus was a bell. Before conditioning took place, the bell did not cause the dogs to salivate; after conditioning, however, the bell consistently elicited salivation. The conditioned response (CR) is a response given to the conditioned stimulus after conditioning occurs. In Pavlov's experiment, the conditioned response was salivating to the bell. After the classical conditioning procedure had paired the food powder and the bell, the dogs were conditioned to salivate to the bell (they acquired the conditioned response of salivating to the bell).

The procedures used to establish a classically conditioned response involve repeatedly pairing the unconditioned stimulus with the conditioned stimulus. The relationship among the components of classical conditioning is shown in the following diagram as it exists before conditioning, during the conditioning procedure, and after conditioning has been completed:

Before conditioning:

$$[UCS] \longrightarrow [UCR]$$

$$[CS] \longrightarrow [No regular reaction]$$

During conditioning:

$$[CS plus UCS] \longrightarrow [UCR]$$

After conditioning:

$$[CS] \longrightarrow [CR]$$

Recall the case of Virginia discussed at the beginning of the chapter. Virginia was involved in an accident in a small car and afterward responded to cars with anxiety. Virginia had been classically conditioned by her experience to fear cars. Her experience could be explained in the following way:

Before conditioning:

$$[Hit by a truck (UCS)] \longrightarrow [Anxiety (UCR)]$$

$$[Sitting in a car (CS)] \longrightarrow [No regular reaction]$$

During conditioning:

$$[Sitting in a car (CS) + Being hit by a truck (UCS)]$$
$$\longrightarrow [Anxiety (UCR)]$$

After conditioning:

$$[Sitting in a car (CS)] \longrightarrow [Anxiety (CR)]$$

Generalization and Discrimination

Once a response has been classically conditioned to a particular stimulus, it may also be produced by other similar stimuli. This effect is called **stimulus generalization.** For example, if you were conditioned to salivate at the sight of an orange, you might also salivate at the sight of a tangerine or even at the sight of an orange balloon. Stimulus generalization occurred for Virginia, who was conditioned to fear a car; her fear response generalized to cars unlike those in which she had her accident.

If stimulus generalization had not occurred, Virginia might feel afraid only in small compact cars like the one she was in during her accident; the response would be elicited selectively, only by certain kinds of cars. This process of selective responding is termed **discrimination.** Discrimination is the opposite of generalization. Discrimination is the process of not responding to stimuli other than the conditioned stimulus. Discrimination can be taught by controlling the classical conditioning procedure. A dog can be trained to salivate to a bell and not to salivate to a buzzer by repeatedly pairing the bell—but not the buzzer—with food powder in the mouth. If one stimulus is paired with the UCS and a second, similar stimulus is not, the first will eventually elicit a conditioned response and the second will not. This is shown in the following:

Before conditioning:

$$[Food powder (UCS)] \longrightarrow [Salivation (UCR)]$$

$$[Bell (CS-1)] \longrightarrow [No regular response]$$

$$[Buzzer (CS-2)] \longrightarrow [No regular response]$$

During conditioning with discrimination training:

$$[Bell (CS-1) + Food Powder (UCS)]$$
$$\longrightarrow [salivation(UCR)]$$

$$[Buzzer (CS-2) presented alone (No food powder)]$$
$$\longrightarrow [No regular response]$$

After discrimination training:

[Bell (CS-1)] $\longrightarrow$ [Salivation (CR)]

[Buzzer (CS-2)] $\longrightarrow$ [No regular response]

Extinction

After a conditioned response has been acquired, how can it be eliminated? After a dog has been conditioned to salivate to a bell, will it go on salivating whenever it hears a bell for the rest of its life?

It is possible to eliminate conditioned responses through a procedure called **extinction.** Extinction is the procedure of repeatedly presenting the conditioned stimulus alone, without the unconditioned stimulus. The result of this procedure is that the conditioned response becomes weaker and weaker, until finally it does not occur at all. The result of the procedure—the elimination of the conditioned response—is also called **extinction.** Thus, the elimination, or extinction, of the response is brought about by following a procedure called extinction.

After a dog has been conditioned to salivate to a bell, if the bell is repeatedly presented without the food powder, the power of the bell to elicit salivation will become weaker and weaker; finally, the bell will cause no salivation at all. The extinction of the conditioned response will have occurred.

Virginia's fear of small cars will eventually weaken and disappear if she continues to see small cars and occasionally sits in them without experiencing further frightening accidents. In this case, the small car (the CS) will be repeatedly presented to Virginia but without the accident (the UCS); this extinction procedure will result in the extinction of her anxiety (CR).

Albert's Problem

Albert was an unusually fearless baby before John Watson decided to use him in his psychology experi-

ment. Watson chose Albert for this experiment on the origins of fear because he appeared to be "stolid and unemotional" and hardly ever cried. When Albert was about one year old, Watson decided to find out whether he could teach Albert to be afraid.

Watson first tested Albert to find out what would make Albert cry. He confronted him suddenly with a white rat, but Albert showed no fear. He presented him with a monkey, a rabbit, a mask, burning newspapers, but Albert showed no fear. But when, unexpectedly, a loud noise was made behind his head, Albert broke into a sudden crying fit. Watson had found the stimulus he needed for his conditioning experiment.

In order to prove that Albert could learn to fear something, Watson had to find something that Albert at first did not fear and then teach him to fear it. Watson chose a white rat because he knew that Albert was not afraid of rats. Watson walked close to Albert, reached into a basket, and suddenly pulled out a large white rat. As Albert smiled and reached for it with his left hand, Watson's assistant suddenly made a loud noise directly behind Albert's head by striking a hammer against a piece of metal. Albert jumped violently and slumped forward, covering his face. The rat and the loud noise were presented to Albert five more times. On the sixth trial the rat was presented alone, without the noise; the instant the rat was shown, Albert began to cry and to turn away.[16] Albert had learned to fear rats.

The procedure Watson used was classical conditioning. The loud noise was an unconditioned stimulus, and the fear reaction to the noise was an unconditioned response. The white rat was the conditioned stimulus, and the fear reaction to the rat was a conditioned response. By repeatedly pairing the CS and the UCS, the CS acquired the power to elicit the CR.

You may be wondering about the ethics of this kind of research with children. This experiment was done more than fifty years ago and would not be consistent with the ethical standards of modern researchers in psychology.

Interim Summary   Classical conditioning is based on the Law of Contiguity: under certain circumstances, a stimulus that repeatedly occurs at about the same time as a response will acquire the power to produce that response.   In the case of Pavlov's dogs, the stimulus was a bell, the response was salivation, and the dogs were conditioned to salivate to the bell.   The following are major concepts in classical conditioning:

1. Unconditioned stimulus—a stimulus that automatically causes a response (for example, food powder in the mouth).
2. Unconditioned response—a response to the unconditioned stimulus (for example, salivating to food powder).
3. Conditioned stimulus—the initially neutral stimulus that is paired with the unconditioned stimulus (for example, a bell).
4. Conditioned response—the learned reaction to the conditioned stimulus (for example, learning to salivate to the bell).
5. Stimulus generalization—a conditioned response to stimuli similar to the conditioned stimulus.
6. Discrimination—responding to certain stimuli but not to others.
7. Extinction—the disappearance of the conditioned response brought about in classical conditioning by presenting the conditioned stimulus without the unconditioned stimulus.

Operant Conditioning

A dog is told to "sit," is encouraged to sit by pressing down on its hindquarters, and then is fed a dog biscuit.   After a few such trials, when the dog is told to sit, it sits.   By rewarding it with grain, a chicken is taught to dance when music is played.   When any behavior is rewarded, it tends to be repeated.   This kind of conditioning by consequences is called **operant conditioning,** or **instrumental conditioning.**

An infant is lying in its crib making babbling noises, and its mother is working nearby.   By chance, the infant babbles "ma-ma, ma-ma"; smiling, the mother picks the baby up and snuggles it.   The baby receives attention and affection as a consequence of babbling in a particular way; such rewards make it likely that "ma-ma" will be said more often in the future.   The response of saying "ma-ma" in the pres-

ence of its mother will be learned through *operant conditioning.*

The key to operant conditioning is controlling the consequences of behavior.   When behavior has favorable consequences, it tends to be repeated.   When behavior has unfavorable consequences, it tends to be abandoned.   Therefore, by controlling the consequences of behavior, the behavior itself can be controlled.

B. F. Skinner

One of the most influential figures in modern psychology is B. F. Skinner, a man who has devoted his life to the study of operant conditioning.   One of Skinner's early contributions was the invention of a special box for studying animal learning (the **Skinner box;** see

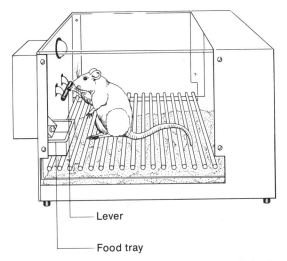

Lever

Food tray

Figure 3-2 Skinner's Study of Operant Conditioning. *In this experiment, a rat was placed in a special cage that has come to be called a* Skinner box. *If the rat pressed a lever, a mechanism automatically delivered a small pellet of food as a reward. The Skinner box has since been used in thousands of studies examining the relationship between responses and their consequences.*

Figure 3-2). When a rat, pigeon, or other small animal is placed in this box and it pushes a lever, a mechanism delivers a small pellet of food to the animal. The Skinner box automatically rewards the animal for pressing the lever; lever pressing is learned through operant conditioning. The Skinner box makes it possible for psychologists to study the effects of various kinds of rewards and reward schedules on the behavior of animals. For example, it has been learned that responses rewarded occasionally but not consistently do not weaken easily. They become very persistent habits.

Superstitious Pigeons • Pigeons have been used extensively in operant-conditioning studies. A pigeon can be put into a Skinner box and taught to peck at a small disk or key in order to receive a reward of grain. In the normal procedure, the pigeon works for its reward by pecking at the key in the box; the reward is not given unless the pigeon pecks at the key.

Skinner wondered what pigeons would do if they were reinforced with grain no matter what they did. Several pigeons were put into Skinner boxes and rewarded every fifteen seconds with a tidbit of grain; the delivery of the grain was not dependent upon what any bird was doing. In effect, these birds were put on welfare; they did not have to work in order to be fed. After some time had passed, Skinner looked into the boxes to see what the birds were doing. He found that each bird was performing some highly patterned act. One bird was turning counterclockwise around the cage, making two or three turns between each feeding; another was repeatedly thrusting its head into the far upper corners of the cage; a third was rocking with a pendulum motion; another bird developed a kind of rhythmic dance. Skinner described the behavior as *superstitious.*[16]

The birds seemed to be repeating what they were doing when they received their reward of grain. Their responses were irrelevant, but they had been conditioned by the reward. The rewards actually appeared by chance and had nothing to do with what the pigeons did.

Human behavior is also sometimes superstitious. Whenever the connection between human activity and significant rewards is uncertain, superstition is fostered. In many parts of the world, rain is a most significant event but is not very predictable to the

B. F. Skinner

average person.   Although the coming of rain does not depend on what people do, rain dances and other ritual ceremonies have evolved to "bring the rain." Skinner speculates that such ceremonies may have origins in some distant time in the past when, by chance, rain followed some human activity.

What are your superstitions?

For many students, receiving a good grade on an exam is a highly important but rather unpredictable event.   By chance, you may have worn a particular shirt one day when you made an unusually high grade; thereafter, this may become your "good luck" shirt. By chance, you may have sat in a particular place one day when you made a high grade on a test; thereafter, you feel more confident taking exams while sitting in that part of the room.   Wearing a certain shirt or sitting in a particular place in the room on exam day are examples of what Skinner would call superstitious behavior—behavior that is acquired because of a past accidental association with reward.

The World Is a Skinner Box   •   Skinner contends that the world is like the Skinner box.   People are like pigeons or rats: their behavior is controlled by the environment, which rewards some activities and not others.   As Skinner put it in an interview:

The world at large is a laboratory.   Take the people in Las Vegas, pulling levers on slot machines.   They are in a laboratory situation, and very willingly.   The slot machines simply use a schedule of conditioning and reinforcement similar to those we use in the laboratory—with money dropping down the chute instead of food.[17]

Skinner argues that in this "Skinner-box" world freedom is an illusion.   People are not free; their behavior is controlled by their environment.   The problem for people to solve is how to gain control over the rewards and punishments in their environment by applying the principles learned in the Skinner box to the design of future society.

To those who are concerned about the excessive control of our lives, Skinner replies, "What we need is more control, not less, and this is itself an engineering problem of the first importance."[18]   Skinner believes that we cannot avoid controls, and that therefore our problem is to design a society with good controls rather than bad ones.   He says:

What is needed is a new conception of human behavior which is compatible with the implications of a scientific analysis.   All men control and are controlled.   The question of government in the broadest possible sense is not how freedom is to be preserved but what kinds of control are to be used and to what ends.[17]

If, as Skinner believes, we are all controlled by external environmental forces, then there is no freedom.   Freedom is only an illusion we have, resulting from our ignorance of the forces that control us.

The Law of Effect

Edward Thorndike, a pioneer in American psychology who worked around the turn of the century, conducted a series of famous experiments using cats and

Edward Thorndike

"puzzle boxes."   A puzzle box was an enclosure from which a confined cat could escape only by clawing at a rope, pushing down on a lever, or moving a peddle.

Thorndike found that after a period of trial and error, a cat would accidentally succeed in opening the box so that it could escape.   The success experience seemed to "stamp in" the behavior which preceded it.   For example, if the box opened after the cat accidentally pressed a lever with its left hind leg, the next time the cat was placed in the box it would repeat the successful act, using its left hind leg.   On the basis of his observations, Thorndike proposed that the association between a stimulus (for example, a puzzle box) and a response (for example, a left-leg press) is either weakened or strengthened as a result of the *effect,* or consequence, of the response.   Successful responses are "stamped in" and unsuccessful responses are weakened.   Thorndike called this principle the **Law of Effect**—responses with favorable consequences tend to be strengthened or repeated, and responses with unfavorable consequences tend to be abandoned.   Operant conditioning is based on the Law of Effect.

If a dog does a trick and is rewarded, it will be more likely to repeat the trick.   If the trick results in punishment, the trick will probably be abandoned.   In either case, the effect of the trick—whether favorable or unfavorable—determines what the animal will do in the future.

Human beings, like animals, are subject to the Law of Effect.   We tend to repeat actions that have proved successful and to abandon actions that are unsuccessful.   Our society applies the Law of Effect by punishing certain undesirable behaviors with fines or imprisonment and by rewarding other behaviors with money, awards, and tax deductions.

Reinforcement and Punishment

Operant conditioning is conditioning by consequences.   **A consequence** of a response is an event occurring after the response and that is contingent on the occurrence of the response (it occurs only when the response occurs).   There are two general types of consequences—favorable consequences and unfavorable consequences.

Favorable consequences are called **reinforcers** because they strengthen, or reinforce, the response they follow.   A reward is a reinforcer.   The procedure of giving rewards or reinforcers following a response is called **reinforcement.**   An example of reinforcement is giving a dog a small piece of meat after it correctly performs a trick.   The meat is the reinforcer; the trick has been reinforced by the meat.

There are different kinds of reinforcers.   Some are directly gratifying, such as food when you are hungry or water when you are thirsty.   These are called **primary reinforcers.**   Primary reinforcers are effective without prior learning or experience with them.   You are born with an appreciation for food.   Another type of reinforcer is only indirectly gratifying, such as the words *thank you* or a smile.   These ae called **secondary reinforcers** or **conditioned reinforcers.**   Secondary reinforcers require prior learning to be effective.   You are not born appreciating the words *thank you.*   The rewarding value of an A+ must be learned.   Such secondary reinforcers acquire the power to affect behavior because they have been associated with direct rewards in the past.   A smile accompanies the caress and feeding; money is associated with satisfying hunger and obtaining comfort.   Because of these associations, smiles and money develop the power to influence behavior.

Unfavorable consequences are called **punishers.**   They weaken the response they follow.   A shock is an example of a punisher.   The procedure of punishing behavior is called **punishment.**   An example of punishment is spanking a child for misbehaving.   To be effective, punishment—like reinforcement—must be contingent upon the response which is to be punished; that is, the punishment must occur when the response occurs and only when it occurs.

There are good reasons to be cautious in using punishment to modify behavior.   One problem with punishment is that it can have undesirable side effects.   If a parent regularly punishes a child, the child may learn to fear the parent. Punishment teaches fear through the process of classical conditioning. Such physical measures as spanking or slapping are unconditioned stimuli that elicit the unconditioned response of fear. When the parent (a conditioned stimulus) becomes regularly associated with physical punishment (the unconditioned stimulus), a conditioned response of fear of the parent may develop. In addition, there are some problem behaviors that, when punished, are made worse instead of better. For example, behaviors involving eating habits, sex, and toilet training, and behaviors stemming from emotional reactions should generally not be punished, since punishment may lead to further problems.

When punishment is used, there are two general principles that should be followed: (1) The punishment should follow the misbehavior without delay. Suppose your dog ran into the street and you called it back to punish it. In this case, the behavior that would be punished is the act of coming to you when called, since this is the behavior that immediately preceded the punishment. If a dog is to be punished for running into the street, it must be punished in the street. (2) A second principle is that behavior should be punished only when an alternative correct behavior is available. A young child, punished for pulling the tail of the family dog, should be immediately shown how to play nicely with the dog. This more appropriate behavior can then be reinforced.

Shaping

New behaviors are learned gradually, not all at once. As people and animals learn how to do something, they typically do it sloppily at first and then better and better.

When you first learned how to make your own bed, your parents probably did not expect perfection from you. At first, they probably reinforced you verbally for any attempt at making the bed. But later, they expected more from you and reinforced you only when the bed looked fairly neat. The procedure your parents were following with you is called **shaping**. Shaping involves reinforcing closer and closer approximations to the desired response.

When a dog is taught to "heel," it is initially reinforced for anything approximating the desired behavior of walking next to the owner's left leg. Later, the dog is reinforced only when it walks exactly right, never leaving the "heel" position until it is released. This procedure, in which a new behavior is acquired through reinforcing behavior more and more similar to the desired behavior, is called shaping.

In the shaping procedure, the criterion for reinforcement—that is, what the person or animal has to

A procedure called shaping is used to teach a whale to jump out of the water on command. Shaping involves reinforcing closer and closer approximations of the desired response. To teach the whale to jump, the whale is initially reinforced for simply breaking the surface of the water. Later, the whale must jump higher to be reinforced. (Len Rue, Jr./© Animals, Animals)

do in order to be reinforced—becomes stricter and stricter as the behavior is mastered. A whale can be taught to jump twenty feet out of the water through shaping. Initially, the whale is reinforced for just breaking the surface of the water. Later, the criterion for reinforcement becomes more strict: The whale must come two feet out of the water before it is reinforced. This criterion is raised gradually as the whale learns the trick. Finally, the whale is consistently jumping twenty feet on command.

People are reinforced for playing slot machines by occasionally winning money. The slot machine is programmed to follow a variable ratio schedule of reinforcement; it pays off after a variable and unpredictable number of plays. (Dave Bellak/Jeroboam, Inc.)

Schedules of Reinforcement

In school, you are not rewarded evey time you give the right answer. At work, you are not paid every minute. The dog is not fed every time it performs a trick. Sometimes a reward is given, sometimes not. To use the technical language, a partial reinforcement schedule is often used.

The term **schedule of reinforcement** refers to how frequently reinforcers accompany responses or how often a reinforcer is given for a correct response. One possible schedule of reinforcement is to give a reinforcer for every single correct response. This is called a **continuous schedule of reinforcement.** An example of continuous reinforcement is reinforcing a dog with a piece of food every single time it performs a trick. Another type of reinforcement schedule is to give reinforcers after some correct responses but not others. This is called a **partial schedule of reinforcement** or **partial reinforcement.** In partial reinforcement, the reinforcer is occasionally withheld after a correct response.

There are different types of partial reinforcement schedules. Some types require a number of correct responses to occur before a reinforcer is given. Other types require a period of time to pass before a correct response is reinforced. The number of responses that must occur, or the amount of time that must pass, before a correct response is reinforced can be fixed or varied. The **fixed ratio schedule (FR schedule)** involves reinforcing the person or an animal after a particular, set number of correct responses have occurred. For example, you could reinforce your dog after it correctly performs its trick twice. You could reinforce your daughter only after she has correctly made her bed for, say, seven days. Factory piecework is reinforced on a fixed ratio schedule: you get paid only after completing a set number of units. A second type of partial reinforcement schedule is the **variable ratio schedule (VR schedule).** In this type of schedule, a response is reinforced after a variable number of correct responses have occurred. For example, the door-to-door salesperson who is selling magazine subscriptions must approach many houses and knock on many doors. After some variable number of approaches, a sale might be made. Sometimes two people in a row might accept the offer. Other times it might take talking to twenty people before an offer is accepted. The salesperson is reinforced on a variable ratio schedule. The slot machines in gambling casinos also follow a variable ratio schedule of reinforcement. The jackpot comes up only after a variable and unpredictable number of plays.

Other reinforcement schedules are defined in terms of the delay that occurs between reinforced responses. A third type of partial reinforcement schedule is a **fixed interval schedule (FI schedule).** The fixed interval schedule involves reinforcing the first correct response to occur after a set period of time has elapsed. Suppose you are paid every week and your paycheck is available every Friday at 2 P.M. You may ask for your paycheck on Tuesday, on Thursday, or at other times, but you are reinforced only for the first request after 2 P.M. on Friday. The act of asking for your paycheck is reinforced on a fixed interval schedule of reinforcement. A fourth type of partial reinforcement schedule is the **variable interval schedule (VI schedule).** This schedule involves reinforcing a correct response after a variable time period has elapsed. If your paycheck was sometimes available at 2 P.M. and other times available at 11 A.M. or 3 P.M., then asking for your paycheck would be reinforced on a variable interval schedule. These four types of partial reinforcement schedules are shown in Table 3-1.

Generalization and Discrimination

According to the principles of operant conditioning, we learn which responses tend to lead to reinforcement and which tend to lead to punishment. Those that are successful are strengthened, and those that are unsuccessful are weakened. But some responses are successful in certain situations and not in others. Approaching the cashier and asking for your paycheck may sometimes be reinforced. Approaching a police-man with the same request will not be reinforced. Asking your spouse for the car keys will sometimes be reinforced. Asking a complete stranger for car keys will probably not be reinforced. The contingencies of reinforcement (the relationship between the reinforcement and the response) are different in different situations.

A pigeon in a Skinner box can be trained to peck at a small plastic disk on the wall of the box. The disk is illuminated from behind by a bright green light. The pigeon is reinforced by a bit of grain after a variable number of correct responses. After the pigeon has learned the task, the experimenter changes the color of the light on the disk as a test to determine the pigeon's reaction. It is found that the pigeon will peck at a blue light even though it was never reinforced for pecking a blue light. This tendency for the response to occur to stimuli other than those associated with reinforcement is called *stimulus generalization.* Stimulus generalization in operant conditioning resembles stimulus generalization in classical conditioning. Both are cases of responses occurring to stimuli different from those presented in training.

If the pigeon is reinforced for pecking at a green disk but is not reinforced for pecking at a blue disk, the pigeon will eventually learn to stop pecking at the disk when it is colored blue. That is, the pigeon will learn to distinguish those circumstances that will lead to reinforcement and those that will not. The pigeon's tendency to respond to certain stimuli and not to others is called **discrimination,** a process of selective responding similar to discrimination in classical conditioning.

Table 3-1 Types of Partial Reinforcement Schedules

Type	Abbreviation	What Must Occur Before a Correct Response is Reinforced
Fixed Ratio Schedule	FR	A set number of correct responses
Variable Ratio Schedule	VR	A variable number of correct responses
Fixed Interval Schedule	FI	A set amount of time delay
Variable Interval Schedule	VI	A variable amount of time delay

Extinction

In operant conditioning, a response that is not reinforced will weaken and eventually stop. The procedure of withholding reinforcement for a response is called **extinction,** and the result of the procedure—the eventual elimination of the response—is also called *extinction.* In operant conditioning, extinction is brought about by removing the reinforcer. In classical conditioning, extinction is brought about by withholding the unconditioned stimulus.

We are often concerned with influencing the behavior of others. We want someone to start doing something or to stop doing something. The principles of operant conditioning can be used to modify the behavior of others. To strengthen someone's response, you can begin to systematically reinforce it. To weaken someone's response, you can remove the reinforcer or reinforce it less. The procedure of eliminating the reinforcer in order to weaken or eliminate the response is called extinction. The response is said to be extinguished (eliminated) when the procedure of extinction has been successfully completed.

In the following case, the problem was to get someone to stop doing something, to get the individual to eliminate a problem behavior. The principle of extinction was used to get a young boy to stop throwing tantrums.

A twenty-one-month-old boy had a tantrum every night at bedtime. If one of his parents left the room after putting him to bed, he would scream and fuss until the parent returned to the room; as a result, the parent could not leave the room until the child was asleep. This required from one-half hour to two hours of time each night.

What could be done about the problem? From the point of view of conditioning, the problem was to *extinguish* the tantrum behavior. One of the principles of conditioning states that a response will extinguish if it has no rewarding consequences. In this case the rewarding consequence of the boy's tantrums was that the parents stayed in his room and gave him attention. Each tantrum was followed by a reward: parental attention. Upon the advice of a psychologist the parents began to put the boy to bed and, after kissing him goodnight, leave the room and close the door. On the first night this was tried the boy screamed and raged for forty-five minutes, but the parents did not reward his behavior by giving him attention. By the tenth night of "no reward," the boy's tantrums had extinguished; when he was put to bed he smiled and quietly went to sleep.[19]

Interim Summary   Operant conditioning is based on the Law of Effect: responses followed by reinforcement will tend to be repeated. In the case of Skinner's rats, when a response (lever pressing) was followed by reinforcement (delivering a small pellet of food to the animal), the response tended to be repeated. Most responses are reinforced according to some type of partial reinforcement schedule. FR, VR, FI, and VI schedules are four types of partial reinforcement schedules.

Primary reinforcers, such as food, have a reinforcing effect without the need for prior learning. Secondary reinforcers, such as money, develop a reinforcing effect as a result of prior learning; the significance of money must be learned. Shaping is a training procedure that involves reinforcing closer and closer approximations to the final desired response. "Superstitious" behavior in animals can develop by occasionally giving them reinforcement regardless of their behavior; under these conditions they may develop rigid, stereotyped actions. Stimulus generalization refers to the tendency to respond to stimuli other than those associated with reinforcement, and discrimination refers to the tendency to respond to certain stimuli but not to others. Using operant conditioning procedures, responses can be extinguished by eliminating their reinforcers or favorable consequences.

Training Animals

Keller and Marian Breland have made a career of training animals with operant-conditioning procedures. In their trained chicken acts, which were exhibited in county fairs in different parts of the country, one chicken was trained to play a five-note tune on a small piano and another performed a tap dance in costume and shoes. They also developed a trained pig show, featuring Priscilla. Priscilla was able to turn on the radio, eat breakfast at a table, pick up the dirty clothes and put them in a hamper, run the vacuum cleaner around the rug, and take part in a quiz program. She would answer "yes" or "no" to questions to her from the audience by lighting up the appropriate signs.[20]

Have you ever taught a dog a trick? If you have, you have used the procedures of operant conditioning. Operant conditioning is an easy and fast method for teaching tricks to all kinds of animals. There are seven easy steps:

1. Get some food that the animal likes and cut it up into a large number of very small pieces.
2. Wait until a time that the animal is hungry—such as right before dinner. To make sure that the animal is really hungry, it may be necessary to withhold one meal.
3. Establish a "secondary reinforcer"—a signal that the animal is conditioned to associate with food. A whistle or a clap will work as a secondary reinforcer. To make a whistle become a secondary reinforcer, you whistle, then immediately give the animal a small tidbit of food; whistle, then feed. This pattern is repeated several times until the whistle becomes a signal for the animal that food is available.
4. Decide on a simple trick you want the animal to perform. Then break the behavior up into a series of simple steps. For example, suppose you want to teach your dog to come to you and sit down by your feet when you say "come." The first step of the trick involves the dog coming toward you. The second step involves the dog going to your right side. The third step requires the dog to orient its body in the same direction as your body, with its head pointing forward. The last step involves the dog sitting down.
5. Shape the desired behavior by gradual approximation or guidance. To do this, you begin by rewarding the animal for completing the first step of the trick. You say "come" and reward the animal if it comes toward you. Sometimes the first step is not something that the animal will naturally do, so you must reward it for doing something approximately like the first step. The technique of reinforcing closer and closer approximations to the desired response is called **shaping**. The way to reward the animal is first to signal it with the secondary reinforcement, then to feed it a tidbit of food. Another way an animal can be helped to perform a physical movement is by guidance; you can help a dog sit, for example, by pressing down gently on its hind quarters. By breaking the trick down into a series of small steps, the animal can gradually learn how to do a complicated trick, but each small step must be fairly easy.
6. Establish a discrimination. Once the animal can perform the trick and is rewarded, you want to train the animal to do it only at certain times; for

example, only when it is told to do so. This is getting the behavior under the control of a verbal stimulus. You do this by providing the stimulus *"Come,"* then rewarding the animal if it performs its trick; if the trick is performed at some other time, when you have not provided the appropriate verbal stimulus, you do not reward it. In this way a discrimination is established; the animal learns to perform the trick only following the appropriate stimulus.

7. Introduce partial reinforcement. After the animal is able to perform the trick perfectly every time, you should begin to withhold the food reward occasionally (but not the secondary reinforcement). At first withhold the food every second or third time the trick is performed; later, withhold the food most of the time, providing the food reward only rarely. This way you won't have to carry dog food with you all of the time. Also, behavior only partially rewarded is less likely to extinguish.

Managing Your Behavior

What is the relation between what you want to do and what you actually do? If you are in control, managing your actions, then what you do and what you want to do are about the same. Sometimes, however, you may do things that you do not want to do. You may bite your fingernails, smoke, or overeat, and you may feel that these behaviors are beyond your power to control. Other times you may want to do certain things, but you do not do them. You may want to exercise or study more and yet have great difficulty in settling down and doing these things. How can you gain control over your actions so that you are able to do what you want to do and you are able to stop doing what you do not want to do?

Analyzing Your Behavior

The first step toward self-control is self-understanding. To change your behavior, you must first understand clearly what you are now doing, when you are doing it, and—if possible—why. In effect, you must become a scientist observing your own behavior.

What about yourself would you like to be able to change? Do you have a bad habit you would like to eliminate? In analyzing your behavior, your first problem will be to specify a problem behavior pre-

cisely, to state exactly what it is, with concrete examples. Rather than stating something general ("I'm too shy" or "I'm too lazy"), try to state the problem in terms of actual examples ("I want to be able to initiate more conversations with members of the opposite sex" or "I want to spend more time studying and less watching television").

Once you have stated precisely the behavior you want to change, the next step is to observe the behavior very carefully in order to determine exactly what you are now doing. In most cases, this careful observation requires counting your behavior. For several days, count the number of times the behavior occurs. This record of the frequency of occurrence of the problem behavior is called the **baseline.** The baseline record should be portable, so that you can carry it about with you during the day and record the problem behavior immediately after it occurs. In the following example a student used a 3 × 5 card for recording baseline behavior:

One of our very bright students reported that he had the bad habit of being rude to his friends. He seemed to insult them and to do it often. He began record keeping by carrying in his pocket a 3 × 5 card with two columns on it, labeled, "Did insult" and "Did not insult." As soon as he had finished some conversation with a friend or acquaintance, he would take out the card and make a check in one of the two columns. For example, he might run into a buddy on campus and stop to talk for a few minutes, then the two would go their separate ways. Our student would immediately make an entry in one of his columns.[21]

Keeping a record of your problem behavior is possible if you are aware of your behavior, but what if you are not conscious of what you are doing? You may bite your fingernails or crack your knuckles without being fully aware of your actions. You may have a cigarette half smoked and be unaware of having put it in your mouth. Some of your "bad habits" are actions that you are not aware of doing deliberately. A procedure for increasing your awareness of your problem behaviors is **negative practice.** Negative practice consists of deliberately doing what you do not want to do; that is, of voluntarily practicing the bad habit. By repeating the habit on purpose, you gain more awareness of it and more control over it.

A man came to a psychologist complaining about headaches, fatigue, and anxiety.[22] An interview with the young man and his wife revealed that he had a bad habit of banging his head into his pillow while asleep. This not only interrupted his sleep but also caused pain in his neck, head, and shoulders. Furthermore, he had apparently been doing this since he was one year old. The man was instructed to use negative practice. Each night just before going to sleep he pounded his head into the pillow on purpose until he was tired. After four nights of negative practice his head-banging habit stopped, and he was able to sleep soundly. And so was his wife.

Antecedents and Consequences

In analyzing your behavior, you will want to study not only what you do but also when, and in what circumstances, you do it. Your behavior does not occur in isolation, out of context, independent of the world you live in. There are events that precede and events that follow your actions. Events that precede your behavior are called **antecedents.** For example, what are the antecedents of nail-biting behavior? If you

have a nail-biting habit, you will find that there are certain situations in which you will bite your nails and others in which you won't. The antecedent situations preceding nail biting may be those situations causing tension or nervousness—for example, a midterm exam.

Events that follow behavior are called consequences. According to the Law of Effect, behavior with good or favorable consequences tends to be repeated. This can sometimes be a problem for bad habits; a behavior may have favorable short-term consequences but unfavorable long-term consequences. Habits of this sort are very difficult to change because the behavior is being rewarded. For example, what is the consequence of eating a banana split? The short-term consequence is good—a satisfying feeling—but the long-term consequences are less favorable—excess weight. To take an extreme example, the short-term consequences of smoking a cigarette may be favorable—good taste—but the long-term consequences—cancer—may be unfavorable.

Think of a bad habit you have. What are its antecedents? What are its short-term and long-term consequences?

Breaking Bad Habits

Once you have analyzed your behavior so that you know what you are doing, how often, and in what circumstances, you are ready to try to change your behavior.

Controlling Antecedents and Consequences • Changing your behavior requires gaining control over the antecedents and consequences of it. To some degree a habit is controlled by its antecedents, but there are ways for you to weaken that control and gain more self-control. One way to weaken antecedent control is to *avoid* the antecedents; that is, avoid the circumstances in which it is likely that the bad habit will occur. For example, what are the antecedents of excessive eating, drinking, and smoking? One circumstance is the presence of other people who are eating, drinking, or smoking. If you want to limit your behavior of this type, you can avoid the social situations that are its antecedents. Eventually the power of the social situations to tempt you into your bad habit will decrease. A second way to weaken antecedent control is to perform an **incompatible behavior**—that is, to do something that would interfere with the bad habit. For example, to some degree, chewing gum is incompatible with smoking; so if you chew gum after meals, you will be less tempted to smoke after meals. If, during periods of tension, you put your hands into your pockets, you will be less likely to bite your nails. By becoming aware of the antecedents of your bad habits and by weakening the control of these antecedents over your behavior, you can increase your self-control.

Habits are also controlled by their consequences. If the short-term consequences of an act are rewarding, the act may become a habit. You can gain more control over your behavior by managing the consequences. For example, if you want to be able to study more, you must make the short-term consequences of studying more favorable. But what is a favorable consequence?

What is rewarding to you? You can best answer this question by noting what you like to do. What makes you feel good, what are your interests, what are the things you frequently do but are not forced to do? These are potential rewards for you; when you make one of these the short-term consequence of some behavior, the frequency of that behavior should increase. If you arrange your study schedule so that after every two hours of study you get to read a chapter in your favorite novel or watch a half hour of television, then the frequency of studying should increase.

A young woman wanted to exercise more but was unable to do it. She decided that one of the things that she liked to do and that was important to her was the opportunity to take a hot shower. In order to increase the frequency of her exercise, she made taking a shower a short-term consequence of exercising. She established a rule that she could not shower until she had exercised for fifteen minutes.[21]

Finding Your Reinforcers: A Checklist • Some people have not given much thought to what reinforces them. It is important to find your reinforcers, because controlling your reinforcers is one of the best ways to gain more control over your life. By making a reinforcer such as a dessert, a movie, or a telephone call to a friend contingent, or dependent, upon the completion of a study task, your study habits will be strengthened. Events, objects, and activities that you can use as effective reinforcers for your behavior have two characteristics: (1) you like them, and (2) you have control over them. Certain things that you like—such as money—you don't control, since you can't get more of it whenever you want. Other things—such as liver pudding—you may not like.

What are your interests or hobbies? What are the things that you do every day or so that you would hate to give up? What do you do just for fun? What makes you feel good? These are your potential reinforcers. Following is a checklist showing what many other people have found to be reinforcing. Check those that are reinforcing to you.

☐ candy	☐ jogging
☐ peanuts	☐ playing basketball
☐ a soft drink	☐ playing Ping Pong
☐ ice cream	☐ going to parties
☐ playing records or tapes	☐ telephoning a friend
☐ listening to the radio	☐ taking a nap
☐ watching television	☐ taking a warm bath or shower
☐ going to a movie	☐ going shopping
☐ reading a book	☐ playing cards
☐ reading a magazine	☐ getting to sleep late

Smoking • What is the reward for smoking? One psychologist reasoned that the reward for the act of reaching for a cigarette and smoking was the experience of smoking; then the reward for smoking could be withdrawn only by preventing the experience of smoking. To withdraw the reward, the cigarettes were put into a special case that had a unique lock allowing the case to be opened only at certain times. A timer could be set that would allow the case to be opened only every hour. The response of reaching for a cigarette would be rewarded only if the case could be opened; thus the response of reaching for a cigarette sooner than once every hour was extinguished.[23] Other psychologists have taken the approach of trying to diminish the rewarding effect of the experience of smoking by getting smokers to overdo it. Just as chocolate might not be rewarding after you had eaten a pound of chocolate, smoking was no reward for persons who were made to smoke almost constantly for a period of several hours. In effect, this procedure attempts to satiate the desire to smoke by overdoing it.[24]

Eating between meals is a habit that has been learned and can be unlearned. One step toward controlling this habit is to control the stimuli for overeating by restricting your eating only to one place. (Joel Gordon)

Overeating • The response of eating is rewarded by food; if the reward could be withdrawn, the response would extinguish. One approach to the problem of overeating is to extinguish attempts to eat between meals. This approach depends upon the removal of the food reward except at mealtimes. When this is accomplished, the attempts to eat between meals will, over a period of time, extinguish.

A conditioning-based approach to the problem of overeating attempts to remove the stimulus for overeating and to strengthen behavior that is incompatible with overeating.[25] Eating, especially the relatively unconscious automatic eating between meals, is a learned behavior, a response that has been conditioned to a variety of stimuli and situations. If you eat in bed for a period of time, for example, the response of eating will be conditioned to the stimulus conditions of the bed. When the stimulus occurs (you are in bed), the response tends to automatically follow (you eat); that is, eating is under the control of the bed stimulus. By restricting your eating to only one place, and only to mealtimes, you will weaken and eventually extinguish the response of eating in bed, in the living room, or in the movies.

A second part of this program depends upon strengthening behavior that is incompatible with overeating. The Law of Effect states that responses followed by rewards will be strengthened and will recur. Staying on a diet is behavior that might be rewarded by attention and approval from your family and friends; if staying on a diet is rewarded, that behavior will be strengthened.

Interim Summary   To change your behavior, you must know what you do, how often, and in what circumstances. Establishing a baseline and negative practice are both methods of increasing your awareness of your behavior. Events that precede (antecedents) and events that follow (consequences) all help support and maintain your behavior. Changing behavior requires gaining control over these antecedents and consequences.

Summary

1. Learning is a change in behavior as a result of experience.

2. Instincts (complex, inborn behavior patterns found in some animals) and reflexes (inborn reactions to certain stimuli) are examples of behavior that is not learned.

3. Changes in behavior resulting from the maturation of muscles and nerves are also not the result of learning.

4. Meaningful human learning involves acquiring sets of organized or related ideas and skills. Learning material from books is easier when the material is organized and is hindered by interference from other learned material.

5. Much of human behavior is learned socially, through observing and imitating adult models.

6. The best method of learning a skill involves a method of practice that reflects whether the skill is organized as a whole or as separate parts. Whole practice is superior for highly interdependent movements, while part practice is superior for relatively independent movements.

7. Massed practice does not work as well for most skills as spaced practice.

8. As several related skills are mastered or as a series of related problems is solved, a learning set is acquired that makes future learning easier.

9. Classical conditioning—or conditioning by association—is based on the Law of Contiguity: Under certain circumstances, a stimulus that repeatedly occurs about the same time as a response will acquire the power to produce that response.

10. In classical conditioning, a previously neutral stimulus (the CS) is paired with a second stimulus (the UCS) that consistently elicits a response (UCR). After repeated pairings, the CS acquires the power to elicit the response (now called the CR).

11. In classical conditioning, stimulus generalization occurs when the CR is produced by stimuli other than the CS. Discrimination is the process of not responding to stimuli different from the conditioned stimulus.

12. In classical conditioning, extinction is the procedure of repeatedly presenting the conditioned stimulus alone, in the absence of the unconditioned stimulus. Extinction results in the elimination of the conditioned response.

13. Operant conditioning—or conditioning by consequences—is based on the Law of Effect: Responses with favorable consequences tend to be strengthened and repeated.

14. A reinforcer is a favorable consequence, such as a reward. Primary reinforcers are effective without prior learning, while secondary reinforcers acquire their reinforcing power through learning. Unfavorable consequences are called punishers.

15. Shaping is a training procedure that involves reinforcing closer and closer approximations to the desired behavior.

16. Four partial reinforcement schedules are the fixed ratio (FR), variable ratio, (VR), fixed interval (FI), and variable interval (VI) schedules.

17. In operant conditioning, stimulus generalization occurs when the response occurs in the presence of stimuli other than those associated with reinforcement. Discrimination occurs when the response occurs to certain stimuli but not to others.

18. In operant conditioning, extinction is the procedure of withholding the reinforce-

ment. The result of extinction is the elimination of the response.

19. Operant conditioning principles can be applied to developing a program to manage your own behavior. Bad habits can be broken by controlling antecedents and consequences of behavior.

Key Concepts

learning A change in behavior or behavior potential as a result of experience.

instincts Complex behaviors present at birth; for example, the nest-building behavior of many birds.

reflex A simple, involuntary reaction occurring to a specific stimulus; for example, a sneeze.

stimulus Anything that is sensed or that produces a reaction.

response Any kind of behavior or reaction that results from a stimulus.

maturation The physical growth and development of the body.

conditioning A form of simple learning: learning by association or learning by consequences.

model A person who is observed and imitated.

whole-part issue The question of whether it is better to practice the whole act every time or to practice one part at a time until it is mastered.

massed-spaced issue The question of whether it is preferable to practice in one long session or in several shorter sessions.

learning set A learned ability to learn, making later learning easier; for example, after learning one foreign language, it may be easier to learn others.

classical conditioning Conditioning by association; a form of conditioning in which a neutral stimulus acquires the power to produce a response by being paired with another stimulus that already consistently elicits the response.

Law of Contiguity Under certain circumstances, a stimulus that occurs about the same time as a response will acquire the power to elicit the response.

unconditioned stimulus A stimulus that automatically elicits a response; for example, food in the mouth elicits salivation.

unconditioned response A response to an unconditioned stimulus; for example, the response of salivating to food in the mouth.

conditioned stimulus The initially neutral stimulus that is paired with the unconditioned stimulus; for example, a bell.

conditioned response The learned reaction to the conditioned stimulus; for example, the reaction of salivating to a bell.

stimulus generalization The tendency to respond to stimuli similar to the conditioned stimulus; in classical conditioning, the tendency to react to stimuli that have not been paired with the UCS; in operant conditioning, the tendency to respond to stimuli that have not been associated with reinforcement.

discrimination Responding to certain stimuli but not to others as a result of learning.

extinction The procedure and result of eliminating a conditioned response; in classical conditioning, brought about by presenting the conditioned stimulus without the unconditioned stimulus; in operant conditioning, brought about by withholding reinforcement.

operant conditioning Conditioning by consequences; instrumental conditioning.

instrumental conditioning Another term for operant conditioning

Skinner box A device developed by B. F.

Skinner for studying animal behavior. The box contains a lever which, when pressed, automatically delivers a small pellet of food.

Law of Effect   Responses followed by reinforcement will tend to be repeated.

consequence   An event occurring after a response that occurs only when the response occurs.

reinforcer   A favorable consequence; for example, a reward.

reinforcement   The procedure of providing a reward or other favorable consequence following a response.

primary reinforcer   An event having a reinforcing effect without the need of prior learning; for example, food.

secondary reinforcer   An event having a reinforcing effect as a consequence of prior learning; for example, money.

conditioned reinforcer   A secondary reinforcer.

punisher   An unfavorable consequence; for example, a shock.

punishment   The procedure of providing a punisher or other unfavorable consequence following a response.

shaping   A training procedure that involves reinforcing closer and closer approximations to the desired response.

schedule of reinforcement   The frequency with which reinforcers accompany responses; how often a reinforcer is given for a correct response.

continuous schedule of reinforcement   Delivery of a reinforcer for every correct response.

partial schedule of reinforcement   Delivery of a reinforcer after some correct responses but not after others.

fixed ratio schedule (FR schedule)   Delivery of a reinforcer after a certain number of correct responses have occurred; for example, factory piecework.

fixed interval schedule (FI schedule)   Delivery of a reinforcer for the first correct response to occur after a set period of time has elapsed; for example, asking for your paycheck at the end of the week.

variable ratio schedule (VR schedule)   Delivery of a reinforcer after a variable number of correct responses have occurred.   For example, a door-to-door sales person is reinforced with a sale after making a variable number of approaches; sometimes only two houses must be visited, and other times twenty houses, before making a sale.

variable interval schedule (VI schedule)   Delivery of a reinforcer for the first correct response after a variable period of time has elapsed; going to the mailbox is occasionally reinforced by a letter from a friend, but such letters arrive at variable intervals.

baseline   The normal level or pattern of a response that occurs before an experiment is conducted; the baseline rate of behavior is the frequency of occurrence of the behavior before any attempt is made to change it.

negative practice   A technique of deliberately practicing a bad habit in order to gain increased voluntary control over it; for example, by practicing knuckle cracking at regular intervals each day, the habit may be controlled.

antecedents   The prior context; the events that precede behavior; for example, studying is an antecedent for success on an exam.

incompatible behavior   Behavior that would interfere with another action.

Chapter 4

The Psychology of Memory

Key Questions   1. How do you remember?
                       2. Where in the brain are memories located?
                       3. Why do you forget?
                       4. How can you improve your memory?

And there was the man who couldn't remember three things: names, faces, and—he forgot what the third was. His wife, however, had the worst memory in the world: she remembered everything.[1]

Memory is often taken for granted, but it is central to the ability to grow. In order to learn from the past, you must be able to remember it.

What would you be like without memory? Even the simplest task would be impossible. For example, you could not repeat your name or find your way home. You could not read this sentence. You would have no knowledge of the beginning of the sentence by the time your eyes reached the end of the sentence. Without memory you would not learn from experience. Without the ability to learn from the past you would begin anew at every moment. In effect, you would remain an infant throughout your life.

Memory Processes

How are you able to remember past experiences and events? Since you do not have a camera in your mind, how can you remember a picture? Since you do not record music with your brain, how can you remember a song once heard? Human memory is still a mysterious process that we know relatively little about. Logically, however, we know that remembering requires at least three processes: getting information in the mind, retaining it, and then getting it out. These processes are called encoding, storage, and retrieval.

Encoding

Memories are not the same as real events; I do not have actual music in my mind; my house is not actually in my head. Memories can be thought of as consisting of information, rather than of physical objects such as houses. **Encoding** is the process of changing physical scenes and events into the form of information that can be stored in memory. This "form" of information used in recording memories is the memory code. Thus the process of encoding consists of changing the physical energy in the environment (for example, a sound) into memory codes.

What is this code? Evidence shows that memories of recent letters or words are often encoded into labels or sounds (see Figure 4-1). In a complex experiment designed to test the capacity of memory, Sperling[2] allowed participants one very brief glance at a group of twelve letters printed on a card, then asked them to name as many letters as they could remember. On the average, they were able to name only about four or five letters. But the errors that they made were very interesting. Although the letters were presented visually, the participants tended to confuse letters that *sounded* alike; for example, they would mix up D and E or B and C. This finding indicates something about the nature of the memory code in this task: people must be encoding what the letters

Figure 4-1 Memory Code.   *Memories of letters seen briefly on a screen are encoded into sounds.*

sound like, and then storing the sound codes. If people encoded what the letters looked like, they would have made more confusions among letters that looked alike than among letters than sounded alike. Other experimenters have confirmed that errors made in recalling visually presented items tend to be acoustically related (related by sound) to the missed item.[3,4] That is, people are more likely to confuse E with C (an acoustic confusion) than they are to confuse E with F (a visual confusion). These brief memories of recent events are sometimes encoded into the spoken sounds of letters or words.

More permanent memories are not influenced so much by sound similarity. The memory for material that is highly practiced tends to be influenced more by semantic similarity—similarity in meaning.[5] Apparently, material that is more permanently stored in memory is encoded into meanings rather than into sounds. Since you can remember pictures of all sorts—even abstract designs—it is clear that the sound code and the meaning code are not the only memory codes we have available. An image code is also used.

Storage

After an event is encoded, the information must be retained. How is it stored? We know that memory **storage** is not a random filing away of information; the information is systematically organized or structured. Things that are related to each other tend to be stored together. This can be shown by the fact that you tend to remember things in clusters. If you put a random list of words into memory, an organized list tends to come out.[6] If you were to read the words: green, north, red, blue, south, yellow, east, you would later tend to recall the directional words in one group and all the color words in another group. Apparently memory storage is organized around units of meaning.

Another type of organization depends not upon meaning but upon the order of occurrence. Events that occur at about the same time tend to be clustered or grouped together. Memorize these numbers:

6   4   9   5   1   7   8   2   3

Chances are, you learned the numbers not as nine individual digits, but as two or three groups of digits, like this:

649   517   823

Memorizing numbers like these is easier when you group them in clusters of three or four.[7] These clusters or groups are called *chunks,* and the process of grouping items into such units is called **chunking.**[8]

Research has shown that our ability to recall material that is presented only once is quite limited, and that our capacity depends upon the number of chunks involved, not the number of individual items of information. On the average, the limit to the amount of material seen once that we can recall seems to be about five to seven chunks.[9] You can increase the amount of information you can recall by increasing the number of items in each chunk. In the example using digits, if you have one digit per chunk you would be able to recall only five to seven digits; if you

How do you remember telephone numbers? Most people repeat them over and over as they walk to the telephone and prepare to dial. Once you stop repeating the number to yourself, you quickly forget it. Thus, a part of the memory system appears to retain material only when it is actively rehearsed. (*Joel Gordon*)

increased the number of digits per chunk to three, you would be able to recall fifteen to twenty-one digits.

This limitation on storage capacity does not hold for all types of learning situations. With adequate time for rehearsal, study, and review, human memory has an essentially unlimited storage capacity.

Retrieval

In order to remember an event, you must first get the information about the event into usable form in memory; this is the encoding process. Then you must retain the information for some period of time until you need it; this is the storage process. The third essential feature of the memory process is **retrieval**: finding and using the stored information. How do you retrieve your memory of the meaning of the word *chunk?* In a sense you have the word and its meaning "on file" and you "look it up"; but your mind is not a dictionary and memory retrieval is not the same as looking something up in a book.

Your Mental Library • If your "filing system" were completely random and mixed up, you would never be able to find what you need. You can retrieve memories because memory storage is organized. It can be compared to a library. Libraries use complex filing systems, typically grouping together the books that are meaningfully related. Different books concerning psychology would be filed in the same general area, for example. Sometimes libraries keep "recent arrivals" separate, so that you can quickly find the newest books in print. Your memory storage and retrieval system in certain ways resembles a library. Your memory is a library of information, organized so that those items are grouped together that are meaningfully related. In addition, the "recent arrivals" (the most recent events) are kept separate, so as to be quickly accessible.

On the Tip of Your Tongue • Sometimes when you try to retrieve from your memory the name of a person, you fail. You know that you have it in memory, but you can't quite locate it. You describe what happened to you by saying that the person's name was "on the tip of your tongue." This frustrating experience has been called the **tip-of-the-tongue phenomenon**. The remarkable thing about the experience is that you often know about how long the word is, you may even know the number of syllables, you may even know the beginning letter of the word, but you cannot recall the word.[10] It is as if you know part of the library "call number" for the book, but not the remainder and therefore cannot find the book. If your memory filing system uses the first letter of words in its indexing system, you would expect that it would be easier to recall a word if you were provided with its first letter, and this has been demonstrated to be the case.[11]

Photographic Memory

Photographic memory is the rare ability to remember in great detail whole scenes or pages from books that were looked at once. Incredibly, such persons are able to retain visual information in memory in a form similar to a photograph. A more technical name for photographic memory is **eidetic imagery.** Children seem to have this ability more often than adults. In one study, 151 children were tested for eidetic imagery and 12 children were found who showed this remarkable memory ability.[12] Although 5 to 10 percent of children have some eidetic ability, almost no adults have been found to have this ability. It is not known why the ability disappears with age, but one possibility is that the culture and the educational system destroy it.[13] This is a "brass-tacks" culture; it is factually oriented, verbally oriented, and distrustful of the visual imagination.

Elizabeth • Rarely is an adult found who possesses this remarkable ability. One of the few documented cases is that of a woman named Elizabeth.[14] Elizabeth showed an amazing talent for remembering visual information in great detail. A demonstration of her memory capacity was her ability to look at one picture of thousands of random dots with her right eye, then, *weeks later,* look at another similar but slightly different picture with her left eye and combine them into a single pattern. Apparently she could take the information given separately to each of her eyes and put together the picture she would have seen if the information had been originally presented to both her eyes simultaneously. She "saw," using her memory, although she had never actually seen with her eyes this complete pattern.

The Case of S. • One of the most carefully documented cases of photographic memory was investigated by A. R. Luria, a famous Russian psychologist. Luria had the opportunity to study the mind of the man he called S. for thirty years. Luria set out to test the limits of S.'s memory.

When I began my study of S. it was with much the same degree of curiosity psychologists generally have at the outset of research, hardly with the hope that the experiments would offer anything of particular note. However, the results of the first tests were enough to change my attitude and to leave me, the experimenter, rather than my subject, both embarrassed and perplexed.

I gave S. a series of words, then numbers, then letters, reading them to him slowly or presenting them in written form. He read or listened attentively and then repeated the material exactly as it had been presented. I increased the number of elements in each series, giving him as many as thirty, fifty, or even seventy words or numbers, but this, too, presented no problem for him. . . .

As the experimenter, I soon found myself in a state verging on utter confusion. An increase in the length of a series led to no noticeable increase in the difficulty for S., and I simply had to admit that the capacity of his memory had no distinct limits. . . . Experiments indicated that he had no difficulty reproducing any lengthy series of words whatever, even though these had originally been presented to him a week, a month, or even many years earlier.[15]

How was S. able to remember so much? When S. was asked how he did it, he described the process as reading off the words or numbers from the paper on which they were originally written; it was as if he continued to see the list. If words were read out loud to him, the sound of each word would produce a visual image; the sounds were changed into colored splotches, lines, or splashes. S.'s visual imagery was very vivid and sometimes bothersome. As S. described it:

To this day, I can't escape from seeing colors when I hear sounds.   What first strikes me is the color of someone's voice.   Then it fades off . . . for it does interfere.   If, say, a person says something, I see the word; but should another person's voice break in, blurs appear.   These creep into the syllables of the words and I can't make out what is being said.[15]

For S. all sounds seemed to be encoded into colored visual images, and it was the images that were remembered.

Interim Summary   Remembering requires three basic processes: encoding, storage, and retrieval.   Encoding involves putting information into memory by changing the physical energies in the world into memory codes that can be retained.   Verbal items like letters and words are initially encoded acoustically; that is, they are changed into labels or sounds.   Storage is the process of retaining information over time.   Memory storage is organized, with similar items linked together by associations; sometimes items are clustered, or chunked.   Retrieval refers to the process of getting at the stored information so that it can be used.   The "tip-of-the-tongue" phenomenon is an example of a failure of retrieval.   Photographic memory, or eidetic imagery, is the rare ability to encode, store, and retrieve whole scenes or pages of information.

Memories in the Brain

Thinking and remembering are activities of the brain, a complicated structure that is composed of billions of nerve cells.   If you were to look at a human brain, what you would see is the outer surface of the brain, the cerebral cortex, a gray wrinkled covering in which many of the most important brain processes occur.   Among other things, the brain is a storehouse of memories.

The Search for the Engram

Where is memory in the brain?   Is there a *place* in the brain where the memory of your name might be located?   Your body has the ability to retain past experience, but where is it kept?   In a series of experiments with rats many years ago, Karl Lashley[16] searched the

Karl Lashley

brain for the physical location of memory. He believed that memories stored in the brain must have a physical form, something he called the **engram.** He reasoned that if he could cut out different parts of the brain he might find where memories are kept. If the memory were cut out with the piece of brain, the animals would not be able to remember. Lashley began by teaching rats to solve a maze, then cutting out particular parts of their brains. He would then test them to see if they remembered how to solve the maze. Surprisingly, Lashley found that in rats memory does not seem to be located in a particular place in the brain; instead, widespread areas of the surface of the brain are involved in each memory. We know today that memory seems to be spread out all through the cortex, but that there are particular brain structures which are essential in order to memorize anything; these structures lie hidden beneath the cortex on each side of the brain.[17]

The Man with Half a Brain

Along the midline of the brain from the front to the back is a deep fold, dividing the brain into two halves called cerebral hemispheres. The left hemisphere controls most of the right side of the body and the right hemisphere controls most of the left side of the body. What do you suppose would happen to you if you lost half your brain?

Small injuries to the brain sometimes produce rapid death; extensive damage to the brain sometimes has little effect. The important factor, of course, is what part of the brain is damaged. You might expect that if you could survive the loss of half your brain, you would wind up with only half a mind. The following case describes what actually happened to one man.[18]

A forty-seven-year-old right-handed man came to the hospital with complaints of being speechless and having seizures in the right arm and face. Five months later a brain operation was performed and a tumor was removed from his left hemisphere. The tumor recurred, so a year later the entire left hemisphere was removed in one piece. Because the left hemisphere was removed and it controls the right side of the body, the operation resulted in paralysis on the right side. The man could not move his right arm and right leg. Remarkably, however, the man's hearing, personality, intelligence, and memory were essentially unaffected by the operation. In this case, half a brain was almost as good as a whole brain. Apparently removing half the brain had little effect on the mind itself.

Brain Chemistry

Recently scientists have proposed that memory may be based on chemical changes in the brain. The search for the physical basis of memory (the engram) has focused on certain kinds of brain chemicals called "protein molecules."[19] Brain cells continuously manufacture protein molecules, a process guided by a substance called **RNA** (*ribonucleic acid*). The physical basis of memory may involve these protein molecules. Interfering with the manufacture of these protein molecules has been shown to produce memory loss in animals.[20] Furthermore, the amount of RNA in the brain seems to increase after learning.[21]

Remembering with the Help of Electricity

A famous brain surgeon, Wilder Penfield, investigated the function of the brain by stimulating the cerebral cortex at different points with a weak electrical current. The current was applied by gently touching the brain surface with a fine wire electrode during a brain operation in which the patient was awake. The operation can be carried out under local anesthesia because the brain itself has no pain receptors and is quite insensitive to pain. Penfield found that electrically stimulating the brain in certain areas occasionally causes past sensory experiences to recur. Old memories are suddenly brought to life again. Penfield described this procedure and the experiences of two of his patients.

Occasionally during the course of a neurosurgical operation under local anesthesia, gentle electrical stimulation in this temporal area, right or left, has caused the conscious patient to be aware of some previous experience. The experience seems to be picked out at random from his own past. It comes back to him in great detail. . . .

A woman heard an orchestra playing an air while the electrode was held in place. The music stopped when the electrode was removed. It came again when the electrode was reapplied. On request, she hummed the tune, while the electrode was held in place, accompanying the orchestra. It was a popular song. Over and over again, restimulation of the same spot produced the same song. The music seemed always to begin at the same place and to progress at the normally expected tempo. All efforts to mislead her failed. She believed that a Gramophone was being turned on in the operating room on each occasion, and she asserted her belief stoutly in a conversation some days after the operation.

A boy heard his mother talking to someone on the telephone when an electrode was applied to his right temporal cortex. When the stimulus was repeated without warning, he heard his mother again in the same conversation. When the stimulus was repeated after a lapse of time, he said, "My mother is telling my brother he has got his coat on backwards. I can just hear them." The surgeon then asked the boy whether he remembered this happening. "O yes," he said, "just before I came here."[22]

The fact that stimulating specific spots on the brain activated specific memories in Penfield's patients does not prove that these memories were located only in these brain areas. To be sure, this is one possibility. Other possibilities are that the electrical stimulation activated not a memory but a retrieval mechanism or that it activated merely one of numerous brain locations involved with each memory.

Wilder Penfield, a brain surgeon, has investigated the memory system in the brain by electrically stimulating the cerebral cortex. (United Press International Photo)

Interim Summary   A particular memory is apparently not located in a particular place in the brain. Instead, as Lashley discovered, widespread areas of the brain may be involved in each memory. Some researchers now believe that certain complex chemicals are produced when learning occurs and that these are the key to the physical basis of memory. The electrical activity of the brain is important also. It has been found that electrical stimulation of certain parts of the brain can bring old memories back to life.

Theories of Memory

A theory of the memory system is an attempt to account for the various facts of human memory that have been discovered. Psychologists have proposed different types of theories of memory. Some focus on a description of hypothetical memory structures, and others focus on the processes that are assumed to take place when material is encoded, stored, or retrieved from memory.

The Duplex Theory of Memory

According to the **duplex theory of memory,** we have two memory systems for storing information, one for remembering something for a short time and a second for remembering something for a long time. (The term *duplex* means having two parts). **Short-term memory (STM)** is the system for storing information for just a few seconds, and **long-term memory (LTM)** is the system for storing information for much longer periods.

Short-Term Memory • Short-term memory appears to be able to hold information for up to thirty seconds or so, but the duration of short-term memory varies under different conditions. By rehearsing the information in short-term memory (repeating it over and over), the items can be retained over long periods of time. The reason is that each time you rehearse an item you give it new life in short-term memory. In effect, each rehearsal puts the information back into short-term memory anew. When you try to remember a telephone number, you are using your short-term memory system, and you probably rehearse the number by saying it to yourself again and again. Short-term memory also has a *limited capacity.* That is, not only does it not hold information for very long, but it cannot hold very much information at one time. You cannot keep fourteen telephone numbers in your short-term memory at one time. Various studies have shown that the capacity of short-term memory is limited to about five to seven new and unrelated items, or five to seven *chunks* of information.

Long-Term Memory • Long-term memory has neither the time limit nor the capacity limit of short-term memory. Information in long-term memory may last for months or decades. Your childhood memories are stored in your long-term memory system. There appears to be no limit to the number of memories that can be kept in the long-term memory system. You already have thousands of different memories in this system. Information enters the short-term memory system and then is either lost or is transferred to the long-term memory system. A process that facilitates this transfer is rehearsal. Unlike short-term memory, long-term memory suffers from retrieval problems. That is, as you may have experienced fairly often, you know that a particular piece of information is in your long-term memory system, but you are unable to locate it when you need it. In fact, you probably had this experience on your last exam.

The Levels-of-Processing Theory

An alternative to the duplex theory of memory, with its STM and LTM, is the **levels-of-processing theory of memory.** This theory denies that there are different parts or systems of memory, and emphasizes instead different memory processes. According to this view, we do not have a short-term memory system with a limited capacity for retaining information; instead, our memory is limited because of the way we process and store information. The central assumption of this theory is that we process information at different levels and that this determines how well we remember it. The first level is that of simple perception: we see or hear or feel the stimulus. A deeper level of analysis occurs when we process the shape of

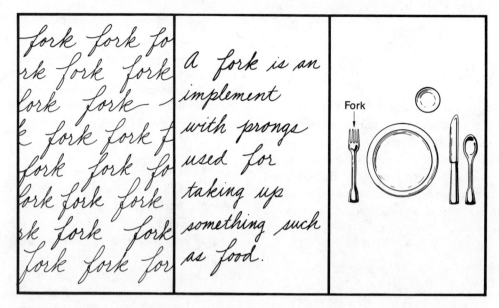

Figure 4-2 Levels of Processing. *According to the levels-of-processing theory, how well we remember something depends upon how deeply it is processed. Noting the shape of the word* fork *represents a shallow level of processing; understanding the meaning of the word represents a deeper level of processing; placing the concept within a context of related ideas represents an even deeper level of processing. The deeper the level of processing, the better.*

the letters of a word or the sound of a word. A still deeper level of processing occurs when we determine the meaning of the word or sentence. The level of processing is even deeper when we not only think of the meaning of the item, but we also form a mental image of it. The deepest level of processing occurs when we think of the meaning of the item within a context of interrelated items. For example, instead of trying to remember the word *fork* out of context, we could try to remember it by making up a story involving it or by thinking of it in relationship to other similar words (*spoon, knife,* and so on). (See Figure 4-2).

Research shows that retention of material processed at "shallow" levels is very poor, but retention of material processed at "deep" levels is good. A way to assure deeper levels of processing is by means of the rehearsal technique. One way to rehearse something you are trying to remember is to say it to yourself over and over. For example, if you are trying to remember a telephone number that you looked up, you will repeat the number to yourself on your way to the tele-

phone. This type of rehearsal does not involve a very deep level of processing, since the number is not placed within a context of meaning. Rote repetition as a method of rehearsal is called **maintenance rehearsal,** because it is effective only in maintaining the item in memory for as long as the rehearsal continues. When you stop saying the telephone number to yourself, you tend to forget it quickly. If you want to remember the number for a longer period, you will need to try a different rehearsal technique. Associating the number with something meaningful and thinking of the number within this context is called **elaborative rehearsal.** For example, how could you remember the telephone number 245-1491 using elaborative rehearsal? The first step would involve thinking of some connections between the number and something meaningful. For example, you might think that the first part (245) is 100 more than your weight, and the second part (1491) is the year before Columbus was supposed to have discovered America. These sorts of connections are examples of elaborative rehearsal.

The Duplicative and Reconstructive Theories

Test your memory for the following sentences.[23] Follow these instructions carefully: Read each sentence, count to five, answer the question on the right, then go on to the next sentence; continue until you have read all of the sentences and answered all of the questions on the right.

Sentence	(Count to Five)	Question
The hill was steep.		What was?
The cat, running from the barking dog, jumped on the table.		From what?
The old car climbed the hill.		What did?
The cat, running from the dog, jumped on the table.		Where?
The car pulled the trailer.		Did what?
The scared cat was running from the barking dog.		What was?
The scared cat jumped on the table.		Did what?
The old car climbed the steep hill.		What did?
The large window was on the porch.		Where?
The car pulling the trailer climbed the steep hill.		Did what?
The cat jumped on the table.		Where?
The car pulling the trailer climbed the hill.		What did?
The dog was barking.		Was what?
The window was large.		What was?

STOP. Cover the sentences above so you cannot see them. Now read the sentences below and mark each as "old" (in the list above) or "new" (not in the list above).

The car climbed the hill.		Old___ New___
The scared cat, running from the barking dog, jumped on the table.		Old___ New___
The window was on the porch.		Old___ New___
The barking dog jumped on the table.		Old___ New___
The scared cat was running from the dog.		Old___ New___
The old car pulled the trailer.		Old___ New___
The cat was running from the barking dog.		Old___ New___
The old car, pulling the trailer, climbed the hill.		Old___ New___
The cat was running from the dog.		Old___ New___
The scared cat, running from the dog, jumped on the table.		Old___ New___
The old car pulling the trailer climbed the steep hill.		Old___ New___
The car climbed the steep hill.		Old___ New___

STOP. Count the number of sentences you judged "old," then read the explanation that follows in order to understand what this means about your memory.

Which sentences did you remember from the first list and mark as "old"? Check the ones you marked as "old" to determine whether they were in fact in the first list. You will find that none of the sentences were actually repeated; every one of them was "new." How can you explain the fact that you "remembered" sentences that you had not read before?

Sometimes your memory plays tricks on you. You think you remember seeing something that you have never seen before. The face of a stranger in a crowd somehow seems familiar.

Memory mistakes are sometimes useful. They

help to show how memory works. Theories of memory are concerned with how past experiences are used in remembering and how they are retained over time. One theory, the **duplicative theory of memory,** proposes a relatively exact storage system, in which the details of past experience are "filed away" and copies later retrieved. From this point of view, memory mistakes might come from misfiling information or failing to retrieve it properly.

A second theory, the **reconstructive theory of memory,** proposes that memory is creative and that duplications or copies of experience are not retained. Instead, what is stored is the meaning and basic facts of experience. According to this theory, remember-

ing involves an imaginative reconstruction made from past experience as a whole. The memory test you have just taken shows that this reconstructive theory has some merit. If you can "remember" things you have never seen before, remembering must involve a creative, or reconstructive, process. Remembering must be more like creating a painting of a past scene than like pulling a photo out of a file. One study of memory used sentences like the ones in the preceding memory tests and found that people were quite sure that they had seen sentences before that were completely new.[24] When a new, complex sentence combined several parts of old sentences, people were especially sure that they had seen it before.

According to the reconstructive theory of memory, remembering involves an imaginative reconstruction of past experience. From this point of view, remembering a face is not like retrieving an internal "photo" but is more like painting a picture. Painting, like memory, is a creative process and does not always duplicate reality. Picasso's painting of Gertrude Stein is an imaginative reconstruction of the reality shown in her photo. (Painting: All rights reserved, The Metropolitan Museum of Art, Bequest of Gertrude Stein, 1946. Photo: The Sophia Smith Collection (Women's History Archive), Smith College, Northampton, Mass.)

Interim Summary   The duplex theory of memory proposes that we have two memory structures or systems: a short-term memory and a long-term memory. The levels of processing theory focuses on *processes* rather than *structures*. It proposes that our memory for information depends upon how we process it. Information processed at a deeper level, through elaborative rehearsal, is retained better than information processed at a shallow level, through maintenance rehearsal. Finally, two theories address how information is stored and retrieved. The duplicative theory proposes a relatively exact storage system, from which information is retrieved intact. By contrast, the reconstructive theory proposes that only the basic *meaning* of experience is stored and that "retrieval" involves a reconstruction of past experience.

Measures of Forgetting

How much do you remember of what you have read in this book? Do you remember more, or less, than the average?

These questions could be answered only if your memory could be measured in some way. Scientists studying memory have devised a number of ways to measure forgetting. Each measure gives a slightly different answer to the question of how much you have forgotten.

The Recall Method

One method that provides a measure of forgetting is the **recall method.** In the recall method you are asked to reproduce exactly what you have read or seen. Can you recall the first sentence of this chapter? If so, you would be able to write it down exactly, word for word. Can you recall the names of all the presidents of the United States? If so, you would be able to write them down.

A pioneer in the study of human memory, the German scientist Hermann Ebbinghaus used the recall method in his experiments in the late 1800s. Ebbinghaus wrote lists of meaningless groups of letters called **nonsense syllables**—for example, FUB, ZID, SEB, HOK, and so on. His procedure was to read through the list of nonsense syllables at a uniform rate and

then, after varying delays, stop to test himself by trying to recall as many items from the list as he could. One of Ebbinghaus's discoveries was that the first and last syllables on the list were typically recalled more easily than the ones in the middle. In a long list, he found that he was more likely to be able to recall the first one or two and the last one or two but was more likely to forget the items in the middle of the list. This effect has been called the **serial-position effect.** Because of the serial-position effect, if you went to the store after memorizing a long grocery list you would be more likely to forget to buy items in the middle of the list than items at the beginning or end.

The Recognition Method

A second method used to measure forgetting is the **recognition method.** In the recognition method you are shown an item and asked whether you have seen it before. Consider this sentence: "Ask not what your country can do for you, ask what you can do for your country." Do you recognize this sentence? Have you experienced it before? You may very well have heard it before or read it somewhere, since it is a famous quotation from President John Kennedy. Have you ever taken a multiple-choice examination? Multiple-choice examinations are recognition tests,

People can recognize thousands of faces they have seen before, even though faces are always changing and expressions are never exactly the same. In one study, students were shown over 600 pictures of faces, then tested to determine how many they could recognize. They recognized 97 percent of the faces seen only once before. (Ellis Herwig/Stock, Boston)

scenes from your childhood, phrases from songs or poems—all in varying degrees are recognized as familiar. In one study, students were presented with 612 different colored pictures; later, they were shown a mixture of these pictures and many new ones.[25] The students correctly recognized an average of 97 percent of the pictures as being those they had seen earlier. The same psychologist showed other people 1,224 sentences, then later tested their ability to recognize them. They were able to recognize correctly 88 percent of the sentences.

The Relearning Method

In the **relearning method** you are first given some new material to learn, and a measure is taken of how long this takes; later you are asked to learn it again (relearn it), and a measure is again taken of how long this takes. Relearning material is usually easier than learning it the first time, because you have not completely forgotten it. If you were to take over again a course that you took last year, it would be easier for you the second time around because you have retained some of the material presented in the course. By measuring how much easier it is the second time around, the relearning method obtains a measure of how much you have retained.

since they present the alternatives and ask you to recognize the correct one.

Your ability to recognize what you have experienced before is extremely large. Faces from the past,

Interim Summary   Three measures of forgetting are the recall method, the recognition method, and the relearning method. The recall method involves reproducing your past experiences. The recognition method requires only that you indicate whether you have experienced something before. The relearning method yields a measure based on how much easier it is to learn a body of material the second time as compared to the first time.

Why You Forget

Often memory fails and you forget. Why do you forget? Can you remember the exact wording of the first sentence of this chapter? You most likely have

forgotten. There are two general possible explanations for the fact that you have forgotten the sentence: first, a certain amount of time has passed, and second, other sentences you have read more recently may have disrupted the memory of the first sentence. These

two general explanations are the basis for prominent theories of forgetting, the decay theory and the interference theory.

Decay

The **decay theory** states that memories weaken spontaneously as time passes; that is, they "decay."[26] According to this theory, you have forgotten the first sentence of this chapter because you read it some time ago; the memory of the sentence decayed or weakened more and more as time passed until the memory was too faint or weak to remember. One way memory decay has been studied is with memories over very short intervals. Evidence shows, for example, that there are brief sensory memories that fade rapidly with time, for both visual events and auditory events.[27] It is difficult to prove that decay occurs, however, in the forgetting of complex material. The problem is the difficulty of deciding whether forgetting was due simply to the passage of time or to interference from activities that occurred in that time period.

Interference

The **interference theory** states that memories weaken because of the action of other memories interfering with them.[28] Learning the name of one new friend is a lot easier than learning the names of ten new friends; the memory of each name may suffer from interference due to the other memories. According to the interference theory, you have forgotten the first sentence of this chapter because you have read many other sentences before it and after it, and the memories of these other sentences create interference.

Two kinds of interference have been identified: proactive interference and retroactive interference. **Proactive interference** occurs when your memory for something you learned recently is interfered with by some previously learned material. In preparing for exams, if you study sociology and then psychology, your memory for the psychological material may be interfered with by the sociological material you learned first, because of proactive interference. Your memory for material in this chapter may be interfered with by material you learned in the previous chapter, because of proactive interference.

A second type of interference, **retroactive interference,** occurs when your memory for something you learned at one time is interfered with by something you learned later.   In preparing for exams, if you study first sociology and then psychology, your memory for the sociology may be interfered with by the psychological material you learned later, because of retroactive interference (see the diagram following). Your memory for material in the previous chapter may be interfered with by your learning of the material in this chapter, because of retroactive interference. When you read Chapters 4, 5, and 6, your memory for Chapter 5 may be interfered with by the material in Chapter 4 (proactive interference) and by the material in Chapter 6 (retroactive interference).

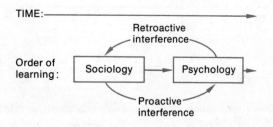

It has proved very difficult to establish which one of the two theories of forgetting, the decay theory or the interference theory, is the best explanation of why we forget.   Probably both theories are right, and some forgetting is due to decay and some to interference.

Repression

When you repress a memory, you block it from consciousness.   It is possible that certain memories are too painful to relive and so are forgotten.   According to Freud, **repression** is a major psychological defense we all use against anxiety; we repress painful experiences in order not to feel the anxiety that would accompany their memories.   A victim of child abuse may repress the painful memories as a means of coping with the traumatic incidents.   Our everyday failures

of memory are sometimes due to repression.   Freud cites the case of a man who repeatedly forgot the name of an acquaintance, and he shows how the forgetting may be explained as repression; it seems that the acquaintance had married a woman whom the man had hoped to marry himself.   His forgetting was a way of dealing with the anxiety of this painful experience.

Amnesia

Amnesia is a loss of memory due to shock or injury. Sometimes the loss of memory is for the immediate past and at other times it is for events in the remote past.   Persons with amnesia cannot remember certain facts of their histories; sometimes they cannot even remember their own names.   What is it like to experience amnesia?   One person described it this way:

With an assurance to my wife that I would be back in a minute or two, I went out and failed to return.   The next thing that I remember is a sound of rifle shots and some short bursts of machine-gun fire coming from the other side of a hill on the right of a road on which I was walking.   I was conscious of being dirty, unshaven and footsore.   I did not seem to be particularly hungry or thirsty.   I had a feeling of puzzlement upon my mind, not unlike that which one may experience on waking from a deep sleep in a strange place.   Where was I?   Who was I?   Something was wrong, but what was it?   I knew my own name and recognized my own writing when I jotted it down on a bit of paper, but everything else seemed uncertain and unstable. . . .   It was some few minutes before I realized fully that I had absolutely no recollection of any course of events which could have brought me to the existing position.   The immediate past seemed to be "a perfect and absolute blank."[29]

Shortly afterward the man went to the police, who located his wife and family.   He still could not remember the events of the past twenty years of his life. Gradually his memory returned, and he wrote a book about his experiences, but he never learned what caused the amnesia.

The human memory has a remarkable capacity for storing and retrieving people, places, and events once experienced. Many older people, however, have a better memory for events in the remote past than for recent ones. (George W. Gardner)

Brain Injury • Sometimes amnesia results from a blow to the head or an injury to the brain. Often when people are knocked unconscious, they fail to remember the blow that did it and also the events occurring just before the blow.[30] Memory for these prior events usually recovers fairly quickly following the return of consciousness, but a memory failure for the events of the few seconds preceding the loss of consciousness may last even after recovery from the head injury.[31] One patient suffered severe memory loss following a brain operation:

He could no longer recognize the hospital staff, apart from Dr. Scovill himself, whom he had known for many years; he did not remember and could not re-learn the way to the bathroom, and he seemed to retain nothing of the day-to-day happenings in the hospital. . . . The same forgetfulness applies to people he has met since the operation, even to those neighbors who have been visiting the house regularly for the past six years. He has not learned their names and he does not recognize any of them if he meets them in the street.[32]

This patient experienced amnesia for events preceding the operation and in addition was unable to retain new information in memory after the operation.

The Case of the Anxious College Student • Occasionally amnesia has an emotional origin. To experience severe loss of memory can be a defense against unbearable anxiety. If you lose all memory of your identity, you start anew, with no painful conflicts. The case of G. R. is an example of amnesia with a psychological origin:

Mr. G. R. was a twenty-four-year-old college student. He was the only son of an extremely ambitious father who was a very successful engineer. His mother was perfectionistic, obsessional, and domineering. The young man was in his third year of university study, struggling to get through a pre-engineering course, in which he was not in the slightest bit interested. However, he felt he had to continue, largely as a result of irresistible parental pressure. He had already failed one year in this course.

His third year was further complicated by the fact that he had made a marriage which had been kept secret, in as far as his parents were concerned. . . .

The marriage had involved emotional and time demands, which had still further interfered with his college performance. He had become extremely anxious about the probable results of examinations, which were due to begin in a few weeks' time. One Friday afternoon, after classes, he took part in a "bull session" in the college dormitory. This left him thoroughly convinced that he would not be able to pass his examinations. This served as the precipitating event.

He started for home, but did not arrive there. Late that evening he was found wandering in the streets of a city some two hundred miles away from the site of his college.[33]

The loss of personal identity is a terrible price to pay for the relief from anxiety. People suffering from anxiety-induced amnesia typically recover from their amnesia and are able to develop less destructive solutions to their conflicts. A trained psychotherapist can sometimes help with this transition.

Interim Summary   Two theories that explain forgetting are the decay theory and the interference theory. According to the decay theory, people forget because memories fade or decay over time. According to the interference theory, people forget because one memory has been interfered with by other memories. This interference can be either proactive (from older memories) or retroactive (from newer memories). Forgetting can also be due to repression, a defensive process in which painful memories are blocked from consciousness. Amnesia is a loss of memory for past events or personal identity resulting from a brain injury or from emotional distress.

Improving Your Memory

The challenge of how to improve memory is an old one. The Greeks invented the "art of memory," creating memory systems by which memory could be improved.[34] Since that time innumerable systems have been invented, most of which depend upon the **principle of orderly association**: items to be remembered are paired with concrete and orderly images. This is a technique for producing a greater depth of processing through elaborative rehearsal. New items to be remembered are matched up with old images already familiar. The set of old images serves as a retrieval aid for the new material.

For one system, you must learn the following rhyme:

One is a bun,
Two is a shoe,
Three is a tree,
Four is a door,

Five is a hive,
Six is sticks,
Seven is heaven,
Eight is a gate,
Nine is wine, and
Ten is a hen.

The rhyme matches a specific image of an object with each number. When you have learned this system, you are able to remember a list of words by combining and associating the words to be remembered with the image from the rhyme. For example, if the first word to be remembered is "wheel," you might imagine a bun with wheels on it speeding around a track. If the second word is "flower," you might imagine a flower growing out of a shoe. The system has been shown to improve memory dramatically.[35] Why don't you try it?

Another popular memory system, using the principle of orderly association, involves imagining items to be remembered in different places. The Russian psychologist Luria studied a man with a photographic memory (mentioned earlier) who went on to become a professional entertainer specializing in feats of memory. One of his techniques for remembering lists of words was to distribute images of them along some roadway or street he visualized in his mind. When it came time to remember the words, he would imagine himself walking along the roadway looking for words. On the rare occasions when S. made an error, it was often attributable to some difficulty in the placement of the word.

I put the image of the pencil *near a fence . . . the one down the street, you know. But what happened was that the image fused with that of the fence and I walked right on past without noticing it. The same thing happened with the word* egg. *I had put it up against a white wall and it blended in with the background. How could I possibly spot a white egg up against a white wall?*[15]

You will not develop the fantastic ability of S. for memorizing material, but your memory can be improved by using the principle of orderly association.

Summary

1. Memory requires three important processes: encoding, storage, and retrieval.
2. Encoding involves putting information into memory by changing the physical energies in the world into memory codes that can be retained.
3. Storage is the process of retaining information over time. Memory storage is organized, with similar items linked by association.
4. Retrieval refers to the process of getting at the stored information so that it can be used.
5. Photographic memory—or eidetic imagery—is a rare ability to remember in great detail whole scenes or pages from books that were seen once.
6. Memories appear not to be located in one spot in the brain but instead to be widespread throughout the cortex.
7. According to the duplex theory of memory, there are two memory systems for storing information—short-term memory and long-term memory.
8. Short-term memory appears to hold information for just a brief time—up to about thirty seconds—and has a very limited capacity. Long-term memory holds material for much longer periods—sometimes for a lifetime—and has an essentially unlimited storage capacity.
9. According to the levels-of-processing theory of memory, memory is limited because of the fact that some information is processed at only a "shallow" level, perhaps through rote rehearsal. Retention is much better for material processed at deeper levels, through elaborative rehearsal.
10. The duplicative theory of memory proposes a relatively exact storage system, while the reconstructive theory of memory proposes that remembering involves imaginative reconstructions of past experience.
11. Three measures of forgetting are the recall method, the recognition method, and the relearning method.
12. Two general explanations have been proposed to account for why people forget: the decay theory and the interference theory.

13. Two special types of interference are proactive interference, in which a memory of something learned recently is interfered with by previous memories, and retroactive interference, in which a memory of something learned at one time is interfered with by something learned later.

14. Most systems for improving memory are based on the principle of orderly association, in which items to be remembered are paired with concrete and orderly images.

Key Concepts

encoding   Putting information into memory by changing the physical energy in the environment into memory codes.

storage   The process of retaining information over time.

retrieval   The process of getting out the stored information so that it can be used.

chunking   Grouping items to be remembered into units or clusters.

tip-of-the-tongue phenomenon   Knowing that a memory is in storage but being unable to retrieve it.

eidetic imagery   A kind of photographic memory in which whole pictures or scenes can be remembered in detail.

engram   The physical basis of memory in the brain.

RNA   Ribonucleic acid; a substance that guides the manufacture of protein molecules.

duplex theory of memory   A theory that there are two memory systems for storing information—one for remembering something for a short time and a second for remembering something for a long time.

short-term memory (STM)   The memory system for storing information for just a few seconds.

long-term memory (LTM)   The memory system for storing information for long periods of time.

levels-of-processing theory of memory   The theory that how well information is remembered depends on how deeply it is processed.

maintenance rehearsal   A shallow level of processing information for memory; the information is rehearsed over and over (rote repetition) without being placed within a context of meaning.

elaborative rehearsal   A deeper level of processing information for memory; the information to be remembered is placed within different contexts of meaning.

duplicative theory of memory   A theory that remembering involves retrieving copies of past experience.

reconstructive theory of memory   A theory that remembering involves an imaginative reconstruction of the past.

recall method   A method of measuring memory in which you are asked to reproduce exactly what you have read or seen.

nonsense syllables   Meaningless groups of letters used in studies to measure memory.

serial-position effect   The tendency to have greater difficulty recalling items in the middle of a list than items at either the beginning or end of the list.

recognition method   A method of measuring memory in which you are shown an item and asked whether you have seen it before.

relearning method   A method of measuring memory in which the length of time you spend learning some new material is compared to the length of time required to relearn that same material at a later time.

decay theory   A theory of forgetting that states that memories fade with time.

interference theory   A theory of forgetting that states that memories are disrupted by newer and older memories.

proactive interference   Older items in memory interfere with the memory for more recent items.

retroactive interference   More recent items in memory interfere with the memory for older items.

repression   A defensive process in which painful memories are forgotten by being blocked from consciousness.

amnesia   A loss of memory for past events or personal identity as a result of brain injury or psychological stress.

principle of orderly association   A rule for improving memory that suggests associating material to be remembered with an organized set of images.

Chapter 5
Academic Learning and Retention

Key Questions
1. How can academic learning be made more efficient?
2. What are some techniques for improving learning from lectures and textbooks?
3. How can memory for academic material be improved?
4. How can motivation and concentration be strengthened?
5. How can time management be improved?

You've taken hundreds of small tests before, but college is the big test—one long test of learning efficiency. Those who don't make it, who fail or drop out, are not so much less intelligent as less *efficient* than the survivors. Those who have problems with learning efficiency have not yet learned how to optimize the learning process.

Debbie made good grades in high school and was president of her class. She was active in school affairs and in many extracurricular activities, including the school annual. She was a serious student but didn't have to work very hard. Most of the time she was able to complete her homework at school. But everything changed when she went to college.

In her first year of college, Debbie was determined to be successful but everything seemed to go wrong. When she made her first "D," she could hardly believe it. When she made her second, she began to wonder if she belonged in college or not. What was the point of it all if she studied all the time and still made bad grades?

Studying long and hard is not the same as studying well. Effective academic learning does require effort, but effort alone does not produce good grades. Effective learning depends upon applying specific skills and techniques for improving efficiency. A good knowledge of learning skills is not inborn and is not an evitable consequence of being reasonably intelligent. These skills must be learned.

You already are an expert learner, having spent a lifetime working at it, and you no doubt can do it rather well. However, you may not be a very efficient learner. In a gas shortage, it's important for automobiles to be tuned up to be maximally efficient; similarly, with a shortage of time, it's important for your learning skills to be tuned up to be maximally efficient. To accomplish this, the first step is to identify your learning problems.

Test Yourself:
An Inventory of Learning Problems

What are your learning problems?

Most of the time you get good grades, but occasionally you don't. Why? Often studying seems to take more time than you have available. Why? As you think about your own experiences of studying and taking exams, you are aware of problems and frustrations, fatigue and anxiety, and sometimes satisfaction or even elation. Could it all be made easier?

In order to understand better the nature of your learning problems and what could be done about them, it would be helpful first to analyze what they are and to categorize them as carefully as possible. On the following list, check off the problems you have.

Problems Learning from Lectures

☐ My mind wanders and I miss important points in lectures.

☐ I don't know how to keep good notes.

☐ I try to write down everything that is said, but it doesn't seem to help.

☐ I can't follow some things that are said in lecture.

☐ The material in lecture is presented too fast for me.

Problems Reading Texts

☐ I read too slowly to get through the assignment.

☐ When I'm reading I sometimes just turn the pages without absorbing anything.

☐ I can't figure out what's important and what is not.

☐ When I'm reading, I feel I understand the concepts fairly well, but actually I don't.

Problems with Memory

☐ I can't seem to remember the major points in a lecture—it's "in one ear and out the other."

☐ When I read the textbook, I often forget the material right away.

☐ Sometimes I memorize definitions and theories word for word, but then I don't recognize them later on the exam when they are changed.

☐ During an exam I often can't remember the material I knew "cold" the night before.

Problems with Concentration or Motivation

☐ I generally have trouble concentrating when I try to study.

☐ My mind wanders and I daydream too much when I study.

☐ Sometimes I fall asleep when I try to study.

☐ I have trouble studying material I'm not interested in.

☐ Studying bores me, and I have to force myself to open my books.

Problems with Time Management

☐ I just can't find the time to get all my homework done.

☐ I procrastinate and keep putting things off.

☐ I have too many interruptions and distractions when I try to study.

☐ I waste too much time—watching television, talking to friends, playing games or sports, going out, or doing other things that won't help my grades.

☐ I have trouble studying without being reminded or prompted by family, friends, or teachers.

Now, check back over the problems that you marked. Do you have any significant learning problems that were not in the list? Do your problems tend to cluster in one or two areas, such as memory or concentration? A recognition and analysis of your learning problems is an important first step in doing something about them. The remainder of this chapter is designed to teach you some of the principles and techniques for effective academic learning that have resulted from basic research by psychologists on human learning and memory.

A Theory of Academic Learning and Retention

One way of conceiving of academic learning is as a *passive process* in which information is transferred from an instructor or textbook to the mind of a student. From this point of view, the student's task is to attend the lectures and read the textbooks in order to permit this process to occur. Students who approach academic learning in this way are often heard complaining, "But I read the entire assignment!" or "I didn't miss a single lecture, but I still failed!"

Learning, however, is not something that happens to you by virtue of exposing your ears to lectures or your eyes to textbooks. The key to effective academic learning is to take an *active* role as a learner. An active role in the learning process involves (1) *questioning* what you hear and read, (2) *taking notes* that summarize main points, and (3) *searching* for relationships between the new—the unfamiliar idea presented in lecture or text—and the known—the ideas and concepts previously acquired and already part of your body of knowledge.

The New and the Known

Why is psychology easier to learn than nuclear physics? An important reason is that nuclear physics, unlike psychology, consists of concepts with which you have little or no familiarity. You have had little experience observing the physical structure of the atom, but you have been observing human behavior all of your life. Because you already know so much about human behavior, additional learning is much easier. You can relate the new to the known.

Meaningful academic learning requires relating new material to what you already know or discovering new relationships among things you have experienced. The term *relationship* is important here. Your knowledge of the world consists, not of lists of unrelated information, but of a body of related facts and rules. Your knowledge of psychology consists of facts, concepts, and their relationships.

A pile of unconnected boards and nails is of little use, but if they are connected and related they form a structure, a house. Ideas are like that. Unconnected ideas or concepts appear meaningless to us, but a set of related or organized ideas can be understood.

Schema Theory

According to the **schema theory of knowledge,** knowledge consists of sets of organized facts, rules, and plans. Just as a house is a physical structure composed of interconnected boards, a **schema** (plural *schemata*) is a mental structure composed of interrelated facts, rules, and plans. You have thousands of schemata, or sets of related facts, about all kinds of things. You have a schema for butterflies—the set of facts and ideas that you have about butterflies. You have a basketball schema, an algebra schema, and an automobile schema.

Without an existing schema or framework for a subject, new information about that subject will not be easily understood. If you know nothing about automobiles, a lecture on the carburetor will leave you confused. If you know nothing about basketball, the description of a particular play won't make any sense. Learning occurs when you are able to relate the new information to previously acquired information or experiences. Figure 5-1 gives other examples.

A joke that was popular in the junior high schools a few years ago went something like this:

Figure 5-1 Organizing Schemata *are sets of related ideas that can be used to organize information and to make sense of it. In the examples above, the irregular black shapes can be organized and made sense of by applying schemata for "triangle", "schema", and "dog."*

Question: "What has horns, a long tail, and flies?"

At this point the listener has been given what appears to be a set of completely unrelated characteristics that cannot be organized into a single image. What is missing in this instance is a schema that can be used to clarify and interpret the facts presented. As the listener, bewildered, is searching for an appropriate schema, the answer is given: "A dead cow."

The task faced by police detectives trying to solve a crime is to obtain a great deal of information and to organize it so that the pieces of the puzzle fit together. The bits of evidence that appear at first to be unconnected are shown later to be related and to be understood once the solution is known. Before they discover the identity of the criminal, the facts and evidence may make no sense at all. Solving a crime, in a sense, is like finding a schema, a set of related ideas that can be used to clarify the facts of the case.

Students, like police detectives, need a schema in order to make sense of the principles and evidence that they encounter in class and in textbooks. Without a set of organized and connected ideas about a topic, the facts presented in a lecture will not be understood.

You have many schemata, or sets of organized ideas, about human behavior. For example, you have a schema for the psychology of academic learning. This schema includes facts about the conditions that facilitate or interfere with college learning, ideas about preparing for exams, and many other related facts and ideas. One of the purposes of this chapter is to add to this schema, to strengthen your knowledge of academic learning and retention.

A Research Example

The implicaton of schema theory is that a certain degree of previously acquired information is essential to understanding new information.[1] A previously existing schema is necessary in order to clarify and interpret new experiences. Without having been clarified by existing knowledge, a new experience may not be understood at all.

Dooling and Lachman[2] conducted an experiment in which students read a paragraph under one of two conditions: (1) no title, context, or previous information about the subject was given, and (2) a brief title was provided, which established a schema. After reading the paragraph, the students were asked to write down as much of it as they could remember. The results showed that having the appropriate schema in advance was essential. Here is the paragraph:

With hocked gems financing him, our hero bravely defied all scornful laughter that tried to prevent his scheme. Your eyes deceive you, he had said, an egg not a table correctly typifies this unexplored planet. Now three sturdy sisters sought proof, forging along sometimes through calm vastness, yet more often over turbulent peaks and valleys. Days became weeks as many doubters spread fearful rumors about the edge. At last, from nowhere, welcome winged creatures appeared, signifying momentous success.[2]

Those students who read the paragraph without the benefit of seeing the title first showed little comprehension of it and were generally unable to recall what it said. Those who read the title first, however, were able to remember it quite well. The title was, "Christopher Columbus Discovering America." With the title in mind, go back and reread the paragraph. The title in this case provides a schema for interpreting and clarifying what is said. Without this schema, the paragraph makes little sense.

In similar studies, other researchers have shown that it is necessay to provide the schema in *advance* of the new information.[3] Providing the schema afterward does no good.

What is the implication of all this for improving your ability to learn from lectures and textbooks? The conclusion from schema theory and the related research is that understanding and remembering new information requires an existing schema, a context or framework of previously acquired knowledge. Understanding and remembering a lecture in a college class requires that you bring to the lecture some previously acquired knowledge about the subject. This means that some preparation is necessary in advance of the lecture, in order to establish a framework. Obtaining the framework afterward will do little good. Understanding a textbook chapter also requires an ex-

isting framework or context of knowledge about the subject. If the textbook does not provide this knowledge, one way to acquire it is through scanning the book to get a general idea of what is going to be discussed. This general idea serves the same purpose as the title of the Christopher Columbus paragraph—it provides a schema for understanding the new information.

Interim Summary   Efficiency in academic learning requires taking an active role as a learner. Questioning, taking notes, and searching for relationships are ways to become actively involved in the learning process. According to the schema theory of knowledge, knowledge consists of organized sets of ideas, rules, and plans. Without an existing schema, you will not understand new information about a subject as well. The implication of this theory is that you could improve learning efficiency by acquiring a schema, or framework, in advance of attending a lecture or reading the text. For example, such a schema could be simply a set of general ideas about the topic to be discussed.

Retaining What is Learned

Many students suffer memory lapses during exams, failing to remember material that they thought they had "down cold." Do you have difficulty remembering what you have read or heard in lecture? Even though you have learned and understand some important principles, retaining them can often be a challenge.

Levels of Processing and Encoding

According to the **levels-of-processing theory** (see Chapter 4), we analyze and process information at different levels—some "shallow" and some "deep"—and this determines how well we can remember things. Shallow levels of processing are involved when we listen to or read material with only half of our attention on the task. Shallow processing also occurs during rote memorization—that is, mindlessly repeating a definition over and over with little thought about

what the words mean. This "shallow" type of study is called **maintenance rehearsal.**

Greater depth of processing is involved when we actively think about what the words mean and when we try to relate new information to already-acquired information. Studying by going over meanings, associations, applications, and relationships requires greater depth of processing. This "deep" type of study is called **elaborative rehearsal.**

Teaching a concept or theory to someone else requires considerable depth of processing; in order to effectively explain an idea to another person, you must understand it fairly well yourself and must be prepared to answer questions about it. One way to improve your memory for material you are learning is to try to teach it to your friend, your mother, or your roommate.

Another way to achieve depth of processing is to paraphrase the definition or theory you are trying to learn. The act of putting it into your own words requires that you process the information deeply, at the meaning level. Try writing down the principle or concept in your own words. This kind of active working with the material ensures adequate depth of processing and thereby strengthens the way the material is encoded in memory.[4]

Encoding Specificity and Retrieval

Suppose you were taking an examination on this chapter and were asked the following fill-in type question:

As a technique for remembering a definition, word-for-word repetition is usually less effective than paraphrasing, according to the _____ theory.

How were you able to remember that the answer called for was "levels of processing?" In answering a question like this, you must retrieve previously learned material from memory. Your ability to retrieve information depends upon retrieval cues. ·A **retrieval cue** is something that helps you find information in memory. In the fill-in question above, the words in the question are retrieval cues because they help point to the answer called for. A problem for students is that the retrieval cues provided by instructors in exam questions are often either too different or too brief to be of much help. Sometimes, however, there is considerable overlap between the material as originally learned and the retrieval cues available at the time of testing. For example, you might have learned that "Psychology is the science of behavior." Later, on a quiz, you may have the test item, "_____ is the science of behavior." In this case there would be a complete overlap between the information available at the time of learning and the information (retrieval cues) available at the time of testing. The words you studied and the words in the exam question are exactly alike and completely overlap.

According to the **encoding-specificity principle,** the effectiveness of retrieval cues depends upon the degree of overlap between the information presented at the time of learning a concept and the information available later when you are trying to remem-

ber it.[5] Memory is best when the information encoded at the time of learning is the same as the information presented at the time of testing.

What are the implications of the encoding-specificity principle for academic learning and retention? As a student in a class, you have little control over the way questions are asked on examinations, and therefore you cannot make sure that exam questions are phrased according to the way you studied the material. You do, however, have control over the way material is encoded during the learning process. You can increase the likelihood of an overlap between the information given during the learning time and that given at testing time by thinking of questions to ask yourself about the material you are learning and by thinking of applications for this material. The questions and the applications you think of are likely to resemble the questions and applications that will appear on exams. Therefore, the exam questions will be more effective retrieval cues, and you will be better able to remember the material learned.

Overlearning

You may have had the experience of having had a principle or theory "down cold" the night before an exam and then failing to remember it during the exam. You apparently had not learned the material as well as you thought you had. This problem results from practicing the material only until you just barely learn it. Material that is just barely learned is vulnerable to forgetting.

Because of forgetting, learning the material is not enough. You must overlearn it. **Overlearning** involves continuing to study material for a while after you feel you have mastered it. You must assume that you will forget some of the material between the time you last study something and the time you are tested on it. When you study something just until you feel you know it, you will often forget it later. By overlearning the material, you give yourself a margin for forgetting.

Interim Summary

The levels-of-processing theory and the encoding-specificity principle point to ways that you can improve your retention of what you read and study. According to the levels-of-processing theory, the information that we encounter as we study is processed at different levels. Information processed at shallow levels—for example, through maintenance rehearsal—is not retained very well. Information processed at deeper levels—for example, through elaborative rehearsal—is retained better and for longer periods. According to the encoding-specificity principle, the ease with which memories can be retrieved for exams depends upon the similarity between the conditions of study and the conditions of the test. Memory is best when the information present at the time of learning a concept is available during the test in the form of a retrieval cue. Finally, memory is better if material is overlearned, since you need a margin for forgetting.

Learning from Lectures

In most college courses, the classroom is the learning center, the focus of instruction. Success in college courses requires certain skills in learning from lectures. Classroom lectures are designed not only to stimulate thought and to provide important facts and principles, but also to present information necessary for progress through the course: what to read and when, when exams are given, what the exams will cover, and so on. For some students, however, coping with lectures can be a serious problem: they have difficulty keeping up, staying awake, or maintaining effective class notes.

Selective Attention and Active Listening

Attending a lecture will guarantee that the words spoken will reach your ears but will not guarantee that these words will be processed, understood, and remembered.

The human mind is limited in its capacity to attend to several things at once. In general, we can attend to only one thing at a time, a process called **selective attention**. Thus, in a lecture, we have the capacity to attend to the person sitting next to us but not—at the same time—to what is being said in lec-ture. We have the capacity to attend to a daydream about a favorite person but not—at the same time—to the context of the lecture.

We can selectively listen to the lecture or to a conversation occurring behind us, but it is extremely difficult, if not impossible, to listen to both. Our ability to tune in to different conversations occurring around us is quite remarkable. Try to remember the last time you were at a party or in a crowded room with everyone talking at once. You were able to attend to any one of several conversations without turning around or otherwise moving. This feature of selective attention is called the **cocktail-party phenomenon.**

The cocktail-party phenomenon works to your disadvantage in a lecture class. It is easy to tune out the lecture and tune in something else. The problem is that you then will not recall what was said in lecture. A research demonstration of this principle can be found in the studies of selective attention that involve **dichotic listening**. Dichotic listening is a procedure in which an individual is given earphones playing two different messages, one in one ear and a different one in the other ear. Such studies show that it is possible to remember one message or the other but not both.[6] Other studies showed that it was not possible to read and listen effectively at the same time; individuals who were asked to try to do both were

Studying with the television on is highly inefficient.   Studies show that people cannot effectively read and listen at the same time, so listening to the television must interfere with your efforts to pay attention to your books.   (Richard Chase)

later able to remember what they read, or what they heard, but not both.[7]

In a large lecture, it's easy for your mind to wander.   On occasion you may even have to struggle to keep yourself from dozing off.   Keeping alert, paying attention, and listening are frequently difficult.   One step toward improving your listening is to recognize that listening is not a passive reaction that you have to a speaker who is somehow responsible for "making you" listen or "capturing" your attention.   Instead, listening is a skill; it is an activity , something that you *do*—either well or poorly.   And it is not a skill you are born with (or without) but is learned, acquired through practice.

The key to *active listening* is to formulate and answer questions as you listen to what the speaker has to say.   For example, you could start at the beginning of a lecture by asking yourself, "What is the lecturer going to talk about today?"   Then you could continue by asking yourself, "What are the major points?"   Or you could ask yourself, "Why did the

lecturer say that?   What evidence is there for believing that?"   Asking the instructor questions during lecture, if appropriate, can also be helpful.   Taking an active approach to listening is also a way of keeping alert and interested during lectures.

The Encoding and Storage Function of Notes

Taking good notes from lecture is an important part of active listening.   Notes serve two main functions: (1) an encoding function, in which the lecture is transformed into material more easily remembered; and (2) an external storage function, in which the content of the lecture is retained for later review.   Aside from the benefit of using lecture notes as an aid to memory when preparing for an exam, taking notes appears to strengthen memory for the lecture material.   The physical act of writing down your version of the main points covered will help you later, even if you never look at your notes again.

One experimenter compared the effect of several note-taking conditions.[8]   One group of students did not take notes, but later reviewed the lecture mentally.   On a subsequent test, this group showed the least recall.   Another group of students took notes and later reviewed them.   This group showed the most recall.   In a second study, students listened to a lecture while (*a*) taking no notes, (*b*) taking notes, or (*c*) having a lecturer-generated summary.[9]   Those students who kept their own notes and later reviewed them had the highest recall scores.

One reason that note taking helps is that it necessitates greater depth of processing.   Research on the levels-of-processing theory shows that material that is dealt with at the meaning level (the semantic level) is better remembered than material dealt with at levels that require less analysis (for example, simply listening to what is said without understanding its meaning).

According to the levels-of-processing theory of memory, taking lecture notes that require paraphrasing main points serves to encode the major ideas of the lecture in memory more deeply and more permanently. Going over the notes by thinking of the relationships between the new material that was presented and what you already know further strengthens your memory. Paraphrasing and placing the new material within different contexts of meaning is a form of elaborative rehearsal, which has been demonstrated to be highly effective for retention.

Some students make the mistake of trying to write down everything that is said in a lecture. In the first place, you really won't be able to do this very well because you can't write fast enough. In the second place, trying to do this would distract you from listening to the lecture. Finally, even if you could do this, you will not have time later to go over the entire lecture word for word. Your notes should be a summary of the major points, facts, and principles that are covered. The best notes are highly selective and are taken in some form of outline.[10] Later, when you review what was said, you should go over these notes and extract from them an even simpler summary of main points. This process of review and summation is also an effective memory aid. Compare the two sets of notes shown in Figures 5-2 and 5-3.

Reading and Comprehending Textbooks

Because the amount of reading that is required in college is enormous, students who can read efficiently have a considerable advantage. How well you read can make a significant difference in the grades you make in your courses. For every hour you spend in class listening to a lecture, you will probably have to spend two to four hours outside class reading and going over your notes.

The Psychology of Skilled Reading

Around the turn of the century, Edmund Huey wrote a book on the psychology of reading, and commented on the difficulty of understanding this complex human ability:

To completely analyze what we do when we read would almost be the acme of a psychologist's achievements, for it would be to describe very many of the most intricate workings of the human mind, as well as to unravel the tangled study of the most remarkable specific performance that civilization has learned in all its history.[11]

Reading is indeed a complicated cognitive activity, and scientists have not yet come to understand very well how it works.

One important aspect of skilled reading is the movement of the eyes. There are three basic types of eye movement: pursuit movements, saccadic movements, and regression movements. **Pursuit movements** are smooth, tracking movements that occur when your eyes follow something that is moving. Look at your finger as you move it back and forth in front of your eyes. The eye movements involved as you follow your finger are called pursuit movements. **Saccadic movements** are the jerky movements that occur when your eyes jump from spot to spot. A single saccadic movement is called a **saccade.** Saccadic movements occur as your eyes move from your desk to your bed and then to your window. Whenever your eyes move from place to place without following a moving target, saccadic movements are occurring. Reading involves looking from place to place on a page and thus involves saccadic movements. **Regression movements** are a type of saccadic movement that moves backwards. As you read, your eyes hop from spot to spot, but sometimes you go back over a sentence again—the jump backwards on the page is called regression movement. If you "get ahead" of yourself, encounter an especially difficult passage, or come to a part that is extremely important, you may look back over the sentence a second time in a regression movement.

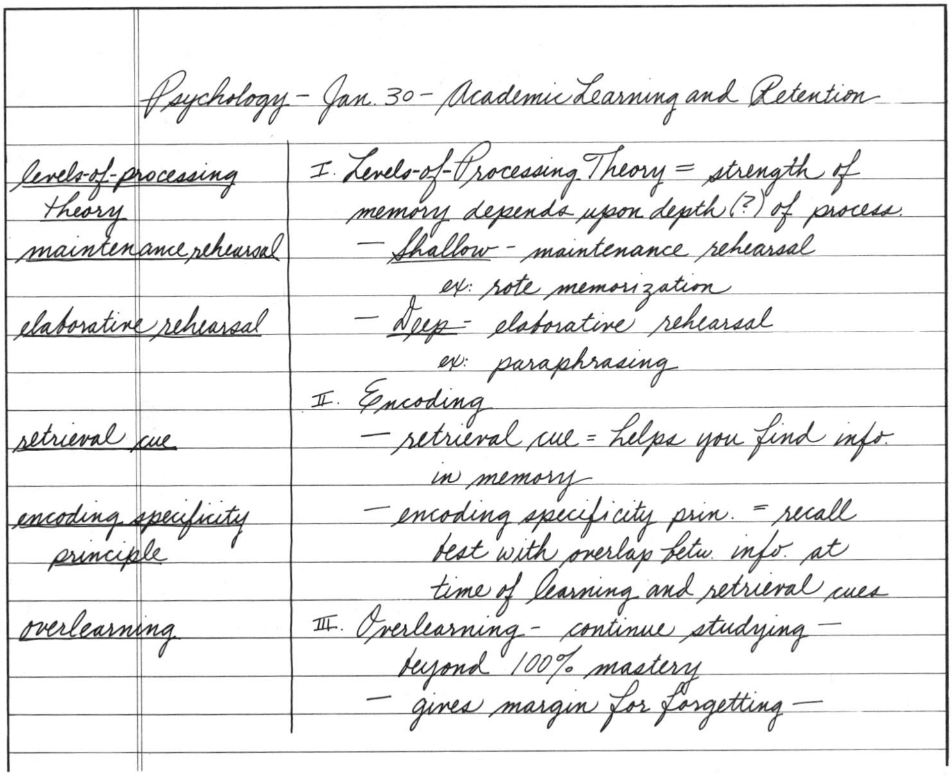

Psychology – Jan. 30 – Academic Learning and Retention

levels-of-processing theory	I. Levels-of-Processing Theory = strength of memory depends upon depth (?) of process.
maintenance rehearsal	– Shallow – maintenance rehearsal ex: rote memorization
elaborative rehearsal	– Deep – elaborative rehearsal ex: paraphrasing
	II. Encoding
retrieval cue	– retrieval cue = helps you find info. in memory
encoding specificity principle	– encoding specificity prin. = recall best with overlap betw. info. at time of learning and retrieval cues
overlearning	III. Overlearning – continue studying – beyond 100% mastery – gives margin for forgetting –

Figure 5-2 Effective lecture notes.

many students suffer from memory lapses – according to the levels-of-processing theory, we process information at different levels – some shallow – some deep. Shallow levels of processing are involved when we

Maintenance rehearsal vs. elaborative rehearsal

Retrieval cue

GET BRAKES FIXED THURSDAY

DON'T FORGET!

645-7332 – Dave

Encoding specificity – degree of overlap is important –

Continue to learn beyond 100% mastery –

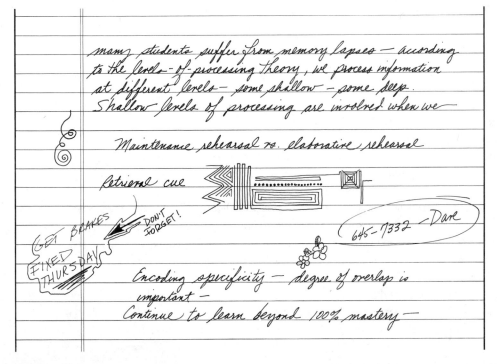

Figure 5-3 Ineffective lecture notes.

At the end of each saccade your eyes stop for a brief moment (for about one-quarter of a second). This small pause is called a **fixation**. Since the eye movements themselves are extremely brief (perhaps two hundredths of a second), most of your reading time consists of fixation. Only during a fixation are you able to pick up information from the page; during a saccadic movement you essentially see nothing.

Good readers differ from poor readers in several ways: (1) Good readers have fewer fixations per line or per paragraph than poor readers; they are able to get as much or more information from fewer pauses. (2) Good readers also have shorter fixations; they are able to pick up the necessary information in a shorter time. (3) Finally, good readers have a regular, economical pattern of eye movements, while poor readers have erratic patterns of eye movements involving many regression movements.[12]

Improving Reading and Comprehension

Although reading speed can be improved by changing the pattern of eye movements, the rate of comprehension depends less on eye movements than on reading strategy. Your goal in reading textbooks is to become efficient in reading. This does not mean simply reading fast; it means reading *effectively*. "Speed reading" is a type of skimming in which only a small portion of the words on the page is read. This type of reading is appropriate for certain types of reading tasks, but not for others. When you need to understand the material in depth and in detail, as in reading a textbook, speed reading alone will not suffice.

Effective reading depends upon comprehending the material efficiently. In reading a textbook, your task is to extract the important information and commit it to memory so that you can later recall it. Sometimes—for example when you have very little background in the subject matter you are reading about—this task of adding new information is difficult and reading progresses very slowly. Other times—for example when you are reading a book the second

Effective reading depends more upon good comprehension than upon high speed. The key to improving comprehension is to read more actively. When some people read, they do little more than move their eyes. Active reading involves interacting with the material, searching for relationships, and questioning what you read. (Frank Siteman/Stock, Boston)

time—there is little new information, and reading is consequently very fast. As one author put it,

The bottleneck [in reading speed] comes from the requirement to add the information on the page to the structures that the reader has in memory, or from the requirement to build new structures. If there is no new information, there is no bottleneck.[13]

Thus, the problem with reading is not improving speed but improving comprehension.

Active Reading

Reading, like listening, must be active in order to be effective. When most people read, they do little more than move their eyes. Active reading requires more work, but it has a payoff: when you are through, you know what you've read.

There are several different kinds of reading, each with its own separate purpose. Reading for pleasure usually involves starting at the beginning and reading through, page by page, without great concentration. When you read a novel for pleasure, you don't want to look ahead because you might spoil the suspense, so you start at the beginning and work through. You also don't want to work very hard at it because that would spoil the fun, so you only apply part of your mind to it. By contrast, skimming and reading with concentration are used when reading a textbook and involve very different processes. Few textbooks are full of suspense, so looking ahead to see how things turn out is to be encouraged.

How do you read your textbooks? Do you read actively? Active reading involves three steps: prereading, skimming, and concentrated reading. When you read actively, you begin by prereading the book. **Prereading** involves examining the text and the chapter you are about to read in order to get a general idea of the structure or organization and to familiarize yourself with the sequence of topics that are covered. You might want to take a few minutes right now to preread this textbook. You will find that the book consists of nine major parts, or sections, with each part having several chapters. You will notice that each chapter begins with a few general questions and ends with a chapter summary. Key concepts are listed after each chapter. Before you continue reading this book, why don't you stop and preread it by thumbing through to see how it was put together?

The second step in active reading is skimming. **Skimming** gives you an overview of what your assignment is about. You skim by reading the chapter subheadings, the interim summaries, and an occasional topic sentence at the beginning of a paragraph. Look for lists of items, definitions of boldfaced words, and emphasized ideas.[14] After you skim a chapter, you should have a rather good idea of what it is all about, and you should already know the major points that the chapter makes. Skimming provides a *schema*—a set of interconnected ideas—which will make comprehending and remembering the details of the chapter much easier.

Concentrated reading is the next step. When you begin to read with concentration, you should stop after key passages and restate the main ideas to yourself. You should try to find relationships between principles presented in the text and your own experiences or information previously acquired. You should try making up questions that are answered in the material you are reading, questions that might appear on an exam. All of these activities serve to encode the material in depth and therefore to improve your retention. These activities are different forms of elaborative rehearsal, which is known to strengthen memory.

During the stage of concentrated reading, you should underline, highlight, or write in the margins of your text. Text marking improves concentration and retention, and focuses later review on major points.[15,16,17] Students who highlight or underline before they preread and skim tend to mark too much of the material. They don't yet know what is important and what is irrelevant because they are reading the material for the first time. But when you wait until after you have skimmed the chapter before you read and mark it, then you will be able to be selective in your emphasis. Only then can text marking be effective in helping you.

By following these steps, your reading will be *active* rather than *passive*. You will continually interact with the material you are reading and code it deeply. Students who read in this way comprehend what they read better and remember it longer. Although this process may take more time than you typically spend in reading your textbooks, it is more efficient and effective and will pay off in terms of greater retention and higher grades.

Interim Summary   Learning from lectures and textbooks requires active listening and active reading.   A problem with listening is that attention is selective—you can pay attention only to one thing at a time.   This means that you will not be able to attend to the lecture and to other things at the same time.   Thinking of questions and writing notes are ways of making listening more active.   Notes have both an encoding function and a storage function.

Active reading involves prereading, skimming, and concentrated reading.   Only in the third stage—concentrated reading—should highlighting or underlining be attempted.   Skilled readers differ from slow readers in several ways.   Their eye movements display fewer regressions, and their fixations are both fewer and shorter than those of poorer readers.   But the major reading problem is not poor speed but poor comprehension.

Improving Motivation and Concentration

Studying in college is hard work.   Whether you do it efficiently—or even do it at all—depends upon your ability to manage and control your own behavior so that you study, with concentration, when you have to study instead of doing something else.   But some students are not motivated to learn.

A student who recently dropped out of college explained that her problem was "willpower":

In the first place, the professors and books were boring. They just couldn't get me interested in all those picky points.   But I guess it was really my fault, because I really didn't study.   I tried, but I couldn't get myself to do it.   I start to study, then I fall asleep.   I start to study, then start thinking about my boyfriend.   I don't have the willpower to stick with it.

The student was wrong.   "Willpower" is not something that you have or don't have.   Instead, it is something that you learn.   Being able to study when you have to study is a skill—and you can learn how to do it.

Motivation and Interest

Many students think that their interest in a subject is something that they were born with or that happens to them, which they can do nothing about.   But your interests are made, not inborn, and are the result primarily of what you do, not what someone else does.   Long-term interest in a subject depends on a number of factors.   One of these is *familiarity*—for the most part, you are more interested in those subjects with which you are generally familiar.   Most students are more interested in a subject after they learn about it than before, although you can probably think of some exceptions to this rule.   Another factor is *competence*—for the most part, you are more interested in those subjects you do well in.   A third factor is *relevance*—you tend to be more interested in those subjects that have some connection to what you already know or to your life and experiences.   A fourth factor is *social support*—you tend to be more interested in those subjects that your friends talk about and are interested in.   To some degree you have control over each of these factors and therefore control over your long-term interests.

You can increase your long-term interest in a

subject by staying with it until you become more familiar with it, by mastering some aspect of it to achieve some degree of competence with it, by deliberately searching for the connections between the new subject and your present knowledge and experiences, and by talking to others who are interested in the subject.

How easily are you bored with your studies? You want to learn the material, but how can you maintain your interest? Your short-term interest in a subject depends a lot on how you approach it. Many students report that they try to study and find that their minds start to wander as they begin to daydream, or that they sometimes fall asleep in the middle of a chapter. The inability to concentrate interferes with college success, because if you can't concentrate, you can't get the information into your mind to begin with. There are three basic strategies for improving your ability to concentrate while studying: (1) create a special place that will stimulate you to study, (2) stop punishing yourself by forcing yourself to study, and (3) make studying more rewarding.

Studying ineffectively. (*Barbara L. Baumann*)

Stimulus Control and Incompatible Behavior: Create a Special Place

Most students try to study in the wrong place, a place that encourages all kinds of behavior except studying. It's easy to lose concentration when you are studying in front of a window with attractive and interesting people outside. It's easy to lose concentration when you are trying to study in front of a loud television set. An open window invites you to look out and watch the world go by. A television set invites you to watch and listen to an entertaining show. Looking out the window and watching television are examples of behavior that is incompatible with studying. **Incompatible behavior** is behavior that interferes with the behavior desired—in this case, studying.

Where do you study? Are there distractions there that encourage incompatible behavior and interfere with trying to study?

Another problem with study places is that they are often multipurpose places. A kitchen table, for example, may be used for studying but also for eating. A bed may be used for studying but also for sleeping. Under most circumstances, the physical setting where you have done things in the past tends to stimulate you to do these things again, as if the stimuli in the setting acquire the power to control your behavior. When you are in the kitchen looking at the refrigerator, you are tempted to eat. When you are lying down in your bed, you are tempted to sleep. If you try to study on your bed, you will be distracted by thoughts of sleeping. If you try to study on the

Studying effectively. (*Barbara L. Baumann*)

do not use it for eating, smoking, or drinking; do not talk to your friends there or write letters there; in fact, do nothing there except study, and you will find that when you are there your mind will become more and more focused on studying. You will have created a place that encourages you to study.[18]

Punishment and Studying: Stop Punishing Yourself

Most students are not able to study with focus and concentration for more than twenty or thirty minutes at a time; yet, when their minds begin to wander, they try to force themselves to go on. This is exactly the wrong approach.

Forcing yourself to study when you have lost concentration and interest is a kind of self-punishment. According to the **Law of Effect,** behavior that has favorable consequences tends to recur and behavior that has unfavorable consequences tends to be abandoned. Associating unfavorable consequences, or punishment, with the act of studying will make studying less and less likely to occur. Try to think of the things you do when you are studying that are unpleasant, frustrating, or boring. These are the things that you should try to avoid.

But what if the unpleasantness and the punishment comes from studying itself? To avoid this kind of punishment, you would have to avoid studying. For most people, however, it is not the studying that is so unpleasant, but the amount of studying and the long hours of reading. To end this kind of punishment, you should stop studying for such extended periods of time. Break your study periods up into smaller sessions. Forcing yourself to go on after you lose concentration should be avoided. After you study efficiently for a while, stop and do something else. If you lose concentration while studying, get up, take a break, and then return to the study task. If you do this regularly, you will find that you will be able to concentrate for longer and longer periods. You will be reducing the punishment associated with studying.

kitchen table, you will be distracted by thoughts of eating. The principle of **stimulus control** states that the stimuli in the environment where you repeatedly do something acquire the power to elicit that behavior. If you have repeatedly used the desk in your room for writing letters to friends, talking on the phone, daydreaming, or doodling, your desk has acquired the power to encourage you to perform these activities.

You can use the principle of stimulus control to your advantage by creating a special study place that will encourage you to study. You can do this by finding a place to study, and do nothing else there—

Reinforcement and Studying: Make Studying Rewarding

Studying is hard work. When you have satisfactorily completed a unit of work, you should try to find a way of giving yourself a reward. Behavior that has favorable consequences is strengthened and tends to recur. Reinforcing yourself for successful studying will strengthen your ability to study with concentration. After you have completed studying this chapter, you might give yourself permission to watch a television program or read a novel for a while. Even such things as taking a short walk, calling a close friend, or buying a soft drink are effective rewards. These rewards build your motivation to study and make studying easier.

Almost anything that you like to do can be used to reinforce your study behavior. It is essential, however, in order for these activities to serve as reinforcers, that they be contingent upon the completion of some unit of studying—that is, the reinforcers can occur only if the unit has been completed. For example, if you enjoy running every day, you could use running as a reinforcer for studying by requiring that you complete a half hour or an hour of concentrated study before you get to run. The completion of larger units of studying could also be reinforced. For example, you could make a kind of "contract" with yourself to the effect that if you stay with your study schedule fairly well all week, then you get to go out on Saturday. Going out, then, becomes a kind of incentive to motivate you to study effectively, and—if you succeed in studying all week—you are reinforced for it.

Interim Summary   Long-term interest depends upon familiarity, competence, relevance, and social support. In general, material in which you have more interest is familiar to you, you are competent working with it, you find it relevant to your life, and your friends are interested in it. Short-term interest can be managed by the way you approach the task of studying. You can concentrate better if you create a special study place, if you stop punishing yourself for studying, and if you make studying more rewarding.

Time Management

Time is life. It is irreversible and irreplaceable. To waste your time is to waste your life, but to master your time is to master your life and make the most of it.[19]

If you could only master your time, think of what you could accomplish! The time you have been wasting could have been spent profitably in any number of constructive ways. Many people can waste time without harmful effects, but college students simply cannot afford to waste time. In order to successfully complete their educations, they must gain control over their time. College survival requires skillful time management.

The Self-Monitoring Effect

College students have devised many creative ways to waste their time.[20] Some students spend so much time worrying about studying and preparing for studying that they never have much time left to actually study. How do you waste *your* time?

- ☐ Too much sleeping
- ☐ Excessive fantasy and elaborate daydreams
- ☐ Nonproductive group "studying"
- ☐ Watching television
- ☐ Playing games
- ☐ "Bull sessions" on irrelevant topics
- ☐ Doing chores (laundry, shopping) during study time

☐ Extending meals for an extra hour after you have finished

☐ Wandering around between classes

☐ Delaying getting up in the morning

☐ Talking on the telephone to friends

☐ Too many parties

☐ An excessive "warming up" routine for getting ready to study that takes so much time that by the time you are ready, your time has run out.

Do you know how much time you study during an average week? You may not even be aware of the time you spend studying and the time you waste. Becoming aware of how you use your time has some important benefits. Research has shown that by simply monitoring yourself and becoming more aware of your study time, you will automatically begin to study more.[21] According to the **self-monitoring effect** your behavior will change if you systematically observe it and keep track of it.

Massed and Distributed Practice

In order to accomplish what you want to in the time you have available, you will probably have to learn to control your time by careful planning. One approach to this goal is to make a list of tasks in two categories—necessary or urgent tasks and less important, secondary tasks. The next step is to determine when each of the necessary tasks must be accomplished. For example, by what date must you be finished reading the first fifteen chapters of this book? Next, you must set up a schedule that shows on which days and at what times you will work on each of your necessary tasks. This schedule should contain eight to twelve hours each week outside class for studying for your present psychology class. Your schedule should also contain time for recreation and play. If you attempt to follow a schedule that takes away all your pleasures, you will soon tire of being punished and will abandon the schedule altogether.

Study time should be distributed, a little each day, not massed into a single long session. Rather than trying to read your psychology assignment in one sitting, try breaking it up into smaller pieces and read it over several days. One problem with cramming (studying all at once—sometimes called **massed practice**) is that it is rather unpleasant and boring. But another, major problem is that material learned in massed practice is easily forgotten. Taking breaks between study sessions (sometimes called **distributed practice**) will improve your retention of what you read.[22]

Procrastination

A special problem many students face is **procrastination**—the tendency to delay working. As one student put it, "Why study today if I can put it off until tomorrow—or, even better, next week?"

Last-minute, frenzied work rarely pays off with good grades. It's difficult to write an "A" term paper the night before it is due. Staying up all night studying before an exam is not only an ineffective way of learning but also tends to cause you to fall asleep during the exam.

Students who procrastinate are often afraid of the task required of them, and they become anxious whenever they think of it. The idea of writing a term paper is overwhelming and frightening. Learning an entire book before the final exam seems an impossible task and therefore provokes anxiety. When students are afraid of writing a paper or of studying, they avoid it as long as possible—until the last possible moment. Then, sometimes, it's too late. Another cause of procrastination is the unrealistic expectation that what you do must be perfect. If you have such high standards for yourself that you will never be able to meet them, your realization of this fact may lead to continual procrastination.

Procrastination can be controlled through **task decomposition**—analyzing the task to be accomplished and then breaking it down into smaller parts. A term paper may seem to be an impossibly large task, but if it is broken down into a number of small parts, it will seem less frightening. (Question: "How do you eat an elephant?" Answer: "Take small bites.")

Taking small bites—working on your large academic tasks a step at a time—will help overcome the problem of procrastination.

Interim Summary   The problem of time management, for many people, is procrastination: putting off completing a study task until the last possible minute. Procrastination can be controlled through the process of task decomposition—breaking down the task to be completed into a number of smaller parts, then tackling each part separately, one at a time. Monitoring how you use your time will help you avoid wasting so much of it. Scheduling your study tasks so that you study a little bit every day—using distributed practice—will work better for you than cramming—using massed practice.

Test Yourself:
An Inventory of Learning Skills

You have been reading about learning problems and ways that some of them can be helped by applying principles gained from basic research on human learning and memory. A theme running through this chapter is that you have control over your study behavior and, if you choose to do so, you can change your approach to learning and become more efficient. What learning skills do you presently have and how do you intend to try to change? On the following checklist of learning skills, indicate for each whether you now practice it ("yes"), whether you intend to start ("will try"), or whether you think you will not be able to adopt it ("no"). Mark each skill with "yes," "will try," or "no."

Learning from Lectures

_____ I read about the lecture topic before going to lecture.

_____ As I listen to the lecture, I try to find relationships between what I am hearing and what I already know or my own personal experiences.

_____ I try to imagine questions about the material as I listen to lectures.

_____ While listening to a lecture, I take outline notes in my own words and then review them later.

_____ I ask questions during or after lecture to clarify and extend my comprehension.

Reading Textbooks

_____ Before reading a textbook, I "preread" it to get an idea of the topics covered and the book's structure.

_____ Before reading an assignment, I first skim it to get an overview of the material.

_____ After reading passages in the text, I summarize them and restate to myself the main ideas.

_____ When I am reading a text, I write down on paper, in my own words, the most important ideas.

Retaining What Is Learned

_____ As I read the text or listen to lectures, I try to think of questions that are answered by the material presented.

_____ While studying for a test, I go over important concepts by explaining them in my own words and teaching them to a relative or friend.

_____ While studying for a test, I make up and give myself practice tests, and then I write out the answers.

_____ After I have learned a concept or theory, I continue to study it to ensure that I won't forget it.

Motivation and Concentration

_____ When I'm feeling bored by what I have to learn, I try to find out more about it.

_____ I have a special place set aside for studying that is fairly free from distractions, and I almost always study there.

_____ I quit studying for a while when I find I have trouble concentrating.

_____ After I have successfully completed a unit of studying, I "reward" myself by doing something I enjoy.

Time Management

_____ I have a schedule for studying, and I follow it fairly well.

_____ I keep a record of when, where, and how long I study.

_____ I study every week and do not depend upon merely cramming before the exam.

_____ I study small units of material frequently, rather than large units less often.

Summary

1. Efficiency in academic learning and retention requires that you take an active role as a learner. Questioning, taking notes, and searching for relationships are ways to become actively involved in the learning process.

2. According to the schema theory of knowledge, you will not understand new information about a subject without a schema, or framework, to clarify and organize the information. This implies that you should gain a general understanding of what is to be covered in a lecture or a chapter before you hear or read the discussion.

3. Material is retained better if it is overlearned, since you need a margin for forgetting.

4. According to the encoding-specificity principle, you should rehearse material in a form similar to the form used on the test. This will increase the likelihood that information available at the time of learning will be available later—on the test—as retrieval cues.

5. According to the levels-of-processing theory, information processed at shallow levels—for example, through maintenance rehearsal—is not retained as well as information processed at deeper levels—for example, through elaborative rehearsal.

6. Learning from lectures and textbooks requires active listening and active reading. Thinking of questions, asking questions, and taking notes are ways to make listening more active. Notes have both an encoding and a storage function. Active reading involves three steps: prereading, skimming, and concentrated reading.

7. Concentration can be improved by creating a special study place (the application of stimulus control), by taking breaks between study sessions (reducing self-punishment), and by increasing the rewards of studying (devising contingent reinforcement).

8. Long-term interest depends upon such factors as familiarity, competence, relevance, and social support. To some degree you have control over these factors and therefore control over your long-term interests.

9. Your study time can be better managed and better used by applying the principles of self-monitoring, distributed practice, and task decomposition.

Key Concepts

schema theory of knowledge   The theory that knowledge consists of sets of organized facts, rules, and plans.

schema (plural, **schemata**)   A mental structure consisting of interrelated facts, rules, and plans.

maintenance rehearsal   A form of rehearsal involving rote memorization; repeating material to be learned over and over without regard for the deeper meaning or context of that material.

elaborative rehearsal   A form of rehearsal involving thinking of meaningful relationships and placing the material to be remembered in different meaningful contexts.

retrieval cue   Something that helps you remember; a stimulus that helps you find information in memory.

encoding-specificity principle   The rule that memory is best when the information encoded at the time of learning is the same as the information presented at the time of testing.

overlearning   Continuing to study the material after you feel you have mastered it.

selective attention   The ability to attend to and perceive only one thing at a time.

cocktail-party phenomenon   The ability to switch your attention to tune in one message and tune out others.

dichotic listening   A procedure in which research subjects are given earphones playing two competing messages, one in the left ear and another in the right ear.

pursuit movements   Smooth tracking movements that occur when the eyes follow a moving target.

saccadic movements   Jerky movements that occur when your eyes jump from spot to spot.

saccade   A single saccadic movement.

regression movements   Saccadic eye movements that jump backwards to reexamine words previously seen.

fixation   A pause between eye movements.

prereading   The process of examining the text you are about to read in order to get a general idea of its structure.

skimming   The process of reading subheadings, summaries, picture captions, and so on to get an overview of the material to be read.

concentrated reading   A type of reading that involves looking for relationships, making up questions, highlighting, and restating main ideas.

incompatible behavior   Behavior that interferes with the desired behavior.

stimulus control   The principle that your behavior is controlled to a degree by the stimuli in the environment in which the behavior has occurred.

Law of Effect   Behavior with favorable consequences tends to recur, and behavior with unfavorable consequences tends to be abandoned.

self-monitoring effect   The principle that behavior will change if it is systematically observed; problem behavior that is monitored tends to decline in strength and frequency.

massed practice   Studying or practicing all at once.

distributed practice   Studying or practicing a little bit at a time.

procrastination   The tendency to delay working.

task decomposition   The process of analyzing the task to be accomplished and breaking it down into smaller parts.

Part III
Mind and Body

Chapter 6
Brain and Behavior

Key Questions
1. What are the common methods for studying the brain?
2. What are the parts of the nervous system and how are they organized?
3. What is the relation between your brain and your behavior?
4. How do your nerve cells influence how you act and feel?

When he was sixteen years old, H. M. developed epilepsy, a brain disorder marked by convulsions and seizures. As he grew, the seizures became worse and could not be controlled by medication. Finally, at the age of twenty-seven, he was operated on and the part of his brain believed to be the source of the seizures was removed. The operation improved his seizures but caused another problem: a loss of immediate memory. His intelligence and personality were unchanged, but he could not learn new material. The immediate past was lost to him—he could not remember what happened a few seconds ago. He experienced everything as new, nothing as familiar. As he explained it,

Every day is alone in itself. You see, at this moment, everything looks clear to me, but what happened just before? That's what worries me. . . . It's like waking from a dream. I just don't remember.[1]

Observations of individuals such as H. M. have made clear that the brain is the biological seat of mind and is the master control organ for behavior. Psychologists have been interested in studying the brain in order to further understand the nature of human behavior. Some of the most exciting recent discoveries in psychology have come from these studies of the relationships that exist between behavior and the brain.

Studying the Brain

Suppose you were given the task of understanding a highly complicated computer—without the aid of a wiring diagram. How might you proceed to unravel not only what the computer could do but also how it managed to do it? One method would involve disconnecting a particular wire and then determining what problems resulted. For example, damaging one wire might interfere with the computer's ability to store material in memory. Another method you could use to study the machine would be to record the electrical activity in one component during different phases of the computer's operation. For example, an oscilloscope could be used to detect and graphically display the electrical signals occurring in one wire. A third method for understanding the computer would involve testing different components of the computer with electrical signals presented through probes, then observing the effects. Finally, the computer could be disassembled and its electronic parts examined. An attempt could be made to trace out its different circuits to determine the connections between the components.

These varied approaches to studying a machine resemble the methods that have been developed to study the human brain.

Ablation, Lesion, and Injury

The oldest method for studying the functions of different parts of the brain involves observing the effects of brain damage. **Ablation** is the surgical removal of brain tissue. The case of H. M., who lost his memory, involved the ablation of a part of the brain. The term **lesion** refers to any kind of damage or injury to brain tissue. For example, cuts or bruises are lesions.

Information concerning a particular part of the brain can be found by ablating that part and then observing the result. If that part of the brain controls memory, then a memory problem should result. If that part of the brain controls vision, then a visual problem should result. In experiments using monkeys, rats, and other animals, psychologists have made many discoveries about the particular functions of the parts of the animals' brains. Because of the resemblance in the basic anatomy of the brains of rats, monkeys, and human beings, the animal findings can be applied to understanding the human brain. These experimental procedures using animals have allowed scientists to discover which parts of the brain are crucial to human functions, so that damage to these parts can be carefully avoided in brain operations.

Sometimes damage to the brain is accidental or is associated with illness. Brain tumors damage specific parts of the brain and cause specific behavioral problems. Studying the relationship between the location of tumors and the nature of the resulting psychological problems provides evidence regarding the function of different parts of the brain.

Mathilde V., a fifty-four-year-old woman, suddenly found herself unable to speak. In addition, she had difficulty swallowing and chewing and the muscles in her right eyelid alternately contracted and relaxed in a convulsive manner. In a subsequent brain operation, a tumor was found and removed from the left part of her brain. Two years after the surgery, she was able to speak with difficulty but displayed many speech problems.

In September 1965 a factory foreman named Joseph V. was attacked by robbers and severely beaten. Joseph was taken to a hospital, and it was discovered that he could not speak a word. In every other respect he was normal: he was intelligent, could read, and could write, but he could not speak. X rays revealed a fracture and brain injury on the left side of his brain in about the same place as Mathilde's tumor. Other people with loss of speech or severe speech problems have been found to have brain damage in the same area of the brain where Mathilde's tumor was located. Apparently, this part of the brain is involved in controlling speech.[2]

Recording Electrical Activity

The cells of the brain operate electrically. The electrical activity of the billions of brain cells can be sensed and detected from the outside of the brain. Electrodes (small metal disks) placed on the skin of the face and head detect changes in the electrical activity of groups of brain cells. These changes—called **brain waves**—are amplified and then displayed for scientists to observe and study. The machine that picks up, amplifies, and displays brain waves is called an **EEG (electroencephalograph)**. Having your brain examined with an EEG involves no pain or discomfort.

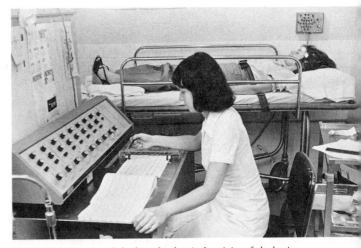

The EEG picks up and displays the electrical activity of the brain by drawing "brain waves" on moving strips of paper. Electrodes are placed on the skin of the face and head and are able to sense the brain's activity with no pain or discomfort. (Judy Sedwick)

Because the level of electrical activity in your brain rises and falls, EEG recordings show waves with peaks and valleys. These brain waves, like sound waves, have different frequencies. The frequency of brain waves is typically different during different mental states and different behaviors. For example, a person who is asleep has a characteristic brain wave that shows up on the EEG. When a person is dreaming, there is a different brain-wave pattern. One type of brain wave that is of particular interest is the **alpha wave.** The alpha wave has a frequency of about ten cycles per second and occurs when a person is relaxed but awake and alert.

A second type of brain wave is the **theta wave.** The theta wave has a frequency of about four to seven cycles per second and is produced by the brain during various conditions. Production of the theta wave appears to be related to learning. In one study with rats, the animals that learned more in the experiment also produced more theta waves. The amount of learning could be predicted by measuring the brain's theta waves.[3]

In addition to measuring the general electrical activity of the brain by means of the EEG, psychologists have also measured the response of the brain to a single stimulus. Imagine yourself in a laboratory, with EEG electrodes on your scalp, looking at a blank screen. A series of pictures flash on the screen. As the information reaches your brain, it responds electrically. This response is picked up by the electrodes, amplified, and displayed so that it can be examined. This electrical response of the brain to a stimulus is called an **evoked potential.** Studies of evoked potentials have aided psychologists in their study of the human brain.

Electrical Stimulation of the Brain

The work of the brain is carried on electrically. The individual nerve cells that make up the brain send and receive tiny electrical impulses; they form brain circuits for processing information and controlling the movements of the body. These circuits can also be made to operate by stimulating the brain with electricity from an external source. This technique is called **ESB,** the **electrical stimulation of the brain.** A fine wire, or *electrode,* that carries an electrical charge can be touched to various brain structures to produce changes in mood, perception, or movements.

Sometimes these wire electrodes are permanently implanted in the brain and rigged so that electrical current can be turned on and off by remote control. One psychologist described, with some exaggeration, what might be possible with ESB:

Docility, fearful withdrawal, and panicked efforts at escape can be made to alternate with fury and ferocity of such degree that its subject can as readily destroy himself by exhaustion from his consuming rage as he can the object of it, whom he attacks, heedless of both danger and opportunity. Eating, drinking, sleeping, moving of bowels or limbs or organs of sensation, gracefully or in spastic comedy, can all be managed on electrical demand by puppeteers whose flawless strings are pulled from miles away by the unseen call of radio.[4]

Happy Rats and Angry Bulls • A well-known study of electrical stimulation of the brain was done by James Olds in 1953. Olds was conducting experiments on electrical stimulation of the reticular formation of a rat's brain. He found that he could implant electrodes in this area of the brain and not interfere with the rat's normal health. One electrode was mistakenly implanted near the hypothalamic region of the rat's brain. Olds found, by accident, that when he sent a mild current of electricity through this electrode the rat acted as if it enjoyed the feeling. It continually returned to that area of the cage where it had been stimulated. Olds concluded that the rat found the stimulation rewarding or pleasurable. He then concluded that there must be **pleasure centers** in the brain which, when electrically stimulated, produce a rewarding and pleasurable experience. The existence of the brain's pleasure centers has since been confirmed in many studies.

The rat's brain is structurally similar to the human brain, so discoveries about the rat's brain often can be applied to human beings. One way of studying the brain is to electrically stimulate particular brain structures through fine wires (electrodes) implanted deep in the brain. The rat in the picture has had a brain operation in which electrodes were placed permanently in the brain. (United Press International Photo)

A pioneer in the study of the electrical stimulation of the brain, José Delgado, implanted electrodes in the brain of a bull and connected the electrodes to a miniature radio receiver. Later the enraged bull charged Delgado but was stopped abruptly when Delgado pressed a button on a small radio transmitter he carried; Delgado had communicated with the bull's brain by radio wave.[5]

"Your Electricity Is Stronger Than My Will"   •   In an attempt to treat certain brain disorders, Delgado has operated on and implanted electrodes in the brains of many individuals. Because so

little is known about the brain, what happens when these electrodes are stimulated is often a surprise. Sometimes the brain stimulation causes body movement, which the patients believe they are causing themselves or which they report they have no control over.

In one of our patients, electrical stimulation of [one part of the brain] produced head turning and slow displacement of the body to either side with a well-oriented and apparently normal sequence, as if the patient were looking for something. This stimulation was repeated six times on two different days with comparable results. The interesting fact was that the patient considered the evoked activity spontaneous and always offered a reasonable explanation for it. When asked "What are you doing?" the answers were, "I am looking for my slippers," "I heard a noise," "I am restless," and "I was looking under the bed." . . .

In one of our patients, stimulation of [another part of the brain] through implanted electrodes evoked a flexion of the right hand starting with contraction of the first two fingers and continuing with flexion of the other fingers. The closed fist was then maintained for the rest of the 5-second stimulation. This effect was not unpleasant or disturbing, and it developed without interrupting ongoing behavior or spontaneous conversation. The patient was aware that his hand had moved involuntarily but he was not afraid. . . . When the patient was warned of the oncoming stimulation and was asked to try to keep his fingers extended, he could not prevent the evoked movement and commented, "I guess, Doctor, that your electricity is stronger than my will."[5]

Electric Sex   •   Stimulation of certain areas of the brain produces feelings of intense pleasure, sometimes sexual pleasure. Two patients were fitted with brain electrodes and were each given a box with buttons with which they could stimulate themselves in different areas of the brain.

The patient, in explaining why he pressed [one] button with such frequency, stated that the feeling was "good"; it was as if he were building up to a sexual orgasm.   He reported that he was unable to achieve the orgiastic end point, however, explaining that his frequent, sometimes frantic, pushing of the button was an attempt to reach the end point.   This futile effort was frustrating at times.[6]

The second patient was also able to stimulate himself.   One of the effects of brain stimulation for him was to alter the subject matter of his conversation, so that he would begin making sexual remarks.

The actual content [of his conversation] varied considerably, but regardless of his baseline emotional state and the subject under discussion in the room, the stimulation was accompanied by the patient's introduction of a sexual subject, usually with a broad grin.   When questioned about this, he would say, "I don't know why that came to mind—I just happened to think of it."[6]

Delgado reports the case of a thiry-six-year-old woman who had electrodes implanted in her brain in an attempt to control a brain disorder.

Electrodes were implanted in her right temporal lobe and upon stimulation of a contact . . . , the patient reported a pleasant tingling sensation in the left side of her body "from my face down to the bottom of my legs."   She started giggling and making funny comments, stating that she enjoyed the sensation "very much."   Repetition of these stimulations made the patient more communicative and flirtatious, and she ended by openly expressing her desire to marry the therapist.[5]

Both before and after the electrical stimulation of her brain, the patient behaved very properly and was not excessively friendly or familiar.

Microscopic Examination

To understand a computer, you might want to take it apart, examine the component parts, and trace the connections among the parts.   To understand the human brain, psychologists have used the same approach.

In a computer or telephone, the wires connecting the parts are clearly visible and, for ease of tracing, are usually different colors.   Unfortunately, the brain is not built that way.   The connecting cells may be too small to see and, in any case, are all about the same color.   The brain contains billions of tiny nerve cells tightly packed together and highly interconnected.   Examined under a microscope, the brain appears as only a dense, milky smear.   How, then, can its parts and connections be studied?

About 1875 an Italian scientist named Camillo Golgi discovered a method of staining certain nerve cells a different color so that they would be clearly visible under a microscope.   Since then, many other methods of staining brain cells have been developed that enable psychologists to identify special cells and to trace their interconnections.   Improved methods of staining brain cells have enabled psychologists to map the brain and its functions.

One of the most recent developments in the study of the anatomy of the brain involves injecting an animal with a radioactive substance that is absorbed by those areas of the brain that are momentarily the most active.   For example, injecting this substance and then stimulating the animal with sound results in the substance being concentrated in that area of the brain most involved with processing sound.   Later microscopic examination of the animal's brain reveals where this area lies because the radioactivity can be traced.[7]

Interim Summary   The brain is the biological seat of the mind and has been of great interest to psychologists who study different aspects of behavior.   Four methods of studying the brain are (1) examining the effects of brain damage, (2) recording and studying the brain's electrical activity, (3) electrically stimulating different parts of the brain, and (4) studying the anatomy of the brain microscopically.

The Organization of the Nervous System

Behavior is the product of the nervous system. Your nervous system permits you to perceive the world, enables you to think and remember, and directs all body movements. Thus an understanding of the nervous system and the way it works is a vital part of understanding human psychology. Many recent advances in explaining psychological problems have been possible because of continued research on the nervous system.

The Pattern of the Nervous System

The nervous system extends thoughout the body, from head to toe, carrying nerve messages. Imagine that you were completely invisible—except for your nervous system. Where your leg was you would see only a network of thousands of nerves, leading eventually to the middle of your back and to the thick rope of nerves called the spinal cord. Where your head was you would now see only your brain, probably the most complicated organ in the world, composed of billions of individual nerve cells. (See Figure 6-1.)

If you could see your nervous system, you would notice that it is all connected. It has unity. One author described this great branching system of nerves as follows:

We see that it is like a tree. Its trunk comprises the intricate, graceful mass of the brain and the slender, tubular spinal cord. The important thing to remember about this tree is its continuity, the stringing together of all parts that allows each part to be in touch with every other. And you might pause to think (in case you had not already thought of it), "This tree inside me—this is where I live."[8]

But the tree of the nervous system, although it works like a single system, has parts. Figure 6-2 shows the organization of these parts.

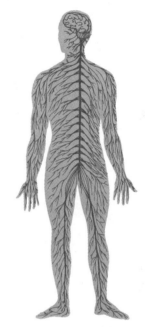

Figure 6-1 The Brain and the Nervous System. *This diagram shows the "treelike" organization of the nervous system, with the main nerves branching off from the spinal cord and terminating in various parts of the body.*

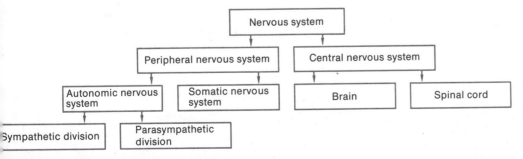

Figure 6-2 Branches of the System. *The nervous system can be broken down into a number of parts. Note that each of the two main divisions of the nervous system (the peripheral and central nervous systems) has two parts.*

The Peripheral Nervous System

The nervous system can be divided into a number of functionally distinct parts. The **peripheral nervous system** and the **central nervous system** (CNS) are the two "largest" parts. The central nervous system consists of the brain and the spinal cord. The peripheral nervous system consists of all the rest of the nervous system—those nerves extending to and from the brain and spinal cord, carrying messages to glands and muscles and bringing information from the eyes, ears, and skin to the brain. The peripheral nervous system can be further divided into two parts: the **somatic nervous system** and the **autonomic nervous system**. The somatic nervous system consists of the nerves going to the major muscles of the body (such as the arm and leg muscles) and the nerves coming from the major sense organs of the body (such as the

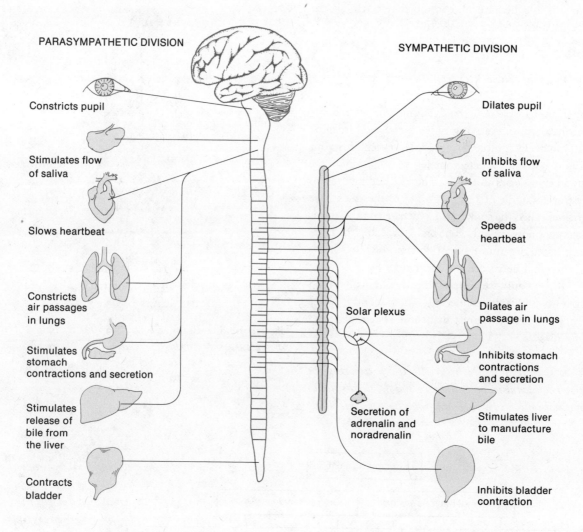

PARASYMPATHETIC DIVISION

Constricts pupil

Stimulates flow
of saliva

Slows heartbeat

Constricts
air passages
in lungs

Stimulates
stomach
contractions and secretion

Stimulates
release of
bile from
the liver

Contracts
bladder

SYMPATHETIC DIVISION

Dilates pupil

Inhibits flow
of saliva

Speeds
heartbeat

Dilates air
passage in lungs

Solar plexus

Inhibits stomach
contractions
and secretion

Secretion of
adrenalin and
noradrenalin

Stimulates liver
to manufacture
bile

Inhibits bladder
contraction

Figure 6-3 The Autonomic Nervous System. *The two divisions of the autonomic nervous system have somewhat different, and opposing, functions. The sympathetic division acts like an accelerator and the parasympathetic division acts like a brake.*

eyes, ears, and skin). The autonomic nervous system consists of nerves going to the internal organs and glands (such as the stomach and salivary glands) and nerves carrying sensory information from the internal organs in the form of feelings of pain, pressure, or warmth. (See Figure 6-3.)

The autonomic nervous system controls many bodily functions that are considered involuntary. When you run, your heart beats faster. When you are cut, your blood vessels constrict to slow the loss of blood. When you get hot, you perspire. These glands, organs, and blood vessels are controlled by the system of nerves called the autonomic nervous system.

The autonomic nervous system has two parts; one is like an accelerator, and the other is like a brake. The **sympathetic division** of the autonomic nervous system is the part that is like an accelerator; when it is active, it tends to increase heart rate, blood flow, and in general prepare the body for action. The **parasympathetic division** of the autonomic nervous system is the part that is like a brake; when it is active, it tends to decrease heart rate, blood flow, and in general prepare the body for rest. Typically, one of the two parts dominates at one time; to some degree the two parts work against each other.

When you are frightened, the sympathetic division of your autonomic nervous system becomes active. It causes your heart to beat faster, your mouth to become dry, and your muscles to gain blood at the expense of your skin and stomach. When you are resting after a meal, the parasympathetic division of your autonomic nervous system becomes active; it causes your heart to slow, your digestive juices to flow, and your stomach and skin to gain blood at the expense of your muscles.

The two divisions of the autonomic nervous system are both involved in sexual arousal and response. The initial stages of sexual arousal seem to be regulated by the parasympathetic division, while the later stages—including orgasm—seem to be regulated by the sympathetic division. Anxiety, like fright, is associated with the activation of the sympathetic division and actually interferes with the parasympathetic divi-

sion. It is not surprising, therefore, that high levels of anxiety typically result in sexual problems.

The Central Nervous System

The central nervous system consists of the brain and spinal cord. The brain is the master control organ for behavior and will be discussed more fully in the next section. For now, think of it as a kind of computer that is encased in the skull at the end of the spinal cord.

The spinal cord lies protected within the bones of the spine. All along its length, nerves join the spinal cord as well as leave it. These nerves are part of the peripheral nervous system. Although most behavior is controlled by the brain, some is controlled by the spinal cord. Very simple reflexes—such as the knee jerk when your knee is tapped—are controlled directly by the spinal cord.

The spinal cord, a kind of nerve freeway, serves mainly to conduct messages to and from the brain. Messages from most of the sensory receptors in the body carry information about the world up the nerves of the spinal cord to the brain. Messages from the brain travel down the nerves of the spinal cord to muscles and glands. If this freeway were blocked or broken, the brain would not be able to communicate with parts of the body. The result of blocking the nerves from the brain to the muscles is paralysis. The result of blocking the nerves from the sense organs in the skin to the brain is numbness.

George C., a twenty-three-year-old soldier in good physical condition, was struck by a shell splinter in the small of the back, slightly to the right of the midline. He was removed to the hospital. On examination, after he had recovered from the immediate effects of the wound, it was noted that he could not move his right leg. . . . In George's case, communication of information along the spinal cord was disrupted by the shell splinter, which cut all the pathways on the right side of the cord.[9]

Interim Summary   The nervous system, like a tree, has both unity and distinct parts. The nervous system as a whole can be divided into the peripheral nervous system (the nerves carrying messages to glands and muscles and from the sensory organs) and the central nervous system (the brain and spinal cord). The peripheral nervous system can be further divided into the somatic nervous system and the autonomic nervous system. The autonomic nervous system, essential for the control of involuntary bodily functions, can be divided into the sympathetic division and the parasympathetic division. In the control of heart beat, digestion, blood supply and distribution, and other involuntary functions, the sympathetic division acts like an accelerator and the parasympathetic division acts like a brake.

The Human Brain

Your brain, although only about three pounds of pinkish-gray material, is far more complicated than the most advanced computer. It is a control center for behavior and experience, made up of perhaps as many as 100 billion nerve cells. These cells are organized into units and circuits serving different functions. Some control the movement of your left hand, others keep you breathing, still others enable you to speak.

The Nature and History of the Brain

The development of the brain of an unborn child during the nine months of gestation shows a consistent pattern. During the first stage of development, the inner core of the brain begins to form. This primitive part of the brain is evolutionarily ancient and is shared by all vertebrate animals. Only later in development does the outer brain form—that part of the brain responsible for thinking, judgment, memory, problem solving, and other "higher" functions.

The development of a rat brain resembles very closely the development of a human brain, up to a point; but the human brain continues to develop before birth, growing a thick outer covering with many wrinkles and convolutions. The evolution of mammals can be traced in the growth and development of this outer covering of the brain. In primitive mammals, such as the shrew, this covering is small and

relatively smooth. In more advanced mammals, such as the cat, it is larger and wrinkled. In chimpanzees or human beings, it is very large and highly wrinkled. The larger this outer covering of the brain, the more intelligent the mammal.

As mammals evolved, the "intelligent" outer covering of the brain became too large to cover the inner core smoothly. The result was an increasingly wrinkled and convoluted covering. Imagine trying to wrap an orange in a piece of paper six inches square; the paper would be small enough so that you could wrap it around fairly smoothly. Now imagine trying to wrap an orange in a piece of paper two feet square; with this large size, the paper could be wrapped around only by wrinkling it. Like the larger piece of paper, the covering of the human brain is too large to fit smoothly around the brain's inner core. As a result it is highly wrinkled.

The human brain comprises only about 2 percent of our total body weight, but it is in complete control of the other 98 percent. Running the machinery of the brain takes a lot of energy. For example, the brain consumes 20 percent of the oxygen used by the body, and it burns a large amount of sugar (glucose) taken from the blood. The brain cells need a constant supply of oxygen and blood sugar. If the flow of blood to the brain stops, consciousness will be lost within ten seconds. Within minutes, permanent damage will be done to brain cells. When a part of the blood supply to the brain is interrupted, such as by a stroke, a part of the brain dies.

The Inner Brain

As nerves travel up the spinal cord, they enter the inner brain. This collection of structures within and at the base of the brain is responsible for regulating such automatic functions as heartbeat, blood pressure, and breathing, as as well as for the control of attention and emotion.

As the spinal cord enters the skull, it enlarges. This enlargement is called the **medulla.** The medulla controls heart rate, blood pressure, breathing, swallowing, and other reflex movements. At the back and bottom of the brain lies the **cerebellum,** a structure that regulates muscle tone and muscle coordination. At the very center of the brain, above the medulla, lies the **thalamus.** The thalamus is a kind of relay station for nerve messages going to and from the outer brain. Sensory information from your eyes or ears and from your senses of touch and temperature is sent to the thalamus, which relays it to higher brain centers. Just below the thalamus is the **hypothalamus,** a tiny but very important structure that regulates sex, hunger, and thirst. It is the master control organ for the autonomic nervous system. The hypothalamus also controls body hormones through its regulation of the endocrine system. Finally, the **limbic system** is a group of structures that lies above and around the thalamus, but also includes certain parts of the thalamus and hypothalamus. (See Figure 6-4.) These interconnected structures form a system for the control of emotional expression and experience. One part of this system, when electrically stimulated, gives rise to the experience of intense pleasure, similar to the pleasure experienced in a sexual orgasm. In the case described earlier in this chapter of a man who could electrically stimulate his own brain by pressing a button, there was an electrode implanted in part of his limbic system; pressing the button stimulated this structure and produced feelings of pleasure. Stimulating other parts of the limbic system causes feelings of anger or rage. Charles Whitman, a mass murderer who killed fourteen people at the University of Texas, was finally shot by the police; a brain autopsy revealed a tumor in part of his limbic system.

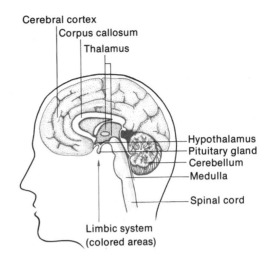

Figure 6-4 The Inner Brain. *If the brain were cut in half, the structures of the inner brain could be seen. The limbic system (colored areas) is a group of structures in the inner brain that control emotion.*

The Cerebrum and Cerebral Cortex

Surrounding the primitive inner brain is an outer brain called the **cerebrum.** The cerebrum is what most clearly differentiates human beings from other animals. The surface of the cerebrum is called the **cerebral cortex.** The cerebral cortex in human beings is like a walnut, with two connected halves and with wrinkled surfaces. The cerebral cortex is responsible for all higher mental functions.

Your Split Brain • From the back to the front, your cerebrum is divided down the middle; the two sides are called left and right **cerebral hemispheres** (see Figure 6-5). Each hemisphere controls one side of your body. But they are "cross-wired": your left hemisphere controls the right side of your body and your right hemisphere controls the left side of your body. For example, if your right foot itches, the "itch" message is sent initially to your left hemisphere; and if you scratch your foot with your left hand, it is your right hemisphere that directs the left hand to move. If one hemisphere is damaged, the opposite

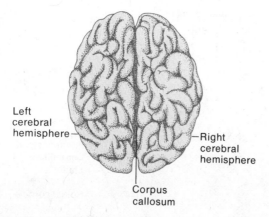

Figure 6-5 The Hemispheres of the Brain. *The left and right hemispheres of the brain are connected by a broad band of nerves called the corpus callosum.*

side of the body may have problems. The left side of your body can be paralyzed from damage to the right hemisphere of your brain.

Your left and right cerebral hemispheres are relatively independent; it's almost like having two brains within one skull. The two brains can stay in touch with one another because they are connected by a broad band of nerves called the **corpus callosum.** This nerve pathway permits the "left brain" to know what the "right brain" is doing, and vice versa. On rare occasions, because of an accident or brain operation, individuals have had their corpus callosum sectioned (cut through). The effect of this was to create

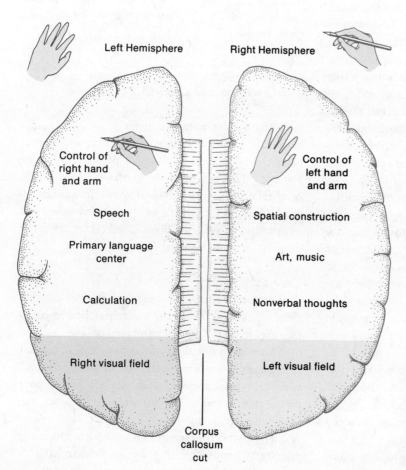

Figure 6-6 The Split Brain. *The two hemispheres of the brain have, to some degree, specialized functions. For example, the left hemisphere controls the right hand and arm and, in most people, contains highly developed language centers. When the connection between the hemispheres is cut, the two halves of the brain lose contact with each other.*

two separate brains within one skull, each out of touch with the other.

What is it like to have two separate brains? One psychologist studied a number of people with "split brains" and wrote a book about them. He said:

Situated dead center in the middle of the brain is the largest and most mysterious information transmission system in the world—the corpus callosum. With it intact, the two halves of the body have no secrets from one another. With it sectioned, the two halves become two different conscious mental spheres, each with its own experience base and control system for behavioral operations.[10]

Other scientists have also shown that people with "split brains" (with the corpus callosum cut) have two completely separate minds; each mind is unaware of what is going on in the other.[11]

Since the two hemispheres are "cross-wired," the left hemisphere controls the right hand and the right hemisphere controls the left hand. Normally, information from one hand can be compared with information from the other; the information is exchanged across the corpus callosum. However, when the corpus callosum has been cut, the two hemispheres are out of touch with each other, like the brains of two separate people. If you reached into a sack of fruit with both hands and felt an apple with one hand and a banana with the other, you could tell that they were different; your corpus callosum allows your two hemispheres to "talk" to each other and compare information. However, if your corpus callosum were cut, you would not have known that your two hands held different fruits; your left hand would not know what your right hand was doing or what it was feeling.

Your two brains (your left and right hemispheres) do not have the same abilities. For most people, the left hemisphere is more competent at speech and writing, math, science, and logic. The right hemisphere is generally more competent at art, music, and perception. Thus, the two brains apparently have somewhat different functions[12] (see Figure 6-6.)

Localized Functions • Different parts of your brain do different things. To some degree, each ability is located in a different area of the brain; the functions of your brain are said to be partially localized. Not only do your two hemispheres have somewhat different abilities or functions, but also different parts of each hemisphere have different functions. In addition, beneath the cerebral hemispheres, at the base and core of the brain, there are different parts that perform different functions.

Each hemisphere can be divided into four regions, or *lobes* (see Figure 6-7). Each region specializes in certain functions, but is involved in other functions as well. At the very back of each hemisphere is the **occipital lobe,** an area that is important for vision. Damage to the occipital lobe can cause blindness. Just forward of the occipital lobe lies the **parietal lobe,** an area important for skin and body sensations. Perceptions of pain, heat, cold, and touch depend upon the parietal lobe. At the very front of the brain is the **frontal lobe,** an area important for planning, abstract thinking, and problem solving. Damage to the frontal lobe can result in a reduced

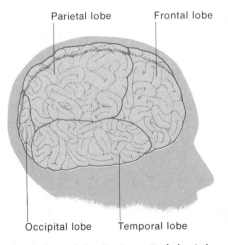

Figure 6-7 Lobes of the Brain. *Each hemisphere of the brain is divided into four lobes, or regions, having somewhat different functions. For example, the occipital lobe specializes in vision.*

ability to plan ahead and to deal with complex situations. Along each side of the brain, above the ear, lies the **temporal lobe,** an area important for memory and for hearing. One part of the temporal lobe is responsible for high tones and another for low tones.

Damage to the temporal lobe can result in difficulties in understanding speech and in memory problems. One patient with a damaged temporal lobe forgot the route to the bathroom and was unable to learn it again.[13]

Interim Summary   The human brain is the master control center for behavior and experience. The brain can be divided into the primitive inner brain, with structures and features shared by all vertebrate animals, and the outer brain, a huge, wrinkled covering responsible for controlling "higher" mental functions. Some important structures of the inner brain are the medulla (which controls heart rate, breathing, and other reflex movements), the cerebellum (which regulates muscle tone and coordination), the thalamus (which relays messages going into and coming out of the outer brain), the hypothalamus (which regulates the autonomic nervous system and the endocrine system), and finally the limbic system (which controls emotional expression and experience). The outer brain contains the cerebrum and the cerebral cortex. The cerebrum is divided into two halves (cerebral hemispheres) that are connected by a broad band of nerves called the corpus callosum. Each hemisphere can be divided into four lobes: the occipital lobe, the parietal lobe, the frontal lobe, and the temporal lobe. To some degree, each lobe has certain specialized functions.

Nerves and Neurons

Your body is composed of billions of tiny cells. Most of these cells have special functions; they have different jobs to do. There are blood cells, bone cells, skin cells, fat cells, hair cells, muscle cells, and many other kinds of cells. One unique kind of cell is specialized for carrying messages: this is the nerve cell, or **neuron.**

Neurons

Neurons are the basic units, or components, from which the nervous system is built. The human brain has recently been estimated to consist of about 100 billion neurons—about the same as the number of stars in our galaxy.[14] Neurons vary greatly in shape and size. Some are tiny, bushy cells, while others are

very long and thin. Some are less than a thousandth of an inch long, while others are over three feet in length. Some neurons are relatively isolated and others are clustered tightly together. A **nerve** consists of a bundle of neurons, like a cord formed from thousands of tiny threads.

Nerves carry messages from one part of your body to another. You are aware of an itch on your foot because a message, in the form of electrical impulses, travels along nerves from your foot to your brain. You are aware of the words on this page because of messages carried by nerves from your eyes to your brain. Your awareness of music on the radio depends upon messages carried by nerves from your ears to your brain. Nerves also carry messages from your brain to other parts of your body, such as muscles and glands. The movement of your hand to scratch your foot is a response to such a message. Each of

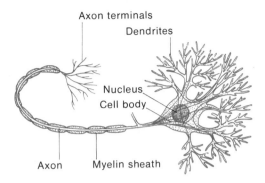

Axon terminals

Dendrites

Nucleus

Cell body

Axon   Myelin sheath

Figure 6-8 A Neuron.   *The neuron, or nerve cell, specializes in carrying messages from one place to another.   The nerve impulse moves from the dendrites to the cell body, then down the axon.*

these nerves consists of bundles of individual nerve cells, or neurons.

Afferent neurons are those that carry messages *to* the brain.   For example, sensory messages concerning sounds or smells are sent to the brain along afferent neurons.   **Efferent neurons** are those that carry messages *from* the brain to muscles or glands.   For example, messages are sent from the brain to your muscles as you pick up this book and turn its pages.   Your brain sends messages to your salivary glands in your mouth as you think about biting into an orange.   These messages sent from the brain to glands and muscles are sent along efferent neurons.   **Interneurons** are those nerve cells that carry messages between afferent and efferent neurons, or between other interconnecting neurons.   The afferent neurons carry "input."   The efferent neurons carry "output."   The interneurons do the rest of the work of the nervous system.   Most human neurons are interneurons, since most of the human nervous system is concerned with neither input nor output, but with such complicated processes as thought, memory, feeling, and problem solving.

All neurons have certain common structures or parts.   The **cell body** contains the **nucleus,** a structure that controls the biological processes of the cell. Numerous small fibers come from the cell body.   One type of fiber is relatively short and branched and is called a **dendrite.**   A second type of fiber is typically long and thin and is called the **axon.**   The neural messages are received by the dendrites and then sent down the axon.   The axon ends in **terminal branches.**   Each terminal branch has a **terminal button** on the tip.   The axons of many neurons are encased in a special tissue called the **myelin sheath.** One of the functions of the myelin sheath is to insulate the axon to prevent electrical interference from neighboring cells.   (See Figure 6-8.)

Nerve Impulses

The messages that neurons carry are pulses of electrical current called **nerve impulses.**   Each neuron is like a tiny electrical generator that creates an electric charge on command.   These electrical nerve impulses can be detected by an electrode with an extremely fine point; when the point of such an electrode touches a neuron, it can pick up the electrical changes in the cell.   These electrical nerve impulses can then be amplified and displayed for study.

Nerve impulses do not vary in size or voltage. Whenever a neuron "fires" (generates an electrical nerve impulse), the size of its response is always the same.   For example, the neurons carrying sensory information from the ear to the brain do not send stronger messages for louder sounds.   The messages sent along these afferent neurons are always the same in size or intensity.   This principle is called **all-or-none law:** whenever a neuron fires, the nerve impulse is always the same size.   In effect, the neuron either responds or it doesn't; and if it responds at all, its response is always the same size.

Differences in sound intensity, or in the intensity of other stimuli, are signaled by differences in rate of firing, not in differences in the size of the nerve impulse.   A loud sound will stimulate a neuron carrying sensory information from the ear to fire many times at a high rate; a soft sound will stimulate the same neuron to fire fewer times at a slower rate.

Neurons receive information on the dendrites and send nerve impulses down the axon to the terminal buttons. The direction of the movement of nerve impulses is the same for all neurons: from the dendrites to the terminal buttons. The speed of these nerve impulses varies, depending primarily upon the size of the axon and the presence or absence of a myelin sheath. Axons that are covered in a myelin sheath and axons that are relatively larger in diameter are able to carry nerve impulses faster.

The Synapse

The nerve impulse does not pass from one neuron to another. The electrical pulse stops when it reaches the terminal button of a neuron, and the form of the neural message changes from electrical to chemical. The chemical message is then passed across the **synapse,** the gap separating the terminal buttons of one

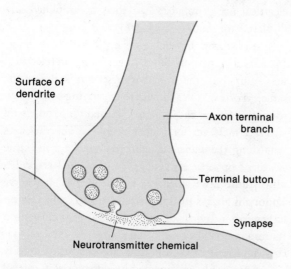

Surface of
dendrite

Axon terminal
branch

Terminal button

Synapse

Neurotransmitter chemical

Figure 6-9 A Synapse. *Messages travel from one neuron to another across a gap called the synapse. When a nerve impulse reaches a terminal button, neurotransmitter chemical is released into the synapse. The chemical stimulates the membrane of a dendrite of a neighboring neuron, causing the neuron to generate a nerve impulse.*

neuron from the dendrites of another neuron. The nature of the chemical communication across the synapse has only recently been understood.

When the nerve impulse travels down the axon and reaches a terminal button, it stimulates the button to release a chemical into the synapse. This chemical, called a **neurotransmitter,** enters the synaptic gap and stimulates the membrane of the next neuron, causing it to fire and generate an electrical nerve impulse. Thus, the message carried down the axon is electrical; the message carried across the synapse is chemical. (See Figure 6-9.)

Neurotransmitters • The neuron is like a gland that secretes chemicals from its tip when it has been stimulated. The chemicals are the neurotransmitters that carry the nerve message across the synaptic gap to the next neuron.

Many different kinds of neurotransmitters have been identified. Some are located primarily in the neurons that serve the muscles and glands, while others are located primarily in the neurons of the brain. Even within the brain there are different types of neurotransmitter chemicals used by the neurons. These different types of neurotransmitters are not distributed randomly but are organized into discrete pathways or circuits.

A number of psychological and medical problems are beginning to be understood as being the result of neurotransmitter problems. Recent research indicates that schizophrenia, the most common type of psychotic disorder, is associated with abnormally high concentrations of a particular type of neurotransmitter, located primarily in the areas of the brain controlling emotion.[15] The most commonly used drugs in the treatment of schizophrenia are the major tranquilizers, such as Thorazine, which work by blocking the action of certain neurotransmitters, and thus reducing the effect of the excessive amount of neurotransmitter available at the synapse (see Table 6-1).

There is evidence that depression may result from an insufficient amount of certain neurotransmitters.[16] The increased tiredness and fatigue, the slow-

Table 6-1 The Effect of Different Substances on the Synapse

Substance	Effect on Synapse	Result
Black widow spider venum	Promotes release of neurotransmitter	Severe cramps and muscular contractions
Amphetamines	Promote release of neurotransmitter	Wakefulness, reduced appetite; a stimulant drug
Cocaine	Prolongs availability of neurotransmitter	Excitement, alertness; a stimulant drug
LSD & mescaline	Mimic neurotransmitter; increases neural firing	Hallucinations; disorientation
Tricyclic drugs (for example, Elavil)	Increase availability of neurotransmitter	Heightened mood; used in treatment of depression
MAO inhibitors	Increase availability of neurotransmitter	Heightened mood; used in treatment of depression
Chlorpromazine (Thorazine)	Blocks neurotransmitter action	Drowsiness, relaxation; used in treatment of schizophrenia
Reserpine	Reduces availability of neurotransmitter	Less constriction of blood vessels; used to lower blood pressure
DFP (nerve gas)	Blocks neurotransmitter action	Respiratory paralysis; death
Curare (a poison)	Blocks neurotransmitter action	Respiratory paralysis; death
Botulinus toxin (poison from spoiled canned food)	Blocks release of neurotransmitter	Respiratory and cardiac paralysis; death in severe cases

ness of movement, the loss of appetite, and the dejected mood found in depression may result from the reduced ability of brain cells to communicate, a condition caused by inadequate neurotransmitter substance and therefore poor synaptic transmission of nerve messages. In one study, samples of fluid were taken from the spinal cords of depressed patients, and the brain tissue of several individuals who had committed suicide was examined.[17] Evidence was found of a reduced level of neurotransmitter in the brains of these depressed individuals. The most commonly used drugs in the treatment of depression are the tricyclic drugs (such as Elavil) and the MAO inhibitors. Both of these drugs work by increasing the availability of neurotransmitter in the synapses of the brain.

Endorphin: The Brain's Own Painkiller • Within the past few years, scientists have succeeded in identifying a chemical manufactured in the brain that bears a surprising resemblance to morphine, the potent painkiller from the opium poppy. The term **endorphin** is a contraction of the words "endogenous morphine," or morphine made within the body, and refers to a group of chemicals produced by the brain that have the ability to suppress pain.

Certain neurons appear to have special receptors for sensing the presence of morphine and the morphine-like endorphins. These neurons are concentrated in those areas of the brain and spinal cord that are involved in the perception of pain. Nearby neurons apparently manufacture and release endorphin.

But how do these neurons suppress pain? One theory is that endorphin inhibits the release of neurotransmitter in neurons involved in pain circuits, thus decreasing the activity of these neurons and ultimately decreasing the perception of pain.[18]

One of the ways in which the effects of endorphins have been studied is by using naloxone, a drug that blocks the action of narcotics such as morphine. One study showed that endorphin injected into the brain produced a powerful suppression of pain and that this effect was reversed when naloxone was also injected into the brain.[19]

Electrical stimulation of certain brain sites produces long-lasting relief from pain. Until recently the reason for this result was unclear. Now there is evidence that the electrical stimulation promotes the release of endorphins, which then affect the neurons involved in pain circuits. The injection of naloxone reverses the effect of the electrical stimulation.[20]

Evidence is accumulating that several of the techniques that reduce pain—for example, hypnosis and acupuncture—have their effect because they somehow stimulate the release of endorphins in the brain. The effectiveness of many of these techniques can be blocked by injecting naloxone, the drug that blocks endorphin.[8]

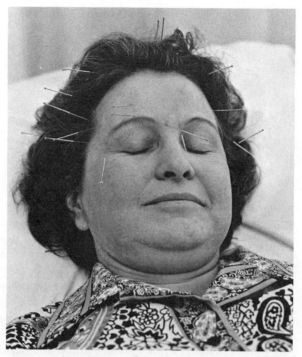

New interest in acupuncture, an ancient method of relieving pain, has been stimulated by evidence that its hair-like needles may promote the release of endorphins in the brain. The group of chemicals called endorphins are manufactured within the brain and resemble morphine in their ability to suppress pain. (Owen Franken/Stock, Boston)

Interim Summary   Afferent neurons carry messages to the brain, and efferent neurons carry messages from the brain. Interneurons do the rest of the work of the nervous system. All neurons consist of three parts: the cell body, with its nucleus; the dendrites; and the axon, with its terminal branches and terminal buttons. Nerve impulses move from the dendrites to the cell body and then down the axon to the terminal branches. According to the all-or-none law, the magnitude of the nerve impulse is always the same, regardless of the amount of stimulation. At the synapse, messages change from an electrical to a chemical form. Neurotransmitters are released into the synaptic gap by one neuron, causing the next neuron to fire. An excessive or insufficient amount of neurotransmitter at the synapse results in a variety of behavioral problems. Endorphin, the body's own painkiller, is concentrated in those areas of the brain involved in the perception of pain. By inhibiting the release of neurotransmitters in neural pain circuits, endorphin reduces the experience of pain.

Summary

1. The brain is the master control organ for behavior and experience. Psychologists interested in studying behavior have found important relationships between the brain and behavior.

2. Four methods of studying the brain are: examining the aftereffects of brain damage; recording and studying the brain's electrical activity by using the EEG; electrically stimulating the brain and observing the effects; and studying the anatomy of the brain through microscopic examination.

3. There are several different divisions of the nervous system. The central nervous system (brain and spinal cord) and the peripheral nervous system (all the rest) comprise the largest of these divisions. The peripheral nervous system is broken down into the autonomic nervous system (which controls involuntary functions) and the somatic nervous system (which controls the major muscles and receives sensory information). The autonomic nervous system is broken down into the sympathetic and parasympathetic divisions.

4. Some of the important structures of the inner brain are the medulla, cerebellum, thalamus, hypothalamus, and limbic system. The inner brain of human beings resembles the brains of more primitive vertebrates and is evolutionarily ancient.

5. The important structures of the outer brain include the cerebrum and the cerebral cortex. The cerebral cortex is responsible for higher mental function.

6. The two halves of the cerebrum—the cerebral hemispheres—are connected by the corpus callosum.

7. Each hemisphere contains frontal, temporal, occipital, and parietal lobes.

8. The nervous system consists of billions of neurons, or individual nerve cells. Afferent neurons carry messages to the brain, and efferent neurons carry messages from the brain. Interneurons do the other work of the nervous system.

9. The parts of the neuron include the cell body, the nucleus, dendrites, and the axon, with its terminal branches and terminal buttons.

10. Nerve impulses are electrical and follow the all-or-none law: the impulse either occurs or does not occur but does not vary in size.

11. At the synapse—the gap separating the terminal buttons of one neuron from the dendrites of another neuron—the electrical nerve message changes to a chemical form. Neurotransmitters are released into the synaptic gap and stimulate the dendrites of the following neuron.

12. A recently discovered substance, endorphin, is produced by the brain and is involved in the control of pain.

Key Concepts

ablation   The removal of brain tissue.

lesion   An injury to brain tissue; for example, a cut.

brain waves   Rhythmic changes in the electrical activity of the brain.

EEG   (electroencephalograph)   A machine that measures the electrical activity of the brain (brain waves).

alpha wave   A type of brain wave associated with relaxed awareness; it has a frequency of about ten cycles per second.

theta wave   A type of brain wave that appears to be associated with learning; it has a frequency of four to seven cycles per second.

evoked potential   The electrical response of the brain to a stimulus.

ESB (electrical stimulation of the brain)   A technique in which a weak electrical current is sent through a part of the brain.

pleasure center   A brain area that, when stimulated with electricity, produces satisfaction or pleasure.

central nervous system (CNS)   That part of the nervous system consisting of the brain and spinal cord.

peripheral nervous system   All nerves that lie outside of the central nervous system; for example, nerves connecting muscles and internal organs with the CNS.

somatic nervous system   The part of the peripheral nervous system consisting of the nerves that connect the CNS, major muscles, and major sense organs.

autonomic nervous system   The part of the peripheral nervous system consisting of the nerves that connect the CNS and internal organs and glands.

sympathetic division   The part of the autonomic nervous system that prepares the body for action; the "accelerator."

parasympathetic division   The part of the autonomic nervous system that prepares the body for rest; the "brake."

medulla   A structure at the top of the spinal cord that controls heart rate, blood pressure, and other reflex movements.

cerebellum   A structure at the back and bottom of the brain that regulates muscle tone and muscle coordination.

thalamus   A structure in the center of the brain that acts as a relay station for nerve messages going to and from the brain.

hypothalamus   A structure immediately below the thalamus that acts as the master control organ for the autonomic nervous system; regulates sex, hunger, and thirst.

limbic system   A group of interconnected structures that are involved in emotional expression and experience.

cerebrum   The outer brain, which, along with its cerebral cortex, is the seat of our higher mental processes, such as learning, memory, intelligence, and thinking.

cerebral cortex   The outer covering of the brain.

cerebral hemispheres   The right and left halves of the brain.

corpus callosum   The broad band of nerves that connects the two hemispheres of the brain.

occipital lobe   A region at the back of each side of the brain that specializes in vision.

parietal lobe   A region at the top of each side of the brain that specializes in skin and body sensations.

frontal lobe   A region at the front of each side of the brain that specializes in planning, abstract thinking, and problem solving.

temporal lobe   A region along the side of each half of the brain that specializes in memory and hearing.

neuron   The nerve cell; the fundamental unit of the nervous system.

nerve   A group of neurons strung together to form a cord.

afferent neurons   Nerve cells that carry messages to the brain.

efferent neurons   Nerve cells that carry messages from the brain to muscles or glands.

interneurons   Nerve cells that carry messages between afferent and efferent neurons.

cell body   The part of a cell that contains the cell's nucleus.

dendrite   A relatively short, branching fiber that extends from the cell body.

axon   A long, thin fiber that extends from

the cell body.

terminal branches   Branching fibers at the end of the axon opposite the cell body.

terminal buttons   The tips of the terminal branches, which contain and release neurotransmitters.

myelin sheath   A special tissue encasing and insulating the axon from the electrical activity of neighboring cells.

nerve impulses   Pulses of electrical current carried by neurons.

all-or-none law   The principle that the size or intensity of a neuron's nerve impulse is always the same; the neuron is either stimulated enough to fire or it is not.

synapse   The gap separating the terminal buttons of one neuron from the dendrites of another.

neurotransmitter   A chemical secreted into the synapse by the terminal buttons of a neuron, which then stimulates the dendrites of other neurons to generate electrical nerve impulses.

endorphin   A group of chemicals produced by the brain that have the ability to suppress pain.

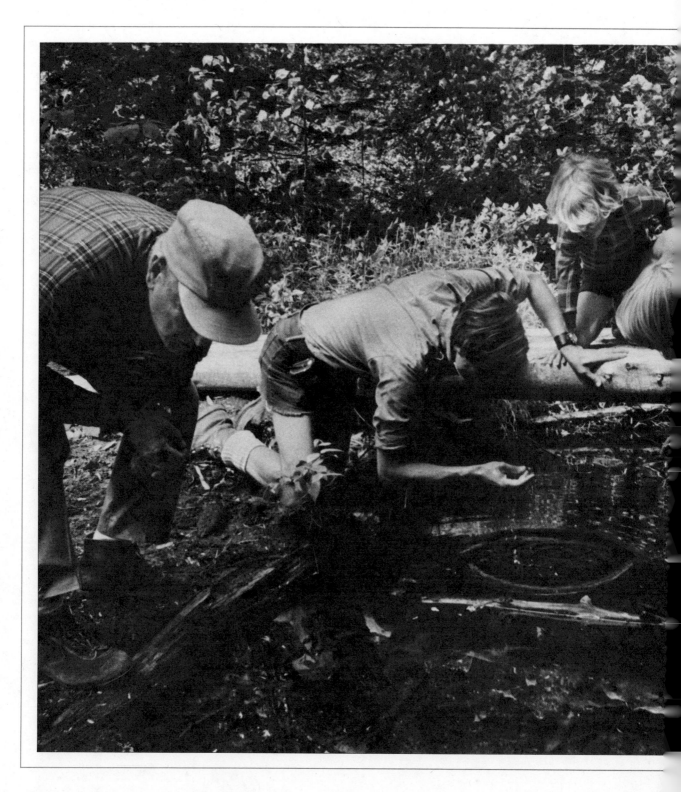

Chapter 7

Sensation and Perception

Key Questions

1. What are the human senses?
2. How do the senses of taste and smell, the skin senses, and the body senses work?
3. How do the ears work, and what are the common hearing problems?
4. How do the eyes work, and what are the common visual problems?
5. How is perception organized?

If you had to give up one of your senses, which one would it be?

Can you imagine living in a world without sight, without sound, or without taste? A world perfectly dark, a world always silent, a world without the taste of orange, without the smell of fresh bread or peppermint? Such a world would be dull, and you would never know about most of what happened in it. But a lack of stimulation is not only dull, it can also be stressful and disorienting.

In order for your mind to work normally, sensory stimulation is necessary. Experiments have shown that it is actually possible to be "bored out of your mind." Without adequate stimulation, you may feel disorganized, fuzzy-minded, and extremely anxious—and begin seeing things that aren't there.[1,2]

The results of the extreme reduction of stimulation have been studied by a number of psychologists. In one case, a woman was waiting in a hospital for an operation on her eyes. Her bed was some distance from the other patients, she was surrounded by screens, and both her eyes were bandaged shut. Soon she became quite restless. Her thoughts became con-

fused, and she began to express fears that she was being poisoned or that she would be smothered. She began to "see" cartoon-like creatures, even though her eyes were completely bandaged. The woman apparently suffered from a lack of sensory stimulation, and her bizarre symptoms were consequences of that fact, since before having her eyes bandaged shut she was completely normal. After the operation, the bandages were removed, and she could see. She also was brought into much closer contact with other patients and with the staff. As a result, within a short while her strange mental and perceptual symptoms disappeared completely.[3]

The human senses are the means we have of gathering information about the world we live in and about our own bodies. Without this information, we would be lost. The pain in your hand tells you to drop the hot pan; the thunder tells you that the rain is coming; the sour taste tells you the milk is spoiled; and the red light tells you to stop. Having all of this sensory information is often taken for granted, but its presence depends upon the complex, and sometimes fragile, sensory systems.

The Human Senses

Aristotle wrote, "Nothing is in the mind which does not pass through the senses." This means that the senses are vital—but what are the senses and how many are there?

Extrasensory Perception

When people count their senses, they commonly come up with five: seeing, hearing, touching, tasting, and smelling. But others believe that there is a sense beyond these five—a "sixth sense" that is psychic, or

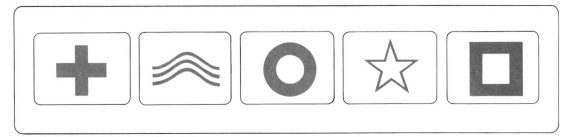

Figure 7-1 ESP Cards.   *In one type of ESP experiment, a deck of cards like the ones shown above is shuffled thoroughly. One person then looks at the cards one at a time while a second person tries to guess the symbol.   A score significantly higher than chance indicates that some communication occurred.*

"extrasensory." The term **extrasensory perception** (ESP) refers to the possibility of sensing information about the world, other people, or the future in ways other than through the normal human senses. **Parapsychology** is the scientific study of ESP. What would it be like to "read" the mind of another person or to "see" into the future? The idea has captured the imagination of millions and has been the subject of intense controversy among scientists for more than a century. The primary controversy has been over the question of whether extrasensory perception exists at all. The problem with demonstrating the existence of ESP is that all other possible sensory information must be ruled out. In order for you to demonstrate that you can read my thoughts, you must prove that your information could not possibly have come from any other sense mode, such as seeing or hearing.

A great deal of research has been conducted to study ESP. Many studies fail to find evidence of the existence of ESP. When the results of a study seem to support the view that ESP is real, the study is typically repeated in order to confirm the evidence. But once-successful studies of ESP generally fail when tried a second or third time. Thus, there is no reliable, consistent evidence supporting the belief in ESP.

Researchers have tried, without consistent success, to find evidence for ESP influences in dreams, to develop methods of training and improving ESP skills, and to identify individuals who display unusual ESP talent. (See the ESP cards shown in Figure 7-1.) But the scientific study of ESP has yet to yield convincing results.

A number of entertainers calling themselves "psychics" perform tricks that they claim can be explained only in terms of their extraordinary "ESP talent." One celebrated psychic convinced a group of scientists that he could read minds,[4] but other, more

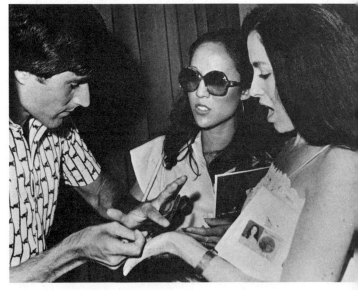

Uri Geller is an entertainer who performs a number of feats that he represents as "psychic." In addition to his mind-reading demonstration, Geller bends spoons and keys while appearing to use only the powers of his mind. (United Press International Photo)

skeptical scientists argued that his feats could be explained by trickery and deception.[5]   Later, a magician showed that he could duplicate the so-called psychic's feats using nothing but ordinary magic and sleight of hand.[6]   Because the results of research on ESP have been inconsistent, and because deception and cheating have occasionally been used by those attempting to demonstrate the validity of the "sixth" sense, most scientists are skeptical and unconvinced that it is real. There appear to be good reasons for withholding judgment on ESP until additional evidence is in.

The Types of Human Senses

There are clearly more than five senses—there are at least seven—and while none of these is "extrasensory," each is quite remarkable in many ways.   For example, over the years many people have claimed the "psychic" power of being able to "read" the color of objects with nothing but their fingertips.   The ability to "see" with the skin of the fingers would indeed be a remarkable feat.   Some have argued that these claims are based completely on cheating, and that sensing different colors with the skin is quite impossible.[7]   One scientist, however, has shown that different colors reflect different amounts of heat from a hand held near colored objects and that our temperature sense is sensitive enough to detect these slight differences.[8]   Our ability to detect changes in temperature is but one of the several senses of the skin.

Our senses can be classified into three basic types that differ in terms of the location of the source of information that is being sensed: those sensitive to far sources, those for near sources, and those for sources inside our bodies.   See Table 7-1.

Two senses provide information about things at a distance from our bodies: vision (sensitivity to light energy) and hearing (sensitivity to sound energy). Three senses provide information about things near or on the surface of our bodies: the skin senses are sensitive to pressure, temperature, and pain; taste is sensi-

Table 7-1 The Human Senses

Sensing Information from a Distance
>   Vision
>   Hearing

Sensing Information from Nearby
>   Skin senses
>   Taste
>   Smell

Sensing Information from Inside
>   Kinesthetic sense (body movement)
>   Vestibular sense (body orientation)

tive to the chemical composition of liquids and foods on the tongue; and smell is sensitive to gases reaching the nose.   The third type of sense includes those that provide information from within the body about the movement, position, and orientation of the body: the **kinesthetic sense** is sensitive to the movement and position of the muscles and joints; the **vestibular sense,** located in the inner ear, is sensitive to body balance and rotation.

Absolute and Difference Thresholds

The senses respond to different aspects of the physical world, allowing us to know the world in many different ways.   But there are limits to how much of the world we can experience: some of the energy in the world is outside our range of sensitivity.   We cannot see some light, we cannot hear some sound, and we cannot feel some touches.

Your eyes, ears, and other senses are extremely sensitive, but there are sounds too quiet and lights too dim for you to detect.   You can hear the ticking of your watch when it is close to your ear, but not when it is fifty feet away.   Your senses require a certain minimum amount of physical energy before they can respond.   This lower limit of sensitivity, or minimum level of energy necessary for sensation, is called the

absolute threshold. A light that is so dim that it cannot be seen is below the absolute threshold; its energy is below the minimum required for the eyes to respond.

The absolute threshold is not a sharp border, with sounds on one side always experienced and sounds on the other side never experienced, but is instead a variable or "fuzzy" border. Sounds near the absolute threshold will sometimes be experienced and sometimes not. Because of this variability, the absolute threshold can be estimated only from repeated tests.

Another important kind of threshold is the limit of sensitivity to a change in the stimulus, or the **difference threshold.** What is the smallest difference between two sounds or colors that you can detect? How sensitive are you to small changes in the world? Like the absolute threshold, the difference threshold is not a clear cutoff point, but instead is a variable point and must be calculated from a series of tests. Try the test presented in Figure 7-2.

People differ in their sensitivity. You may be more or less sensitive to sounds than other people; that is, your absolute threshold for sound may be above or below average. Scientists have estimated the average absolute threshold for different senses. For example, they estimate that the absolute threshold for vision is the amount of light that would come from a

candle thirty miles away on a dark night; the absolute threshold for hearing is the amount of sound from a ticking watch twenty feet away in a very quiet room; the absolute threshold for touch is the amount of pressure felt from the wing of a bee falling on your cheek from a height of about half an inch; the absolute threshold for smell is about one drop of perfume diffused throughout a six-room apartment; and the absolute threshold for taste is about one teaspoon of sugar dissolved in two gallons of water.

Adaptation and Aftereffects

Your sensitivity to a stimulus depends upon the history of your experience. Your experience at one moment influences and shapes your experience at the next moment. After cold water, lukewarm water feels rather warm, but after hot water, it feels cool. An object feels heavy after you have recently lifted light objects, but it feels very light after you have recently lifted heavy objects. In addition, your sensitivity to weight, heat, and other qualities declines with repeated stimulation. After a period of less stimulation, sensitivity is eventually restored. This change in sensitivity is a type of adjustment called **adaptation.**

When you walk into a movie theatre, you can see very little at first because your eyes have been continuously exposed to the bright light outside the theater—they are adapted to the light and are therefore not very sensitive to low levels of light stimulation. After a few minutes in the darkened theater, you begin to be able to see the faces of the people around you as your eyes become more and more sensitive. As you lose your adaptation to the light and become more sensitive, you achieve what is called **dark adaptation.** If you then walk out of the theater into the afternoon sun, your eyes are dazzled by the light—everything seems very bright and intense because your eyes are extremely sensitive to light.

Because of the process of adaptation, objects that you have just seen leave their prints on your eyes for a

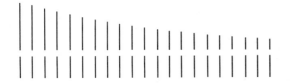

Figure 7-2 Absolute and Difference Thresholds. *The difference threshold is the smallest change in a stimulus that can reliably be detected. What is your threshold for detecting differences in line lengths? Examine the lines in the illustration and try to determine which of the top lines are different in length from the bottom lines. As the difference approaches your threshold, the task becomes difficult.*

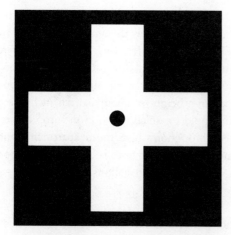 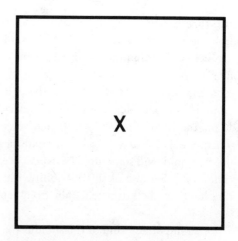

Figure 7-3 The Negative Afterimage.   *Find your negative afterimage by focusing on the dot in the center of the white cross for about one minute, then look at the X in the middle of the square.   A dark cross should be visible.*

few seconds. You may remember seeing a flashbulb go off when someone took your picture and afterward seeing a black spot wherever you looked. A strong white light leaves an aftereffect that is black. After looking at a black spot, you may experience an aftereffect of a ghostly white spot. These aftereffects are called **negative afterimages.**

How can negative afterimages be explained? They result when adaptation occurs in one part of the eye more than in another. A flashbulb adapts a small part of the eye and makes it very insensitive to light. Afterwards, when you look at a wall, you see a black spot resulting from this area of insensitivity on the eye.

You can demonstrate this effect for yourself, using Figure 7-3. Hold this book in bright light and fixate on the dot in the center of the white cross. Focus on the black dot without moving your eyes while you slowly count to fifty. Then look at the X in the center of the white square. The negative afterimage—a black cross—should be visible. If it isn't, blink your eyes a time or two and it will appear. The negative afterimage results from the fact that adaptation has occurred in the area of the eye focused on the white cross. The pigment in the visual cells in this region of the eye is bleached by light and takes a while to recover. During this recovery period the area that is bleached is less sensitive and gives rise to the perception of a gray image in the shape of the bleached area.

Interim Summary   The basic human senses are vision, hearing, the skin senses, smell, taste, and the kinesthetic and vestibular senses (body senses). The lower limit of sensitivity is called the absolute threshold, and the limit of sensitivity to stimulus changes is called the difference threshold. Sensitivity changes with repeated stimulation, an effect called adaptation. One example of adaptation is the negative afterimage.

The Minor Senses

Historically, the skin and body senses, taste, and smell have been studied less than vision and hearing and have been termed "the minor senses." But these senses are by no means minor when you consider the interest, energy, and dedication that people invest in the pursuit of these unique sensations.

Taste

Consider the gustatory sense—taste. Throughout recorded history, the search for new, more exciting flavors has stimulated great discovery and adventure. Christopher Columbus and Marco Polo set out on dangerous voyages to strange lands in search of the spices of the East. Today, men and women train for years in cooking academies to learn the art of gourmet cooking. All of this energy and dedication is focused on various combinations of only four possible tastes: sour, salty, sweet, and bitter.

How are these tastes sensed? The tongue contains groups of cells sensitive to the chemicals in food. These groups of cells are called **taste buds** and are distributed all over the top surface of the tongue, with the exception of the center. A remarkable feature of taste buds is that they are replaced every few days, so that a particular taste bud has a very brief life span. Not all parts of the tongue are equally sensitive to the different tastes. The tip is especially sensitive to sweet and salty tastes, the sides are more sensitive to sour tastes, and the front and back are more sensitive to bitter tastes.

Taste combinations are especially important in preparing foods. One rule of taste mixture is that of *flavor independence*. For the most part, different tastes retain their qualities when combined. For example, a combination of sweet and sour (as in sweet-and-sour sauce) does not result in a combination that is neutral, or some compromise between the two, but instead

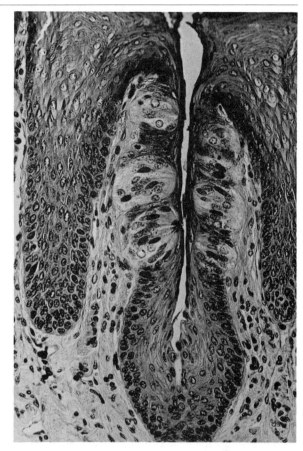

Tastes are sensed by special cells on the tongue called taste buds. This photo shows a crevice on the surface of the tongue that has several taste buds opening onto it. (Manfred Kage/Peter Arnold, Inc.)

results in a combination in which both flavors are independently present. A second rule of taste mixture is that of *mutual suppression*.[9] Combined flavors interact so that the stronger overwhelms the weaker. A mild bitter taste in vegetables may be overcome by the addition of a small amount of sugar. An excessively salty taste in soup may be slightly suppressed by the addition of a small amount of sugar.

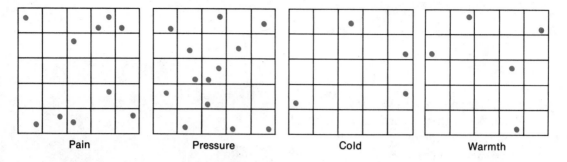

Figure 7-4 A Skin Grid. *To test the skin senses, a tiny grid is drawn on the surface of the skin. When a hair-like probe is used to touch different parts of the grid, different sensations are reported. The type of sensation—pain, pressure, cold, or warmth—depends upon which part of the grid is touched.*

Smell

Perfumes to please the sense of smell sometimes cost thousands of dollars an ounce. The stimulus for smell is, of course, airborne molecules of various chemical substances. Many scientists have attempted to classify the variety of odors by reducing them to a system of four or more basic or primary odors, but no general agreement about such a system has yet developed. In fact, much less is known about the sense of smell than is known about the sense of taste.

How are odors sensed? The nose contains cells sensitive to smell, clustered in two small patches high up in the nasal passages. In normal breathing, air does not pass directly across these cells, since they are not located in the main air passages. They are reached in a minor way by deflected air and they can be reached directly by sniffing, which sends currents of air into the upper regions of the nasal passages that contain the odor-sensitive cells.

Odors combine in several ways. Sometimes they *blend* and produce a single odor that combines the properties of the ingredient odors; this blending effect is more likely to result from the combination of similar odors. A second common result of combining odors is *masking,* in which the stronger odor completely or almost completely suppresses the weaker. One way to get rid of unpleasant odors is through masking. This principle explains why air fresheners work.

The Skin Senses

The skin senses convey information about pressure, temperature, and pain. Contact with the skin produces the sensation of touch when the nerve endings in the skin have been stimulated. Warmth and cold are sensed from the skin, as well, when contact is made with objects significantly above or below body temperature. The sensation of pain may be elicited in a variety of ways: through pressure or extreme temperature, or with electrical or chemical stimulation.

The skin is not uniformly sensitive. It is, instead, a mosaic of small, sensitive spots, each of which is sensitive to pressure, warmth, cold, or pain. When researchers have explored the sensitivity of the skin by touching it with a fine point, they have found that touching certain spots results in a cold sensation, regardless of the temperature of the probe. You can confirm this for yourself by touching various spots on your skin with a sharp pencil point or stiff hair. For reasons not clear, your lips and the end of your nose have a large number of "cold spots," so if you touch different spots on the tip of your nose or lips with a pencil point, you are likely to find at least one that feels quite cold. Figure 7-4 shows the typical results of exploring a small area of skin with a probe. The sensitive points for pain, pressure, cold, and warmth are distributed differently in different regions of the body. For example, the back of the hand has about one-seventh as many pressure spots as the tip of the nose but has over four times as many pain spots. The chest has more cold spots than the forehead, but only about half as many warmth spots.

The Body Senses

You know where your body is and how its parts are arranged. You can sense the position of your arms and legs, and even in the dark you know where the floor and ceiling are. As you swing a tennis racket, you can feel the movement and position of your arm. You are, in other words, in contact with your body. This knowledge of your body does not come from vision, hearing, smell, taste, or touch, but is instead a result of your special body senses—the kinesthetic sense and the vestibular sense.

The **kinesthetic sense** provides knowledge of body position and body movement. Nerve endings in the joints, tendons, and muscles monitor what is happening in the body and keep you in constant contact. Try this test of your kinesthetic senses: Close your eyes, hold out both arms in front of you, then bring your hands together so that your forefingers are touching. Chances are, you will miss the first time you try this—but you won't miss by far, and with a little practice, you will be able to do it easily. This task would be impossible without precise knowledge of the position of your hands. Baseball, basketball, swimming, dancing, and other physical activities that depend upon careful and skilled muscular movements depend upon the feedback provided by your kinesthetic sense.

The **vestibular sense** provides knowledge of body orientation. It tells you, by responding to gravity cues, which way is down and which way is up. The vestibular sense organ lies in an area of the inner ear called the **semicircular canals** (see Figure 7-5) and consists of a liquid that is disturbed whenever you change your orientation. This liquid stimulates special hair receptors that line the semicircular canals and thereby provide you with feedback about the orientation of your own body. Without this knowledge,

Your ability to walk a tightrope or a balance beam depends upon how sensitive you are to changes in the orientation of your body. Knowledge of body orientation is provided by the vestibular sense organ, a part of the inner ear. (Cary Wolinsky/Stock, Boston)

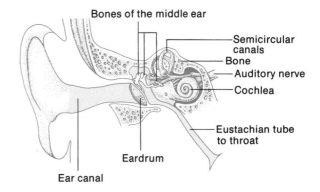

Figure 7-5 The Human Ear. *Vibrations are carried through the ear canal to the eardrum, then along the bones of the middle ear to the cochlea. The cochlea contains a structure called the basilar membrane that transforms vibrations into nerve impulses.*

you could not maintain your posture or your ability to walk upright in the dark; you certainly could not walk a tightrope without this special knowledge of body orientation.

Dizziness results from a disturbance in the semicircular canals. When the head is rotated, the fluid in the semicircular canals flows against the hair sensors in the canal walls. After prolonged rotation, or violent and sudden changes in head position, dizziness or nausea may result. Some people get motion sickness from boats, planes, automobiles, or even from riding camels. This disorder largely depends upon head movement when the body is experiencing varying acceleration. One way to reduce motion sickness is to restrict head movements. Drugs such as Dramamine can also help.

Interim Summary   There are only four basic tastes: sour, salty, sweet, and bitter. Groups of cells called taste buds, located on the tongue, are sensitive to the chemical composition of foods and are responsible for sensations of taste. The upper regions of the nose contain clusters of cells sensitive to odors. The skin senses provide information about pressure, temperature, and pain. The kinesthetic sense provides information about body position and movement from special cells located in the muscles and joints. The vestibular sense provides knowledge of body orientation from cells in the inner ear.

Hearing

Any vibration that reaches the ear within the right range of frequency and with adequate intensity will produce the sensation of sound. Sound waves, or vibrations, typically reach the ear by means of the air, but vibrations conducted to the ear by the bones of the head will also produce sensations of sound.

Sound and the Ear

Sound has many sensory qualities, but three are primary: loudness, pitch, and timbre. The sensory quality of *loudness,* or sound intensity, results primarily from the physical quality called the *amplitude* of the sound wave, or the intensity of the vibration. The sensory quality of *pitch* (the highness or lowness of sound) results primarily from the physical quality of the *frequency* of vibrations. High-frequency sound waves are perceived as high tones, and low-frequency sound waves are perceived as low tones. The human ear is sensitive to sound waves ranging from about 20 vibrations to about 20,000 vibrations per second. Middle C on the piano is 256 vibrations per second. The sensory quality of *timbre* (the richness or complexity of sound) results primarily from the *purity* or *complexity* of different tones. The flute produces a relatively pure tone, while the trumpet produces a much more complex tone.

The ear is divided into three general regions: the outer ear, the middle ear, and the inner ear. The outer ear is the externally visible portion of the ear that gathers the sound and concentrates it on the sensitive parts of the middle ear. Many animals, such as dogs or cats, can move the outer ear to gather the sound more efficiently and channel it toward the middle ear. The eardrum, or **tympanic membrane,** separates the outer ear from the middle ear and transmits the sound energy to the tiny bones of the middle ear. The middle ear contains three small bones that conduct the vibrations to the inner ear. The inner ear contains the **cochlea,** a canal coiled like a snail's shell, which contains the receptors sensitive to sound vibrations. The sound waves set up regular movements of the fluid in the cochlea. These movements are transmitted to a structure in the cochlea called the **basilar membrane** and finally stimulate special cells on the membrane that lead to the auditory nerve. Again see Figure 7-5.

Theories of Hearing

It is not yet known precisely how the stimulation of the basilar membrane results in the experience of sounds of different frequencies. There are, however, two influential theories of pitch discrimination, the place theory and the frequency theory.

According to the **place theory,** sounds of different frequencies stimulate different places on the basilar membrane. High-frequency tones are known to displace the narrow end of the basilar membrane, and tones of lower frequency stimulate the broader end of the membrane. The theory assumes that the experience of pitch results directly from the region of the membrane that is displaced by the sound. While the place theory accounts fairly well for high and intermediate tones, it works less well in accounting for the experience of low tones. Low tones have been observed to activate and displace the entire basilar membrane, rather than a particular region, and this fact complicates the place theory.

A second theory of pitch discrimination is the **frequency theory.** According to this theory, sounds of different frequency stimulate the basilar membrane to cause different frequencies of nerve impulses to travel to the brain from the ear. It has been found that sounds of 500 cycles per second result in 500 nerve impulses per second. The rate of nerve impulses from the ear is about the same as the rate of vibration per second associated with sound. There is a limit, however, to the rate at which individual nerve cells can fire—about 1,000 impulses per second.

It appears likely that sounds of frequencies below 1,000 cycles per second are coded in terms of frequency of nerve impulses (frequency theory), while sounds

above 1,000 cycles per second are coded in terms of the region of the basilar membrane that is most displaced (place theory). Thus, both the place theory and the frequency theory appear to be correct.

Hearing Problems

Loss of hearing can result from several different kinds of problems. There are three basic kinds of deafness: conductive deafness, neural deafness, and central deafness. **Conductive deafness** results from problems in the outer or middle ear that block the passage of sound waves and prevent sound energy from reaching the sensitive structures of the inner ear. One type of conductive deafness comes from perforation of the tympanic membrane, or eardrum. If the eardrum is broken (by a hairpin, explosion, slap, or other injury), the sound waves will not be carried efficiently to the bones of the middle ear. With proper medical attention, however, most perforated eardrums heal, and little permanent loss of hearing results. Infections and other diseases of the middle ear can also produce conductive deafness.

Neural deafness results from problems in the inner ear or with the auditory nerve. Some degree of neural deafness is common with advancing age. As the body ages, the hair cells in the cochlea and the nerve cells in the auditory nerve slowly deteriorate, and hearing becomes poorer and poorer. Not all individuals show loss of hearing with age, but the reasons for this are not well understood. Neural deafness also results from exposure to noise. Prolonged exposure to the noise of jet airplanes, to industrial noise, or to amplified music can result in permanent hearing loss.

Central deafness results from problems with the auditory centers of the brain or from certain abnormal psychological conditions. Injury or damage to the portions of the brain responsible for hearing will produce central deafness. For example, a brain tumor or a cerebral hemorrhage may destroy some of the brain cells necessary for processing auditory information, and central deafness may result. Central deafness may also result from psychological trauma, as a result of severe psychological stress. This type of psychological reaction is described in Chapter 20 and is termed a **conversion reaction.**

Interim Summary

The three sensory qualities of sound are loudness, pitch, and timbre. These result primarily from the amplitude, frequency, and purity of the sound waves. A structure called the basilar membrane in the cochlea, an organ located in the inner ear, is responsible for transforming sound energy into nerve impulses. The experience of pitch can best be explained by a combination of two theories—the place theory and the frequency theory. Three types of deafness are conductive deafness, resulting from problems in the outer or middle ear; neural deafness, resulting from problems in the inner ear or auditory nerve; and central deafness, resulting from problems with the auditory centers of the brain or from psychological stress.

Vision

The stimulus for vision is a form of energy called *electromagnetic radiation.* Only a small part of the electromagnetic spectrum is visible to the eye, a part referred to as *light energy.* Gamma rays, X rays, and ultraviolet rays are parts of the electromagnetic spectrum whose wavelengths are shorter than visible light; infrared rays, radar, and radio and television waves are all longer than visible light.

Color and Brightness Vision

Like sound energy, light energy has three basic sensory qualities: hue, brightness, and saturation. *Hue* (apparent color) results primarily from the physical characteristic of the *wavelength* of the light. Blue and green have shorter wavelengths than yellow and red. *Brightness* (light strength) results primarily from the physical characteristic of *intensity.* *Saturation* (color purity) results primarily from the physical characteristic of *complexity.* Light of a single wavelength will appear as pure or highly saturated; light of mixed wavelengths, or a color with added gray, will appear duller, less saturated.

The Duplicity Principle • The light-sensitive part of the eye is called the **retina.** The retina is a mosaic of unique light sensors that covers the back of the eye. Light focused on the cells of the retina stimulates the optic nerve, which carries visual information to the brain.

According to the **duplicity principle** of vision, there are two kinds of light-sensitive cells in the retina, and their function accounts for the variety of visual effects that we all experience. **Rods** are specialized cells that respond to differences in light intensity but not to differences in wavelength. If all you had on your retina were rods, you would see everything only in terms of black and white—no color. Though rods are color-blind, they are extremely sensitive to small amounts of light. The second kind of light-sensitive cell in the retina is the cone. **Cones** are specialized cells that respond to differences in wavelength as well as, to a lesser degree, differences in light intensity. Although the cones do not respond well in dim light, in bright daylight they are extremely sensitive to differences in wavelength and are wholly responsible for the rainbow of colors that make up your visual world. You may have noticed that in dim light—in the very early morning or just before dark—most colors just fade away. This is because your cones do not work very well in dim light, and you become essentially colorblind.

Theories of Color Vision   •   There two basic theories of color vision, and each of them partially explains how we see colors. Modern research has not yet resolved the question of which is correct, but a combination of the two theories appears to be the best answer. The **trichromatic theory**, also known as the Young-Helmholtz Theory, assumes that we have three types of cones, each sensitive to a different primary color: red, green, and blue-violet. The theory further assumes that all color experiences result from different combinations of these three basic receptors being stimulated. In fact, it is true that all colors can be produced by different combinations of these three colors. In addition, microscopic examinations of the eye have discovered three types of cones, each sensitive to a different wavelength of light.[10]

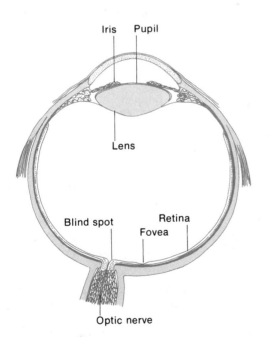

Figure 7-6 The Eye. *The human eye is a complex, specialized organ that in some ways is like an extension of the brain. This horizontal cross-section of the eye shows the different structures important for vision.*

A second theory, the **opponent-process theory,** also known as the Hering Theory, proposes that there are four primary colors: blue, green, yellow, and red. The theory assumes that red and green are opposite and opponent processes, that blue and yellow are a second pair of opponent processes, and that black and white are a third opponent pair. These three opponent processes are believed to occur, not in the cones of the retina, but in the brain itself. There is some evidence that supports this view. Prolonged fixation on a red color will result in a green negative afterimage; prolonged fixation on a yellow color will result in a blue negative afterimage; and the negative afterimage from a white object is black. In addition, studies of the electrical activities of visual cells in the brain indicate that certain cells respond in a manner consistent with the opponent-process theory.[11]

These two theories of color vision describe different parts of the perceptual system. The trichromatic theory appears to be a good description of the color receptors in the eye, and the opponent-process theory appears to be a good description of the color system in the brain. Thus, a combination of the two theories is necessary for a complete explanation of color vision.

The Eye

Your eye is a wonderful device. In some ways it is like an extension of your brain and has a kind of intelligence of its own. It is not simply a passive receiver of light, but is actively involved in seeking and processing information. Figure 7-6 shows a cross-section of the human eye.

The Eye Is Not a Camera   •   Sometimes we think of our perceptual experiences as if they were pictures inside our heads. You may think that the eye is like a camera. There is some validity to that analogy, as the following points indicate:

1. Both the eye and the camera collect light and focus it upside down on a light-sensitive surface. The camera uses film containing a chemical that changes when exposed to light. The back of the eye consists of a coating of small cells, the **retina,** also containing a chemical that changes when exposed to light.

2. The image in a camera can be focused by adjusting the lens. The image in the eye is focused by an adjustment of the **lens** made by small muscles in the eye. Muscles connected to the lens tighten to increase its curvature, causing nearby objects to come into focus. You can feel the tension of these tightened lens muscles by bringing this book close to your eyes.

3. The amount of light entering the camera is controlled by enlarging or contracting a hole behind the lens called the aperture. The size of the aperture is indicated by an arbitrarily acquired number called the *f-stop.* The amount of light entering the eye is controlled by enlarging or contracting a small hole in front of the lens called the **pupil.** In bright light the pupil is small and looks like a black dot in the center of the eye. In the dark the pupil enlarges to admit more light to the eye. The pupil is surrounded by a muscle called the **iris;** the iris is the part of your eye that makes you blue, brown, or green eyed.

But the eye is not a camera; perceptions are not copies of the external world. You cannot know my perception by knowing only the external world, although that knowledge is a start. Cameras are passive receivers of information; the eye actively searches for information. Cameras record; the perceptual system constructs. The camera registers all, but perception is highly selective. The camera has no memory, but perception learns from the past.

Your Blind Spot • Our perceptual worlds are personal constructions, not copies of the physical world. A simple demonstration of this fact can be made by considering the **blind spot.** Although many people are never aware of it, the field of vision for each eye has a rather large blind area. Because the visual fields of the two eyes overlap somewhat, when we look at the world with both eyes, there is not a large area in which we are blind. But looking with only one eye, there is a large "hole" in the perceptual world, an area in which we are absolutely blind. The blind spot results from the fact that there is on the retina of each eye a small spot where the *optic nerve* from the brain joins the eye. This spot lacks visual receptor cells and is therefore insensitive to light.

You can find your blind spot by looking at the X in Figure 7-7 with your right eye only (close your left eye) from a viewing distance of about ten inches. When you are focused on the X, an image of the X is projected on the **fovea** of the eye, the part of the retina that is most densely packed with light-sensitive cells. When you have done this, move the book back and forth, closer and farther from your eye, while keeping your eye focused on the X. At the right distance from your eye, you will notice that the spot on your right will disappear completely—it will be in your blind area. If the book is brought either closer or farther away from your eye, the spot will reappear as it leaves the blind area. When the spot has disappeared, what do you see in its place? Oddly enough, not a hole in the page, but paper, as if we could see underneath the spot. When the spot has disappeared, many people even see the black line as continuous through the blind area.

If you have a large blind area in your visual field, why is it that you do not see a "hole" in the wall of the room when you look at it with one eye only? If

Figure 7-7 The Blind Spot. *To find your blind spot, close your left eye and look at the X with your right eye. Then move the book nearer and farther from your face until the round spot disappears. This will happen when the image of the spot falls on your blind spot.*

you have a large blind area in your visual field, why is it that you did not see a large "hole" in the page of this book when the spot on the page disappeared? Somehow you "fill in" this void. You repair the hole, in a sense. And the material used for the patch has the same appearance and color as the surrounding field. Apparently, your perceptual world is different from the physical world; it is in part your own construction.

Visual Problems

The most severe visual problem is, of course, blindness. The term *legally blind* refers not only to those who are completely without sight, but also to those who have lost 80 percent or more of their sight and therefore cannot read or easily get about. Blindness can result from specific problems with the structures in the eye, the optic nerve, or the visual area of the brain.

One source of blindness is **cataracts,** a loss of transparency in the lens of the eye. Cataracts can come about from a variety of causes, including diabetes, advancing age, or exposure to an excess of ultravi-

olet radiation from the sun. A baby may be born with cataracts if the mother contracted German measles during her pregnancy. Without a transparent lens, of course, light cannot be focused on the retina, and thus sight is impossible. Cataracts can be successfully removed in most cases by a simple operation.

Color blindness is an inherited condition that results in varying degrees of difficulty in discriminating different colors. Total color blindness, or **monochromatism,** is a rare disorder in which only blacks, whites, and grays can be seen. Much more common is partial color blindness, in which the individual may have some difficulty seeing the difference between red and green or between yellow and blue.

By far the most common visual problem is a difficulty in focusing the eye. People who are *nearsighted,* with a condition called **myopia,** are able to see nearby objects in focus but cannot focus on those at a distance. Myopic vision can be corrected with glasses that have a *concave* lens. People who are *farsighted,* with a condition called **hyperopia,** can focus on distant objects but not on nearby objects. Hyperopic vision can be corrected by wearing glasses with a *convex* lens.

Interim Summary   The three sensory qualities of vision are hue, brightness, and saturation. These result primarily from the wavelength, intensity, and complexity, respectively, of the light. There are two kinds of light-sensitive cells on the retina—rods (which specialize in detecting changes in light intensity) and cones (which specialize in detecting changes in wavelength). Two theories that explain color vision are the trichromatic theory (Young-Helmholtz theory) and the opponent-process theory (Hering theory). Important structures of the eye include the iris, pupil, lens, retina, fovea, and blind spot. Common visual problems include cataracts, color blindness, and problems in focusing.

The Organization of Perception

Perception goes beyond the information provided by the senses. We experience a world of objects and people, not a world of points of light and patches of color. We experience a world of structure and relationship, not a world of unconnected surfaces. The raw material given by the senses is used to build the world of our experience. We not only *sense* the physical energy in the world, we struggle to *make sense* of it by organizing it into meaningful experiences and interpreting them in the context of our other experiences.

The Principles of Organization

In order to see and make sense of an object, you must first be able to distinguish it as an object; you must be able to separate it from its background. As you look at this book, you see an object separated from the table, wall, or floor that is its background. As you read this page, you see black words standing out against a white background. Perception requires that you separate figures (books, people, words) from their background. You tend to organize what you see into figure and ground. This is the **figure-ground principle** of perception. (See Figure 7-8.)

How perception is organized was an important issue for psychologists at the turn of the century.

Max Wertheimer

Figure 7-8 Vase or Face?   *Do you see a vase or two faces? What you see depends upon whether you perceive the colored area as figure or as ground. If you see it as the figure, you see a vase; if it is the ground, you see two faces.*

Some argued that perception could be understood only be breaking it down into its elements, by analyzing it into its separate parts. Others argued that perception is an organized whole, and is more than the simple sum of its parts. This latter view was stressed by Max Wertheimer, a German psychologist interested in perception.

One day in 1910, while on a train trip, Wertheimer had a sudden insight: if two lights blink on and off in rapid succession, you see continuous movement. Wertheimer got off the train at the next stop, at a city he had not intended to visit, and went in search of a flashing light to test his idea. After two years of experimenting with this illusion, he published a paper describing his discovery. The illusion of movement was called the **phi phenomenon,** and is the foundation of the movie industry: a rapid succession of "still" pictures creates an illusion of continuous movement. For Wertheimer, a gentle man with a walrus moustache, the discovery provided a new framework for psychology—*the whole is different from the sum of the parts.* The parts of a movie consist of a series of frames, each without movement; the sum, however, consists of movement. This insight was the beginning of a new school of psychology, the **Gestalt movement,** which stressed the significance of wholes, patterns, and relationships among elements.

The Gestalt movement showed that all perception was organized and patterned. Rather than seeing random and unrelated patches of light, you tend to organize what you see into patterns and relationships. The separate figures that you see are themselves organized and structured. Objects that are similar in form or size and those that are close to each other are seen as belonging together. In fact, you tend to see patterns even when no actual patterns exist.

The tendency to see patterns was studied in great detail early in this century by the Gestalt psychologists. They observed that ambiguous collections of elements tended spontaneously to form subgroups; this grouping followed certain rules of organization (see Figure 7-9 for examples):

- **Rule of Proximity**   The term *proximity* means closeness; the proximity rule of organization is that things that are close together seem to go together or belong together; close things are grouped.
- **Rule of Similarity**   According to the similarity rule, things that resemble each other or are similar are grouped together; groups or classes tend to be formed of similar elements.
- **Rule of Closure**   The term closure refers to being closed or complete; according to the closure rule, areas tend to be seen as closed or bounded; patterns tend to be seen as complete or closed. For example, a broken circle that is almost closed—but not quite—will be seen as completely closed and unbroken.

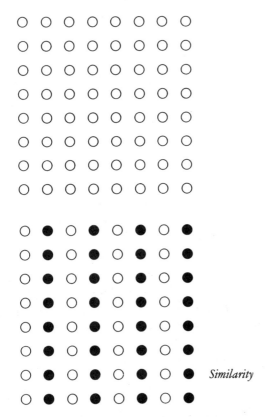

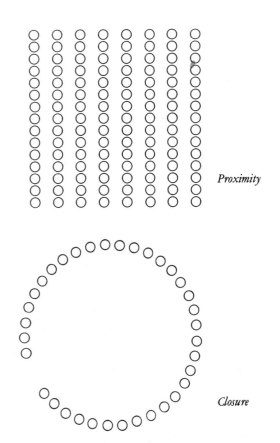

Figure 7-9 Organized Dots.   *Perception is organized; the arrangement of dots shown at upper left can be organized according to the rules of proximity, similarity, and closure, so that they appear to spontaneously form into patterns or subgroups, as shown.*

Illusions

Perceptions are organized and go beyond the information given by the senses.   Perceptions are not copies of reality; indeed, perceptions are often distorted interpretations of the external world.   Perceptual distortions are common and are collectively called **illusions.**

Look at the arrow illusion shown below.   The two straight lines consisting of the shafts of the arrows are in fact the same length, but they appear to almost everyone as different in length.   The wings of the arrowheads are responsible for causing the illusory difference in length.   In the railway illusion two horizontal parallel lines are in fact the same length, but to almost everyone they appear different in length.   The slanting lines on each side cause the two lines to appear different in length.

Why are your eyes fooled by these simple line drawings? Psychologists have proposed many different theories over the years to explain the phenomena of illusions, but none is completely satisfactory.   Whatever the process is, learning must be involved.   Psychologists have found that people living in different cultures experience the illusions differently;[12] for example, people who have not experienced railways are much less likely to experience the railway illusion.[13]   Perhaps the illusory drawings are seen as depicting real objects, like railroad tracks.   The lines of the drawings would suggest parts of the objects—like crossties—that would be located at different distances from the observer.   This sense of depth in the drawings could produce the distorted perceptions.

Expectancy and Learning

The world of our experience is always in the past, since a fraction of a second always passes between an event and our perception of it.   But perception is linked to the past in a more significant way.   What we see now is always compared with what we have seen.   To *recognize* an object or event is to categorize it as something familiar, known, seen before.   Thus without the effect of past perception there would be no recognition.   Furthermore, our perception of something right now is affected by what we expect to see, in addition to what we have learned to see and what we have just previously seen.   Thus there are several reasons for believing that perception is, to a degree, a personal construction.

The Red Six of Spades   •   Research shows that people tend to see what they expect to see.[14]   In a perception experiment using a tachistoscope—a machine capable of presenting pictures for just a fraction of a second—people were briefly shown pictures of different playing cards.[15]   Some of these playing cards were not true to life.   For example in a real deck of cards spades are black, so when individuals were shown a picture of a *red* six of spades, some reported that they saw a black six of spades, some said they saw a red six of hearts, and some said they saw a purple six of spades.   Seeing a purple six of spades is a kind of compromise between the reality of the red and the expectancy of the black.

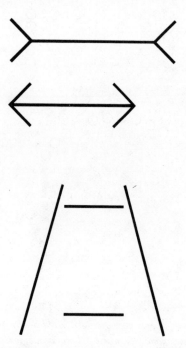

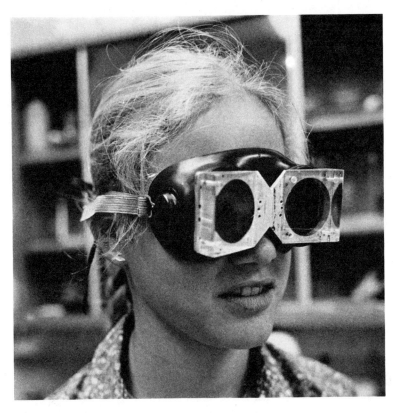

Special eyeglasses containing distorting prisms cause the perceptual world to shift. When you first put these glasses on, you miss doorknobs and bump into things; as you continue to wear the glasses, you adapt and the world looks normal again. (Ken Robert Buck)

The World Is Upside Down • To some extent what people see is what they have learned to see. If you have ever worn cracked eyeglasses for any length of time, you know that initially the crack in the glasses causes a distortion, a wave, in the visual field. With time, however, you adapt to the distortion and the perceptual world seems normal.

Specially made distorting lenses have been worn by some psychologists in an attempt to test the extremes of perceptual adaptation. For example, when they wore prisms over their eyes, shifting the visual field a few degrees to the left, they initially had trouble picking up objects and grasping doorknobs. They kept reaching and missing, grasping for the object to the left of where it really was. Eventually they adapted.

For nine days one man wore special lenses that turned the world completely upside down.[16] At first it was very difficult for him to move about in the world without bumping into things; everything looked upside down. When he turned his head up he

saw his feet, and when he turned his head down he saw the ceiling. Eventually he adapted so that the world no longer looked upside down. At the end of nine days when the glasses were removed, he experienced a strange reaction: *without the glasses* the world looked upside down! After not wearing the prisms for a time, his perceptual system adapted and the world again looked normal.

Correct . . . vision was achieved by subject M. after wearing the experimental spectacles for nine days. . . . After the spectacles were removed, however, objects appeared to revert to their previous upside-down position—this without any apparatus covering the eyes or in any way obstructing the visual field.

For a few minutes people and furniture seemed suspended from the "ceiling," head downward. . . . Short periods of disorientation and inverted vision occurred for several days after the experiment proper, particularly soon after awakening in the morning.[16]

Interim Summary

Sensory information is organized into meaningful experience. Two principles of perception are that you organize what you see (1) into figure and ground, and (2) into patterns or groups. Illusions demonstrate that perceptual experiences are organized constructions that go beyond the information provided by the senses. Perception is, to some degree, a personal construction. What you see depends upon what you *expect* to see and what you have *learned* to see.

Summary

1. The human senses are the means we have of gathering information about the world we live in and about our own bodies. We have at least seven different senses: the sense of vision, the sense of hearing, the skin senses, the sense of taste, the sense of smell, the kinesthetic sense, and the vestibular sense. The weight of the evidence does not support the existence of ESP, a psychic sense.

2. The lower limit of sensitivity is called the absolute threshold, and the limit of sensitivity to a stimulus change is called the difference threshold.

3. The change in sensory sensitivity with repeated stimulation is called adaptation. Dark adaptation is an adjustment to dim light, which results in an increase in sensitivity.

4. Tastes are sensed by groups of cells on the tongue called taste buds. There are only four possible basic tastes: sour, salty, sweet, and bitter. Taste mixtures follow the rules of flavor independence and mutual suppression.

5. Smells are sensed by cells located in patches high up in the nasal passages. Odor mixtures follow the rules of blending and masking.

6. The skin senses convey information about pressure, temperature, and pain, as nerve endings in the skin are stimulated. The skin contains a mosaic of small spots, each sensitive to different information; some convey sensations of cold, others of warmth, and still others of pain.

7. The body senses convey information about the position and movement of the body. The kinesthetic sense provides knowledge of body position and movement from nerve endings in the joints and muscles. The vestibular sense provides knowledge of body orientation from cells in the inner ear.

8. Important structures of the ear include the tympanic membrane (eardrum), the cochlea (in the inner ear), and the basilar membrane (the organ in the cochlea that responds to different sounds).

9. Two theories of hearing are the place theory and the frequency theory. The place theory assumes that the experience of pitch arises when different regions of the basilar membrane are displaced by sounds. The frequency theory assumes that different pitches result from the nerve cells on the basilar membrane firing at differ-

ent rates, or frequencies.   The best explanation of pitch involves a combination of both theories.

10. Three types of hearing problems are conductive, neural, and central deafness.

11. Important structures of the eye include the retina, with its fovea and rods and cones, the lens, the pupil, and the iris.

12. Two theories of color vision are the trichromatic theory, which assumes that color sensations result from three types of cones, and the opponent-process theory, which assumes the existence of three types of opponent processes in the brain—a red-green process, a blue-yellow process, and a black-white process.   Research evidence supports both theories, and both theories are needed for a complete explanation.

13. There are several types of visual problems.   One source of blindness is cataracts, a loss of transparency in the lens of the eye.   Color blindness is an inherited disorder that in its pure form (monochromatism) is quite rare.   Myopic people are nearsighted (able to see nearby objects but not those far away), and hyperopic people are farsighted (able to see faraway objects but not those nearby.)

14. Sensory information is organized into meaningful perceptual experiences on the basis of several principles.   Perceptions are organized into patterns or groups and by figure and ground, and are affected by learning and expectations.

Key Concepts

extrasensory perception (ESP)   The sensing of information about the world, other people, or the future in ways other than through the normal human senses of seeing, hearing, touching, tasting, smelling, and the body senses.

parapsychology   The scientific study of ESP.

kinesthetic sense   The sense that responds to body movement and the positions of muscles and joints.

vestibular sense   The sense, located in the inner ear, that responds to body orientation and rotation.

absolute threshold   The lower limit of sensitivity; the minimum level of energy necessary for sensation.

difference threshold   Lower limit of sensitivity to a *change* in the stimulus; the minimal change in a stimulus that can be detected.

adaptation   Changes in sensitivity with repeated stimulation.

dark adaptation   Adjustment to reduced light; this results in increased sensitivity to low levels of light.

negative afterimages   After viewing a stimulus, then looking at a neutral background, the persisting image of the stimulus can sometimes be seen in complementary colors.

taste buds   Groups of cells on the tongue that are sensitive to the chemical composition of food and liquids.

semicircular canals   Area in the inner ear filled with liquid and lined with special hair receptors that provides us with information regarding the orientation of our bodies.

tympanic membrane   The eardrum; transmits the sound energy to the tiny bones of the middle ear.

cochlea   The inner ear structure containing the receptors sensitive to sound vibrations.

basilar membrane   A structure within the cochlea that contains the special cells that transform sound energy into nerve impulses.

place theory   A theory of pitch discrimination that theorizes that sounds of different frequencies stimulate different areas of the basilar membrane; our experience of a sound depends on which areas are stimulatd by that sound.

frequency theory   A theory of pitch discrimination that theorizes that sounds of different frequencies stimulate the basilar membrane to transmit different frequencies of nerve impulses to the brain.

conductive deafness   Deafness resulting from problems in the outer or middle ear that block the passage of sound energy to the inner ear; for example, a perforated eardrum.

neural deafness   Deafness resulting from problems in the inner ear or with the auditory nerve.

central deafness   Deafness resulting from problems with the auditory centers of the brain or from certain psychological disorders such as conversion reaction.

conversion reaction   Sensory or muscular problems that exist without a physical cause.

duplicity principle of vision   The principle that the eye has two types of light-sensitive cells, each specializing in a different type of visual task.

retina   The light sensitive part of the eye; a layer of light-sensitive cells on the back of the eye.

rods   Specialized cells in the retina that respond only to differences in light intensity and not to differences in wavelength.

cones   Specialized cells in the retina that respond to differences in wavelength as well as, to a lesser extent, to differences in light intensity; responsible for "color vision."

trichromatic theory   A theory of color vision that assumes that all color experiences result from different combinations of three types of cones, each sensitive to a different primary color: red, green, and blue-violet.

opponent process theory   A theory of color vision that proposes that there are three pairs of color processes in the brain: a black-white pair, a red-green pair, and a blue-yellow pair.

lens   The structure in the eye that focuses light on the retina.

pupil   The hole in front of the lens through which light enters the eye.

iris   The muscle surrounding the pupil that gives color to the eye.

blind spot   The blind area in the field of vision resulting from the absence of receptor cells on the retina where the optic nerve leaves the eye.

fovea   The center of the retina; a small area densely packed with light-sensitive cells.

cataracts   A visual disorder resulting from a loss of transparency in the lens.

color blindness   An inherited condition that results in varying degrees of difficulty in discriminating different colors.

monochromatism   Total color blindness in which only blacks, whites, and grays can be seen.

myopia   A condition in which the eye can focus on nearby objects but not on those at a distance.

hyperopia   A condition in which the eye can focus on objects far away but not those nearby.

figure-ground principle   The rule that perceptual experiences are organized into two parts: objects and their background.

phi phenomenon   An illusion of movement created by flashing still pictures; the basis of apparent movement in "moving pictures."

Gestalt movement   A school of psychology that stressed the significance of pattern and organization in perception; founded by Max Wertheimer.

Rule of Proximity   The principle that things that are close together appear to belong together; close things are grouped in perception.

Rule of Similarity   The principle that things that resemble each other appear to belong together; similar things are grouped in perception.

Rule of Closure   The principle that areas of figures tend to appear as whole or closed, even if they are incomplete or broken.

illusions   Distorted or untrue perceptions.

Chapter 8

Drugs and Consciousness

Key Questions   1. What is consciousness?

2. How can consciousness be altered?

3. What problems are associated with the use of different drugs?

4. What are the effects of alcohol and marijuana?

What's on your mind?

What are your thoughts, feelings, and perceptions at this moment? You are aware of the book, the room around you, and your body; you may be aware of feelings of hunger, pleasure, or fatigue; you may be remembering what happened yesterday or planning what you will do tomorrow. Your private awareness of your thoughts, feelings, and perceptions is called your **consciousness.**

Your state of consciousness changes with hypnosis, sleep, meditation, biofeedback, and drugs. These experiences change your consciousness by influencing the physical basis of consciousness in your body. Some of the most exciting recent discoveries in psychology are those revealing the physical basis of consciousness.

Body and Consciousness

Your consciousness and body are not separate, independent parts of you. Changes in one are usually accompanied by changes in the other.

Your body affects your mind. Your mental life—your consciousness—is possible because of the activity of your brain and nerves. Your awareness of the world and your self requires that your eyes, ears, nerves, and brain be working properly. Even though your heart may be working normally, you can be declared legally dead, in some states, if your brain has stopped working.

You can lose consciousness from a concussion, or violent blow to the head. One woman fell off her bicycle and struck her head. She lost consciousness and was taken to a hospital. About five days later she gradually began to regain her awareness of the world around her. But it took several weeks for her mind to return to its normal level of consciousness.[1]

Your body affects your mind, but your mind also affects your body. Fear can cause your heart to pound and your hands to tremble. Even when you are not afraid, you can change the rate of your heartbeat simply by thinking different thoughts.[2] Your blood pressure is increased when you are excited and decreased when you are feeling relaxed.[3] Anger, frustration, and anxiety can cause headaches.[4] Prolonged emotional stress can sometimes cause muscle cramps, asthma, heart attacks, and ulcers.

Ulcers result from an excessive flow of digestive juices (hydrochloric acid) in the stomach. Prolonged stress increases the flow of hydrochloric acid in the stomachs of both animals and humans. Psychologists have studied the relation between ulcers and emotional stress in laboratories. Ulcers in rats can be produced experimentally by causing rats to experience psychological conflict.[5] Monkeys trained to make rapid decisions to avoid shock eventually get ulcers, apparently because of the psychological stress involved.[6]

Prolonged psychological stress in humans causes a variety of physical problems. One such problem is a skin disorder called hives. The case of Anna illustrates the consequences of stress for one young woman.

Anna A., a twenty-seven-year-old nurse, was engaged to be married and was somewhat anxious and uncertain about this adventure. A week before her wedding day she developed a severe attack of [hives]: most of her body was covered with raised white, intensely itchy wheals. Two weeks after her marriage, she reappeared at the hospital, radiantly happy and with quite clear skin.[7]

Anna's skin problem probably resulted from anxiety related to her coming marriage. The anxiety affected her skin by causing an allergic reaction to develop, and this led to the skin disorder. Her honeymoon changed her psychological mood and lowered her anxiety, allowing her body to return to normal. Changes in her mind were accompanied by changes in her body.

Interim Summary   Your mental life, or private awareness, is called your consciousness. Your consciousness requires a working brain. A brain injury such as a concussion can result in loss of consciousness. Your state of mind can also affect your body. For example, fear and anxiety can result in temporary problems involving heartbeat or blood pressure and also in more lasting problems such as ulcers and hives.

Altered States of Consciousness

Your state of consciousness at this moment is a normal waking consciousness; you are reasonably alert and aware of yourself and the world around you. But there are other states of consciousness, in which your awareness is either higher or lower than it is now. One of the first American psychologists, William James, put it this way:

Our normal waking consciousness, rational consciousness as we call it, is but one special type of consciousness, whilst all about it, parted from it by the filmiest of screens, there lie potential forms of consciousness entirely different. . . . No account of the universe in its totality can be final which leaves these other forms of consciousness quite disregarded.[8]

These other forms of consciousness—or **altered states of consciousness**—can result from hypnosis, meditation, biofeedback, and drugs. With each of these, your awareness and experience are different from that of normal consciousness. Changes in conscious-

ness are typically accompanied by physical changes in your body. In some cases there are changes in heartbeat, blood pressure, and breathing. Changes in the electrical activity of the brain can be recorded on a machine called an **EEG**. EEG recordings show that some states of consciousness are related to different states of the brain. Studies of these altered mental states help us to understand the physical basis of consciousness.

Meditation

Meditation is an ancient practice used for altering consciousness and acquiring inner peace. It involves controlling attention by concentrating the mind fully on one object or event, free from all distractions. Meditation is a way to calm the mind, to make it more aware, relaxed, and receptive. In **Yoga meditation** (such as "TM," or transcendental meditation), you concentrate on a special word that you repeat silently to yourself over and over again; an example of such a word is "OM." In **Zen meditation,** you concentrate on your breathing; you think of nothing but the air moving in and out of your body.

One procedure of Zen meditation, used in Japan, involves a special way of concentration on breathing. You can try a simplified version of Zen meditation by following these instructions. First, sit in a comfortable position and relax your muscles. Rest your hands in your lap and let your head fall forward. Breathe through your nose in a normal way; do not force the air in—let it come in naturally. Then exhale slowly, letting all the air out of your lungs. Each time you exhale, slowly count to yourself—"one," with the first out-breath, then "two," and continue counting for ten breaths. The next time you exhale, begin again at "one." One session of meditation should last twenty or thirty minutes.

This technique of meditation will be accompanied by a physical change in your brain, and with practice may result in an altered state of consciousness. Both Zen and Yoga meditation result in an increase in a type of brain activity associated with relaxed awareness—**alpha waves.**[9,10,11] Techniques of meditation are effective in promoting relaxation and have been used successfuly in psychotherapy, although exactly why meditation is beneficial is not yet known.[12]

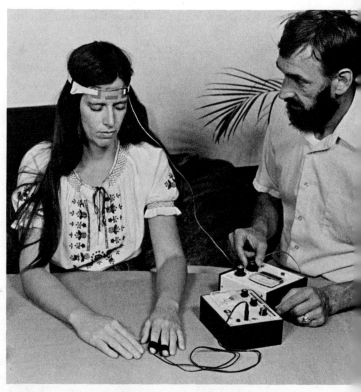

Biofeedback allows you to monitor the states of your body and to gain more control over them. In one type of biofeedback, a machine produces a tone whenever it detects alpha waves, a brain wave that is associated with relaxed awareness. (Judy Sedwick)

Biofeedback

You are ordinarily unaware of changes in the activity of your brain. These changes can, however, be measured by using an EEG. By observing the EEG records, you can become aware of the pattern of your brain waves. An EEG machine can be connected to turn on a light or a tone whenever your brain produces alpha waves. In this way, you can be given feedback about your brain's electrical activity.

Biofeedback is a technique that measures what is going on in your brain or other parts of your body and provides you with knowledge, or feedback, of that activity. Feedback about heart rate, blood pressure, muscle tension, and brain waves are examples of bio-

feedback that have been studied. With biofeedback, people can learn to control these physical responses.

Because biofeedback techniques enable people to gain greater control over their inner processes, these techniques have both medical and psychological benefits. For example, biofeedback can promote deep relaxation and has been used as a form of therapy for people with certain neurotic disorders.[10]

When muscles are tense, the muscle cells are electrically very active. This electrical activity can be sensed by electrodes placed on the skin. The signal from the electrodes controls an audible tone, which provides feedback about muscle tension. By learning to keep the tone off, the individual learns deep muscle relaxation.

Alpha waves have been claimed to reflect a distinct state of consciousness, similar to that of meditation. When your mind is relaxed and alert, it tends to produce alpha waves; but the EEG pattern changes if you begin to worry about something or to concentrate on a problem. During alpha-wave production, people describe their state of consciousness as "relaxed awareness" or "inner peace"; one person described it as "a lovely serene feeling of being in harmony with the universe."[13]

Hypnosis

Hypnosis is an altered state of consciousness in which a person is highly responsive to suggestion. People who are hypnotized seem to be in a dreamlike trance. Their experience of the world and themselves can be easily influenced by the hypnotist; they seem unable to act on their own, following instead the suggestions of someone else. One author described what a hypnotized man would look like:

His eyes are closed, the muscles of his face are rather loose, his entire body is quite relaxed and, if he is sitting in a chair, he often will have slumped down it. The head falls forward on the subject's chest, sometimes far backward or, again, sideways over his shoulder. The arms and hands usually rest limply on a support or hang limply by his sides.[14]

The movement of a hypnotized person has a kind of "slow motion" quality, and the eyes, if they are open, may have an unfocused stare.

Inducing Hypnosis • Hypnosis can be produced by a variety of methods. Most involve techniques for focusing attention and increasing relaxation. To focus attention, the hypnotist may tell the subject to concentrate on a single object, such as a thumbtack on a wall or a candle on a table. To produce relaxation, the hypnotist may tell the person to relax and suggest that the person is feeling sleepy. Not all people can be hypnotized; those who can, gradually respond to

the repeated suggestions and enter a hypnotic trance.

Methods for hypnotizing someone usually begin with a procedure for producing deep relaxation. In a typical procedure, the subject is asked to sit in a comfortable chair and look at a small light. The hypnotist then talks to the subject. The following passage shows examples of some of the things that are typically said in the early stage of this procedure.

Keep your eyes on the light and listen carefully to what I say. Your ability to be hypnotized depends entirely on your willingness to cooperate. It has nothing to do with your intelligence. As for your will power—if you want to, you can pay no attention to me and remain awake all the time. . . . On the other hand, if you pay close attention to what I say, and follow what I tell you, you can easily learn to fall into a hypnotic sleep. . . .

Now relax and make yourself entirely comfortable. Keep your eyes on that little light. Keep staring at it all the time. . . .

Relax completely. Relax every muscle in your body. . . . Let yourself be limp. Relax more and more, more and more. . . .

Your legs feel heavy and limp, heavy and limp. Your arms are heavy, heavy, heavy as lead. . . . You feel tired and sleepy, tired and sleepy. . . .

Your eyes are tired from staring. . . . The strain in your eyes is getting greater and greater, greater and greater. You would like to close your eyes.[15]

The Effects of Hypnosis • You may have read stories or seen television programs about people who were hypnotized against their will and turned into human robots willing to do whatever the hypnotist ordered. Scientific studies have exposed this view of hypnosis as a myth. In fact, to be hypnotized, you must cooperate with the hypnotist and agree to the procedure. If you don't want to be hypnotized, you can't be.

A more complicated question is whether people can be hypnotized and made to do something harmful, immoral, or criminal. The answer seems to be

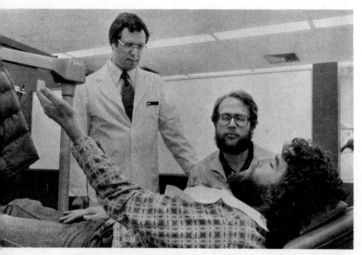

Hypnosis is a method of altering consciousness that has a number of practical uses. For example, hypnosis is used in dentistry to relax patients and to make them less sensitive to pain. (United Press International Photo)

yes, but only under certain special conditions. Studies show that people who are hypnotized will do harmful acts when (a) they are given strong, repeated suggestions to do so, and, in addition, (b) they are in an experimental or laboratory situation.[15]

In one study that met these two conditions, hypnotized individuals acted in ways they would normally be unwilling to act. College students were hypnotized and told to pick up a poisonous snake with their bare hands; others were told to throw deadly acid at the experimenter. The results were astonishing: they did what they were told. The hypnotized students reached for the snake but, at the last minute, were prevented from picking it up. Other students threw what they thought was acid at the experimenter (it was, in fact, a harmless liquid). In a later interview, these students reported that they felt they would not be harmed by their actions because it was just an experiment.[16]

Hypnosis, in some ways, resembles sleep; in fact, the word "hypnosis" comes from a Greek word meaning sleep. EEG studies have shown, however, that sleep and hypnosis involve different states of consciousness.[17] The brain waves during sleep and hypnosis are quite different. In terms of brain activity, hypnosis closely resembles waking consciousness. At one time it was thought that the hypnotized brain produced more alpha waves than the brain in normal waking consciousness; more recent studies have shown that the amount of alpha waves produced in hypnosis is not unusual.[17]

The influence of the mind on the body appears strengthened in hypnosis. Hypnotized subjects have a remarkable capacity to control bodily responses that are typically considered involuntary. For example, hypnotized persons can raise or lower their skin temperature on command. In one experiment subjects were able to cool down one hand and warm up the other so that there was a four-degree difference in temperature between them.[18] Heart rate can also be influenced by hypnosis.[18] There is evidence that hypnosis can produce such an insensitivity to pain that surgery can be performed without anesthetic.[19] Hypnosis is a powerful tool for controlling consciousness and behavior and has been used extensively in psychotherapy.

Interim Summary   An altered state of consciousness is one in which your level of awareness is higher or lower than normal. Meditation, biofeedback, hypnosis, and drugs are techniques for producing altered states of consciousness. Meditation is a procedure for controlling attention and making the mind more aware, relaxed, and receptive. Biofeedback is a technique for measuring subtle changes in your body and revealing them to you. With biofeedback you can learn to control responses, such as brain waves, that are normally considered involuntary. Hypnosis is a state of heightened suggestibility. To be hypnotized, a person must cooperate with the hypnotist. Under special conditions, a person can be hypnotized to act in harmful or immoral ways. Meditation and biofeedback can be used to increase the production of EEG alpha waves; hypnosis, however, does not affect the EEG. Meditation, biofeedback, and hypnosis have been successfully used in psychotherapy.

Drugs and Behavior

This has been called the age of anxiety. It is a time when more and more people are searching for ways to change their consciousness to reduce their levels of stress. The most popular solution has been to turn to drugs, to reach for the instant "high."

Our society apparently believes in chemicals. Each year new chemicals that can change emotions, perceptions, or personality are developed and marketed. Millions of dollars are spent by drug manufacturers to persuade us that their new drugs are the ideal solutions to our problems. Television peddles aspirin as the royal road to psychological health: husbands who cannot cope with their wives, mothers who snap at their children, employers who lose their tempers, nervous teachers—all are advised to reach for some brand of aspirin for instant relief. Drugs to make you sleep, drugs to wake you up, drugs to calm you down—all are sold on television through miniature dramas, all ending happily in romance, money, or fame.

Using Drugs

You use drugs.

Coffee and tea contain a drug, caffeine, which is a stimulant. Wine and beer contain alcohol, a sedative drug. Cigarettes, tranquilizers, diet pills, and sleeping pills all contain drugs that affect the mind. Some drugs—LSD, marijuana, and heroin, for example—profoundly change human behavior and consciousness. See Table 8-1 for a list of commonly abused drugs.

Table 8-1 Catalog of Drugs

Amphetamines	A stimulant drug; sometimes called "uppers," "pep pills," "whites," "bennies," or "speed." Heavy use may produce a psychotic reaction.
Cocaine	A stimulant drug; sometimes called "coke," "gold dust," or "snow." Extended use may produce episodes of drug psychosis. Itching under the skin may result from heavy use.
Caffeine	A stimulant drug found in coffee and tea.
Nicotine	A stimulant drug found in tobacco. Physically addictive.
Alcohol	A sedative drug found in beer, wine, and whiskey. Physically addictive.
Barbiturates	A sedative drug; sometimes called "downers," "reds," "blue heavens," or "yellow jackets." Physically addictive.
Morphine	A narcotic drug made from the opium poppy. Physically addictive.
Heroin	A narcotic drug made from morphine; sometimes called "horse," "junk," or "smack." Physically addictive.
Codeine	A narcotic drug similar to morphine but less potent. Physically addictive.
LSD	A psychedelic drug producing hallucinations; sometimes called "acid."
Marijuana	A psychedelic drug that is smoked or eaten; sometimes called "grass" or "pot." A more concentrated form is hashish or "hash." Marked tolerance develops with high doses.

Almost every adult has used drugs, through experiences with cigarettes, coffee, or alcoholic beverages. The use of other drugs is also widespread. In recent years, 6 to 10 percent of all medical prescriptions were for tranquilizers to relieve tension and depression. Close to 50 million prescriptions for barbiturates are filled each year in America.[20] Recent studies show that about 30 percent of high school students and 50 to 75 percent of college students have used marijuana.[21,22,23] More and more college students are using marijuana, although there is some evidence that this trend will not continue.[24]

How do people become users of drugs? Because drugs such as heroin and marijuana are illegal, many people do not have these drugs easily available. In order to become a user of illegal drugs, you must have access to them. Heroin and marijuana also involve a period of learning how to use them; it is not just a matter of taking them and waiting for the effect. Thus, most people who use illegal drugs have friends who provided the drugs and who taught them how to use them.[25] For people not now using illegal drugs, the best way to predict whether they will become users is to count the number of friends they have who are users; the more friends who are users, the greater the chance they have of eventually becoming users themselves.[26]

Drugs and the Brain

Mind-altering drugs work by changing the chemistry of the brain. Whether these drugs are injected, inhaled, or swallowed they eventually are absorbed into the bloodstream and carried to the brain. The brain is composed of billions of individual nerve cells (neurons), and the activity of these cells control behavior and consciousness. Mind-altering drugs change consciousness by changing the activity of these brain cells.

Your level of arousal ranges from high, when you are excited and alert, to low, when you are drowsy. During these times the level of activity of your brain is also either high or low. Certain drugs act, in a sense, to slow down the brain. For example, alcohol and barbiturates reduce the activity of the brain cells and make you less aware, alert, and active. These drugs are called **sedative drugs** because they reduce your level of arousal and calm you down. On the other hand, nicotine, caffeine, and amphetamines speed up the brain and make you more alert and energetic. These drugs are called **stimulant drugs** because they increase your arousal and energy levels. The effect of LSD and marijuana is more complicated and not as well understood. EEG studies show that these drugs alter the activity of only certain brain structures.[27,28] It is believed that these drugs affect special parts of the brain that are involved in controlling and processing information from the senses; because of this effect, these drugs often result in sensory or perceptual distortions or hallucinations.[29] LSD and marijuana are called **psychedelic drugs** because of their ability to change consciousness and experience.

Drug Problems

Under certain circumstances drugs can lead to mental disturbance, drugs can induce an uncontrollable craving for more drugs, and drugs can kill. Because of these concerns, many drugs are outlawed in this society. Addiction, mental disturbance, and flashbacks are drug problems of particular psychological interest.

Tolerance and Toxicity

Any drug can kill you if the dose is high enough. Why should a person take a dose that high? The answer is that most drugs produce a **tolerance** for themselves, so that increased doses are necessary in order to obtain the desired psychological effects. After you have taken the drug for a while, you must begin to take more and more of it in order to experience the same initial effect. While the amount required to produce the desired effect increases with use, the amount required to kill you—the **toxicity level**—does not change. With continued use the amount of the drug required to produce the desired effect equals the amount required to kill you, and death results.

A moderate amount of tolerance develops to continued use of alcohol or barbiturates. An experienced drinker of alcohol may be able to drink twice as much as a novice before appearing drunk. Heroin, morphine, and codeine require larger and larger doses with continued use. Profound tolerance for these drugs develops, so that in order to ward off withdrawal symptoms, the user must take increasing doses. An increased dosage of the amphetamines is required by most people in order to maintain the initial stimulating effect.

The question of tolerance with continued usage of LSD and marijuana is complicated. For LSD, with daily usage, tolerance develops rapidly, so that higher doses are required to produce the same effects.[30] But the tolerance disappears following a few days without using the drug. Thus, LSD does produce tolerance, but it is a temporary effect. Marijuana does not produce much tolerance at low doses (those typical among many users in this country).[31] With frequent high doses, however, marked tolerance for marijuana does develop.[32]

Dependence and Addiction

Some people become dependent upon certain drugs so that they feel they need to have them. **Psychological dependence** results in a strong craving for the drug and a feeling of anxiety when it's available. A psychological dependence results from the continued use of tobacco; a craving, a feeling of urgency, and even a mild panic may develop when cigarettes are withdrawn. Cigarettes contain a stimulant drug, nicotine. Heroin, alcohol, amphetamines, and barbitu-

Heroin users become physically addicted to the drug and continue to take it in order to avoid painful withdrawal symptoms. Failure to continue injecting the drug may produce sweating, watering nose and eyes, diarrhea, severe muscle cramps, and vomiting. (Joel Gordon)

rates all produce psychological dependence. A regular user of one of these drugs who is denied access to it often becomes quite anxious. Marijuana and LSD do not produce psychological dependence in most people. However, certain individuals become compulsive users of marijuana and develop a psychological dependence on the drug.[33]

Certain drugs produce **physical addiction,** so that when the drug is not taken, withdrawal symptoms develop in the body. A drug addict, in order to prevent the painful withdrawal symptoms, must continue to take the drug. Some heavy drinkers become physically addicted to alcohol. When they stop drinking, they experience severe withdrawal symptoms. Nausea, anxiety, agitation, confusion, tremors, and sweating occur first; then cramps, vomiting, hallucinations, and convulsions develop. Death can occur in the latter stages of severe alcohol or barbiturate withdrawal.[33] Withdrawal from heroin addiction is also painful:

Withdrawal sickness, in one with a well-developed physical dependence, is a shattering experience. . . . About 12 hours after the last heroin dose, the addict begins to grow uneasy. He yawns, shivers, and sweats, while watery discharge pours from inside his nose. . . . For a few hours, he falls into an abnormal restless stupor known among addicts as "yen sleep." On awakening 18 to 24 hours after his last drug dose, the addict enters the lower depths of his personal hell. Yawning may violently dislocate his jaw. More watery mucous pours from his eyes and nose. . . . The hair on his skin stands erect, and his skin shows that typical goose flesh called "cold turkey" in the parlance of the addict. . . . His bowels act with violence. Great waves of contraction pass over the stomach walls, causing explosive vomiting frequently stained with blood. . . . The surface of his abdomen appears corrugated and knotted and abdominal pain is severe.[34]

Alcohol, barbiturates, heroin, morphine, and codeine can all produce physical addiction, a state in which the body itself becomes dependent upon the continued presence of the drug. LSD and the amphetamines do not seem to produce addiction. Physical withdrawal symptoms do not develop from quitting the use of one of these drugs.[33] In the case of marijuana, frequent high doses can result in symptoms of a mild addiction. Abruptly discontinuing a pattern of heavy marijuana use results in such withdrawal symptoms as weight loss, sweating, irritability, sleep disturbances, and intestinal upsets.[35]

Drug Psychosis

Certain drugs can cause a psychotic reaction, or **psychosis,** a severe mental disturbance. Where a mental disturbance is associated with drug taking, it is sometimes found that a history of mental instability existed before the drug experience; in other words, drugs may exaggerate a previous mental condition.

The psychotic reaction brought on by drugs is typically characterized by **hallucinations** (seeing things that aren't there), **paranoid delusions** (false beliefs that people are out to "get you" and that you are all-powerful), and experiences of nightmarish terror. LSD can cause psychotic reactions lasting months or even years in some individuals,[36] although most investigators believe that such individuals were psychologically disturbed before the drug experience. The exact frequency of psychotic reactions from LSD is unknown, although the evidence indicates that the incidence is less than 1 percent.[37]

Psychotic reactions from marijuana use are also rare: most reports of extreme adverse reactions come from individuals who are inexperienced with the drug, who take a large amount, and who have a history of previous psychological problems.[38,39,40] These psychotic reactions, although frightening, tend to be temporary.

In contrast, psychosis resulting from the heavy use of amphetamines is not rare. The psychotic reaction caused by prolonged and excessive use of amphetamines is indistinguishable from the most common mental illness, schizophrenia. The similarity between amphetamine-produced psychosis and schizophrenia may be due to the fact that individuals who use the drug heavily may be disposed toward schizophrenia before their drug experiences.[41]

Flashbacks

In users of LSD and marijuana, sometimes the drug experience recurs without the drug; this spontaneous recurrence of the drug effect has been called a **flashback.** Flashbacks may happen as long as a month or even a year after taking the drug.[42] They may happen at any time—walking down the street or driving a car—and they consist of images and illusions resembling those experienced under the influence of LSD. One estimate of the frequency of flashbacks is that one out of twenty regular users of LSD has the flashback experience.[43] One person's LSD flashback involved seeing inanimate objects as weird animals; another consisted of auditory hallucinations.[44] Flashbacks following marijuana use are much rarer, although a few cases have been reported.[45, 46]

The problem with flashbacks is that they are not under your control. To have an LSD experience when you want it and plan on it is serious enough; to have an LSD experience when you have not taken the drug and don't expect it, is worse. You do not control the drug experience; the drug controls you. Worse yet, flashbacks may recur even years after taking the drug.

Drugs and the College Student

Among college students, the two most commonly used nonmedical drugs are alcohol and marijuana. Both are used socially to relax and to alter mood and consciousness. A great deal of publicity has been given reports of the dangers of using these drugs. One hears warnings that occasional use of alcohol will cause alcoholism and that marijuana turns people into criminals or damages the mind. While there is essentially no evidence supporting these extreme claims, there is good reason to be cautious with these drugs.

Alcohol

Alcohol is the most commonly used—and abused—drug for altering consciousness. A sedative that slows down the central nervous system, alcohol results in feelings of relaxation, warmth, and well-being in moderate use. Aches and pains are dulled, reaction times are slowed, and alertness is reduced.

Psychological Effects • The effects of alcohol depend upon the amount of alcohol reaching the bloodstream. Unlike other foods and drinks, alcohol requires no digestion and is absorbed into the bloodstream directly from the stomach and small intestine. The faster it is absorbed, the sooner its effects will be felt. The rate of absorption is slower in a full stomach than an empty one, and wine and beer are absorbed more slowly than whiskey or gin. Six ounces of whiskey, six glasses of wine, or six cans of beer—consumed within an hour or so—are enough to raise the blood alcohol level of a 150-pound man to 0.15 percent, a level defined as legally drunk in every state. In many states, a blood alcohol level of 0.10 percent is sufficient to be declared legally drunk. A small person could reach this level after two drinks or glasses of wine in one hour; a 150-pound man would probably reach this level after about four drinks in an hour.

One of the effects of alcohol is to slow reaction times and interfere with critical judgment. As a result, driving under the influence of alcohol is especially dangerous. According to recent studies, alcohol is involved in more than 25,000 deaths on the highway each year. In one study of single-car accidents in which the driver died, blood tests showed that 70 percent of the males and 40 percent of the females had blood alcohol levels of 0.10 percent or more.[47]

Alcohol is one of the drugs for which a tolerance develops with continued use. Novice drinkers require less alcohol to produce particular effects than do experienced drinkers. Heavy drinkers are able to consume more alcohol before passing out or becoming stuporous than moderate or light drinkers. The toxicity level, however, does not rise with continued alcohol use. The minimum level required for death is about 0.35 percent (the result of consuming about fourteen ounces of whiskey in one hour).

Alcoholism • **Alcoholism** is a disorder involving repeated and uncontrolled use of alcohol, resulting in interference with social and occupational behavior and with health. There are 5 to 10 million teenagers and

3. **Crucial phase.** This stage is marked by the inability to stop drinking once it is started. Although the individual has control over taking the first drink, once it is taken, drinking will continue until the individual is too intoxicated or sick to continue. At this stage the drinker will experience withdrawal symptoms if alcohol is not taken every day.

4. **Chronic phase.** In this stage the individual drinks constantly, and becomes intoxicated every day. The drinker's entire life becomes organized around the problem of obtaining enough to drink—and anything containing alcohol will be drunk. Personal hygiene and diet are neglected. Resulting malnutrition may produce a number of physical symptoms, even death.

An increasing number of teenagers are victims of alcoholism, a disease associated with cultural, psychological, and genetic factors. (George W. Gardner)

The causes of alcoholism are not yet well understood. There appear to be both cultural and psychological factors involved in the development of the disorder. For example, there are significant differences in rates of alcoholism among different ethnic groups, but these differences tend to be reduced as the ethnic groups become assimilated into the culture. For example, first-generation Irish-Americans have higher rates of alcoholism than second- or third-generation Irish-Americans while first-generation American Jews have lower rates of alcoholism than second- or third-generation Jews. Apparently, cultural differences in alcoholism tend to converge as the different cultural groups become Americanized.

There is also evidence that tendencies toward alcoholism can be inherited. The children of alcoholic parents have higher rates of alcoholism than other children. This holds true even for the children of alcoholic parents who were adopted at an early age by nonalcoholic parents. In addition, identical twins tend to be either both alcoholic or both nonalcoholic. These facts support the importance of genetic factors in the development of alcoholism.

adults in the United States who are alcoholics. Although there are different types of alcoholism, many alcoholics seem to progress through four stages in the development of the disorder:[48]

1. **Prealcoholic symptomatic phase.** This stage involves regular drinking as a means of avoiding problems and dealing with stress, with increasing reliance on alcohol to the point of daily heavy drinking.

2. **Prodromal phase.** In this stage the drinker begins to have periods of amnesia or "blackouts," in which the activities of the evening before cannot be recalled the next day. The individual becomes preoccupied with alcohol and begins to worry about having enough on hand to get through the evening or the day.

Marijuana

Marijuana is a mixture of the flowers, leaves, seeds, and stems of the Indian hemp plant. The active drug in the plant, THC, may vary considerably in concentration from one batch of marijuana to another. On the average, about 5 percent of marijuana consists of THC. The most potent concentration of THC is found in the sticky resin secreted by the plant, a substance called **hashish (hash).** Hashish consists of up to 12 percent THC.

Subjective Effects • The effect of marijuana depends upon whether the smoker is naive or experienced with the drug. First-time users often do not feel much affected by the drug.[49] Feeling "high" or "stoned" on marijuana may require learning what aspects of behavior and experience should be attended to. In a sense, marijuana smokers must learn how to get high.

The marijuana high involves a feeling of relaxation, a sense of well-being, and an impression that your senses have been sharpened. Some people, however, experience a markedly different state, ranging from mild anxiety to acute panic. Marijuana distorts the sense of time. The experience of time may be changed so that minutes seem like hours, as if some internal, subjective "clock" were greatly speeded up. Visual imagery and sensory experience generally seem to be enhanced, although this is entirely a subjective effect.

Behavioral Effects • Like LSD, marijuana can trigger a temporary psychotic reaction in mentally unstable individuals. Such reactions, although rare, involve a break from reality, with delusions and hallucinations. Although these psychotic reactions usually end within a few days, some have lasted for several months.[50]

The capacity for sustained attention, for problem solving, and for estimating the passage of time are reduced by marijuana.[49] Marijuana interferes with the ability to concentrate and to perform simple tasks that require full attention. Individuals under the influence of marijuana are less able to count backwards, to perform serial mental arithmetic, and to react quickly by pressing the correct button on a panel when a light comes on; they are easily distracted and less able to shift attention voluntarily.[51]

Individuals under the influence of marijuana often have difficulty carrying on coherent conversation. They often forget what they are saying and lose their place in their own sentences. This effect can be explained by studies that show the influence of marijuana on short-term memory. Memory of recent events (short-term memory) is significantly worse under marijuana intoxication.[52,53]

Although the long-term effects are not known definitively, researchers agree that marijuana adversely affects short-term memory. It also probably presents a high risk of lung cancer, especially to heavy users, since it contains more tar than tobacco does. (Read D. Brugger/The Picture Cube)

From experimentation with animals, there is evidence that long-term exposure to doses of marijuana equivalent to those of very heavy human users can cause changes in brain-wave activity and a reduction in the ability to learn.[35] These effects persist for several months after the use of marijuana is discontinued. The effect of marijuana on the biological and psychological development of young people is not known. It is known, however, that individuals are less able to attend, to learn, and to remember while they are intoxicated with marijuana. Since marijuana is used extensively by some students during school, it appears likely that the level of acquired knowledge and skills will be lower for these students.

Medical Hazards • There is now convincing evidence that the heavy use of marijuana is dangerous to your health. Marijuana cigarettes produce much more tar and other known cancer-causing substances than regular cigarettes. Two to three marijuana "joints" a day are equivalent—in terms of the risk of lung damage—to one pack of cigarettes.[35] The tar from marijuana cigarettes has been tested for the risk of cancer with mice. It has been found that the tar, painted on the skin of mice, produces cancerous changes very similar to those produced by tobacco tar.[35] By the age of about forty heavy tobacco smokers begin to develop cancerous changes in the tissue of their bronchial passages. In heavy users of hashish and tobacco, these changes have been found by the age of twenty. Because of this evidence, there is reason to believe that frequent smoking of marijuana involves a risk of lung cancer.

There is evidence that marijuana suppresses the production of sex hormones.[54] Men who are heavy users typically show a decreased sperm count and lower levels of testosterone, the male sex hormone.[35] This effect has also been shown experimentally in male animals. In addition, marijuana appears to suppress the immune reaction—the biological process that creates the body's resistance to infection.[35]

The evidence on the hazards of frequent use of marijuana is not yet conclusive. Much additional research is needed before the long-term effects of heavy marijuana use can be known for certain. The bulk of recent research, however, strongly suggests that regular, heavy use will increase the risk of lung damage, will interfere with reproductive and endocrine functions, and will lower resistance to infection. These dangers and the present illegality of the drug seem to be good reasons to use caution until the facts—all the facts—are in.

Interim Summary   Drugs are a powerful method for altering consciousness. Psychedelic, or mind-altering, drugs work by changing the level of activity of the brain cells. Sedatives decrease and stimulants increase brain activity. Psychedelic drugs affect parts of the brain involved in controlling and processing sensory information. All drugs have a toxicity level (an amount that will kill), and most drugs produce a tolerance for themselves. Drug tolerance leads to ever-increasing doses, with death resulting when the toxicity level is reached. Continued use of some drugs leads to either a psychological dependence (a strong craving for the drug when it is not taken) or physical addiction (severe withdrawal symptoms when it is not taken) or both. Drug psychosis and flashbacks are other dangers of drug abuse. Alcohol and marijuana have profound effects on the mind and body. They distort perception and experience and disrupt most mental activity.

Summary

1. Your mental life, or private awareness, is called your consciousness. Your consciousness can be lost through a brain injury such as a concussion. Your state of mind can also affect your body. Prolonged psychological stress produces a variety of physical problems, such as ulcers, high blood pressure, headaches, and skin problems.

2. Meditation, biofeedback, hypnosis, and drugs are techniques for producing altered states of consciousness. Meditation and biofeedback can be used to increase the production of EEG alpha waves—an activity of the brain associated with relaxed awareness.

3. Drugs are a powerful—and dangerous—way to alter consciousness. All drugs have a toxicity level (an amount that will kill), and most drugs produce a tolerance for themselves with continued use.

4. Continued use of some drugs leads to either a psychological dependence (a strong craving for the drug when it is not taken) or a physical addiction (severe physical withdrawal symptoms when not taken).

5. Alcohol is the most commonly used—and abused—drug for altering consciousness. Alcohol slows reaction time and interferes with critical judgment; as a result driving under its influence is especially dangerous.

6. With continued use, a tolerance for alcohol develops. In addition, alcohol is an addictive drug.

7. Many alcoholics progress through four stages in the development of alcoholism: the prealcoholic symptomatic stage, the prodromal phase, the crucial phase, and the chronic phase.

8. Marijuana comes from the Indian hemp plant, and its active ingredient is THC. The subjective effects of the drug typically include a sense of well-being and relaxation and a distorted perception of time.

9. Marijuana interferes with short-term memory, attention, and learning.

10. Recent evidence indicates that smoking marijuana regularly increases the risk of lung cancer, interferes with endocrine functions, and lowers resistance to infection.

Key Concepts

consciousness   Mental life; the private awareness of thoughts, feelings, and perceptions.

altered states of consciousness   A level of awareness that is higher or lower than normal; a state of mind different from normal waking consciousness.

EEG (electroencephalograph)   A machine that measures the electrical activity of the brain (brain waves).

meditation   An ancient procedure for controlling attention and making the mind more aware, relaxed, and receptive.

Yoga meditation   A type of meditation in which one's concentration is focused on a special word which is repeated silently over and over.

Zen meditation   A type of meditation in which concentration is focused on one's breathing.

alpha waves   A type of brain wave associated with relaxed awareness; it has a frequency of about ten cycles per second.

biofeedback   A technique for measuring subtle changes in the body and revealing them; this technique can be used to provide people with knowledge of their heart rate, blood pressure, and brain waves.

hypnosis   A state of heightened suggestibility in which a person is under the influence of someone else.

sedative drugs   Drugs that reduce the level of arousal.

stimulant drugs   Drugs that increase the level of arousal and make people feel more energetic.

psychedelic drugs   Drugs that change perceptions and consciousness.

tolerance   An effect resulting from some drugs in which ever-increasing doses are needed to obtain the same impact.

toxicity level   The amount of a drug that will kill.

psychological dependence   An effect produced by some drugs in which—if the drug is not available—there is a strong craving for it and a feeling of anxiety.

physical addiction   An effect produced by some drugs in which—if the drug is not taken—there are physical withdrawal symptoms, such as nausea and sweating.

psychosis   A severe mental disorder characterized by loss of contact with reality, accompanied by disturbances in emotions, ideas, or perceptions.

hallucinations   A disturbance in perception in which something that does not exist is seen, heard, or felt; for example, seeing things that are not there.

paranoid delusions   False beliefs that one is being victimized—for example, believing that others are "out to get you."

flashback   A spontaneous recurrence of the drug effect at a time when the drug has not been taken.

alcoholism   A disorder involving the repeated and uncontrolled use of alcohol that results in interference with social and occupational behavior and with health.

prealcoholic symptomatic phase   The first stage in the development of alcoholism in which regular drinking is used as a means of avoiding problems and dealing with stress.

prodromal phase   The second stage in the development of alcoholism, marked by periods of amnesia or "blackouts."

crucial phase   The third stage in the development of alcoholism, marked by the inability to stop drinking once it is started. In this stage the drinker will experience withdrawal symptoms if alcohol is not taken every day.

chronic phase   The fourth and final stage in the development of alcoholism in which the drinker's entire life is organized around the problem of obtaining alcohol.

amphetamines   A stimulant drug (sometimes called "speed" or "uppers"); heavy use may produce a psychotic reaction.

cocaine   A stimulant drug (sometimes called "coke" or "snow"); extended use may produce episodes of drug psychosis.

caffeine   A stimulant drug found in coffee and tea.

nicotine   A stimulant drug found in tobacco; physically addictive.

alcohol   A sedative drug found in beer, wine, and whiskey; physically addictive.

barbiturates   A sedative drug (sometimes called "reds" or "downers"); physically addictive.

morphine   A narcotic drug made from the opium poppy; physically addictive.

heroin   A narcotic drug made from morphine; physically addictive.

codeine   A narcotic drug similar to morphine but less potent; physically addictive.

LSD   A psychedelic drug producing hallucinations; sometimes called "acid."

marijuana   A psychedelic drug that is smoked or eaten; marked tolerance develops with high doses.

hashish ("hash")   A more concentrated form of marijuana, containing a higher percentage of THC.

Chapter 9

Sleep and Dreaming

Key Questions
1. Is sleep necessary?
2. How can you tell when someone is dreaming?
3. Does everybody dream?
4. What do your dreams mean?

Once upon a time I dreamt I was a butterfly. . . . Suddenly I awakened, and there I lay, myself again. Now I do not know whether I was a man dreaming I was a butterfly, or whether I am now a butterfly dreaming I am a man.

Chuang Tzu, Chinese philosopher, 350 B.C.

Sleeping and dreaming have always been a source of fascination and mystery. Why do we sleep? Why do we dream? Some societies, for example the Eskimos of Hudson Bay and the Pantani Malay people, believe that a person who is asleep has entered another world and is no longer physically present. Acciden-

tally awakening a sleeping person is dangerous because the soul may be forever lost from the body. The ancient Greeks and Egyptians used dreams to predict the future and to diagnose illness. They developed complex systems of dream interpretation.[1] A dream interpretation book written in India in the fourth century A.D. advised that if you dreamed of being swallowed by a fish, of being surrounded by crows, or of eating salt, then you would become ill or die.[2] Arguments about sleep and dreams have lasted for thousands of years, but modern science has recently begun to understand these mysteries that have plagued humanity for centuries.

Your Need to Sleep

Everyone has experienced the strength and power of the need to sleep. You can resist the need for a while, but you must eventually give in. Your determination and willpower are no match for your need to sleep.

You may have heard that everyone needs to sleep eight hours a night. There is no evidence to support this belief. What is clear from the existing data is that, while on the average adults sleep seven to eight hours a night, there is tremendous variability in the length of time people typically sleep. No one has been tested who does not need to sleep at all, but some people need only three to four hours per night, and others need ten or twelve hours per night. Newborn babies sleep most of the time—perhaps as much as sixteen or more hours a day; older adults sometimes sleep only five or six hours per day.

Sleep Deprivation

One way of examining the need to sleep is to observe the effects of going without sleep. Studies of sleep deprivation show that it is relatively easy for many people to stay awake for twenty-four hours.[3] During the first night without sleep, the person may experience drowsiness, particularly between 3 A.M. and 6 A.M., and may feel an unpleasant itching of the eyes when they are open. During the second night, staying awake is much more difficult and is possible only with continued muscular activity. The person may experience visual distortions and is able to sustain attention only for brief periods. With continued loss of sleep, the person may experience irritability, double vision, and confusion. In some cases, delusions (false and bizarre ideas) and hallucinations (unreal perceptions) may develop.

Sleep is part of a daily biological cycle called the circadian rhythm. Each of us has a kind of internal clock that reminds us when it is time to go to sleep.   (Arthur Tress/Photo Researchers, Inc.)

Peter Tripp was a disk jockey who stayed awake for two hundred consecutive hours to raise money for the March of Dimes.[3] He was able to perform his duties in a normal way until toward the end of the eight-day period when he began to show some unusual symptoms. His speech was very slurred, he began to see things that were not there, and he developed several paranoid ideas. A psychologist described his condition as a "nocturnal psychosis." Randy Gardner was a seventeen-year-old high school student who stayed awake for eleven days as part of a science project for school.[3] Sleep researchers studied him throughout the period. Aside from a great desire to go to sleep, he experienced no serious problems. After the experiment, Randy went to bed and slept for fourteen hours.

Circadian Rhythms

Many animals, including all mammals, experience daily cycles in a number of biological processes. Human beings, as well, show these biological cycles.

It is as if our bodies can tell the time of day and adjust their activities accordingly. Body temperature and sleep are two such processes that follow a daily cycle. These daily cycles are called **circadian rhythms.** (The term *circadian* means "almost daily.")

To some degree we are at the mercy of our internal clocks. It is not easy to switch our cycle of sleeping and waking and to begin sleeping all day and staying awake all night. Of course, many people can and do make this switch as they go to work on a night shift. A somewhat more disturbing shift is the effect known as "jet lag." Following an airplane trip that involves a large change in time zones, a considerable adjustment is necessary. There is a temporary feeling of fatigue, depression, low energy, and mental sluggishness that disappears after several days. One study showed that ten to twelve days were needed for full recovery from a jet lag.[4] Apparently, jet lag results when your body clock is not synchronized with your wristwatch. Diplomats flying from country to country pursuing "jet diplomacy" suffer particularly from jet lag.

Although circadian rhythms seem to be tied to cycles of day and night, they do not depend upon the sun for their timing. When humans or animals have been experimentally kept in constant light or in constant dark, their circadian rhythms continued on a cycle of about twenty-four hours. Apparently, we have some kind of internal body clock set on a twenty-four hour schedule.

Where is this body clock? The cockroach displays twenty-four-hour cyclic patterns of activity and rest, and a timing mechanism—a biological clock— has been located in the cockroach brain.[5] In sparrows, there is also a clear twenty-four hour activity cycle. This circadian rhythm is timed by a "biological clock" located in a tiny structure in the bird's brain called the pineal. Experiments show that one bird's "clock" can be surgically transplanted and given to another bird, which will then begin an activity cycle at precisely the point where the "donor" bird's cycle stopped.[6] The biological clock in the nervous system of human beings has not yet been located.

Sleep Stages

What happens when you fall asleep? Being very drowsy and on the edge of sleep can sometimes be a pleasant experience. As sleep begins, you lose your awareness of the world around you, but you can easily be wakened. You are not yet deeply asleep. Later in the night you will be deeply asleep and can be wakened only with difficulty. Studying the changes that occur during sleep has been possible only recently, with the development of the means to measure sleep.

Measuring Sleep

The depth of sleep can be measured by monitoring the brain, eyes, and muscles of the sleeping person. As muscles become tense or move, they become more electrically active. This increase in electrical activity can be detected on the surface of the skin above the muscles. The movement of the eyes is accompanied by changes in the electrical activity of the eye muscles, and these changes can be detected on the skin around the eyes. The electrical activity of the brain generates changes in voltage called brain waves that can be detected on the surface of the scalp.

By means of electrodes attached to the scalp, face, and arms, tiny electrical signals can be picked up and amplified by a machine called the **polygraph.** On a moving sheet of paper, the polygraph makes continuous records of the electrical activity sensed by each electrode. The record of the electrical activity of the eye muscles reflects eye movements and is called an **electrooculogram (EOG).** The record of the electrical activity of other muscles, such as arm or shoulder muscles, is called an **electromyogram (EMG).** The record of the electrical activity of the brain is called an **electroencephalogram (EEG).**

The gross electrical activity of the brain, as measured on the surface of the skin, is displayed on the EEG as up-and-down fluctuations in voltage. The brain generates several different types of these brain waves. Brain waves vary in both frequency and amplitude. The frequency of a brain wave is its number of up-and-down cycles per second (cps). (The electricity in your home has frequency of sixty cycles per second.) The amplitude of a brain wave is its voltage level, indicated by the height of the wave on the EEG. The amount of voltage generated by the brain and sensed by the EEG electrodes is very small. As the brain's state of consciousness changes, the frequency and amplitude of its brain waves also change. Table 9-1 describes the most common types of brain waves.

Depth of Sleep

Characteristic changes occur when a person falls asleep, and further changes occur as deeper stages of sleep are reached. As sleep deepens, the heart beats more slowly, the rate of breathing declines, the blood pressure drops, and body temperature drops. In addition, there are systematic changes in brain waves.

When you are awake, preparing for sleep, your brain is producing **beta waves,** a fast, low-voltage rhythm. As you lie down and close your eyes, feeling drowsy, your brain produces **alpha waves.** When you fall asleep, you move into what is called *stage one* of sleep. In this stage the brain produces **theta**

Table 9-1 Brain Waves

Wave	Frequency	Description
beta	13–28 cps	high-frequency, irregular, low-amplitude wave
alpha	8–12 cps	a slower, more regular, low-amplitude wave
theta	3–7 cps	a still slower, fairly low-amplitude wave
delta	½–2 cps	a very slow, very high-amplitude wave

to flutter back and forth very rapidly. For this reason, this period of sleep is called rapid-eye-movement sleep **(REM sleep).** Other changes at this phase include a twitching of the face and fingertips, irregular breathing, and a cessation of all body movement—the large muscles of the body are completely paralyzed. The electrical activity of the brain changes as well to the pattern of brain waves characteristic of wakefulness—the beta wave.

This pattern of moving from stage one to deeper stages of sleep and returning again to lighter stages and then to a period of REM sleep repeats itself, with variations, four or five times a night. There are four or five periods of REM sleep each night, constituting perhaps 20 percent of total sleep time.

Dreaming tends to occur only during REM sleep. When a person is awakened during REM sleep, about 80 percent of the time a dream will be reported. When a person is wakened during some other phase of sleep, a dream will be reported only about 15 percent of the time.

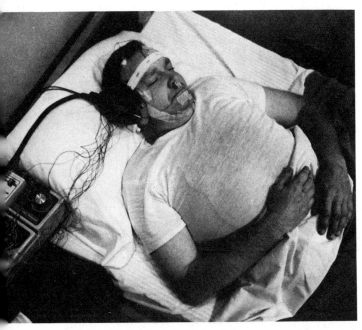

Depth of sleep can be studied by monitoring eye movements, muscle tension, and brain waves. Biological measurements show that there are four levels of sleep in addition to REM sleep (dream sleep). (Janet Knott/The Boston Globe)

waves, with voltage fluctuations of three to seven cycles per second. As sleep deepens in *stage two,* the brain begins to produce **sleep spindles**—brief bursts of higher-voltage waves ranging from twelve to sixteen cycles per second. As sleep becomes even sounder, and *stage three* is achieved, the brain begins to produce **delta waves**—slow fluctuations of one-half to two cycles per second—although the delta rhythm does not yet dominate. In *stage four,* the deepest level of sleep, delta waves dominate, and there are fewer sleep spindles. In stage four it is very difficult to waken the sleeper. (Figure 9-1 shows the typical patterns of the different kinds of brain waves.)

After you initially fall asleep, it takes thirty to forty minutes to reach stage four. Shortly after reaching stage four, you move back through the stages again—first to three and then to two. At the end of this cycle, some remarkable changes occur in the brain and body. One of these changes is that the eyes begin

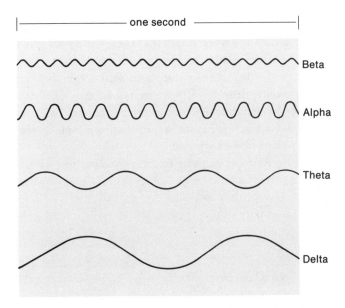

Figure 9-1 Brain Waves. *A simplified illustration of human brain waves. The four types shown are the beta wave (13–28 cycles per second), the alpha wave (8–12 cps), the theta wave (3–7 cps), and the delta wave ($\frac{1}{2}$–2 cps).*

Perception and Learning During Sleep

There is no doubt that perception is possible during sleep. How else could a parent hear the cry of a child and wake up? If you could not hear when you were asleep, you would not wake up when your alarm rings in the morning, and you would not awake with the occurrence of an unusual noise in the middle of the night.

But not all noises cause you to wake up. You get accustomed to some noises, even fairly loud ones, and learn to tune them out. Broadbent[7] and Treisman[8] proposed a theory of selective attention, which attempts to explain how we are able to tune in to certain sounds and tune out others. The **filter theory of attention,** initially developed by Broadbent and later modified by Treisman, assumes that we somehow set different thresholds for detecting different sounds, depending upon the significance of the sounds to us. One sound that is particularly significant to each of us is the sound of our own name. We can hear our name spoken even when we are asleep, and we will often wake up. Even when we are not paying attention to a conversation across the room, if our name is used we will often notice it. Thus, our names and a few other sounds have very low thresholds for our hearing them; we notice them even when they are spoken quietly or when we are fast asleep. The basic idea is that the process of selective attention somehow "filters out" irrelevant sounds and lets only a few through for recognition.

An experiment by Treisman[9] showed that we can hear our own names and other relevant sounds when we are asleep. The subjects of this experiment were told that when they were asleep (in the psychology laboratory), a number of names would be played over a speaker system; furthermore, they were told that if they heard their own names or a second specified name, they were supposed to close one fist—even though they were asleep. The results of the experiment showed that they were able to do this, although each subject's own name produced more fist clenching than any other name.

Since you clearly can hear when you are asleep, sleep learning would seem to be a possibility. There are many claims made about the possibility of learning while you are asleep. You may have seen advertisements for equipment or programs aimed at sleep instruction. Since we spend a third of our lives sleeping, the idea of learning while asleep instead of just lying there is very compelling. Unfortunately, the claims about the effectiveness of sleep learning are not supported by evidence.[10] Apparently what is possible is to learn during the night in those periods when you are not asleep. One experiment monitored depth of sleep with an EEG and presented information to subjects at each stage of sleep, including those transitions into sleep marked by relaxation and drowsiness.[11] They found that 50 percent of the information could later be recalled when the EEG record indicated that it had been presented during a relaxed and drowsy state, but *no* information could be recalled when the EEG indicated it had been presented during sleep. The results of this experiment and others show that attempting to learn during sleep is neither effective nor practical.

Sleep Disorders

When we are awake, we seem to have many different kinds of problems—but we are awake only two-thirds of our lives. During the remaining one-third, when we are asleep, we can also have problems. What can go wrong?

One problem is **insomnia,** chronic difficulty in getting to sleep or in staying asleep. A common cause of insomnia is depression or anxiety. But insomnia can also be aggravated by drugs, most commonly the sleeping pill. Sleeping pills apparently work initially to help people get to sleep, but after they have been used for a while, they begin to disrupt sleep. A response is often to take more sleeping pills. And thus a pattern of drug dependency develops.

Another problem—one that in a way is the opposite of insomnia—is **narcolepsy,** the inability to stay awake in the daytime. Narcolepsy is not merely daytime drowsiness, but is the sudden overpowering need to sleep, regardless of the situation, as the following examples make clear:

A woman starts to laugh. She topples as if clubbed and her flaccid body seems almost to bounce as it smashes to the ground. A man is playing softball. He is at bat. He takes a terrific cut at the ball and goes suddenly limp; the bat drops from his hands. His body slumps and falls.[3]

The cause of narcolepsy is not well understood, although an abnormal brain process is believed to be involved. No cure has been found, although certain drugs may relieve some of the symptoms of narcolepsy.

A third sleep problem is **apnea.** People with sleep apnea are able to breathe only when awake, and therefore are unable to get a single night's rest. They are able to sleep only a few seconds at a time; then they must wake up to gulp some air, then fall asleep again. This pattern occurs hundreds of times a night and thoroughly interferes with the normal sleep cycle.

Interim Summary   Individuals vary greatly in the amount of sleep they need. Temporary problems may result when our circadian rhythms are disturbed, as in jet lag. There are four stages of sleep, with stage four the deepest, each defined by a different pattern of brain waves, muscle action, and eye movements. These patterns can be detected with the polygraph. REM sleep is a special phase of sleep marked by irregular breathing, rapid eye movements, and dreaming. Perception is possible during sleep, and the sound of your own name spoken quietly can wake you up—an effect explained by the filter theory of attention. Sleep learning does not appear to be a realistic possibility. Insomnia, narcolepsy, and apnea are three sleep disorders.

Dreaming

Are you a dreamer? Many people report that they never dream or that they dream only rarely. These reports can now be checked. The new science of dream monitoring has made it possible to discover who dreams and who does not. The polygraph, with its record of brain waves and eye movements, reveals when REM sleep occurs, and thus when dreaming is likely to be experienced.

Does Everybody Dream?

Among the hundreds of subjects who have been studied using the REM method, not a single person has been found who does not dream. Everybody dreams, even those who believe that they do not. Furthermore, everybody dreams several times every night. REM periods (and dreams that accompany them) occur about every hour and a half throughout the night. There is a cycle of about four or five REM periods each night. When people are wakened during one of the REM periods, they will almost always report being in the middle of a dream (even those who "never dream").

How often do you dream? Although we have about four or five REM periods each night, we have more than four or five dreams. During a single REM period we may have several short dreams. The best estimate of the number of dreams ordinarily occurring per night is ten to twenty.[12] Within one REM period the boundary between one dream and the next is marked by body movements. If you observe sleepers and notice that their eyes are twitching, they are probably dreaming; if they then move their body, one dream is probably ending and a new one beginning.

How long are dreams? At one time it was thought that dreams only lasted a few seconds, that the sense of time within the drama of the dream was condensed into a mere moment of real time. We now know that this is false. The REM records suggest that for adults one to two hours are spent dreaming each night if all the REM periods are added together. Since we have several dreams each night, some are apparently short and some longer; some dreams of over thirty minutes have been recorded. These longer dreams tend to occur in the morning before waking.

The Dreams of Children

A psychologist observed his sleeping daughter when she was less than two years old:

I went into her room one morning before she awoke and saw her eyes moving. Suddenly she said, "Pick me! Pick me!" I woke her and she immediately said, "Oh Daddy, I was a flower." [13]

The REM method of monitoring the occurrence of dreams has been used with infants and children.[14] The results show that newborn infants spend about half of their total sleeping time dreaming (or about nine hours per day); young children spend about 25 percent of their sleeping time in dreams (or about two and a half hours); adults spend about 20 percent of their sleeping time in dreams (or about one and a half hours); and adults over age fifty spend about 15 percent of their total sleeping time in dreams (or about one hour). The proportion of sleeping time each night that is spent in dreaming gradually decreases with age. The psychological basis for this remains unknown.

The Dreams of Animals

You may have watched a dog or cat sleeping quietly and breathing regularly; then suddenly the whiskers twitch, the tongue and paws move, and the eyelids flutter. The animal is probably dreaming.

All mammals that have been studied show cycles of REM activity during sleep; this includes people as well as the cat, dog, monkey, rat, rabbit, goat, mouse, opossum, and guinea pig.[15] While we know that animals experience REM activity during sleep, we do not know for certain whether they experience dreams as we do. There is, however, some evidence that they do dream. One scientist studied the electrical activity in the brains of cats while they were sleeping.[16] He found that the area of the cat's brain responsible for vison was particularly active during REM periods, as if the cats were having visual experiences. Another investigator kept monkeys in a totally dark environment and conditioned them to press a lever near their paw whenever a visual image was presented to them.[17] During REM periods at night the monkeys would sometimes press the lever in their sleep, as if they were having visual experiences.

Remembering Your Dreams

If everybody dreams several times every night, why is it that many people report dreaming only about once a month and other people report that they never dream? One group of persons who reported that they almost never dreamed was studied in a dream-monitoring laboratory.[18] They showed the same REM cycle as other subjects; furthermore, when they were wakened during a REM period, they reported being in the middle of a dream. These results and the findings from similar studies[19] indicate that everybody dreams, even those who claim that they don't. The evidence leads to the conclusion that while everybody dreams every night, many dreams are forgotten. There are no nondreamers, but there are people who do not recall their dreams.[20]

A number of studies have found personality differences between people who do and do not recall their dreams.[20] For example, one study[21] found that people who frequently recall their dreams tend to be more sensitive, conservative, shy, stable, and self-assured. People who recalled their dreams less often were found to be more liberal, conscientious, adventurous, and worrying.

Your Need to Dream

If dreams are nothing more than the "confused results of indigestion," as Socrates believed, then it would make little difference whether you dreamed or not; but if dreaming serves an important psychological function, then a certain amount of dreaming may be necessary.

Do you need to dream? Psychologists have studied this question by preventing people from dreaming, then observing the consequences. In one study an attempt was made to prevent subjects from dreaming without interfering with the length of their sleep periods.[30] Each time subjects began to dream, as indicated by REM activity, they were awakened,

kept awake for a few minutes, and then allowed to go back to sleep. This procedure for preventing dreaming is called **dream deprivation.** For each of three to seven consecutive nights subjects were prevented from dreaming, and then for several following nights they were allowed to sleep normally. At a later period the subjects came back to the laboratory and underwent another series of awakenings; this time, however, they were wakened at times when they were not showing REM activity.

What was the effect of dream deprivation? First, on their "recovery" nights following their nights of dream deprivation, they showed a "rebound effect"—the amount of time spent dreaming increased greatly. It was as if the subjects had to make up for the lost dreams by dreaming overtime. This suggests that a certain amount of dreaming is psychologically necessary. Similar results have been shown for animals.[31] A second result of dream deprivation is the stress it imposes on subjects. Some subjects showed anxiety, irritability, and difficulty in concentrating; five subjects developed a substantial increase in appetite during the period of dream deprivation; another subject became agitated and quit the study in a panic. The psychological changes observed in the subjects disappeared as soon as the subjects were allowed to dream.[30]

Why do we need to dream? Why should dream deprivation cause psychological problems? No one knows for sure, but one dream researcher, Charles Fisher, believes that dreaming is the normal person's journey into insanity or psychosis:

The dream is the normal psychosis and dreaming permits each and every one of us to be quietly and safely insane every night of our lives.[32]

Interim Summary   People dream ten to twenty times each night during four or five REM periods. The passage of time in dreams is not condensed into a moment; most dreams last several minutes. Although everybody dreams, people differ in their ability to remember dreams. The tendency to remember dreams is associated with certain personality characteristics.

Dreaming is psychologically necessary. People prevented from dreaming show anxiety, irritability, and stress; then, when they are permitted to dream, they show a rebound effect by dreaming overtime.

What You Dream About

Although each dream is a unique event, there are similarities among the dreams of different people. Certain kinds of dreams are fairly common: dreams of falling, of being attacked, of being chased, of appearing nude in public, of being lost, of getting married, and of making love.[22]

Dream Content

What do people dream about? Thousands of dreams have been analyzed and their contents studied.[23,24] The results of these studies show that most dreams do not take place in bizarre settings; most dream settings are commonplace—a living room, an automobile, a street, a classroom, or a field. Half the time, the characters in dreams have been found to be either the dreamer or friends and acquaintances of the dreamer; the remainder of the time the characters are strangers. What do people do in their dreams? Passive activities occupy a large part of dreams—talking, sitting, watching, or thinking; strenuous, work-related activities are less common. What are the emotions experienced in dreams? The most common type of emotion is fear and anxiety; anger, excitement, and happiness are the next most common emotions felt. Although unpleasant emotions are more common in dreams than pleasant ones, they are usually not intense.

Dreams in Color

I dreamed I was floating in the air, carried by blue, red, and yellow balloons. Then the balloons became large black birds.

Some dreams appear to be in full natural color, and others appear to be entirely in black and white. Can you recall experiencing a "technicolor" dream? In a study of 3,000 dreams 29 percent were colored or had some color in them.[23] Women reported color in dreams more than men. There seemed to be no experienced difference between the color dreams and the black-and-white dreams. The relatively low percentage of color dreams may be somewhat surprising; a recent study, however, sheds some light on the puzzle. One researcher, studying dreams from persons wakened in REM periods, found that color was mentioned about 25 percent of the time.[25] Upon further questioning, however, the dreamers revealed that color was experienced in over 80 percent of the dreams. Apparently, color is experienced in most dreams, but is often not reported.

Nightmares

Nightmares often contain frightening events in which the dreamer is the victim of unpreventable psychological or physical harm. Often the dreamer is helpless in the terrible drama but awakens suddenly just before the final danger.[26] Particularly common nightmares are dreams of falling and of being attacked. A survey found that 80 percent of males and 81 percent of females have had both types of nightmares.[22] The following dreams are the nightmares of two young women.[27]

Crazy-Woman Dream • *I am in this house. It's a nice house, by a park. I'm alone in the house with this crazy woman. She's acting wild and unreasonable. I don't know exactly like what, something in an insane asylum. It was a very nice house set in a park that was*

Have you ever had a nightmare in which you dreamed of running away from some terrible, but unknown, danger? Nightmares are frightening dreams that occur during stage four of sleep. (Peter Laytin)

very nice. *She was very hostile and at the same time she wanted to hold me. I felt she wanted to hold me, to crush me, to kill me. She hated me very much. I dropped my keys and she wouldn't let me look for them. I found them again and dropped them again, and because I had lost them I had to stay in this house with her. . . . The situation is too horrible. My feelings were great horror, disgust, and fear of this crazy woman.*

Tiny-Cobras Dream • *There were many tiny cobras. They were about a foot long and sandy colored. This was all in a room, and there were bookshelves. . . . The cobras were concealed everywhere. They came up everywhere I went. They could come out of a book. There were other people around and I was pleading with them not to do it. They had something to do with having these snakes come out. I pleaded with them not to do it because I was so scared of snakes. I didn't kill the snakes. I was too scared to touch them. I was pleading with the people. They were doing it on purpose. They were hiding the snakes. I was tense and scared, I woke up petrified. I kept waking up and I was too frightened to go to sleep again. I kept waking myself up lest I dream about the snakes again.*

There are two different kinds of frightening dreams. One kind—the nightmare—involves a series of dream images, accompanied by some anxiety. A second kind—the "night terror"—involves at most a single image and is accompanied by intense anxiety. With a night terror, the heart rate may double, breathing comes in gasps, and screaming may occur. Nightmares and night terrors typically occur in two different stages of sleep. The nightmare occurs during REM sleep, and the night terror occurs during stage four of sleep.

Sleepwalking

Most sleepwalking occurs in childhood, but it sometimes recurs in later years. The sleepwalker behaves like a robot, moving slowly and with apparent purpose. Most sleepwalking is not remembered upon wakening. This may result from the fact that sleepwalking does not occur during the normal dreaming cycle of sleep, when REM activity is present.[28] Sleepwalking, like night terrors, tends to occur during stage four of sleep. Sleepwalkers often will return to bed if gently interrupted, but if abruptly wakened they will experience a period of extreme confusion. An extraordinary case of sleepwalking is described below:

A twenty-two-year-old man was subject to repeated episodes of sleepwalking. One night while asleep he climbed from the window of his apartment, twelve stories above the ground, and walked on a narrow (eighteen-inch wide) outside ledge to another window. He returned to bed without waking.

A horrified roommate awoke in time to watch the latter part of this performance and his friend's return to the room. He had been afraid to move or to comment for fear of awakening the patient, who might have become startled and fallen to the street below.

When the sleepwalker was awakened, he had no recollection of the incident. He refused to believe it as described, until confronted with his sooty feet and, in the morning, by the clear footprints which he had left on the ledge.[29]

Interim Summary   Most dreams are fairly commonplace, even dull, and involve familiar settings and characters. Although many people do not remember experiencing color in their dreams, studies show that most dreams are in color. Nightmares are far less common than normal dreams, but most people occasionally experience them. Sleepwalking, unlike dreams, does not occur during REM sleep.

What Your Dreams Mean

Do you believe that your dreams are just scrambled images, or do you believe that they are revealing and meaningful? According to the Talmud, "A dream which is not explained is like a letter which has not been read." The idea is that dreams are messages that should be understood. By way of contrast, a famous psychologist of the last century wrote that dreams made no sense and could be compared to the ten fingers of a man who knows nothing about music, wandering over the keys of a piano.

If dreams are meaningful, some basis for interpreting their meaning must be developed; the language of dreams must be studied in order to be understood. The first systematic theory of dreams was developed by Sigmund Freud and published in his book *The Interpretation of Dreams*.[33]

Freudian Theory

In Plato's *Republic* Socrates says that dreams reveal our hidden desires: "In all of us, even in good men, there is a lawless, wild beast nature, which peers out in sleep." That, in essence, is Freud's theory of dreams. According to the **Freudian theory of dreams**, dreams reveal unconscious wishes, and these wishes are represented symbolically.

Wish Fulfillment • According to Freud, many of our wishes—particularly those concerning sex and aggression—are inhibited or suppressed. We are not conscious of their existence; their presence in our unconscious is made known only when they "peer out" when we sleep. Freud's principle of **wish fulfillment**

states that unconscious wishes are revealed and satisfied in dreams. Dreams, Freud believed, were the "royal road to the unconscious"; by understanding dreams we can know the contents of the unconscious mind. Wishes that we could not imagine acting out in our waking state are played out in the drama of our dreams. It is "safe" to dream our wishes, because in sleep we cannot act on the basis of them. Freud wrote:

No matter what impulses from the normally inhibited unconscious may prance upon the stage, we need feel no concern; they remain harmless since they are unable to set in motion the motor apparatus by which alone they might modify the external world. The state of sleep guarantees the security of the citadel that must be guarded.[33]

Nightmares do not seem to support Freud's wish-fulfillment principle; it is hard to believe that the frightening events of the nightmare express an unconscious wish. Try to recall a nightmare you have had. Do you think you wanted the frightening events actually to happen?

Dreams do not seem to reflect needs or wishes in any clear fashion. Researchers have tested the wish-fulfillment theory. Participants in one psychology experiment reported their dreams on nights following a period of at least twenty-four hours with no intake of fluids whatsoever.[34] The subjects had dry lips and mouths, had difficulty salivating, and were extremely thirsty. In the fifteen dreams that were recorded, there was no instance of a dream involving drinking or an awareness of thirst. These results are not very consistent with Freud's wish-fulfillment principle of dreaming.

Hidden Meanings • Freud believed that a hidden psychic censor prevented unconscious impulses from reaching awareness; this same censor disguised the impulses and wishes revealed in dreams so that they appeared only symbolically. Dreams could be interpreted at two different levels: the **manifest content** of the dream consists of the events of the dream as they were experienced and reported by the dreamer; the **latent content** of the dream is the true meaning that is hidden behind the dream images. The manifest content is the surface content of the dream, and the latent content is the hidden meaning of the dream. The same hidden, or latent, meaning could be represented in many different manifest dreams, just as, for example, the literary theme of sin and salvation has been represented in many different plays and novels. The underlying theme of these novels (the latent content) is the same, but the actual plots and characters (manifest content) are different.

The following three dreams were experienced by one man in the same night and seem to be united by a common theme.[35] The dreamer was awakened by a bell when his eyes showed REM activity.

Dream One

I was dreaming something about a woman. The last scene was something about some kind of involvement where she's trying to do something about an inheritance and I'm trying to thwart her. I must have thwarted her pretty well, but she still has something she can do, and I'm saying—we're in some kind of dining room—"Let me see your trump card. Let me just look at you." I went over and looked at her in the face and I said, "How can I possibly be afraid of you?" She wouldn't let me look her in the eye. She just kind of turned away a little., And just as the bell went off I was chasing her out and I shouted, "You god damn bitch." The woman was a woman I'd never seen before.

Dream Two

I was watching a guy standing in the street. Suddenly he raised his gun and shot a woman in the back. I'm sure it was a woman. And I ran. There was a little frame house sitting on the street. Just a few rooms, five or six. I ran in the front door and started running out the back. I was afraid this guy would come out the back door. Somehow I knew he was on my side, yet I was afraid he would come after me. I felt frightened and anxious when I woke up.

Dream Three

This dream started out at a—no, it didn't. Oh, Lord, it started out with Sara Smith (pseudonym). She seduced me. That's how it started. I don't remember how we got undressed or anything, but we got undressed and she was kind of neurotic and I had a queer feeling I was being manipulated. She scorned any way of conventional intercourse. I'd try to do it conventionally and she'd just sneer at me. . . . Finally I got mad and left.

Although the characters and the story line of each dream differ, the underlying attitude of conflict toward women runs through each dream. These dreams therefore could be seen as different ways of expressing the same basic meaning.

Dream Symbols • Since the true meaning of dreams, according to Freud, is expressed symbolically, understanding the language of dreams requires symbolic interpretation. For example, a woman reported a frightening dream of "tiny winged men who wanted to come in through my window." The dream was interpreted, from a Freudian point of view, to have the following latent meaning: "The tiny men as the penis, the wings as the erection, and the window as the female genital are all clear."[36] An object that represents or symbolizes the penis is called a **phallic symbol**. Many objects in dreams Freud interpreted to be phallic symbols representing the penis; for example, the penis may be disguised as a stick, umbrella, gun, plowshare, knife, snake, fish, or any object that is relatively elongated. Freud interpreted any hollow object or container—such as a box, chest, oven, or cave—as a disguised vagina. A young married woman experienced the following dream a few days after she had, for

What would Freud say about the latent content of this dream?

the first time, experienced a completely loving acceptance of the sexual act.

I saw a dark brown fertile field in which a plow was cutting large furrows. Suddenly I myself became the field and the sharp steel plow went easily through the length of my body and cut me into two halves. Although it hurt, it was indescribably beautiful. I experienced myself as the plowed-up field, and the furrow as my own flesh, but it was not bleeding.[37]

Cognitive Theory

An alternative to the Freudian theory of dreams is the **cognitive theory of dreams,** which considers dreams to consist of thought and memories similar to mental activity when awake. When we are asleep, information from the environment is not available and action toward the environment is not possible; in this state we periodically construct thought and images from stored information and old memories, and these constructions are called dreams. Not all memories are constructed into dreams. Only those memories that have been recently "activated" by emotions are formed into dreams. Excitement, fear, anger, and other emotions bring certain memories to life. From this point of view the connection between the concerns of the day and the dreams of the night can be explained by assuming that memories from the day which have been associated with emotional arousal are those most available for construction into dreams.[38] Calvin Hall, a proponent of the cognitive theory of dreams, characterizes a dream as "a highly private showing of the dreamer's thoughts."[39] Hall writes:

Dreaming is thinking that occurs during sleep. It is a peculiar form of thinking in which the conceptions or ideas are expressed not in the form of words or drawings, as in waking life, but in the form of images, usually visual images. In other words, the abstract and invisible ideas are converted into concrete and visible images. By an odd process which we do not understand, the sleeping person can see his own thoughts embodied in the form of pictures.

When he communicates his dream to another person, he is communicating his thoughts, whether he knows it or not.[23]

Evidence for the cognitive theory of dreams comes from the observation that dreams sometimes involve productive mental activity, similar to mental activity when awake. For example, the poem "Kubla Khan" was composed in a dream by Samuel Taylor Coleridge; the plot of the story *Dr. Jekyll and Mr. Hyde* was dreamed by Robert Louis Stevenson; and the structure of the benzene molecule was discovered in a dream by Friedrich Kekulé, a German chemist.[13]

Contact with the Spirit World Through Dreams

A Malaysian people called the Senoi use dreams as tools to understand themselves and to obtain contact with "the powers of the spirit world."[40] Every morning at breakfast the family members share their dreams. Elders analyze the dreams of children and the art of dream interpretation. The Senoi believe that the dreamer can actively enter and change a dream while it is in progress. For example, a dream of falling may be changed into a dream of flying. Children are taught that their dreams are their own property and they control what happens in them.

For the Senoi all dreams have a purpose, and the purpose must be understood. Dreams of falling are believed to be the quickest way to get in contact with the powers of the spirit world. In such dreams the "falling spirits" are attracting you to their spiritual universe, and you should learn from the journey. If a child reports a frightening dream of falling, an elder may answer, "This is wonderful. It is one of the best kinds of dreams. Now, where did you fall and what did you discover?"[40]

Interim Summary

Two major viewpoints about dreams are the Freudian theory and the cognitive theory. According to the Freudian theory, dreams are an example of the principle of wish fulfillment; that is, dreams represent unconscious wishes. Freud believed that dreams have two levels of meaning: the manifest content (the dream images as experienced) and the latent content (the hidden meaning of dreams). According to the cognitive theory, dreams are constructed from thoughts and memories that have made an emotional impression on the dreamer; they are similar to waking mental activity.

Summary

1. Studies of sleep deprivation show that, while it is easy to go for twenty-four hours without sleep, continued loss of sleep produces psychological problems such as irritability and confusion.

2. Sleep follows a daily cycle called a circadian rhythm, timed by some internal biological clock. Although this "clock" has been located in the brains of certain animals, the human body clock has not yet been found.

3. Sleep can be measured using a polygraph that records the EOG, EMG, and EEG. Such records show the activity of the eye muscles, the arm or shoulder muscles, and the brain.

4. Four types of brain waves are the beta wave (13–28 cps), the alpha wave (8–12 cps), the theta wave (3–7 cps), and the delta wave ($\frac{1}{2}$–2 cps). These brain rhythms are characteristic of different states of alertness and sleep.

5. There are four stages of sleep that vary in depth and are characterized by different patterns of brain waves. In addition, there is a type of sleep called REM sleep which is associated with dreaming.

6. Perception is possible during sleep, and the sound of your own name spoken quietly can wake you up—an effect explained by the filter theory of attention. Sleep learning is neither effective nor practical.

7. Insomnia (chronic difficulty in falling asleep or in staying asleep), narcolepsy (a sudden, overwhelming desire to sleep), and apnea (the inability to breathe when sleeping) are three types of sleep disorders.

8. Evidence indicates that everybody dreams, although not everybody can remember their dreams. The tendency to remember dreams is associated with certain personality characteristics.

9. Most dreams are relatively commonplace in setting and plot. The characters in dreams are typically either the dreamer or friends or acquaintances of the dreamer. Color is experienced in most dreams but is often not reported.

10. Nightmares (extended, anxiety-provoking dreams) typically occur in REM sleep.

Night terrors (brief images associated with intense anxiety, gasps, or screams and an accelerated heart rate) typically occur in stage four, the deepest phase of sleep. Sleepwalking also occurs in stage four.

11. The effects of dream deprivation are anxiety, irritability, and stress. Later, when permitted to dream, people show a rebound effect by dreaming overtime.

12. The Freudian theory of dreams assumes that dreams represent unconscious wishes. Freud distinguished the hidden meaning of dreams (the latent content) from the dream images as experienced (the manifest content).

13. The cognitive theory of dreams assumes that dreams are constructed from thoughts and memories that have some emotional significance. From this point of view, dreaming is like thinking, except that it occurs during sleep.

Key Concepts

circadian rhythms   Daily cycles of certain biological processes such as sleep and body temperature.

polygraph   A machine that detects, amplifies, and records the electrical activity of the body.

electrooculogram (EOG)   A record of the electrical activity of the eye muscles.

electromyogram (EMG)   A record of the electrical activity of muscles, such as in the face or shoulders.

electroencephalogram (EEG)   A record of the electrical activity of the brain.

beta waves   Brain waves produced when you are awake, with your eyes open; voltage fluctuations from thirteen to twenty-eight cycles per second.

alpha waves   A type of brain wave associated with relaxed awareness; voltage fluctuations from eight to twelve cycles per second.

theta waves   Brain waves produced in stage one of sleep; voltage fluctuations from three to seven cycles per second.

delta waves   Brain waves produced in stages three and four of sleep; voltage fluctuations are from one-half to two cycles per second.

sleep spindles   Brief bursts of voltage fluctuations ranging from twelve to sixteen cycles per second.

REM sleep   A period of sleep marked by periodic rapid eye movements and dreaming.

filter theory of attention   A theory of attention that assumes that we somehow set different thresholds for detecting different sounds, depending upon the significance of the sounds to us.

insomnia   Chronic difficulty in getting to sleep or staying asleep.

narcolepsy   The inability to stay awake in the daytime.

apnea   The inability to breathe when asleep.

dream deprivation   A condition caused by waking people each time REM begins, in order to prevent dreaming.

Freudian theory of dreams   The theory that dreams reveal unconscious wishes that are expressed symbolically in dream images.

wish fulfillment   The idea that unconscious wishes are revealed and satisfied in dreams.

manifest content   The events of the dream as they are experienced.

latent content   The hidden "true" meaning of dreams.

phallic symbol   A dream image—such as a pencil or snake—that symbolically represents the penis.

cognitive theory of dreams   The theory that dreams consist of fragments of thought and memories that have been associated with emotions.

Part IV

Life-Cycle Development

Chapter 10
The Family

Key Questions

1. How is behavior inherited?
2. What methods are used to study the relative effects of heredity and environment on behavior?
3. What are some common types of families?
4. What are the results of not having a family?
5. How do children and parents influence each other?

Could you have been someone else?

Suppose some family in another part of the world had adopted you at birth. Your home and experiences would have been entirely different. Would you be similar to the person you are now? You would look about the same. Your eye, hair, and skin color are physical characteristics you were born with; they were determined genetically. But are there aspects of your behavior, your personality, your *identity,* that were not formed uniquely by your life experiences but were inherited from your parents?

How did you become what you are today? Some would stress the importance of heredity, while others would stress the effects of experience or learning. The debate about the relative effects of learning and heredity in shaping human behavior is called the **nature-nurture issue.** Your personality may result from "nature" (you were born that way) or from "nurture" (you were brought up that way).

The seventeenth-century philosopher John Locke believed that all aspects of human character resulted from learning; he argued that babies are born with a **tabula rasa,** a "blank slate," or empty mind. The eighteenth-century philosopher Immanuel Kant disagreed. He wrote that people are born with certain inborn ways of perceiving the world, that babies' minds are not blank but instead hold **innate ideas.** For example, Kant believed that we are born with the ideas of time, space, cause, and effect. During the first half of this century psychologists strongly emphasized the effects of learning in human development—that is, the "nurture" side of the issue. Today psychologists tend to take a more balanced approach in which the effects of heredity are also emphasized.

The Inheritance of Behavior

To some degree your behavior and personality are inborn; some aspects of your behavior you inherited from your parents. **Genetics** is the study of inherited characteristics, and **behavioral genetics** is the study of the inheritance of behavior.

Scientists typically separate two general influences on behavior, heredity and the environment. Some characteristics are influenced strongly by heredity; like hair color they are primarily inborn. Others are strongly influenced by the environment, that is, by what happens in the womb and after birth. However, all behavior involves both hereditary and environmental influences; both must be considered to understand behavior.

Human beings are, of all animals, the least determined by hereditary influences. The most important forces affecting your behavior come from your experiences in the world and with the people around you.

Simple animals like insects and fish, however, are under much stronger hereditary control.

Instincts

Behavior can be inherited: the migration of birds at the change of seasons; salmon returning from the sea to spawn; the spider building its complex web; the bee storing its honey; the moth flying to its death in the flame. Complex unlearned behaviors such as these are called **instincts.** These behavior sequences are as characteristic of a particular animal species as is its physical appearance and hence are called **species-specific behaviors.** Typically, an instinctual behavior pattern appears to be adaptive and purposeful, in that it contributes to the capacity of the species to survive. Human beings, however, do not appear to be born with instincts.

The male satin bower bird of Australia builds a small structure of twigs and branches in which to court the female bower bird. To attract a mate, the bower bird places small colored shells and stones on the ground around this structure, giving the appearance of a garden. (See Figure 10-1.) To complete his work, he paints the inside of his love house with charcoal from a burnt twig or purple juice from a berry held in his mouth. This elaborate courtship display is apparently an inborn behavior.[1]

A pregnant rat that is kept in a cage will begin to build a nest just before her litter is born. After she gives birth, she cleans her tiny babies carefully and allows them to nurse. When the young begin to scatter about the cage, she carries them back to the protection of the nest. This sequence of behavior is inborn, not learned. The instinctive behavior is the same for a rat's first litter as it is for its fifth; it is not dependent upon previous experiences and is displayed in exactly the same fashion by rats reared completely apart from other rats.[2]

Chromosomes and Genes

The instinctive behavior just described follows a genetic blueprint or program; the program is set to go into operation when the conditions, either body chemistry or external stimulation, are exactly right. How does a species-specific sequence of behavior continue, generation after generation?

Genetic programming of behavior is transmitted from parent to young in **chromosomes,** small rodlike structures within the nucleus of each cell of the body. (See Figure 10-2.) Each chromosome consists of a sequence of thousands of **genes**—the basic units of genetic information. Genes are composed of **DNA,** a complex molecule that has the capacity to duplicate itself. Half of your chromosomes came from your mother, and half from your father.

You began when a sperm cell from your father united with an egg cell from your mother—a chance meeting of two cells from each parent's population of reproductive cells. The sperm and egg each brought twenty-three chromosomes to the union. The result-

Figure 10-1 Bower birds. *The male Australian bower bird builds a house, paints it, and carefully decorates it with ornaments—all controlled by instinct. (American Museum of Natural History)*

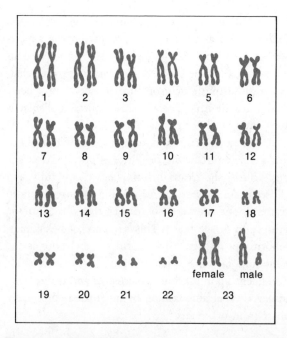

Figure 10-2 Human Chromosomes. *Normal human beings have 46 chromosomes, small rod-like structures within the nucleus of each cell of the body. Chromosomes are the carriers of genetic information. Babies with two X chromosomes are female; babies with an X and a Y chromosome are male.*

ing fertilized cell (you), containing forty-six chromosomes, began its growth through a long process of multiplying by dividing. During cell division each chromosome duplicates itself, so that the resulting two cells each contain exactly the same genetic information. On rare occasions two individuals, each having the same forty-six chromosomes, result from a single fertilized egg. These babies will be **identical twins.** Identical twins look almost exactly alike because they have the same genetic structure. **Fraternal twins** result from two eggs being fertilized by two sperm cells at about the same time; the genetic structure of fraternal twins may be similar but it is not identical. Fraternal twins are no more similar than other brothers and sisters.

Because of the enormous number of possible combinations of genetic structures, human beings are very different from each other. The single exception

is the case of identical twins, the individuals who share the same genetic structures as a consequence of originating from a single egg. Identical twins are always of the same sex and look very much alike. They also show similarity in measures of respiration rate, motor performance,[3] and patterns of brain-wave activity.[4] Findings such as these indicate the genetic basis for these characteristics.

Your sex was determined by one pair of your chromosomes known as **X and Y chromosomes.** If you are a female, this pair consists of two X chromosomes; if you are a male, this pair has an X and a Y member. About half of the male sperm cells contain an X chromosome and the other half contain a Y chromosome. All female egg cells contain X chromosomes. If a sperm containing an X chromosome unites with the egg, the resulting cell will have two X chromosomes, one from the sperm and one from the egg, and a female baby will result. If a sperm containing a Y chromosome unites with the egg, a male will result.

Research Methods for Studying the Inheritance of Behavior

Several different research methods are used in the study of behavioral genetics. Each has the goal of discovering the relative hereditary influence on some aspect of human or animal behavior. Family history studies, selective breeding, and twin studies are common research approaches in trying to unravel the hereditary and environmental origins of behavior.

Family History Studies • Behavioral tendencies that are hereditary should run in families—that is, children should resemble their parents on these traits. **Family history studies** examine the resemblance of family members on some particular trait. For example, a number of family history studies have shown that intelligence and musical ability tend to be found to a high degree in some families and to a low degree in others. The Bach family, for example, had a large number of very talented musicians. Records of other family trees show that certain families have a large number of criminals. Drawing conclusions about hereditary influences from family resemblances, however, should not be attempted without additional supporting data. A disadvantage of the family history method is that it fails to account for the *basis* of family resemblance; it could be heredity or it could be environment, since members of the same family usually share the same environment.

As a general rule, the children of bright parents are bright and the children of dull parents are dull. The extent of this relationship was examined in a study comparing the IQs of parents and children in 428 father-child pairs and 538 mother-child pairs. In general, the children's IQs resembled the IQs of their parents.[5]

What accounts for the intellectual resemblance of children and their parents? One possibility is that intelligence, like physical appearance, is inherited. If this were true, bright parents would tend to have bright children for the same reason that tall parents tend to have tall children—they pass this trait on through their genes. However, a second possibility is that intelligence is a consequence not of heredity but of the child's home and school environment. If this were true, bright parents would tend to have bright children because they rear their children in homes that are intellectually more stimulating. Which of these two possibilities is correct? To put the question more generally, what are the relative effects of heredity and environment on intelligence?

In an attempt to separate the effects of heredity from the effects of environment, psychologists have compared the intelligence levels of adopted children with that of both their biological and adoptive parents. Although adopted children share their genetic makeup with their biological parents, their home environments are entirely the products of their adoptive parents. Therefore, evidence for genetic or hereditary effects on intelligence would be found if the adopted children's intelligence levels were more similar to that of their biological parents. For example, finding a bright child whose biological parents were bright—but whose adoptive parents were dull—would support the argument that intelligence has a genetic basis. By contrast, finding a bright child whose biological parents were dull—but whose adoptive parents were bright—would support the argument that intelligence is primarily determined by the home environment. Thus, the relative effects of heredity and environment on intelligence can be examined in a study of adopted children.

A study of this kind was made using 194 children who were placed in foster homes before the age of six months and another 194 children living with their biological parents.[6] The IQs of the parents and children were tested and compared. It was found that the IQ of a child resembles more closely the IQ of biological parents than the IQ of adoptive parents. A child born of bright parents but living with dull adoptive parents is more likely to be bright than dull. This shows the important effect of heredity on intelligence.

Selective Breeding • People breed horses, dogs, and cats to enhance certain traits and to reduce others. Horses are sometimes bred for speed; a fast horse is bred, and a slow horse is neutered. Since fast horses have many offspring and slow horses have fewer, the trait of speed is selectively bred. The Shetland sheepdog was bred to be a small active dog that could learn quickly to carry out commands in controlling sheep. Dogs that could do this especially well passed on their genes to many offspring. Dogs that could not do this task very well were neutered, and their genes were lost. This process of breeding for certain traits is called **selective breeding.**

One problem with the selective breeding method is that it takes many generations of the animals in order to find an effect. A second problem with this method is that it is limited to studying animal behavior, since experimentation with human breeding is obviously not acceptable.

This method of selective breeding has been used successfully to develop a strain of bright rats, a strain of aggressive dogs, and a strain of alcoholic mice. The fact that strains with these characteristics have been developed indicates that, in these animals, these traits have a genetic basis.

Additional evidence on the genetic basis of intelligence comes from attempts at selectively breeding more intelligent animals. Using a population of rats, it is possible to mate the brights to the brights and the dulls to the dulls. The brightest offspring of the brights are mated with each other and the dullest offspring of the dulls are mated. This procedure of *selective breeding* will, over a period of a few generations of rats, produce two strains—one strain of bright rats and one strain of dull rats.

Using a maze as an intelligence test, one psychologist was able to develop a maze-bright strain and maze-dull strain of rats in ony six generations. The brights had only half as many errors as the dulls in solving the maze.[7] These rats were found to be bright only at solving mazes, not bright in general. Such experiments, of course, are not possible for human beings. But since mate selection is not random but often involves consideration of traits such as intelligence, selective breeding in effect does take place among humans as well.

Twin Studies • Since identical twins have identical genes, a behavior with a genetic basis should be found in either both twins or in neither. **Twin studies** compare the behavior and personality of identical and fraternal twins. If both fraternal and identical twins were found to be equally likely to share a particular trait, the trait would likely have an environmental basis, since twins of both types live together in the same homes. By constrast, a trait that tended to be shared much more by identical twins than by fraternal twins is one that probably has some genetic basis. For example, the fact that identical twins tend to be much more similar in intelligence than fraternal twins is seen as evidence for the genetic basis of intelligence.

A problem with this method is that it ignores the unique psychological context that develops for identical twins. For example, they are typically assumed by family and peers to be psychologically identical, because of their physical identity. This assumption undoubtedly influences the way people respond to them and the way they develop. Identical twins also tend to share more than fraternal twins as they grow up. Thus, the environment in which they grow up may contribute to the psychological resemblance of identical twins.

Twin studies have clarified the role of heredity in personality characteristics. There are personality similarities among family members. Identical twins are more similar than fraternal twins or other siblings, although their similarity in personality is not so great as their similarity in physical characteristics or in intelligence.[8] This similarity in temperament of identical twins can be seen even during the first year of life.

One psychologist studied twenty pairs of twins over this one-year period.[9] Each baby was observed at home by independent judges and was rated on the extent of social smiling and on the extent of fear of strange persons and objects. The nine pairs of identical twins were more alike, or concordant, than the eleven pairs of fraternal twins.

In the second month, it usually took some external stimulation to elicit smiling. . . . This was the case with Arturo, a fraternal twin, who was a sleepy-head and rarely wide awake. His fraternal brother, Felix, was a remarkable contrast. He was wide eyed and very watchful—but he was unremittingly sober and rarely smiled. This difference in amount of smiling persisted throughout the first year.

While infants under 5 months of age will usually smile at any person, after this age they become increasingly discriminating, and smiles are increasingly reserved for familiar persons. Discrimination turns to wariness some time in the third or fourth trimester of the first year, and most infants begin to react with fear when with a stranger. . . . Lori and Lisa, an identical pair, were both very wary of strangers from 5 months of age through 8 months, when fear gave way to rather easy acceptance. As in the majority of identical pairs, the timing and intensity of their reactions were very similar over the entire period.[9]

Even infants who are deaf or blind from birth exhibit patterns similar to those of their normal twin in the development of social smiling. Yvonne, congenitally blind from cataracts, smiled and consistently turned her blind eyes toward the person holding her. Smiling seems to be a response under strong biological control. The study of infant twins concludes:

Heredity plays a role in the development of positive social orientation (including smiling) and in the fear of strangers. Our evidence for this is that identical twins show greater concordance than fraternal twins in these two areas of behavior over the first year of life. There seems to be no reasonable alternate explanation of these results.[9]

Interim Summary   Behavioral genetics is the study of the inheritance of behavior. Behavior can be inherited, but the behavior of human beings is not as influenced by genes as is the behavior of insects, fish, and birds, which display many instincts. The inheritance of behavior occurs through chromosomes that are passed on from parents to their children. Each chromosome has many genes, the basic unit of heredity that is composed of molecules of DNA. Family history studies, selective breeding studies, and twin studies are common methods used to examine the relative effects of heredity and environment on behavior.

Family Influences on Behavior

From her studies of families in many different cultures around the world, the anthropologist Margaret Mead concluded:

The family is, as far as we know, the toughest institution we have. It is, in fact, the institution to which we owe our humanity. We know no other way of making human beings except by bringing them up in a family.[10]

Not only are we born into the family, we are also shaped by the family to be the adults we are. We learn in the family to be human.

The family is a universal form of social organization, a type of grouping seen in every culture and society that has been studied. The joys and conflicts of family life have been celebrated by novelists and playwrights throughout history. Shakespeare's *Hamlet* and *King Lear* are examples of dramas focusing on the dynamics and violence in family relationships. Freud, the founder of psychoanalysis, believed that the human personality was determined by crucial events in family life. He focused on conflicts between family members and also conflicts within the minds of individuals. Freud argued that we are born with basic instinctual and animalistic drives for sex and aggression and that these impulses are tamed within the family. One goal of the family, from his viewpoint, is to teach us to repress antisocial impulses and thus become human. More recent theorists have stressed the role of parents as models that children observe and imitate and thereby acquire social attitudes and behaviors.

Socialization

Your own family is special to you, and you can think of many ways in which they have influenced you. Because of your genes and your unique experiences, you are a unique person; there is no one else just like you. You may have inherited your mother's hair color or your father's build. But you received much more than physical characteristics from your parents. You learned to speak their language, you learned to

Parental Expectations

You have felt the weight of parental expectations, both spoken and unspoken. What did your parents expect of you? What kind of person did they expect you to be? You may or may not have been able to live up to their expectations, and their expectations may or may not have been realistic. Realistic or not, parental demands for conformity begin in infancy. Even before the child is born, parents may have hopes and expectations about what the child will be.

Often before the infant is born adults may have decided what sex the infant should be, and also have a number of other expectations that may or may not be congruous with or appropriate for the actual child who arrives.[11]

Parental expectations have persisting effects on the personality. Children internalize the expectations of their parents and make them their own. These expectations then live on, long after the parents are gone. You may be reading this page—a small part of your effort to be educated—in order to satisfy an expectation your parents have of your future. These expectations are communicated in a variety of different ways.

A Hopi Indian Child • Hopi parents expect their children to be peaceful and nonaggressive. An autobiography of a Hopi Indian gives an idea of how this cultural value is communicated to the young.

As soon as I was old enough to take advice, he (my grandfather) taught me that it was a disgrace to be called kahopi *(not Hopi, not peaceful). He said, "My grandson, old people are important. They know a lot and don't lie. Listen to them, obey your parents, work hard, treat everyone right. Then people will say, 'That boy Chucka is a good child. Let's be kind to him.' If you do these things you will live to be an old man yourself and pass away in sleep without pain. That is the trail that every good Hopi follows."*[12]

We learn in the family to be members of the human community through a process called socialization. Parents shape the behavior of their children through the use of rewards and punishments. In addition, children observe their parents and imitate them. (Bill Owens/Jeroboam Inc.)

use their manners, you learned to adopt their values and prejudices. Your parents actively prepared you to become a member of their culture, and you may or may not accept the invitation to join.

This process of learning how to be a member of the human community is called **socialization.** From earliest infancy children begin to learn how they are to act as they relate to others. These parent-child interactions can have great significance. Because of the dependence of children on their parents, emotional bonds develop that invest the parents with enormous powers of reward and punishment. Parents use these powers in enforcing their expectations through the use of discipline. For example, parents may reward children for their achievement with praise, love, or even money; withholding such rewards can be punishing.

The Hopi Indians place great significance on peace. The grandfather ensures the continuity of his culture by transferring his values and expectations to the coming generation.

The Case of the Teenage Thief • The following paragraph shows how a boy became what his mother expected of him.

A middle-class family's 15-year-old son stole a car. His mother told the psychiatrist that she had anticipated something of the kind ever since the boy had stolen, six years earlier, a pack of cigarettes. She had disciplined him at the time, but . . . she had never really expected her son to stop stealing. Instead, the mother classified him in her mind as a potential thief. . . . From then on, whenever anything was missing from the house she immediately questioned him about it. The boy soon realized that his mother expected him to steal.[13]

Parental expectations are experienced as pressure to conform to whatever standard of behavior is expected. When expectations are high, there is pressure to do better; when expectations are low, there is pressure to do worse.

Obedience and Achievement

A recent study of adolescents shows the influence of parental expectations.[14] Three groups of teen-agers were compared: those who were classified as independent, those who were dependent, and those who were rebellious. The study revealed that children in these different groups came from different types of families. The independent adolescents tended to grow up in homes where parents expected independent thinking, where rules were consistent and explanations for rules were freely given. The adolescents who were dependent tended to have another type of parents. Their mothers and fathers tended to expect respect for authority and absolute obedience above all. Rules in these homes were not made and enforced consist-

ently. The rebellious adolescent group had parents remarkably like those of the dependent adolescents. That is, the parents of the rebellious adolescents expected absolute obedience—but their children, rather than submitting, rebelled and failed to conform to this expectation. Think about your parents. Did they expect you to be independent, or did they expect you to submit to their absolute authority? Did you turn out to be independent, dependent, or rebellious?

Most parents, particularly those in a competitive society, expect their children to achieve success. The children eventually accept this expectation and make it their own. Psychologists have called this motive the **need for achievement.** You probably know people who have an unusually high need for achievement—they seem driven to succeed. This need for achievement is highly influenced by parental expectations. Mothers of boys with a high need for achievement tend to expect and encourage independence and accomplishment. Such mothers also expect achievement of their sons at an earlier age than mothers whose sons have a low need for achievement.[15] Your need for achievement and success probably reflects the expectations of your parents.

Discipline

Many parental expectations are imposed on children through the use of discipline. When children violate their parents' expectations, they are scolded; when they conform, they are praised. This is how parents teach their children to become acceptable members of their culture. Try to recall the last time you were punished as a child. What parental expectation did you violate? Is this an expectation that you now have of yourself?

The Law of Effect • Discipline is a powerful tool of socialization. Using it, parents, in effect, shape the behavior of the child through interactions involving rewards and punishments. Sometimes the rewards and punishments are obvious, such as giving candy or a spanking; more often less direct techniques are employed. The smiles or frowns of your parents, their praise or criticism, the raising of an eyebrow or a quick penetrating glance, the subtle sound of the voice—these have acquired powers of reward and punishment for you. The meaning of these subtle signs, and thereby their rewarding or punishing power, is learned in the family situation. The frown, infants learn, precedes the spanking; the smile, they eventually discover, precedes the caress or the candy. After a period of learning, the smile and frown themselves can reward or punish behavior.

Children's behavior occurs, not in isolation, but in a responsive system: the family unit. Occurring in this responsive system, children's behavior is typically followed by some kind of a reaction. The reaction or **feedback** has the effect of modifying the children's later behavior. Children adjust their behavior to make it adaptive to their family system. When a particular behavior is followed by rewarding feedback, children tend to repeat it; when a behavior is followed by punishing feedback, children under certain circumstances tend to abandon that behavior. The principle shown here is called the **Law of Effect:** acts followed by rewards tend to be repeated and acts followed by punishment tend to be abandoned.

Punishment • Patterns of discipline characterized by domination, rigidity, and excessive control through physical punishment typically produce children who are submissive, inhibited, and respectful to authority.[16] Punishment, however, often does not eliminate the behavior that is being punished. A study by Sears compared the childrearing practices of 379 suburban New England mothers in two different towns and assessed the consequences of parental punishments and rewards.

In our discussion of the training process we have contrasted punishment with reward. Both are techniques for changing the child's habitual ways of acting. Do they work equally well? The answer is unequivocally "no." . . .

Punitiveness, in contrast with rewardingness, was a quite ineffectual quality for a mother to inject into her child's training.

The evidence for this conclusion is overwhelming. . . . Mothers who punished toilet accidents severely ended up with bed-wetting children. Mothers who punished dependency to get rid of it had more dependent children than mothers who did not punish. Mothers who punished aggressive behavior severely had more aggressive children than mothers who punished lightly.[17]

But the Law of Effect states that behavior that is rewarded should increase in frequency, and behavior that is punished should be abandoned. In this case, however, the punishment of aggression caused aggressive acts to increase. Why would a child tend to repeat what he or she has been severely punished for? Sears explains:

Parents teach their children to become acceptable members of their culture by using rewards and punishments. Different patterns of discipline have lasting effects on the personality of the child. (Michael Weisbrot and Family)

Punishment [of aggression] seems to have complex effects. While undoubtedly it often stops a particular form of aggression, at least momentarily, it appears to generate more hostility in the child and lead to further aggressive outbursts at some other time or place. Furthermore, when the parents punish—particularly when they employ physical punishment—they are providing a living example of the use of aggression at the very moment they are trying to teach the child not to be aggressive. The child, who copies his parents in many ways, is likely to learn as much from this example of successful aggression on his parent's part as he is from the pain of punishment. Thus, the most peaceful home is one in which the mother believes aggression is not desirable . . . but who relies mainly on nonpunitive forms of control.[17]

The use of physical punishment can also have effects unrelated to the behavior punished. Harsh and arbitrary punishment has been shown to precede later prejudice[16] and also delinquency.[18] An important part of this problem is whether the strict discipline occurs within a context of rejection and hostility or whether it occurs within the context of acceptance and love.

Children Influence Parents

Parents shape the personality of their children and teach them to become members of their culture, but they are part of a relationship. Obviously, children are more than lumps of clay molded by their parents. Children can also influence their parents.[19] The family is an interacting system of relationships in which each member affects, and is affected by, other members.

The fact that troubled children tend to have troubled parents does not necessarily mean that the parents are at fault. It could be that troubled children are so hard to live with that their parents develop mixed attitudes of love and anger. Perhaps troubled children produce troubled parents, or, what is more likely, each influences the other.

The impact of children on parents begins before birth. Mothers may experience nausea, anxiety, or depression with pregnancy; and complications of pregnancy sometimes result from an abnormal fetus.[20] These experiences may shape the attitudes of mothers toward their infants. Different infants behave differently from birth; some are easier to care for than others because of their lower activity levels and their better reactions to being held. Mothers of infants that are easy to care for develop strong positive feelings toward their infants more often than mothers of infants that are difficult.[21] Thus, while parental behavior and attitudes may influence the personality and development of children, the personality of children likewise influences the behavior and attitudes of their parents.

Interim Summary   Parents actively prepare their children to be members of their culture; this process of learning is called socialization. Children internalize parental expectations and make them their own. Expectations for obedience and achievement are particularly strong in this culture. Most parents expect their children to be successful; the acceptance of this expectation results in children with a strong need for achievement. Parents differ in their expectations for obedience and in their patterns of discipline. Harsh and arbitrary punishment in childhood has been shown to precede a variety of adult personality problems. While parents influence their children in a variety of ways, it is also true that children influence their parents. The impact of children on parents begins before birth and continues throughout childhood.

Babies Without Families

Babies are helpless and must have their physical needs satisfied in order to live. They need caretaking, or **parenting,** by mothers, fathers, or both. But parenting is more than meeting basic physical needs—parenting is also holding, hugging, caressing, loving the infant. Remarkably enough, these other aspects of caring for children are also matters of life or death.

Infants who lack adequate loving, who suffer from **love deprivation,** may develop a condition called **marasmus.** Marasmus is a condition of increasing physical weakness, loss of appetite, and apathy.

Cases of Extreme Isolation

Anna was found in an attic room when she was six. She had skeleton-like legs and a bloated abdomen. She could not talk or walk and appeared as a wild animal, without human intelligence. Anna had lived her life without care and attention and with only enough food to be kept barely alive. She was removed from her mother's house by the authorities and placed in a county institution; no special treatment was provided her. Two years later she could walk and she had achieved the mental age of an infant of about one year old.[22]

Isabelle was discovered when she was six and a half years of age. Her mother was a deaf mute, and they had lived together since her birth in a dark room completely isolated from the rest of the mother's family. Isabelle acted like an infant; she was unable to relate to people or care for her own needs. She made only a strange croaking sound. She was given an IQ test and scored close to the zero point of the scale. The authorities removed her from her room and put her under the care of a psychologist and a speech specialist. Within two months she was using sentences; nine months later she began to read and write. By the time she was eight and a half she was intellectually and psychologically normal.[22]

These and similar cases show the terrible consequences when children are raised in extreme isolation, away from a normal human family.[23,24] Because they are deprived of human contact, these children do not learn to be human. Interaction with loving adults, usually in the context of a family, is necessary for healthy development. Sometimes, as in the case of Isabelle, the damage of early neglect can be undone; sometimes the damage is more permanent.

Love Deprivation

Orphans in institutions have no real families, and so orphanages have tried to provide loving care. Because of overcrowding and lack of money, some institutions are unable to provide more than the basic physical requirements for their children. Cases of gross neglect are fairly rare now, but conditions used to be much worse.

The Nursery and the Foundling Home • Some years ago, a scientist named Spitz studied infants in two institutions. The two places equally met the physical needs of their babies for food and warmth, but differed in the amount of emotional interchange offered.[25]

In one institution, the "Foundling Home," the infants were attended by overworked nursing personnel who had minimal contact with each child. In the other institution, the "Nursery," the children were cared for by their own mothers with much emotional interchange. Spitz was particularly interested in determining the effect of warm interactions between mother and infant, under conditions where other differences between infants might be small. He described the results.

While the children in "Nursery" developed into normal healthy toddlers, a two-year observation of "Foundling Home" showed that the emotionally starved children never learned to speak, to walk, to feed themselves. With one or two exceptions in a total of 91 children, those who survived were human wrecks.[25]

The infants cared for by their own mothers developed normally. On the other hand, the unloved infants failed to develop normally (inferior intelligence and motor ability). Among the unloved infants, about one child in three died during its first two years of life. Furthermore, the early experience of love deprivation for the infants in the "Foundling Home" affected their adult personalities. Those who survived grew up to be maladjusted and neurotic adults.[26]

The Case of Paul and His Mother • Fortunately most orphans in this country are now placed in foster homes as early as possible, where they usually receive the love and care they need to develop normally. It is important that such placement occur as soon as possible, because in the early years of childhood parenting is especially important. The case of Paul shows some of the effects of the lack of love.

Paul's parents were separated before his birth. As a small child, he scarcely had any contact with his father. . . . As for Paul's mother, she had always been a profoundly unhappy woman. Paul never knew a family life. He scarcely knew what being loved meant. . . . From the maternity ward of the hospital in which he was born, Paul went directly to a nursery, where he lived out his first four years of life. . . . The occasional night spent with his mother meant very little to Paul. She worked so late that when she did bring him home he was half asleep, and in the morning she deposited him again at the nursery before he was really awake. . . . When he was not yet six, his mother . . . placed him in an orphanage.[27]

Paul's mother, an extremely disturbed woman, was ridden by guilt for having neglected him, yet could not cope with the responsibility of functioning as his mother. Her confused feelings toward her son can be seen in the fact that she would plan grand birthday parties for him and then forget his birthday. Paul did not do well at the orphanage, becoming more

and more violent. During his last several months there, Paul—screaming that he wanted to die—made several suicide attempts. He was referred to the Orthogenic School for emotionally disturbed children.

When we met him, Paul was ten years old. The psychiatric examination that was given him when he entered the School did not so much reveal murderous and depressive phantasies—as might have been expected from his suicidal and homicidal attempts—as emptiness, great flatness and instability of emotion, inability to relate, extreme detachment, and markedly infantile behavior.[27]

After years of care in the controlled environment of the school for emotionally disturbed children, Paul was able to achieve a relatively good adjustment and was placed in a foster home.

Monkeys Without Mothers

The need for love is not unique to human children; infant monkeys need love, too. Infant monkeys are helpless and dependent at birth, as are human infants, and monkey mothers show much affection and care for their babies. The infants of monkeys and humans show about the same pattern of development—infant monkeys just mature more rapidly. The similarities of humans and monkeys make the study of monkeys relevant to the understanding of human behavior.

Mothers Made of Wire and Wood • Psychologist Harry Harlow raised monkeys both with and without mothers.[28] Harlow wanted to investigate the love bond between mother and infant in order to see the effects of love deprivation on adult behavior. Many scientists believed that a baby loves its mother because the mother feeds the infant; according to this view, the rewarding effects of being fed result in the infant's positive reactions to the mother. Harlow, however, suspected that the stimulation of warmth and holding was responsible for the development of the love bond. He tested this idea by building a **surrogate**

mother, an artificial "mother" made of wire and cloth.

We had . . . discovered . . . that a baby monkey raised on a bare wire-mesh cage floor survives with difficulty, if at all, during the first five days of life. If a wire-mesh cone is introduced, the baby does better; and, if the cone is covered with terry cloth, husky, healthy, happy babies evolve. It takes more than a baby and a box to make a normal monkey. . . .

We built a surrogate mother . . . from a block of wood, covered with sponge rubber, and sheathed in tan cotton terry cloth. A light bulb behind her radiated heat. The result was a mother, soft, warm, and tender, a mother with infi-nite patience, a mother available twenty-four hours a day, a mother that never scolded her infant and never struck or bit her baby in anger. . . . It is our opinion that we engineered a very superior monkey mother, although this position is not held universally by the monkey fathers.[29]

Harlow gave the infant monkeys a choice of two surrogate mothers: one was made of bare wire mesh but contained a bottle from which the infant received all its meals; the other, containing no bottle, was constructed of wire mesh covered with soft terry cloth. Harlow observed the infant monkeys to find which type of mother they preferred. He found that, except at meal times, the baby monkeys spent all their time clinging to the terry-cloth mother. The infant monkeys reacted to their terry-cloth surrogates very much as they would have reacted to their real mothers.

When the cloth mother was present . . . the babies rushed to her, climbed up, clung tightly to her, and rubbed their heads and faces against her body. . . .

During the last two years we have observed the behavior of two infants raised by their own mothers. Love for the real mother and love for the surrogate mother appear to be very similar. The baby macaque spends many hours a day clinging to its real mother. If away from the mother when frightened, it rushes to her and in her presence shows comfort and composure. As far as we can observe, the infant monkey's affection for the real mother is strong, but no stronger than that of the experimental monkey for the surrogate cloth mother, and the security that the infant gains from the presence of the real mother is no greater than the security it gains from a cloth surrogate.[29]

The Infant Monkeys Grow Up • The comfort offered by the soft surrogate mothers is sought by the infant monkeys, but the artificial cloth mothers are not an adequate replacement for real mothers. Motherless monkey infants tend to grow up to be aggressive and isolated; they often do not mate, or if females do mate, they are poor mothers. Sometimes

Harry Harlow investigated the love bond between mothers and infants by raising baby monkeys with artificial (surrogate) mothers of different types. (Harry Harlow, University of Wisconsin Primate Laboratory)

they are brutal and rejecting to their own infants.[30] They behave as if they do not know how to be a loving parent.   On the other hand, infant female monkeys raised by their own mothers develop normally and usually grow up to be mothers who love, protect, and care for their babies.

Substitute Families

The warmth and affection of parenting are important for the development of the healthy personality.   Love deprivation in the early years of infancy often has persisting effects on adult personality.   Can these effects be undone?   Can the emotional damage be repaired? Yes—to some extent, but it is not yet clear exactly what rehabilitation program works best.

Foster Homes • Institutionalized children who have suffered love deprivation make considerable gains when placed in foster homes.[31]   Thirty children who had experienced extreme love deprivation up to age two and one-half were placed in foster homes with special programs designed to make up for the lack of loving relationships that they had experienced.   Most of these children showed rapid growth and a healthy potential.[32]

Enrichment Programs • If foster parents are not available, special enrichment programs may be helpful.[33]   In one early study a psychologist transferred a group of orphan babies diagnosed as mentally retarded from their own overcrowded institution to a nearby institution for retarded older girls.   The brighter girls were selected to care for the infants.   During a two-year period the orphans cared for by the retarded girls experienced an average gain in IQ of over twenty-five points, while a similar group of infants left in the orphanage experienced a drop of over twenty-five points in IQ.[34]   What became of the orphan babies? Thirty years later they were located as adults.   All the infants cared for by the retarded girls were found to be normal adults, while most of those left in the orphanage were still institutionalized as mentally retarded.

Even small amounts of loving in infancy may have long-lasting positive effects on the development of personality.   One psychologist selected twelve six-month-old babies from an institution and provided extra loving to half of them each day for a period of eight weeks.[35]   The six babies she did not visit were cared for normally by the institutional staff.   At the end of the experimental eight-week period, the psychologist measured how all twelve babies responded to people, using a series of specially designed behavioral tests.   For example, in one test a baby received a high score for "social responsiveness" if it smiled when the experimenter stood by its crib.   The social responsiveness score was high when a baby reacted positively to people.   The responsiveness of the twelve babies to strangers was also tested.   The psychologist found that the experimental babies who were given extra loving were more responsive, both to the experimenter and to strangers.

You might wonder about the six "control" babies who did not receive the extra attention.   Were they treated fairly?   In order to find out whether this kind of "short-term loving" was beneficial, a comparison had to be made between some infants who got it and some who did not.   Because it was discovered that short-term loving was effective, programs are now being designed to provide this kind of care to all institutionalized children.   Effective enrichment programs, however, are only short-term solutions, designed to fix the problems that result from troubled families.

Interim Summary   Babies are helpless.   To survive they must have someone provide for their physical needs, but they also must receive love.   Infants suffering from love deprivation may develop marasmus, a condition of extreme weakness.   The need for parental love was studied in monkeys by Harry Harlow. He provided motherless infant monkeys with a wire and cloth surrogate, then observed the effect on them as adults. He found that the motherless monkeys grew up to be aggressive and poor parents. Studies show that foster homes and certain enrichment programs can reverse the bad effects of love deprivation.

Family Types

Each family is different, because the family is a system composed of unique individuals. But similar families can be grouped together for the purpose of study and description. In this way we can talk about family types.

Nuclear, Extended, and One-Parent Families

In different cultures and societies around the world, the pattern of family grouping varies. But almost everywhere, the basic unit is the **nuclear family**—two adults of opposite sex, living in some socially approved relationship with their children. How universal is the nuclear family? Some researchers have argued that the Nayar people, a caste in southern India, represent an exception to the rule. Nayar households consist not of husbands and wives and their children, but of brothers and sisters and the children of the sisters and their daughters. Husbands and wives are completely separated. The recent trend among the Nayar, however, is to establish nuclear family residences and abandon the older tradition.

Most people, at different times in their lives, are members of two different nuclear families. They are born into one family, joining their parents, and this one is termed the **family of orientation**. When they are grown, they typically leave, marry, and create their own nuclear family; this one is termed the **family of procreation.**

Sometimes the family of orientation and the family of procreation live together, forming what is called the **extended family.** An extended family consists of a married couple with their children, together with the parents of the husband or the wife. In extended families, three generations live under the same roof. The nuclear family is one unit in the extended family.

Some nuclear families are incomplete, with the father or the mother not present. The **one-parent family,** consisting of children living with a single parent, is becoming much more common in this country than ever before. In 1976, about 20 percent of all children under eighteen were not living in an intact nuclear family. There are many reasons for the one-parent families: divorce, death, imprisonment, and separation are some of the causes, and never having been married is another. Since many single parents remarry, the one-parent family is often a temporary arrangement that evolves into an intact nuclear family. About one-third of all two-parent families are reconstituted, having experienced a period with only a single parent before remarriage. Thus, a substantial proportion of children (almost half) either are now in a one-parent home or have recently experienced such a condition.

Many studies have been conducted to examine the effect of marital separation and divorce on children. There is no doubt that the tension and stresses generally occurring at such times negatively affect the children. One study found that divorce disrupted children's lives and influenced their behavior for one to two years following the separation.[36] Family habits, discipline, and organization tended to be inconsistent and chaotic after the divorce, but the breakdown in the family appeared to last only a year or two in most cases. During this period of disturbed family life, the children were found to be more upset, defiant, and negative.

A difficulty in studying the long-term effects of divorce is the problem of separating the possible effects of the divorce itself from the effect of the family fighting and conflicts that so frequently accompany divorce. In general, studies that have carefully examined one-parent families and intact nuclear families have found that conflict—but not divorce itself—is harmful to children's self-concept and to their social and personality development. Parental separation and the family structure itself (one-parent or two-parent family) have been found to have no harmful effect on children.[37] One study examined adolescents from several different types of families and found no systematic differences in personality traits, grades, or school attitudes.[38] There appeared to be no significant differences among the children of families with both mothers and fathers present, of mother-only families, and of mother-and-stepfather families.

Typical Families

From birth until death we seek love, for not to be loved is to be separate and alone. For most people love is provided within the living environment of a family. The family serves the important functions of overcoming separateness and fostering strength and growth.

Love begins in the family when we are infants. The experience of unconditional acceptance, warmth, caressing, food, and security provides an environment of trust within which the personality can grow. As one author put it:

When the baby is genuinely loved and given much-needed, warm, reassuring mothering, with consideration for his helpless dependency and also his individuality, he begins to develop an image of the self, with feelings and expectations toward the world, that evokes his many capacities and latent potentialities. This prepares him for the experience of being transformed into a personality, the core of which is the image of the self that becomes symbolically expressed as I, me, my and mine.[39]

In other words, when babies are genuinely loved by their family, their identity begins developing and they are given the freedom to grow.

Most families have their good and bad times, but to the developing child what seems to matter is the predominant pattern. Even though a family may have occasional problems, an overall pattern of love will foster the development of the growing personality of the child. In these typical families the pattern of relationships with the children is characterized by several positive features:

1. Love, affection, and warmth
2. Attention and interest
3. Unconditional acceptance of the child as an individual
4. Stability and reliability
5. The encouragement of independence
6. Clear parental expectations
7. Validation—acceptance of the experiences and feelings of the child
8. Consistent discipline within a context of love

The families of outstandingly successful persons have been studied in search of the origins of health. One psychologist studied the childhood histories of twenty eminent geniuses. He hoped to find a consistent pattern of experiences to help explain their intellectual achievements.[40] He concluded that most of the twenty had received in early childhood a large amount of loving and intellectually stimulating attention from their fathers and mothers. Families that are loving and democratic not only have children who are brighter than families that are cold and autocratic, but also tend to have children whose IQs *increase* while in school rather than decrease.[41]

Attention and interest also affect a child's feelings of worth. A study of adolescents showed that parents who are relatively indifferent toward their children tend to have children with low self-esteem, while parents who are relatively interested in their children tend to have children with high self-esteem.[42] The self-esteem of the child is affected much more by the interest and attitudes of the parents than by the social position or income of the family, the physical attractiveness of the child, or the child's ability in academics or sports.[43]

In other parts of the world parents interact with their children differently from the ways typical to American society. Studying families in other cultures sometimes shows the consequences of different family patterns. In a comparison of forty-eight other societies, it was found that the frequency of theft by adults was low when the cultural pattern for child rearing included a high level of parental indulgence and affection.[44] Similar effects have been found for individuals within our culture. Those parents who show affectionate warmth toward their children have children with a lower incidence of juvenile delinquency.[18] Interest and affectionate warmth in the home are important for the growing personality.

Disturbed Families

Some families have an emotional climate of rejection and hostility and are centered around unhappy parents. Such disturbed families may be unable to provide the love and stability generally needed for the normal development of a child's personality. Disturbed families are more likely to produce children who are unhappy, troubled, or disturbed.

One or both parents in some disturbed families are victims of alcoholism, a disorder that greatly disrupts family life. Some parents are involved in constant verbal and physical fights, which is frightening and confusing to children. Other parents, because of their own personal problems, or through lack of understanding, are unable to establish and maintain affectionate and supportive relationships with their children. In disturbed families, the pattern of relationships with children is characterized by several negative features:

1. Rejection and hostility
2. Lack of interest in the child's accomplishments
3. Conditional acceptance; parental acceptance must be "earned"
4. Instability and unreliability
5. Domination, overprotection, or indifference
6. Confused communications; mixed signals
7. Invalidation—rejection of the child's experiences and feelings
8. Inconsistent or harsh and arbitrary discipline

The children of disturbed families typically have more psychological problems than the children of loving families. Children who are runaways, have drug problems, have behavior problems at school, have emotional problems or have serious social problems are more likely to come from families with disturbed patterns of interaction.

The most common type of severe mental disturbance is **schizophrenia.** Schizophrenics withdraw from reality into a world of their own and often show bizarre thought processes and perceptual disturbances. It has been found that children and adults suffering from schizophrenia often were raised in disturbed families. They tend to come from homes with emotional climates that differ in specific ways from the homes of healthy individuals. In some cases one parent dominated the family, and the other parent withdrew completely. One study showed that male schizophrenics, as compared with normal males, more often had a weak father and a strong, dominant mother. These women rejected their sons but encouraged their dependency, a combination of attitudes that put the sons in a **double-bind** with no way to please their mothers.[45] The sons were given a double message: come close but stay away. They could not do both.

The Son of Mr. Lamb—A Case Study • The parents of some schizophrenics compete for the affection of the child; the mother wants all of the child's love, but so does the father. These parents may also use inconsistent discipline, giving the child two conflicting sets of expectancies and standards.[46] Here is an account of the family history of one such schizophrenic patient.

Mr. Lamb (the father of the patient) was a very successful businessman but a most inadequate parent. As a young adult he had been an outstanding athlete but had to leave his school for disciplinary reasons. . . . From the time of the son's conception on, he made every possible effort to retain all of his wife's attention and affection, and to keep her away from his son, who later was our patient. . . . Instead of standing up to the father and objecting to his behavior, she tended to look at times to the son for emotional support that the husband could not give her. Moreover, she encouraged the talented son to fulfill her own artistic tendencies. These were entirely lost on her husband, who openly criticized the son as effeminate, weak, and unathletic, after having thwarted the son's earlier efforts to be physically active by sneering at the child's performance in games or sports.[47]

In the Lamb family all the relationships among the family members were disturbed. The relationship of the parents was not one of confidence and love. The father was jealous of the child and was hostile and rejecting toward him, while the mother turned away from the father to seek a close relationship with the son. In turning toward the son for the love she could not find with the father, the mother in a sense was relying on the son to be the lover that her husband never was. The son could not meet the demands made by his disturbed family; he became schizophrenic.

Only autistic withdrawal seemed open to him. To live up to his father's "expectations," he had to be weak and passive in one sense, and an athlete in another; to please his mother he had to be artistic; but to assume a male role in any area carried the threat of incestuous closeness to his mother and indeed constituted a threat to his father's shaky masculinity.[47]

An unhappy family life, however, does not doom a child to be schizophrenic. Most children are remarkably resilient and able to endure great hardships without lasting harm. Many children of disturbed families receive psychological help in coping with their difficulties, but even those who receive no help are often able to work out their relationships with their families. Disturbed families contribute to the psychological problems of children, but not all children from disturbed families are themselves disturbed.

Interim Summary   The basic unit of most societies is the nuclear family—two adults of opposite sex living in some socially approved relationship with their children. The family of your parents is called your family of orientation. When you marry and have children, the family you start is called your family of procreation. An extended family consists of the family of orientation and the family of procreation living together. Families do not need two parents in order to have normal children. Studies show that the children of one-parent families are not substantially different from the children of two-parent families. Disturbed families display an emotional climate of hostility and rejection, while typical, more loving families show caring, attention, and acceptance. The children of disturbed families are more likely to be disturbed and troubled than the children of the typical families.

Can the Family Survive?

The family is the basic social unit of society, but the American family is in trouble. The signs of trouble have been widely publicized. The divorce rate is increasing; now about one out of every three marriages ends in divorce. Increasing numbers of young people express the determination never to get married. Family conflict is increasing: runaway teenagers, child beating, and even murder are becoming more common occurrences in American families.

The traditional family structure has been changed by the changing roles of men and women in family life. Women used to do a great deal of menial work in the home, serving the men and children; now women want the same choices as men. A large proportion of women work but find that their families still expect them to play the role of "homemaker" full time, an impossible job. Family structure has been changed by families moving from place to place. Families used to settle and remain close to grandparents and other relatives, but the new mobile family leaves relatives behind.

Family structure has been weakened because the traditional functions of the family unit have been taken over by other social agencies. The education of children is increasingly done by schools. Child care is being taken over by child-care centers. Welfare and security needs are increasingly met by government. Families used to serve many important purposes, but these purposes are diminishing. Do you think the family unit can survive these changes?

Anthropologist Margaret Mead was optimistic. She had studied families in different cultures all over the world and was convinced that the family will survive. She wrote:

As more and more women go to work, either for personal satisfaction or to add to the family income, the traditional family structure has to change to accommodate itself to the new conditions. Many families, like the one shown here, are adjusting schedules and roles, and seem to be managing quite nicely. (© Bruce Roberts 1975 / Rapho-Photo Researchers)

If we go back into history we find over and over again, in moments of revolutionary change, that people start talking about the family, and what they're doing to it, and what's wrong with it. They even predict it's going to disappear altogether. It is in fact the only institution we have that doesn't have a hope of disappearing.[48]

Summary

1. Genetics is the study of inherited characteristics, and behavioral genetics is the study of the inheritance of behavior.
2. Animals inherit complex, species-specific behavior patterns called instincts, such as

the spider's ability to build a web or a bee's tendency to build a hive and store honey.

3. The inheritance of behavior results from chromosomes within the nucleus of each cell of the body. Chromosomes consist of genes and genes consist of DNA. Identical twins have identical chromosomes.

4. Research methods in behavioral genetics include family history studies, selective breeding, and twin studies. The family history method involves examining the degree to which different members of families are similar in their personality or behavior. The selective breeding method involves mating animals that show a desired trait in an attempt to produce different strains of animals which consistently show that trait. Twin studies involve comparing fraternal and identical twins in order to determine their similarity.

5. Parental expectations have persisting influence on the personality of children. Children internalize these expectations and make them their own. For example, parents expect their children to be successful, and the children, influenced by this expectation, develop a need for achievement.

6. Parental discipline influences children in more than one way. In addition to affecting the behavior that is punished, the personality of the child is also influenced. Harsh and arbitrary punishment is associated with later prejudice, delinquency, and other problems.

7. Children are powerful influences on their parents. Even before birth, children begin to affect the behavior and feelings of their parents.

8. Infants who suffer from love deprivation may develop a condition called marasmus, involving physical weakness, loss of appetite, and apathy. Infants deprived of love may grow up to have severe psychological problems or may not survive at all.

9. Harry Harlow studied motherless monkeys and found that they grew to be aggressive and inadequate parents.

10. Three types of families are the nuclear family, the extended family, and the one-parent family. The nuclear family consists of two adults of opposite sex living in some socially approved relationship with their children. The one-parent family is an incomplete nuclear family. The extended family consists of a married couple and their children living with the parents of the husband or wife.

11. Two types of nuclear families are the family of orientation (the family you grew up with) and the family of procreation (the family you form when you marry).

12. Although divorce causes some short-term problems in children, there are no substantial long-term effects resulting from the separation itself.

13. The typical family, though experiencing occasional problems, has a pattern of positive relationships characterized by love, attention, validation, and other features favorable to the growth and development of the child.

14. Disturbed families, though experiencing occasional good times, have a pattern of negative relationships characterized by rejection, hostility, instability, and other features that interfere with the growth and development of the child.

Key Concepts

nature-nurture issue   The debate about the relative effects of heredity and learning in determining human behavior.

tabula rasa   A "blank slate," or empty mind; according to Locke, the state of the mind before any outside impressions.

innate ideas   Ideas, concepts, or ways of perceiving the world that are inborn or present at birth.

genetics   The study of inherited characteristics.

behavioral genetics   The study of the inheritance of behavior.

instinct   A complex, unlearned behavior sequence, such as nest building in some birds.

species-specific behavior   A behavior pattern that is characteristic of a species and distinguishes it from other species; for example, in a bird species, the inborn tendency to build a particular type of nest; an instinct.

chromosome   A rodlike structure within the nucleus of each cell in the body that carries hereditary information.

genes   The basic units of genetic information found on chromosomes.

DNA   The complex molecule that makes up the genes.

identical twins   Twins resulting from a single fertilized egg, each having exactly the same genes; they are therefore always of the same sex and of very similar physical appearance.

fraternal twins   Twins resulting from two eggs being fertilized by two sperm cells at about the same time; their genetic structure is no more similar than that of other siblings.

X and Y chromosomes   Chromosomes determining sex; an XX pair is female and an XY pair is male.

family history studies   A research method consisting of examining the resemblance on particular traits among family members.

selective breeding   A procedure for strengthening a trait in a population by mating only those animals from each generation which show the trait in the extreme.

twin studies   A research method consisting of comparing fraternal and identical twins on particular traits; greater resemblance among identical twins is viewed as evidence that the trait is hereditary.

socialization   The process by which children are shaped to become members of their culture.

need for achievement   The motivation to succeed or win.

feedback   Knowledge of results; knowing whether an action was or was not successful.

Law of Effect   The principle that actions with favorable consequences tend to be repeated, while actions with unfavorable consequences tend to be abandoned; for example, an action followed by reward is more likely to recur than an action followed by punishment.

parenting   Taking care of children; serving as a caretaker.

love deprivation   For children, the condition of experiencing inadequate love.

marasmus   A condition of extreme weakness, loss of appetite, and apathy found in infants experiencing prolonged love deprivation.

surrogate mother   A fake or artificial mother; for example, in Harlow's work, a "mother" made of wire and wood.

nuclear family   A social grouping consisting of two adults of opposite sex, living in some socially approved relationship with their children; usually a married couple and their children.

family of orientation   The family consisting of you, your parents, and your siblings.

family of procreation   The family consisting of you, your spouse, and your children.

extended family   A social grouping consisting of a married couple with their children living with the parents of either the husband or the wife.

one-parent family   Children living with a single parent.

schizophrenia   The most common type of severe mental disturbance; characterized by disturbances in thought processes, perceptions, and communication.

double-bind   A condition in which two opposing attitudes have been communicated; a double message, such as, "I love you" and also "I hate you."

Chapter 11
Childhood

Key Questions

1. What is the relation of maturation and learning?
2. What is unique about the mind of a child?
3. How can the growth of personality be described?
4. How does our sense of morality develop?

Four-year-old Billy invented a new game to play with his baby brother. When the baby was sitting on the floor playing with his blue rattle, Billy walked up and made some funny noises—"woogie, woogie, woogie." The baby looked up. Billy leaned down and quickly covered the rattle with his handkerchief. Then the baby looked down but didn't search for the hidden rattle at all. It was as if, in those few seconds of distraction, he forgot all about it. After a minute or two, Billy went over and slowly pulled the rattle out from under the handkerchief. The baby was delighted, waved his hands in the air, and made little gurgling noises.

A few weeks later the game didn't work at all. When Billy covered the rattle with the handkerchief, the baby just reached under the handkerchief, grasped the rattle, and pulled it out. Billy just couldn't understand how his brother had changed so quickly.

Psychologists studying infants and young children have made remarkable discoveries about the world of childhood—including discoveries that provide insight into Billy's game with his brother. During the first several months of life, babies like Billy's

brother seem to believe that objects cease to exist when they are hidden. As they grow a few months older, infants understand that objects exist whether they can see them or not. This is but one of the many ways that infants change during the first year of life.

Many studies have examined how children change with age. Some of these studies have focused on the rapid growth of intelligence during the first few months of life. Other studies have focused on the common challenges faced by children at different stages of growth. This chapter is concerned with these studies and others exploring the psychology of child development. It discusses what psychologists have learned about the physical, mental, personality, and moral development occurring during childhood.

In *Paradise Lost*, John Milton wrote, "The childhood shows the man, as morning shows the day." Patterns established in childhood show up in adult behavior. Understanding the world of childhood is an important step in understanding yourself. By tracing your journey from infancy, you can better understand where you came from, where you are now, and perhaps where you are going.

Physical Development

Human infants are truly remarkable. Although newborns typically sleep about twenty hours a day, they can be quite active. They cry, suck, cough, spit, sneeze, burp, turn away, and move their arms, legs, and fingers; they react to light, sound, touch, smell, and taste. Some of the actions of infants are auto-

matic and are responses to specific stimuli. For example, the **rooting reflex** occurs in response to the infants' cheek being touched; if a finger or nipple touches their cheek, they will turn and try to contact the object with their mouth. This simple inborn reaction is soon modified by learning; the infant rapidly becomes better and better at locating the nipple.

As children grow older, they become capable of

more and more complex behavior. These changes result both from learning and from maturation. The term **learning** refers to changes in behavior or potential that result from experience; the term **maturation** refers to developmental changes that are relatively independent of experience. Maturation is a genetically programmed growth process in which muscles, bones, and nerves become increasingly mature. Walking seems to depend very little on learning or practice. Children walk, on the average, by about twelve to fourteen months whether or not they have been trained in the art of walking; walking follows a schedule based on maturation rather than learning. Individual differences in the age of walking depend primarily on individual differences in maturation. (See Figure 11-1.)

Although children from different cultures have widely different early experiences, most begin to walk at about the same age. The Hopi Indians restricted their infants' movements by tying them to cradle boards until about nine months of age. A study compared two groups of Hopi Indian infants—one group was confined to cradleboards and the other was not.[1] Cradleboards prevent babies from moving their bodies. Although the infants of one group spent much more time moving about, both groups walked at the same age. Apparently the age of walking depended more on the level of maturation than on practice.

Learning many motor skills is possible only after an appropriate level of maturation is reached. The ability to type or ride a bicycle depends upon delicate muscular coordination not available to infants. Con-

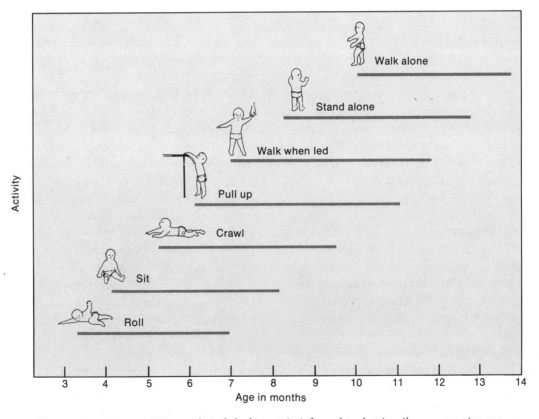

Figure 11-1 Motor Skills. *Physical development in infancy depends primarily on maturation, not learning. As the infant's bones, muscles, and nerves mature, different physical skills become possible.*

trol of bladder or bowels requires the maturation of muscles and nerves to a level typically reached only in the second year of life; before this level of maturation is reached, toilet training will be unsuccessful.

To study the effect of learning and maturation on the development of a simple skill, a psychologist observed two groups of young children, two to three years of age.[2] One group was allowed to practice climbing a small ladder each day for twelve weeks. These toddlers slowly got better and better at the task until at the end they were able to climb it well. The second group of children had no opportunity to climb the ladder until the first group had finished their twelve-week practice period; then the second group was allowed to practice. Rather than taking them twelve weeks to master the task, it took them only one week. Less practice was required because they had reached a more advanced stage of maturation.

Interim Summary   At birth infants are already capable of a wide range of behavior. Some skills, however, require a later stage of maturation before they can be mastered. For example, the age of walking is primarily dependent upon physical maturation and is little influenced by practice.

Cognitive Development

While your body matured and your skills increased with age, your intelligence and knowledge also increased. The word **cognition** refers to such activities as thinking, perceiving, knowing, and understanding. The study of **cognitive development** is the study of how these activities change with age; it is the study of the growth of the mind.

Perceptual Development

What did the world look, sound, and feel like when you were young? What kind of world does an infant perceive? The senses of the infant are working from birth, or in some cases, even before birth. For example, there is evidence that the fetus in the womb can hear and can respond to touch, temperature, and pain.

The visual world of the infant is different from the visual world of the adult. At birth, the infants' ability to discriminate fine lines or points is rather poor; even if they knew how to read, their vision is not well enough developed at birth to see the differ-ence between the letters. They also have difficulty adjusting the focus of their eyes to see things at different distances; the eyes of infants are like fixed-focus cameras set at about eight inches, so that things closer or farther are out of focus.

Depth perception is the awareness of the distance between yourself and objects in the world; it is the ability to see things in three dimensions. There has been a long debate in the history of philosophy and science on the question of whether depth perception is innate or learned. If depth perception is innate, then infants at birth can see things in three dimensions. But infants can't talk, so how could you ever find out how they see the world?

One way of studying depth perception in infants is by using an apparatus called the **visual cliff**. This consists of a large sheet of very heavy glass suspended a foot or two above the floor, to form a kind of table. A checkered cloth is attached to the undersurface of half of the glass; under the other half of the glass the material is placed on the floor below. An infant is placed in the middle of the glass. To one side the glass appears solid; to the other side it appears to drop off, like a cliff. Infants old enough to crawl (six

The visual cliff apparatus is used to study depth perception in infants. A large sheet of heavy glass covers a checkered surface at two different depths. Infants old enough to crawl typically show that they can discriminate the depth of objects by refusing to crawl on the glass over the deep part of the apparatus. (University of Denver)

months) tend to be willing to crawl across the "shallow" side but not the "deep" side of the glass; apparently, by this age infants are able to see in depth.[3] A follow-up study showed that infants respond to depth even before they are able to crawl. Infants that were fifty-five days old were placed on either the shallow or the deep side of the visual cliff.[4] Their heart rates were monitored and it was found that there was a significant difference in the heart rate on the two sides. This evidence shows that human infants can see things in three dimensions at a very early age. Depth perception is either innate or it is learned within the first few months of life.

Language Development

Have you tried to learn a foreign language? For some of us this is a painfully difficult task. How easy it would be if you were born with the ability to speak and comprehend the language, rather than having to spend time in painstaking study. Yet, remarkably enough, there is evidence that you were born with such an ability.

The general sequence of language development appears to be universal, as if reflecting a genetic program that is unfolding. Although different children proceed through these stages at different rates, all seem to follow the same order in moving from stage to stage.[5] The first stage begins with the birth cry of the newborn; for the next three weeks or so the infant is limited to variations on this basic cry. From about three weeks to about five months of age, in the second stage, the infant begins making vowel-like sounds, often through a partly open mouth. These sounds appear to indicate comfort or pleasure. In the third stage, during the last half of the first year, the infant begins "babbling," a continual stream of articulated vowel-like sounds. These sounds appear to be independent of what the infant hears, since they are very similar across cultures with different languages. By the end of the first year, in stage four, the beginnings of patterned speech are heard as the infant begins to use single words meaningfully. Initially, these words may simply accompany actions ("bye-bye"); later, they may involve commands ("Cookie!"). Finally, at around two years of age, in stage five, the infant begins to use two-word phrases and sentences. These two-word sentences are not simply random pairings of words; they are put together according to certain rules; that is, they follow a grammar. **Grammar** is a term referring to the rules that people follow when they construct sentences.

As the child grows older, longer and more complex sentences are constructed. An interesting paradox is that children are able to construct grammatical sentences that they have never heard before; they are able to create correct new sentences that they could not possibly have learned by imitation. This fact suggests that a basic competence in language is inborn.[6]

Jean Piaget

Intellectual Development

How does intelligence grow? The author A. A. Milne, who wrote the delightful children's book *Winnie the Pooh,* gave a child's perspective on this question in *Now We Are Six.*

> When I was One,
> I had just begun.
>
> When I was Two,
> I was nearly new.
>
> When I was Three,
> I was hardly Me.
>
> When I was Four,
> I was not much more.
>
> When I was Five,
> I was just alive.
>
> But now I am six, I'm as
>   clever as clever.
> So I think I'll be six now
>   for ever and ever.[7]

According to some psychologists, you were very clever indeed by the age of six; they find that six-

year-olds have attained about two-thirds of the adult level of intelligence.[8] Other psychologists would argue that it is not so much a matter of *how much* intelligence is acquired, but rather of *what kind.*

The late Swiss psychologist Jean Piaget was the best-known child psychologist in the world. He devoted his life to the careful study of the minds of children. According to Piaget, in each stage of development the quality of intelligence is somewhat different. Piaget's **theory of cognitive stages** states that intellectual development occurs through a sequence of stages, the order of which remains constant, although for different individuals, the rate of development may vary. (See Table 11-1.)

Piaget's Theory of Cognitive Stages

According to Piaget, children in the first stage of cognitive development, the **sensorimotor stage,** live in a world of sensation and motor movement. From birth until about age two, the life of the infant is dominated by sucking, sniffing, tasting, and moving arms and legs. During the early part of this stage, infants lack the concept of **object permanency;** as far as they are

Table 11-1 Piaget's Stages of Cognitive Development

Stage	Approximate Age	Description
1. Sensorimotor	0–2	World of sensation and motor movement; learns object permanency
2. Preoperational	2–7	Learns language, can represent things symbolically; is egocentric
3. Concrete operations	7–11	Achieves conservation; becomes capable of logical thought
4. Formal operations	11–up	Capable of abstract and hypothetical thinking

concerned, objects that are not perceived simply do not exist. If a ball rolls out of sight behind a chair, the ball, for the infant, ceases to exist. Later in this stage, the infant learns object permanency, so that objects are considered to continue to exist even though they may not currently be seen.

The **preoperational stage,** from about age two to seven, begins with the emergence of language; now children can represent objects by words. Children in this stage can think, but cannot think very abstractly. An important feature of this stage is the child's **egocentrism,** the tendency to see things only from his or her own point of view. Egocentrism does not mean "selfish," but refers instead to a limitation on perspective so that a child cannot see the world from someone else's point of view. For example, children in the

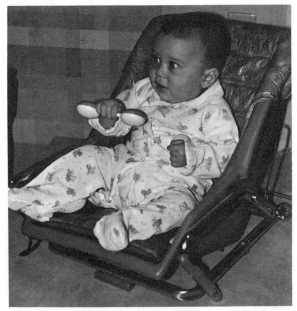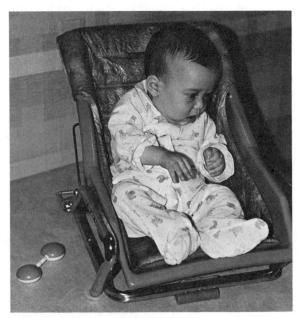

In the early part of the sensorimotor stage, it's "out of sight, out of mind." During the last part of the sensorimotor stage, infants will search for objects that drop out of sight; they have acquired the concept of object permanency. (John Young)

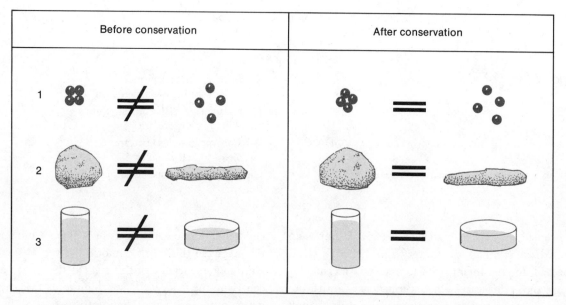

Figure 11-2 Conservation.   *Before infants acquire the concept of conservation, the quantity, mass, and volume of things are seen as changing with shape or appearance. For example, before conservation, the amount of clay is seen to change as its shape changes.*

preoperational stage may think that the sun follows them as they travel; from their point of view, the world revolves around them.

In the **concrete operations stage,** from about seven to eleven, children are able to think logically for the first time, but only about fairly concrete things. During this stage children develop the concept of **conservation**—the idea that things retain their general character even though their appearance may change. Before the concept of conservation is acquired, children believe that the number of things in a collection changes just because they are spread out; for example, before conservation, children believe there are more marbles if they are scattered than if they are in a pile. Before the concept of conservation is acquired, children believe that a ball of clay, when rolled

out in a snake, becomes more clay. After conservation, children believe that number, weight, mass, volume, and other properties of objects remain unchanged when the shape of the object is changed. (See Figure 11-2.)

In the **formal operations stage,** from about eleven on up, children acquire their adult level of intelligence. During this stage children become capable of abstract and hypothetical thinking. The child can design and conduct scientific experiments; hypothetical possibilities can be imagined and then systematically tested. In this stage the child develops the capacity to think about thinking, to examine and evaluate personal thoughts as well as thoughts of others. You have acquired these capacities for abstract thinking and are now in the formal operations stage.

Interim Summary   Babies have all their senses at birth, but their perceptual worlds are different from the perceptual world of an adult. They have less ability to focus their eyes at different distances and to see fine lines and points. We do not know whether they have depth perception at birth, but we do know, from studies using the visual cliff, that they have depth perception at two months of age.

It appears that language competence is inborn. The development of language follows a sequence of stages that is similar for people in different cultures. According to Piaget, intellectual development also follows a set sequence of stages for children everywhere. Children's view of reality and way of thinking are different in each stage.

Personality Development

Your **personality** is your unique way of reacting to the world and relating to the people around you; it is your psychological self. Although there is some evidence that personality characteristics can be influenced by heredity, for the most part you are who you learned to be. Your personality developed through a history of experiences with the world and with people. There are different views of how personality development can best be understood.

Freud's Psychoanalytic Theory

One of the most influential theories of child development is that developed by Sigmund Freud. According to Freud's **psychoanalytic theory,** behavior and development are strongly influenced by ideas, impulses, and memories that are unconscious. Even though we are not aware of them, they influence our attitudes and behavior.

Id, Ego, and Superego • The personality, Freud believed, consists of three basic structures: the id, the ego, and the superego. The **id** is a storehouse of unconscious impulses and memories. It is that part of the mind that, in a sense, always remains infantile, ignoring logic and seeking instant gratification. The **ego** deals with reality and strives to adjust behavior to achieve long-term satisfaction. The **superego,** or conscience, is the internalization of our parents' values and moral beliefs; the superego restrains us from violating a moral principle.

Freud believed that the personality is fixed or determined at an early age, as a consequence of certain crucial experiences. Social practices centering around food habits and cleanliness training are important learning experiences early in life. Freud considered these experiences to be significant in determining the adult personality.

Weaning • Weaning is the procedure for changing the infant from nursing to drinking and eating. The transition from dependence on sucking to the ability to drink or eat from a spoon can be a difficult period of adjustment both for the infant and the mother. There are wide cultural differences in how and when weaning occurs, but in this society it usually begins between six and ten months of age. In some societies weaning does not occur until the child is several years old.

Toilet Training • Another critical period in an infant's early life, according to Freud, is toilet training. This period involves one of the first major learning tasks for the child that requires performance (doing something).

Many parents attempt toilet training before the infant is capable of acquiring the necessary control. Such attempts lead to failure and frustration for both the infant and the parent. The average age at which a baby has the physical maturity to achieve good control over the bladder and bowels is about eighteen months. Toilet training is easiest and least frustrating when the child is about twenty months of age.[9] Yet American parents, with their drive for performance, typically attempt toilet training when the child is about eleven months of age, long before the average infant has the capacity for success.[9]

Oral and Anal Characters • Weaning plays an important role in Freud's psychoanalytic theory. Freud believed that sucking was more than a way to get food; it was a basic need and a source of sexual pleasure for the infant. The frustration of this need, according to Freud, led to an adult personality disturbance, a pattern of traits called the **oral character.** This pattern includes traits of excessive dependency, passivity, sarcasm, and pessimism. Furthermore, because the need to suck was frustrated and ungratified, adults having "oral characters" would be expectd to chew, smoke, and talk excessively in order to achieve oral compensation. While Freud's hypothesis is an intriguing one, the idea that early and severe weaning causes adult personality maladjustment has not been substantiated.

Freud believed that elimination, like sucking behavior, produced sexual gratification for the infant. He argued that the blocking or frustration of this need led to later personality disturbance, a pattern called the **anal character.** Freud described the anal character as consisting of traits of stinginess, stubbornness, compulsive cleanliness and punctuality, and extreme orderliness. If Freud were right about the origins of the anal character, we might expect these traits to characterize the "American personality," since we in this culture employ relatively harsh toilet-training practices.

Harsh toilet training has a variety of unpleasant consequences in the development of the personality.[10,11,12,13] Freud's hypothesis, that frustrations associated with toilet training will lead to the development of such "anal" traits as stinginess and excessive orderliness, has not, however, been substantiated. A review of research on this problem shows that the evidence does not generally support the Freudian position.[14]

It is clear, however, that the interactions of parents and infants are especially significant for the development of the personality, especially during certain periods in the early life of the infant. Infants with harsh weaning and with severe and early toilet-training experiences are more likely to become poorly adjusted adults. Infants with close and warm contact with their parents, with gradual and permissive weaning, and with bladder and bowel training attempted only when such control is easy and natural, tend to develop more healthy adult personalities.

Erikson's Psychosocial Theory

A second theory of personality development, Erikson's **psychosocial theory,** assumes that personality is shaped by the demands of the social world. Unlike Freud, who believed that the personality was fixed early in childhood, Erik Erikson believes that the personality continues to develop throughout life. Erikson identified eight stages of development, from birth to death.[15] These **psychosocial stages** describe the progressive development of a person's orientation to society. During each of the eight stages, individuals face a crisis in their relationship to the social world—a crisis that can be resolved either positively or negatively. If it is resolved positively, a new dimension of social interaction becomes possible. If the crisis is resolved negatively, progress to further stages will be slowed or blocked.

Four of Erikson's eight stages describe important developments during childhood and are discussed in the following paragraphs. The remaining four stages describe development during adolescence and adulthood and are discussed in the next chapter.

In the first stage—*Trust versus Mistrust* (age 0–1)—infants learn to trust other people if adequate care and loving are provided. If their needs are not met, they develop attitudes of suspicion and mistrust toward the world.

In the second stage—*Autonomy versus Doubt* (age 2–3)—infants begin to explore and manipulate their world and gain an increasing sense of independence (autonomy) and self-control. With overly critical or impatient parents, children develop an excessive doubt

Erik Erikson

about their abilities to control the world and themselves.

In the third stage—*Initiative versus Guilt* (age 4–5)—parents either support the self-initiated activities of their children by allowing them relative freedom to act and to think, or they inhibit their initiative by telling them that their activities are stupid, silly, or bad. With the former, the children gain a stronger sense of freedom and initiative; with the latter, they develop a sense of guilt over their activities.

In the fourth stage—*Industry versus Inferiority* (age 6–11)—children learn how to do things in the world and become concerned with how things are made and how they work. When children are encouraged in productive activities, their sense of competence is strengthened; when their efforts are discouraged, they develop a sense of inferiority. During these elementary school years the school contributes to the children's sense of competence or inferiority.

Social-Learning Theory

A third theory of personality development, the **social-learning theory,** assumes that personality is learned within the social environment. According to this theory your personality results from your experiences interacting with your environment and with other people. In other words, your personality consists of learned behavior patterns. Unlike psychoanalytic theory, social-learning theory does not focus on a few "crucial" early experiences but regards all experiences as significant. Furthermore, social-learning theory assumes that people continue to grow and to change throughout life. Unlike Erikson's psychosocial theory , social-learning theory rejects the notion of universal stages of personality development and stresses the wide range of individual differences.

The Inconsistent Woman • Social-learning theory rejects the idea that individuals have a set personality trait or character that is displayed in all situations. Instead, the pattern of your reaction will be different in different situations; that is, your behavior is situation-specific. How you act depends on the situation.

People act differently at different times and in different situations. In one situation a man may be aggressive, and in another he may be submissive and dependent. As one author wrote, a woman can be inconsistent; she can be

a hostile, fiercely independent, passive, dependent, feminine, aggressive, warm, castrating person all in one. Which of these she is at any particular moment would not be random and capricious; it would depend on . . . whom she is with, when, how, and much more. But each of these aspects of her self may be a quite genuine and real aspect of her total being.[16]

Imitating Models • The different ways that people have of reacting to the world are learned. Much of this learning results from watching other people and imitating them. Do you remember being told that you acted just like your father or that you were the image of your mother? Because you were closest to them as you grew up, you observed them and in many instances imitated what you saw.

In addition to imitating your parents, you also identified with them. The process of **identification** involves incorporating the values and attitudes of others as well as imitating their mannerisms and behavior. Boys are taught to identify with their fathers and girls with their mothers. Children learn from their parents of the same sex what is expected of them and how they are to act as males or females.

What is learned—that is, what is not biologically determined—is influenced by a particular culture. Sex-role learning appears early in childhood. Indications of masculine identification are present in boys as young as three.[17] The process of identification serves the function of transferring the values and behaviors of a culture from one generation to the next.

How does this process of identification work? As you grew up, you copied a parent, who served as your **model.** You learned by observation; you acquired new behaviors simply by watching your parents behave. Sometimes the act of imitating or copying the parent is itself rewarded by the parent, and the act of imitating may thereafter increase. Sometimes, however, a kind of secondhand reward system seems to be working; the child receives a kind of indirect reward by observing the parent receive a direct reward.

The more a child envies the status of another with respect to the control of a given resource, the more he will covertly practice that role. By covert practice we mean that he will indulge in phantasy in which he sees himself as the envied person, controlling and consuming the valued resources of which he has been deprived. It is the phantasy of being someone other than himself that we would like to define as identification.[18]

A boy observes a parent act and obtain rewards and the child indirectly enjoys the reward himself. A boy, in his fantasy, becomes his father, has competence, and is rewarded.

The Girl Who Limped • Children imitate the parent with whom they identify. The process can be seen in the following example. A psychologist visited a poor Puerto Rican family near San Juan to interview the mother about one of her several children.[19] One

There are several theories of personality development, and possibly all of them contain elements of truth. What does seem clear, however, is that children develop widely varying personalities but also have some characteristics in common across all cultures—such as the ability to play. (Cary Wolinsky/Stock, Boston)

child, a small three-year-old girl, remained quite close to the mother throughout the visit. The mother, a woman in her early thirties, walked with a slouch and a slight limp. She made a noise—a loud whispered "ooph"—whenever she had to bend over to pick up something from the floor. The little girl was perfectly healthy but also walked with a slouch and a limp, and each time she bent down she uttered a loud "ooph." The mother said to the psychologist, "I don't know what drives her to make that awful sound every time she bends down."

Interim Summary   According to Freud's psychoanalytic theory of personality, an individual's personality is fixed at an early age; weaning and toilet training experiences are of particular significance in personality development. According to Erikson, personality continues to develop throughout life and follows a sequence of stages; each stage describes the development of a person's orientation to society. According to social-learning theory, personality is learned, and results from interactions with other people and the environment. Observational learning and imitation of adults are the ways that children develop traits and habits similar to their parents.

Moral Development

What is moral behavior? How do we learn to do what is right? Although science cannot tell us what is moral, it can study morality and can observe the moral choices we make.

As the mind grows, our sense of morality grows, and many psychologists, including Piaget and Freud, have been interested in studying how our views of morality change with age. Brian was a dark-eyed and mischievious child. His conception of right and wrong was different when he was three than when he was nine. When he was three years old, Brian was observed hitting a cat with a stick. His mother punished him for this and told him that it was wrong. When Brian was nine he became extremely angry at his little sister for hitting the same cat. Why had Brian changed?

The Psychoanalytic Theory of Moral Development

One explanation of moral development was offered by Sigmund Freud. Freud's **psychoanalytic theory of moral development** assumes that moral behavior results from children identifying with their parents and incorporating their values and standards. As a girl identifies with her mother, she assimilates aspects of her mother's personality and ethical principles, and thus acquires a conscience, or superego. Boys identify with their fathers and thus develop a superego. The superego is the child's internalized set of parental standards and values.

According to Freud, the strength of a child's conscience depends upon the severity of the parents' discipline. Severe parents train their children to inhibit their impulses more completely, and this training, Freud believed, strengthens the superego. According to this theory, boys have stronger impulses than girls, are treated more harshly by their fathers, and therefore develop stronger superegos than girls.

In general, research has not supported the psychoanalytic theory of moral development. For example, severe and harsh parents tend to produce children who are *less* able to control their impulses and are more aggressive, instead of producing children with stronger superegos.[19] Furthermore, studies show that girls exhibit *more* self-control than boys—in contrast to Freud's prediction.[9]

The Social-Learning Theory of Moral Development

A second explanation of the growth of morality with age is the **social-learning theory of moral development**. This theory assumes that moral behavior, like all behavior, emerges from the interaction of the individual with the environment. These interactions have favorable or unfavorable consequences that shape future behavior. When a child does something that is valued and is regarded by the parents as right and good, the child is rewarded. When a child does something that the parents regard as bad or immoral, the child is scolded or punished. Thus the child learns to avoid punishment and to act in ways that are regarded as good or "nice." According to this theory, children also learn good from bad by observing and imitating their parents.

Direct rewards can teach children generosity, empathy, and altruism. Consistent with the social-learning theory, a number of studies have shown that generosity in children can be increased through reward. In one study, four-year-old children were given bubble-gum rewards for sharing their marbles with other children.[20] The results showed that sharing behavior increased significantly following the rewards. A second way that children acquire moral behavior is through imitating adult models. According to the social-learning theory, children observe adult behavior, then imitate it. In one experiment, third-grade and fifth-grade children observed an adult model donate half of a collection of marbles to poor children.[21] In a subsequent test, the children imitated the model whom they had observed. From this point of view, parental generosity and morality are the most important determinants of generosity and morality in children.

The Cognitive Theory of Moral Development

A third explanation of the changes in moral behavior with age is Kohlberg's **cognitive theory of moral development**. This theory, based on Piaget's more general theory of cognitive development, has stimulated a great deal of research not only in this country, but in many other countries around the world.

Kohlberg argues that moral development follows an invariant sequence consisting of six stages, each of which is characterized by a particular kind of moral reasoning.[22] The notion of "invariant sequence" means that the order in which a child moves through the six stages is fixed: Stage One is always

first, followed by Stage Two, and so on. Kohlberg also believes that the stages are universal; that is, that children everywhere, in all societies, experience the same stages and in the same order. Kohlberg's six stages of moral development are:

- *Stage One: The punishment-and-obedience orientation.* In this stage, children defer to their parents and are concerned primarily with physical consequences of acts and with avoiding trouble. Children focus on avoiding punishment.
- *Stage Two: The instrumental-relativist orientation.* In this stage, children are concerned with self-satisfaction. Children follow a rule only if they think it will bring them something good in return. What they regard as right and good is what satisfies their needs.
- *Stage Three: The "good boy-nice girl" orientation.* In this stage, children conform in order to obtain the approval of others. They focus on pleasing adults, on doing what older people want. Being well intentioned and not selfish are very important to children at this stage.
- *Stage Four: The law-and-order orientation.* In this stage, individuals follow rules in order to maintain the social order. The social stability of the larger group—the society as a whole—not just the stability of the neighborhood is what is valued. Respect for authority and doing your duty as a citizen are held to be important values at this stage.
- *Stage Five: The social-contract legalistic orientation.* In this stage, individuals regard right behavior as that which conforms to the general standards and values for individual rights that have been agreed on by the members of society as a whole. Since different points of view are recognized, an emphasis is placed on the procedures that are used to arrive at a consensus. The law is regarded as a set of principles reflecting what people generally believe to be good.
- *Stage Six: The universal-ethical-principle orientation.* In this stage, individuals follow personally chosen ethical principles because of their universality and

consistency.   An example would be the Golden Rule: Do unto others as you would have them do unto you.   A "wrong" act is regarded as one that is inconsistent with one's own personal ethical principles.

Kohlberg has been criticized for failing to define the stages of moral development with precision and for permitting his own personal point of view to bias his theory.   The kind of reasoning and behavior that constitute the highest morality depend upon your point of view.   Some do not agree with Kohlberg's definition of what should constitute "Stage Six." What do you think?

Interim Summary

Freud's psychoanalytic theory of moral development assumes that moral behavior results from children identifying with their parents and incorporating their values and standards.   This internalized set of parental values and standards becomes the conscience or superego.   Social-learning theory assumes that moral behavior results from the children's interaction with their environment.   This theory emphasizes the roles of punishment and rewards, and the imitation of adult role models.   Kohlberg's cognitive theory organizes moral development into a fixed succession of six stages that are believed to be universal.

Summary

1. The change in behavior potential with age results partly from learning and partly from maturation.   Walking and climbing stairs depend very little on practice; these abilities emerge when the infant achieves the necessary level of physical maturation.

2. The perceptual world of the infant is different from the perceptual world of the adult.   Babies are less able to focus their eyes and to see fine lines and points. Depth perception is either present at birth, or it develops by two months of age.

3. Language competence is inborn.   The development of language abilities follows a sequence of stages that is similar for people in other cultures speaking other languages.

4. According to Piaget, intellectual development also follows a set sequence of stages for children everywhere: the sensorimotor stage, the preoperational stage, the stage of concrete operations, and the stage of formal operations.

5. Freud's psychoanalytic theory of personality development assumes that behavior and development are strongly influenced by ideas, impulses, and memories that are unconscious.   According to this theory, personality is determined at an early age.

6. Freud believed that the personality consisted of three basic structures: the id, ego, and superego.

7. Erikson's psychosocial theory of personality development assumes that the personality continues to develop throughout life.   Erikson described eight stages that all individuals were believed to pass through.   During each stage, individuals confront and resolve a crisis in their relationship to the social world.

8. The social-learning theory of personality development assumes that personality results from experiences of interacting with other people and the environment.

Unlike the psychoanalytic and psychosocial theories, the social-learning theory rejects the notion of universal stages of personality development and stresses the wide range of individual differences.

9. The psychoanalytic theory of moral development assumes that moral behavior results from children identifying with their parents and incorporating their values and beliefs; in this way, children develop a superego, or conscience.

10. The social-learning theory of moral development assumes that moral behavior develops in the child because it is rewarded and because children imitate moral behavior in adults.

11. Kohlberg's cognitive theory of moral development assumes that all children progress through six stages as they grow older. Each stage is characterized by a particular kind of moral reasoning.

Key Concepts

rooting reflex   An automatic response of infants to being touched on the cheek; they turn toward the source of stimulation and try to take it into their mouths.

learning   Changes in behavior or potential that result from experience.

maturation   Developmental changes that are relatively independent of experience, but result instead from genetically programmed growth processes.

cognition   Mental activities such as thinking, perceiving, knowing, or understanding.

cognitive development   The changes that occur with age in cognitive activities.

depth perception   The ability to see in three dimensions; the awareness of the distance between yourself and objects.

visual cliff   An apparatus used for studying depth perception in infants; consists of a piece of heavy glass covering shallow and deep surfaces.

grammar   The rules that people follow when they construct sentences.

theory of cognitive stages   Piaget's theory that intellectual development proceeds through a succession of qualitatively different stages.

sensorimotor stage   The first of Piaget's cognitive stages, from birth until about age two.

preoperational stage   The second of Piaget's cognitive stages, lasting from two to seven.

concrete operations stage   The third of Piaget's cognitive stages, lasting from about seven to eleven.

formal operations stage   The fourth and last of Piaget's cognitive stages, beginning about eleven and continuing throughout adulthood.

object permanency   The concept that objects continue to exist even when they cannot be perceived.

egocentrism   The tendency to see things only from one's own point of view.

conservation   The idea that things retain their properties of weight, number, and volume, even though their surface appearance may change.

personality   A person's unique way of reacting to the world and relating to people.

psychoanalytic theory   Freud's theory of personality; according to this theory, personality is determined at an early age.

id   According to Freud, the storehouse of unconscious memories and impulses; a part of the mind that remains infantile, rejecting reason and morality and demanding instant gratification.

ego According to Freud, that part of the personality that deals with the demands of reality; unlike the id, it strives for long-term satisfaction and adjustment.

superego According to Freud, that part of the personality that determines right from wrong; the internalization of parental standards and values; the conscience.

oral character A personality pattern of excessive dependency, passivity, sarcasm, and pessimism.

anal character A personality pattern of stinginess, stubbornness, compulsive cleanliness and punctuality, and extreme orderliness.

psychosocial theory Erikson's theory of personality development that assumes that personality is shaped by the demands of the social world and continues to develop throughout life.

psychosocial stages Erikson's description of the eight stages of personality develop-

ment, beginning with birth and ending with death.

social-learning theory The theory that a person's pattern of behavior is learned and results from experiences with other people and the environment.

identification The process by which children observe and imitate adults and incorporate their values and beliefs.

model An observed and imitated person.

psychoanalytic theory of moral development Freud's theory that moral development results from the development of the superego, or conscience, through identification with the parents.

social-learning theory of moral development A theory that assumes that moral behavior results from rewards, punishments, and the imitation of parental models.

cognitive theory of moral development Kohlberg's theory that describes moral development in terms of a succession of stages that are believed to be universal.

Chapter 12

Adolescence and Adulthood

Key Questions

1. What are the stages of adulthood, and how are they studied?
2. What are the physical changes occurring in adolescence and adulthood?
3. What are the psychological changes occurring in adolescence and adulthood?
4. How can longevity be predicted and increased?

For much of our childhood we wait impatiently to be "grown up," to be a teenager or an adult. From the perspective of a child, being grown up means being free, independent, and without worry. But we know that it is not quite so simple as that.

What is your view of adulthood? Some high school students were asked when they thought they would be adults and what it meant to be an adult. These were some of their answers:

I'll be an adult when I'm living away from home and earning my own living. Adults are people who are responsible for themselves.

I feel like I'm already an adult. I make most of my own decisions and am not treated like a child. I live at home, *but so do some people who are 25 or 30.*

In some ways my parents still treat me like a child, but I feel that I am mentally and physically grown up and should be treated like an adult. I will probably get married next fall and my parents will still treat me like a child.

Being an adult means different things to different people. For some, adulthood starts with marriage and a job; for others, adulthood means having a driver's license, being able to vote, having sexual experience, living away from home, or being economically independent. There is no general agreement on what being an adult really means or on what age or event marks the end of childhood.

Adult Development

Although we will spend less than 20 percent of our lifetimes as a child, psychologists have devoted much more energy to the study of childhood than to the study of adolescence and adulthood. Freud's theories of development focused almost entirely on young children, and later psychologists showed the same bias in favor of the very young. In fact, only recently have psychologists begun to study seriously the developmental changes that occur in adolescence, adulthood, and old age. Perhaps this is because more and more of us are adults and are surviving to the ages of seventy, eighty, or beyond.

Studying Adult Development

Psychologists study adult development in two basic ways: the longitudinal method and the cross-sectional method. The **longitudinal method** involves the study of individuals as they grow older. For example, the psychologist may observe and test a group of individuals when they are twenty, thirty, and forty years old. This approach allows psychologists to note how similar an individual is at different times and also to note the changes that occur with age. A problem with this method is that it takes several decades to complete the study—you have to wait for the people to grow older.

A second method, the **cross-sectional method,** avoids this difficulty because the researcher does not have to wait.   This approach involves studying groups of people who are of different ages.   For example, a psychologist may study one group of twenty-year-olds, another group of thirty-year-olds, and a final group of forty-year-olds.   This approach allows the scientist to observe how people of different ages are alike or different.   A problem with this method is that the groups being compared may not be strictly comparable.   For example, the group of forty-year-olds were born twenty years before the group of twenty-year-olds and grew up at a different time in our culture.   Because of this problem, comparisons among such groups must be made cautiously.   But when different methods are used and similar conclusions are reached, confidence in the conclusion is stronger.   As a result of applying these and other research methods, psychologists have begun to learn a great deal about adolescence and adult life.

Theories of Adult Development

There is growing evidence that adulthood is not a single, unbroken journey, but instead occurs through a series of stages, with new choices and challenges presented at each stage.   As we live our lives as adults, we pass through these stages, one by one, changing and growing as we meet new problems along the way.   The stages of adult life have been conceptualized by Erik Erikson and, more recently, by life-span researchers Levinson and Gould.

Erikson's Psychosocial Stages • Erikson assumed that from birth to death we passed through a series of stages of psychological development.[1]   Unlike Freud, Erikson believed that we progress through stages of development even in adulthood.   At each stage we face an important developmental task and also confront what Erikson calls a **psychosocial crisis.**   A psychosocial crisis is the stress or tension produced by a set of demands that the social world places on the individual.   For example, in adolescence, we experience pressures to integrate various roles and put together a firm identity.   According to Erikson, the psychosocial crisis of adolescence is **identity versus role diffusion.**   We resolve the crisis positively by defining ourselves and achieving a sense of identity or resolve it negatively by experiencing a state of confusion called "role diffusion," in which we do not have a firm sense of who we are.   After adolescence, we pass through three additional stages of psychosocial development, according to Erikson.

In young adulthood, individuals experience the psychosocial crisis of **intimacy versus isolation.**   In this state the major tasks are typically centered around work, marriage, childbearing, and the establishment of a life-style.   During this stage we are called upon to establish close and enduring ties with persons outside our original families.   We attempt to develop deep relationships with a mate or friends.   This kind of intimate relationship is possible only after we have a firm sense of personal identity and are confident about who we are, for to be open, giving, and supportive to another person, we cannot be fearful of losing our own identity.   Most people are able to achieve a close and intimate relationship with others, but some are not.   The consequence of being unable to achieve intimacy is isolation and loneliness.   Those whose sense of self is threatened by intimacy are doomed to live a lonely and separate life until they are able to resolve the crisis and establish close relationships.

After young adulthood, in middle age, individuals experience the psychosocial crisis of **generativity versus stagnation.**   In this stage of life the major tasks are centered around child rearing and managing a career and household.   During this stage (middle age) we are called upon to become concerned about our communities, society at large, and the future world.   Erikson uses the term *generativity* to refer to this concern for future generations by improving the quality of life of others.   Toward the end of middle age, after we have successfully managed a household, career, and family, we are called upon to make contributions to others by offering money, time, or guidance to institutions concerned with benefiting society. Most people are able to look beyond their own homes and careers and achieve "generativity," but a few continue to focus only on their own selfish needs and suffer what Erikson terms "stagnation." As old age is approached, the self-absorbed, stagnated individual faces great difficulties in adjusting and may experience serious emotional crises.

In the final stage, old age, individuals experience the psychosocial crisis of **integrity versus despair.** In this stage the major tasks are typically centered around developing new roles appropriate for retirement, accepting one's life, and developing a point of view toward death. Individuals in this stage reflect on their lives and the coming of death. Acceptance of life and a feeling of satisfaction with it lead to a sense of integrity or completeness. Despair is experienced by individuals who see their lives as missed opportunities and who sense that it is too late to start over.

Levinson and Gould's Passages • In 1976 Gail Sheehy published a book called *Passages: Predictable Crises of Adult Life* based primarily on the research of Levinson and Gould concerning the stages of adult life.[2,3,4,5,6] The book became a best-seller and generated wide interest in the developmental psychology of adulthood.

Levinson and Gould describe the stages of adult life in terms of different concerns and challenges.

They point out that in the early twenties we are in a transition between adolescence and adulthood, still experimenting with and testing various adult roles that we may wish to play. In the mid-twenties we are focused on beginning a family and a career; typically we are independent and confident. In the late twenties and early thirties we are increasingly dissatisfied and self-reflective. Changing careers or changing marital partners is somewhat more common at this stage of life. According to Levinson and Gould, the period from the mid-thirties to the early forties marks for many people a time of quiet desperation. We recognize that our lives are about half over, and we worry that we may not be able to achieve the high goals we once aspired to. At this stage many people experience a **mid-life crisis,** a time of doubt, reassessment, and—sometimes—depression. It is a time of questioning and probing, as expressed in the following:

What have I done with my life? What do I really get from and give to my wife, children, friends, work, community and self? What is it I truly want for myself and others? What are my greatest talents and how am I using or wasting them? What have I done with my early dreams and what do I want with them now?[3]

In the final stage studied by Levinson and Gould, the late forties, individuals often become more involved with their spouse, their children, and their friends, and they become more accepting of things rather than wishing for them as they might have been.

Interim Summary   Adult development is studied in two basic ways: by studying the same individuals as they grow older (the longitudinal method) and by studying groups of people of different ages (the cross-sectional method). Two theories of adult development have proposed that people pass through distinct stages of life as they grow older. Erikson's theory of psychosocial stages assumes that people face a different psychosocial crisis at each stage. Levinson and Gould also described adult development in terms of a series of stages characterized by different concerns and challenges. They note that many people experience a mid-life crisis—a period of doubt, reassessment, and depression.

Approaching Adulthood

At around the age of twelve, childhood ends with the onset of adolescence. The term **adolescence** literally means "becoming an adult." But most people use it to refer to the period of growth approaching adulthood, between **puberty** (the period when the body becomes sexually mature and capable of reproduction) and the late teenage years, or from about twelve to seventeen years of age.

The years from twelve to seventeen are, for some people, full of confusion, conflict, and turmoil. From the perspective of adults, adolescence is one of the least desirable phases life—both childhood and adulthood are preferable.[7] As the humorist Richard Armour put it, "Adolescence is a disease. . . . Like the common cold, there is no cure for it."[8]

But this stereotyped view of the teenage years may be misguided. People in adolescence are just as varied and different as they are later in adulthood. Some are in turmoil, but many are not. Some are confused, but others are quite clearheaded. The view of adolescence as a "disease" is simply not supported by studies of adolescents. One researcher concluded:

Consider the images that so often come to mind in response to the word "adolescent": rebellious toward parents, peer-oriented, restless, emotionally turbulent, intense, impulsive. The implicit picture of the young offered in those adjectives, though compelling, is essentially untrue—though, of course, it does apply to some youngsters some of the time. If we examine the studies that have looked fairly closely at ordinary adolescents, we get an entirely different picture.[9]

Adolescence is not a disease, but it is a time of special challenges to the young person, challenges which require the use of new skills and resources. The biological changes of puberty, the strivings for independence, the development of peer-group relations, and the search for personal identity create for the adolescent many problems, but also many opportunities for learning and self-discovery.

The psychology of adolescence and adulthood has only recently received the concentrated attention of developmental psychologists. In their study of adult development, researchers use two basic methods: the longitudinal method and the cross-sectional method. (Margaret Thompson)

Physical Development in Adolescence

Physical changes occur rapidly during adolescence, and some of these can be unsettling. Within a period of just a few years, the adolescent's body changes dramatically in size, shape, and appearance. The image that they see of themselves in the mirror changes noticeably within a few months. Adjusting to these rapid changes can be a challenge. The changes are brought about by hormones.

Hormones   Certain glands in the body secrete their chemicals directly into the bloodstream. They are carried to other organs and glands where they exert their influence. Glands that secrete chemicals into the bloodstream are called **endocrine glands,** and the chemicals that they secrete are called **hormones.** Because hormones are released in one part of the body and have their effect on another part of the body, they are a kind of "chemical messenger" enabling the body to communicate with itself.   Some of the endocrine glands are:

- **adrenal glands**   Endocrine glands located just above the kidneys; regulate physical response to stress and strong emotion; also play role in growth and metabolism.
- **pituitary gland**   Endocrine gland that controls the functions of other endocrine glands; located at the base of the brain just below the hypothalamus; the "master gland" of the endocrine system.
- **thyroid gland**   Endocrine gland in the neck that controls metabolism and is important in regulating growth.
- **ovaries**   Endocrine glands in females that produce sex hormones as well as egg cells.
- **testes**   Endocrine glands in males that produce sex hormone as well as sperm cells.

The rapid physical changes in adolescence are triggered by the sudden increase in the flow of sex hormones into the bloodstream.   This comes about when the **hypothalamus**—a brain structure involved in the regulation of motivation and emotion—signals the pituitary gland to release its hormones into the bloodstream.   Hormones from the pituitary gland serve as chemical messengers stimulating the ovaries or testes to release sex hormones into the bloodstream. Pituitary hormones also stimulate the adrenal glands to produce and release sex hormones into the blood. Two of the sex hormones that are particularly influential at puberty are **estrogen,** a female sex hormone, and **testosterone,** a male sex hormone.   Estrogen, produced by the ovaries, and testosterone, produced by the testes, are largely responsible for the changes in body size and shape at puberty.   Figure 12-1 shows the location of the various endocrine glands.

Changes in Size •   One of the dramatic changes associated with puberty is the sudden increase in height and weight.   Between the ages of ten and thirteen most girls begin a "growth spurt" in which each year for a few years they may gain as much as two to

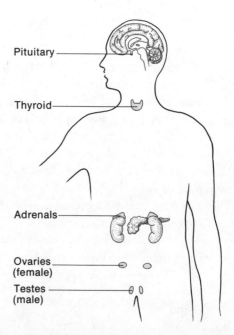

Figure 12-1 Endocrine Glands.   *The physical changes of adolescence are brought about by chemical messengers called hormones that are secreted by the various endocrine glands, shown in the diagram above.*

three inches in height and ten to twelve pounds in weight.   About two years later, on the average— between twelve and fifteen years of age—most boys begin a similar "growth spurt."   Boys may gain as much as four to five inches in height and twelve to fifteen pounds in weight per year.

During the growth spurt, not all parts of the body are growing at the same rate.   Initially, growth in leg length is more rapid than growth in the length of the body's trunk; later, as leg growth slows down, growth in the trunk continues.   Different parts of the face also grow at different rates, with noses growing before jaws.   These differences in growth result in a rapidly changing physical appearance and, frequently, feelings of awkwardness.

Sexual Development •   Puberty is the beginning of sexual maturity.   For girls, one of the important physical changes is **menarche** (the first menstrual period), which occurs on the average at about twelve years of age, but for different girls may occur as early as ten or as late as sixteen. Fertility, with the possibility of bearing a child, usually develops several months after menarche.

The flow of sex hormones into the bloodstream stimulates the development of physical changes that are called **secondary sex characteristics**—breasts and rounded thighs in girls, facial hair, deep voice, and broad shoulders in boys. The hormones also produce changes in the **primary sex characteristics**—the sex organs themselves—which grow to adult size.

There is a large range of individual variation in physical development during adolescence. Some girls may have adult breast development by the age of twelve, and others may not yet be mature at eighteen. Some boys may have experienced a rapid increase in height by the age of ten or eleven, and others are still short at seventeen. These wide differ-

ences in physical maturation are normal but cause difficulties for some people. Both the adolescents who are ahead of their peers and those who are behind their peers in development are often very preoccupied with their appearance, are self-conscious about their bodies, and may feel embarrassed by the changes that have (or have not) taken place.

In terms of your own physical development, were you ahead of or behind your peers? Do you remember how you felt about yourself and your body during early adolescence?

Cognitive Development in Adolescence

It is no accident that the study of geometry, algebra, and physical science usually occurs after the onset of puberty. These academic subjects seem to require a certain level of intellectual maturity that is reached at adolescence.

Piaget described the changes in cognitive development that occurred with age. According to Piaget, the final and highest stage of intellectual development was reached at about the age of eleven, with the beginning of adolescence. Piaget called this the **formal-operations stage.** The concept of a "formal operation" refers to a mental process, such as complex logical reasoning, that can take place entirely in the head. This ability to perform complex mental operations is the greatest cognitive achievement of adolescence.

Unlike the younger child, the adolescent is able to reason abstractly and draw logical inferences. Adolescents for the first time invent systems of beliefs and begin to speculate and theorize about the world. Bull sessions, idealism, and intense arguments about ideas are characteristic of the adolescent's emerging ability to think abstractly. The capacity to do science depends upon the ability that develops at adolescence to do complex and hypothetical reasoning.

Piaget developed a test of logical reasoning that can be given to children of five as well as to adolescents. The test involves finding the right combination of liquids that will produce a particular yellow

Adolescents of about the same age may vary greatly in size. Some experience the "growth spurt" before others. Those who are ahead of their peers as well as those who are behind their peers in physical development are often self-conscious about their appearance. (Margaret Thompson)

Figure 12-2 Test of Formal-Operations Ability.   *In one of Piaget's tests of formal operations, the problem is to mix an "indicator liquid" with one or some combination of four different liquids to produce a liquid with a bright yellow color. How would you solve this puzzle? Adolescents who have achieved formal operations typically procede to systematically test all possible combinations of the liquids until they find the correct combination.*

color. Children in the stage of formal operations are consistently able to solve the puzzle and to use an orderly strategy in reaching a solution. Consider the problem presented in Figure 12-2.

Adolescent children typically pause, consider a strategy, and then procede to test all possible combinations of the liquids systematically. First, they mix the indicator liquid with each of the flask liquids. Then, they add the indicator to the mixture of 1 and 2, to 1 and 3, to 1 and 4, and so on. Younger children are more likely to begin without developing a plan, and to try mixing the flasks in a random fashion. The adolescent's ability to go through all possible combinations requires the level of cognitive maturity that Piaget called formal operations.

Personality and Social Development

Adolescence is a time of transition from childhood to adulthood, a time in which an individual's developing skills are tried and tested in the world outside the family. As adolescents test themselves in the world, they redefine their concepts of themselves. Some individuals emerge from adolescence with a relatively positive self-concept and others with a relatively negative self-concept. Do you have a positive or negative self-concept?

One measure of self-concept is a personality scale

designed to evaluate a person's feelings of self-worth. The following items are examples from such a scale.[10]   Indicate whether you strongly agree (SA), agree (A), disagree (D), or strongly disagree (SD) with each statement.

	SA	A	D	SD
On the whole I am satisfied with myself.	☐	☐	☐	☐
I feel that I have a number of good qualities.	☐	☐	☐	☐
I am able to do things as well as most other people.	☐	☐	☐	☐
I take a positive attitude toward myself.	☐	☐	☐	☐

A positive self-concept is indicated by agreement with these items. Adolescents with relatively negative self-concepts have been found to have poor relations with siblings and peers and to have been harshly and inconsistently treated by their parents.[11]

Identity Formation   •   One of the major psychological tasks during adolescence is to discover who you are, a sense of yourself, or way of looking at yourself. You wonder about yourself and seek to define who you are. You evolve a sense of personal **identity**. How would you answer the question, Who are you? A sixteen-year-old high school student answered it this way:

I'm a girl. I'm a cheerleader. I go to W. high school. I'm tall. My grades are O.K. but not great. I hate history. I love to dance. I'm very friendly but sometimes lose my temper. I love L.—he's a senior. I have three sisters. I'm intelligent. I can't draw.

Who are you? Most people answer the question by referring to groups—formal or informal—to which they belong, by describing their physical appearance, by mentioning their likes and dislikes, and by describing their strengths and weaknesses. These ideas and attitudes form our sense of personal identity.

Adolescents are typically self-conscious and are preoccupied with questions about their identity. According to Erik Erikson, adolescents experience an **identity crisis**: they face the difficult problem of answering the question of who they are and developing a firm sense of self.   In their efforts to define themselves, they rely heavily on their feeling of identification with their parents, the attitudes of their parents toward them, and the parents' evaluations of their character and abilities.   They must integrate their diverse roles of son or daughter, student, friend, socializer, worker, and independent thinker into a single self-concept, a unified identity.   If the identity crisis is resolved positively, the adolescent emerges with a firm sense of self.   If the crisis is resolved negatively, the adolescent is left in a state of **role diffusion,** in which the sense of self is confused and the diverse roles that must be played are not integrated.   An individual with role diffusion has been unable to evolve a coherent sense of personal identity and may fall into a kind of meaningless drifting through life until a sense of personal identity is established.   This feeling of role diffusion is described by a woman named Dolores, an unemployed college dropout:

I have two sisters, and my father always told me I was the smartest of all, that I was smarter than he was, and that I could do anything I wanted to do . . . but somehow, I don't really know why, everything I turned to came to nothing. . . .   (She looked off into space for a moment and her eyes seemed to lose the train of her thought.   Then she shook herself and went on.)   I've always drifted . . . just drifted. . . .   I had every opportunity to find out what I really wanted to do.   But . . . nothing I did satisfied me, and I would just stop. . . . Or turn away. . . . Or go on a trip. . . .   (Her voice grew more halting.)   I feel my life is such a waste.[12]

Research has shown that children who have been able to identify positively with their parents and who have had the opportunity to participate in family decisions develop stronger senses of personal identity.[13,14]

Independence •   During adolescence children begin spending more and more time away from home.

They learn to drive and spend an increasing proportion of time involved with school and social activities.   The direct influence of parents declines.

Adolescence can be a time of conflict.   Parental values and expectations are not always consistent with the strong adolescent desire for freedom and independence.   Parents begin preparing their children at birth to be competent adults, to be able to make responsible decisions for themselves, and to form their own attitudes and opinions.   But parents are not always prepared when, as teenagers, their children begin to assert themselves and to act independently.

During adolescence peer groups replace parents as a major source of influence for many decisions concerning fashions and behavior.   For many adolescents, it is not just having friends that is important, but also being accepted by and being part of a group.   Acceptance and approval by a group of teenagers can be based on ethnic group membership, a sense of humor, owning a car, dressing in the "right" clothes, or on a variety of other factors.   But primary factors determining popularity in high school seem to be sports ability and physical attractiveness.   Highly attractive or athletic students usually have a choice of belonging to several peer groups.

Peer groups provide opportunities for teenagers to try out new roles, to test them for effect, and to learn how to be adults.   Adolescence is a practice period, a time for developing a personal identity separate from parents, and a time for acquiring the social competence required of mature adults.

Sex-Role Development •   From an early age, children begin to adopt the patterns of dress, mannerisms, interests, and behaviors that society regards as appropriate for males or females.   Male children are encouraged to be relatively more independent and aggressive; female children are encouraged to be relatively more nurturant and dependent.   By observing and imitating their parents of the same sex, children learn to adopt an appropriate **sex role**—the behaviors expected of their sex.   Sex roles were once more narrowly defined; yet, there is still a clearly different set of expectations for how male and female children should act. Learning about one's sex role begins early in life and continues in adolescence.

In early adolescence children are typically involved in close relationships with others of their same sex. These close peer relationships provide important learning experiences in which group expectations about sex-role behavior are communicated. The hormonal changes of adolescence bring sexual maturity and the possibility of adult sexual behavior. The acceptance of one's sexuality at this age is an important step in developing adult sex roles.

Adolescents also begin trying out various aspects of their adult sex roles. For example, the sex-role behaviors expected in adult men include providing for a family through holding a steady job. The sex-role behaviors expected of adult women include homemaking and maternal skills. Adolescent boys are often encouraged to work part-time and girls are encouraged to help with the cooking or the house. These experiences facilitate the development of mature sex roles.

Women of three generations within the same family face different challenges and are at different stages of adult development. Because of this, conflicts and misunderstanding can easily develop between family members at different ages. (John R. Maher/ EKM-Nepenthe)

The Generation Gap

The world is changing, and we are changing with it. Although we have many stable values and beliefs that have been passed on from previous generations, certain attitudes have changed. Attitudes toward sex, the environment, and the role of women are significantly different now as compared to years past. To some degree, your attitudes depend upon how old you are. While some adolescents share all or most of their parents' values, others do not agree at all. In addition, both parents and teenagers perceive their differences as greater than they actually are. These differences—both perceived and real—in values, opinions, and beliefs are frequently referred to as the **generation gap.**

The generation gap leads to a certain degree of generational conflict, an example of which is the occasional conflict between adolescents and their parents. When this conflict is extreme, the parents feel that the adolescent's values are wrong or nonexistent, while the adolescents feel the parents' values are old fashioned and inappropriate. As one comic put it,

Sons and daughters in their teens
Think their parents don't know beans.
This is bad enough, although,
Even worse, it's often so.[12]

The late anthropologist Margaret Mead argued that there is now a great gulf, a permanent division, between the younger and older generations.[15] From Mead's point of view, however, the generation gap is not necessarily bad; she saw in this division between parent and child a guide to the future, a future composed of a new form of culture. Mead identified three kinds of culture: **postfigurative,** in which children learn primarily from their parents; **cofigurative,** in which children and adults learn from their peers; and **prefigurative,** in which adults learn from their children. Mead found that we are changing into a pre-figurative culture, in which children will serve as scouts, exploring the frontiers of knowledge and experimenting with new life-styles.

Why should we be moving toward a prefigurative culture? It may be the natural result of having a highly industrialized, technological society. Advanced industrialization has been accompanied by urban migration as the place of work shifted from the farm or shop to the office or factory. In the city families work together less often, so family ties have been weakened. Industrialization has also brought an increased need for professional and technical labor; the specialized training necessary to support this work has required prolonged schooling, and this has further weakened family ties. As the youth have tended to be isolated from their families, they have depended more on their peers and less on their parents for guidance. The increased freedom from parental traditions has made it possible for young adults to experiment and innovate with forms of dress, music, and life-styles, which the older generation increasingly has begun to adopt. Thus, children become the "scouts" exploring the frontiers, and their parents follow.

Interim Summary   Adolescence, the transition between childhood and adulthood, is marked by many changes. Physically, the body enters puberty and becomes sexually mature; production of the sex hormones results in the development of secondary sex characteristics, which in turn produce the physical aspects of maleness or femaleness. Intellectually, the final stage of cognitive growth—formal operations—is achieved. Adolescence is also a period of developing independence; peer groups replace parents as a major source of influence. A major psychological task is the formation of a sense of personal identity through the resolution of the identity crisis. According to Margaret Mead, the culture is changing into a prefigurative society, in which children lead and teach their parents.

Early and Middle Adulthood

The years from eighteen or twenty to sixty or sixty-five constitute the bulk of the human life span; yet, these are the least-studied years of life. From the perspective of adolescence, the adult years may seem to involve nothing but problems: shouldering responsibility, worrying about money, making compromises, getting into a rut, and growing old. To be sure, sometimes these are involved, but the adult years are also times of excitement, years of accomplishment and productivity, and a period of growth. In early adulthood, individuals choose a career and begin to develop a life-style; most marry and have children and begin to build for the family's future. In middle adulthood, individuals typically become less self-absorbed and find meaning in life through contributing to society.

Physical and Cognitive Development

The peak of physical fitness is typically reached in early adulthood. Maximum physical strength is reached on the average between twenty-five and thirty years of age. Between thirty and sixty people generally lose strength, mostly in the legs and back muscles, but strength can be maintained through regular exercise. Maximum height is also reached at about twenty-five to thirty; after this age height slowly declines, so that by the age of sixty two or more inches may be lost. During early and middle adulthood there is also a redistribution of body weight. On most people the waist thickens and the chest recedes. These physical changes have little effect on overall physical ability and physical health. Most people remain vigorous and healthy through early and middle adulthood.

Adults continue to learn as they grow older and continue to expand their body of knowledge and skills. In this sense, the adult mind improves with age. Tests of verbal and mathematical reasoning tend to show little decline with age, but certain intellectual functions apparently decline with age. Tasks that require quick reaction time or that depend upon short-term memory are performed less well with age. However, active and healthy adults show little or no intellectual decline.[16,17]

Transitions and Crises

Moments of potential crisis occur in adult life when the ground shifts and your world suddenly changes in some significant way. Some of these changes are predictable, such as the changes that occur when you gain or lose an important aspect of your identity because you add or subtract a significant role.

The birth of the first child is such a change, for it brings with it new, demanding roles for both the mother and the father. Life after the first birth is quite simply a different life, and the parents are, to a degree, different people. They must adopt the new roles of caretakers, educators, and providers, and some new parents are not well prepared to assume these responsibilities.

A second potential crisis in adult life occurs when the children leave home. At this point, the parents are usually in their forties and have for perhaps twenty years settled into the parental roles. These roles are lost when the children leave; suddenly the house is empty and life becomes quite different. This is an unsettling change and requires considerable adjustment, particularly for those parents who have centered their lives around their children. It's hard to give them up. According to one study, the low point of life for parents—the time that is least satisfying—is the time when the children leave home.[18]

A third time of change and potential crisis for women is **menopause,** the phase of life, usually in the middle to late forties or early fifties, when menstruation stops. Women experience both physical and psychological changes at menopause, the result of a sudden decrease in the production of estrogen, a female sex hormone. One of the accompanying physical changes is the loss of fertility. For some women, the inability to bear more children can be extremely disturbing, especially if they have built their sense of personal identity around the view of themselves as mothers. Other physical symptoms that sometimes occur at this time are hot flashes, dizziness, and headaches. Psychological problems may include irritability, depression, crying spells, and the inability to concentrate. Menopause (sometimes called "the change of life") is an emotionally significant change in the life of a woman. This change may be seen as either good or bad, and the psychological effects vary accordingly. Menopause signals freedom from the menstrual cycle and freedom from childbearing, seen by some women as very positive changes. The loss of the ability to bear children may symbolically represent for some women the loss of femininity, and this will be seen as very negative. In any event, menopause is often a very real "change of life."

A fourth potential crisis in adult life is retirement. For both men and women who have spent a lifetime at work, stopping working can be a traumatic change. Part of the problem is that your role changes on retirement; in a sense, you lose a part of your personality, an aspect of yourself that may have provided a lot of satisfaction. If this part of yourself is not replaced by other satisfactions, then retirement can create adjustment difficulties. Another problem with retirement is the economic change that results. Often a result of retirement is a sudden drop in income and standard of living, and this requires some adjustment. By contrast, for those who are thoughtful and plan ahead, retirement offers expanded opportunities and increased satisfactions. There are opportunities to go places never before seen and to do things you may have wanted but lacked the time to do. A person's satisfaction with retirement thus depends highly on the planning done for it during the person's working life.

Interim Summary   Early and middle adulthood are, for most people, periods of health and productivity. Certain physical changes occur during this time—strength declines slightly, height declines slightly, and there is a redistribution of weight. Although certain mental abilities decline with age, most do not, and active and healthy adults show no overall decline in intelligence. Four crises of adult life are the birth of the first child, the time when the children leave home, menopause in women, and retirement.

Later Adulthood

"You are old, Father William," the young man said,
And your hair has become very white;
And yet you incessantly stand on your head—
Do you think, at your age, it is right?"

"In my youth," Father William replied to his son,
"I feared it might injure the brain;
But now I'm perfectly sure I have none,
Why, I do it again and again."

Lewis Carroll

We have a negative view of old age; aging, in the minds of many people, is equivalent to deterioration, and the loss of youth is equivalent to the loss of brainpower and muscle power. But research shows that the process of aging is neither so negative nor so simple.

Physical Changes in Aging

We do not yet know why we change as we grow old. One theory is that our bodies just get worn out, like machines; but this "wear and tear" theory has not been supported by recent research. Aging and longevity appear, rather, to be genetically programmed processes, just as the basic aspects of growth and development during childhood are. Longevity is, however, affected by life-style.

Many of the changes with age are visible to any observer. Your hair slowly changes color and becomes white; it thins on top and some people become bald. The skin loses some of its elasticity, becomes drier, and develops sags and wrinkles. But other changes may not be so obvious.

The eyes change, so that changing focus from far objects to near ones becomes increasingly difficult. Some older people require bifocal glasses because of this problem. There is a loss in the ability to hear high-frequency sounds. Balance and coordination are somewhat poorer, and muscle strength and suppleness may decline. The heart and circulatory system do not function as well in the old as in the young. This is partly due to a cumulative thickening of the arterial walls.

Many people believe that older men and women have no interest in sex, or even if they do, they are not capable of doing anything about it. Comedians often turn to the topic of sexuality in old age for material to entertain us:

Definition of old age: The time of life when a man flirts with girls but can't remember why.[19]

But the facts are that, in most adults, sexual interest and activity continue well into the seventies and eighties. The problem for many older adults in not a lack of interest, but a lack of opportunity. Many people, particularly women, lose their marriage partner with many years of life left to them. Establishing a new intimate relationship is difficult because of the attitudes of our society toward sexual expression in older people.[20] Fortunately, these attitudes are changing.

Cognitive Changes in Aging

Which are smarter—the old or the young? This question is not easy to answer. In fact, there are two answers, depending upon the meaning of the question. One answer, based on cross-sectional studies of intelligence, is that, on the average, young people today are more intelligent than old people today.[21] The peak overall intelligence score is usually achieved by those in the late teens or early twenties. People between the ages of thirty and fifty typically score slightly lower on IQ tests than those who are twenty

years old, and people in their sixties or older typically score significantly lower still. But this is not the whole answer. Another way of answering the question is to conduct a longitudinal study, testing the same individuals at different ages, as they grow older. With this type of study, intelligence is found to remain the same or to increase slightly during adulthood, up to the age of at least fifty.[22,23]

Thus, the best answer to the question of whether the young are smarter than the old is that there appears to be a generational difference: the average young person is smarter than the average older person; however, people do not lose their intelligence as they grow older.

Other studies of mental changes with aging tend to show that, although there is wide individual variation, people do not mentally deteriorate with age. Basic, long-term memory ability does not decline; thinking and problem-solving abilities remain about the same as you grow older; and verbal skills tend to increase with age. The ability to learn does not weaken with age—old dogs can learn new tricks, as one author wrote:

Old dogs can learn new tricks, but they may be reluctant to do so, particularly when they are not convinced that the new trick is any better than the old tricks which served them so well in the past. They may not learn new tricks as rapidly as they did in the past. But if they started out as clever young pups, they are very likely to end up as wise old hounds.[24]

Dying

People die without aging, as in a fire or automobile accident, and many age for a long time without dying; but the inevitable end of the aging process is dying. Psychologists recently have studied attitudes toward death and the stages of dying in order to learn how to help the living. Those who are left behind must somehow cope with the loss, and this adjustment is usually very hard.

Most people do not deteriorate psychologically with age. Long-term memory, thinking and problem-solving, and verbal skills do not decline with age. Furthermore, in most adults, sexual interest and activity continue well into the seventies and eighties. (George W. Gardner)

As one author put it, "A person's death is not only an ending; it is also a beginning—for the survivors."[25]   Learning to live without a husband, a mother, or close friend can be difficult for many and apparently is impossible for some, who remain behind plagued by guilt, shame, depression, or even hatred. A woman who has recently lost her husband is more likely to die or to become emotionally disturbed than other women of similar age and physical health who have not lost a husband.[26]

Adjusting after the death of a member of your family or close friend would be one thing, but what if you were facing death yourself?   In a large national survey, 30,000 people responded to the question, "What does death mean to you?"[25]   Here's how they answered:

The end; the final process of life	35%
The beginning of a life after death; a transition, a new beginning	13%
A joining of the spirit with a universal cosmic consciousness	12%
A kind of endless sleep; rest and peace	9%
Termination of this life but with survival of the spirit	17%
Don't know, or other answers	14%

How would you have answered the question?

Suppose you were facing certain death from a terminal illness, but you had some time left.   What would you do?   How would you react?

Elisabeth Kübler-Ross, after observing and conducting frank interviews with hundreds of dying patients describes five stages that occur in one's awareness of certain death.[27]

1. *First stage: denial and isolation.*   The person says, "No—not me!   It can't be true!   There's been some awful mistake!"   The initial evidence and opinions concerning the death are rejected, and the person denies that death is imminent.   Some patients attack the evidence, arguing that the X rays or lab tests got mixed up; others "shop around" for a different opinion, going from doctor to doctor.

There is finally a partial acceptance of the facts.

2. *Second stage: Anger.*   When the denial cannot be maintained, it is replaced with rage and resentment.   The person says, "Why me?   I don't deserve this.   Why couldn't it have been someone else?"   In this stage, the patient is often very difficult to deal with, is irritable, and sometimes irrational; the anger about the impending death is released against those people who happen to be in the vicinity.

3. *Third stage: Bargaining.*   In this stage the dying person seems to strive to postpone the inevitable by attempting to enter into certain agreements.   In effect, the person says, "If you (doctor, family, God, fate) will agree to extend my life, I'll agree to whatever you wish."   The patient may offer all kinds of promises, if only he or she will be permitted to live a little longer, perhaps to see a son's wedding or the birth of a grandchild.

4. *Fourth stage: Depression.*   Denial, rage, and bargaining are soon replaced with a sense of great loss and a feeling of intense depression.   The patient seems to be experiencing a period of self-mourning and feeling what Kübler-Ross calls ". . . the preparatory grief that the terminally ill patient has to undergo in order to prepare himself for his final separation from this world."[27]   In this condition, the individual should not be "cheered up," for being allowed to express this grief and sorrow is necessary in order to achieve the final acceptance of death.

5. *Fifth stage: Acceptance*   In this stage, the dying person is neither angered nor depressed about the approaching death, but instead is able to accept it, not happily, but peacefully.   During this period the patient's interest in the outside world diminishes.   Increasingly, the patient prefers to be left alone and is often tired and weak.

Finally, according to Kübler-Ross, throughout each of the stages toward death, the one feeling that persists is *hope.*   Even though death may be realistically accepted, many patients at each stage leave open the remote possibility of a cure or a miracle.   As

Kübler-Ross says, "It is this glimpse of hope which maintains them through days, weeks, or months of suffering. . . . No matter what we call it, we found that all our patients maintained a little bit of it and were nourished by it in especially difficult times. . . . If a patient stops expressing hope, it is usually a sign of imminent death . . . All these patients died within twenty-four hours."[27]

Preventing Aging

Aging begins at birth, and the changes that it brings—physical, social, and psychological—while inevitable, are not completely beyond our control. Death rates have steadily declined as our health has improved. In the Middle Ages in England, life expectancy was about thirty years. In 1900 in the United States it was forty-seven years. Today it is more than seventy. By the end of this century, it is likely to be eighty. Research on heart disease, cancer, and the aging proces itself are certain to result in increased longevity during the coming decades.

Increasing Longevity

But longevity is also under individual control. As people become more aware of how to live more healthful lives, they can delay death. More and more people are striving to maintain good diets and moderate levels of activity and to avoid tobacco and other carcinogens. By making these choices, people are, in effect, deciding to live longer.

Psychological stress is another important factor related to longevity that is under individual control. The frustrations, anxieties, and shocks of our fast-paced modern lives result in psychological stress, and chronic levels of stress result in what are called the diseases of modern civilization. Coronary heart disease and high blood pressure are more common among hard-driven, competitive, and tense people who do not easily relax. The rate of heart attacks among women has increased as more women have moved into what used to be the male's domain—the high-pressured, competitive job.

Life-style is, however, a matter of choice. People can choose to relax more often, just as they can choose to avoid smoking. As our knowledge about the forces influencing longevity increases, our ability to shape healthful life-styles for ourselves will also increase. Will you choose to prevent aging and delay death or to lead a more frenzied (and shorter) life?

Predicting Longevity

According to one researcher, the following chart provides a guide for predicting how long you will live.[28] To calculate your expected longevity, start with your basic life expectancy—sixty-seven for males, seventy-five for females. For each factor listed in the chart, add to or subtract from this basic value the number indicated. When you are through, you will have an estimate of how long you will live.

_____ 1. Your basic life expectancy.

2. Family history

_____ Add five years if two or more of your grandparents lived to eighty or beyond.

_____ Subtract four years if any parent, grandparent, sister, or brother died of heart attack or stroke before fifty. Subtract two years if anyone died from these diseases between fifty and sixty.

_____ Subtract three years for each case of diabetes, thyroid disorders, breast cancer, cancer of the digestive system, asthma, or chronic bronchitis among parents or grandparents.

3. Marital status

_____ If you are married, add four years.

_____ If you are over twenty-five and not married, subtract one year for every unwedded decade.

4. Physique

_____ Subtract one year for every ten pounds you are overweight.

_____ For each inch your girth measurement exceeds your chest measurement deduct two years.

_____ Add three years if you are over forty and not overweight.

5. Exercise

_____ For regular and moderate exercise (such as jogging three times a week), add three years.

_____ For regular and vigorous exercise (such as long distance running three times a week), add five years.

_____ Subtract three years if your job is sedentary. Add three years if it is active.

6. Smoking

_____ If you smoke two or more packs of cigarettes per day, subtract eight years.

_____ For one to two packs per day, subtract four years.

_____ For less than one pack, subtract two years.

_____ Subtract two years if you regularly smoke a pipe or cigars.

7. Disposition

_____ Add two years if you are reasonable and practical.

_____ Subtract two years if you are aggressive, intense, and competitive.

_____ Add one to five years if you are basically happy and content with life.

_____ Subtract one to five years if you are often unhappy, worried, and often feel guilty.

8. Education

_____ Less than high school, subtract two years.

_____ Four years of school beyond high school, add one year.

_____ Five or more years beyond high school, add three years.

9. Environment

_____ If you have lived most of your life in a rural environment, add four years.

_____ Subtract two years if you have lived most of your life in an urban environment.

_____ Add two years if your home's thermostat is set at no more than 68° F.

10. Health care

_____ For regular medical checkups and regular dental care, add three years.

_____ If you are frequently ill, subtract two years.

_____ = Estimate of my life expectancy.

Interim Summary   A variety of physical changes occurs as we grow old, including changes in the heart, the muscles, the skin, and the sensory systems. Research on intelligence suggests that most people do not decline mentally in later adulthood. As individuals approach death, they experience five stages in their attitudes toward dying. The single feeling that persists in each stage is hope. Longevity is to some extent under individual control. Longevity can be predicted from a knowledge of your life-style.

Summary

1. Two methods of studying adult development are the longitudinal method (studying the same individuals as they grow older) and the cross-sectional method (studying different groups of people of different ages).

2. According to Erikson, the life span can be conceived as a series of different stages of development, each characterized by a unique psychosocial crisis (stress produced by the demands of the social world).

3. According to Erikson, the psychosocial crisis of adolescence is "identity versus role diffusion," in young adulthood the crisis is "intimacy versus isolation," in middle age the crisis is "generativity versus stagnation," and in old age it is "integrity versus despair."

4. Levinson and Gould have proposed a similar theory describing the stages of adult

life in terms of a series of different concerns and challenges. Between the mid-thirties and the early forties, many people experience a mid-life crisis—a time of doubt and quiet desperation.

5. Adolescence is a period of transition between childhood and adulthood, which begins with puberty—the time when the body becomes sexually mature.

6. The onset of puberty is triggered by the hypothalamus, which signals the pituitary gland to secrete hormones into the bloodstream; pituitary hormones stimulate the ovaries or testes to release sex hormones into the blood. These sex hormones (estrogen and testosterone) are responsible for many of the physical changes in adolescence.

7. Intellectually, the final stage of cognitive development is reached during adolescence—the stage of formal operations, in which people are able to reason abstractly and do science.

8. According to Erikson, adolescents experience an identity crisis, in which they must integrate their diverse roles, define themselves, and discover who they are.

9. Adolescence is also a time of developing independence from parents and increasing dependence on peer groups. Peer groups provide opportunities for teenagers to try out new roles and to learn how to be adults.

10. The differences—both perceived and real—between parents and children in opinions, values, and beliefs are called the generation gap.

11. Early and middle adulthood—from eighteen or twenty to sixty or sixty-five years of age—is typically a period of accomplishment and productivity when most marry and begin to build for their family's future. There is some physical decline, but it has little effect on overall health and physical ability.

12. Four predictable crises of adult life are the birth of the first child, the time when the children leave home, menopause for women, and retirement.

13. In later adulthood, the aging process affects the skin, hair, senses, the heart and circulatory system, and other organs of the body. Although certain mental functions decline with age, healthy people do not lose their intelligence as they grow older.

14. According to Kübler-Ross, there are five stages in approaching death that are experienced by many people: denial and isolation, anger, bargaining, depression, and acceptance.

Key Concepts

longitudinal method   A method of studying developmental changes by examining individuals as they grow older—for example, studying a group of women when they are twenty and again when they are forty.

cross-sectional method   A method of studying developmental changes by comparing different groups of people who are of different ages.

psychosocial crisis   According to Erikson, the stress produced by a set of demands that the social world places on individuals at different ages.

identity versus role diffusion   Erikson's psychosocial crisis of adolescence in which the individual strives to achieve a firm sense of self.

intimacy versus isolation   Erikson's psychosocial crisis of young adulthood in which the individual seeks to establish deep relationships with friends or with a mate.

generativity versus stagnation   Erikson's psychosocial crisis of middle age in which the individual becomes concerned with others outside the immediate family—with society and future generations.

integrity versus despair   Erikson's final psychosocial crisis of old age in which the individual reflects on life and the coming of death.

mid-life crisis   According to Levinson and Gould, a period in middle age when individuals may experience doubt, reassessment, and depression regarding their lives, directions, and goals.

adolescence   The period of growth between childhood and adulthood, or from about twelve to seventeen years of age.

puberty   That age at which the body becomes sexually mature, typically around the age of eleven or twelve.

endocrine glands   Glands in the body that secrete chemicals (hormones) into the bloodstream.

hormones   "Chemical messengers" secreted by the endocrine glands; these chemicals circulate in the bloodstream and cause changes in specific bodily tissues.

adrenal glands   Endocrine glands located just above the kidneys; play role in growth and metabolism, response to stress and strong emotion.

pituitary gland   Endocrine gland located at the base of the brain; "master gland" which controls functions of all other endocrine glands.

thyroid gland   Endocrine gland located in the neck; controls metabolism and is important in regulating growth.

ovaries   Endocrine glands in females that produce sex hormones as well as egg cells.

testes   Endocrine glands in males that produce sex hormones as well as sperm cells.

hypothalamus   Small brain structure that regulates drives and controls the auto-nomic nervous system; involved in the regulation of motivation and emotion.

estrogen   A female sex hormone; produced by the ovaries.

testosterone   A male sex hormone; produced by the testes.

menarche   A girl's first menstrual period.

secondary sex characteristics   Those physical characteristics which classify a body as "male" or "female." Male secondary sex characteristics include facial hair, deepened voice, more developed musculature. Female secondary sex characteristics include breasts and rounded thighs.

primary sex characteristics   The sex organs themselves (penis, vagina).

formal-operations stage   The fourth and last of Piaget's cognitive stages, beginning at about age eleven and continuing through adulthood, in which a person develops abstract reasoning ability.

identity   A sense of who you are, often in terms of social roles, relationships, goals, activities, interests.

identity crisis   According to Erikson, a period in adolescence marked by great uncertainty about one's identity.

role diffusion   A state in which the sense of self is confused and the diverse roles that a person plays are not integrated.

sex role   The styles and mannerisms typical of members of one sex.

generation gap   The difference between parents and their children in values, opinions, and beliefs.

postfigurative culture   A culture in which children learn primarily from their parents.

cofigurative culture   A culture in which children and adults learn from their peers.

prefigurative culture   A culture in which parents learn from their children.

menopause   That stage in a woman's life when menstruation stops due to a decrease in the production of estrogen. This "change of life" results in both physical and psychological changes.

Part V

Interpersonal Relationships

Chapter 13
Relationships

Key Questions

1. What are the types of interpersonal communication?
2. What is nonverbal communication?
3. What is the basis of friendship?
4. What are the characteristics of good and bad relationships?
5. What are realistic and unrealistic expectations of marriage relationships?

We need other people, and we need close personal relationships. Without others we are lost, confused, lonely.

A prisoner who had been placed in solitary confinement wrote, "Gradually the loneliness sets in. Later I was to experience situations that amounted almost to physical torture, but even that seemed preferable to absolute isolation."[1]

You spend a lot of time with other people, talking with them, working with them, or simply being together. Most of your behavior is social—it occurs in interaction with others. The way you act in the presence of others is different from the way you act when you are alone; what you do is modified and influenced by what others do. In turn, you affect the behavior of persons you are with.

Many of our personal problems are actually *interpersonal*—they stem from our difficulties in relating to other people. Understanding the nature of interpersonal relationship is a step toward social growth.

Communication

Relationships require communication. When you try to communicate to your friends how you feel, sometimes you are understood and sometimes not. Have you ever felt when talking to a friend that the two of you were "on the same wavelength"?

Can you remember the last conversation you had with someone? What was it about? Were real feelings and ideas exchanged, or did you talk about the weather? Perhaps you communicated something with your facial expressions instead of just your words—communication can be both verbal and nonverbal. Verbal communication uses words. But if information or feelings are to be transmitted from one mind to another, both talk and listening are required. Sometimes we communicate when we talk, and sometimes we do not.

Most personal problems are really interpersonal, arising from difficulties in relating to and communicating with other people. Parallaction, mystification, and games are three types of communication that interfere with the goal of a true exchange of feelings and information. (© Erika Stone 1978/Photo Researchers)

Parallaction

Parallaction is pseudo-interaction in which two or more people *appear* to be having an exchange, but there is no real involvement with each other.[2] It is termed *parallaction* because the action is going on in parallel, independently, with no intersection. Parallaction occurs in our ritual greetings to each other. These rituals serve the function of a nod of recognition but their form is verbal. They consist of words but they have no meaning—they are a form of non-communication.

John: Hello! How are you?
Sue: Fine, thanks. How are you?
John: Just great.
Sue: Nice day, huh?
John: Sure is.
Sue: Warm enough for you?
John: You bet. Think it'll rain?
Sue: I don't know—maybe.
John: Well, see you later.
Sue: Okay, don't work too hard.
John: Yeah, be good now.
Sue: Be seeing you.
John: Bye bye.
Sue: So long.

This parallaction is a greeting ritual in which neither information nor feelings are exchanged. There is no intention of conveying information, only of recognizing the presence of each other.

Another common form of parallaction occurs when two persons are talking but neither person is listening. Joe talks, and while he is talking Ellen is thinking only what she will say when he is through; when Joe finishes, Ellen talks, and Joe starts thinking about what he is going to say when she is through. Rather than listening to each other, they act independently; they are having a pseudo-interaction.

Joe: I got a letter from my father today. All he seems to care about is whether my grades are up and how much money I'm spending.
Ellen: I got the craziest letter you ever saw today! Came from Susie, my friend who is in Europe. She writes hysterical letters.
Joe: So my father sends me ten dollars in the letter and says to spend it on good books and not the movies.
Ellen: Susie says that the movies over there are just terrible. She just can't wait to come home so she can see the ones she's missed.

Mystification

While parallaction is *non*communication, mystification is *mis*communication. **Mystification** occurs when two people are talking but one or both are hiding or falsifying their true feelings or intentions. Sometimes we mystify people because we do not want to hurt their feelings.

Jim: Hello, Laurie. I've been wanting to see you. I tried to phone you. Did you get the message to return my call?
Laurie: Yes, and I was just about to call you.
Jim: But I left a message every day this week.
Laurie: Gee, I've been real busy.
Jim: Are you mad at me or something?
Laurie: Oh, no. I've been real busy.
Jim: How about a movie tomorrow night?
Laurie: I'm sorry Jim. I'm real busy tomorrow night.

Sometimes we mystify people in order to manipulate them for our own selfish reasons. For example, a man comes to the door and asks you to participate in a survey that he is taking; in fact, he is a salesman and is trying to sell you magazine subscriptions.

Games People Play

Games are another example of pseudo-interaction. Sometimes two people appear to be communicating when in fact they are playing a game—having a ritualized, stereotyped encounter, the object of which is to win, not to exchange information or feelings. Games in social interaction are basically dishonest, because each player has an ulterior motive in playing. In the game entitled "Why don't you—Yes but"[3] one player (Bill) tries to help another player (Mary), but for Mary winning is more important than solving her problem.

Mary: My husband always insists on doing his own repairs, and he never builds anything right.

Bill: Why doesn't he take a course in carpentry?

Mary: Yes, but he doesn't have the time.

Bill: Why don't you buy him some good tools?

Mary: Yes, but he doesn't know how to use them.

Bill: Why don't you have your building done by a carpenter?

Mary: Yes, but that would cost too much.

Bill: Why don't you accept what he does the way he does it?

Mary: Yes, but the whole thing might fall down.

In this game, Mary will win if she can hold off every solution with a "Yes, but . . ." response. The game ends in silence when all suggestions have been rejected as inadequate. Mary's reward for winning the game is the feeling that the other person is inadequate, not she. The other person is regarded as inadequate because he has tried to think of an acceptable solution to Mary's problem but has failed.

Authentic Communication

Not all meetings end in parallaction, mystification, or games: some involve a true exchange of feelings and information. **Authentic communication** is occurring, not ritual. It is not easy for two people to talk to each other and communicate. In order to communicate you must be open with your thoughts and feelings, and that is difficult and sometimes scary. To reveal yourself to other people gives them the power to hurt you if they want to do so; but it also makes it possible for them to know you and to like you. If you do not communicate and therefore do not allow yourself to be known by another, you have little chance of developing fulfilling relationships.

There is much evidence that indicates that healthy relationships are based on self-disclosure. If you hide how you are reacting to the other person, your concealment can sicken the relationship. . . . Being silent is not being strong; strength is the willingness to take risks in the relationship, to disclose yourself with the intention of building a better relationship.[4]

If you do communicate, if you do disclose who you are to another, you will find in most cases that your disclosure is reciprocated. If you trust me enough to reveal yourself to me, I may trust you enough to reveal myself to you. This reciprocation of self-disclosure is called the **dyadic effect**.

It is not easy to communicate things that are truly meaningful to you. That is why so much of our conversation amounts to nothing more than parallaction or mystification. It is also often more difficult to talk about the present than the past. The order of disclosures, from least difficult to most difficult, appears below:

I tell you how Jane felt about John, neither person being present.

I tell you how Jane feels about John, neither person being present.

I tell you my past feelings about Sam, who is not present.

I tell you my present feelings about Sam, who is not present.

I tell you my past feelings about you.

I tell you my present feelings about you.[4]

Why is it so difficult for you to tell me how you feel about me? One reason is that you fear that I will hurt you by using the information against you, or by rejecting you, or by not understanding you. But if you don't tell me how you feel, I may never know you in any depth.   Although disclosure is necessary for a truly close relationship, it does not guarantee one. Sometimes disclosure to unsympathetic people can cause you great hurt.   While it is necessary to take risks to be close, it is also necessary to use common sense in self-disclosure.

Interim Summary   Relationships are based on communication.   Authentic communication, involving a true exchange of feelings and information, is difficult.   It requires that you be open and honest and have the courage to disclose yourself.   A consequence of openness is the dyadic effect, or reciprocation of self-disclosure.   Parallaction (noncommunication), mystification (miscommunication), and games (communcation with ulterior motives) are common types of interaction.   When these are present, the possibility for true communication is remote.

Body Talk

Hands talk and smiles talk.   Communication consists of more than words.   You communicate with your facial expression, with the clothes you choose to wear, with the inflection and loudness of your speech, with your posture, and with your body movements.   This type of communication is called **nonverbal communication.**   In two-way conversations words have been estimated to carry less than 35 percent of the total meaning communicated.[5]   You already know how to read the language of the body fairly well, but you can learn how to read it better.   The body is like a book, and each part of the body communicates information.   The meaning of the message that is sent is sometimes the feelings or intentions of the sender. Sometimes body talk consists of signals or regulators used for controlling the pacing of conversations.

Regulators

Regulators are body signals sent between two people when they are talking that signify that communication and comprehension are occurring.[6]   In a two-way conversation the speaker signals the listener to indicate

Can you read the language of the body?   In two-way conversations, body language has been estimated to carry over 65 percent of the total meaning communicated.   Regulators and body messages are two types of nonverbal communication.   (Philip Jon Bailey/Jeroboam Inc.)

when it is permissible to answer by using tonal variations and pauses in speech and by moving head and eyes in certain ways.   An upward tonal inflection (as in a question) or a downward tonal inflection (as in a declarative sentence), when accompanied by an extended pause, is a signal that the speaker is temporarily finished and that it is now permissible for the listener to respond.   However, if the extended pause is accompanied by the speaker moving eyes upward, then the signal is different: the listener should not interrupt, because the speaker wishes to continue.[7]   The listener also uses body signals to communicate with the speaker.

1. The listener maintains eye contact with the speaker and slowly nods the head up and down.   This is a signal that the listener understands what is being said and that the speaker may continue.
2. The listener maintains a quizzical or blank look, sometimes accompanied by a slight frown.   This is a signal that the listener is not understanding the message and that the speaker should repeat it in different words.
3. The listener moves the eyes upward without speaking.   This is a signal that the speaker should stop talking so that the listener can respond.
4. The listener raises the eyebrows or frowns.   This is a signal that the listener disagrees with or is skeptical about what is being said.   The speaker then usually elaborates on the point or strengthens the case with additional evidence.
5. The listener extends a hand, palm forward, toward the speaker.   This is a signal that the speaker should stop abruptly so that the listener can respond.

Messages

There are many meaningful messages that can be sent with the body.   Unlike regulators, **body messages** convey actual information.   In effect, these body messages replace words and sentences; sometimes words cannot communicate the subtle feeling carried by a facial expression or the complex information about size or direction carried by appropriate hand gestures.

Talking Without Words • Body language is often used to communicate direction, distance, and size. The hands point, the arms stretch out, or the thumb and forefinger are held a certain distance apart—all of these gestures carry important meanings.   The hitch-hiker's thumb tells drivers that a ride is wanted.   I use my hand to say "Come," "Go," "Look," or "Good-bye."   I cup my hand behind my ear to ask you to speak louder; I put my forefinger in front of my lips to ask you to be quieter.   I rub my hand in a circling motion on my stomach to tell you that your food tastes good.   I hold my nose to say "You stink!"

Feelings You Cannot Hide • Body language is particularly useful in communicating emotion. Words often fail when it comes to expressing feelings, but the body talks clearly, sometimes saying more than we want it to.   The face is ever changing, with the muscles around the mouth and eyes communicating subtle feelings.   People all over the world smile when happy and frown when sad.   Charles Darwin suggested that the facial expression of emotion was an inborn signal, and presented as evidence the similarities between the facial expressions of people and other animals, such as monkeys.   While there are clearly differences among societies in the details of emotional expression, there are great similarities also.   Research shows that observers in the United States, Brazil, Japan, New Guinea, and Borneo all showed remarkable agreement about the emotion being expressed in photographs of faces.[8]

Posture, too, expresses emotion.   When you are slumped forward, head down, with your arms tightly crossed in front of you, you communicate depression and withdrawal.   When you are interested in someone, you will often turn your body toward that person and may lean forward.   The hands also express feelings.   You cover your face with your hands to express shame.   When you are angry, your fists are clenched.

You hunch your shoulders and turn your palms up to express puzzlement. You may strike your palm against your forehead to express surprise or forgetfulness. How you move your hands—slowly or rapidly—communicates how you are feeling.

What you say with words can be controlled fairly well. You can tell the truth, or you can lie or you can choose not to talk. It is much harder to control body language. Often your body will communicate how you are feeling when you choose not to reveal your feelings with words. Sometimes your words will say one thing and your body another. We have learned to trust body language more than word language because it is harder to lie with the body. A person may say "I like you" with words but say "Stay away" with the body; a person may say "I feel fine" with words but say "I feel terrible" with the body. These contradictory messages are sometimes the result of insincerity (deliberate deceit) and sometimes are the consequence of not knowing how you feel.

Territories

One way in which we communicate nonverbally is by means of the physical distance that we maintain between ourselves and other people. Many animals, including humans, seem to have **territories**—geographical areas in which they live and which they defend against the intrusion of strangers. In many species of birds the males claim an area surrounding the nest and attack members of their species that intrude into this territory. Dogs and cats have territories with specific boundaries.

You have a portable territory, a zone around your body called your **personal space.** Your personal space is like an imaginary bubble surrounding you that keeps you at a distance from others. You can locate the boundary of your personal space by asking someone to stand still, then walking closer and closer until you begin to feel uncomfortable. Imagine yourself walking up to someone and standing only one foot away; you would feel distinctly uneasy and would have a strong desire to back off. This is because the other person has violated your personal space.

It is also possible for you to stand too far away. Imagine yourself walking up to someone in order to talk and stopping about fifteen feet away. Interacting at that distance just would not feel comfortable. Thus, it is possible to be either too close or too far away from someone else. There is an intermediate distance that is most comfortable; this optimal distance is called the **optimal interpersonal distance.** The optimal interpersonal distance is the distance that two people typically maintain between themselves; it is the distance that violates neither person's personal space yet is also close enough for comfort. This distance is less between friends than between strangers.

How is the optimal interpersonal distance maintained? You can test this by the following methods. The next time you are talking with someone, take a step forward and observe what happens; later take a step backward and notice the consequences. When you step forward, the other person will probably step back in order to regain the best interpersonal distance; when you step back, the other person will probably step forward. People are motivated to maintain a comfortable interpersonal distance.

Shyness and Assertiveness

Relating to others is a frightening or painful experience for some people. The television actor Robert Young reported, "I've always been shy. As a kid, I was even afraid of the teacher."[9] Comedienne Phyllis Diller said, "Teachers who knew me as a child told my parents I was the most painfully shy youngster they'd ever seen."[9]

Shyness can be defined as discomfort in the pres-

People who are extremely shy feel alone in a crowd. Surveys have shown that over 40 percent of high school and college students describe themselves as shy. Shyness can be overcome by learning to be more assertive. (© Joel Gordon 1978)

ence of others, a feeling of tension and awkwardness in social interactions, and difficulty confronting others with requests, demands, or disagreements. In a recent survey of high school and college students, more than 40 percent indicated that they were shy and of these, most reported that they did not like being that way.[10] Shyness results in difficulty in making friends, extreme self-consciousness, and problems in standing up for your own beliefs, feelings, and rights. Shyness also results in loneliness and isolation. A painfully shy businesswoman confessed,

I am lonely beyond belief. I live in complete solitude without a friend in the world, neither male nor female. . . . I spend the holidays in complete solitude.[11]

Each of us is sometimes a little shy. In certain situations, or with certain people, we feel shy, uneasy, and awkward. What makes you shy?

☐ Being the center of attention
☐ Talking to a person of the opposite sex
☐ Meeting new people
☐ Asking a stranger for directions or assistance
☐ Small social groups

One way to overcome shyness is to become more assertive. **Assertiveness** involves the honest expression of how you feel, standing up for your own rights without violating the rights of others. Assertiveness can be contrasted with both aggressiveness and shyness. **Aggressiveness** involves violating the rights of others, hurting others by putting them down, attacking them, or demanding that your own needs be met at their expense. The assertive person is able to express thoughts and feelings, to look people in the eye, to talk to them directly, to make requests, and to refuse requests without belittling others or injuring them. The shy person is unable to make requests of others and is unable to refuse the requests others make. Unlike the assertive person, the shy person is not able to stand up for his or her rights. Shyness, assertiveness, and aggressiveness can be thought of as on a line, or a continuum, with assertiveness in the middle:

| Shyness | Assertiveness | Aggressiveness |

Imagine that you were in a restaurant and had ordered breakfast, including whole wheat toast and scrambled eggs. When the waitress brings your food, you find white toast and poached eggs. What do you do?

☐ *The aggressive response:* You tell the waitress off, sarcastically pointing out that the order may have been too complicated for someone of limited intelligence to understand.

☐ *The shy response:* You say, "OK," and eat the food you were given.   You grumble to yourself, thinking that you will not come back to this restaurant.   When the waitress asks how your food is, you say "Fine, thank you."

☐ *The assertive response:* You call the waitress over, point out the mistake, and ask that it be corrected.   When the waitress brings the correct order, you thank her, and then eat your breakfast.

Shy people can become more assertive by trying certain physical and verbal techniques.   Physical techniques for increasing assertiveness include looking people directly in the eye more often, increasing the loudness of your voice somewhat, and holding your head erect.   Verbal techniques for increasing assertiveness include the "broken record" technique, the "fog-

Aggressiveness involves attacking others and demanding that your needs be met at their expense; by contrast, assertiveness involves standing up for your own rights without violating the rights of others.   (Paul Conklin)

ging" technique, and the "negative assertion" technique.

The **broken-record technique** involves calmly repeating your main point until the other person understands it.   A persistent magazine salesman can be handled by saying, "I'm sure your offer is a good one, but I do not want to subscribe at this time."   As the salesman pushes you for a sale, you repeat again and again, "I'm sure your offer is a good one, but I do not want to subscribe at this time."   The broken-record technique can also be used in making requests.   It can be used effectively in asking a store manager for a refund for something you bought.   In this case, the technique involves repeating over and over that you understand the manager's problems, but you want your money back.

The **fogging technique** is a way of coping with someone who continuously nags.   The technique involves expressing understanding and agreeing in principle with at least a portion of what the other person is saying, but still maintaining your own rights.   The following conversation illustrates the use of fogging.[12]

Jeff: I see you are dressed in your usual sloppy manner.

Carl: That's right.   I am dressed in my usual way. (Fogging)

Jeff: Those pants!   They look like you stole them off the Goodwill rack without pressing them.

Carl: They are a bit wrinkled, aren't they. (Fogging)

Jeff: Wrinkled is the understatement of the week.   They are positively dreadful.

Carl: You're probably right.   They do look a bit worse for wear. (Fogging)

The **negative-assertion technique** involves acknowledging a mistake or agreeing with criticism—even hostile criticism—without agreeing that you are a bad or worthless person.   This technique should be used only when you have in fact made a mistake or done something wrong.   Instead of apologizing for your stupidity or feeling bad or guilty about yourself, you accept the fact of your mistakes.

Interim Summary   Most information in conversations is exchanged nonverbally, in "body talk." Two types of nonverbal communication are regulators and body messages. Regulators are nonverbal signals that indicate that communication and comprehension are occurring. They regulate the flow of the conversation. Body messages convey actual information; for example, facial expressions send body messages about emotion. Another way in which we communicate nonverbally is through the distance that we maintain between ourselves and others, reflecting the zone around our bodies called personal space.

Shyness is a discomfort in interacting with and confronting others. Shyness can be overcome by becoming more assertive. Assertiveness can be increased through such techniques as the broken record, fogging, and negative assertion.

Friendship

Will Rogers once said, "I never met a man I didn't like." Most of us, however, like some people and dislike others. You have met a lot of people in your life, but only a few of them became your friends. Why did those particular people become your friends and not others? How do you feel about them?

A Friendship Scale

Can friendship be measured? One psychologist has developed what he calls a "liking scale," a way of measuring how well one person likes another.[1] Think of a good friend of yours, and check the items below that reflect your attitudes toward that person.

☐ When I am with this person, we are almost always in the same mood.
☐ I think that this person is unusually well adjusted.
☐ I would highly recommend this person for a responsible job.
☐ In my opinion, this person is an exceptionally mature person.
☐ I have great confidence in this person's good judgment.
☐ Most people would react very favorably to this person after a brief acquaintance.
☐ I think that this person and I are quite similar to each other.
☐ I would vote for this person in a class or group election.

☐ I think that this person is one of those people who quickly wins respect.
☐ I feel that this person is an extremely intelligent person.
☐ This person is one of the most likable people I know.
☐ This person is the sort of person I myself would like to be.
☐ It seems to me that it is very easy for this person to gain admiration.

Now go back and answer the questions again—this time, from the point of view of your good friend thinking about *you*. The items in the "liking scale" reflect three aspects of liking: respect for the other person, a positive evaluation of the other person, and the perception that the other person is similar to you. Do these correspond to what it means to you to like someone?

Similarity and Complementarity

Think about yourself and your friends, then try to decide which of the following is true:

1. Birds of a feather flock together.
2. Opposites attract.

Are you and your friends similar, or are you opposite in many ways? When you think about it, you will realize that you and your friends are similar in some ways and different in others, so neither of these general rules is probably totally true for you.

Birds of a Feather • In certain ways, you and your friends are similar. According to the **principle of similarity,** birds of a feather should flock together; people who are similar ("of a feather") should be friendly ("flock together").

Who your friends are depends in part on which people you meet, since you cannot make friends with people you never heard of. But the people you meet are often similar to you in various ways: they may be similar geographically if they live in the same general area; they are often similar economically and similar in age. One study of engaged couples found similarities in many background dimensions, including religious affiliation, income and social status of parents, and the type of family relationship in which they were raised.[13] Persons tend to select marriage partners of similar intelligence level[14] and of similar educational attainment.[15] A series of studies has shown that the degree of interpersonal liking is related to the proportion of agreement in attitudes and beliefs between couples.[16,17]

Why should we be attracted to persons who are similar to us in attitude and belief? One possibility is that we respond to those who support us when they express agreement with our ideas, and this validation is a rewarding experience.

Opposites Attract • A common theory of friendship and love is that "opposites attract." This is called the **principle of complementarity.** If you and a friend are *complementary,* you are opposite but each supplies what the other lacks. The idea is that you like people who are mirror images of yourself— their strengths are your weaknesses or their needs and your needs are opposite and therefore do not compete.[18] For example, a socially awkward person may particularly value a person who is socially at ease. A person who needs to dominate may value a person who needs to be submissive. A person who is dependent may be attracted to a person who tends to take charge. This theory would be supported by evidence showing that people who like each other have personality characteristics that are opposite. Although some studies have found a tendency toward opposing personalities between friends,[19] most studies find couples to have similar, not opposite, personalities.[20,21,22] Thus, while there is some evidence that opposites attract, most of the evidence supports the idea that birds of a feather flock together.

Reinforcement and Exchange Theories

Our relationships are a source of rewards and punishments for us. Some relationships are highly rewarding, others are punishing, and still others are rather mixed. According to the **reinforcement theory of friendship,** we tend to like those people who reward or reinforce us; the more they reward us, the better we like them.[23] According to operant conditioning and the Law of Effect, the social interactions that have rewarding consequences should be repeated and strengthened. There are many potential rewards in relationships: praise, approval, agreement, and uncritical acceptance are all rewarding. This idea was expressed by a character in one of Disraeli's novels when he said, "My idea of an agreeable person is a person who agrees with me."

The best-selling book by Dale Carnegie, *How to Win Friends and Influence People,*[24] argues that people like to be appreciated, and they tend to like those who express this appreciation. Many psychological studies have confirmed that people like those who reward them through praise or other positive evaluations.[25,26,27]

An alternative view of how people become close is the **exchange theory of friendship.**[28] According to this theory, there is an "interpersonal marketplace" and each person has a "market value." Physical attractiveness, high status, wealth, wit, and other characteristics add to our market value. Those with high market values have high capacities for rewarding others. We estimate our own desirability, then try to form relationships with those with equal or greater value. If we overestimate our value, we risk rejection. People who are extremely attractive, according to this theory, tend to associate with others who are extremely attractive (or wealthy) because they are after the best deal they can get in the "marketplace."

One experiment manipulated the estimations people had of their own value.[29] The experimenter gave a group of men an IQ test, then told half of them that they had done exceptionally well and told the remaining half that they had done exceptionally poorly. These results, of course, were faked; what the men were told was unrelated to how they actually scored on the test. The subjects of the experiment were then placed in contact with a young woman who was made up to look either extremely attractive or quite plain. The men who had been told that they did well on the IQ test were more likely to make romantic advances to the attractive woman; the men who had been told that they did poorly were more likely to make advances to the plain woman. The faked IQ results apparently had raised or lowered the estimates the men had of their own social desirability, or market value, and this—in turn—influenced their subsequent selection of a romantic partner with a high or low market value.

To think of friendship in terms of reinforcement and market values is to have, it seems to me, a particularly limited and pessimistic view of friendship. While there is certainly some truth in these two theories, most of us have experienced close friendships that cannot adequately be described in these economic terms. What do these theories leave out? They fail to discuss commitment, loyalty, and sensitive understanding, and these, I believe, are more important than ego reinforcement. What do you think?

Interim Summary   Why do two people become friends? One possibility is that people like those who are similar to them (principle of similarity); a second possibility is that people like those with opposite needs (principle of complementarity). Most available evidence supports the principle of similarity. Two theories to account for the formation of friendships are the reinforcement theory and the exchange theory. According to the reinforcement theory, we like those people who reward us with praise, agreement, or validation. People who are similar to us are more likely to be agreeable and therefore more likely to be reinforcing. According to the exchange theory, we estimate our own "market value," then try to form relationships with those of equal or higher value.

Close Relationships

We are social creatures; much of life consists of relating to others. We have close interpersonal relationships with family, friends, lovers, and others in our society with whom we come in frequent contact. The quality of these relationships significantly contributes to the quality of life. Persons who are psychologically healthy have the capacity to develop deep and satisfying relationships with others. This does not mean that your health is measured by the number of your friends. Quite the contrary is true; studies of particularly healthy individuals have shown that they tend to have only a few intense relationships. Thus, the quality, not the quantity, of human relationships is the key factor.

Relationships that Promote or Block Growth

Human relationships are opportunities for growth. Good relationships foster self-understanding, self-confidence, and self-acceptance; they provide us with the chance to exercise our most positive human traits—love, commitment, and trust.

Martin Buber has described two forms of interpersonal relationship.[30] The **I-Thou relationship** is a relationship between the being of one and the being of another; it is a relationship in which each person *confirms* the other by recognizing, validating, and accepting the other's nature. By contrast, the **I-it relationship** occurs between an observer and an object; one person is treated as a thing, not a unique being. Perhaps in some relationship you have felt treated as an object, a thing to be manipulated, instead of a separate being with your own feelings, needs, and perceptions. I-Thou relationships promote growth, but I-it relationships block growth.

Test Your Relationships

Think about the different interpersonal relationships in which you are involved. You have relationships with members of your family, with neighbors, with friends in school, and with peers of the opposite sex. What is the quality of these relationships? Good interpersonal relationships have special characteristics, some of which are listed below. You can test each of your relationships against this list to judge its quality.

☐ *Is it honest?*   Each of you can risk being honest with the other. You are not afraid to tell the other person what you are thinking and how you feel.

☐ *Is it supportive?*   You are mutually supportive and accepting of the other. You express your approval, praise, and appreciation of the other. You accept and value the other person just the way he or she is.

☐ *Is it deep?*   The relationship is between two "real" selves, not between the social or public impressions you try to create. Each of you feels you really know and understand the other in a personal, not superficial, way.

☐ *Is it meaningful?*   The relationship is a significant part of your life. What happens to the other and how he or she feels are matters of concern for you.

☐ *Is it transcendent?*   Each of you is involved with the life of the other in an unselfish way. You are not self-centered or egocentric in the relationship; you are not in it for what you can get out of it. The relationship transcends, or goes beyond, your selfish needs.

Sources of Difficulty

Few interpersonal relationships have all of the ideal features just listed. Healthy relationships do not just happen but have to be actively built. It takes commitment and work on the part of both people. Why are your relationships not ideal? Some of the sources of difficulty in interpersonal relationships are presented here for you to consider.[31] Which are your stumbling blocks?

☐ *Egocentricity*   A concern with one's own interests to the extent of being insensitive to the welfare and rights of others.

☐ *Deceitfulness*   A tendency, often accompanying egocentricity, to take an exploitative approach to interpersonal relationships. Sometimes deceit extends to outright lying and stealing, but more commonly it shows itself in the efforts of an "operator" to manipulate people and situations to his or her own advantage.

☐ *Overdependency*   A tendency to lean excessively upon others for either material aid or emotional support and to rely upon them for making decisions.

☐ *Hostility*   A tendency to be antagonistic and suspicious toward other people.

☐ *Inferior feelings*   A basic lack of self-confidence or self-esteem which may be expressed either in oversensitivity to "threat" or in exaggerated efforts to prove one's own adequacy and worth by such techniques as boasting, showing off, and being hypercritical of other people.

☐ *Emotional insulation*   An inability to make the necessary emotional investment in a relationship, for fear of being hurt.

Interim Summary   Some relationships promote personal growth while others do not. Buber's I-Thou relationship promotes growth because participants confirm and validate each other. By contrast, the I-it relationship blocks growth because one person treats the other as an object to be manipulated.

Marriage

For most people, the longest and most intimate relationship they will ever have is with a spouse. The deep, long-term relationship of marriage offers a means for self-fulfillment and for growth. The value of marriage is widely recognized. In a recent survey, thousands of high school seniors were asked to rate the importance of a list of major life goals.[32] Some rated

What are your expectations about marriage? Difficulties result when people enter marriage with false and unrealistic expectations. Marriage does not solve all problems, rarely makes an unhappy person happy, and is not a good cure for loneliness. (© Mike Malyszko 1977/Stock, Boston)

as very important the goals of "having lots of money" or "finding purpose and meaning in my life" or "making a contribution to society." But the goal rated highest in importance was having "a good marriage and family life."

Why Marry?

Most people eventually will marry, but they will marry for different reasons—love, companionship, children, a home life, or money. A study of husbands and wives reported that 56 percent of the wives and 39 percent of the husbands indicated that they married for love.[33] As one wife expressed it,

We fell in love, we wanted to be together. After 31 years of marriage my heart still skips a beat when he enters the room. There is no other person I would rather spend my life with than him.

A husband who was asked why he married responded, "Nothing but love. Full of love." Other husbands and wives interviewed in the study reported different reasons for marrying. One wife said, "I decided to marry because I wanted security." Another wife reported, "I was young and I wanted sex with him all the time but felt guilty outside of marriage." A husband said, "I thought I was lonely. My first wife had left me. And all my friends were married and I just felt lonely."

What will be (or were) your reasons for marrying? Check off the three or four reasons in the list at the top of page 281 that you regard as most important:

☐ love
☐ security
☐ children
☐ sex
☐ companionship
☐ a home life
☐ parental expectations
☐ social pressure
☐ religious beliefs

Readiness for Marriage

When is someone "ready" for marriage? For some people, readiness is determined by the calender: at age eighteen, for example, or upon graduating from high school or college. For others, readiness for marriage is determined by economic readiness: when a particular income or level of savings is achieved. But psychological readiness for marriage is determined by the maturity of the two individuals involved.

According to Erik Erikson, each person passes through different stages of life as one moves from birth, to maturity, to death. In late adolescence, in Erikson's fifth stage of psychosocial development, individuals face a crisis of identity. Their task is to build a firm sense of distinct identity, to define themselves, to discover their essential character. Without a sense of identity, individuals are unable to form close and committed relationships with others. One test of readiness for marriage is whether the two potential partners have each achieved a firm sense of identity.

Marriage requires work to be successful, and certain interpersonal skills and a certain level of maturity are essential for success. Readiness for marriage depends upon how mature you are and how skilled you are in working out interpersonal problems. According to one author,[34] you should ask yourself the following questions before you marry:

Yes No

____ ____ 1. Are you in touch with your feelings? Are you aware, for example, of your own feelings about your dependency needs, or your needs to be mothered or fathered?

____ ____ 2. Can you accept your feelings? Are you able to accept your needs to be dependent, dominant, passive, or nurturant?

____ ____ 3. Can you live with yourself? Can you make yourself happy? Can you be alone in a room and enjoy your own company? Or are you seeking someone else to define your identity for you?

____ ____ 4. Can you communicate your needs? Do people know what you really want? Or are you afraid to express what you want?

____ ____ 5. Can you face your problems instead of blaming them on someone else? Are you mature enough to acknowledge your own problems?

____ ____ 6. Can you see your future mate as he or she really is? Or are you seeing things that aren't there? Do you need someone so desperately that you can't see straight?

____ ____ 7. Can you really share? Do you feel that you can't belong to someone without losing your identity? Do you feel threatened by the prospect of another person's presence in your life?

____ ____ 8. Are you aware of the influence your parents may have had on you and your expectations? Are you able to distinguish between your problems and those of your parents that may have influenced you?

If you are able to answer most of these questions "yes," you have a sense of your own identity, an acceptance of yourself, and an ability to communicate and to share. These are important achievements for those considering marriage.

Marriage Myths

Movies, novels, television, and fairy tales present many different views of marriage and what being married is like. Many of these are completely unrealistic, but they nevertheless strongly affect our expectations about what our marriages will be like. From the point of view presented in fantasy, being in love is the central issue of marriage; the problems, conflicts, and hard work are typically ignored. It is no surprise, then, that so many young people enter into marriage with the wholly unrealistic expectation that, because they are in love, they will have no problems. What are your expectations about marriage? What do you think it will be like? Some of the more common false expectations—or marriage myths—are the following:[35,36]

☐ 1. If a couple is in love, all problems will be solved easily. (In fact, all married couples face problems, and solving many problems requires skill and hard work.)

☐ 2. If you can just find the right person to marry, all problems will take care of themselves. (No problems take care of themselves. Problems are taken care of only when they are confronted and discussed and dealt with.)

☐ 3. If my spouse really loves me, he or she will intuitively know what I want or need and will make sure my needs are met. (Relying on good and deliberate communication, not ESP, works much better. People who don't say what they want generally don't get what they want.)

☐ 4. In a good marriage, the romance of the honeymoon continues forever. (This happens only in the movies. A good marriage may occasionally recapture the romance of the honeymoon, but involves a lot more than constant romance.)

☐ 5. In a good marriage, your spouse can satisfy all your needs. (Few people could tolerate the burden of being responsible for satisfying all the needs of someone else, even a spouse.)

☐ 6. My marriage relationship will be completely different from other relationships that I have had that have not worked. (It is most unlikely that everything will suddenly change. It is much more likely that your marriage will suffer some of the same problems found in your other relationships.)

☐ 7. When you get married, you become an adult. (Growing up is not so easy. It is wiser to become an adult first, then marry.)

☐ 8. Marriage will make an unhappy person happy. (Marriage is not a cure-all. The problems you had before marriage will likely continue.)

☐ 9. Marriage is a good cure for loneliness. (If you were unable to establish and maintain close relationships before marriage, you may have difficulty establishing such a relationship with your spouse.)

☐ 10. You can become a "complete" or "whole" person through marriage. (Marriage is not a good way to resolve an identity problem. When half a person marries half a person, the result is not a whole person; the result is half a marriage.)

Sex Roles in Marriage

What are the appropriate roles (expected behaviors) for husbands and wives? Who should make the decisions, and how should the labor of the marriage be divided? In a recent survey of 759 married couples, husbands and wives were asked a series of questions about sex roles in marriage.[37] How would you have answered the survey questions?

- Who should provide the income?
  - ☐ Husband entirely
  - ☐ Husband more
  - ☐ Husband and wife equally
  - ☐ Wife more
  - ☐ Wife entirely

- Who should do the housekeeping?
  - ☐ Husband entirely
  - ☐ Husband more
  - ☐ Husband and wife equally
  - ☐ Wife more
  - ☐ Wife entirely

- Who should take care of preschool children?
  - ☐ Husband entirely
  - ☐ Husband more
  - ☐ Husband and wife equally
  - ☐ Wife more
  - ☐ Wife entirely

The results of the survey showed a range of different views about how the labor of marriage should be divided. Eighty-eight percent of wives and 88 percent of husbands believed that husbands should either be more responsible or entirely responsible for producing the family income. Ninety-one percent of wives and 87 percent of husbands believed that wives should either be more responsible or entirely responsible for doing the housekeeping. And 88 percent of wives and 83 percent of husbands believed that wives should either be more responsible or entirely responsible for the care of preschool children.

One of the most common views of sex roles in marriage is the **traditional marriage model.** In this type of marriage, the roles and responsibilities of husbands and wives are distinct, with husbands supporting the family while wives take care of the house and the children. This model has been criticized recently for not providing wives with adequate opportunities for personal growth and self-fulfillment. From the point of view of some critics, wives in the traditional model are little more than slaves working for room and board. But supporters of this model argue that traditional wives can lead highly rewarding lives. As one woman put it, "I'm a mother and a housewife—and I'm proud of it!"

A second view of sex roles in marriage is expressed in the **egalitarian marriage model.** In this type of marriage, the roles and responsibilities are shared (the term "egalitarian" means "promoting human equality.") In the egalitarian marriage, husbands and wives share the household chores as well as the task of proving the family income. Unfortunately, as increasing numbers of women are having to work, many wives find themselves thrust into a mixed marriage model that combines the worst of both the traditional and the egalitarian models: they have to do all the housework and also provide part of the income.

A third view of sex roles in marriage is expressed in the **reversed-roles marriage model.** In this type of marriage, the traditional roles and responsibilities of the husband are performed by the wife, and vice versa. The reversed-role arrangement can come about because of a basic conviction on the part of the couple involved, or, more likely, comes about when the husband loses his job and the wife continues to work. Reports from such arrangements suggest that "househusbands" with working wives are perfectly capable of learning how to cook, to care for the house, and to provide loving care for preschool children.

As more women join the work force and gain more power outside the home, sex roles in marriage will probably change. Modern marriage often is a compromise between the traditional marriage model and the egalitarian marriage model, with husbands sharing portions of the housework and wives sharing the burden of providing family income. The marriage of the future will probably involve greater sharing and will more closely resemble the egalitarian model.

Interim Summary

Readiness for marriage requires that both individuals have established a firm sense of identity, that they are able to communicate effectively, and that they have the skills needed to work out interpersonal problems. Our expectations of marriage are affected by many unrealistic ideas, such as that love solves all problems or that the romance of the honeymoon should continue forever. Different views of the sex roles in marriage are expressed in the traditional marriage model, the egalitarian marriage model, and the reversed-roles marriage model.

Summary

1. Relationships are based on communication. Authentic communication involves an actual exchange of information and feelings, but to disclose yourself to others involves some risk.
2. If you disclose your true feelings to another person, the other person will often reciprocate by revealing important feelings to you; this reciprocation of self-disclosure is called the dyadic effect.
3. Parallaction occurs when two people talk without listening or when no real meaning is exchanged. Mystification occurs when one or both of the two people talking

attempt to hide the truth or falsify their true feelings.   Games are dishonest interactions in which the object is to win rather than to communicate.

4. Regulators and body signals are two types of nonverbal communication.   Regulators control the flow of the conversation, while body messages communicate actual information just as words do.   Another way we communicate nonverbally is through the physical distance we maintain between ourselves and others.

5. The optimal interpersonal distance is the distance between two people that is most comfortable (usually less for friends than for strangers).   When two people walk toward each other, their personal spaces eventually intersect; at this point, they have reached their optimal interpersonal distance.

6. Shyness is discomfort in the presence of others, a feeling of awkwardness in social interactions, and difficulty confronting other people.   At the opposite extreme of the social continuum is aggressiveness (attacking others or violating their rights).   Between shyness and aggressiveness is assertiveness.   Assertiveness is the honest expression of how you feel, standing up for your own rights without violating the rights of others.

7. The broken record, fogging, and negative assertion are three techniques for increasing assertiveness.

8. The principle of similarity (birds of a feather flock together) and the principle of complementarity (opposites attract) are two explanations of friendship.   Most of the evidence supports the principle of similarity.

9. According to the reinforcement theory of friendship, we tend to like those people who reward or reinforce us.   An alternate view is the exchange theory of friendship, which assumes that we strive to form relationships with those of equal or greater desirability or status.

10. Buber's I-Thou relationships promote growth because the participants support and confirm each other; by contrast, the I-it relationships block growth because one person treats the other as an object.

11. Readiness for marriage depends upon psychological maturity: the individuals must have established a clear sense of personal identity, must be able to communicate effectively, and must have the skills necessary to solve the interpersonal problems that will arise.

Key Concepts

parallaction   A pseudo-interaction, without real involvement, in which each participant acts independently and does not exchange information.

mystification   A form of miscommunication in which the participants are hiding their real feelings or intentions.

games   Stereotyped interactions in which the hidden motive is to win, not to exchange information or feelings.

authentic communication   A true exchange of information and feelings involving openness and self-disclosure.

dyadic effect   The tendency for self-disclosure to be reciprocated; when one person is open and honest in a relationship, the other person is encouraged to be open and honest in return.

nonverbal communication   Communication through facial expression, posture, speech inflection, and body movements; that is, communication that does not depend upon the meaning of words.

regulators   Body signals sent between two people that indicate whether comprehension is occurring and that control the flow of the conversation.

body messages   Nonverbal communications, such as hand gestures or emotional expressions, that convey actual information.

territory   Geographical area that a person or animal lives in and defends against invasions.

personal space   The immediate area surrounding the body that a person defends from invasion; the person's portable territory.

optimal interpersonal distance   The physical distance between two people at which they feel most comfortable; close enough for comfort, but far enough away so that personal spaces are not violated.

shyness   Discomfort in the presence of others; inability to express oneself openly and honestly.

assertiveness   The honest expression of how you feel and the standing up for your own rights without violating the rights of others.

aggressiveness   Violation of the rights of others, hurting others by putting them down, or demanding that your own needs be met at the expense of others.

broken-record technique   A technique for increasing your assertiveness that involves calmly repeating your main point over and over until the other person understands it.

fogging technique   A technique for increasing assertiveness that involves expressing understanding and agreeing in principle with some portion of the other person's criticism while still maintaining your own rights.

negative-assertion technique   A technique for increasing assertiveness that involves acknowledging a mistake or agreeing with criticism without agreeing that you are a bad or worthless person.

principle of similarity   The idea that people like others who are similar to themselves in values, beliefs, and background; in other words, that "birds of a feather flock together."

principle of complementarity   The idea that people like others who are unlike themselves, and that one looks for someone to supply what the other lacks; in other words, that "opposites attract."

reinforcement theory of friendship   The theory that you like those people who reward you.

exchange theory of friendship   The theory that you form friendships by estimating your "market value," then forming relationships with those with equal or higher value.

I-Thou relationship   A relationship in which each person confirms the other by recognizing, validating, and accepting the other's nature.

I-it relationship   A relationship in which one person is treated as an object, a thing to be manipulated, instead of as a unique being.

traditional marriage model   One of the most common views of sex roles in marriage; the roles and responsibilities of husbands and wives are distinct, with husbands supporting the family while wives take care of the house and children.

egalitarian marriage model   In this type of marriage the roles and responsibilities are shared.

reversed-roles marriage model   In this type of marriage the traditional roles and responsibilities of husband and wife are reversed, with wives supporting the family and husbands caring for the house and children.

Chapter 14

Male and Female

Key Questions

1. How masculine or feminine are you?
2. How did you develop your masculine or feminine identity?
3. What does it mean to be a homosexual?
4. What are the origins of homosexuality?

How feminine are you? How masculine are you?

The term *masculine* does not mean simply having a male body—it refers to the many, often subtle, qualities and behaviors usually associated with men. Although you might make a few mistakes, you can generally tell a man from a woman without knowing *any* physical characteristics; you can make judgments based on behavior alone, because men tend to behave differently from women. Consider your behavior: do you ever go shopping in a dress? Do you like to play football? Do you open car doors for your date? Do you sometimes wear lipstick? You can guess a person's sex if you know how the person answers these four questions.

Masculinity-Femininity

Because football is a game more often played by men than by women, playing football is considered a *masculine* activity. It is more characteristic of men than of women. The two sexes differ not only in behavior but also in personality. For example, on the average, men tend to be more dominant and aggressive than women. Personality traits like dominance and aggressiveness are therefore considered masculine characteristics.

A Test to Take

Some traits are more characteristic of men and some more of women. A group of two hundred college freshmen taking my psychology class checked those adjectives below which best described their personalities. Of the sixteen traits in the list, half were checked significantly more often by men and half more often by women. Those eight checked more often by men can be called masculine traits and the eight checked more often by women can be called feminine traits. Can you tell the difference? Mark each trait with an M or F to indicate whether you think it is masculine or feminine. Then, circle the traits which describe you.

—— 1. Scientific	—— 9. Emotional
—— 2. Romantic	—— 10. Sensitive
—— 3. Domestic	—— 11. Wise
—— 4. Logical	—— 12. Mechanical
—— 5. Competitive	—— 13. Sincere
—— 6. Affectionate	—— 14. Intuitive
—— 7. Sensible	—— 15. Brave
—— 8. Vulgar	—— 16. Delicate

You will probably discover that you, like most people, have a combination of masculine and feminine traits. Those traits checked more often by male students were 1, 4, 5, 7, 8, 11, 12, and 15. The remaining traits were checked more often by females. On the whole, the feminine traits were checked more often than the masculine traits. For example, even though 90 percent of the females considered themselves "sensitive," nearly three-fourths of the males also checked "sensitive." What does it mean if you consider yourself a sincere and sensitive male or a sensible and logical female? You are not alone. Many of the male and female college students in my study described themselves in that way.

"Masculine" and "feminine" are not opposites. A person can have both masculine and feminine traits. One psychologist recently developed a test similar to the one above; it consists of a list of such masculine traits as "aggressive," "competitive," and "dominant," and such feminine traits as "affectionate," "compassionate," and "gentle."[1] The psychologist found that about one-third of the men and women tested scored about equally masculine and feminine; that is, they rated themselves as having about the same number of masculine and feminine traits. Individuals having both masculine and feminine traits are called **androgynous**. Androgynous individuals have a broader range of options and can adapt to a wide range of situations. Unlike people who are exclusively masculine or feminine in their behavior, androgynous individuals can be both sensible and sensitive, both competitive and affectionate.

Human sexuality is expressed in polarity: male and female. Your identification with one of these poles was in important step in your childhood. With that identification came a **sex role**—the requirement to adopt the attitudes, to wear the clothes, and to engage in the behavior appropriate for males or females. Sex roles, however, which once were clearly defined, are now more blurred. Women are demanding more active roles and men are developing more emotional roles than ever before. In some places, men and women are even beginning to look alike; most of us have had the experience of passing persons on the street without knowing whether they were male or female.

What are your ideals of male and female roles? Do you support the traditional idea that men should be decision-makers and women should be helpers? (© Joel Gordon 1978)

Three New Guinea Tribes

Ideas of masculinity and femininity are different in different cultures. The anthropologist Margaret Mead, in studying the people of the island of New Guinea, described a remarkable tribe of lake dwellers called the Tchambuli.[2] Tchambuli men, it seems, are emotionally dependent and sexually passive. They like to gossip and spend time decorating their bodies. They are sensitive persons who enjoy painting, music, and drama. On the other hand, Tchambuli women are responsible for obtaining food for the family and are impersonal and businesslike. They are more dominant and sexually aggressive than the Tchambuli men. Typical behaviors characterizing many American men and women appear reversed for Tchambuli men and women. That is, typical sex *roles* are reversed. The Tchambuli children learn what is appropriate for their sex *in their culture*. How well would you fit in the Tchambuli culture?

Mead describes two other New Guinea cultures. For one culture, the Mundugumor, both men and women are described as violent, aggressive, and competitive—in other words, characterized by "masculine" traits according to American standards. In a neighboring culture, the Arapesh, both men and women are gentle, loving, and cooperative—what we would call "feminine" traits.

Apparently behavior typical of men and of women is not exclusively biologically determined but is highly influenced by cultural norms. The older members of a given culture pass on to the younger members of that culture characteristic patterns of behavior; these patterns are different in different cultures.

The Norm Is Not the Ideal

It is important for you not to confuse the psychological concepts of masculinity and femininity with other ways in which these words are sometimes used. The concept of **masculinity** in psychology refers to how much a person acts the way men act in their culture or how closely behavior conforms to the norm for men. The concept of **femininity** refers to how much a person acts the way women act or how closely behavior conforms to the norm for women. **Norms** are standards based on the way people do in fact behave in a particular society at a particular time in history.

Psychology uses a **normative model** of masculinity-femininity, a standard based on the norm. There is no implication that people should conform to this model, although you may experience social pressure to do so.

A different meaning of these terms is involved when they are used in a *prescriptive* sense, an attempt to define how you should act. To be masculine—in the sense of a "real man"—refers to conformity, not to a behavioral norm, but to an **idealized model**, a standard based on the ideal. Each society has a concept of what the ideal man or the ideal woman should be like, and these concepts differ among different societies. Individuals within a society disagree about what is ideally feminine or ideally masculine. Thus, while some fathers cheat on their income tax, they tell their sons that it is not "manly" to cheat on their school examinations. Some people believe that being ideally masculine includes being sensitive and that being ideally feminine includes being sensible. What are your concepts of being ideally masculine and ideally feminine?

The women's liberation movement is changing our concept of what is "feminine"—in the sense of the idealized model. From the women's liberation point of view, the submissiveness, the sexual passivity, and the dependency expected of women lead to a kind of "slavery" that prevent full human development. Unfortunately, the degree to which women are sexually attractive is for many men dependent upon the degree to which they conform to the feminine idealized model for this society.

Men are also shackled by an idealized model of masculinity that requires them to be decisive, dominant, and aggressive. These idealized models severely limit alternative choices and the unique expression of individuality in both men and women. There is, however, some indication that this is changing as the sex roles blur. Both men and women seem to be experiencing less pressure to conform to narrowly defined ideal models.

Interim Summary   Behavior that is typical of men and women in one culture may be quite different in another culture. The ideals of male and female behavior also differ among cultures. You are called masculine or feminine to the degree that your behavior conforms to what is typical of your culture. However, in American society the pressure for people to conform to these standards seems to be decreasing.

Sex-Role Acquisition

What are the origins of your masculinity or femininity? How did you acquire the attitudes, mannerisms, preferences, and behaviors that are characteristic for persons of your sex? You began to learn at an early age that the behavior appropriate for men was often inappropriate for women and vice versa. Evidence shows that the majority of children by the age of three are aware of their sexual identity and—to some extent—begin to act accordingly.[3] Preference for the masculine or the feminine sex role also begins to emerge early in life, probably by the age of three or four.

In this society the male sex role seems to be more narrowly defined than the female sex role. While girls can engage in activities more appropriate for the male role without being considered abnormal, this is not true for boys. Girls can wear shirts and pants and can play with trucks and guns with little or no social disapproval; boys, however, cannot wear dresses or play with dishes and sewing materials without parental disapproval.

The Freudian Theory

You may think that your pattern of sexual behavior began suddenly with adolescence, but it is unlikely that this is so. Most of your behavior has roots in your childhood.

At the beginning of this century Sigmund Freud shocked his contemporaries by asserting that children not only have sexual desires, but they have incestuous sexual desires for their own parents. According to Freud's **principle of infantile sexuality,** sexual gratification is obtained throughout childhood from a variety of sources. Freud thought of personality development in terms of a progression of **psychosexual stages,** periods of development defined by different sources of sexual pleasure.

The Oral Stage • According to Freud's theory, during the first year of life, in the **oral stage,** the infant gains sexual pleasure from sucking and biting. Freud wrote:

The infant's first sexual excitations appear in connection with the other functions important for life. Its chief interest, as you know, is concerned with taking nourishment; as it sinks asleep at the breast, utterly satisfied, it bears a look of perfect content which will come back again later in life after the experience of the sexual orgasm. . . . We perceive that infants wish to repeat, without really getting any nourishment, the action necessary to taking nourishment. . . . The action of sucking is sufficient in itself to give it satisfaction. . . .

Sucking for nourishment becomes the point of departure from which the whole sexual life develops, the unattainable prototype of every later sexual satisfaction, to which in time of need phantasy often enough reverts. . . .

This assessment of the nature of pleasure-sucking has now brought to our notice two of the decisive characteristics of infantile sexuality. It appears in connection with the satisfaction of the great organic needs, and it behaves auto-erotically, that is to say, it seeks and finds its objects in its own person.[4]

The Anal Stage • After the oral stage the infant enters a second stage of psychosexual development, the **anal stage.** Freud believed that in this second stage sexual pleasure centers around the eliminative functions, the urinary and bowel habits. Of this stage, Freud wrote:

What is more clearly discernible in regard to the taking of nourishment is to some extent repeated with the process of excretion. We conclude that infants experience pleasure in the evacuation of urine and the contents of the bowels, and that they very soon endeavor to continue these actions so that the accompanying excitation of the membranes in these ero-

togenic zones may secure them the maximum possible gratification.[4]

The Phallic Stage •

From ages three to about six, in the **phallic stage,** the source of sexual gratification for the child is masturbation—the manipulation of the penis or the clitoris. Many parents are aware of their child's masturbatory activity that begins during this period.

Toward the end of this stage, a crisis called the **Oedipus complex** develops in which the child experiences conflict because of sexual desire for the parent of the opposite sex. This incestuous desire causes the child to compete for the affection of the parent but also to fear retaliation from the parent's mate. This conflict is resolved when the child identifies with the parent of the same sex. The child's sex role is determined when the identification is complete. Thus in the case of a boy, Freud assumed that he desired his mother and wished to displace his father. The boy's ambivalent feelings of fear, hostility, and love for his father that accompany his sexual desire for his mother end with the resolution of the Oedipus complex. The boy identifies with his father, strives to resemble him, and develops a masculine identity. In effect, the boy has decided, "If I can't fight him, I should join him."

The Latency Stage •

From Freud's point of view, the resolution of the Oedipus complex was achieved, first, as the boy repressed sexual desire by pushing it from awareness, and, second, as he began identifying with the father. The repression of sexual desire initiates the **latency stage,** a period of little sexual interest that precedes adolescence. During the latency stage sexual thoughts and impulses seem to be forgotten.

The Genital Stage •

The onset of puberty, at about twelve or thirteen years of age, marks the beginning of the **genital stage** of psychosexual development. This final stage in sexual maturation marks the occurrence of the expression of adult sexuality, in

Table 14-1 Stages of Psychosexual Development

Stage	Approximate Age	Source of Sexual Pleasure
Oral	0–1	Sucking, biting
Anal	1–3	Feces expulsion and retention
Phallic	3–6	Masturbation
Latency	6–12	Little or none
Genital	12–	Masturbation and intercourse

which gratification is found in masturbation and sexual intercourse.

From Freud's viewpoint, the development of sexual identity is the result of passing through a fixed series of stages and successfully resolving the Oedipus complex. The stages are defined in terms of biological processes, such as sucking, urinating, or masturbating. In Freud's theory, the sex role that is finally achieved by the developing child depends upon sex drive and its repression. Table 14-1 summarizes the stages of Freud's theory.

The Social-Learning Theory

In contrast to Freud's stage theory of psychosexual development, social-learning theory assumes that sex roles result not from biological forces or sexual conflicts but from learning. **Social-learning theory** is a general theory of behavior that focuses on the relation between behavior and the environment. It also emphasizes the influence of other people whose behavior is observed and imitated.

According to this theory of personality development, sex roles are learned through a combination of two basic processes: (1) observation and imitation of models, and (2) rewards and punishments. Boys observe and imitate the behavior of their fathers and other male figures who serve as **models;** girls observe and imitate their mothers and other female figures. In addition, children are explicitly taught masculine and feminine behaviors. Boys are complimented for "acting like a man" and girls are rewarded for displaying "feminine grace." Boys are punished for playing with dolls or wearing dresses, and girls are scolded when they act tough. In these ways, children learn appropriate sex-role behaviors.

The Stability of Sex Roles

The Stability of Sex Roles • Social-learning theory argues that "social learning"—learning by observing, imitating, and being rewarded by other people— begins in infancy and continues throughout life. By contrast, Freud's theory assumes that children identify with their parents primarily at the end of the phallic stage of psychosexual development as part of the resolution of the Oedipus complex.

Learning is a life-long affair, and sex-role learning is no different. Even as adults, we are rewarded for displaying certain types of sex-role behavior and punished for displaying others. For example, to some degree adult women are punished for aggressiveness and adult men are rewarded for this same trait. Often the pattern of social forces that react to our behavior remains quite stable, and when this is true our sex-role behavior also remains stable. However, if a child's environment changed—for example, from one rewarding masculine behaviors to one punishing these same behaviors—the boy or girl would begin to act differently. This illustrates a central difference between the psychoanalytic and social-learning theories: Psychoanalytic theory assumes that the personality is fixed at an early age, while social-learning theory assumes that the personality changes throughout life. Since, from the point of view of social-learning theory, sex-role behavior is maintained by changing forces *external* to the individual, sex-role behavior is assumed to be able to change in childhood or even later; by contrast, since psychoanalytic theory assumes that sex-role behavior reflects a stable *internal* personality trait, sex-role behavior is assumed to be acquired during childhood and then to remain unchanged during adult life.

According to the social-learning theory, sex roles are learned— through observation, imitation, and reinforcement—rather than genetically imprinted. Unlike the mother shown here, many women are now teaching their daughters that they need not choose the traditional female role. (© Erika Stone 1973/Photo Researchers, Inc.)

Imitating Models

Imitating Models • Another difference between social-learning and psychoanalytic theory is that psychoanalytic theory assumes that your achievement of sexual identity is entirely dependent upon the parent of the same sex. Boys identify with their fathers and girls with their mothers. In this way they acquire masculine and feminine traits. Social-learning theory, however, assumes that children learn sex-role behavior from many sources. While the parent of the same sex is an important source, other sources are available as well. There are other adults with whom the child comes into contact. There are older brothers and sisters and film and television stars who are regarded with admiration and are imitated in certain respects.

Furthermore, mothers are quite capable of teaching their sons how to behave in a masculine way, and fathers reward their daughters for behaving in feminine ways.

When children perceive their models as exercising power, displaying mastery, and receiving affection, identification takes place more readily because children desire these same experiences and attributes. Children copy success.[5] The extent to which children identify with their parents varies. For example, boys identify with fathers who are nurturant and supportive more than with fathers who are not.[6,7] For boys without a father, appropriate role models are usually found in older brothers, grandfathers, or friends of the family. Most children eventually achieve sexual identification with an adult of the same sex, but some do not.

Interim Summary   According to Freud, everyone passes through a fixed set of psychosexual stages, defined by their different sources of sexual pleasure. These stages are the oral (with sexual pleasure from sucking), anal (from urinary and bowel activities), phallic (from penis or clitoris), latency (from nothing), and genital (from penis or clitoris again). The Oedipus complex develops toward the end of the phallic stage and, according to Freud, results in the identification with the same-sexed parent. By contrast, social-learning theory assumes that the process of identifying with others occurs throughout life; from this point of view, the achievement of sexual identity results from observing and imitating others.

Sexual Variations

Although most children grow up to acquire typical masculine and feminine roles and to be attracted to members of the opposite sex, some do not. In some cases the variation from the typical involves adopting certain behaviors appropriate to the opposite sex. Others cases involve a variation in sexual identity.

Transvestism is the act of dressing in the clothes of the opposite sex in order to achieve sexual gratification. Transvestites are usually not homosexuals, and many are married. The overwhelming majority are males who cross-dress secretly, usually in front of a mirror, often as a prelude to masturbation or intercourse. Studies of the backgrounds of transvestites show that many as children were forced to wear girls' clothes or were rewarded for wearing feminine clothes by their parents.

Transsexualism is an intense discomfort with one's biological sex and an identification with members of the opposite sex. Transsexuals believe that they were born the "wrong sex"—a man in a woman's body or a woman in a man's body. The transsexual male, unlike the transvestite, views himself as a woman trapped in a man's body. The intense denial of their biological sex typically begins early in childhood. As children they insist on dressing as members of the opposite sex, and they view with disgust the signs of sexual maturity that emerge at puberty—breasts for girls, beards for boys—because these seem to confirm publicly some kind of mistake made in their sexual identity.

The cross-sex identity of transsexuals begins in early childhood. Adult males seeking help for transsexualism often report wanting to be girls as far back as they can remember. They like to play with girls and to dress up as girls and they tend to avoid playing with trucks, cars, and other "masculine" toys. The parents of one effeminate boy reported that he would dress up with a towel on his head and call himself "batgirl."[8] When he was thirteen months old he began wearing his mother's high-heeled shoes. His mother reported that he thought of himself as a girl:

When he was two, you know how the other boys say, "What do you want to be when you grow up?" He will say he wants to grow up to be a mommy. We just kind of laughed at it at first. . . . He plays with the little girls all the time. He likes to play house, and he's the mama when he plays house. One day they were over playing and I said, "Why don't you be the daddy?" and he said, "No, I'll be the little sister."

Sex-change operations are occasionally used to treat transsexuals in order to bring their anatomical sex in line with their inner sense of sexual identity. Hormone treatments are also used. But these radical medical treatments are given only to those who pass a careful screening process. For some, these treatments are successful. One transsexual, a man born James Morris who became Jan Morris after a sex-change operation, wrote:

I was born with the wrong body, being feminine by gender but male by sex, and I could achieve completeness only when the one was adjusted to the other.[9]

Often, however, the unhappiness and problems of the transsexual are not eliminated by the sex-change operation.[10]

Homosexuality

Although encouraged and accepted in ancient Greece, the homosexual in American society has often been treated as an outcast and sometimes suffers the punishment of the law. In many states homosexual activities are a crime. The American fear of homosexuality is, by comparison with other nations in the world, extreme. The charge of homosexuality is sufficient to ruin a person's reputation and career. Any gesture such as the male embrace that might remotely suggest homosexual interests is carefully avoided. But who is a homosexual? The answer depends upon what is meant by homosexuality.

Who Is a Homosexual?

If a "homosexual" is defined as someone who has engaged in homosexual activities at some time, then nearly half of the people in this country would be "homosexuals." Toward the end of the latency stage of psychosexual development, many boys participate in sex play with other boys. Kinsey, in his *Sexual Behavior in the Human Male* and *Sexual Behavior in the Human Female,* reported that 60 percent of preadolescent boys and 33 percent of preadolescent girls engaged in homosexual activities.[11,12]

For this discusson a **homosexual** is defined as someone who seeks sexual satisfaction exclusively—or almost exclusively—from members of the same sex. **A heterosexual** is defined as someone who is attracted to and finds sexual satisfaction primarily from members of opposite sex. Not many people are exclusively homosexual. According to Kinsey's report about 4 percent of American men and less than 2 percent of American women fall into this category; there are only about one-third as many female homosexuals as male homosexuals. Homosexual behavior occurs in all mammals and always is more common in the male of the species than in the female.[11]

Homosexuality refers not to appearance but to sexual preference. Most homosexual men do not appear feminine and most homosexual women, or **lesbians,** do not appear masculine. The "queen"—feminine, lipstick-type male homosexual—and the

Homosexuality is a form of sexual preference and is not currently regarded as either unhealthy or abnormal. Research on the origins of homosexuality shows support for three different theories: the psychoanalytic theory, the biological theory, and the social-learning theory. (Left: Rose Skytta/Jeroboam Inc. Right: Rick Grosse/EKM-Nepenthe)

"butch"—a masculine-type female homosexual—are the exceptions rather than the rule.

Until recently, homosexuality was frequently regarded as unhealthy and abnormal. Modern studies have shown, however, that homosexuals are, on the average, as psychologically healthy as heterosexuals.[13,14] Homosexuality is now regarded by most psychologists and psychiatrists as a form of sexual *preference,* not as an illness. In recognition of this modern view, the American Psychiatric Association recently removed homosexuality from its list of psychological disorders.

It is important for you to understand that having a homosexual experience, or even several such experiences, does not make you a homosexual. Almost half the people in the country have such experiences and yet remain heterosexual. Neither do you become a homosexual because you feel attracted to people of your own sex. Furthermore, sexual identity is subject to change, and people can experience changes in their sexual preferences.

The Origins of Homosexuality

No one knows for sure what causes homosexuality. The causes of heterosexuality are equally unclear. It is certain, however, that no single explanation can apply to all cases. In the matter of sexual preference, there are many different paths to the same end.

One theory of homosexuality that appears to have little basis in fact is the **seduction theory.** The seduction theory holds that homosexuality results when a child is seduced by a homosexual at an early age. In order for this theory to be true, one would have to believe that (1) homosexuals regularly seduce young children, and (2) a child with a single homosexual experience will likely become a homosexual. Both of these assumptions are false. Homosexuals are no more likely than heterosexuals to be sexually attracted to children. And a homosexual experience in early life does not determine one's sexual preference. In view of the large number of people who have homosexual experiences early in life, there seem to be relatively few homosexuals. Most people who have homosexual experiences are not permanently conditioned by them to become homosexuals. Furthermore, engaging in occasional homosexual acts does not mean that one is a homosexual. Three theories of homosexuality that have greater support are the biological, psychoanalytic, and social-learning theories.

The Biological Theory • The **biological theory of homosexuality** assumes that homosexuals are biologically different from heterosexuals. This difference, it is argued, can be seen both in the genes and in the hormones. The genetic explanation of homosexuality considers homosexuality as an inherited condition; according to this view homosexuals are "born that way." Sometimes several children in the same family are homosexual. Evidence of homosexuality has on occasion been traced over several generations.[15] Further evidence consistent with this explanation comes from twin studies. If one fraternal twin (with different heredity) is homosexual, the other twin has about a 4 percent chance of being a homosexual. This chance is about the same for the general population. But if the co-twin is an identical twin (identical heredity), the chance of both being homosexual rises to about 70 percent.[16]

This evidence suggests a possible genetic basis for homosexuality; however, since identical twins have more similar home environments than fraternal twins, it is difficult to determine whether the increased rate of homosexuality results from the similarity in genes or the similarity in environment. Furthermore, this form of sexual preference may spread by association, which would explain its overrepresentation in some families without the need of referring to a genetic theory.[17] Thus, the evidence for the genetic explanation is not very conclusive.

A second biological explanation of homosexuality focuses on sex hormones. The hormone-imbalance explanation asserts that male homosexuality results from an excess of female hormones, and female homosexuality results from too much male hormone.

Although this possibility has often been raised, there is little evidence supporting it.[18,19] A study of thirty male homosexual students found them to have significantly lower levels of male hormones than a comparable group of heterosexual males; however, there was no evidence to show that their sexual preferences were *caused* by their lowered hormone level.[20] Sex hormones seem to affect sexual development and sex drive but not sex preference. One group of male homosexuals who were administered dosages of male hormones showed increased sexual arousal—but toward their homosexual partners.

The Psychoanalytic Theory • Freud believed that everyone was born **bisexual** (relating equally to both sexes) and was capable of responding to sexual stimulation regardless of the source. In the course of normal development, however, sexual preference becomes focused on members of the opposite sex.

According to the **psychoanalytic theory of homosexuality,** normal psychosexual development can be distorted by certain disturbed family interactions. If parent-child relationships interfere with the child's ability to resolve the Oedipus complex, the child may be blocked from progressing normally through the stages of development. In such circumstances, male children might not identify with their fathers, and female children might not identify with their mothers.

What kind of parents might provoke such a reaction? According to the psychoanalytic theory, the male child is frightened of his dominant but seductive mother because he fears that she will castrate him. His fear of her generalizes to a fear of all women and leads to the avoidance of heterosexual contact. A cold and distant father, according to this view, leads to the boy's desire to win his father's love, a desire which may generalize and influence his relationship with other males. Freud's explanation of female homosexuality was not well developed, but in general the psychoanalytic theory accounts for lesbianism in the same way as it accounts for male homosexuality. A dominant and seductive father, with a hostile and distant mother, produces a fear of men and a stong desire to obtain love from women.

Studies of the families of homosexuals report results partially consistent with the psychoanalytic prediction.[21,22,23] Male homosexuals tend to come from families with controlling dominant mothers, who maintain an unusually close and intense relationship with their sons; their fathers tend to be distant, passive, and rejecting. According to some researchers, the relationship between the mothers and fathers of homosexual men tends to be disturbed. The mothers seem to rely on the son for the closeness and comfort that is lacking from the husband.

Studies of the families of female homosexuals show a somewhat different pattern. While parent-child relations in these families were found to be consistently poor,[24] there was particularly intense hostility between fathers and daughters.[25] The father's hostility apparently creates the same response in the daughter as the mother's dominance and seduction: fear. Female homosexuals report that they were afraid of their fathers and that their fathers were irresponsible, incompetent, and weak.[25]

A problem with this type of research is that most of the studies of homosexuals have been conducted by therapists who are reporting on their own clients. Homosexuals seeking therapy are probably not representative of homosexuals in general, so the results may be biased. In addition, it cannot be determined from these findings whether the fear of the father or mother preceded and caused the homosexuality or whether it was a result of homosexual tendencies.

The Social-Learning Theory

The Social-Learning Theory • A third explanation of homosexuality is based on principles of learning. According to the **social learning theory of homosexuality,** it is neither a biological condition nor the result of a failure to resolve the Oedipus complex. It is acquired through the processes of observation and imitation of models and receiving rewards and punishments.

If heterosexual relationships are repeatedly punishing, unpleasant, or distasteful, they may be avoided, to be replaced by homosexual experiences. Rape or other negative heterosexual experiences may lead to a fear of men and a turning toward women for emotional and sexual support.[26]

Parents reward certain sex-role behaviors and punish others. Usually, parents would not reward a boy for wearing his mother's dress. In the case of one five-year-old boy, adults actively supported such inappropriate behavior.[27] The boy was encouraged to dress up frequently in his mother's clothes, including her cosmetics and jewelry, and even adopted a girl's name that his mother suggested. In another case, after a sixteen-year-old girl formed a homosexual attachment to a teacher, it was learned that her mother had for many years encouraged mutual stroking of the breasts and other sexual activities.[27]

Not all sex-role behavior is explicitly taught. Much of it is acquired from observing and imitating adults. According to social-learning theory, children observe adult models and copy them. If a boy's father is weak, distant, and hostile, the father may not succeed in modeling appropriate masculine sex-role attitudes and behaviors. The evidence for the social-learning theory is mixed. The following case of a homosexual man who came to a psychiatrist for help with his sexual adjustment reflects this problem with adult models.

Patient gives a history of homosexuality of nine years duration. Previous to that time he had what he considered a normal adolescence and young manhood, showing the same interest in girls as his associates. He recalls, however, developing an interest in the male body, particularly the genitalia, and then a fascination for the sexual functions of the male, when he was between the ages of sixteen and twenty years. . . . He never was aggressive in seeking homosexual contacts, but on an average of every two to three months he would put himself in a position to be approached. Between these experiences he would suffer greatly from shame and remorse and would stay strictly away from such localities.

What happened in this case was that the young man had been brought up in a small town. His father was weak and ineffectual, and his mother was over-protective. What sort of masculine attitudes could he absorb?[28]

The psychiatrist interprets this case in terms of a learning or modeling theory, writing that the patient had insufficient opportunity in which to learn the male role.

Interim Summary

A homosexual is someone who seeks sexual satisfaction exclusively—or almost exclusively—from members of the same sex. Although many people are at different times attracted to those of the same sex and may even have had a homosexual experience, very few people are exclusively homosexuals. Although the seduction theory of homosexuality has little support, the biological, psychoanalytic, and social-learning theories all have some evidence supporting them. It is likely, however, that no single theory can account for the diversity seen in human sexual behavior.

Summary

1. The terms "masculine" and "feminine" refer to the characteristics typical of males and females in this society. Individuals having both masculine and feminine traits are called androgynous.
2. Behavior expected of men and women (sex roles) differs among different cultures. Behavior typical of men and women is apparently not exclusively biologically determined but is highly influenced by cultural norms.
3. People acquire masculine and feminine identities early in life. By the age of three children evidence an awareness of their sexual identity and begin to act accordingly.
4. Freud assumed that sexual identity was achieved through a series of stages of sexual development, each characterized by a different source of sexual gratification. According to Freud's principle of infantile sexuality, infants acquire sexual satisfaction from a variety of sources.
5. Freud believed that all people progress through the oral, anal, phallic, latency, and genital stages of psychosexual development.
6. Children face the crisis of the Oedipus complex at the end of the phallic stage. This crisis involves a conflict between the child's incestuous desire for the parent of the opposite sex and the fear of retaliation from the parent of the same sex.
7. According to social-learning theory, sex roles are learned through interactions with the environment. This learning occurs by observing, imitating, and being rewarded by other people. Social-learning theory assumes that sex roles are shaped throughout life and that learning is a life-long affair.
8. One type of sexual variation is transvestism, or dressing in the clothes of the opposite sex in order to achieve gratification. A second variation is transsexualism, an intense discomfort with one's biological sex and an identification with members of the opposite sex.
9. A homosexual is one who seeks gratification exclusively or almost exclusively, from

members of the same sex.   Homosexuality is regarded by a form of sexual preference, not as an abnormal or unhealthy disorder.

10. According to the biological theory of homosexuality, the origins of the preference are to be found in the genes and hormones.   There is little evidence supporting the claim of a hormonal difference between homosexuals and heterosexuals.   There is some evidence that homosexuality is an inherited condition, but the evidence is not conclusive.

11. According to the psychoanalytic theory of homosexuality, the condition results from disturbed patterns of family interactions and the child's failure to resolve the Oedipus complex.   The evidence for this theory is mixed.

12. According to the social-learning theory of homosexuality, the condition is acquired through the processes of observing and imitating models and receiving rewards and punishments for masculine or feminine behavior.   If a boy's father is weak and distant, he may not succeed in modeling appropriate masculine sex-role behaviors. This evidence for this theory is mixed.   It is likely that no single theory can account for the diversity of human sexual behavior.

Key Concepts

androgynous   Possessing both masculine and feminine traits.

sex role   The style and mannerisms typical of members of one sex.

masculinity   The degree to which an individual conforms to behavior typical of men in a culture.

femininity   The degree to which an individual conforms to behavior typical of women in a culture.

norms   Standards based on the way people typically behave in a particular society.

normative model   A standard of masculinity and femininity based on the norm.

idealized model   A standard of masculinity and femininity based on what is considered perfect or ideal.

principle of infantile sexuality   Freud's idea that sexual gratification is obtained throughout childhood.

psychosexual stages   According to Freud, periods of development in childhood defined by the different sources of sexual pleasure that dominate.

oral stage   The first psychosexual stage during which the infant gains sexual pleasure from sucking and biting.

anal stage   The second psychosexual stage during which the infant gains sexual pleasure from urinary and bowel activities.

phallic stage   The third psychosexual stage during which the child gains sexual pleasure from manipulating his penis or her clitoris.

latency stage   The fourth psychosexual stage during which sexual interests are repressed.

genital stage   The fifth and final psychosexual stage during which sexual pleasure is gained from masturbation and intercourse.

Oedipus complex   A crisis occurring at the end of the phallic stage resulting from a conflict between the child's desire for the parent of the opposite sex and fear of the parent of the same sex.

social-learning theory   A general theory of behavior that emphasizes the importance of observing and imitating others as a basis of learning.

model   Someone who is copied or imitated.

transvestism   The act of dressing in the clothes of the opposite sex in order to achieve sexual gratification.

transsexualism   A condition of cross-sex identity; an intense discomfort with one's biological sex.   Sex-change operations are sometimes used to adjust the body so that it conforms to the inner sense of sexual identity.

homosexual   A man or woman who seeks sexual satisfaction exclusively—or almost exclusively—from members of the same sex.

heterosexual   A man or woman who seeks sexual satisfaction primarily from members of the opposite sex.

lesbian   A female homosexual.

seduction theory   A theory that assumes that homosexuality results from early homosexual experiences.

bisexual   An individual who can achieve sexual gratification equally from both sexes.

biological theory of homosexuality   The theory that homosexuals are biologically different from heterosexuals.

psychoanalytic theory of homosexuality   The theory that homosexuality results from the failure to resolve the Oedipus complex; this failure comes about from disturbed parent-child relationships.

social-learning theory of homosexuality   The theory that homosexuality results from observing adult models, from imitation, and from rewards and punishments that encourage the homosexual role.

Chapter 15

Love and Sex

Key Questions	1. What is love?
	2. How does the body become sexually aroused?
	3. What is sexually normal?
	4. How does society regulate sexual behavior?

Remember your first love?

You must think of it now as an infatuation or a silly crush, but it was extremely important at the time and is important still. The most famous young love is that of Shakespeare's Romeo and Juliet. Romeo says:

> *Did my heart love, till now?*
> *Forswear it, sight!*
> *For I ne'er saw true beauty*
> *Till this night.*

Your first love was a kind of rehearsal and preparation for later more meaningful loves; it was a learning experience in relationship.

Love is often a source of intense delight, and sometimes intense pain, but it is rarely neutral. It is necessary to life in infancy, and it releases our potential in adulthood. It is the source of much talk and much confusion. This chapter will discuss love, sex, and how they are related; sexual arousal and expression; and the social control of sex.

Love

Ashley Montagu wrote a book about love[1] and concluded that love is a general creative principle that must guide our future. In his view, love is a form of behavior that contributes to the healthy growth of both the lover and the loved. Everyone agrees that love is good—but what is love?

Dictionary and Operational Definitions

Much of the poetry, music, literature, and art of the world is concerned with love. "Love" is a common word, a word you use often when you are talking to friends, but what does it mean? The Greeks had more than one word for it: **agape** ("ah-*gah*-pay"), spiritual love, or love as giving and caring; and **eros**, erotic or passionate love, represented by Cupid and his arrows. The anonymous author of *The Ladies Dictionary* of 1694 tried to define love, but finally had to give up:

Love, *what is it? Answ. Tis very much like light, a thing that everybody knows, and yet none can tell what to*

make of it. . . . 'Tis extremely like a sigh.

Webster's New Collegiate Dictionary of 1979 does considerably better, which suggests some progress:

love: *strong affection for another arising out of kinship or personal ties (maternal love for a child); attraction based on sexual desire . . . ; affection based on admiration, benevolence, or common interests . . . ; unselfish loyal and benevolent concern for the good of another.*

Yet even this definition somehow is unsatisfactory. Perhaps no set of words on a page can possibly match the quality and intensity of the subjective feeling we all have felt.

Rather than trying to develop a dictionary definition of love, psychologists have tried to define love in terms of behavior. Many psychologists believe that in order to study love scientifically, it must be possible to measure it. From their point of view, the methods or operations used in measuring love provide the best definition of love. Definitions based on methods of measurement are called **operational definitions**. An advantage of using an operational definition of love is that it avoids confusion about what you mean; if you agree with the operational definition of love, you can objectively determine whether you are or are not in love.

Operational definitions require a method of measurement. But how can love be measured? One approach is by using a "love scale"—a questionnaire asking people to report their behavior and attitudes toward another person. Such a questionnaire consists of a number of items reflecting loving attitudes; the person answering the questionnaire responds to each item by reporting whether or not it correctly describes his or her attitudes. The result is a score that is interpreted as a measure of love. For example, the following items appear on one love scale:[2]

_____ *You feel he (she) understands you.*
_____ *You take his (her) suggestions seriously.*
_____ *You enjoy taking care of him (her).*
_____ *He (she) is sexually attractive to you.*
_____ *You feel more secure when you are with him (her).*

The operational definition of love, on the basis of this love scale, would be your total score, reflecting your degree of agreement with each of the items.

You may feel that trying to define love in terms of a score from a love scale is an inappropriate way to understand love. Your score, a single number, just does not seem equal to the depth and complexity of your feeling of love. You may disagree with the validity of the operational definition of love. This is a perfectly reasonable reaction; nevertheless, the development of operational definitions of love has stimulated a great deal of research on love that otherwise would not have been possible.

The Need for Love

Why do psychologists study love? The need for love is deeply rooted in the human psyche. Love is a way of overcoming separateness; and separateness, according to Erich Fromm, is the source of all anxiety. Being separate means being cut off, helpless, unable to use our powers. Fromm says:

The deepest need of man, then, is the need to overcome his separateness, to leave the prison of his aloneness. The absolute failure to achieve this aim means insanity, because the panic of complete isolation can be overcome only by such a radical withdrawal from the world outside that the feeling of separation disappears—because the world outside, from which one is separated, has disappeared.[3]

To overcome separateness you must be known. To be known, to be accepted as you really are, and to be prized for who you are, you must risk being open with another; you must disclose yourself in order to be known. Furthermore, it is in a close relationship with another person that we can best learn about ourselves. The other person, in a sense, acts like a mirror in which we can see ourselves more clearly.

Theories of Love

There are different kinds of love: love can be selfish and possessive or unselfish and giving. In order to understand these differences, theories of love have been developed by psychologists such as Abraham Maslow and Erich Fromm.

Being-love and Deficiency-Love • Maslow distinguished between two kinds of love: B-love (**being-love**—love for the being of another person; an unselfish love not dependent upon your needs) and D-love (**deficiency-love**—a selfish possessive love based upon someone's ability to satisfy your needs). B-love does not diminish from being gratified; it is generous and pleasure-giving; it makes possible the truest, most penetrating perception of the other person.

B-love in a profound but testable sense, creates the partner. It gives him a self-image, it gives him self-acceptance, a feeling of love-worthiness and respect-worthiness, all of which permit him to grow.[4]

D-love is conditional; it depends upon whether personal needs continue to be met. But B-love is unconditional; it depends not upon what you do but upon who you are. And because it depends upon who you are, it is possible only when you allow yourself to be known.

Mature Love and Immature Love • Fromm also distinguishes between two types of love, **immature love** and **mature love**. Immature love is based on the satisfaction of needs and is similar to Maslow's concept of D-love. An example of immature love is a relationship between two persons, one of whom needs to dominate, command, and exploit the other; the other needs to submit, to be dependent, and to be dominated. The relationship will work only so long as each satisfies the other's needs.

In contrast to immature love, mature love is a relationship that allows individuals to retain their independence, their identity, and their integrity. In mature love people can overcome their sense of separateness yet continue to be themselves. Mature love is not just a pleasant sensation, it is an activity.

Love is an activity, not a passive affect; it is a "standing in," not a "falling for." In the most general way, the active character of love can be described by stating that love is primarily giving, not receiving. . . . Giving is more joyous than receiving, not because it is a deprivation, but because in the act of giving lies the expression of my aliveness.[3]

Erotic Love

Some love involves strong sexual feelings and some does not. Erich Fromm in his book *The Art of Loving* describes some of the varieties of love:

Brotherly love is love among equals; motherly love is love for the helpless. . . . In contrast to both types of love is erotic love; it is the craving for complete fusion, for union with one other person. It is by its very nature exclusive and not universal.[3]

Sex and love are sometimes clearly separable feelings: the love of a mother for a child is a sexless love, and the experience of masturbation can be a loveless sexual activity. When love and sex are joined in **erotic love,** a high point of human experience is possible, a joy in which the whole is greater than the sum of the separated parts.

One of the best-known lovers of literature, Cyrano de Bergerac, wrote to the woman he loved:

> *Love, I love beyond*
> *Breath, beyond reason, beyond love's own power*
> *Of loving! Your name is like a golden bell*
> *Hung in my heart; and when I think of you,*
> *I tremble, and the bell swings and rings—*
>
> > *"Roxane!"*
> *"Roxane!" . . . along my veins, "Roxane!"*

Unfortunately, Cyrano was never bold enough to declare his love in person, but his love for Roxane was erotic love, or sexual love, a feeling that combines adoration and tenderness with sexual desire.

Love and sex interact. Love can stimulate sexual desire, and the experience of sex is changed by love. Sexual behavior in erotic love involves freely giving and taking and can be a lusty and wholesome expression of the joy of living. As Maslow wrote:

Sex and love can be, and most often are, very perfectly fused with each other in healthy people. While it is perfectly true that these are separable concepts, . . . still it must be reported that in the life of healthy people they tend to become completely joined and merged with each other.[5]

Even outside of marriage, when intimate sexual behavior such as intercourse occurs, it most often occurs within the context of a loving relationship.[6] A sex survey showed that the overwhelming majority of women who have engaged in premarital intercourse report that they were in love.[7]

Sex is one way for two people in relationship to interact and communicate; as such, it is profoundly affected by feelings and personal meanings, attitudes, and social and cultural customs, as well as biological urges. This form of love is the foundation of the human family, upon which our society is built.

An understanding of human behavior must include an understanding of sexual behavior. Sexual interests and sexual expression are not only biological processes but are also significant parts of our emotional and spiritual experience. Sex is a major part of life. In a recent survey of college students, over 90 percent reported experiencing urges to engage in sexual activity.[8]

| Interim Summary | Operational definitions, unlike dictionary definitions, are based on ways of measuring the concept to be defined. An operational definition of love is "the score made on a love scale." Maslow and Fromm observed that there was more than one kind of love; being-love and mature love are terms referring to unselfish love, while deficiency-love and immature love are terms referring to selfish love. Love and sex often interact and are fused in erotic love. |

Sexual Arousal

What is sexually arousing? How does the body respond to sexual excitement? Researchers studying the psychology of human sexual behavior have examined these questions in numerous scientific studies. The study of human sexuality is a major theme in the history of psychology, going back to Sigmund Freud, the founder of psychoanalysis, who was especially concerned wth sexual conflicts. Although an understanding of human sexuality is impossible without considering questions of belief, values, and morality, the biological foundations of sex and the relationship between the sexual stimulus and the sexual response can be isolated and studied.

Biological Foundations

The biological basis of sexual arousal consists of the brain, nervous system, hormones, and body surfaces sensitive to touch. Your capacity for sexual arousal depends upon these structures, but it also depends upon your physical condition; for example, fatigue, poor health, and intoxication all reduce the capacity for arousal. This is not to say that your sexual feelings are controlled exclusively by your bodily structures and chemistry. Sex is clearly not "just a physical thing"—it's also mental.

Bodily Changes • The primary source of sexual stimulation is tactile—pressure applied either to the sexual organs themselves or to other **erogenous zones** (sexually sensitive areas) such as lips, breasts, or thighs. Although touch, or **tactile stimulation,** is a primary source of sexual stimulation, sexual thoughts, images, and perceptions are also important. People give and seek tactile stimulation in a variety of ways, and they use their creative talents to produce books, movies, and paintings that stimulate sexual thoughts. Someone you love may touch you, talk to you, send you a letter, or sing you a song. This information is received by your senses of hearing, feeling, and seeing, reaches your brain, and subsequently may arouse you.

How does your brain signal sexual arousal to your body? The **autonomic nervous system** is a network of nerves connecting the brain to the organs and glands of the body. It is responsible for regulating many automatic functions such as blood pressure

erogenous zone

Sex is not just physical—it's also mental. The physical changes in the body that accompany sexual arousal are controlled by the autonomic nervous system and by a small brain structure called the hypothalamus. But thoughts, memories, and personal meanings are also important in sexual arousal.

and heart rate. The physical changes in the body that accompany sexual arousal are controlled by the autonomic nervous system.

What physical changes occur with sexual arousal? The pattern of changes that occurs is remarkably similar for men and women. From observing many different cycles of arousal and orgasm, Masters and Johnson, the well-known researchers in sexual behavior, have concluded that the basic physiological responses to sexual stimulation in both men and women are twofold: first, tissues become congested with blood, and, second, general muscle tension increases.[9]

Sexual arousal and response in men and women

involves many separate components, among which are increases in heart rate and blood pressure; congestion of blood in the sexual organs, causing swelling; deeper breathing; and a generalized body flush. These bodily responses result from the stimulation of the autonomic nervous system.

There are certain differences in male and female response to sexual stimulation. Women are more likely than men to need continuously applied stimulation in order to reach orgasm, but the female orgasm typically lasts longer than the male's and involves more contractions. Women typically need more time than men to climax in intercourse, but not in masturbation. Finally, the female capacity for multiple orgasm is greater that the male's.

The Sexual Control Center of the Brain • The brain is a master control center for regulating behavior—including sexual behavior. Sexual arousal is turned on or turned off by the activity of the brain. Damage to certain areas of the brain has resulted in **hypersexuality** (continuous sexual activity) and in **hyposexuality** (no sexual activity of interest).[10,11] Feelings of sexual pleasure can result from the stimulation of certain brain structures with a tiny current of electricity.[12]

Behavior that is directed toward some goal is called *motivated,* and motivations that serve biological needs are called **drives.** The need for water, food, and sex are three biological drives. These drives energize and instigate behavior. One area of the brain is particularly important in regulating drive level, the **hypothalamus,** a small structure at the base of the brain (see Figure 15-1). Following damage to certain areas of the hypothalamus, some animals no longer show any sexual interest;[13] stimulating other areas of the hypothalamus has been found to produce sexual behavior in animals.[14]

When different parts of the hypothalamus are stimulated with a weak current of electricity, various emotions may result, including rage, fear, and pleasure. Some of these hypothalamic regions have been called **pleasure centers.** If given the opportunity,

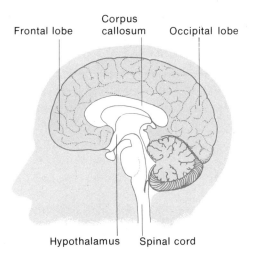

Frontal lobe Corpus callosum Occipital lobe

Hypothalamus Spinal cord

Figure 15-1 The Brain, Showing the Hypothalamus. *The hypothalamus helps regulate sexual drive and sexual behavior. This tiny structure lies at the heart of the brain and is present, not just in humans, but in all mammals.*

animals will work to stimulate themselves and will continue until they are exhausted.[15] Another "pleasure center" of the brain is the **septal area;** like the hypothalamus, the septal area is a small structure deep in the brain. Human patients whose septal areas were stimulated reported that the resulting feeling resembled that preceding a sexual orgasm.[16]

The hypothalamus in rats seems to be similar to the human hypothalamus. An area has been found in the hypothalamus of rats which, when electrically stimulated, causes sexual activity.[17] The sexual behavior of male rats can be turned on and off by turning a switch on and off which controls the electric current reaching their hypothalamus. Studies like this one demonstrate the power of the brain to regulate and control sexual arousal and sexual behavior.

Sex Hormones • What makes the two sexes different? Partly, it's a matter of body chemistry. **Sex hormones** are chemicals released directly into the blood by specialized sex glands—in the male, the *testes,* and in the female, the *ovaries.* Puberty begins with a great increase in the production of these hormones

and their subsequent release into the bloodstream. This flood of sex hormones spurs the rapid development of the sexual organs and the so-called secondary sexual characteristics such as body hair. In the male, this change of body chemistry leads to an enlargement of the genitals, and in the female it leads to an enlargement of the ovaries and the onset of menstruation along with the gradual enlargement fo the breasts. Additional information about sex hormones appears in Chapter 12. At the same time that these biological changes are occurring, most adolescents experience increased interest in the opposite sex. Do you remember when you first became interested in the opposite sex?

The Role of Learning

Although the primary source of sexual stimulation is pressure applied to erogenous zones, there are other, secondary sources that are important. The type of clothing, jewelry, perfume, hairstyle, the quality of the voice, the eyes, the smile, the shape of the body—all these, for different people, are sources of sexual arousal.

What do you find attractive? There are wide variations among individuals, among different cultures, and among different times in history as to what is regarded as sexy. These variations suggest that secondary sources of sexual arousal are learned, acquired through particular experiences in a culture.

The hairstyle, mode of dress, and physical appearance that are regarded as sexually attractive by men and women are the products of a particular culture and, to some extent, even a particular decade in history. What the men of one decade find sexually exciting, the men of another decade may find neutral. The sight of the female ankle used to excite men; today it rarely does. The sexually ideal woman from the average man's point of view, used to be plump and small-breasted; today she is thin and large-breasted. This change is associated with changes in our society, not with basic biological changes in men; therefore it

Sexual attractiveness is culturally learned rather than inborn. The characteristics that are considered attractive and highly erotic in one culture may be neutral or even repulsive in another. For example, this woman's decorative scars, lip plug, and nose rings are ways of enhancing feminine beauty in her own culture but not in ours. (George Rodger/Magnum Photos, Inc.)

is a change of learned, not inborn, responses. There are, of course, many individual differences in sexual preference. This diversity also suggests the importance of different learning experiences.

What the people of one society find erotic, the people of another may find repulsive. Different cultures endow different bodily features with erotic properties. Black pointed teeth, deformed ears or nose, long swinging breasts, rolls of fat—these are sexually exciting in some cultures but not in ours. The male movie idol in this society looks different from the male movie idol in Japan. Clearly, these cultural preferences are not inborn but learned.[18]

Classical Conditioning • How does this learning take place? The process is called **classical condition-**

ing, an elementary type of learning in which simple emotional responses are acquired. When sexually neutral stimuli (such as pictures) are associated with the occurrence of direct tactile sexual stimulation, these neutral stimuli acquire arousal properties in and of themselves. The sexual response becomes *conditioned* to these other stimuli. For example, many different mammals become sexually aroused when they approach places in which they have had previous sexual experiences; through conditioning the place has acquired the power to produce sexual arousal.

Is there something other than the human body that you find sexually exciting? The odor of certain perfumes or the feel of silken lingerie are conditioned sexual stimuli for some men because they have become associated with sexual arousal and response.

Fetishes • It is believed that sexual fetishes are the result of early learning experiences. A sexual **fetish** is an object that a person comes to associate with sexual activity, objects as unlikely as shoes, crutches, or furniture. Female underclothing is somewhat erotically arousing to many men; for the fetishist, however, the underclothing itself may be a primary sexual object, having greater sexual significance than the person who wears it.

The first sexual feelings that a thirty-year-old Dutch author reported occurred early in his childhood when he saw a young boy on crutches. Over the years following puberty he masturbated to the fantasy of a lovely woman dressed in furs hobbling on crutches. He made and bought several pairs of crutches, using them at night to walk about his room. He referred to the crutches as his "wives." He eventually married but required his wife, during intercourse, to take a pair of crutches to bed with her.[19]

Pornography

Erotic fantasies are often stimulated by sexy books, magazines, or films; in fact, many sexually explicit novels are erotic fantasies written down. Books, pictures, or films that are intended to be sexually arousing are called **pornography**. The word "pornography" means something different from the word "obscenity," which means material that is offensive or disgusting. There is considerable disagreement about the relationship between these two words. Some people believe that all pornographic material is obscene; other people find some pornography enjoyable. There is also a long history of attempts to control the availability of pornography legally. But in recent years erotic material has been more and more generally available.

What is the effect of exposure to pornography? Most studies report that sexually explicit pictures and films are sexually arousing for both men and women. In one study 200 men and women viewed films of a couple engaging in oral-genital contact and intercourse.[20] After the films, the audience reported their feelings on a questionnaire. Both men and women reported being sexually aroused, although men reported more arousal than women. Most men reported partial erection while viewing the films. Most women reported varying degrees of genital sensations; some reported breast sensations and vaginal lubrication.

A concern of many people is the easy availability of pornography to young people. Some argue that these materials will distort impressionable minds and may lead to rape or other forms of sexual deviance. In a follow-up to the study just discussed, the researcher wanted to find out what effect watching these films had on later sexual activities.[20] He found that there was essentially no effect at all.

If exposure to pornography leads to sex crimes, then it could be assumed that sex criminals have had a

Is pornography obscene? Books, pictures, or films intended to produce sexual arousal are called "pornography." Material that is offensive or disgusting is called "obscenity." (Eric Kroll/Taurus Photos)

greater exposure to pornography than normal individuals. One researcher checked out this idea and found that, contrary to common belief, sex criminals had significantly less exposure to pornography during adolescence than did normal individuals.[21] Conclusions about the long-term effects of exposure to pornography are simply not available; but these effects appear to be less harmful than many people once believed.

Interim Summary The biological foundations of sexual arousal involve various structures in the brain, the autonomic nervous system, sexual hormones, and skin receptors. Sex hormones control sexual development and are responsible for the physical changes associated with puberty. Sexual arousal is primarily dependent upon tactile stimulation but also involves the mind.

Sexual arousal is not just physical; it is also mental. Through the process of conditioning, a person associates a variety of stimuli—words, perfume, music—with arousal. These stimuli then become sexually exciting themselves. The intent of pornography is sexual arousal. Pornographic films, while sexually arousing, have been shown to have little long-term effect on sexual activity.

Forms of Sexual Expression

What is normal sexual behavior? Behavior that may be considered to be sexually motivated includes all sorts of human activities, ranging from dancing to sexual intercourse. Some psychologists, notably Freud, have argued that the motivation for most human behavior is sexual—if not explicitly, then in more hidden ways. The discussion here, however, will be confined to direct sexual acts that may culminate in **orgasm,** the climax of sexual feeling, accompanied by intense muscle tension and repeated involuntary contraction. Human sexuality has a variety of outlets to orgasm, and some of the more common forms of expression will be discussed here. Two of these, sex dreams and masturbation, are generally solitary forms and two others, petting and intercourse, are interpersonal forms. Psychologists consider all of these to be quite normal.

The study of human sexual behavior has only recently become acceptable in our society. The first large-scale sex study was a survey of sexual behavior conducted by Kinsey about thirty years ago. Kinsey and his associates interviewed thousands of men and women in different parts of the country and summarized their findings in two books, *Sexual Behavior in the Human Female* and *Sexual Behavior in the Human Male.*[9,22] Many other sex studies have been published since Kinsey's study that reveal how common different kinds of sexual behavior are.

Sex Dreams

Sex dreams, some involving orgasm, are common for both males and females, although more males have these experiences than females. According to Kinsey's sample, 83 percent of males and 37 percent of females have sex dreams to orgasm at some time in their lives. Sex dreams are more common in adolescence but may occur at any age. A common explanation of these dreams is the **compensation theory,** which states that orgasms in dreams compensate, or make up, for a lack of orgasms when awake. If this theory were true, you would expect to find more sex dreams during periods of reduced sexual activity when awake.

Kinsey reports that his survey data do not support this theory, since the frequency of sex dreams is not closely related to the occurrence of orgasms from other sexual outlets.[9] Sex dreams do not increase when other sexual activity decreases.

Masturbation

Masturbation, or self-stimulation, is a widespread sexual practice both in this culture and among other cultures, as well as among other mammals.[23] As such, it can be considered a natural and normal form of sexual expression.

Masturbation typically involves some form of genital manipulation and for both men and women results in orgasms over 90 percent of the time.[9] The "efficiency" of masturbation, however, does not mean that it is the preferred form of sexual expression; masturbation is not only discouraged by some social and religious customs, but as a solitary activity it lacks the profound personal significance and feeling attached to sexual relationships.

According to Kinsey's data, by the age of fifteen 82 percent of males and 20 percent of females have masturbated to orgasm; by the age of twenty these figures have increased to 92 percent for males and 33 percent for females.[9]   More recent studies confirm that between 30 and 40 percent of college-age women, and almost all men, masturbate.[8]   Eventually, over 90 percent of males masturbate to orgasm, and almost 60 percent of females do so.[9]

Although masturbation is very common, there are still many misconceptions about it.   Because of the social controls concerning masturbation, it is a subject rarely talked about; as a consequence, those who practice masturbation often believe that they are strange, different from others, and weak-willed.   Many persons suffer unnecessarily because of inappropriate guilt and anxiety associated with their own masturbation activity.

Henry: A Case History • *Henry, a sophomore, was referred to the college psychiatrist by his counselor after the two had discussed Henry's difficulties with his studies.   He reported himself unable to concentrate and to "get down to work."   Instead of reading his assignments, he found himself aimlessly leafing through pulp magazines, cheap novels, and the daily paper.   He soon began to describe himself as lacking will-power.   After considerable hesitation, obvious discomfort, and embarrassment, he revealed that he lacked will-power not only in his studies, but also in controlling his, as he put it, tendency to indulge himself.   Finally he admitted that he masturbated from time to time.   Henry hastily explained that of course he knew everyone masturbated, but he felt that at his age he should have outgrown the habit and that, even if it was all right to masturbate occasionally, he did it too much.   He felt caught in a vicious circle.   When unable to concentrate on his work he frequently felt the urge to masturbate, but if he gave in he felt depressed and even less able to work.*[24]

It was clear that Henry's problem was not masturbation itself, but rather the way he felt about his practice of masturbating.   Henry was plagued by a number of myths about masturbation.

Masturbation Myths • Society and parents are responsible for passing on to children many myths about masturbation.   The problem with masturbaton is the anxiety and stress caused by these false beliefs, some of which follow:

1. *Teen-agers do it but not adults—it is a habit that is outgrown.*   This is false—adults of all ages masturbate, as Kinsey has shown, although the frequency declines with age.[9]
2. *It can be practiced to "excess."*   This is false—the only consequence of frequent masturbation is the fatigue lasting for a few minutes.[25]
3. *It causes sexual problems later, such as impotence or frigidity.*   This is false—there is no known effect of masturbation on later sexual capacities.   In fact, those who suffer least from sexual problems later are those who masturbated in adolescence.[9]   (This does not prove a cause-and-effect relationship however.)
4. *It is harmful, either psychologically or physically.*   This is false—there is no evidence that masturbation is in any way harmful either psychologically or physically.[26]   On the other hand, anxiety and guilt about masturbation can be a problem.

Petting

Petting, sexually stimulating another person by touching, is practiced extensively in other cultures and among other mammals.[9]   In this society ultimately over 90 percent of both men and women have petting experiences, and over 30 percent have petting experiences to orgasm.[9]   The rate of heavy petting—genital stimulation without clothing barriers—apparently is increasing in frequency.   While Kinsey reported that about 50 percent of college women experienced heavy petting twenty-five years ago, recent surveys typically obtain a higher percentage, from 60 to 90 percent.[27,28,29]   The techniques of petting that are most commonly used are kissing, both simple and deep; breast stimulation, both manual and by mouth; and stimulation of the male and female genitals, both manually and orally.   In some cases petting may be preliminary to intercourse.

Intercourse

Premarital intercourse is quite common in most societies in the world. In the majority of primitive societies limited adolescent intercourse is permitted for both males and females. In one study of 158 primitive societies, it was reported that 70 percent did not prohibit premarital intercourse.[6] The majority of people engage in premarital intercourse in spite of societal prohibition. Kinsey showed in his survey that about 50 percent of the females and about 70 percent of the males had engaged in premarital intercourse.

The rates of nonvirginity among college students are changing. More than twenty-five years ago Kinsey reported that about one in five college women

and somewhat over half of the college men had experienced sexual intercourse.[9] About ten years ago, another survey of 8,000 college freshmen and juniors found that 29 percent of the freshman women and 36 percent of the junior women were nonvirgin, while 42 percent of the freshmen and 59 percent of the junior men were nonvirgin.[29] More recent studies have found that 20 to 40 percent of freshmen men and women and 70 percent or more of seniors are nonvirgin.[30] People are more active sexually and are beginning their sexual lives earlier than before. Changing sexual standards and the availability of reliable methods of contraception have played important roles in the recent changes in sexual behavior and in the social mores that govern it.

Interim Summary   There is great variety in the forms of sexual expression and in the individual patterns of sexual behavior. Sexual behaviors such as sex dreams, petting, masturbation, and intercourse are common and can be considered normal. Premarital intercourse appears to have increased somewhat for both men and women during the past few decades.

The Social Control of Sex

All societies exercise some form of regulation of sexual behavior; our society follows fairly strict social control, even of private sexual acts. Legal controls are imposed not only on sexual activities, such as premarital intercourse or homosexuality, but also on stimuli assumed to be sexually arousing, such as pornography and sex education materials. Most adults have been exposed to one or more of these activities and stimuli. According to one report, nine out of every ten Americans is a sex criminal, having violated some sex law.[31] Sexual "crimes," however, are rarely punished.

Sexual Standards

How should you behave? Just because a practice is common or normal does not necessarily mean that it is

proper or right. What is proper? Schools, churches, and parents are all responsible for communicating the forms of socially acceptable behavior; children are socialized by these agents of society and given standards of behavior. People who do not conform to these social norms suffer punishing consequences. They may be jailed, ostracized, or labeled "promiscuous," "slut," "prude," or "queer."

Children begin to learn sexual standards when very young. The following is a case history of a young woman whose parents were harsh and punishing in their attempt to make her conform to their concept of proper sexual behavior.

At about age four I was accused of playing with myself and was slapped with a metal spatula and made to stand up against a wall. . . . When I was in high school all hell broke loose when I began dating boys. Suddenly there seemed to be no other topic in the minds of my parents but sex. It was a constant flow of accusations. And the situation became worse each year. I was called every name, but the favorite was slut. *When I was 16 I was accused of being pregnant and hounded about it, although no attempt was made to take me to a doctor. Every boy I dated was insulted by my father and accusing and insinuating remarks were made to them. Finally during the summer before I was married my mother informed me that I had no right to wear white on my wedding day, that red would be more appropriate for me. I was a virgin at the time.*[32]

There are differences among people in the types of standards for premarital sex that they accept. One common sexual standard is **abstinence before marriage**—the rule that intercourse is acceptable only between married adults. This principle has strong historical roots within both the Judaic and the Christian traditions. A second common sexual standard is the rule of **permissiveness with love.** According to this standard, intercourse is acceptable before marriage, but only between those who are deeply in love or are engaged to be married. A third sexual standard is the **hedonistic standard.** According to this principle, no limitations should be placed on intercourse between consenting adults. Premarital sex between those who feel attracted to each other is consistent with the hedonistic standard. The hedonistic principle aims at achieving the greatest possible short-term pleasure. A fourth standard, the **double standard,** states that women, but not men, must be virgin at marriage. According to the double standard, the rules of sexual behavior that should apply to men are different from those that should apply to women.

According to recent studies, the majority of young men and women consider premarital intercourse as acceptable if the participants are seriously in love or engaged.[33,34] The double standard is still operating, since both men and women place less value on male virginity than on female virginity at marriage.[8] Have you observed different attitudes held by men and women regarding their sexual behavior? What are your attitudes?

The Individual's Response

Guilt is a common feeling resulting from violating a behavior standard of your group or society. Since the majority of people in our society violate the stated sexual standard, most experience feelings of guilt in varying degrees with new sexual experiences. Guilt over sexual activities, however, typically diminishes as the sexual activities continue; one study showed that over three-fourths of those studied were not in any way restrained from sexual activities by feelings of guilt.[7] Most people begin their active sexual lives with some minor behavior such as masturbation or kissing and then gradually advance through stages to sexual intercourse. As each new stage of intimacy is reached for the first time, guilt feelings may occur, then diminish with continued experience.[39]

Many people, however, refrain from sex before marriage, preferring to maintain a sexual standard of abstinence, prohibiting premarital intercourse. Such standards are often based in moral or religious principles. For these people, violation of these principles could lead to serious and prolonged feelings of anxiety and guilt.

Interim Summary   The most common standard of sexual behavior held by young people today is permissiveness with love; they feel that intercourse is acceptable between those who are in love, even though they are not married. Attitudes are still, however, influenced by the double standard. There has been a great change in sexual attitudes and some change in sexual behavior during the past few decades. People today are more sexually active and are beginning their sexual lives earlier.

Summary

1. Operational definitions are definitions based on methods of measurement. One operational definition of love is the total score made on a scale designed to measure love.

2. Maslow distinguished between two kinds of love: B-love (being-love)—love not dependent upon the satisfaction of selfish needs—and D-love (deficiency-love)—a selfish love, based on a person's ability to satisfy your needs.

3. Fromm distinguished between two similar kinds of love: immature love (similar to D-love) and mature love (similar to B-love).

4. The primary source of sexual stimulation is touch—pressure applied to erogenous zones—but sex is also mental, involving beliefs, imagination, perceptions, and thoughts.

5. The physical changes in the body that accompany sexual arousal are controlled by the autonomic nervous system, but the brain is the master control center for all behavior, including sexual behavior. A small brain structure called the hypothalamus is especially important in regulating sexual interest and behavior.

6. The fact that there are historical, cultural, and individual differences in what people find sexually arousing suggests that the stimuli for sexual arousal are learned, not inborn.

7. The term *pornography* refers to materials that are produced to stimulate sexual excitement. Conclusions about the long-term effects of pornography cannot be made with confidence because of the lack of evidence; the effects, however, appear to be less harmful than many people once believed.

8. Psychologists regard both sex dreams and masturbation as normal, in the sense that they are very common, particularly among adolescents and young adults, and they are harmless, both physically and psychologically.

9. Recent evidence indicates that people are more active sexually and are beginnng their sexual lives earlier than before. Premarital intercourse has increased for both men and women during the past few years.

10. Four sexual standards are the abstinence-before-marriage standard, the permissiveness-with-love standard, the hedonistic standard, and the double standard. Although the double standard is still influential, the most common standard among young men and women is permissiveness with love.

11. Guilt feelings typically accompany new sexual experiences, since—as a new level of intimacy is initiated—there is often a violation of a personal or group-held standard of behavior.

Key Concepts

agape   The Greek word for spiritual love; love as giving and caring.

eros   The Greek word for erotic or passionate love.

operational definition   A definition of a concept based on a description of the method of measuring it.

being-love (B-love)   Maslow's term for an

unselfish love; the person does not require the satisfaction of his or her own needs.

deficiency-love (D-love)   Maslow's term for a selfish possessive love; the person's love is conditional upon the satisfaction of his or her own needs.

immature love   Fromm's term for a selfish love that lasts only as long as needs are satisfied.

mature love   Fromm's term for love based primarily on giving; an unselfish love that allows people in relationship to maintain their independent identities.

erotic love   A feeling that combines adoration and tenderness with sexual desire.

erogenous zones   Sexually sensitive areas of the body, such as lips, breasts, or genitals.

tactile stimulation   Sensations resulting from touch or pressure.

autonomic nervous system   The network of nerves connecting the brain to the glands and organs of the body; responsible for regulating automatic functions such as blood pressure.

hypersexuality   An extremely high level of sexual drive resulting in almost continuous sexual activity.

hyposexuality   An extremely low level of sex drive resulting in little or no sexual activity.

drive   A motivation that serves a biological need, such as the need for food or sex.

hypothalamus   A small brain structure that regulates drives and controls the autonomic nervous system.

pleasure center   A brain area which, when stimulated with electricity, produces satisfaction or pleasure.

septal area   A brain area near the hypothalamus which contains a pleasure center.

sex hormones   Chemicals released into the bloodstream by the male and female sex glands, the testes and the ovaries.

classical conditioning   An elementary type of learning by association in which simple emotional responses are acquired.

fetish   An object that a person associates with sexual activity and requires for sexual gratification; for example, a shoe.

pornography   Sexually stimulating books, pictures, or films.

orgasm   The climax of sexual feeling, associated with high levels of muscle tension and contraction.

compensation theory   The theory that orgasms in sex dreams make up for a lack of sexual activity while awake.

abstinence before marriage   A standard of sexual behavior stating that intercourse is acceptable only after marriage.

permissiveness with love   A standard of sexual behavior stating that intercourse is acceptable before marriage only for those who are deeply in love or engaged to be married.

hedonistic standard   A standard of sexual behavior stating that no limitations should be placed on intercourse between consenting adults.

double standard   A standard of sexual behavior stating that premarital intercourse is acceptable for men but is not acceptable for women.

Part VI

Personality and Growth

Chapter 16

Personality

Key Questions   1. What is personality?
                       2. How can you describe and measure personality?
                       3. What are theories of personality?
                       4. Are you normal?

Who are you?

You will spend most of your life, one way or another, trying to answer this simple question. Each day you learn more and more about yourself; you have a growing understanding of what you are like, where you are going, and why you do the things you do. An important goal of this book is to add to this understanding.

Your concern for who you are is a search for your *self*. Awareness of self is learned early in life; a baby girl discovers the boundaries of her body, what is and what is not *self*, by playing endlessly with her hands and feet. She learns where she stops and where the world begins. But learning about your self does not stop with the discovery of the boundaries of your body; it continues throughout life, focusing on understanding your particular pattern of thinking and acting—the discovery of your psychological self, your *personality*. This chapter discusses personality, its assessment, normality, and various theories of personality.

What Is Personality?

Who are you? You could answer this question by describing your typical pattern of behavior in the world—perhaps you are a person who is "aggressive," "lazy," "intelligent," or "cheerful." You would be describing your personality.

The word "personality" comes from the Latin word *persona*, which meant the mask worn by actors to signify their role in the drama. Today however the word refers to more enduring personal qualities. Your **personality** is your typical way of reacting to the world and relating to the people around you. To say that you are "cheerful" means that in many different situations and at many different times you express joy or optimism rather than gloom or pessimism. The "you" of today here in this room is similar in certain ways to the "you" of yesterday somewhere else; both were "cheerful."

Personality characteristics describe consistencies both at different times and in different situations.

Although there are differences between your behavior today and your behavior last month, there are similarities and consistencies, too. Although there are differences between your relationship to your mother and your relationship to other women, there are also similarities. These similarities and consistencies in your way of behaving are what characterize your personality.

Seeming and Being

Appearances are not always what they seem; seeming and being are different. The "self" that we present to the world is often false, a personal construction behind which we hide our real selves.

A choice that confronts every one of us at every moment is this: Shall we permit our fellow men to know us as we now are, or shall we seek instead to remain an enigma, an uncertain quantity, wishing to be seen as something we are not?

This choice has always been available to us, but throughout history we have chosen to conceal our authentic being behind various masks. . . . We conceal and camouflage our true being before others to foster a sense of safety, to protect ourselves against unwanted but expected criticism, hurt, or rejection. This protection is purchased at a steep price. When we are not truly known by the other people in our lives, we are misunderstood. When we are not known, even by family and friends, we join the all too numerous "lonely crowd." [1]

The way we *act* and the way we *are* often are different. We may present different selves to different people: the self we present at home may not be the self we present to close friends. Think of yourself as having three different faces: a social face, a personal face, and a real face.

The *"self"* that we present to the world is often false—a mask that we hide behind. We have different "social faces"—aspects of ourselves that we present in public. Like the clown, we create a false image to show the world. (George W. Gardner)

Social Face • Your **social face** represents how you act in public. Like a wig, this face may have several interchangeable styles, depending upon whom you wish to impress. Imagine yourself making an appearance at a party where there are many strangers in the room. As you enter the room, you strive to appear unconcerned, cheerful, and "cool"; you strive to hide your nervousness and inexperience.

You strive to create good first impressions. In public, you wear a kind of false face—a mask—in order to present yourself at your best. You have learned that people often judge you on the basis of your physical appearance, clothes, voice, cosmetics, and mannerisms. You use these superficial aspects to create for yourself a public image, a social face.

Personal Face • Your **personal face** represents your **self-concept,** or the way you see yourself. Your personal face is the person you think you are. This private vision could be a grandiose idea or a rather harsh judgment and may or may not correspond to reality. The feelings you have about yourself are reflected in this private vision.

Your self-concept can be positive or negative. If you have a positive self-concept, you may think of yourself as competent, worthy, likable, and intelligent. If you have a negative self-concept, you may think of yourself as inadequate, inferior, and worthless. What is your self-concept? In the following list, which of the statements do you feel best describe you? [2] Check the ones that fit you best.

What kind of a personal face do you have? How positive is your self-concept? Your idea of yourself and the impressions others have of you are often different; your personal face and social face are rarely the same. You can discover this difference by asking a friend to check the statements below that correspond to the image others have of you.

Positive Self-Concept

☐ I am intelligent
☐ I am self-reliant
☐ I am satisfied with myself

☐ I am tolerant
☐ I am sexually attractive
☐ I am optimistic
☐ I usually like other people
☐ I am a responsible person
☐ I am emotionally mature

Negative Self-Concept

☐ I feel hopeless
☐ I am worthless
☐ I am insecure within myself
☐ I just don't respect myself
☐ I am shy
☐ I don't trust my emotions
☐ I am a hostile person
☐ I often feel humiliated
☐ I have few values and standards of my own

Real Face • Your **real face** represents what you are in reality. This is how you would appear if you could see yourself clearly. This is the self referred to in the poet's line "To thine own self be true." If you could be peeled like an onion, with your outer shell of pretense and pride removed, your naked core—your real self—would be exposed. This is not a rigid plaster mask but is changing, becoming, as you grow. If you are on a journey in search of your self, this is the reality awaiting you at the end of your trip.

A Test to Take

If I were to ask you who you are, how would you describe yourself? Which mask would you wear? Would you pretend to be something that you are not? Which of the following characteristics describe you the way you really are? Which describe the impression you try to create at parties? Check off the alternative for each number below that corresponds to your real self. Are your social face and real face ever the same? How well do you know your friends? Which of the following characteristics describe your best friend? Do you think you know the "real face" of your best friend?

1 ☐ I am sometimes careless and impulsive
☐ I am always self-controlled

2 ☐ I am sometimes very depressed
☐ I am always cheerful

3 ☐ I am sometimes lonely
☐ I am never lonely

4 ☐ I am sometimes selfish
☐ I am always generous

5 ☐ I am sometimes shy
☐ I am always friendly and sociable

6 ☐ I am sometimes nervous and anxious
☐ I am always cool and calm

7 ☐ I am sometimes naive and ignorant
☐ I am always experienced and knowledgeable

8 ☐ I am sometimes embarrassed
☐ I am never embarrassed

9 ☐ I am sometimes dumb
☐ I am always intelligent

10 ☐ I am sometimes angry
☐ I am never really angry

How do you see yourself? Our perceptions of ourselves, being extremely subjective, vary greatly from one person to another. But would it be to our liking to have, as the poet Robert Burns wrote, ". . . some Power the giftie gie us,/To see oursels as ithers see us!". . .? (Ellis Herwig/Stock, Boston)

Interim Summary   The word "personality" comes from the Latin word for "mask" and refers to your typical way of reacting to the world and the people around you. You have aspects to your personality, or three "faces": a social face, a personal face, and a real face. Your social face is your public self; your personal face is your private image of yourself, or your self-concept; your real face is what you are in reality.

Describing Your Personality

What kind of a person are you? How would you describe yourself? Are you friendly, shy, nervous, idealistic, talkative, selfish, cheerful, dominant, suspicious, reserved, jealous, intelligent, lazy, considerate, inquisitive, forgetful, creative, modest, sensitive, enthusiastic, moody? How many different words can you think of that accurately describe who you are? We have developed thousands of words to describe ourselves. Trying to understand ourselves, trying to understand others, and trying to communicate this understanding are among the most significant of human activities. Psychologists have over the years developed many systematic ways to describe personality.

Personality Types

What type of person are you? Do you think that people can be classified into different personality types? It is certainly possible to classify people. Just as trees or cats can be classified into different types, people can also be classified into different types. A **personality type** is a set of personality characteristics that one group of people has in common that makes them different from another group.

Carl Jung, an early disciple of Freud, developed a theory of personality types. Jung was born in 1875 in a small country town in Switzerland and was the son of a Protestant clergyman. Early in his studies Jung showed an interest in religion, ancient languages, and archaeology, but after a dream he had while in college,

he abruptly switched to natural science and worked for an M.D. degree.

Jung was a close friend and follower of Freud, but broke with the founder of psychoanalysis after criticizing Freud's emphasis on sex. Jung viewed the motivating force for people not as primarily sexual as Freud did, but as a creative energy, shared by all.

Jung introduced his book *Psychological Types*[3] by contrasting the opposing natures of Plato and Aristotle. Plato was a poetic visionary and mystic for whom ideas were more real than the world of objects. Aristotle was a scientist, concerned with studying and classifying the forms and events of the external world. According to Jung, Plato and Aristotle represent two fundamentally different tendencies in

Carl Jung

the human personality: Plato, concerned with the inner world, was an introvert and Aristotle, focusing his energies on the outer world, was an extrovert.

Introverts turn inward, seek isolation, and tend to withdraw from social engagements. They are reflective and introspective, absorbed with self-searching thoughts. They are self-critical and self-controlled, giving an outwardly cold appearance. They prefer to change the world rather than to adjust to it. **Extroverts** seek social contacts and are outgoing and accommodating. They appear friendly and outspoken and make friends easily. They are tolerant of others but relatively insensitive to the motivations and moods of their friends. They prefer to experience things rather than to read about them. Can you apply one of Jung's two personality types to yourself? How do you appear to others, as an introvert or an extrovert?

Most people are a mixture of introvert and extrovert, being neither wholly one nor the other. This is one of the problems of classifying people into types. Unlike rocks, few people can be easily sorted into boxes according to type. We are just not that simple; each of us has the potential for behaving in different ways in different circumstances.

A second theory of personality types was developed by W. H. Sheldon. Sheldon noted that there appeared to be a relationship between the shape of the body and the nature of the personality. His theory of **somatotypes** (body types) classified people into one of three categories: (1) **mesomorph,** a person with a narrow pelvis, broad shoulders, and muscular build; (2) **endomorph,** a person who is short and plump with a short neck and broad hands; and (3) **ectomorph,** a person who is tall and thin, with flat chest, long limbs, and narrow face. (See Figure 16-1.) These three physical types, Sheldon believed, corresponded to three basic personality types: (1) the mesomorph personality—assertive, direct, competitive, aggressive, bold, ruthless, and adventuresome; (2) the endomorph personality—tolerant, social, extroverted, emotionally even and easy going, enjoys

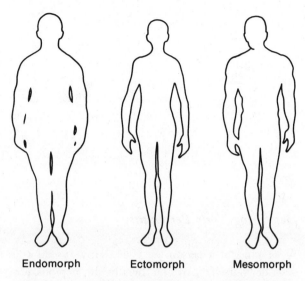

Endomorph   Ectomorph   Mesomorph

Figure 16-1 Sheldon's Somatotypes. *According to Sheldon's theory of somatotypes, people can be classified into three physical types—the endomorph, ectomorph, and mesomorph—which are associated with three personality types. From this point of view, your personality type can be determined by the shape of your body.*

physical comfort, and has a high need for the approval of others; (3) the ectomorph personality—self-conscious, antisocial, emotionally restrained, has very fast reactions, intense, loves privacy, sensitive to pain, and sleeps poorly. Studies of the relationship of bodily type and personality type do not show consistent support for Sheldon's theory. Where there are correlations between physical and psychological characteristics, the question left unanswered is whether the psychological characteristics resulted from the physical characteristics, or whether the existence of a relationship is due to some other factor.

Personality Traits

An alternative way of describing your personality is to think of yourself not as a type but as a collection of traits. A **personality trait** is a relatively permanent personality dimension or characteristic that makes you different from someone else. For example, "aggressiveness" is a personality trait; you can have varying degrees of this trait, from extremely aggressive to only slightly aggressive. Your personality can be described by listing the degree to which you have each of many different personality traits.

Dominance is another trait; it is characteristic of both humans and animals. Some individuals tend to be very dominant; they seem confident, independent, are often argumentative, and they seek leadership positions that enable them to direct and control the activities of others. The dominant person finds it easy to initiate interactions with others and to resist pressures to conform. The opposite of dominance is **submissiveness.** The submissive person tends to be timid, dependent, and conforming. Such a person suppresses personal dissatisfactions and follows the lead of others.

Animals as well as humans show this personality trait. Groups of chickens that have been together for some time establish a "pecking order" among themselves; a pecking order is also known as a **dominance hierarchy.** At the top of this hierarchy is a bird that can peck at and dominate all the rest without getting pecked back. The second bird in the pecking order can peck at all those below it on the hierarchy, but is pecked at by the most dominant bird. The unfortunate bird on the bottom is pecked by all the others and can peck none in return.[4]

In human groups there are dominance hierarchies, too. Individuals are dominant with some people and submissive with others. That is, in the human "pecking order," some people are above us (they dominate us) and some people are below us on the hierarchy (we dominate them). Where are you in the human pecking order? Do you tend to be dominant or submissive in most of your relationships? How do you act in a group of your peers? Do you usually lead or follow? What if a woman is dominant and a man submissive? What if a child is dominant and a parent submissive? Is it "natural" for certain kinds of people to be dominant and "natural" for others to be submissive?

Security is another important personality trait. Secure people have a firm sense of their own identities. They relate easily to other people, and in their involvement with them generally feel accepted. They are usually optimistic, seeing other people as friendly and having good intentions; they are adventurous, striking out on their own and expecting the best.

Insecurity is the opposite of security. Insecure people may lack an overriding sense of personal identity. The ordinary events of living often threaten their feeling of security or safety, and they are preoccupied with preserving themselves. Such people often feel isolated, unloved, and discontent. Insecure people are generally pessimistic, seeing other people as hostile and rejecting. They often feel discouraged and expect the worst from the world, as if some disaster were always about to happen. Few individuals are wholly secure or wholly insecure; most of us are somewhat between the two extremes. How would you describe yourself? How do you pretend to be?

Situational Differences

The idea of personality types and traits suggests that people have relatively permanent and consistent ways of behaving in different situations and at different times. But recent studies of personality have questioned this idea.[5] How consistently do you behave? You are not the same at school and at home. You are not the same alone and with friends. You are not the same with your parents and with strangers. You behave differently in different situations.

This does not mean that the concept of personality traits is useless. It does mean that, in considering your personality traits, you should take into account different situations and how you behave in them. You may be consistently outgoing in certain types of situations and consistently shy in others. You may be dominant in some circumstances and submissive in others. To describe your personality accurately, these situational differences must be considered.

Interim Summary   Personality can be described in many different ways.   One way is by classifying people into types, such as introvert or extrovert.   A second way is to think of people as having different dimensions or traits, such as dominance or insecurity.   A problem with both the type and trait descriptions is that they assume that people behave consistently over time and in different circumstances; but in fact there are important situational differences in personality.

Personality Assessment

We all have informal impressions of other people. Often our first impressions have a powerful influence that shapes our relationships.   But these impressions are often not very accurate.   Psychologists are concerned with objective and accurate descriptions of personality and have devised special instruments to measure aspects of personality.

You are unique.   But how can your uniqueness be described?   The ways in which your personality differs from other people's could be listed and verbally described, or these differences could be measured. Can the dimensions of your mind be measured?   To some extent, yes.   Psychological tests are "rulers" attempting to do just that.   These tests are designed to measure one or more psychological traits—for example, an IQ test is a psychological test measuring intelligence.

A Test to Take

There are thousands of different personality tests. Some attempt to measure many different aspects of the personality, while others are designed to measure a single trait.   The following items are a version of a scale intended to assess a single facet of the personality.   Read each pair of statements, then circle either "a" or "b" to indicate which corresponds best to your beliefs.

1. (a) Promotions are earned by hard work and persistence.
   (b) Making a lot of money is mostly a matter of getting the right breaks.
2. (a) Many times teachers' reactions seem haphazard to me.
   (b) In my experience I have noticed that there is usually a direct connection between how hard I study and the grades I get.
3. (a) The number of divorces indicates that more and more people are not trying to make their marriage work.
   (b) Marriage is mainly a gamble.
4. (a) Getting promoted is really a matter of being a little luckier than the next guy.
   (b) In our society anyone's future earning power depends on ability.
5. (a) I have little influence over the way other people behave.
   (b) If you know how to deal with people, they are really quite easily led.
6. (a) Sometimes I feel I have little to do with the grades I get.
   (b) The grades I make are the result of my own efforts; luck has little or nothing to do with it.
7. (a) People like me can change the course of world affairs if we make ourselves heard.
   (b) It is only wishful thinking to believe that you can really influence what happens in society at large.
8. (a) I am the master of my fate.
   (b) A great deal that happens to me is probably a matter of chance.

The items in the personality test above were designed to measure how much control you feel you have over your life.[6] Similar items are used in a common personality test, the **I-E Scale.** People who make a very low score on this scale are called "internals" (I) and people who make a very high score are called "externals" (E). Internals are people who believe that they are responsible for what happens to them, that the control of their life is located inside of them, or that they have an internal "locus of control." Externals are people who believe that they can't control what happens to them, that things external to them are responsible for what happens, and that they have an external locus of control. To score your own answers to the sample items above, give yourself one point for each answer corresponding to the following: 1(b), 2(a), 3(b), 4(a), 5(a), 6(a), 7(b), 8(b). A high score (7 or 8) indicates you are probably an "external" person, while a low score (0 or 1) indicates you are probably an "internal" person. Scores in the middle range indicate you are between the two extremes and do not have a uniform set of beliefs about locus of control.

Psychological tests require you to respond to questions or pictures and are typically brief, rarely lasting more than an hour or two. How can something as complex as your personality be assessed in such a brief time? Such tests are designed to sample aspects of your personality and behavior and then come to a conclusion about your personality as a whole.

Sample and Population

A **sample** is a subset of, or selection from, the population as a whole. The term **population** refers to the entire group in which you are interested. A good sample is both large enough and representative enough to "stand in" for the whole population, so that the results obtained from surveying the sample may be assumed to hold for the population as well. When you come to a conclusion about a population (all students or all voters) on the basis of evidence from a sample (some students or some voters), you are **generalizing.** To generalize is sometimes warranted and sometimes not.

After meeting one person from New York with red hair, you may mistakenly conclude that everybody from New York has red hair. Your *sample* (one red-haired person) from the *population* (New York residents) was neither large enough nor representative enough to warrant your *generalization* that all New Yorkers have red hair.

Suppose you wanted to estimate the proportion of Americans who have consulted a psychiatrist or clinical psychologist. You conduct a survey of patients in a nearby mental hospital, finding that all have received psychological help, and conclude that everybody in the country has received psychological help. Your *sample* (patients in the hospital) was not representative of the population (all Americans); it was therefore a *biased sample.* It was biased because not all people live in hospitals and those who do may be different in some way from the general population. A **biased sample** is an unrepresentative sample.

A representative sample of American adults is sometimes formed by selecting persons from many different geographic regions, races, occupations, and economic and educational levels. The characteristics and opinions of such a sample are assumed to reflect the characteristics and opinions of the population as a whole.

A psychological test is a method of obtaining a selected sample of a person's behavior. On the basis of that sample a psychologist may generalize and draw a conclusion about *all* of the person's behavior. On the basis of a paper-and-pencil test of intelligence (a one-hour sample of behavior), a psychologist is able to reach a conclusion about the person's intelligence in general.

Such a test serves *descriptive, diagnostic,* and *predictive* purposes. A test is descriptive insofar as it helps to precisely characterize the ability or personality of an individual. ("Joan has an IQ of 60.") A test is used diagnostically when a psychologist **diagnoses,** or classifies, an individual's psychological problem on the

basis of test results. ("Joan is mentally retarded.")
A test is *predictive* when it is used to predict, or
forecast, future behavior. ("Joan can be expected to
have serious academic difficulties in school.") Research concerning individual differences in ability or
personality often relies upon the descriptive, diagnostic, and predictive functions of psychological tests.

Reliability and Validity

Any ruler or other measuring device is useful only to
the degree that it yields dependable results and to the
degree that it actually measures what it claims to measure. **Reliability** means consistency or dependability;
useful psychological tests and surveys are reliable in
that they yield consistent results on repeated measurements. A rubber ruler is an unreliable measure of
height; each time I measure your height I would obtain a different figure. Similarly, if a psychological
test given on one day shows that you are a genius and
on the next day shows that you are a moron, the test is
unreliable, or inconsistent.

Validity refers to how well a test or survey measures what it is supposed to measure; useful psychological tests and surveys are valid in that they are appropriate and effective instruments for describing or
predicting some aspect of behavior. A ruler is a valid
measure of height but an invalid measure of time;
different marks on the ruler are just not related to
different amounts of time.

If you invent a new test of intelligence that
proves to be of no value in predicting academic success, reading comprehension, mathematic ability, or
competence in the world, your test of intelligence will
be called invalid; it does not seem to measure what it
claims to measure. If your final exam in psychology
class consisted exclusively of a series of questions
about Latin or geology, the test would be invalid,
since it would not measure the amount learned
in psychology. To check on the validity of a test,
first you must know exactly what it is supposed to
measure.

Types of Personality Tests

Psychologists have developed many types of personality tests designed to assess individual differences in
personality. These tests do not have right or wrong
answers. Instead, the way you answer is used to characterize your personality.

Projective Personality Tests • A **projective personality test** consists of a standard set of ambiguous
stimuli which are presented to the individual for interpretation. Since the pictures presented have no objective meaning, the viewer is encouraged to "project"
his or her own private meanings into the picture, just
as you might see your own private images in a great
white cloud in the sky.

*The Thematic Apperception Test is a projective personality test
that consists of pictures similar to the one shown in this illustration. As you look at the ambiguous picture and relate a story
about it, you are assumed to "project" your own personality into
the picture and to reveal the important themes of your personality. (© Harvard University Press, 1943, 1971)*

Figure 16-2 Rorschach Inkblot. *The Rorschach is a projective personality test that consists of cards with inkblots similar to the one shown in this illustration. As you look at the ambiguous picture and talk about what you see, you are assumed to reveal aspects of your personality.*

The **Thematic Apperception Test (TAT)** is a projective test consisting of a set of pictures of persons and scenes. As each picture is shown to the individual being tested, the person is asked to make up a story about the situation presented in the picture. The idea is that the viewers will reveal basic needs, concerns, and problems in the themes of the stories that are told, that when they interpret ambiguous social situations, they will expose their personalities. The psychologist listens to the stories that are stimulated by the pictures, then scores them according to certain standard scales; one such scale is the need for dominance. The reliability and validity of the TAT have been questioned by researchers.

The **Rorschach** inkblot test consists of ten cards, each with a picture of a different inkblot. Persons taking this projective test are asked to look at each card and describe what they see. The way subjects respond to a card is used to describe and to diagnose their personality. The test is very controversial, and its usefulness has been seriously questioned by many psychologists who consider it unscientific. Figure 16-2 shows an example of a Rorschach inkblot.

Personality Inventories • The **personality inventory** is a personality test consisting of a questionnaire asking a large number of personal questions. The answers are usually structured like a true-false or multiple-choice test, so that the person taking the test has only to check the most appropriate response. The questions may concern what you like or dislike, what you feel, or what you typically do in various situations.

One example of the personality inventory is Raymond Cattell's 16 PF, the **Sixteen Personality Factor Questionnaire.** This inventory consists of more than one hundred questions that are answered "yes" or "no." The questions define sixteen basic personality traits—what Cattell calls **source traits**—that all individuals possess to varying degrees. These underlying traits were not selected on the basis of Cattell's personal preference or intuition, but were the result of a complicated statistical analysis that found the ways in which groups of the hundred questions on Cattell's test tended to cluster together. The sixteen source traits can be characterized by sixteen pairs of descriptive terms, for example, reserved–outgoing, submissive–dominant, trusting–suspicious, relaxed–tense, and so forth.

A second example of a personality inventory is the Minnesota Multiphasic Personality Inventory **(MMPI).** The MMPI was developed to measure those traits which commonly characterize psychological disorders, but it has often been used to describe the personalities of normal people. The test consists of hundreds of true-false questions concerning various subjects such as physical health, sexual adjustment, religious and political attitudes, fears, fantasies, delusions, and hallucinations. The MMPI is an objective test in that the answers have standard interpretations based on empirical evidence. This test can be scored by a computer. Below are some examples of questions similar to those asked on the MMPI; each consists of a statement that is related as either "true," "false," or "cannot say."

☐ There are people who are plotting against me.
☐ I am frequently troubled by unusual feelings in the pit of my stomach.
☐ My hands shake most of the time.

☐ Love is only for persons who are weak.
☐ I am afraid to step on cracks in the sidewalk.
☐ Nobody could possibly like someone like me.
☐ I always do what I want no matter what happens.
☐ I am afraid of losing my mind.
☐ Someone has control over my mind.
☐ Most of the time I wish I were dead.
☐ Almost every day something happens to frighten me.
☐ I am a special agent of God.
☐ It is safer to trust nobody.

Problems with Personality Tests

The use of personality tests is sometimes controversial. Certain tests have been charged with being racially biased. The validity of personality inventories has been questioned on the grounds that they seem to depend upon the honesty of those answering the questions, and people are not always honest about themselves. When personality tests have been used in industry to help in the selection and hiring of personnel, the argument has been raised that asking such highly personal questions constitutes an invasion of the privacy of the people being tested.

The attempt to measure psychological traits using tests involves certain difficulties. In interpreting your responses on a personality test, for example, a psychologist must assume that you are answering honestly. But what if you were faking your answers, trying to appear as an especially well-adjusted individual? All personality tests depend to some extent on the basic honesty of the people who are taking them, but some tests have special protections against faking. For example, the MMPI has a special, built-in "lie-scale," a way of scoring certain items that detects an attempt to fake answers.

A second problem with tests is whether psychologists have the right to ask highly personal questions. Some personality tests include questions about political, religious, and sexual attitudes. The charge has been made that such tests constitute an invasion of privacy. Tests, like knives, are tools that can be used for good or for ill. Although the issue has not yet been perfectly resolved, psychologists take their responsibility very seriously and follow a strict code of ethics designed to prevent the misuse of test results.

A third problem arising from the use of tests is the issue of cultural and racial bias in tests. IQ tests, for example, although designed to measure general intelligence, in fact consist of verbal questions having specific content. The subject matter of some questions concerns food, clothing, or housing habits more common to some members of our society than to others. Persons from different subgroups in our society have different familiarity with the items discussed in certain IQ questions; the experience of middle-class white America is not shared by all citizens. Test items referring to that experience are biased against other groups. Additionally, different subgroups of people use different languages or dialects; tests written in standard English are often biased against students from Spanish-speaking homes. The problem of cultural and racial bias in tests has been of great concern to psychologists in recent years, and much effort has been devoted to the development of tests that are less biased.

Interim Summary   Psychological tests serve descriptive, diagnostic, and predictive purposes. They must be reliable—give consistent results on repeated measurements, and they must be valid—measure what they are supposed to measure. Two types of personality tests are the projective tests, such as the TAT, and personality inventories, such as the MMPI.

Personality tests do have problems. They have been criticized as being culturally and racially biased. The validity of all tests has been questioned, and the personal nature of such tests has raised the matter of invasion of privacy.

Theories of Personality

A theory of personality is a comprehensive explanation that describes how some individuals are different from others. Personality theories typically identify the important ways in which personalities vary and may offer an explanation of how these personality differences originate. Different theories view personality differently. Three major views of personality are represented in the psychoanalytic, social-learning, and humanistic theories of personality.

Psychoanalytic Theory

Sigmund Freud, the founder of psychoanalysis, believed that people could be understood only by understanding their inner thoughts and feelings. Some thoughts and feelings are conscious while others are unconscious. According to Freud's **psychoanalytic theory,** certain memories and impulses are repressed—pushed into the unconscious—and we are thereafter unaware of them. Painful thoughts and feelings are repressed in order to avoid anxiety; if we are unaware of them, we can't be frightened by them. Have you ever forgotten that you were to see the dentist or to take a test on a certain day? Such lapses of memory could be explained in terms of repression.

Freud believed that painful memories and frightening impulses are repressed and made unconscious. These unconscious ideas and memories, though we are unaware of them, continue to influence our behavior. Individual differences in personality, according to psychoanalytic theory, result from differences in the content of the unconscious mind and from differences in coping with these unconscious feelings and ideas.

Freud distinguished three levels of consciousness: the conscious level, the preconscious level, and the unconscious level. For Freud, the **conscious level** of the mind was a small part of mental life, consisting only of whatever we are currently aware of, our immediate thoughts and feelings. The **precon-

scious level** consists of thoughts and images not now in consciousness but accessible to it; those things we are not now thinking of but could recall—for example, our date of birth. The **unconscious level** consists of a storehouse of impulses, drives, and memories that we are not aware of and that we could not recall; yet they influence our lives. Some of this unconscious material was never conscious, and some of it was conscious at one time but was repressed, pushed into the unconscious mind. Memories that were extremely painful or impulses that are threatening and unacceptable are kept under lock and key in the unconscious mind.

Freud conceived the total personality as consisting of three parts—the id, ego, and superego—which, in the healthy person, work together cooperatively. The totally unconscious **id** consists of basic biological drives such as the avoidance of thirst and hunger or the need for sex and is with us at birth. The id has a special way of thinking and operates according to a special rule when it selects a path of action. The id's way of thinking is called **primary process thinking.** This way of thinking is characteristic of unconscious mental activity and involves the illogical demand for the instant satisfaction of all impulses and needs. In addition, the id operates according to a rule called the **pleasure principle:** the seeking of maximum immediate pleasure and minimum pain.

The second part of the personality, according to Freud, is the **ego,** the executive of the personality, responsible for voluntary processes such as thinking, judgment, and remembering. The ego develops from the id as we develop through interaction with the environment. The ego perceives the needs of the individual, evaluates the environment, and finds ways of satisfying personal needs within the environment. The ego takes into account the reality of the world as well as the demands of the id and tries to devise constructive ways to achieve satisfaction. Like the id, the ego also has a special way of thinking and operates according to a rule. The ego's special way of thinking is called **secondary process thinking.** This way of thinking is characteristic of conscious mental activity and involves plans, logic, and realistic thinking in order to achieve some goal. The ego operates according to a rule called the **reality principle:** the seeking of maximum pleasure *in the long run,* not immediate gratification at all costs. Following the reality principle may require enduring some short-term discomfort in order to gain long-term satisfaction. (Going to the dentist is consistent with the reality principle, but not with the pleasure principle.)

The third part is the **superego,** the moral area of the personality. Initially, children depend upon the guidance of their parents for determinations of good and bad, for what is moral and what is sinful. As children become older, they adopt their parents' ethical standards as their own; they assimilate or "internalize" this moral code. The superego is this internalized moral code. Eventually children no longer need their parents for moral judgments; they are controlled by their superegos. At this time the child is said to have a conscience.

The id is full of "wants"; the superego is full of "shoulds"; the ego is the "me" that seeks the compromise between the "wants" and the "shoulds." How do you see yourself in terms of these personality concepts? Do you have struggles between the impulsive demands for instant pleasure coming from your id and the moral judgments of conscience coming from your superego?

Social-Learning Theory

A second major theory of personality is the social-learning approach. The **social-learning theory of personality** stresses the ways in which patterns of behavior are learned through interaction with other people and with the environment. As you grow up, your personality is shaped and molded by the experiences you have. You learn to behave differently under different conditions. From this point of view, individual differences in personality result from different histories of learning experiences.

You learn by doing and also by observing.

When you were young, if you struck another child, you were punished for it. This is an example of **direct learning,** or learning by doing. Many of your actions as a child resulted in rewards or punishments, approval or disapproval. You learned to do things leading to rewards and approval, and you learned to avoid doing things leading to punishment and disapproval.

Much of your learning, however, resulted not from doing but from observing others. When you were young, you learned to play certain games by watching others play. This is an example of **observational learning,** or learning by watching and imitating others. People around you—your parents, an older brother, or your friends—were **models** whose behavior you observed and copied.

Unlike the psychoanalytic theory, the social-learning theory of personality assumes that the personality is always changing as new learning experiences occur. There are several ways in which models may affect the observer. The **modeling effect** is the way in which novel responses are acquired through observation. For example, a child who observes an aggressive adult model may later display a number of precisely imitative aggressive responses, exactly copying behavior that was observed. The **inhibitory effect** is a type of observational learning resulting in a reduced tendency to perform some behavior. For example, a child who observes an adult being punished for an aggressive action is less likely to perform similar aggressive actions later; these actions have been inhibited. The **eliciting effect** occurs when observing a model releases, or elicits, some previously learned response. The difference between the modeling effect and the eliciting effect is that the modeling effect describes how new responses are learned through observation, while the eliciting effect describes how previously learned responses are elicited or released through observation. For example, you may learn a particular dance through observing others perform it (an example of the modeling effect). However, once you have learned it, your tendency to perform this dance at a party may be increased by observing others perform it

According to the social-learning theory, children observe and imitate the behavior of others.   The influence of television models on personality is a controversial and unresolved issue.   (© Joel Gordon 1979)

(an example of the eliciting effect).

Because observational learning is so effective, many people are concerned with the aggression and violence shown on television.   By watching others display violence, children may learn to become more violent themselves.   Are there parts of your personality that you acquired by observing and copying your parents?

Humanistic Theory

The psychoanalytic theory of the personality focuses on the importance of unconscious memories and impulses, while the social-learning theory focuses on learned behavior.   Both of these theories conceive of personality as determined by past events, either by old memories that are now repressed or by your past history of learning.   By contrast, the **humanistic theory** of personality focuses on the role of your present experience and your future plans and goals.   This theory assumes that the personality can be understood as a process of growth, a process of becoming more and more your "real" self.

Carl Rogers and Abraham Maslow, two humanistic theorists, stressed the way people viewed themselves and their world and explored the conditions of personal growth.   Both believed that openness to experience and self-acceptance fostered growth and led to fulfillment, or what they called *actualization.*   According to humanistic theory, our primary motivation is neither the reinforcement proposed by social-learning theory nor the unconscious impulses proposed by psychoanalytic theory but is instead an inborn drive for self-fulfillment, or actualization.

An important idea in humanistic theory is the *self-concept,* the image you have of yourself.   The self concept develops as you grow older and consists of the sum of all your perceptions of your physical and psychological characteristics.   Your perceptions of your intelligence, musical ability, social skills, generosity, and physical appearance are all part of your self-concept.   Often the perception you have of yourself is

Carl Rogers

distorted, so that your self-concept does not match objective reality. This is an example of type of mismatch that Rogers called **incongruity**—a lack of consistency between your awareness and reality.

Sometimes we have feelings or experiences that we are unable to accept, and so we deny their existence. For example, we may feel angry yet at the same time deny that we are angry. People who were punished as children for expressing anger may have difficulty as adults in fully experiencing their anger. This is another example of the mismatch between awareness and reality that Rogers called incongruity. Humanistic theory argues that growth toward greater actualization involves an expanded awareness of the full range of feelings and experiences together with an unconditional acceptance of these experiences.

How clearly can you see yourself? How aware are you of your feelings in most situations? Can you accept your feelings? Or do they make you feel guilty or upset?

Interim Summary   A personality theory attempts to give a complete explanation for why people behave as they do. The psychoanalytic theory of personality focuses on how unconscious impulses and memories influence behavior. The personality is assumed to consist of three parts: the id, ego, and superego. The social-learning theory of personality stresses the influence of learning on behavior. From this point of view, your typical way of behaving is the result of both direct and observational learning. The humanistic theory of personality focuses on how people experience themselves and their worlds. According to this view, people are oriented toward the future and seek fulfillment.

Being Different

No two people are alike. Even twins from the same egg, with identical genetic structures, are different as a consequence of differences in their experiences. In the English language there are more than 1,000 words to describe individual differences in personality. The number of combinations possible of those thousand words, according to one estimate, exceeds by far the total number of atoms in the universe! The possible varieties of personality are equally numerous.

What does being different mean for you? Your body, your needs, your memories, your thoughts, your personality—all are unique. There has never been someone like you, there is no one quite like you now in the world, and there never will be. Your individuality does not make you worse or better than anyone else: everybody is in the same boat.

Try *feeling* your difference. Imagine that your eyes were orange and you had green spots on your nose and you were the tallest person in the world. How would you feel at a party?

Why does being different, or even the thought of being different, cause so much worry? Imagine looking the way you look right now in a world where everybody else was eight feet tall with orange eyes and green spots on their noses. You might feel like painting green spots on your nose to hide your difference. Even now, at this moment, you are trying not to be different. The clothes you wear, to some extent, follow the fads or fashion of the day for your age group. Why, in fact, are you wearing clothes at all? We seem to have a basic desire not to stand out in the crowd, not to be very different. There is security in joining the crowd, but there is something lost, too: the possibility to be truly yourself, to be entirely free. Suppose you did not try to cover up the ways you were different from other people; suppose you did not hide your differences in body, feelings, desires, thoughts, and personality. Would you still be normal?

Are You Normal?

Have you ever wondered whether certain of your thoughts, feelings, or behaviors were normal or not?

Perhaps you have feared that in some ways you are not normal. Deciding whether you or someone else is normal is not at all easy to do. Here is a personality description of an individual written by a psychologist. Would you say that the person described here is normal or abnormal?

You have a strong need for other people to like you and for them to admire you. You have a tendency to be critical of yourself. . . . Your sexual adjustment has presented some problems for you. Disciplined and controlled on the outside, you tend to be worrisome and insecure inside. At times you have serious doubts as to whether you have made the right decision or done the right thing. . . . You have found it unwise to be too frank in revealing yourself to others. At times you are extroverted, affable, sociable, while at other times you are introverted, wary, and reserved. Some of your aspirations tend to be pretty unrealistic.[7]

What kind of person has just been described? Is it possible for a person who has those kinds of problems to be a *normal person?* The description was invented by a psychologist, then given to college students. Surprisingly, a survey showed that over 90 percent of the college students rated the personality description given as a "good" or "excellent" interpretation of their own individual personalities.[7] Some of the comments made by the students were: "I agree with almost all your statements and think they answer the problems I may have"; "On the nose! True without a doubt"; "This interpretation applies to me individually"; "Unbelievably close to the truth." Almost all of the students accepted the *same* statement as a description of themselves.

Normal Problems

"Normal" does not mean "having no problems." Everybody has problems that worry them to some ex-

tent. The typical student in high school or college has doubts and worries about physical attractiveness, ability to love and be loved, the control of anger, the sex drive, and sexual behavior. The secret fears we all have are, remarkably enough, very similar; what you fear and what I fear are not that different. Many of the weaknesses you see in yourself are felt by almost everyone else; your feelings of guilt or shame about the things you have done are felt by almost everyone, for almost everyone has done the things you have done.

What is the normal person like? Psychologists who have tried to study the normal person can't agree among themselves. One psychologist, after studying seventy young persons selected because of their normality, concluded: "The vast majority of our subjects exhibit some anxiety about sexual role function. . . . Our subjects demonstrate specific struggles with anxiety, depression, shame, and guilt."[8] Another psychologist selected 50 men from over 1,900 men on the basis of their being "most normal." His testing of them showed that over 50 percent of them had neurotic symptoms, although the disorders were mild.[9] The elected student councils from three colleges were tested in another study.[10] One college president commented, "It is as normal a group as you'll ever get." The psychologist found that some of the "normal" students had alarming problems, such as extreme depression, withdrawal, coldness, sadism, and other symptoms of neurosis. He concluded that 57 percent could benefit from mental health services and 14 percent urgently needed psychiatric care. Obviously, being normal does not mean being without problems.

Normality Is a Value Judgment

What does it mean to be normal? The word **normal** is used in more than one way; sometimes it means good, and sometimes it means typical or average. It is used both evaluatively and descriptively. When it is used *evaluatively,* a value judgment is made; in this sense "normal behavior" means "good behavior," what you ought to do, what is acceptable or desirable. "Abnormal behavior," then, means what is bad, undesirable, immoral, or bizarre. Thus certain sexual practices are referred to by some people as "abnormal acts," even though the majority of people have participated in them. Masturbation is one such sexual act. What people mean when they call masturbation abnormal is that in their opinion it is not good or desirable. You are justified in asking what are the criteria, standards, values, and hidden assumptions behind the use of the words *normal* and *abnormal*.

Cultural Differences

What is "good" and "acceptable" behavior in one culture may not be "good" in another culture. The Tchambuli tribe of New Guinea has different standards of normality than we do. A businesslike and sexually aggressive Tchambuli man or an emotionally dependent and sexually passive Tchambuli woman would be considered "abnormal" in their society.

Being Kind Is Being Crazy • The anthropologist Ruth Benedict cites an extreme example of cultural differences:

The most spectacular illustrations of the extent to which normality may be culturally defined are those cultures where an abnormality of our culture is the cornerstone of their social structure. . . . A recent study of an island of northwest Melanesia describes a society built upon traits which we regard as beyond the border of paranoia. . . . Their preoccupation with poisoning is constant; no woman ever leaves her cooking pot for a moment untended. . . . Fear and distrust pervade the culture. . . . They have even rigorous religiously enforced customs that forbid the sharing of seed even in one family group.[11]

In this island society where suspicion, mistrust, and fear were "normal," where no one could work with another or share food with another, there was one man who was regarded by all his fellows as crazy.

He was not one of those who periodically ran amok and, beside himself and frothing at the mouth, fell with a knife

upon anyone he could reach. . . . But there was one man of sunny, kindly disposition who liked work and liked to be helpful. Men and women never spoke of him without laughing; he was silly and simple and definitely crazy (according to the people of his island society).[11]

The point is that what is normal is normal *for some group*. For some comparisons, the group is an entire culture. There can also be great differences within a given culture.

The Case of the Ozark Preacher • As you move from place to place within our country, you encounter differences in what is socially acceptable behavior.

In an isolated rural area of the Ozark Mountains a man received a revelation from God, and a "call" to preach that revelation to his neighbors. He did so successfully. Later he was "called" to preach in the neighboring communities, and with equal success. He soon achieved great prestige in the area as a highly respected charismatic leader. But then he received a "call" to go to the city. Soon after arriving in St. Louis he was arrested for preaching on the street in the business district during the rush hour. Subsequently he was diagnosed by a psychiatrist as a paranoid schizophrenic, because he had delusions of grandeur and hallucinations. Here a man who conforms to a rural, lower-class subculture seems to be a deviant from the point of view of an urban, middle-class subculture.[12]

Normal Means Typical

One of the ways the word *normal* is used is evaluatively, referring to behavior that is acceptable. The second way that "normal" is used is *descriptively*. From this perspective an act is "normal" if it is typical of a group, if it is conventional or ordinary for that group. An act is abnormal if it is unusual or unconventional for that group. Defining "normal" in this way, it is correct to say that masturbation is normal, since it is typical for this culture. From this point of view, a person who has an IQ of 130 is just as unusual, and therefore abnormal, as a person who has an IQ of 70; both are equally far away from the average IQ of 100. Psychologists use the term *normal* in a descriptive sense, to refer to behavior that is typical.

It is not necessarily undesirable to be deviant; being different from what is typical can be either good or bad. All people of unusual talent or intelligence are "abnormal" in the sense of being different from the usual. Are you normal? Many things that you do, many thoughts and feelings that you have, many fears and fantasies you dwell on are normal—in many ways you are not that different from other people. But you are unique; no one else is quite like you, and because you are different in some ways from all other people, you are in these ways "abnormal."

Interim Summary

Being normal does not mean being without problems. The word "normal" is used in different ways. Sometimes it is used evaluatively, to refer to behavior that is regarded as good. Other times it is used descriptively, to refer to behavior that is typical or average for a culture.

Summary

1. Personality refers to a person's typical way of reacting to the world and to other people.
2. Three aspects of your personality, or "faces," are your social face (your public self), your personal face (your private image of yourself), and your real face (what you are in reality).
3. According to Jung, there are two basic personality types: introverts, who turn inward and withdraw from social contact, and extroverts, who turn outward and seek social contact.
4. According to Sheldon, the shape of the body is related to different personality types. He classified people as either mesomorphs, endomorphs, or ectomorphs.
5. People can also be described as possessing different personality *traits* or characteristics such as dominance or insecurity.
6. One problem with describing personality in terms of "types" and "traits" is that such descriptions assume that people behave consistently over time and in different circumstances. In fact, there are important situational differences in personality.
7. Psychological tests serve descriptive, diagnostic, and predictive purposes.
8. Psychological tests must be *reliable*—giving consistent results on repeated measurements, and *valid*—measuring those aspects of behavior they are supposed to measure.
9. Two types of personality tests are the projective tests, such as the TAT, and personality inventories, such as the MMPI.
10. The use of psychological tests is not without controversy. Certain tests have been charged with being culturally and racially biased. The validity of all tests has been questioned, and the personal nature of such tests has raised the question of invasion of privacy.
11. Freud's psychoanalytic theory of personality focuses on how unconscious impulses and memories influence behavior. It assumes that the personality consists of the id, ego, and superego.
12. The social-learning theory stresses the influence of learning on behavior. It assumes that personality is the result of both direct and observational learning.

13. The humanistic theory of personality assumes that personality can be understood as a process of growth, the result of both present experience and future goals.
14. The word "normal" is used both evaluatively, to refer to behavior that is regarded as good, and descriptively, to refer to behavior that is typical or average for a culture. Psychologists use the word in this latter sense.

Key Concepts

personality An individual's typical way of relating to people and reacting to the world.

social face A public image; the false front that is presented to other people.

personal face A private image; an individual's self-concept.

real face The true self; what an individual is in reality.

self-concept A private image of oneself; an individual's personal face.

personality type A set of personality characteristics that one group of people has in common that makes it different from other groups.

introvert A personality type that turns inward, withdraws from social engagements, is introspective, self-controlled, and reflective.

extrovert A personality type that turns outward, seeks social contacts, is friendly, outspoken, and tolerant.

somatotypes Body types, such as mesomorph, endomorph, and ectomorph.

mesomorph A body type which has a muscular build, with a narrow pelvis and broad shoulders.

endomorph A body type which is short and plump, with a short neck and broad hands.

ectomorph A body type which is tall and thin, with a flat chest, long limbs, and a narrow face.

personality trait A characteristic or dimension of personality that each person possesses in varying degrees, such as aggressiveness, dominance, or insecurity.

dominance A personality trait describing the tendency to be confident, independent, and controlling.

submissiveness The opposite of dominance; refers to the tendency to be timid, dependent, and conforming.

dominance hierarchy A group that can be ordered from most dominant to most submissive; an individual in this group dominates those below and is dominated by those above; a "pecking order."

security A personality trait describing the tendency to relate easily to other people, to feel accepted, to be optimistic and self-confident; individuals with this trait have a firm sense of their own identities.

insecurity The opposite of security; refers to the tendency to feel threatened by living, unloved, pessimistic, and discontented.

I-E scale A personality test designed to measure how much control you feel you have over your life.

sample A subset, or selection, from a larger group.

population An entire group; the set being sampled.

generalization Reasoning from evidence obtained from a sample to a conclusion about a population.

biased sample An unrepresentative sample; a sample with characteristics systematically different from its population.

diagnosis The classification, or labeling, of a problem.

reliability Consistency or dependability.

validity The degree to which an instrument actually measures what it is supposed to measure.

projective personality test A test to assess

personality that consists of a set of ambiguous stimuli, often pictures, which the individual is encouraged to interpret according to his or her own private meanings.

Thematic Apperception Test (TAT) A series of pictures about which the individual being tested is asked to make up stories.

Rorschach A test of personality using "inkblots" on cards.

personality inventory A personality test consisting of a large number of personal questions concerning what you like or dislike, what you feel, or what you typically do in various situations.

Sixteen Personality Factor Questionnaire A personality inventory designed to assess an individual in terms of Cattell's source traits.

source traits Cattell's term for basic personality traits.

MMPI A personality test, consisting of hundreds of true-false questions, designed to measure abnormal personality traits.

psychoanalytic theory Freud's theory of personality; according to this theory, personality is fixed at an early age.

conscious level That level of consciousness consisting of immediate thoughts and feelings; one's current awareness.

preconscious level That level of consciousness consisting of thoughts and images not now in the conscious level but accessible to it; those things we are not now thinking about, but could recall.

unconscious level That level of consciousness consisting of those impulses, drives, and memories that we are not aware of and that we could not recall.

id According to Freud, that part of the personality that is the unconscious storehouse of basic biological drives.

ego According to Freud, that part of the personality that deals with reality and is responsible for voluntary processes of thinking, perceiving, and remembering.

superego According to Freud, that part of the personality that is the internalized moral code or conscience.

pleasure principle The principle that governs the operation of the id, namely, the seeking of pleasure and the avoiding of pain.

reality principle The principle that governs the operation of the ego, namely, the delaying of instant gratification for the maximum gain of the long run.

primary process thinking A way of thinking whose sole aim is the immediate gratification of pleasure and the avoidance of pain; utilized by the id.

secondary process thinking A way of thinking that is in line with the reality principle; utilized by the ego.

social-learning theory of personality A theory that stresses the ways in which patterns of behavior are learned through interaction with other people and the environment; assumes that personality is always changing as new learning occurs.

direct learning Learning by doing.

observational learning Learning by watching and imitating others.

models People whose behavior is observed and copied.

modeling effect The way in which novel responses are acquired through observation.

inhibitory effect A type of observational learning which results in a reduced tendency to perform some behavior.

eliciting effect A type of observational learning which results in the increased tendency to perform some behavior.

humanistic theory A theory that views personality as a process of growth or becoming, rather than as something determined by the past.

incongruity A lack of consistency between your awareness and reality; for example, a lack of consistency between your awareness of how you feel and what your feelings actually are.

normal Refers to behavior that either is good or is typical for a culture.

Chapter 17

Motivation and Emotion

Key Questions   1. How can the varieties of human motivation be described?
2. What is the relation between behavior and arousal?
3. What theories of motivation are important in psychology?
4. What are the effects of emotion on the mind and body?
5. What theories of emotion are important in psychology?

On August 1, 1966, Charles Whitman, twenty-five years of age, climbed to the observation deck of the Tower Building at the University of Texas. In two hours, he killed fourteen people and wounded twenty-four others before he himself was slain by the police.

Many people thought him a fine young man. He liked children, worked hard, and had been an Eagle Scout at the age of twelve. He was humorous and most of his friends and acquaintances seemed to regard him highly. But there were ominous undercurrents.

In various notes left behind, he described a deep hatred toward his father, even though it was his mother he killed—to save her from embarrassment, he said. He also left a written request that his brain be autopsied. And, indeed, a tumor the size of a walnut was found in the amygdaloid area of his brain.[1]

Why did Charles Whitman murder his mother, his wife, and twelve other people? Was it because of his hatred for his father, his frustration from not doing well in school, his brain tumor, or some unconscious urge arising from childhood conflicts? In this tragedy, the answer will never be known. But the basic question—why?—continues to be posed by those who are interested in studying human motivation. This chapter will discuss various aspects of motivation.

The Concept of Motivation

Why do people act the way they do? The behavior of others is often a puzzle, a challenge to our understanding. Even your own behavior is occasionally a puzzle. Sometimes after you do something, you stop and ask yourself, "Now why in the world did I do that?" You are trying to understand the reasons or causes for your behavior. You want to understand the behavior in terms of your desires, plans, urges, goals, impulses, needs, or intentions. You want to understand your motivation. The term **motivation** refers to the forces which determine the arousal and direction of purposeful behavior.

Motives, Incentives, and Drives

When you are hungry, you are likely to do something to obtain food—going to the refrigerator, stopping at a restaurant, or putting money into a machine to buy candy or an apple. Hunger is a **motive,** something which arouses behavior and directs it toward a specific goal. Thirst is also a motive, since it arouses you to act in a way that obtains something to drink. In addition to the biological motives of hunger, thirst, and sex, you have many social and psychological motives that move you to act in different ways.

Motives can be viewed either as forces that push you into action or as forces that pull you into action.

Motivation refers to the forces that determine the arousal and direction of behavior. What is the runner's motivation for striving to win? This motivation can be viewed as a drive (a force pushing him into action) or as an incentive (a force pulling him toward the goal). (© Gerry Cranham/Photo Researchers, Inc.)

When motives are viewed as forces that push you into action, they are called drives. **Drives** are needs that arouse behavior and push people into action. For example, a person with a strong sex drive is strongly motivated to engage in sexual activity in order to satisfy a need. Your hunger drive goads you into action to obtain food, so that your hunger may be satisfied.

Motives viewed as forces that pull you into action are called incentives. An **incentive** is a goal or condition that you strive to obtain. Food, praise, and money are examples of incentives. As you struggle across a desert toward an oasis, the water serves as an incentive that motivates your action. Incentives are said to "pull" you into action because they occur in the future; they are goals that have not yet been reached. Of course, goals effectively motivate behavior through present plans and anticipation. Future events do not actually control present behavior directly.

Unconscious Motivation

How successful are you at identifying your own motives? Are you generally aware of the motives that cause you to act the way you do? You may be aware of some of your motives but unaware of others. According to some theorists, answering the question of why people act the way they do must take account of the importance of **unconscious motivation**. An unconscious motive is a force or goal that affects our behavior but is not accessible to the conscious mind.

Are we controlled by unconscious motives? According to Freud's theory, the answer is yes. Freud believed that unconscious impulses and urges—primarily sexual and aggressive in nature—powerfully affected our day-to-day behavior. In modern psychology, the role of unconscious motivation is controversial. There are differences of opinion about the importance of this concept in understanding human motivation. While there is no doubt that we are all sometimes unaware of the reasons for our actions, some psychologists explain this in terms of a simple lack of knowledge instead of something as complicated as unconscious forces.

Intrinsic and Extrinsic Motivation

As you observe the behavior of other people, you note that most things people do are in some way rewarded. People work, apparently in order to earn money. People perform, apparently because they find the audience's reaction rewarding. Most of the things people do, they do in order to get something. There are external, or extrinsic, reasons for these behaviors. **Extrinsic motivation** refers to forces outside the person, such as rewards, that motivate behavior.

By contrast, certain things that people do are rewarding in and of themselves. There are tasks that are inherently or intrinsically interesting and enjoyable, such as games, artwork, and puzzles. The concept of **intrinsic motivation** refers to the factors that make these tasks interesting. If you are extrinsically motivated to perform some action, you are doing it to obtain some kind of reward or to avoid some kind of punishment not inherent in the task itself. If you are intrinsically motivated to perform some action, you are doing it in the absence of any reward other than the rewards available simply from completing the action itself.

Under certain circumstances, providing extrinsic rewards for tasks that are inherently interesting tends to *decrease* future performance on those tasks. This is an exception to the Law of Effect, which states that rewarded acts will be repeated. It has been shown with children who draw and with adults who solve puzzles that attempting to reinforce these activities decreases the likelihood of their continued participation in these activities.[2] Apparently, introducing extrinsic rewards sometimes reduces intrinsic motivation.

Why are certain tasks intrinsically motivating? According to some theorists, people are motivated to solve problems and to seek out and to conquer challenges.[3] For each person, there is an ideal difficulty level in problems that presents an optimum challenge—neither too easy nor impossibly hard. Our need to be and to feel competent is satisfied when we confront such a challenge and meet it.

What Were Your Motives for Attending College?

Some students are intrinsically motivated to attend college, and others are extrinsically motivated. The list below contains what some other students have said were their motives for attending college. Which of these are closest to your motives?

- ☐ I wanted to get away from home.
- ☐ My career goals require college.
- ☐ I have a strong desire to learn.
- ☐ I wanted to please my parents.
- ☐ I wanted to be more independent.
- ☐ I wanted to meet interesting people.
- ☐ I am competitive and have a strong need for achievement.
- ☐ People who have gone to college have more status.
- ☐ People who have gone to college make more money.
- ☐ I wanted to improve some of my skills.
- ☐ Most of my friends were going to go to college.
- ☐ I enjoy encountering new ideas.
- ☐ I wanted to avoid having to work full time.
- ☐ I wanted to participate in the social and cultural life on campus.
- ☐ My parents gave me no other choice.

Interim Summary   The forces that determine the arousal and direction of purposeful behavior are called motivations. Drives are needs that arouse behavior and push people into action, while incentives are goals or conditions you strive to obtain.

Some motives may be unconscious, not accessible to the conscious mind. Motivations are either extrinsic (forces outside the person) or intrinsic (factors inherent in the activity itself). Under certain circumstances, an individual's intrinsic motivation for a task may be reduced by providing some form of extrinsic reward.

Motivation and Activation

One of the ways psychologists have studied motivation is by examining the relation between behavior and activation or arousal. People who are aroused or excited are typically more active than people who are not. Without some level of tension or arousal, you will fall asleep. Yet extreme states of arousal or tension seem to interfere with behavior, and people find them unpleasant. People appear to be motivated to avoid the extremes of both understimulation and overstimulation. What happens when you experience prolonged periods of understimulation?

Sensory Deprivation

Have you ever been confined to bed for several days? The experience is notably unpleasant. You feel bored and irritable and may feel disoriented and weak. You feel more and more restless and want to become active. Stimulation is necessary in order to maintain an acceptable level of arousal and activation.

The extreme absence of stimulation is called **sensory deprivation**. People who are deprived of adequate levels of stimulation for long periods suffer a variety of psychological problems. Psychologists studied hospital patients confined to bed for long periods of time and found that a number of them developed unusual symptoms of anxiety, delusions, and hallucinations. These symptoms vanished when the patients were allowed to experience a more varied sensory environment.[4]

Bored Monkeys and Rats • Monkeys and rats also prefer a varied sensory environment. In one study, a monkey was confined to an enclosed box, with a small window that the animal could open. The monkey quickly learned to open the window in order to look outside. The experimenter then rigged the window so that it would open only after many separate at-

In a sensory deprivation experiment, an individual is put into a darkened room on a soft bed while brain waves are monitored. Sensory deprivation experiments show people need a moderate level of stimulation to be able to function. (© Van Bucher 1970/Photo Researchers, Inc.)

tempts to open it; still the monkey was willing to work hard for a peek outside.[5] Apparently the opportunity to look outside was rewarding.

Other studies with monkeys show that stimulation is not only rewarding to animals—it is necessary. One experimenter deprived chimpanzees of all visual stimulation from birth on. Later examination revealed that the optic nerve fibers leading from the eyes to the brain shriveled and became useless. Some stimulation is necessary for the continued functioning of nerves and cells in the sensory system.

Given a choice, rats demonstrate a preference for more complex environments rather than environments with little sensory variation.[6] Rats growing up in less complex environments show poorer abilities at solving problems,[7] which suggests that an environment lacking sensory stimulation may reduce thinking capacity. Rats growing up in less complex environments have also been shown to have smaller (lighter) brains than rats growing up in more stimulating environments.[8] What is a stimulating environment for a rat? In the above study the rats were provided with little toys, such as ladders, wheels, boxes, and platforms; in addition they were allowed to explore a larger cage with novel patterns of barriers on the floor each day.

The Understimulated Mind • "Bored to tears," "bored to death," "bored out of your mind"—how do you react to boredom? How do you feel when your world is very dull? Without normal environmental stimulation, you may tend to feel that your mind is slow, confused, or "fuzzy."

Without continual stimulation, thinking is more difficult. Laboratory experiments have shown that sensory deprivation interferes with human thought. College students volunteered as subjects in most of these experiments and were shut off from most stimulation for periods of hours or days. A common procedure used to isolate subjects from environmental stimulation was to place them in a dark quiet room on a soft bed; earplugs and blackened goggles were worn to block sounds and light further.

In one experiment subjects were tested before isolation, after two, twenty-four, and forty-eight hours of isolation, and then on the two days following isolation.[9] The battery of tests consisted of problems in simple arithmetic, number series, and anagrams. The subjects who experienced sensory deprivation showed poor performance on all tests, as compared to another group of students who took the same tests without sensory deprivation. Tasks involving logical reasoning seem to be particularly affected by an environment that is not stimulating.[10] Other studies show that memory,[11] attention,[12] and concentration[13,14] are all poorer for persons experiencing inadequate stimulation.

A lack of sufficient stimulation from the environment not only is boring and mind-dulling, it also is stressful. The subjects in sensory-deprivation experiments commonly express feelings of fear, anxiety, and even panic as the period of isolation continues.[15]

In a dim twilight world shadows play tricks on the mind. With a prolonged lack of environmental stimulation, both illusions and hallucinations may develop. **Illusions** are distortions of reality. One person reported (after six days of sensory deprivation), "the wall bulged toward me and then went back . . . the whole room is undulating, swirling."[16] **Hallucinations** are perceptual experiences of things that are not there. Hallucinations are a common experience arising from lengthy sensory-deprivation experiments. Sometimes these hallucinations resemble those induced by certain drugs, such as LSD and mescaline.

In one study each of eight subjects was required to lie on a bed in a quiet room for eight hours; the subjects wore goggles with a frosted glass so that light was admitted but no forms could be discriminated.[17] In addition they wore cotton gloves to reduce stimulation of the hands. Several of these subjects reported hearing music, buzz saws, voices, or the chirping of birds. Several visual hallucinations were also reported, including the following:

The herd of elephants. Oh, that was pretty. That came very spontaneously. It was just sort of elephants in black, with pink and blue and purple. . . . They were moving.[17]

When there is little to see in the world, it seems that the mind makes up things to see.

Sensory Overload

Sensory overload is an excess of stimulation, the opposite of sensory deprivation. The extreme of overstimulation is also psychologically disturbing and motivates people to reduce their level of arousal. If you stand on a crowded downtown street corner at five o'clock in the evening, you receive a lot of sensory information. There is a chaos of intense sounds and images, more than you could possibly respond to. As the world becomes more complicated and we move at a faster and faster pace, we become overloaded.

The Effects of Overload •

According to one scientist our society suffers from an excess of stimulation, and as a consequence, "Overstimulated and bewildered parents bring up overstimulated and bewildered offspring unable to cope with overstimulation."[18]

Bombarded with rapidly changing sights and sounds from the environment, individuals may be confused by the abundance of choices for responding; this creates a kind of conflict, which may result in stress. Studies have shown that as information multiplies and mental load increases, a variety of emotional and bodily changes occur: the rate of blinking decreases[19] and blood pressure increases.[20]

One important study compared the effects of eight hours of sensory deprivation with the effects of eight hours of sensory overload.[21] The sensory deprivation consisted of silence and darkness, and the sensory overload was provided by strobe lights going off at random intervals, two tape recorders playing simultaneously, a filmstrip projector showing random scenes, and two slide projectors. The results showed that both overload and deprivation increased hostility and certain physiological measures of stress and anxiety. In addition the sensory overload condition increased both the heart rate and the breathing rate.

Another investigator created an overload condition by requiring subjects to work at an unnaturally rapid pace on certain psychological tests.[22] Subjects in the overload condition performed more poorly than subjects who worked at a normal speed; moreover the type of errors they made resembled the type of errors made by patients that were mentally disturbed. Another experiment using only a short exposure to sensory overload (twenty minutes) showed essentially no effects of overload.[23] These studies confirm that prolonged exposure to sensory overload has similar effects to prolonged exposure to sensory deprivation: overload disturbs thought processes and creates anxiety and stress.

Noise Pollution •

Listen to the noises of modern civilization: the jet airplane overhead, an ambulance siren, a jackhammer, the screech of chalk on a blackboard, a gum-chewing neighbor, amplified rock music, a motorcycle speeding by. Noise, especially in cities, is reaching such an intensity that scientists and politicians talk about **noise pollution** in our environment. Noise pollution is an excess of unwanted noise and is a special case of sensory overload.

Noise is annoying. Loud sounds, high-pitched sounds, discordant sounds, unpredictable or uncontrollable sounds, and sounds associated with danger, pain, or fear are particularly bothersome. The intensity of noise increases each year because we invent larger and more powerful machines while we live closer and closer together. A recent survey of residents of Detroit and Los Angeles revealed that about 25 percent of the women and about 33 percent of the men were regularly annoyed by noise at home or at work.[24] Residents near airports or under paths of supersonic flights are often particularly annoyed by noise; their houses rattle, their sleep is interrupted, and their attempts to communicate with other people are often blocked.[25]

Noise does more than annoy; it causes stress reactions, it interferes with memory and attention, and it can damage the ear itself. Persons briefly exposed to loud noise suffer a temporary reduction in the ability to hear; if the noise exposure is prolonged, permanent damage to the ear and permanent loss of hearing can result. Airport workers exposed to the loud noise of jet aircraft become increasingly deaf over the years.[25] Performers of rock music and their audience suffer hearing losses.[25]

The evidence for the effects of noise on thinking is unclear. Some studies find that noise interferes with memory,[26] and others find that it has little effect.[27] Noise does seem to interfere with attention and concentration.[28] Whereas unpredictable loud noises probably interrupt thinking briefly, most tasks do not suffer from brief time-outs from thinking; most tasks therefore are not interfered with by noise. The more complex the task, the more likely that it would be interfered with by loud noise.

Noise causes stress reactions. When a sudden noise strikes your ear, your heart starts beating more rapidly, your blood pressure increases, your muscles are tensed, you skin turns pale due to constricting blood vessels, your pupils get larger, and you experience other stress reactions.[25,29] Persons who are exposed to loud noises experience frequent stress reactions. A variety of other physical and psychological problems soon follows. Prolonged exposure to noise has been linked with chronic fatigue,[30] headaches,[31] physical illnesses,[25] irritability, frustration, and emotional upsets.[32,33] People living near noisy airports have a significantly higher rate of admission to mental hospitals than people living in quieter residential areas.[34] Since our whole society is becoming noisier, these problems will probably increase.

The Optimum Level of Arousal

Somewhere between the extremes of sensory deprivation and sensory overload is an intermediate level of stimulation and activation that is psychologically more healthful. With extremely low arousal, when you are bored and understimulated, your mind becomes fuzzy and you can't think very clearly. With extremely high arousal, when you are tense and overloaded, you also can't think very clearly.

Some psychologists believe that people need an intermediate level of stimulation, not too much and not too little, and that we avoid both extremes if we can. We are strongly motivated to maintain an **optimal level of arousal,** a level that is best for human functioning.[35,36] When the environment is not stimulating enough, we begin to explore, to investigate, or to manipulate it in order to increase the variation of stimulation reaching our brains and become more aroused. When the environment is too stimulating, we withdraw or begin focusing on one thing at a time in order to reduce the overload. Many people also adjust their level of arousal with the use of drugs, such as caffeine, alcohol, and other stimulant and depressant chemicals.

Studies of aesthetic preference are consistent with the concept of an optimal level of arousal. In several studies, people have been offered the choice of looking at pictures of low, intermediate, or high complexity. Pictures of intermediate complexity are rated as more pleasant than those of low or high complexity.[37,38] Apparently, pictures of intermediate complexity provide a preferred level of stimulation—neither too much nor too little.

Your level of performance on different tasks depends upon your level of arousal. The **Yerkes-Dodson law** describes the relationship between arousal and performance. The Yerkes-Dodson law makes two claims about the way performance is affected by different levels of arousal: (1) performance is best at an intermediate level of arousal, and (2) the optimal level of arousal is higher for easy tasks than for difficult tasks. The first point is that all tasks suffer from extremely high or extremely low levels of stimulation or arousal and that some level in between works best. The second point is that tasks having different levels of difficulty require different levels of arousal for optimum performance. A simple, dull task is performed best at moderate to high levels of arousal—without a fair amount of stimulation, you may lose concentration or fall asleep. By contrast, a complicated, difficult task is performed best at relatively low levels of arousal; moderate to high levels of arousal will interfere with your performance.

Individual Differences

Not only is the optimal level of arousal different among different tasks, but it is also different among different people. Some people perform best at relatively low levels of arousal and others at relatively high levels of arousal. Those who function best at high levels of arousal are motivated to seek additional stimulation in order to increase their level of excitement and activation. Those who function best at low levels of arousal are motivated to avoid excitement and reduce their arousal.[39,40]

What kinds of experiences increase levels of

Are you a sensation-seeking person? Those who perform best at high levels of arousal seek challenges, changing stimulation, excitement, and new experiences. Individual differences in the need for stimulation can be measured by the Sensation-Seeking Scale. (Pamela R. Schuyler/Stock, Boston)

arousal? To some degree the intensity of stimulation is a factor. Loud noises, very bright lights, and other intense stimuli all increase levels of activation. Change in stimulation is another factor. Rapidly changing stimulation is more arousing than constant stimulation. New experiences are more arousing than old ones. Personal meaning is another factor involved in determining how stimulating different events may be. One person may be afraid of dogs while another person is indifferent to them. One person may be excited by a baseball game while another is bored by the same game.

What type of person are you? Are you a high-activation person—someone who seeks sensation, excitement, and change—or are you a low-activation person—someone who avoids situations that might increase arousal levels? The following Sensation-Seeking Scale will help you to determine what type of person you are.[41] Each item in the test presents a situation with two choices. For each item, pick the choice that best describes the way you feel or the way you tend to act.

Sensation-Seeking Scale

1. ☐ (a) I like seeing movies I've seen before.
   ☐ (b) I find it boring to see any movie for the second time.
2. ☐ (a) Routine work bores me.
   ☐ (b) I find that routine work can be fun.
3. ☐ (a) I would like to sky dive.
   ☐ (b) Skydiving is too dangerous a sport to try.
4. ☐ (a) I like people who are predictable.
   ☐ (b) I like people who are unpredictable.
5. ☐ (a) When in a restaurant, I would prefer to order dishes I know well.
   ☐ (b) When in a restaurant, I would prefer to order something I've never had before.
6. ☐ (a) I often wish I could be a deep-sea diver.
   ☐ (b) I can't understand people who risk their necks deep-sea diving.
7. ☐ (a) On a vacation I would like to go to some relatively unexplored place, even if it involved some danger.
   ☐ (b) On a vacation I like to go places where I can find a good hotel, good food, and no danger.
8. ☐ (a) I avoid arguments at all costs.
   ☐ (b) Arguments can be exciting and interesting at times.
9. ☐ (a) I would like to walk into a room filled with new, unfamiliar people.
   ☐ (b) I would like to walk into a room filled with old, familiar friends.
10. ☐ (a) I can't stand to take cold showers.
    ☐ (b) I am invigorated by a brisk, cold shower.

Score your answers per the footnote following the Key Concepts at the end of the chapter. The higher your score, the higher your need for arousal.

Interim Summary   People are motivated to avoid the extremes of both overstimulation and understimulation, to seek an optimal level of arousal.   The extreme absence of stimulation (sensory deprivation) can interfere with thought and produce anxiety, panic, and hallucinations.   The extreme excess of stimulation (sensory overload) can also produce psychological problems.   For example, excessive exposure to noise causes stress reactions, chronic fatigue, and emotional problems.   According to the Yerkes-Dodson law, performance is best at an intermediate level of arousal and, in addition, the optimal level of arousal is higher for easy tasks than for difficult tasks.   Individual differences in need for arousal can be measured by the Sensation-Seeking Scale.

Theories of Motivation

A theory of motivation is a systematic attempt to account for the known facts concerning human motivation.   From the Greeks Plato and Aristotle to the English philosophers of the early nineteenth century, the theory that was most popular was that what motivates human behavior is knowledge and rational thought.   In the nineteenth century, several important new ideas emerged that permanently changed our views of motivation.   Jeremy Bentham and John Stuart Mill, English utilitarian philosophers, argued that people everywhere were motivated by a single urge: the desire to achieve the greatest possible pleasure (**hedonism**).   Charles Darwin, author of *The Origin of Species* and the theory of evolution, showed that human beings are closely related to animals.   Sigmund Freud, the founder of psychoanalysis, showed that people were often motivated by irrational, animalistic impulses.   Freud's theory, and two other theories, are still influential today.

Freud's Psychoanalytic Theory

Sigmund Freud's **psychoanalytic theory of motivation** assumed that people have inborn needs, which, when unsatisfied, produce states of tension that motivate behavior.   Behavior is both initiated and organized in order to reduce these states of tension.

For Freud, all of our inborn needs fall into two main categories: the life instincts and the death instincts.   The **life instincts** are those innate biological and psychological needs that serve the purpose of the survival of the individual and the human species.   Hunger, thirst, and sex are life instincts.   The life instincts also constitute a form of psychic energy Freud termed the **libido**.   **Psychic energy** is the total amount of energy your system has available to it, including the energy used for thinking, moving, breathing, coping with problems, and eating.   The **death instincts** are those innate needs that serve destructive purposes, the most important of which is aggression.   Freud was much less detailed about this type of instinct and had no name for the form of psychic energy involved with the death instincts.

The **id** is the depository of all the inborn sexual and aggressive needs.   The totally unconscious id consists of everything that is inherited and is completely removed from the constraints of reality.   The id operates according to the **pleasure principle**: the avoidance of pain and the seeking of pleasure at any cost.

Since the id is unconscious, the basic needs and impulses that arise from the id and motivate behavior are typically inaccessible to our conscious mind.   In fact, as we become socialized, these needs are seen as increasingly unacceptable, and we strive to disown them by repressing them.   Although they are repressed, they nevertheless find means of expression.   In dreams, for example, the experienced dream images are camouflaged expressions of sexual and aggressive needs, according to Freud. Our day-to-day behavior, Freud argued, similarly reflects hidden unconscious motives. Thus, the concept of unconscious motivation played an important role in Freud's theory of motivation.

Hull's Drive Theory

Like Freud, Clark Hull developed an all-encompassing theory of behavior that has been very influential in American psychology. Hull's work, based mostly on research with rats, was a systematic mathematical theory attempting to account for all learning and motivation. A central concept in Hull's theory was *drive*.

In his famous book, *Principles of Behavior,* published in 1943, Hull argued that any kind of deprivation—for example, deprivation of food, water, or sex—increased the general drive level. The concept of a **generalized drive** refers to the idea that there is only one kind of drive and that it is increased similarly by any kind of deprivation. This drive serves to energize or activate habits and response tendencies. Consider, for example, a rat that has been trained to run a maze in order to obtain a reward of food. If a trained rat is deprived of food for several hours, it will run the maze quickly. If the rat has just eaten a full meal, it may not run at all. The difference is due to different levels of drive produced by different degrees of food deprivation.

Hull's view was that drive activated, or aroused, behavior but did not direct it or steer it toward any particular goal. But you respond to hunger by eating and to thirst by drinking. Apparently there is something about being hungry that not only activates your behavior but also directs it toward food. Hull accounted for this obvious fact with the concept of a **drive stimulus.** Hull argued that each condition that increased drive produced certain bodily changes (for example, stomach contractions when you are hungry) that are distinctive stimuli associated with the drive condition. Specific behavior—eating, for exam-

ple—becomes conditioned to these stimuli. Thus, two things happen when you are deprived of food: (1) an increase in generalized drive, which activates behavior, and (2) the production of drive stimuli, which serve as cues for specific conditioned responses (such as eating), with the effect of reducing the drive level.

According to Hull's theory, the source of the drive makes little difference. All sources add drive to a general pool that energizes behavior. If this idea were correct, rats trained to make certain responses when hungry would be even more likely to make these responses if they were both hungry and thirsty. Research on this issue has shown rather clearly that Hull's notion of generalized drive is, in fact, incorrect. For the most part, drives from different sources do not summate; they have different effects on behavior.

Maslow's Humanistic Theory

Abraham Maslow's **humanistic theory of motivation** assumes that people strive for self-fulfillment. According to Maslow, everyone is born with a desire to achieve their maximum potential and competence. Sometimes the circumstances of life block this growth toward fulfillment, as with individuals trapped in poverty. For example, children who are hungry may not be able to benefit fully from school and may be blocked from achieving their potential.

Maslow believed that there are five levels of needs that motivate human action, and that the lower levels must be satisfied before needs at higher levels can motivate behavior. In other words, there is a hierarchy of human needs, and the ones at the bottom must be satisfied first. The most basic needs, those at the bottom of the hierarchy, are physiological needs (for warmth, food, water, and sex). Only when these are reasonably satisfied do people seek to satisfy needs at the next higher level, the safety needs (for security, stability, and order). When safety needs are met, people can seek to satisfy their need for belongingness (for affection, love, and acceptance). When belongingness needs are met, people can seek to meet their need for esteem (for prestige, self-respect, and success). When all lower levels of need are met, people can seek to satisfy the highest level—self-actualization (for self-fulfillment and personal growth). Maslow's hierarchy of human needs (in ascending order, from lowest level on the bottom to highest on the top) is shown in Figure 17-1.

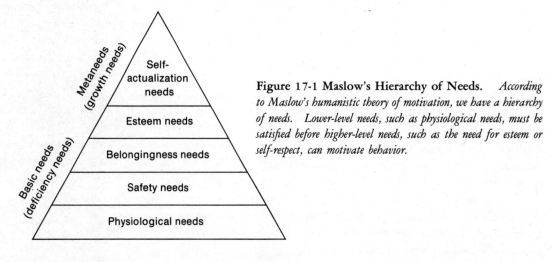

Figure 17-1 Maslow's Hierarchy of Needs. *According to Maslow's humanistic theory of motivation, we have a hierarchy of needs. Lower-level needs, such as physiological needs, must be satisfied before higher-level needs, such as the need for esteem or self-respect, can motivate behavior.*

Interim Summary   Three important theories of motivation are Freud's psychoanalytic theory, Hull's drive theory, and Maslow's humanistic theory. Freud's theory assumed that behavior is both initiated and organized in order to reduce states of tension from certain inborn needs. Two of these needs are the life instincts and the death instincts. The id is the depository of all inborn needs, but since the id is unconscious, our behavior is influenced by motives of which we are unaware. Hull's theory assumed that any kind of deprivation (1) increased a general drive level, which energizes behavior, and (2) produced "drive stimuli," which direct behaviors toward specific actions. Maslow's theory assumes that people have an inborn need for self-fulfillment and that lower-level needs must be satisfied before higher needs could be satisfied.

The Concept of Emotion

What were the most significant, memorable events in your life during the past two years? A birth, a death, getting a job, losing a job, falling in love, graduating—whatever the important events in your life, one feature is common among them: you reacted emotionally to them.

Our emotional experiences enrich our lives.

The feelings of excitement, joy, sorrow, or anger add depth and meaning to our experiences. Without emotion, life would be extremely dull. But sometimes our emotions get out of hand. Feelings of intense anger, anxiety, or depression can be painfully unpleasant and difficult to control.

What is emotion? On the one hand, you know it very well, you know it intimately from the inside, as part of your experience. On the other hand, you can only guess about the emotional experience of other people. You look for clues to their emotional experience in their posture, in the words, in the tone of their voice, and particularly in their facial expressions. Psychologists define **emotion** as a subjective feeling accompanied by changes in behavior and in the physiology of the body.

The Expression of Emotion

Whenever you talk to someone else, you are constantly expressing how you feel and you are constantly observing and monitoring how the other person is feeling. The person you are talking to is doing the same. Each of you is trying to "read" the feelings of the other.

What are the observable signs of emotional reactions? As you try to read the feelings of someone else, you search for certain clues to help you categorize the apparent emotion. Here are some of those clues:

How sensitive are you to emotions expressed in the faces of friends? Sometimes, when seen out of context, facial expressions are hard to "read." But people are surprisingly accurate in judging the emotions expressed on faces—even when the faces are those of members of a different culture. (Paul Conklin)

1. Smiling
2. Sneering
3. Biting lip
4. Trembling chin
5. Clenching jaw
6. Blushing
7. Blanching
8. Intensity of voice
9. Speed of talking
10. Sighing
11. Laughing
12. Moaning
13. Silence
14. Tears
15. Hands trembling
16. Wringing hands
17. Clenching fist
18. Biting nails
19. Sweaty palms or brow
20. Tensing of shoulders or neck
21. Tapping foot
22. Staring
23. Looking away
24. Frowning
25. Raising eyebrows
26. Wrinkling nose
27. Fidgeting
28. Shaking head

What additional clues to emotional reactions can you think of? What emotions are signified by each of the above behaviors?

Studies show that people are remarkably accurate in judging emotion from photographs of faces, even when the faces are those of individuals from a totally different culture.[42] In one study, people from New Guinea who had had little contact with Westerners were asked to judge the emotions expressed in photographs of Westerners.[43]   They were able to infer the emotion correctly in most cases.   Such studies support the view that the forms of emotional expression are at least partly innate and therefore similar across different cultures.

The Physiology of Emotion

There clearly are important bodily changes that occur in emotion.   Some of these are observable—crying, laughing, and shouting are obvious examples of bodily changes occurring in emotional reactions.   But other changes, changes inside the body, are not observable without special instruments.

The **autonomic nervous system,** that part of the nervous system connecting the brain and spinal cord to the smooth muscles and glands, plays an especially important role in emotion.   The autonomic nervous system has two major divisions: the **sympathetic nervous system,** which becomes active when you are threatened, and the **parasympathetic nervous system,** which becomes active when you are at rest or preparing for rest.

The sympathetic nervous system responds during fear, anger, or anxiety by increasing blood pressure and heart rate, increasing blood flow to the brain and to the major muscles, releasing sugar stored in the liver to the blood for quick energy, and releasing adrenalin into the blood.   The blood flow to the skin and to the stomach and other internal organs is reduced.   The flow of digestive juices and saliva is reduced.   The bodily changes during the experience of fear result from sympathetic activity: the blanching (from reduced blood flow to the skin), the cold hands or feet (also from reduced blood flow to the skin), the dry mouth (from reduced saliva flow), the "knot in the stomach" (from reduced blood flow to the stomach), the increased alertness (from increased blood flow to the brain, from added sugar in the blood, and from adrenalin), and the "pounding heart" (from increased blood pressure).

The parasympathetic nervous system serves essentially the opposite functions as the sympathetic nervous system.   The parasympathetic system is active when the body is at rest and is involved in restoring the stores of energy so that they can be used again when a threat occurs.   The parasympathetic system reduces blood pressure and heart rate and increases blood flow to the stomach and skin.

The particular brain structures involved in the experience of emotion have not been identified with certainty.   However, a group of structures called the **limbic system** is known to play an important role in emotion.   The limbic system is a group of structures deep in the brain that forms a kind of emotional circuit.   These structures include the hypothalamus (the master control organ for the autonomic nervous system), the amygdala (the brain structure with the tumor in the case of mass murderer Charles Whitman, discussed at the beginning of this chapter), the hippocampus, the septum, and a number of other small structures.   Some limbic structures in the brain appear to produce intense pleasure when stimulated with a small electric charge.   Violent and aggressive behavior can be reduced by surgically removing the amygdala.   Electrical stimulation of certain parts of the hypothalamus produces aggressive reactions.   The limbic structures appear to be especially important in the control and expression of emotion.

Interim Summary   Emotion is the subjective feeling that accompanies changes in behavior and physiology. People are remarkably accurate in judging emotional expressions, even of those from different cultures.   This suggests that emotional expression is at least partially innate. Bodily structures important in emotion include the brain's limbic system and the autonomic nervous system, with its sympathetic and parasympathetic divisions.

Theories of Emotion

How can our emotional reactions be explained? Theories of emotion are attempts to account systematically for the feelings, the bodily changes, and the behavior that are involved in emotions.

The philosopher Descartes in the seventeenth century argued that emotional reactions result from seeing or hearing something in the world and the resulting activity of "animal spirits" in the brain and nerves. Descartes believed that there were only six basic emotions: admiration, love, hate, desire, joy, and sadness. Other feelings were various combinations of these primitive feelings.

Charles Darwin's book *Expression of Emotions in Man and Animals* argued that emotions were innate and that they have evolved with a purpose—the purpose of promoting the survival of the species. Darwin focused his attention on the similarities among species in emotional expression in order to show the biological relationships between animals and human beings. Darwin was also interested in the relationship between the expression of emotions and the experience of emotions, a theme that later became the key to several important theories of emotion. In 1872 Darwin wrote, "The free expression by outward signs of an emotion intensifies it. . . . He who gives way to violent gestures will increase his rage; he who does not control the signs of fear will experience fear in a greater degree."

This statement set the stage for three classic theories of emotion: the James-Lange theory, the Cannon-Bard theory, and the Cognitive theory. See Figure 17-2.

The James-Lange Theory

William James, the first American psychologist, was a contemporary of Wilhelm Wundt, the German psychologist who established the first psychological laboratory. The older brother of Henry James, the famous

William James

novelist, William James tried his hand at a number of professions—painting, chemistry, medicine, and biology—then finally settled on psychology and philosophy. He achieved worldwide fame in each.

In 1884, twelve years after the publication of Darwin's book on emotion, James published an article in which he claimed that emotions such as fear are really based on the perception of bodily changes, such as trembling and sweating. According to this theory, later called the **James-Lange theory of emotion,** fear does not cause trembling—trembling causes the experience of fear. James wrote that the sequence of seeing a bear, feeling afraid, and then running away is wrong. Instead, what happens is that we see the bear, begin to run, and then feel afraid. The experience of running away results in fear, according to James.

James argued that no emotion was possible if the bodily experience of it was removed. Since the emotional experience resulted from the perception of bodily changes in the viscera (internal organs) and muscles, an interruption in the nerve pathways which carry information from the body to the brain would, according to James, interfere with the experience of emotion.

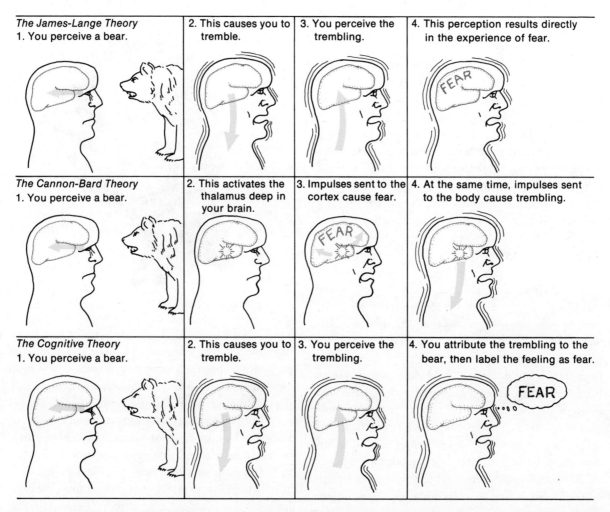

The James-Lange Theory
1. You perceive a bear.

2. This causes you to tremble.

3. You perceive the trembling.

4. This perception results directly in the experience of fear.

The Cannon-Bard Theory
1. You perceive a bear.

2. This activates the thalamus deep in your brain.

3. Impulses sent to the cortex cause fear.

4. At the same time, impulses sent to the body cause trembling.

The Cognitive Theory
1. You perceive a bear.

2. This causes you to tremble.

3. You perceive the trembling.

4. You attribute the trembling to the bear, then label the feeling as fear.

Figure 17-2 Three Theories of Emotion. *According to the James-Lange theory, different emotions result from the perception of different bodily reactions such as trembling. According to the Cannon-Bard theory, emotions do not depend upon perceiving bodily reactions. According to the cognitive theory, emotions follow the labeling of bodily reactions.*

The Cannon-Bard Theory

The James-Lange theory became very influential in psychology. Although it was extremely controversial, since its claims opposed common sense, it was also a testable theory. As evidence began to accumulate, it came under increasing attack.

In 1927 Walter Cannon proposed five arguments against the James-Lange theory: (1) The James-Lange theory requires that the perception of visceral changes results in emotion, but research shows that artificially inducing visceral changes does not lead to emotional feelings. (2) The James-Lange theory requires that different emotions result from perceptions of different patterns of visceral changes, but research fails to show any clear differences in pattern of visceral response in emotion. (3) The James-Lange theory requires that differences in emotional feelings result from the perception of subtle differences in visceral response; but research shows that the viscera are relatively insensitive structures, and we are aware only of gross changes in them. (4) The James-Lange theory requires visceral feedback for the experience of emotion, but if the nerve pathways from the viscera to the brain are cut, emotional reactions still occur. (5) The James-Lange theory requires the perception of visceral changes before an emotional reaction; but visceral changes occur very slowly, taking several seconds, while emotional reactions occur very quickly.

Cannon's objections to the James-Lange theory did not destroy the theory but have succeeded in stirring a controversy which even now has not been completely resolved.

Cannon not only attempted to refute the James-Lange theory, but he proposed an alternative, a theory that has since become known as the **Cannon-Bard theory of emotion.** Cannon argued that bodily changes were independent from emotional experience and followed these experiences rather than preceded them. This theory assumed that the perception of a dangerous bear would have two independent results: (1) the experience of fear, and (2) the bodily changes that accompany fear. The experience of fear would occur whether or not the bodily changes were perceived. Thus, emotions were regarded as resulting directly from the perception of environmental objects and events (such as bears). Cannon believed that a brain structure called the thalamus sent impulses to the cortex to be experienced as emotion, and later sent impulses to the viscera and muscles to produce the bodily changes seen in emotion. More recent research has shown that Cannon was wrong about the role of the thalamus in emotion; instead, the key brain structures for emotion are those in the limbic system.

The Cognitive Theory

Neither James nor Cannon was much concerned with the role of cognition—thinking, evaluating, appraising, and other mental activities—in emotion. For James, emotion resulted directly from the perception of bodily changes; for Cannon, emotion resulted from the perception of environmental events.

The Interpretation of Arousal • In the 1960s Stanley Schachter developed a **cognitive theory of emotion** that assumed that the perception of both bodily changes and environmental events were essential to emotion.[44] According to the cognitive theory, emotional experience results from an interpretation of perceived bodily arousal. We encounter a bear and become physiologically aroused. We perceive this arousal and refer to environmental events for an interpretation of it—in effect, we attribute it to some environmental circumstance ("I am aroused because I just encountered a bear"). As the arousal is thus labeled *fear,* we experience a fear reaction.

The cognitive theory assumes that there is little difference between the states of arousal that result from different emotion-producing situations. The arousal resulting from fear, rage, and sexual excitement, Schachter argues, is essentially the same. What makes the emotional experience different in these cases is our interpretation of the arousal. If we perceive this arousal while sitting next to an attractive person of the opposite sex, we will attribute the arousal to sexual excitement and will then experience it that way. If we perceive the bodily arousal while climbing a cliff, we will attribute it to fear and will experience it that way.

The Schachter-Singer Experiment • According to Schachter, the actual source of the arousal is irrelevant to the emotional experience; what defines the nature of the emotional experience is the interpretation made of the arousal, not its source. This was shown in a classic experiment by Schachter and Singer.[45] In this study, male college students were given injections of adrenalin to produce states of heightened arousal. Adrenalin causes the sympathetic nervous system to become active, with the resulting increase in blood pressure, heart rate, and other physiological changes common in emotion. All of the students were told that the injection was a vitamin shot ("Suproxin"). One group of subjects was then told that the shot would have certain side effects such as increased heart rate and the other effects produced by the adrenalin; a second group was told nothing about possible side effects.

At this point in the study, the experimenters had artificially increased bodily arousal in all the student subjects and had given half of them reason to believe that their arousal was due to the injection. After receiving the adrenalin injection, each student was placed in one of two situations designed to influence the interpretation of the arousal. In one situation, the student was placed in the same room with someone acting silly, clowning around, throwing paper airplanes and shooting paper-wad basketballs into a wastebasket. In a second situation, the student was placed in a room with someone acting angry and irritable. The first situation was designed to provoke happiness, and the second was designed to provoke anger.

What was the effect of the two situations on the students who had been told that the shot would cause side effects? These students apparently attributed their states of arousal to the drug, not to the situations in which they were placed, and they rated their resulting emotional feelings as relatively neutral. By contrast, the students who were ignorant of the drug's effects reacted differently. They apparently attributed their states of arousal to the situations in which they were placed; they labeled their arousal as "happiness" or "anger" and rated their emotional experience accordingly. With the same state of bodily arousal (produced by the shot of adrenalin), students placed into the happiness-provoking situation labeled their arousal as due to feelings of happiness, while students

placed into the anger-provoking situation labeled their arousal as due to feelings of anger. The Schachter-Singer study, then, confirmed the cognitive theory's assumption that emotional experience results from a cognitive interpretation of bodily arousal.

Three Explanations of Fear

1. The James-Lange Theory of Emotion

    1. We perceive a bear.
    2. This perception results directly in specific patterns of visceral and muscular changes associated with fear ("knot" in stomach, rapid heartbeat, running away, and so on).
    3. We perceive these changes in our bodies.
    4. This perception of specific bodily change results directly in the subjective experience of fear.

2. The Cannon-Bard Theory of Emotion

    1. We perceive a bear.
    2. This perception activates the thalamus, which releases impulses to the cortex where they are experienced as fear.
    3. The thalamus also sends impulses to the viscera and muscles, where they produce certain bodily changes.

3. The Cognitive Theory of Emotion

    1. We perceive a bear.
    2. This perception results directly in visceral and muscular changes associated with a state of general emotional arousal.
    3. Other events contribute to this same pool of undifferentiated arousal—for example, a thunderstorm or being lost in the woods.
    4. We perceive our state of general arousal.
    5. We attribute this arousal to a likely cause—for example, the bear.
    6. This interpretation of the reason for the arousal results in the specific emotional experience of fear.

Interim Summary   Three theories of emotion are the James-Lange theory, the Cannon-Bard theory, and the Cognitive theory. The James-Lange theory assumes that emotions result from the perception of bodily changes in the internal organs and muscles. From this point of view, the emotion of fear results from the perception of such effects as muscular trembling, increased heart rate, a "knot" in the stomach, and running away. The Cannon-

Bard theory assumes that emotional experience results directly from the perception of environmental events and does not require an awareness of bodily changes. The cognitive theory assumes that emotional experience requires the perception of both bodily change and environmental events. In effect, we first perceive that we are aroused, then attribute this arousal to some likely environmental event.

Summary

1. Motivation refers to those forces which determine both the arousal and direction of purposeful behavior; for example, hunger and thirst are motives.

2. Drives are motives that arouse behavior and push people into action, while incentives are goals that you strive to attain.

3. Motivations are either extrinsic or intrinsic. Extrinsic motivation refers to those factors outside the person, such as rewards, that motivate behavior. Intrinsic motivation refers to those factors inherent in the task or activity itself that makes it rewarding. Under certain circumstances, an individual's intrinsic motivation for a task may be reduced by providing some form of extrinsic reward.

4. Both the extreme absence of stimulation (sensory deprivation) and the extreme excess of stimulation (sensory overload) can interfere with thought processes and create high degrees of anxiety and stress. People are motivated to avoid these extremes and seek an optimal level of arousal.

5. According to the Yerkes-Dodson law, performance is best at an intermediate level of arousal, and in addition, the optimal level of arousal is higher for easy tasks than for difficult tasks.

6. Freud's psychoanalytic theory of motivation assumed that behavior is both initiated and organized in order to reduce states of tension from inborn needs such as the life instincts and death instincts. All such inborn needs are contained within the id, but since the id is unconscious, our behavior is influenced by motives of which we are unaware.

7. Hull's theory of motivation assumed that any kind of deprivation (1) increases a general drive level, which activates behavior, and (2) produces "drive stimuli," which direct behavior toward specific actions that have the effect of reducing the drive level.

8. Maslow's theory of motivation assumes that people have an inborn need for self-fulfillment and that lower-level needs must be satisfied before higher needs can be satisfied.

9. Emotion is the subjective feeling that accompanies changes in behavior and physiology.

10. Bodily structures important in emotion include the brain's limbic system and the autonomic nervous system, with its sympathetic and parasympathetic divisions.

11. The James-Lange theory of emotion assumes that emotional experiences result directly from the perception of bodily changes in the internal organs and muscles. The perception of the "knot in the stomach" results directly in the subjective

experience of fear.

12. The Cannon-Bard theory of emotion assumes that emotional experiences result directly from the perceptions of environmental events and do not require any awareness of bodily changes. The sight of the bear results directly in the subjective experience of fear.

13. The cognitive theory of emotion assumes that emotional experiences require the perception of both bodily changes and environmental events. In effect, we first perceive that we are aroused, then attribute this arousal to some likely environmental event. Such assumptions have been supported by the Schachter-Singer experiments.

Key Concepts

motivation   The forces that determine the arousal and direction of purposeful behavior.

motive   Something that arouses behavior and directs it toward a specific goal; for example, hunger results in behavior directed toward obtaining food.

drive   A need (or motive) that arouses behavior and "pushes" a person into action; for example, the hunger drive pushes you to obtain food.

incentive   A goal or condition that you strive to obtain; something that "pulls" a person into action.

unconscious motivation   Needs and impulses that have been repressed so that a person is unaware of them.

extrinsic motivation   Forces outside the person that motivate behavior, for example, money, applause, or punishment.

intrinsic motivation   Factors that make an activity enjoyable or rewarding in and of itself—for example, participation in some tasks such as games, puzzles, or artwork is enjoyable and interesting.

sensory deprivation   An extreme reduction in stimulation.

illusions   Distorted or incorrect perceptions.

hallucinations   A disturbance in perception in which something is seen, heard, or felt that does not exist—for example, hearing voices when no one is near.

sensory overload   An extreme excess of stimulation.

noise pollution   An excess of unwanted sound.

optimal level of arousal   The best or ideal level of arousal or stimulation for human beings, neither too high nor too low.

Yerkes-Dodson law   The principle that performance is best at an intermediate level of arousal and that the optimal level of arousal is higher for easy tasks than for difficult tasks.

hedonism   The desire to achieve the greatest possible pleasure.

psychoanalytic theory of motivation   Freud's theory that behavior is motivated by the tension created from unsatisfied inborn needs.

life instincts   According to Freud, those inborn needs that serve the purpose of the survival of the individual and the human species, for example, hunger, thirst, and sex.

death instincts   According to Freud, those inborn needs that serve destructive purposes; for example, aggression.

psychic energy   According to Freud, the total amount of energy available to the human system.

libido   A form of psychic energy constituted by the life instincts; sexual energy.

id   According to Freud, that part of the personality that is the unconscious storehouse of basic biological drives.

pleasure principle   The principle that governs the operation of the id, namely, the seeking of pleasure and the avoidance of pain.

generalized drive   According to Hull, the idea that there is only one kind of drive and that it is increased similarly by any kind of deprivation.

drive stimulus   According to Hull, certain bodily changes (associated with different drive conditions), which serve as cues for directing behavior toward the desired goal.

humanistic theory of motivation   Maslow's theory that all people are born with a desire to achieve their maximum potential.

emotion   A subjective feeling accompanied by changes in behavior and in the physiology of the body.

autonomic nervous system   The network of nerves connecting the brain to the glands and organs of the body; responsible for regulating automatic functions such as blood pressure.

sympathetic nervous system   The part of the autonomic nervous system that prepares the body for action; becomes active when the body is "threatened."

parasympathetic nervous system   The part of the autonomic nervous system that is active when the body is at rest.

limbic system   A group of structures deep in the brain that is important in the control and expression of emotion.

James-Lange theory of emotion   According to this theory, the experience of emotion results from the perception of bodily changes.

Cannon-Bard theory of emotion   According to this theory, bodily changes are independent from emotional experience and follow these experiences rather than cause them.

Cognitive theory of emotion   According to this theory, emotional experience results from an interpretation of perceived bodily arousal.

Answers for the Sensation-Seeking Scale (give yourself one point for each answer corresponding to the following): 1. (b)   2. (a)   3. (a)   4. (b)   5. (b)   6. (a)   7. (a)   8. (b)   9. (a)   10. (b). The higher your total score, the greater your need for high levels of arousal.

Chapter 18

Intelligence, Creativity, and Potential

Key Questions

1. What is intelligence, and how is it measured?
2. What is creativity, and how can it be fostered?
3. What are the conditions that increase or reduce your sense of freedom?
4. What is psychological health?
5. What is your stage of growth?

What is your potential for growth? Can you improve your personality and the quality of your relationships? You *can* change; you can become more healthy than you are. Human personality and human behavior are not fixed. They are flexible, modifiable; they hold the potential for growth. This potential for growth is one of the most important differences between human beings and the lower animals. The behavior of an ant is rigidly fixed by a genetic program, but you can change yourself and grow. The intention or desire for growth is an important ingredient for the process of growth itself; your decision to change is itself a step toward growth.

The limits of human potential are unexplored. A number of psychologists have claimed that we use only 10 percent of our capacity and that the challenge of our time is to release the vast, unused potential that we have.[1] At present, this claim cannot be confirmed because we just don't know the limit of our powers. If you could, how would you choose to grow? Which of your present capacities would you choose to expand? Perhaps you would strive to increase your intelligence and creativity, and to realize, as fully as possible, your potential.

Intelligence

Your **intelligence** is your ability to learn and to solve problems. Your abilities to reason, to remember, to read, to think abstractly, to work with numbers, and to take care of yourself all reflect your level of intelligence. There are disagreements about what the concept of intelligence refers to and how—and even whether—it should be measured. These disagreements result from two important facts about intelligence: (1) The concept of intelligence has been invented and in different cultures in the world means different things, and (2) This society highly values intelligence and allocates resources to its citizens partly on the basis of measures of intelligence. Because of the vagueness and importance of the concept, many controversies about intelligence have arisen.

The Measurement of Intelligence

Tests of intelligence have taken many forms, but they all have in common the production of a quantitative measure of intelligence called the IQ. The **IQ,** or **intelligence quotient,** is a score that is computed from the answers on an intelligence test.

The Stanford-Binet Intelligence Scale • One of the earliest and most widely used tests of intelligence is the **Stanford-Binet Intelligence Scale.** This test was devised more than sixty years ago and has been revised several times since. It is based on two assumptions about intelligence: (1) Intelligence consists of many different kinds of abilities and must therefore be measured with many different kinds of questions, and (2) Intelligence grows with age. The items on the

Stanford-Binet test require reading, writing, arithmetic, and judgment. There are different questions for each age level. The difficulty level of the questions written for a particular age child is such that on the average, about half the problems could be correctly answered by children of that age. If a ten-year-old child (a child with a chronological age of ten) correctly answered half the questions written for ten-year-olds, the child was said to have a mental age of ten. A child's **mental age** is equal to the chronological age of an average child with similar intelligence. If a ten-year-old has the intelligence of a fifteen-year-old, the child has a mental age of fifteen.

For the Stanford-Binet intelligence scale, a child's IQ reflects the relationship of chronological age (age in years) to mental age (age of a child of equal intelligence). For children, the IQ can be obtained from the following formula:

$$IQ = \frac{\text{Mental Age}}{\text{Chronological Age}} \times 100$$

If a child of ten has a mental age of twelve, he or she will have an IQ of 120:

$$120 = \frac{12}{10} \times 100$$

An IQ of 100 means average intelligence (chronological age equals your mental age). An IQ of 70 is much lower than average, and an IQ of 130 is much higher than average.

Because mental capacity ceases to increase much beyond the middle teens, the concept of "mental age" applied to adults is not meaningful. For the sake of convenience, tables have been developed so that the IQ score can be found directly, without computing the ratio of mental age to chronological age.

The Wechsler Intelligence Scales • Two other commonly used intelligence tests are the **Wechsler Adult Intelligence Scale (WAIS)** and the **Wechsler Intelligence Scale for Children (WISC)**. The Wechsler IQ tests assume that intelligence consists of a limited number of specific abilities, both verbal and mathematical. The test consists of a number of subtests, each measuring one of the component abilities. For example, the **digit-span test** is a test of ability to repeat, both forward and backwards, a series of numbers that are read out loud. The **block-design test** is a test of ability to construct particular given designs from a number of colored blocks.

The Wechsler intelligence tests do not yield an IQ measure based on an estimate of mental age. Instead, the scores on each of the subtests are statistically combined to produce what is called a **deviation IQ.** The deviation IQ is based on the distribution of intelligence test scores and reflects how far a particular score deviates from the average score made by other people of similar age. Like the IQ score produced by the Stanford-Binet test, the Wechsler IQ score has an average of 100. An IQ of 70 is considerably below average, and an IQ of 130 is quite high.

If your IQ is 100, you would expect that about 500 people out of 1,000 would have IQs higher than yours. If your IQ is 110, you would expect that about 270 people out of 1,000 would have IQs higher than yours. If your IQ is 120, you would expect about 110 people out of 1,000 would have IQs higher than yours. If your IQ is 140, you would expect about 7 people out of 1,000 would have IQs higher than yours.

Genius and Retardation

In past centuries, the mentally dull were regarded as being insane, as freaks, or as workers of Satan. They were either killed in infancy or subjected to ridicule and neglect. In this century we have taken a more enlightened view.

The term **mentally retarded** is applied to individuals with three characteristics: (1) their IQs are below 70 (the lowest 2 or 3 percent of the population); (2) compared to others of their age, they show significant failures in adaptive behavior (in acting responsibly and functioning independently); and

(3) their mental dullness must have initially appeared in childhood (individuals who become mentally dull later in life, as adults, are said to suffer from **dementia,** a progressive deterioration of mental functioning that sometimes occurs in older persons).   A boy of fifteen, with an IQ of 40, who was unable to take care of his own personal cleanliness, his physical appearance, and his clothing would be called mentally retarded.

Mental retardation is not something that one either has or does not have but is part of the continuum of intellectual and social competency that is seen in human beings.   There are different levels of mental retardation, ranging from mild to profound.   Those with **mild retardation** (IQs from about 50 to 70) are typically able to take care of themselves and can develop skills in reading and arithmetic to a third- to sixth-grade level.   Another term for the mildly mentally retarded is the **educable mentally retarded (EMR).**   Most mildly retarded children attend special education classes in public school.   Mildly retarded adults are typically able to support themselves partially or wholly in simple, undemanding jobs.

The next level, for those who are somewhat more retarded, is called moderate retardation.   Those with **moderate retardation** (IQs from about 35 to 50) typically cannot be entirely self-sufficient, although they are able to perform simple manual jobs. With training, many are able to eat, bathe, and dress by themselves and may need only minimal supervision.   They can learn to communicate verbally, but usually cannot learn to read.   Individuals with **severe retardation** (IQs from about 20 to 35) require special training to learn how to talk and to take care of their simple personal needs.   Academic learning is usually not possible for them, and continual supervision is needed.   Severely retarded adults have a mental age of four to six.   Another term for the moderately to severely retarded (IQs from about 20 to 50) is the **trainable mentally retarded (TMR).**

Those who are most retarded, with **profound mental retardation,** have IQs below 20.   The profoundly retarded often have severe medical problems. They require total care and are unable to learn how to

Mental retardation in some cases has a genetic basis.   Children with Down's syndrome have 47 chromosomes (instead of the normal 46) and typically are mentally retarded.   (Judy Sedwick)

take care of even their simple needs.   Profoundly retarded adults have a mental age of three years or less. Many, but not all, are able to walk and some can learn to speak a few words.   The profoundly retarded require continual supervision in a protective environment, such as a special home or institution.

Individuals with IQs above 130 are called **mentally gifted.**   Only about 2 percent of the population has IQs as high as 130.   The term **genius** is sometimes applied to individuals with extremely high IQs (above 140, or the highest 1 percent), but is more accurately used to refer to those with exceptional originality and creativity.   One of the myths about geniuses is that they are able to accomplish their work with hardly any effort.   This is entirely false, as the study of the lives of different geniuses shows.

It has been estimated that John Stuart Mill (1806–1873) had an IQ of about 190.[2]   An IQ that high is so rare that in the entire population of the

United States, you might expect to find only one or two persons with an IQ of 190. John Stuart Mill began hard intellectual work before the age of three, by which time he had learned to read some Greek. By the age of eight Mill had read extensively in philosophy and history, written both in English and Greek, and had begun the study of Latin, algebra, and geometry. Mill was educated exclusively by his father, a strict disciplinarian who taught Mill to be skeptical and to think for himself. A study of the early life of John Stuart Mill suggests that an important part of being a genius is extremely hard work.

Michelangelo, the Italian sculptor and painter; Newton, the English physicist and mathematician; and Gauss, the German mathematician and astronomer, all clearly were geniuses. All describe the secret of their genius as concentrated labor. Michelangelo wrote, "I strain more than any man who ever lived." Newton, when asked how he was able to solve so many problems, replied, "By always thinking about them." Gauss wrote that he spent four years brooding about a single problem before he was able to solve it.[3]

Heredity and Environment

Differences in intelligence are due to a variety of sources. It can be shown that part of the difference among individuals in intelligence is due to inherited characteristics. Studies show, for example, that the more similar two persons are genetically, the more similar they tend to be in intelligence.[4] Brothers are more similar in intelligence than cousins, and cousins are more similar in intelligence than persons not genetically related. Identical twins are not only extremely similar in their physical features but are also extremely similar in intelligence level.

Environment also contributes to differences in intelligence. An extreme case is the individual who has been deprived of the opportunity to learn to read and write the language; such a person would make a low score on a written IQ test. The more opportu-

nity children have for learning in the home and the more encouragement they are given for intellectual accomplishment, the higher their IQs tend to be.[5]

Teachers can influence the IQs of students through their expectations. In one study elementary school teachers were led to believe that certain students would be "bloomers"; that is, that they would experience rapid gains in IQ during the years.[6] In fact, the children designated as "bloomers" were chosen at random, but the teachers did not know this. Over the period of a school year, the students showed a significant increase in IQ, apparently caused by the expectations of their teachers.

IQ Is Not Intelligence

IQ does not *equal* intelligence. IQ is only one measure of intelligence. Although it may be the best measure we have, in some ways it is a relatively poor one. First, different IQ tests yield different IQ scores for the same individual. According to one IQ test score, a person may be categorized as below normal in intelligence, whereas a second test may categorize the person as above normal. If yardsticks were like that, you wouldn't trust them very much. Furthermore, the same IQ test given at different times yields different scores. In one study of two hundred children who were tested twice, 85 percent of the group changed up or down 10 or more points from the first IQ test to the second, and 10 percent changed 30 or more points in IQ.[7]

IQ tests may not measure the ability we think of as "intelligence." When we call a woman *intelligent* what do we mean? We do not mean simply that her English vocabulary is large, that she is familiar with mathematical thinking, and that she can analyze and solve problems that might be encountered in the lives of white middle-class American people—yet these skills are primarily those which IQ tests measure. On the basis of an IQ test, some intelligent students from Spanish-speaking homes have been classified as "retarded," because of their unfamiliarity with the language used in the IQ test. The available IQ tests are probably inappropriate measures of the intelligence of black Americans, since the average black person grows up in an environment with substantial differences in language and culture as compared to the average white person. Since the items on IQ tests were largely developed and standardized on white middle-class children, the tests may be biased against Chicano and black children.[8]

The IQ test is a useful predictor of grades in school. Many studies have shown that students with high IQs make better grades,[9] because IQ tests and classroom tests require similar kinds of skills.[10] But neither IQ[11] nor school grades[12] are useful predictors of nonacademic achievement. Success in life is not related to success in school or to success on IQ tests, except insofar as certain jobs require academic degrees. David McClelland, a Harvard University researcher, has recently proposed that the term "intelligence" be dropped from IQ tests and that they be named to reflect what they are: scholastic achievement tests.[10]

Interim Summary   Your intelligence is your ability to learn and to solve problems. Tests of intelligence yield a score—the IQ, or intelligence quotient. A score of 100 reflects average intelligence, while a score above 130 indicates that the person is mentally gifted. Mentally retarded individuals have three characteristics: (1) an IQ below 70, (2) below average adaptive behavior, and (3) a dullness of childhood origin. Both heredity and environment contribute to intelligence.

Creativity

One of the most highly valued human characteristics is creativity. All of us are creative. We are creative to the degree that we behave or respond creatively. What is a creative response? There is general agreement that a creative response has two important features: (1) uniqueness or unconventionality, and (2) appropriateness or fit. The garbled language of the schizophrenic and the language of the poet are similar in that both are unconventional; they are different in that the language of the poet seems appropriate, while the language of the schizophrenic is simply confused. Thus, **creativity** is the ability to respond uniquely and appropriately.

How Creative Are You?

You are creative. You have original ideas; you sometimes come up with unusual solutions to problems.

Perhaps you have some talent in creative writing, painting, crafts, or music. But how much creativity do you have? The measurement of creativity is very difficult, and many different tests have been developed. One test, the "Uses Test," requires people to think of unusual uses for common objects like bricks or paper clips. "Building a fireplace" would be a common use for a brick; "as a paperweight" would be an uncommon, and therefore creative, use for a brick. Another test that has been used to identify creative individuals requires people to choose which designs they like best. Figure 18-1 is a brief test for creativity.

Psychologists have found that artists and other creative persons prefer designs that are highly complex, asymmetrical, freehand rather than ruled, and restless and moving in their general effect.[13] Preference for complexity seems to go along with artistic interests, unconventionality, and creativity. Do you prefer complex asymmetrical designs or simple ruled ones?

What are the characteristics of the creative per-

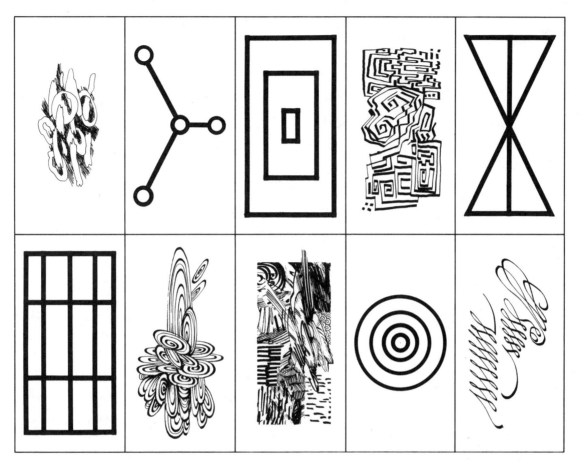

Figure 18-1 Creativity Test. *Which design do you like best? When you look at paintings or other works of art, what kind do you prefer? Studies show that highly creative people tend to prefer complex and assymetrical art.*

son? The creative person is not necessarily extremely intelligent. Although a minimal level of intelligence is necessary for a person to be creative, many highly intelligent persons are not particularly creative. Studies have shown that the relationship between measured creativity and measured intelligence is rather small.[14,15] Apparently the capacity to get the conventionally "correct" answer to a problem, on the one hand, and the capacity to devise a unique but fitting solution, on the other hand, are two different capacities. A person can have one of these talents without the other or the person might have both.

What kind of people are creative people? One psychologist compared a group of highly creative architects with a group of average architects in order to discover how the creative individuals were different.[16] The relatively uncreative architects tended to see themselves as responsible, sincere, reliable, sociable, and cooperative. By contrast, the creative architects tended to see themselves as imaginative, independent, individualistic, sensitive, and committed. Personality studies of creative architects,[16] creative writers,[17] and creative research scientists[18] agree that creative individuals tend to be highly independent, self-accepting,

Creative people tend to be independent, self-accepting, and open to experience. Although a minimum level of intelligence is necessary for creativity, many creative people do not achieve high scores on traditional tests of intelligence. (Jean-Claude Lejeune/Stock, Boston)

and spontaneous or impulsive. Creative people are more independent both in their attitudes and in their social behavior; they are more introverted, more open to experience, more self-accepting, more flexible, and more intuitive.[19]

Creativity and Conformity

Creative persons are more healthy, psychologically, than uncreative persons. Contrary to the folk myth of the "mad genius," creativity is inhibited and reduced by neurosis or madness. Current investigators of creativity tend to agree that creativity is an expression of the psychologically healthy person.[20] Creative persons are more open to experience[19] and are less anxious.[21]

Creative people are not afraid of being themselves; they have courage.

The courage of the creative person . . . is the courage to be oneself in the fullest sense, to grow in great measure into the person one is capable of becoming, developing one's abilities and actualizing one's self. Since the creative person is not preoccupied with the impression he makes on others, and is not overly concerned with their opinion of him, he is freer than most to be himself. . . .

Creative persons are not conformists in the realm of greatest importance to them, the area of their creative striving, but on the other hand they are not deliberate nonconformists, either. Instead, they are genuinely independent.[16]

It takes courage to be creative in the face of all the pressures toward conformity that we encounter at every turn. Teachers in the school system tend to reward intelligence and conformity, but not creativity.[13] To be the same—same clothes, same goals, same thoughts—is safe. To be the same means not to be singled out; to go along with the crowd means to be safe. But every person is unique; you are different from every other human being on earth. To be most truly yourself is to make the most of your uniqueness. You cannot actualize yourself and also conform to the crowd. Clark Moustakas compared the creative and the conforming person:

To be creative means to experience life in one's own way, to perceive from one's own person, to draw upon one's own resources, capacities, roots. It means facing life directly and honestly. . . .

When a person's involvement in a situation is based on appearances, expectations, or the standards of others; when he acts in a conventional manner, or according to prescribed roles and functions, when he is concerned with status and approval; his growth as a creative self is impaired. When the individual is conforming, following, imitating, being like others, he moves increasingly in the direction of self-alienation. . . . Gradually the conforming person loses touch with himself, with his own real feelings.[22]

Conditions Fostering Creativity

What does it take to be in touch with yourself, to face life directly and honestly, to be a creative person? Certainly, conditions that promote conformity tend to interfere with creativity. Several important conditions that foster creativity have been identified by Carl Rogers.[23] Rogers described three conditions in the person (inner conditions) and three conditions in the person's environment (outer conditions) that tend to increase creativity.

According to Rogers, the inner conditions fostering creativity are openness to experience, internal standards, and the ability to "toy" with ideas. A person who is open to experience is sensitive to things as they really are, and does not jump to conclusions based on prior expectations. A person who is open to experience is not quick to label people or events, but postpones conclusions until all evidence is in. A person with internal standards strives to satisfy personal goals and expectations rather than someone else's. A person with internal standards decides what is good or bad on the basis of an internal standard of evaluation rather than on the basis of external standards established by others. A person with the ability to "toy" with ideas enjoys exploring new combinations of concepts and can see problems in fresh ways.

The outer conditions fostering creativity are unconditional acceptance, absence of external evaluation, and empathetic understanding. Unconditional acceptance fosters creativity; people who are valued by those around them and accepted without reservations are more likely to be creative. The absence of external evaluation fosters creativity by permitting people to develop their own internal standards. Empathetic understanding fosters creativity; when people are truly understood by those around them, they are encouraged to be fully themselves. These conditions together provide the optimim climate for creativity.

Interim Summary   Your creativity is your ability to respond uniquely and appropriately to problems. Although a minimal level of intelligence is required to be creative, high intelligence is not related to creativity. Creative people have been found to be more independent, more self-accepting, more spontaneous, more introverted, more open to experience, and more intuitive. According to Carl Rogers, creativity can be promoted by fostering certain inner and outer conditions.

Freedom

What does it mean to be free? Erich Fromm distinguished two types of freedom: freedom *from* and freedom *to*. The first type involves the avoidance of problems, while the second type involves the availability of opportunities. Freedom from restrictions, freedom from poverty and disease, freedom from injustice, freedom from pain—this is one type of freedom. Freedom to vote, freedom to say what you want, freedom to dress as you please, freedom to read and learn—this is another kind of freedom.

Freud, the founder of psychoanalysis, was concerned primarily with the first type of freedom; he emphasized the limitations imposed by unconscious controls. For Skinner, the behaviorist, the concept of freedom is an illusion; all that can be hoped for is to be relatively free *from* aversive (unpleasant) consequences. By contrast, Maslow and Rogers emphasized the significance of the freedom *to* act and feel; in their view, psychologically healthy people have more freedom to act consistently with their feelings, to be authentic, and to make free choices.

Unfree People

Freedom is not something that you either have or do not have. Some people are more free than others; and sometimes you feel more free than at other times. There are degrees of freedom.

Certain people are regarded as relatively unfree. For example, when people are drunk or intoxicated with drugs, they and others feel that they are not responsible for what they may do; they are not in control of themselves and are therefore not free. An individual who is hypnotized is not in control and is therefore not free.

The **obsessive-compulsive neurosis** is a type of psychological disorder involving uncontrollable thoughts and actions. Obsessive-compulsive neurosis limits freedom; individuals suffering from this problem feel a loss of voluntary control. For example, a man may feel a compulsion to wash his hands over and over again; he does not want to do it and tries to resist doing it, but is not successful.

Certain types of compulsive actions are called **irresistible impulses,** because they suddenly appear and have the force of commands. For example, **kleptomania** is a compulsion to steal. Individuals with this disorder steal repetitively, often taking small or useless items, and feel unable to resist their impulses. Other types of compulsive impulses are **pyromania,** a compulsion to set fires, and **exhibitionism,** a compulsion to expose the sexual organs. Each of these disorders involves a great loss of voluntary control over behavior; individuals feel that they simply cannot help what they do.

Free People

Whom do you regard as relatively free?

Chances are, you regard most *other* people as freer than you are. Imagine yourself in an argument with your mother. If she does something you don't like, you may get angry with her because you think that she can control herself and stop doing it. By contrast, if *you* do something that *she* doesn't like, you feel that you can't help yourself and therefore she should not be angry. For example, if while you are talking with her she repeatedly interrupts you, you may feel that she is acting by choice; however, if you repeatedly interrupt her, you may feel that you were too excited to control

yourself. To consider another example, if someone else is overweight, you may feel that the person lacks "willpower"; but if *you* are overweight, you may feel that the situation is beyond your control—you cannot control yourself.

Why do you regard other people as having more freedom? One reason is that you see yourself "from the inside" and you see them "from the outside." You are aware of the forces influencing your own behavior, but you are relatively ignorant of the pressures operating on other people. You therefore assume that their choices are freer from pressure and influence. You assume that they have more voluntary control.

Your Freedom

When do you personally feel most free?

Sometimes your behavior is relatively automatic. You may be walking or driving without really being aware of what you are doing. You may brush your teeth in the morning without even remembering later whether you have done it. One author describes his automatic behavior as an "inner robot":

I am writing this on an electric typewriter. When I learned to type, I had to do it painfully and with much nervous wear and tear. But at a certain stage a miracle occurred, and this complicated operation was "learned" by a useful robot whom I conceal in my subconscious mind. Now I only have to think about what I want to say; my robot secretary does the typing. He is really very useful.[24]

When you are behaving automatically, you don't feel free; you don't feel that you are making free choices.

You feel free when you are aware of what you are doing, when you are fully conscious and "in touch" with your feelings. Freedom requires awareness. But you must also be able to do what you want to do. You must feel relatively free from external controls; you must feel under internal rather than external control.

Psychological Health

Are you psychologically healthy? How can you tell? It depends upon what is meant by "psychological health." There is no absolute, objective definition of "health," just as there is no absolute definition of "good," or "beautiful." Different cultures and different individuals have different views of what is "good," "beautiful," and "healthy." The definition of health, in other words, involves human values, and different groups have different values. Generally speaking, those aspects of behavior and experience which are positively valued are considered "healthy."

Healthy Personalities

At one time many people considered mental health to be equivalent to "good social adjustment." Individuals were regarded as "mentally healthy" if they were well adjusted in their society. To adjust to your society, you must conform to the expectations of that society. However, today we recognize that adjustment to many aspects of our society may be disease-producing. Social pressures contribute to ulcers, anxiety, and mental illness.

Being healthy is not the same as being "normal." The normal person is not a person who has no problems, who is perfectly healthy. The normal person is instead a person who is more or less average—average in the number of colds suffered per year and average in the severity of emotional problems.

Psychological health has often been defined negatively, in terms of the absence of disease. This tendency has led psychology to focus on human deficiency instead of human potential. Many of the concepts used in describing the normal personality are derived from symptoms of the mentally ill. The psychological description of a normal person, in effect, specifies how similar the individual is to a mentally ill person rather than to a mentally healthy person. But psychologists recently have begun to use concepts based

on human potential rather than on human disease. A positive view of mental health can be developed by considering those aspects of human behavior and experience which we highly value and toward which we want to grow. Try to imagine an ideal person, one who is perfectly healthy psychologically. What kind of abilities and traits would such a person possess?

Being psychologically healthy is similar to being physically healthy: both involve the capacity to function well and both involve a feeling of well-being. Feeling well and functioning well are positively valued. The details of this ideal concept of health have been described by the psychologists Rogers[23] and Maslow.[26]

Rogers: The Fully Functioning Person

Carl Rogers describes the healthy person as a **fully functioning person,** one who is happy, creative, and socially effective. An important aspect of the fully functioning person, according to Rogers, is **congruence.** A person is congruent if inner feelings, awareness of those feelings, and outward expression of feelings all correspond, or are congruent with one another. Most of us lack congruence in some way. We may lack congruence because we do not express the feelings we are aware of, or we may lack congruence because we are not entirely aware of the feelings we have. A friend, noticing your abrupt manner and scowling face, asks, "What are you so mad about?" You reply, "Who me? I'm not mad about anything!" But you are angry; sometimes you know it at the time and just don't want to admit it, and sometimes you are not aware that you were angry until later. Your inner feelings were not congruent with the feelings you expressed.

Maslow: The Self-Actualized Person

Abraham Maslow described the ideally healthy person as a **self-actualized person,** one whose basic needs are satisfied and whose potential is fulfilled. From Maslow's point of view, self-actualization cannot take place until fundamental human needs have been met: basic needs of belongingness, affection, respect, and self-esteem; freedom from pain, fear, and hunger; being safe and secure.[27]   Persons who are self-actualized, Maslow discovered, are better able to experience life fully, vividly, with full concentration and total absorption, and without self-consciousness; they are able to take risks and to be spontaneous; they have the courage to be honest and to be different, even if that means being unpopular.[28]   All the self-actualized persons whom Maslow studied were devoted to some task, call, vocation, or beloved work—a cause "outside" themselves in which they found meaning and satisfaction.

According to several studies[29,30] people who are more self-actualized are more likely to agree with the following statements. Check the ones you agree with.

- ☐ I can like people without having to approve of them.
- ☐ People are basically good.
- ☐ The truly spiritual person is sometimes sensual.
- ☐ My moral values are self-determined.
- ☐ I trust the decisions I make spontaneously.
- ☐ I am able to risk being myself.
- ☐ For me, work and play are the same.
- ☐ I enjoy detachment and privacy.
- ☐ I have had an experience where life seemed just perfect.
- ☐ I am self-sufficient.

All people have *moments* of self-actualization in their lives during which this state of ideal health is briefly achieved. These moments Maslow calls **peak experiences**. Peak experiences are moments of great joy, wonder, or awe when a person seems to surrender to a great experience; fears and inhibitions are replaced by a feeling of great power and well-being. In some peak experiences, of a mystical or religious nature, the world is felt as a great unity, while in other peak experiences, particularly the love experience or the aesthetic experience, one small part of the world and one moment in time are experienced as all of reality.[26]

Most people have had moments of great joy or wonder called peak experiences. According to Maslow, the psychologically healthy person has more of these moments of self-actualization. (© Ken Robert Buck)

Can you remember a peak experience you have had in your life? When have you felt moments of ecstasy or wonder? Can you remember moments of intense well-being when everything felt vividly real? Perhaps it was when you fell in love, one day when you looked at the ocean or a sunset, or when you fulfilled some great ambition. These peak experiences are moments of self-actualization. These are the times that you are most healthy.

Allport: The Mature Person

Gordon W. Allport described a state of psychological health which he called **maturity**. Maturity, in this sense, is not an automatic result of age but is a process of becoming, working toward life's goals, and developing a unique philosophy and style of life.

Gordon Allport

One aspect of maturity is self-acceptance. Mature people know their strengths and weaknesses; they understand themselves, they are aware of their feelings, and they are able to accept these feelings without either rejecting them or allowing them to rule their lives. Allport wrote,

Irritations and thwarting occur daily. The immature adult, like the child, meets them with tantrums of temper, or with complaining, blaming others, and self pity. By contrast, the mature person puts up with frustration, takes the blame on himself if it is appropriate to do so. He can bide his time, plan to circumvent the obstacle, or, if necessary, resign himself to the inevitable. His moods come and go, but he has learned to live with his emotional states in such a way that they do not betray him into impulsive acts, nor interfere with the well-being of others.[31]

Allport stressed the future orientation of human beings. Unlike Freud, who believed that people were primarily motivated by biological drives, Allport emphasized the importance of goals and values in human motivation. People who are absorbed in work, curi-

osity, or play often forget about their hunger. Values and goals, Allport argued, take precedence over hunger. Have you ever been so involved in something you valued that your forgot about lunch?

Maturity, according to Allport, is characterized by seven qualities: (1) *Self-extension*—active involvement in meaningful activities such as those associated with the church, school, clubs, country, or career; (2) *warm relationships*—such as in strong friendships or in a good marriage; (3) *emotional security*—including self-acceptance and the ability to tolerate frustration and stress; (4) *realistic perception*—the ability to see things as they are, without distortion or denial; (5) *competency*—basic skills in one or more areas of life; (6) *self-awareness*—an awareness of your strengths and weaknesses, an understanding of what you can do as well as what you can't do; and (7) a *unifying philosophy of life*—a system of values or sense of purpose to guide choice and to give meaning to life.

Being Healthy: A Checklist

The psychologically healthy person is one who has many positively valued behaviors and experiences and has few negatively valued behaviors and experiences. Following is a list of positively valued traits, based primarily on the writings of Rogers and Maslow. Look at the list and check off each item that is generally true for you. How many can you check? Few persons are honestly able to check all of these. In fact, if you are able to check even half of these "ideal" traits, you are probably healthy.

You Feel Good; Most of the Time
You Have a Feeling of Well-Being.

☐ You feel secure and safe; you are rarely anxious.
☐ You have feelings of belongingness and rootedness; you do not usually feel outcast and isolated.
☐ You feel loved and love-worthy; you rarely feel rejected, worthless, unlovable, or inferior.
☐ You feel competent; you are relatively self-confident about your own abilities; you have self-esteem and self-respect.

☐ You trust and you are open to your own feelings; you are immediately aware of your feelings and can act on them; you can be spontaneous.

☐ You have "peak experiences"—ecstatic, intensely satisfying moments when all seems vividly real.

You Can Do Things; You Function Well.

☐ You can do most of the things you want to do; you can take care of yourself.

☐ You are committed to and intensely involved in some work or cause "outside of your own skin."

☐ You can accept yourself and others; you can disclose yourself to others.

☐ You can experience fully, without self-consciousness.

☐ You can show spontaneity and also self-control.

☐ You have the capacity for forming and maintaining intimate interpersonal relationships; you can love.

☐ You can be self-directed; you are relatively independent from the expectations of others.

☐ You are creative.

Interim Summary   Psychological health refers to those aspects of behavior and experience that are positively valued and toward which we want to grow.   According to Carl Rogers, the psychologically healthy person can be described as "fully functioning."   One characteristic of fully functioning people is that they are congruent—that is, they are aware of their feelings and express them accurately.   According to Abraham Maslow, the ideally healthy person can be described as "self-actualized."   Self-actualized people have met their basic needs and fulfilled their potentials.   While few of us are completely self-actualized, most of us have occasionally experienced that state in moments of great joy, wonder, or awe.   Maslow calls these moments peak experiences.   According to Gordon Allport, the psychologically healthy person can be described as "mature."   Some of the characteristics of maturity are self-awareness, involvement, and a unifying philosophy of life.

What Is Your Stage of Growth?

Few persons can truly be described as ideally healthy, as self-actualized or fully functioning. Most of us are at some stage of development below the ideal. What stage are you at?

The following description of stages of growth represents one of several possible views of what constitutes "ideal health." As you read this to determine your stage of growth, remember that this is not the final word but is only one theory.

Stage One •   You are unwilling to talk about yourself; you talk only about externals—about facts, not feelings. You don't recognize your own feelings; you lack congruence. You see yourself as static, constant, unchanging. Close personal relationships with others you find dangerous and threatening. You maintain personal distance and tend to see others as objects. You live by external rules, values, and expectations; you are a conformist. You don't believe you have any problems.

Stage Two •   You talk about yourself, but you see your *self* as an object, as separate from you. You are able to talk about personally meaningful feelings and experiences but always in the past or future, never in the present; you cannot communicate how you are feeling right now. You recognize your feelings, but you don't accept them; you tend to see your feelings as shameful or abnormal. You begin, with great self-consciousness, to risk relationships with others. You begin to search for your own internal rules and values, but you still basically conform; you don't trust yourself yet. You recognize that you have problems, but you don't feel responsible for them.

Stage Three • You can communicate your feelings and experiences in the present; your feelings seem to "bubble up" in spite of your still-remaining fears and distrust. Although you have these immediate experiences of feelings, you are often surprised and frightened by them, rather than pleased. You begin to have lengthy periods of selfless absorption, of unself-consciousness. You experiment with being nonconforming. You feel greater effectiveness in handling problems and in making choices. You recognize the central importance of close personal relationships and can identify the problems you have in this area. You accept greater responsibility for your own problems.

Stage Four • You can communicate your feelings and experiences freely, both verbally and nonverbally, at the time they are happening. You are very aware of your own feelings; you accept them as being you. You trust you own impulses. You live very much in the present, experiencing what *is,* not trying to interpret and explain what is in terms of the past. You see yourself as changing, as growing. Close, open relationships with other persons are highly valued. You can be independent even at the risk of being unpopular. You have strong feelings of competence and well-being and participate fully in the richness of life.

Stage Four is equivalent to being self-actualized or to being a fully functioning person. Few people have achieved this stage of growth, although you will recognize aspects of yourself there; at moments you have been at this stage, when you have had peak experiences. Most of us are at Stages One, Two, or Three most of the time.

How can you move from Stage One to Stage Two? How can you grow and eventually become fully functioning? How can you achieve that ideal stage of psychological health? You cannot be healthy simply by trying to be healthy; you cannot be happy simply by deciding to be happy.

The pleasure principle is self-defeating. The more one aims at pleasure, the more his aim is missed. In other words, the very "pursuit of happiness" is what thwarts it. . . . This is due to the fact that pleasure, rather than being a goal in itself, is and must remain a side-effect, or by-product, of attaining a goal. Attaining a goal . . . is the reason why I am happy. This is why it is not necessary to pursue happiness.[25]

Pleasure, happiness, and self-actualization cannot be effectively *pursued;* instead, they *ensue,* or automatically result, from your having satisfied a need, attained a goal, or grown toward health. Your deciding to be happy will not make you happy; happiness follows from what you *do.*

You have unpleasant feelings sometimes, and this is quite natural. But if your unpleasant feelings are severe, unending, and tend to color your whole emotional life, then you want to stop feeling so bad. We are all sometimes blue, but if you are blue most of the time, then you want to change. As you grow toward health, you tend to experience fewer and fewer persistent unpleasant feelings.

What you do and what happens to you are under your control. You are in charge. And what you do will determine whether you grow toward health or whether you stay as you are now. While you cannot attain psychological health by pursuing it directly, you can grow in the direction of health through certain kinds of experiences and these experiences are under your control. Some experiences move you toward health; some move you away from health. To learn about yourself and others, to love and be loved, and to live actively and productively—all are growth-producing experiences.

Interim Summary   Early stages of psychological growth are characterized by conformity, failure to recognize your own feelings, fear of close relationships with others, and the tendency to live by external standards.   Later stages of growth are characterized by recognition and acceptance of your own feelings, trust of your impulses, living in the present, and a tendency to see yourself as changing and growing, not static.   Learning about yourself and others, loving and being loved, and living actively and productively are all growth-producing experiences.

Helping Others to Grow

You do not need to be a professional therapist in order to help others grow—any close and open relationship with another can be health-producing.   You can help others to grow, and they can help you to grow.   Because you control the kind of relationships you have, you can choose to have relationships that promote growth or ones that inhibit growth.

Qualities of Effective Helpers

What kind of people are effective helpers?   Are you someone who can help others to grow?

Effective helpers are people with several characteristics.[32,33]

1. *Self-awareness.*   People who are self-aware are able to separate their own perceptions, feelings, and needs from those of the person they are trying to help.   People who understand themselves are also more likely to understand others.
2. *Honesty.*   People who are open, genuine, and honest are liked, respected, and trusted more by those whom they are trying to help.   When people are honest, what they have to say is taken seriously; they are not ignored.
3. *Congruence.*   People are congruent when their words are consistent with their actions and when their emotional feelings are consistent with their emotional expressions.   People who are congruent

are seen as sincere and are more likely to be trusted.

4. *Regard for people.*   People with a high positive regard for others help others to have a high regard for themselves.   People who are very interested in others and concerned about them are more effective as helpers.   Such people enjoy helping others.   As one author wrote,

Just as some persons experience pleasure after creating a poem or playing a musical composition, so helpers experience a glow of satisfaction in experiencing human growth before their eyes and realizing that they had some part in facilitating this growth.[33]

5. *Empathy.*   This is the fundamental quality of those who are concerned with helping others.   **Empathy** is the ability to participate in the perceptions and feelings of other people, to see the world the way they see it and to feel with them the subtle qualities of their emotional feelings.

Helping Behaviors

What can you do to help someone else who is in a crisis or who is having a problem?   The underlying skill is effective communication.   This means being able to listen to what people are really saying, to give them your full attention, to understand the way they are feeling, and to respond both verbally and nonverbally.

Some ways of responding to others are helpful,

Table 18-1 Helping and Nonhelping Behaviors

Helping Behaviors

Verbal	Nonverbal
Clarifies statements of other	Maintains eye contact
Paraphrases statements of other	Uses varied facial expressions
Identifies and responds to the feelings of the other	Has a relaxed posture
Encourages the other to talk about his or her feelings	Communicates warmth by smiling and by other gestures
Shares own feelings with other	Leans body toward the other

Nonhelping Behaviors

Verbal	Nonverbal
Gives advice or preaches	Frowns or scowls
Blames or criticizes	Yawns
Talks about self too much	Closes eyes or keeps turning away
Questions and interrogates extensively	Sits far apart
Strays from topic	Speaks in unpleasant tone of voice

in that they promote growth, and other ways are not helpful at all and may even be harmful. Table 18-1 shows a few helpful and nonhelpful ways of responding to others:[32]

Other people encourage you to grow toward health, too. You can probably remember a friend, a parent, or a teacher who has served this important function in your life. Remember one time when someone encouraged you to act exactly the way you felt? That was a growth experience. Remember when someone encouraged you to express your feelings—to talk about your fears, doubts, hopes? That was a growth experience. Remember when someone told you very frankly exactly how he or she felt abut you? That was a growth experience. Remember when someone accepted you and loved you just the way you were? That was a growth experience. You can help others toward health by encouraging them to be "real," by helping them to know and to experience their feelings, by accepting them the way they are, and by prizing them. Naturally it is important to let them know that you accept and value them for themselves.

Summary

1. Intelligence is the ability to learn and solve problems.
2. Tests of intelligence yield a score called the IQ, or intelligence quotient. The Stanford-Binet Intelligence Scale and the Wechsler intelligence scales are widely used tests of intelligence.
3. An IQ score of 100 reflects average intelligence, while a score above 130 indicates that the person is mentally gifted. Both heredity and environment contribute to intelligence.

4. Mentally retarded individuals have three characteristics: (1) an IQ below 70, (2) below average adaptive behavior, and (3) a dullness of childhood origin. There are various degrees of mental retardation ranging from mild to profound.

5. Creativity is the ability to respond uniquely and appropriately to problems.

6. Creative people have been found to be more independent, more self-accepting, more spontaneous, more introverted, more open to experience, amd more intuitive.

7. According to Carl Rogers, creativity can be promoted by fostering certain conditions both within and outside the individual.

8. You have a heightened sense of freedom when you are aware of what you are doing and are in touch with your feelings. A diminished sense of freedom is associated with certain psychological disorders such as the obsessive-compulsive neuroses.

9. Psychological health refers to those aspects of behavior and experience that are positively valued by a particular culture.

10. According to Carl Rogers, the psychologically healthy individual can be described as "fully functioning" and can be characterized as congruent.

11. According to Maslow, the psychologically healthy individual can be described as "self-actualized" and can be characterized as able to experience life fully, to take risks, and to be spontaneous.

12. According to Allport, the psychologically healthy individual can be described as "mature" and can be characterized as self-aware, involved, and possessing a unifying philosophy of life.

13. Early stages of psychological growth are characterized by conformity, failure to recognize one's own feelings, fear of close relationships, and the tendency to live by external standards. Later stages of growth are characterized by recognition and acceptance of one's own feelings, trust in self, and a tendency to see oneself as changing and growing, not static.

14. Effective helpers have several characteristics: self-awareness, honesty, congruence, regard for people, and empathy.

Key Concepts

intelligence   The ability to learn and to solve problems.

intelligence quotient (IQ)   A score on an intelligence test that reflects a person's level of intelligence compared to others of the same age.

Stanford-Binet Intelligence Test   One of the earliest tests of intelligence; assumes that (1) intelligence consists of many different kinds of abilities, and (2) intelligence grows with age.

mental age   Equal to the chronological age of an average child with similar intelligence. A ten-year-old child with the intelligence of a fifteen-year-old has a mental age of fifteen.

Wechsler Adult Intelligence Scale (WAIS) and Wechsler Intelligence Scale for Children (WISC)   Tests of intelligence that assume that intelligence consists of a limited number of specific abilities; yield deviation IQ scores.

digit-span test   Test of ability to repeat, both forward and backwards, a series of numbers that are read aloud.

block-design test   Tests ability to construct a particular design with blocks.

deviation IQ   A measure of intelligence that reflects how far a particular score deviates from the average score made by people of similar age.

mentally retarded   Individuals with IQ's below 70 who are below average in adaptive behavior and have a dullness of childhood origin.

dementia   A progressive deterioration of mental functioning that sometimes occurs in older persons.

mild retardation   The least severe level of retardation; the mildly retarded have IQ's of 50 to 70 and are typically able to care for themselves.

educable mentally retarded (EMR)   Another term for the mildly retarded, as they are able to learn reading and math skills up to a sixth-grade level.

moderate retardation   A more severe level of retardation; the moderately retarded have IQ's from 35 to 50 and can perform simple manual jobs. Although able to speak, they usually cannot learn to read. Only minimal supervision is required.

severe retardation   The severely retarded have IQ's of from 20 to 35 and require special training to learn how to talk and perform simple tasks. Continual supervision is required.

trainable mentally retarded (TMR)   Another term for the moderately to severely retarded.

profound mental retardation   The most severe level of retardation; they have IQ's below 20 and require total care.

mentally gifted   Individuals with IQ's above 130.

genius   The term sometimes applied to individuals with IQ's over 140, but is more accurately used to refer to those with exceptional creativity.

creativity   The ability to respond uniquely and appropriately.

obsessive-compulsive neurosis   A type of psychological disorder involving uncontrollable thoughts and actions.

irresistible impulses   A sudden strong compulsion to do something socially unacceptable or unlawful.

kleptomania   A compulsion to steal.

pyromania   A compulsion to set fires.

exhibitionism   A compulsion for bodily exposure, usually exposure of the sexual organs.

fully functioning person   Rogers's term for the psychologically healthy person; one who is happy, creative, and socially effective.

congruence   A condition in which inner feelings, awareness of feelings, and outward expression of feelings all correspond.

self-actualized person   Maslow's term for the ideally healthy person, one whose needs have been met and whose potential is fulfilled.

peak experiences   Moments of great joy, wonder, or awe; moments of self-actualization.

maturity   Allport's state of psychological health characterized by such things as self-awareness, involvement, and a unifying philosophy of life.

empathy   The ability to participate in the feelings and perceptions of others.

Part VII

Conflict and Disorder

Chapter 19

Anxiety and Stress

Key Questions
1. What is stress?
2. What is anxiety?
3. What causes anxiety?
4. How do you react to anxiety?

Have you been feeling nervous, worried, and unhappy?

At this moment you may feel emotionally upset and unable to concentrate; you may feel frustrated because you have been unable to satisfy some of your needs; you may feel anxious and depressed when you think about the days or years ahead. What are you worried about?

☐ Parents
☐ Friends
☐ Ability to love

☐ Being independent
☐ Grades
☐ Health

☐ Physical appearance
☐ Feeling inferior

☐ Sex
☐ Money

Tension and worry commonly accompany the problems and conflicts we encounter every day. Most of our problems are small ones, resulting only in momentary upset: a dog's barking wakes us in the night, someone drives too close behind us, a friend is late for a meeting, the toast burns. But some of our problems are larger ones: we are challenged to respond, and our minds and bodies react to that challenge in a number of different ways.

Stress

Our environment threatens us in many ways. We are in physical danger from speeding cars, airplanes, storms, poisons, and other aspects of the physical world that are harmful. We are in social and psychological conflict with other people and with ourselves. Our lives are full of tests, deadlines, personal difficulties, and problems to be solved. The challenges, demands, threats, and other conditions in our lives that produce tension are called **stress.**

Most of us live in chronic mild stress. The complexities and the pace of modern life confront us with daily problems. In our struggle for increasing opportunities, our academic and vocational lives become more and more competitive and stressful.

General Adaptation Syndrome

Many physical and emotional problems result from stress.[1] Physical and psychological stress have been shown to precede heart disease, arthritis, ulcers, infections, and skin disease.[2] Illness often follows the stress associated with important changes in life, such as a death in the family, the birth of a child, moving, or divorce.[3,4] Stress also diminishes sexual activity both in animals and in people.[1]

The body reacts to environmental stress in certain standard ways. The pattern of response to prolonged extreme stress has been labeled the **general adaptation syndrome.**[1] The general adaptation syndrome consists of three stages. The first stage is the **alarm reaction,** during which heart rate increases, blood is directed to the skeletal muscles to prepare for a "fight-or-flight" reaction, and other bodily changes occur. The second stage is **resistance,** during which the body seems to return to normal and all the bodily resources are consumed adapting to the stress. The third stage is **exhaustion,** when the body is unable to continue resisting the stress. If the stress continues, the bodily reactions of the alarm stage may recur, and death is likely.

Stress and Life Changes

Any change in your life or circumstances requires some adjustment. Both pleasant changes, such as marriage or the birth of a child, and unpleasant changes, such as divorce or the loss of a job, demand responses on the part of the individual. These demands can be stressful.

People have been found to respond to extremely stressful single events in similar ways. The death of someone you love is a source of sudden stress. The death of a spouse, parent, or other loved one, personal injury resulting from an accident, surgery, rape, or other stressful event all have aftereffects. Life has changed for a while. Common responses from those experiencing such events are shown below.[5]

- I had waves of strong feelings about it.
- Other things kept making me think about it.
- Pictures about it popped into my mind.
- I tried not to talk about it.
- My feelings about it were kind of numb.
- I felt as if it hadn't happened or it wasn't real.

Attempts to measure the degree of stress associated with life changes have been made by a number of researchers. Researchers have found that measures of life change are related to the incidence of a variety of physical and psychological disorders. Coronary heart disease, for example, is more common among people who have recently experienced a number of life changes.[6] Depression and other psychological disorders are more common after a period of important changes in life.[6] The academic performance of students is lower following periods of numerous life changes.[7]

Certain life changes would be expected to have greater impact than others. One measure of cumulative life change takes account of this difference by assigning each potential change a different number of points, called *life-change units*.[8] People with a high number of life-change units (or LCUs) have been found to have a greater likelihood of physical and psychological disorders. To find your total LCUs add up your points from the **Life-Change Scale** (see Table 19-1).[8] Give yourself the points indicated only if you have experienced the life event described within the past year.

Interim Summary	The conditions in our lives that produce tension are called stress. Modern life has become increasingly stressful. Extreme stress results in a variety of psychological disorders and physical diseases and may even contribute to death. The pattern of response to prolonged extreme stress is called the general adaptation syndrome. One measure of the total amount of stress in your life is the Life-Change Scale.

Anxiety

Anxiety is a feeling similar to fear, an experience of alarm, as if something unpleasant were about to happen. Although you are consciously aware of the unpleasant feeling, you are often unable to identify its source; you know you feel worried, nervous, moody, and tense, but you don't know why.[9]

What Is Anxiety?

When anxiety is severe, your body reacts: increased heart rate, fast and shallow breathing, perspiration, muscular tension (especially in the back of the neck), and muscle tremor. Additional physical reactions are sometimes continuous fatigue, stomach upsets, and constipation or diarrhea.

Table 19-1 Life-Change Scale

Events	LCU Values	Your Points
Death of a spouse	100	____
Divorce	73	____
Marital separation	65	____
Jail term	63	____
Death of close family member	63	____
Personal injury or illness	53	____
Marriage	50	____
Fired at work	47	____
Marital reconciliation	45	____
Retirement	45	____
Change in health of family member	44	____
Pregnancy	40	____
Sex difficulties	39	____
Gain of new family member	39	____
Business readjustment	39	____
Change in financial state	38	____
Death of a close friend	37	____
Change to different line of work	36	____
Change in number of arguments with spouse	35	____
Mortgage over $10,000	31	____
Foreclosure of mortgage or loan	30	____
Change of responsibilities at work	29	____
Son or daughter leaving home	29	____
Trouble with in-laws	29	____
Outstanding personal achievement	28	____
Wife begins or stops work	26	____
Begin or end school	26	____
Change in living conditions	25	____
Revision of personal habits	24	____
Trouble with boss	23	____
Change in work hours or conditions	20	____
Change in residence	20	____
Change in schools	20	____
Change in recreation	19	____
Change in church activities	19	____
Change in social activities	18	____
Mortgage or loan less than $10,000	17	____
Change in sleeping habits	16	____
Change in number of family get-togethers	15	____
Change in eating habits	15	____
Vacation	13	____
Christmas	12	____
Minor violations of the law	11	____
Your total number of LCU's:		____

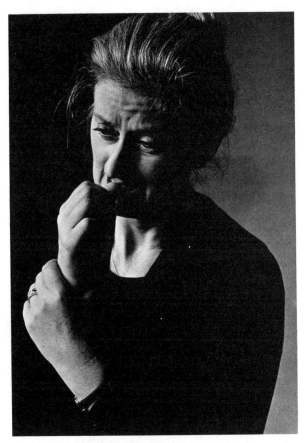

Anxiety is a signal of psychological danger. Physical signs of anxiety include increased heart rate, perspiration, muscular tension, fatigue, and stomach upset. (© *Jean-Claude Lejeune*)

☐ Coldness in the hands or in the feet
☐ Stiffness across the back of the shoulders
☐ Tightness in the back of the neck
☐ Feeling you cannot "catch" your breath
☐ Dryness in the mouth
☐ Hands shaking or trembling
☐ Feeling your stomach is tied up in knots
☐ Feeling your heart beats irregularly
☐ Feeling a tight band around your head
☐ Thinking that you're falling apart
☐ Feeling frightened for no reason that you can identify
☐ Feeling that the world is caving in around you
☐ Feeling that something dreadful is about to happen
☐ Feeling tense and irritable
☐ Worrying about "every little thing"
☐ Thinking that you cannot cope with your problems

Just as pain serves as a signal of a bodily problem, anxiety serves as a signal of a psychological problem. A severe pain in your foot indicates to you that your foot is in trouble and should be moved. A feeling of anxiety signals a kind of psychological danger. Anxiety can serve as a signal that you have a problem or conflict that needs to be resolved. You may then take action to reduce the danger and anxiety. Often when an important conflict is resolved, the feeling of anxiety is greatly reduced. Think of when you solved a personal problem or resolved conflict. Did you then feel more relaxed and less tense?

Anxiety and Conflict

What are your conflicts? What are the forces pulling you in different directions? You have many different wants and needs. Sometimes one need you have is opposed to another need you or someone else may have; you cannot satisfy both needs, so you have a **conflict.** When you have two opposing needs within yourself, you have an **internal conflict.** When you have a need that is opposed to the need of someone else or of society, you have a **social conflict.** Both internal conflicts and social conflicts are sources of much human suffering.

You live with other people and you are sometimes in conflict with them. Even if your family and

Everyone experiences anxiety at some times in life. Taking an important test, making a speech in front of a lot of people, or walking alone on a dark street away from home can be moments of anxiety for many people. For some people, anxiety is not just an occasional uncomfortable feeling, but is an overwhelming and frequent problem. Below are some of the signs of anxiety.[10] How frequently do you have these experiences? Check those you commonly have.

☐ Light-headedness or faintness
☐ Sweating heavily when you have not exerted yourself
☐ Feeling you have a "lump" in your throat
☐ Numbness in the hands or legs

your society are democratic, you cannot always have your own way; what you want and what the group wants are sometimes opposed. Social conflict can arise between individuals as well as between an individual and a group. I may want you to be or to act in a particular way, and you may want to be or to act in another way: this puts us in conflict.

When one of your needs is incompatible with another one of your needs, you have an internal conflict. You want to be able to speak French, but you don't want to learn it: you have a conflict. You want to be slim, but you also want to eat sweets: you have a conflict. You want to go out with the opposite sex, but you shrink away when you have the opportunity: you have a conflict. Other examples are numerous: you want to pass the test, but you want to watch television instead of studying; you want to be entirely independent of your parents, but you don't want to support yourself; you want to be sexually satisfied, but you cannot at this time without violating your beliefs about morality. Which of these are *your* conflicts?

Approach or Avoid • Internal conflict can be classified into three categories: approach-approach conflict, avoidance-avoidance conflict, and approach-avoidance conflict. The term "approach" refers to a positive reaction toward something or a liking of it; the term "avoidance" refers to a negative reaction toward something or a tendency to dislike it. You have an **approach-approach conflict** when you like two different things but can only have one. It's time to order dessert—will you have ice cream or pie? It's time to go to college—will you go to this one or to that one? It's time to choose a career—will you be a teacher or a lawyer? There are moments in life, "choice points," when different paths can be taken, when decisions can be made about different possible futures, or, on a smaller scale, when decisions must be made about what to do in the next few minutes. When both alternatives that you must choose from are attractive and desirable, you are in conflict (an approach-approach conflict).

Sometimes the alternatives from which you must

The feeling of overwhelming anxiety is portrayed in Edvard Munch's lithograph, "The Cry." Anxiety is a feeling of worry and apprehension, as if something unpleasant were about to happen. (Courtesy Museum of Fine Arts, Boston)

choose are negative, unwanted, and undesirable, and you are placed in an **avoidance-avoidance conflict.** You don't like either choice, but you must choose anyway. Do you pay taxes or go to jail? Do you study all weekend or do you flunk the final? Do you go to the dentist or do you continue to have toothaches? When you try to avoid one of these undesirable alternatives, you find that you must accept the other undesirable alternative; you cannot avoid both. You are thus in a dilemma and experience a conflict.

Sometimes the same choice is both desirable and undesirable; it has both attractive and unattractive aspects. When these two tendencies operate at the same time, you have an **approach-avoidance conflict.** You want it, but you don't want it. Another piece of pie would taste very good, but it might give you a stomachache—should you have a second helping? You think that being a doctor would be very satisfying, but you fear you might fail some of the difficult academic courses that are required—should you try to become a doctor? You want very much to receive the attention and affection of a certain person of the opposite sex, but you fear that you would not make a favorable impression and would be humiliated or rejected—should you try to go out with that person? An example of an approach-avoidance conflict is the young man who sat in the telephone booth for an hour. He wanted to call a particular woman to whom he was very attracted, but the prospect of talking to her made him nervous. Fearing that he would be rejected, he finally left without calling. The conflict was resolved in favor of fear. Approach-avoidance conflicts like this have been studied experimentally with animals.

How to Drive Your Cat Crazy • Approach-avoidance conflicts sometimes have serious psychological consequences. Psychologists have known for many years how to induce mental disturbances in animals such as rats,[11] dogs,[12] and cats.[13] The experimenters who work with these animals are not cruel; they feel that the study of abnormal behavior in animals might contribute to our understanding of psychological problems in humans. If we can understand how animals become neurotic and how to treat them, then we might be able to develop treatments for human problems. An experimental technique used in many of these studies with animals involves presenting the animal with an approach-avoidance conflict and observing the consequences of the conflict on the animal.

In one study,[13] several cats were first taught to open the hinged lid of a food box in order to eat. Each cat gradually learned to get at the food by lifting the lid with its head or paws and eagerly worked for its food in this way for several months. One day without warning each cat was given a mild blast of air at the moment of feeding. The physically harmless air blast was delivered to the cat's head just as it was

about to eat. This mild stimulus had very strong effects. The typical reaction of a cat was to rush to the far side of the cage and crouch in fear, making no further attempt to feed in spite of its hunger. The next day, hungrier than ever, a few cats tried again to feed and received another air blast. For almost every cat one or two such experiences were enough to cause them to refuse to eat, regardless of extreme hunger. In order to be kept alive they had to be forcibly tube-fed.

The cats experienced an approach-avoidance conflict. On the one hand they were hungry and food was readily available; on the other hand they feared the mild air blast. In almost every cat this conflict produced a general "mental breakdown," which, because it was produced in the laboratory, has been called **experimental neurosis.** For months afterward, previously quiet cats treated in this way tended to be tense and nervous, trembling frequently, with sweating, raised blood pressure, and irregular breathing. These are common reactions to intense anxiety. Other cats seemed to lose their tameness, becoming vicious and aggressive and attacking other cats in their cage. One cat put its head inside the food box and remained fixed in this position without eating, despite extreme hunger from several days of starvation.

These "neurotic" cats were treated with a variety of procedures in an attempt to make them well again. Prolonged rest away from the food box, reassurance by stroking and petting, and watching other normal cats eat all proved to be somewhat effective procedures in getting the cats to eat again on their own. Some psychologists believe that approach-avoidance conflicts, similar to those induced in experimental neurosis, underlie human cases of intense anxiety.

Basic Anxiety

According to psychiatrist Karen Horney, there is a basic anxiety, developed in childhood, that underlies a variety of adult anxieties. She believed that when children grow up under threatening or hostile conditions, they feel isolated and helpless in a threatening world. The conditions producing basic anxiety are disturbed interpersonal relations between children and adults, as evidenced by excessive domination, indifference, overindulgence, erratic behavior, lack of reliable warmth, or overprotection.

Horney proposed that children, in trying to cope with these unfavorable conditions, will follow one or more of these three strategies: (1) moving *toward* people—they accept their own helplessness and become submissive and dependent, thereby gaining a feeling of belonging that makes them feel less weak and less isolated; (2) moving *against* people—they accept the hostility around them and determine to fight for their own protection; (3) moving *away from* people—they accept their isolation and distrust and build up a world of their own. Conflicts occur in adults when they use combinations of two strategies. The combination of strategies (1) and (2), for example, results in a conflict between being helpless and dependent on others, on the one hand, and being hostile, defiant, and angry, on the other hand. Hostility and dependency don't work well together, so the person is likely to exhibit inconsistent and contradictory behavior.

Interim Summary   Anxiety is an unpleasant feeling of tension and worry, typically accompanied by a variety of physical reactions, and may signal the presence of a conflict which needs to be resolved. Three types of internal conflict are approach-approach conflicts, in which you must choose between two desirable alternatives, avoidance-avoidance conflicts, in which you must choose between two undesirable alternatives, and approach-avoidance conflicts, in which the same choice is both desirable and undesirable. Approach-avoidance conflicts can produce experimental neurosis, a type of mental disturbance that can be produced in laboratory animals. According to Karen Horney, adult anxiety begins in childhood as basic anxiety, caused by disturbed interpersonal relations in the family. The child reacts by adopting a strategy of moving toward, against, or away from people.

Defense Against Anxiety

The experience of anxiety is extremely unpleasant, and we avoid it when we can. According to Freud, the self is relatively fragile and must be protected from excessive anxiety. We use various strategies for defending the self from anxiety, and these strategies are called **defense mechanisms.** Defense mechanisms typically operate unconsciously to ward off anxiety; we usually are not aware that we are using a defense. Here is a list of some defense mechanisms. Do you recognize any that you might have used today?

Repression

"I can't remember ever having a sinful thought."

Repression, or selective forgetting, is the most fundamental defense against the anxiety resulting from emotional conflict. Thoughts, impulses, and experiences that produce severe anxiety are "forgotten" or pushed from awareness, so that the anxiety that accompanies them will not occur. In our society sexual and aggressive impulses are responsible for the most common internal conflicts and are most subject to repression.   People in conflict have two opposing tendencies; if they repress one or both of them, the conflict is temporarily resolved.

To be successful as a defensive strategy for guarding against anxiety, repression must be continuous and complete.   This as a matter of fact is rarely possible.   People who have been punished severely for the expression of anger may become extremely anxious whenever they begin to get angry.   They may repress their anger in order to avoid conflict and anxiety.   But repression of anger might fail in extreme circumstances, and as their anger threatens to become conscious, their anxiety will increase.   People who have repressed sexual impulses will feel anxious whenever sexually tempted, due to the increased difficulty of keeping sexual feelings from awareness.

Reaction Formation

"I've never been afraid of anything."   (*trembling*)

Reaction formation is a defense mechanism that consists both of repressing how you actually feel and insisting thay you feel the opposite way.   Suppose for a moment that you hate your father.   To accept these hostile feelings may produce too much threat and anxiety; therefore you repress them and insist that just the opposite is true: you dearly love your father; he is the best father in the world.

Reaction formation is suspected to underlie many forms of extreme behavior.   Psychologists have proposed, for example, that men who always display extreme stereotyped "masculine" behaviors may be reacting against underlying repressed homosexual impulses.   Some mothers have a conflict between the social expectation that they should love their child and the simple fact that they do not.   A mother who feels hostile toward her child may be made so anxious by this feeling that she not only "forgets" it but also insists that she loves the child intensely, continually demonstrating this "affection" in an exaggerated fashion.

The cowardly lion, a character from The Wizard of Oz, *insists that he is afraid of absolutely nothing.   A psychologist might call this a* reaction formation—*a defense mechanism that involves repressing your true feelings and insisting that you feel the opposite way.   (The Museum of Modern Art Film Stills Library.   Courtesy of Metro-Goldwyn-Mayer)*

Projection

"Nobody at this school likes me."

Projection is a defense against anxiety by which you attribute to others certain thoughts, feelings, or impulses that you have but can't admit.   In order to guard against anxiety, you may repress feelings of anger and hostility toward other people and "project" these unacceptable feelings onto them, so that you come to believe that *they* feel angry and hostile toward *you.* People with repressed homosexual impulses may "project" these feelings onto others, believing that the persons around them are making subtle homosexual advances toward them. People who feel that everybody dislikes them may simply be projecting their own hostility, which, if they admitted, might give them intolerable anxiety.

Rationalization

"The teacher flunked me because I'm a . . ." (*woman, black, athlete, radical*)

Rationalization is a defense against the anxiety that results from personal failures or disappointments. Anxiety can be reduced if the failure can be made acceptable, if it can be explained away so that our self-esteem is not damaged. We rationalize a failure by inventing a logical, but fictitious, excuse for it.

Suppose you failed a test because you had not mastered the material; you rationalize your failure by saying that the teacher had a grudge against you. You didn't win the class election because you didn't get enough votes; you rationalize your failure by saying that you really didn't want to be elected anyway. You weren't accepted at the college of your choice; you rationalize your failure by saying that the college probably isn't any good anyway. College students are very good at rationalization and can usually figure out an explanation for almost any failure. How did you rationalize the last bad grade you made?

Displacement

Father spanks son, who kicks the dog, who chases the cat.

Displacement is the shifting of a response from one object to another. The boss has yelled at the father; the father is angry at the boss but can't express it safely, so he displaces his anger to his son and spanks him. The son is angry at his father but can't express it safely, so he displaces his anger to the dog and kicks it. The dog is "angry" at the son but can't express it safely, so he displaces his "anger" to the cat and chases it. In displacement, a feeling is displaced to a safer substitute. The displacement of aggression is as well known among animals as it is among people. One psychologist trained two rats to attack each other. Then he removed one of the rats and replaced it with a rubber baby doll. The doll was viciously attacked by the rat in a displacement of aggression.[14]

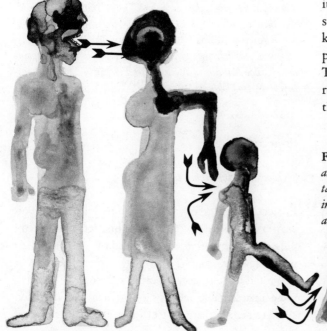

Figure 19-1 Displacement.   *Displacement is a defense mechanism in which an aggressive reaction is shifted from its true target to a safer substitute. The child feels anxious when thinking about responding aggressively to the parent, and reduces the anxiety by displacing the aggression and attacking the dog.*

Scapegoating is a kind of displacement of negative feelings in which a person or group of people is unfairly blamed for a problem. The number of lynchings in this country was high during economic depressions and was low during more prosperous times. Blacks in the South may have served as "scapegoats," convenient substitutes toward which the rest of society could vent its frustrations.

Robert: A Case History

We all use defense mechanisms. The following case shows a college student whose underlying conflicts were so severe that he experienced intense anxiety in spite of his use of several defense mechanisms.

Robert went to his college counselor for help. He had been having increasing difficulty sleeping and would awaken in the middle of the night with acute anxiety reactions. During these anxiety attacks he would have a terrible fear that he was going insane. He would wake up trembling and fearful, with his heart beating rapidly. His counselor eventually discovered that when Robert was about five his mother, trying to stop his frequent masturbation, told him that it would make him insane. This threat caused Robert to suffer a severe conflict between his increasing biological urges and his fear of insanity. Robert was now a college freshman, and was afraid to masturbate; his sole sexual outlet consisted of wet dreams from which he awakened in acute anxiety. Robert's reaction to this conflict was complex: (1) He renounced sex in all its forms, emphasizing the "wholesome cleanness" of his feelings toward his friends; (2) he did not remember ever having masturbated as a child; (3) he was irritated because he felt that a couple of his female classmates kept watching and following him and had nothing on their minds but sex; (4) he said that he had thought about getting married and having a family, but that his chosen profession required that he give up sex and dedicate himself to his work.

Each of Robert's four reactions represents a defense mechanism. Can you identify which reaction corresponds to which defense? (The correct answers appear at the end of the chapter, following the Key Concepts.)

Interim Summary   Freud proposed that we develop strategies for protecting ourselves against the experience of anxiety, unconscious strategies called defense mechanisms. In repression, the fundamental defense mechanism, thoughts and impulses that threaten to produce anxiety are pushed from awareness and forgotten. Reaction formation involves repressing how you actually feel and then insisting that you feel the opposite way. Projection consists of attributing to others certain thoughts or impulses you have but cannot admit. Rationalization is the attempt to explain away failure so as to protect your self-esteem. Displacement involves shifting a reaction from one person to a safer substitute.

Managing Anxiety and Stress

What can be done about stress and anxiety? There are many approaches to this problem. People experiencing high levels of stress often take drugs to calm down—alcohol, barbiturates, or tranquilizers all work in reducing some of the symptoms of stress, but they each have side effects that may not be so welcome. Professional psychotherapy is available for some and is often recommended as an answer to chronic states of anxiety that interfere with functioning. College counseling centers offer short-term assistance to students experiencing a life crisis. A change in life-style is the answer for some, since many stresses in life can be avoided.   Another approach is to learn how to manage your own states of tension by using certain psychological principles to calm yourself.

Relaxation

You can learn to relax.   The anxiety and nervousness that you feel produces tension in the body, muscular tension; by relaxing your muscles, you can change your mental state.

A method called **progressive relaxation** is used by psychologists who treat clients with extreme tension and anxiety; progressive relaxation induces deep muscular relaxation by contracting and relaxing the muscles of the body in a step-by-step fashion.   When a muscle is contracted or tightened, you feel a **tension sensation**.   The object of the progressive-relaxation method is to become highly sensitive to your tension sensations, to become aware of all the bodily tensions you may have, then to relax them.

Some students use jogging as a way to relax.   Psychologists use such techniques as progressive relaxation (a way to reduce muscular tension) and desensitization (a way of reducing fear).   (Peeter Vilms/Jeroboam Inc.)

By alternately tightening and relaxing the muscles in your body, you can become completely relaxed.   Try it now.   Sit in a quiet and comfortable place.   Tighten the muscles in your feet and the calves of your legs; then relax them.   Notice the difference between the way the muscles feel tensed or relaxed.   Tighten the muscles in your thighs; then relax them.   Tighten the muscles in your stomach, noticing the tension sensations; then relax them.   Continue to tighten and relax the muscles in your body in a step-by-step fashion.

When you are through, relax everywhere, breathing slowly and deeply, letting your body feel loose and heavy.   Imagine the tension flowing down your body and out your toes.   Focus on finding tension spots and relaxing them.

This method of relaxation is somewhat similar to the practice of meditation.[15]   In **Zen meditation** the individual sits in a quiet and comfortable place and breathes in an effortless way; the person focuses intently on an internal sensation—that accompanying breathing—while relaxing.   A goal is to observe yourself without reaction or evaluation.   The technique of progressive relaxation developed by psychologists during this century differs little from meditation techniques used for thousand of years.

Self-Desensitization

To manage your emotional reactions, you need to learn to relax in the presence of what has been upsetting you; you need to learn to relax while taking a test or while observing a spider; you need to relax while giving a speech or asking someone for a date; you need to relax in thunderstorms or in the dark; you need to relax while driving in traffic or traveling in an airplane.   A technique for learning to relax in such situations is desensitization.   **Desensitization** involves systematically pairing the feared situation with relaxation.

Fear can be overcome by degrees much better than all at once.   A person who is afraid of the water should not be thrown suddenly into the lake, but rather gradually exposed to small amounts of water under nonthreatening conditions. Repeated gradual exposure is the basis of the method of desensitization.

How can you use desensitization yourself? First, think of an irrational fear you have—for example, fear of public speaking. Next, think of a number of examples of the fear. Some examples should be ones that elicit only minor anxiety, and others should be ones that elicit stronger fears. The example situations (ten to twenty of them) should then be arranged in order of their ability to elicit fear—from ones that are only slightly feared to ones that are very feared. This arrangement of situations, ranked from the least to the most threatening, is called an **anxiety hierarchy.**

The process of desensitization consists of imagining, as vividly as possible, the first situation (least feared) while relaxing. The method of progressive relaxation can be used to maintain complete relaxation while imagining a situation from the hierarchy. The tension aroused by imagining the feared situation should be released by the relaxation procedure; by pairing an image of the feared object or event with the relaxation response, you increase your ability to relax in the presence of the real object or event. There is a transfer of the ability to relax from the imagination to reality. A basic principle of desensitization is that progress up the hierarchy (toward imagining more threatening situations) is made only after complete success at earlier levels of the hierarchy; you don't move on to a second feared situation until you are able to imagine the first situation while remaining completely relaxed.

Meditation has been found effective in reducing fear and anxiety.[16,17] The effectiveness of meditation may come from its resemblance to desensitization.[15] Both methods involve systematic relaxation, focusing on an internal event, and repeatedly maintaining relaxation while imagining or thinking of worries or fears.

Interim Summary You can learn how to relax and how to get rid of irrational fears. Progressive relaxation is a method of deep muscular relaxation that helps you control bodily tension. Control over irrational fears involves first learning how to relax, then using desensitization to reduce the fear. Desensitization is a method of reducing fear that involves pairing relaxation with the feared object or stimulus. The process of desensitization begins with imagining a slightly threatening situation while remaining relaxed.

Positive Anxiety

Anxiety can be a source of great suffering and pain but it has a positive side as well. Not all anxiety is bad. Some anxiety is a normal and even necessary part of life. As the late anthropologist Margaret Mead wrote:

It is clear that we have developed a society which depends on having the right amount of anxiety to make it work. . . . People who are anxious enough keep their car insurance up, have the brakes checked, don't take a second drink when they have to drive, are careful where they go and with whom they drive on holidays. People who are too anxious either refuse to go into cars at all—and so complicate the ordinary course of life—or drive so tensely and over-cautiously that they help cause accidents. People who aren't anxious enough take chance after chance, which increases the terrible death toll of the roads.[18]

Anxiety is a fact of life in the modern world. Moderate levels of anxiety energize behavior, motivating us to act, plan, and take care of ourselves.

Anxiety is a sign of conflict and stress. But conflict means the opportunity for choice, and choice is necessary for growth. Your anxiety may be a sign that you are extending yourself, reaching out, becoming more independent. Each new stage of life is typically accompanied by anxiety: the first day at a new school, your first date, your first job, leaving home, graduation, or marriage. To face conflict and confront anxiety is to engage life and promote personal growth and self-understanding. The poet Kahlil Gibran described this feeling when he wrote, "Your pain is the breaking of the shell that enclosed your understanding."

Summary

1. Conditions in our lives that produce tension are called stress. Extreme stress results in a variety of psychological and physical disorders, and may even contribute to death.
2. The pattern of response to prolonged extreme stress is called the general adaptation syndrome.
3. Anxiety is an unpleasant feeling of tension and alarm, typically accompanied by a variety of physical reactions. It often signals the presence of a conflict that needs to be resolved.
4. Three types of internal conflict are approach-approach, avoidance-avoidance, and approach-avoidance. Approach-avoidance conflicts can produce experimental neurosis.
5. According to Karen Horney, adult anxiety has its roots in a basic anxiety, which develops during childhood as the result of disturbed interpersonal relations within the family.
6. Freud proposed that we develop unconscious strategies called defense mechanisms for protecting ourselves against the experience of anxiety. These defense mechanisms include repression, reaction formation, projection, rationalization, and displacement.
7. Repression is "selective forgetting," the pushing from consciousness of anxiety-producing thoughts and impulses.
8. Reaction formation is the repression of a feeling and the insistence that its opposite is true.
9. Projection is the attribution to others of thoughts and impulses that an individual cannot admit to having personally.
10. Rationalization is the attempt to explain away failure so as to protect self-esteem.
11. Displacement is shifting a reaction from one person to a safer substitute.
12. Progressive relaxation is a method of deep muscle relaxation that helps control the bodily tensions produced by anxiety and stress.
13. Desensitization is a method for reducing fear and anxiety that involves pairing the feared object or stimulus with relaxation. This process consists of imagining increasingly threatening situations while remaining relaxed.
14. Not all anxiety is bad; moderate levels of anxiety are quite positive, energizing behavior and signaling opportunities for growth.

Key Concepts

stress   The changes, demands, threats, and other conditions in life that produce tension.

general adaptation syndrome   A patterned response to prolonged extreme stress in the environment.

alarm reaction   First stage of the general adaptation syndrome, in which heart rate increases to prepare for a "fight-or-flight" response.

resistance   Second stage of the general adaptation syndrome, in which bodily resources are consumed adapting to the stress.

exhaustion   Third stage of the general adaptation syndrome, in which the body is unable to continue resisting the stress.

anxiety   A feeling of tension, worry, and alarm.

conflict   A struggle between opposing wishes, needs, or forces.

internal conflict   A struggle between two opposing wishes or needs within an individual.

social conflict   A struggle between the needs of one person and the opposing needs of someone else or of society.

approach-approach conflict   A conflict involving a choice between two desirable alternatives.

avoidance-avoidance conflict   A conflict involving a choice between two undesirable alternatives.

approach-avoidance conflict   A conflict involving a choice that is both desirable and undesirable.

experimental neurosis   A mental disorder in laboratory animals caused by an approach-avoidance conflict.

defense mechanism   An unconscious strategy for protecting ourselves against the experience of anxiety.

repression   A defense mechanism in which thoughts and impulses that threaten to produce anxiety are pushed from consciousness and forgotten.

reaction formation   The repression of a feeling and the insistence that its opposite is true.

projection   Attributing to others certain thoughts or impulses an individual may have but cannot admit.

rationalization   The attempt to explain away failure so as to protect self-esteem.

displacement   Shifting a reaction from one person to a safer substitute.

scapegoating   A displacement of negative feelings in which a person or group of people is unfairly blamed for a problem.

progressive relaxation   A method of producing deep muscular relaxation by alternately tightening and relaxing sets of muscles.

tension sensation   The feeling associated with a tightened muscle.

Zen meditation   A practice that involves sitting in a comfortable place and focusing on breathing.

desensitization   A technique for reducing fear by pairing relaxation with the feared situation.

anxiety hierarchy   An arrangement of feared situations, ranked from the least to the most threatening.

Answers to question about defense mechanisms (p. 397): (1) reaction formation; (2) repression; (3) projection; (4) rationalization.

Chapter 20

Psychological Disorders

Key Questions

1. How is psychosis different from neurosis?
2. What are the types of neurotic disorders?
3. What are the types of psychotic disorders?
4. What causes psychological disorders?

Psychologist Milton Rokeach studied three men—a farmer, a clerk, and an electrician—who denied their real identities.[1] Each of them insisted that he was Jesus Christ. At one remarkable meeting Dr. Rokeach brought the three men together in a small room and asked them to introduce themselves. Their real names were Joseph, Clyde, and Leon.

Joseph was fifty-eight and had been hospitalized for almost two decades. Of medium height and build, bald, and with half his front teeth missing, he somehow gave the impression of impishness . . .

"My name is Joseph Cassel."
"Joseph, is there anything else you want to tell us?"
"Yes, I'm God."

Clyde introduced himself next. He was seventy and had been hospitalized for seventeen years. Clyde was over six feet tall and, despite the fact that he was all but toothless, stated, whenever asked, that he was in excellent health—and he was. He spoke indistinctly, in a low, rumbling, resonant voice. He was very hard to understand.

"My name is Clyde Benson. That's my name straight."
"Do you have any other names?"
"Well, I have other names, but that's my vital side and I made God five and Jesus six."
"Does that mean you're God?"
"I made God, yes. I made it seventy years old a year ago. Hell! I passed seventy years old."

Leon was the last to introduce himself. Of the three, he looked the most like Christ. He was thirty-eight and had been committed five years before. . . . Leon denied his real name vigorously, referring to it as his "dupe" name, and

refusing to co-operate or have anything to do with anyone who used it in addressing him. We all called him Rex. "Sir, it so happens that my birth certificate says that I am
    Dr. Domino Dominorum et Rex Rexarum, Simplis
    Christianus Pueris Mentalis Doktor. . . . It also
    states on my birth certificate that I am the reincarnation
    of Jesus Christ of Nazareth . . . and it so happens that I
    was railroaded into this place because of prejudice and
    jealousy and duping that started before I was
    born. . . . I do not consent to their misuse of the frequency of my life."
"Who are 'they' that you are talking about?"
"Those unsound individuals who practice the electronic imposition and duping."[1]

How can we understand people who seem to have totally irrational beliefs and who talk and behave in unconventional or bizarre ways? Some people appear to be extremely unhappy and in great personal distress. Others have irrational fears, fears that dominate their lives. Other people see or hear things that aren't there and appear to be out of touch with the real world. A woman whose father died withdraws from life and becomes so depressed that she can no longer manage to care for herself. A young boy develops a powerful and overwhelming fear of school, which his parents cannot understand. A famous actress finds suddenly that she cannot leave her house; the thought of being outside terrifies her. An engineer becomes more and more suspicious of other people and finally comes to believe that they are trying to poison him and steal his inventions. These are examples of what psychologists call abnormal behavior or psychological disorders. The concept of abnormality is discussed more fully in the following pages.

Abnormal Behavior

All of us have troubles—problems of adjustment—at different times in our lives, and sometimes these problems are severe enough to require help. According to a recent estimate, 15 to 25 percent of the population of the United States is in need of help for psychological problems.[2] The scope of the problem, therefore, is enormous.

So far as is possible to determine, a proportion of the people in every society and in every age in history has displayed abnormal behavior. At one time, abnormal behavior was explained in terms of **demonic possession,** the assumption that an evil spirit, witch, or god was somehow inhabiting the body and controlling the individual's behavior. Beatings, bleedings, magic, and prayers were used to expel the demon who was believed to be in the victim's body. Later there were other beliefs about the origins of the problem. For example, the word "lunatic" comes from the belief that abnormal behavior resulted from the influence of the moon (being "moonstruck"). Constipation, masturbation, and blood bile were all mistakenly believed to provoke mental disorders.

Abnormal behavior is inappropriate, unusual, maladaptive, and usually associated with anxiety. You would need more information about the man in the picture before you could decide whether to classify his behavior as "abnormal." (Michael Weisbrot and Family)

Defining Abnormal Behavior

To distinguish "normal" and "abnormal" behavior suggests that there are two kinds or types of behavior—one type is normal, and a different type is abnormal. But the concept of abnormality is far more complex than this distinction suggests. First, different people have different ideas about what abnormal behavior is. A behavior that one person would call normal, another person might call abnormal. Second, behavior does not fall into two clear categories, but lies on a continuum or range in which everything is a matter of degree.

Abnormal behavior is defined as behavior that is inappropriate, unusual, and maladaptive and that is typically associated with distress and anxiety. Each of these four characteristics is important in understanding abnormal behavior. Any one of them used alone is insufficient as a definition.

Abnormal behavior is inappropriate. Compared to generally accepted social standards, abnormal behavior violates our expectation of how people should act. A person who walked down the street nude, who frequently set fires in buildings, or who masturbated in public would be violating the cultural norms or standards for acceptable behavior. A problem with this concept as a sole definition of abnormality is that it would equate abnormality with any behavior judged unacceptable by a particular culture. For example, in this society one behavior which you are not "supposed" to do, but which most people do, is to pick your nose. Yet it does not seem reasonable to call people who pick their noses "abnormal." Thus, other characteristics must also be considered in the definition of abnormality.

Abnormal behavior is unusual. In a statistical sense there are certain behaviors that are infrequent.

It is rare for a person to see visions or hear voices when nobody is there. Having an IQ below 70 is rare (statistically, less than 3 percent have IQs that low) and would be regarded as abnormal. A problem with statistical rarity as a sole definition of abnormality is that many behaviors are rare in a positive direction—for example, IQs above 130 are just as rare as IQs below 70. Acts of extreme generosity, courage, or self-sacrifice are rare. But it does not seem reasonable to call heroes and the mentally gifted "abnormal." Other characteristics must be considered in defining abnormality.

Abnormal behavior is maladaptive. Behavior that does not work, is ineffective, or is harmful to the individual is maladaptive. For example, extreme hostility and suspicion toward others is maladaptive because it interferes with the possibility of normal human relationships and the many satisfactions that result. People who have an intense fear of leaving their homes are unable to shop, to visit friends, and to go to work; thus, such a fear would be regarded as maladaptive. A problem with this as the sole definition of abnormality is that some people are able to compensate for their problems and continue to function reasonably well. A person may be extremely suspicious and bitter, yet continue to be a productive worker. Thus, in defining abnormality, other characteristics must be considered.

Abnormal behavior is associated with distress and anxiety. People may feel anxious, unhappy, depressed, agitated, upset, and miserable; these feelings both accompany and are part of the pattern of abnormal behavior. A problem with using subjective distress as a sole definition of abnormality is that there appear to be some conditions (such as a conversion reaction, discussed later in the chapter) in which little subjective anxiety is experienced. Another problem is that there are some conditions (such as schizophrenia) in which the individual is so disturbed that meaningful communication may not be possible; thus, the schizophrenic may be unable to report subjective feelings.

Although not all abnormal behavior is characterized by all four of the defining conditions that have just been discussed, in most cases this four-point definition works. The four characteristics, in combination, describe what is commonly referred to as abnormal behavior. An issue not yet discussed is the importance of the difference between the occasional occurrence of an unusual or upsetting behavior and the frequent occurrence of the same behavior. The intensity and frequency of the behavior are important in categorizing it as abnormal. A mild, occasional fear would not be regarded as abnormal; the same fear, felt intensely and frequently, might be regarded as abnormal.

Types of Psychological Disorder

In a sense, every example of abnormal behavior is unique and different from any other. But there are similarities as well; examples of abnormal behavior sometimes share certain features. The young boy who has an overwhelming fear of school and the actress who is terrified of leaving her house are both experiencing intense but irrational fears. The engineer who believes that his neighbors are trying to poison him and the farmer who insisted that he was Jesus Christ both have manifestly false beliefs about reality.

Researchers concerned with studying abnormal behavior have developed several different ways of classifying it. The first systematic method for classifying psychological disorders was published in 1883 by Emil Kraepelin, a German psychiatrist. Kraepelin considered psychological disorders to be diseases resulting from basic biological problems. Kraepelin's system has been changed over the years but still forms the basis of the modern scheme for classifying mental disorders. The current classification system (DSM III), published in 1980, reflects the latest research concerning the categories of mental disorder and is a careful and comprehensive framework for understanding the types of disorders. Since many of the terms in the new classification system are technical diagnostic terms not yet commonly used, this chapter will use the more common descriptive terms. For example, the most recent classification system essentially abandons the term "neurosis," but the term is still commonly used and will be used in this chapter.

DSM III, the most recent system for classifying abnormal behavior, groups together disorders that are behaviorally similar and carefully describes the behavioral symptoms for each of the disorders it names. It is designed to increase the reliability of the diagnosis of abnormal behavior. Some of the categories of DMS III and its numbering system are shown in the following list:

I. Disorders Usually First Evident in Infancy, Childhood, or Adolescence
   A. Mental retardation—for example, severe mental retardation (318.1)
   B. Conduct disorder—for example, undersocialized aggressive (312.0)
   C. Anxiety disorders of childhood or adolescence—for example, separation-anxiety disorder (309.21)
II. Organic Mental Disorders
   A. Substance induced—for example, amphetamine delusional disorder (292.11)
   B. Organic brain Syndrome—for example, dementia (294.10)
III. Substance-Use Disorders—for example, alcohol abuse (305.0)
IV. Schizophrenic Disorders—for example, paranoid schizophrenia (295.3)
V. Paranoid Disorders—for example, Acute paranoid disorder (298.3)
VI. Affective Disorders—for example, recurrent major depression (296.3)
VII. Anxiety Disorders
   A. Phobic disorders—for example, agoraphobia with panic attacks (300.21)
   B. Anxiety states—for example, obsessive compulsive disorder (300.30)
VIII. Somatoform Disorders—for example, conversion disorder (300.11)
IX. Dissociative Disorders—for example, multiple personality (300.14)
X. Psychosexual Disorders—for example, transsexualism (302.5)
XI. Disorders of Impulse Control—for example, kleptomania (312.32)
XII. Adjustment Disorders—for example, adjustment disorder with anxious mood (309.24)

Interim Summary   Abnormal behavior differs from normal behavior in several ways. Abnormal behavior is inappropriate (it violates social expectations and standards). It is also unusual (it occurs infrequently) and maladaptive (it interferes with human relationships and happiness). Finally, it is typically associated with distress and anxiety.

Neurotic Disorders

A soldier, about to be sent on a dangerous mission to the front lines, suddenly became paralyzed; he was now unable to walk and therefore would not have to fight. An eight-year-old girl washed her hands twenty to thirty times every day, until they were red and bleeding; if she was prevented from doing so, she panicked. A business executive was so terrified of germs that she would not leave home without wearing rubber gloves. A college student felt extremely tense, pressured and on edge and was afraid he was losing control. Each of these is an example of neurosis.

Neurosis is a psychological disorder characterized by the presence of anxiety, either experienced directly or controlled in ways producing abnormal symptoms. In some types of neurosis, the individual experiences anxiety directly and feels upset, nervous, or panicked. In other types of neurosis, the individual adopts special strategies for controlling the intense anxiety, strategies that are maladaptive and that interfere with living a normal life; an example of this type is the eight-year-old girl, described above, who felt compelled to wash her hands repeatedly.

Neurosis is a part of normal life. In its mildest forms, we all experience neurotic episodes. Periods of excessive anxiety or depression are examples of mild neurotic episodes. Most often we recover from these periods with no professional help, although we may be supported by family and friends through rough times. Because college is a highly pressured and stressful environment, many college students experience psychological problems, and many seek assistance from counseling centers or psychiatric clinics. Most of these psychological problems experienced in college are mild neurotic reactions. In the extreme, however, neurosis can be so incapacitating that it interferes with school and work.

There are many types of neurotic disorders. Different people display different patterns of neurotic behavior or reactions. These types are not totally different from the normal behavior and everyday reactions that all people show. The difference is a matter of degree. Neurotic reactions are extreme and exaggerated forms of reactions common in normal individuals. For this reason, as you read about the types of abnormal behavior, you are likely to see a resemblance to your own behavior. A description of different types of neurotic disorders follows.

Anxiety Reactions

The experience of intense anxiety, with all of its bodily reactions, can interfere drastically with normal functioning. Thought and judgment deteriorate, self-control becomes increasingly difficult, concentration is impossible, and the mind is overwhelmed by unpleasant feelings of despair and alarm. The neurotic **anxiety reaction** involves the experience of excessive and uncontrollable anxiety.

Occasionally a feeling of intense anxiety will come on suddenly, as in the case of the young woman who described her experience as follows:

It was just like I was petrified with fear. If I were to meet a lion face-to-face, I couldn't be more scared. Everything got black and I felt I would faint, but I didn't. My heart was beating so hard and fast it would jump out and hit my hand. . . . My hands got icy, and my feet stung. My head felt tight, like someone had pulled the skin down too tight, and I wanted to pull it away. . . . I couldn't breathe I was short of breath. . . . I don't know what I'll do. . . . I can go along real calmly for a while. Then, without any warning, this happens. I just blow my top.[3]

This woman experiences **acute anxiety reactions,** feelings of extreme anxiety that come quite suddenly and then disappear.

Anxiety can also be experienced almost continuously, rather than suddenly coming and going. A continuous feeling of intense anxiety is called a **chronic anxiety reaction** and can interfere seriously with everyday life, as the following example shows. A man describes the way he feels:

I feel tense and fearful much of the time. I don't know what it is. I can't put my finger on it. I am frightened, but don't know what I fear. I keep expecting something bad to happen. I just get all nervous inside. . . . I fear I might go all to pieces, maybe become hysterical.[3]

Phobic Reactions

Sometimes a person shows great fear of something that is relatively harmless; this neurotic reaction is called a **phobia.** A person with a phobia will make a great effort to avoid the object or situation that is feared. Many persons have mild phobias of some sort; you may have unreasonable fears of elevators, garden snakes, or small spiders. Sometimes, however, these fears are extreme and interfere with living.

An intense irrational fear is called a phobia. Claustrophobia is the irrational fear of closed-in spaces, such as closets or elevators. (© Peter Laytin 1977)

One man, a chemist, was terribly afraid of flowers. This phobia interfered with his work because certain chemicals that smelled like flowers also made him very anxious.

The sight or smell of flowers, particularly bouquets, sprays, and cut flowers, brought on intense fear, dread, and anxiety. This might be even more intense if the flowers were beginning to whither. Flowers had become for him an external threatening object which had to be avoided at all costs.[4]

Persons have developed phobic reactions to many different kinds of objects and situations. Some of the different phobias have been named. Following is a list of some of these names:

- *Acrophobia* fear of heights
- *Agoraphobia* fear of open spaces
- *Arachnophobia* fear of spiders
- *Ailurophobia* fear of cats
- *Brontophobia* fear of thunder
- *Claustrophobia* fear of closed spaces
- *Cynophobia* fear of dogs
- *Nyctophobia* fear of the dark
- *Ophidiophobia* fear of snakes

What are you afraid of? Are these fears realistic or are they phobic?

Obsessive-Compulsive Reactions

An **obsession** is an idea or desire that intrudes, unwanted, into your mind over and over again. We all experience some minor obsessions. When we leave on a trip we may be obsessed with the thought that we have forgotten to pack something or that we have left the door unlocked. In neurotic obsessions, however, unwanted and recurrent thoughts force themselves into the person's mind and interfere with normal thinking.

A **compulsion** is an irrational repetitive act over which you seem to have little control. Compulsions, like obsessions, intrude, unwanted, into a person's life. We also all experience some minor compulsions. As children many of us compulsively avoided stepping on cracks in the sidewalk, and as adults we have particular set ways of dressing in the morning or taking baths. These compulsive rituals do not interfere with living; but in neurotic compulsions, unwanted acts occur over and over again and prevent the person from doing other things.

One man had obsessive thoughts about cleanliness; he kept thinking about germs on his body. He also had a compulsion to wash his hands.

His hands were reddened and sensitive from the thorough scrubbing received on a daily average of twenty-five times or more. Occasionally when his level of anxiety or internal pressure became quite high, even this frequency of washing greatly increased. . . . He could not stand to brush against another person, and if this happened, dry-cleaning of his garments was often a necessity. . . . He usually had to wear a special pair of gloves when dressing or undressing.[4]

Clearly, this man's neurotic reaction handicapped him in his attempts to live a satisfying life.

Notice the difference between the mild obsessions and compulsions that we experience in our normal behavior and the severe neurotic reaction of this man, a reaction that seriously interfered with his life.

Depressive Reactions

Depression is the feeling of despair, worthlessness, and sadness that often occurs in response to actual or imagined loss, failure, or misfortune. **Neurotic depression** is different from normal depression. It is much more intense and lasts longer. The person who is neurotically depressed feels persistently sad, worthless, unlovable, inadequate, and lonely. Eating and sleeping habits are often changed; at times the person will sleep excessively, at other times there will be difficulty sleeping. Fatigue and apathy become continual facts of life. Sometimes the person will consider suicide as the only way to end the misery.

Sometimes the neurotic reaction is quite severe, as in the following case of a woman who was severely depressed after she and her boyfriend stopped seeing each other.

Angela Savanti was 22 years old, lived at home with her mother, and was employed as a secretary in a large insurance company. She stated that she had had passing periods of "the blues" before, but her present feelings of despondency were of much greater proportions. She was troubled by a severe depression and frequent crying spells, which had not lessened over the past two months. Angela found it hard to concentrate on her job, had great difficulty falling asleep at night, and had a poor appetite. She said her depression had begun after she and her boyfriend Jerry broke up two months previously. . . . It became difficult for her to initi-

ate a conversation with others, and many times her lips felt as if they were stiff, and she had to make an effort to move them in order to speak. . . . She felt constantly tired, and loud noises, including conversation or the television, bothered her. She preferred to lie in bed rather than be with anyone, and she often cried when alone.[5]

Although each of us has felt depressed at different times, a person suffering from a neurotic depression finds constant difficulty in life, love, and work. Great sadness, feelings of worthlessness, and lack of self-esteem make it difficult to live a satisfying life.

Dissociative Reactions

Dissociation means separation or splitting apart. In a **dissociative reaction,** one aspect of the personality is isolated from the remainder, resulting in a loss of memory and personal identity. People forget who they are and even where they live. Two types of dissociative reactions are amnesia and multiple personality.

Loss of Memory • **Amnesia** is a loss of memory for certain parts of your past life. In many cases individuals do not know their own name, work, family, or home; they lose all memory for personal identity. Amnesia is often associated with psychological stress or trauma, and can be considered as a way to escape from unbearable emotional conflict. Here is a case history showing the background of an amnesia victim:

Donald G. was 22 and attended college at night while working in the daytime to support himself and his mother. Donald had a girlfriend whom he wanted to marry, but his mother disliked her. It was clear that he could not support himself, a wife, and his mother while going to college. Finally his girlfriend told him that he must make a choice between her and his mother, giving him one month to decide. One week before the decision was due, Donald disappeared. Two weeks later he was discovered in another state, and could remember neither his name nor his home. Amnesia had solved his problem; he no longer had to make a choice.[6]

Donald G.'s personal identity was lost over the conflict. This seems to be an unreasonably large price to pay for avoiding the anxiety associated with the decision and certainly did not lead to a satisfactory resolution of the problem. The response of amnesia is therefore a neurotic reaction and is self-defeating.

The Three Faces of Eve • In the case of **multiple personality,** individuals seem to have two or more distinct personalities and identities, only one of which is present at a time. Individuals with this rare disorder change from one personality to another, as in the case of "Dr. Jekyll and Mr. Hyde." People with such a "split personality" may be in conflict over two opposing patterns of behavior. They solve the problem by essentially becoming two people. At one time they are person A, at another time they are person B. Multiple personality is a rare condition, but cetain dramatic cases have been reported.

One of the best-known cases of multiple personality was reported in a book and movie entitled *The Three Faces of Eve,* based on the life of a real person.[7] Eve White was a twenty-five-year-old woman who suffered from severe headaches followed by blackouts. During one therapy session Eve suddenly changed her pattern of behavior and introduced herself to the doctor as "Eve Black." While Eve White was quiet, sweet, and industrious, Eve Black was mischievous, vivacious, and irresponsible. Eve White's blackouts were actually periods in which Eve Black was in control. Eve White was not aware of Eve Black's existence, although they shared the same mind. After months of therapy a third personality emerged—Jane—who was mature and competent.

Conversion Reactions

An individual with a **conversion reaction** has sensory or muscular problems without a physical cause. A woman became blind upon seeing her husband with another woman; a soldier became paralyzed when ordered to the front lines. These persons have, in a sense, converted their mental conflicts into the bodily symptoms of blindness and paralysis. In addition to blindness and paralysis, conversion reactions may include deafness, inability to taste or smell, inability to speak, visceral problems such as hiccups, vomiting, or diarrhea, seizures, anesthesia, and even the physical conditions of a pregnancy. These symptoms are real. Victims are not faking but suffer from them as much as if they had a physical basis.

Problems with a physical basis and problems resulting from a conversion reaction may differ in that conversion reactions often do not make sense in terms of what we know about the anatomy and physiology of the body. For example, a conversion reaction resulting in a loss of feeling in an arm or leg may affect an area of the skin that might be covered by a glove or stocking; nerve damage, however, would affect a very different area because of the way the nerves are distributed. Because of their psychological nature, conversion reactions may be cured by a treatment such as psychotherapy.

The physical problems of a conversion reaction often seem to have two types of benefits: first, the problem allows people to escape their conflicts, thus reducing their anxiety; second, people often receive sympathy and attention because of the problem. The second benefit is called a **secondary gain** and can serve the function of encouraging the problem to continue once it occurs. The conversion reaction results in a secondary gain for a person to the extent that other persons are stimulated to respond with sympathy, affection, and attention. The following case illustrates a secondary gain brought about by a neurotic conversion reaction:

A middle-aged married woman had to nurse her mother-in-law, who was paralyzed in both legs. Her husband forced her to do this, and seemed to become concerned only with his mother, forgetting his wife. One day the wife took a walk, feeling rebellious, but at the same time very anxious as she became dimly aware of angry wishes that the old lady would die. She felt faint and sat down on a park bench. A moment later she tried to rise, only to discover that both her legs were paralyzed and that she now needed as much of her husband's attention as did his mother.[8]

Traumatic Reactions

Everyone has a breaking point. Under conditions of extreme shock or injury, an emotional collapse may occur. A trauma is a physical or psychological injury or shock and a **traumatic reaction** is a neurotic disorder resulting from such a shock. This reaction may involve intense anxiety, phobias, dissociation, depression, or other types of neurotic problems. Traumatic reactions can result from any kind of overwhelming stress, such as war, accidents, or natural disasters.

A War Trauma • Soldiers in combat face extreme stress, and some may break down. Continued expo-

A traumatic reaction is a neurotic disorder resulting from an overwhelming crisis or stress, such as a flood or earthquake. (United Press International Photo)

sure to rifle fire, mines, and bombing had both immediate and long-term psychological consequences for soldiers who fought in Vietnam. After returning from the war, many veterans suffered from recurrent nightmares, jumpiness, and depression, and experienced great difficulties in interpersonal relations.

One soldier had been pinned down by enemy fire for twelve hours and had seen most of his platoon killed. He had a temporary traumatic reaction and was flown directly from the battlefield to a hospital.

No information accompanied him, he had no identifying tags on his uniform, and he was so completely covered with mud that a physical description of his features was not possible. His hands had been tied behind him for the flight, and he had a wild, wide-eyed look as he cowered in a corner of the emergency room, glancing furtively to all sides, cringing and startling at the least noise. He was mute, although once he forced out a whispered "VC" and tried to mouth other words without success. He seemed terrified. . . . His hands were untied, after which he would hold an imaginary rifle in readiness whenever he heard a helicopter overhead or an unexpected noise. . . .

Soon after his arrival at the hospital the patient was given tranquilizers to calm him and keep him asleep for approximately 40 hours. When he was allowed to wake, the medication was discontinued. Although he appeared somewhat dazed and subdued, his response to ward activities was dramatic. Within 72 hours after his admission to the hospital, the patient was alert, oriented, responsive, and active. Although still a little tense, he was ready to return to duty. He was sent back to his combat unit on his third hospital day.[9]

Disaster at Buffalo Creek • Tornadoes, hurricanes, fires, floods, and earthquakes are natural disasters resulting in extraordinary psychological stress. They injure the mind as well as physical structures. For example, one year after a tornado struck San Angelo, Texas, about 50 percent of the townspeople who were examined reported they still suffered from emotional problems caused by the storm.[10] While the immediate psychological response to disaster is shock and confusion, there may be long-term, and even permanent, traumatic reactions. These problems have been observed in the residents of a mountain valley in West Virginia.

The Buffalo Creek valley in West Virginia had fourteen small towns with a population of four to five thousand people. On February 26, 1972, disaster struck. An enormous dam broke and released a tidal wave of water and mud which destroyed everything in its path. More than 100 people were killed and 4,000 were left homeless. Two years after the disaster, more than 90 percent of the survivors who were examined showed anxiety, depression, nightmares, phobias, and other psychological problems.[11] Many of these were diagnosed as showing a traumatic neurosis. The survivors sued the company that owned the dam and received $6 million for psychological damages.[12]

Are You Neurotic?

When you read about neurotic reactions, you may notice that your own behavior in some ways resembles neurotic behavior. You recognize *yourself* in some of these descriptions of neurotic persons. Does this mean that you are neurotic?

We are all very similar; you, me, a neurotic person. To classify people as neurotic is not to claim that they are extremely different from normal persons. Your behavior and the behavior of neurotics differ mainly in degree. You are different from obsessive-compulsive neurotics not because they have recurring obsessive thoughts and you do not but because they are more bothered by obsessive thoughts than you are. In fact, they are so bothered that they have grave difficulties functioning in life. You are different from depressive neurotics not because they have periods of depression and you do not but because their depressions are severe and persistent and yours are not. Their depressions are so severe that they interfere with their ability to function in life. You are different from phobic neurotics not because they have unreasonable fears and you do not but because their fears interfere seriously with their life and yours do not. If, despite your problems, you are able to function fairly well in life, you are probably not neurotic. If you have further questions about yourself that you want answered, you should see your teacher, a counselor, or a psychologist.

Interim Summary	Neurotic reactions appear in a variety of forms: intense anxiety (anxiety reaction); an unreasonable fear (phobia); recurring, unwanted ideas (obsessions); irrational, repetitive actions (compulsions); a splitting apart of the personality (dissociation) resulting in loss of memory (amnesia) or alternating distinct personalities (multiple personality); sensory or muscular problems without a physical cause (conversion reaction); and a neurotic reaction to a physical or psychological shock (traumatic reaction). Each of these forms of neurosis involves anxiety, either experienced directly or controlled in ways producing abnormal symptoms.

Psychosis

Have you ever wondered what it is like to be insane? Madness, or—to use the technical term—**psychosis,** is a major psychological disturbance involving a disorga-nization of the personality and a loss of contact with reality. It affects hundreds of thousands of persons in this country. More than half of all the hospital beds in America are occupied by persons who are suffering from psychosis.

What is it like to be psychotic? One psychotic person described his own experience:

I call attention to a great crime, which has hardly its equal in history. . . . A conspiracy was inaugurated against me, unparalleled by anything heard of before. . . . Now, wherever I go, these diabolical agents are following me. They not only injure me in business, but are molesting everyone who may come in contact with me. They place chemical odors in every room where I may be. The effects of these odors upon my system are as numerous as they are painful. Now and then I lose, almost, my consciousness, and only with the utmost efforts can keep my eyes open. Often, again, I experience a feeling as if my whole body was pierced with needles. At night especially these merciless agents pour such chemical odors or gases into my room that I have a choking sensation, and I am unable to breathe. Pain seems to squeeze my eyes out of the sockets, and visions arise before me.[13]

This individual was forced to leave one job after another because of his continuing problems, and he finally wrote a letter to the district attorney, demanding police protection from the "evil agents" he believed to be following him.

People who are psychotic are rarely a danger to others; they are instead people who have problems coping with the stressful requirements of their everyday life. They may be so disturbed that they are incapable of carrying on everyday activities, such as eating and going to the bathroom. They are often withdrawn and isolated and find it impossible to communicate with others and to relate to them emotionally. Psychotics are out of contact with the reality of the world and other people. They are unable to deal with it effectively or to communicate about it.

When you see psychotic people, you may see them acting or talking in strange and bizarre ways. These bizarre ways of talking and acting are *symptoms* of psychosis. A **symptom** is a sign or indication of a disorder. Psychotics may have one or a combination of several types of disordered behavior or symptoms,

among which are disturbances in perception, in ideas, in emotions, and in the movement of the body. Disturbances in perception and ideas are common psychotic symptoms.

Hallucinations

Disturbances in perception are called **hallucinations**. A person who hallucinates sees or hears something in the absence of any external physical source. A hallucination resembles a waking dream in which you experience something that is not there but that seems very real to you. Sometimes these hallucinations take the form of seeing a dead relative or religious figure such as the Virgin Mary or Jesus Christ; sometimes they take the form of smelling nonexistent odors or hearing voices.

Voices from Another World • Hearing voices is a more common form of hallucination than seeing something that is not there. One man described his hallucinations as follows:

The "voices" manifest themselves in me as nervous impulses, and always have the character of soft lisping noises sounding like distinct human words. . . . For about seven years—except during sleep—I have never had a single moment in which I did not hear voices. They accompany me to every place and at all times; they continue to sound even when I am in conversation with other people.[3]

Strange Visions • Another man, hospitalized because of his psychosis, had come to believe that his hospital attendant was in reality Jesus Christ. One day while walking around the hospital grounds he experienced the following visual hallucination.

I became aware of something remarkable happening in the air only a very short distance in front of me. It seemed to me that there had been some big air waves, and then through them the well-known form of [my attendant] appeared, facing me, and coming towards me. I thought for a second that he had been rendered invisible by ordinary heat waves that had happened to be between us, and that he had just walked through them. As soon as I thought this, he seemed to disappear for a second; once again he became clearly visible, firm, and solid, all but his feet, which seemed lost in vibrating air; an instant afterwards they became visible, and I heard the gravel crunch under his tread as he took four or five paces up to me.[14]

Delusions

Disturbances in ideas are called **delusions.** Not all false ideas are delusions; we all sometimes have false ideas, but people with delusions have bizarre, irrational ideas of what is going on around them in the world, and no amount of evidence will persuade them that they are wrong. If you insist that you are Napoleon, you have a delusion. Common types of delusions are **delusions of grandeur** (in which people believe themselves to be a famous person or one who has magical powers), **delusions of persecution** (in which people believe that various people or organizations are "out to get them" by killing or torturing them), and **delusions of reference** (in which people believe that random events occurring around them are all concerned with them in some way—for example, the belief that people are always whispering about them on the bus).

My Weird Powers • One psychotic patient was obsessed with feelings of guilt and with a belief in his own personal power. He had delusions of grandeur.

I am causing a lot of people to become insane, accidentally, by reason of the power that leaves me and comes back. . . . This power causes railroad accidents, which is awful. My presence in the world is injurious to many people—I don't understand how. . . . People's voices change when talk-

ing; sometimes they appear pale and drowsy, again peppy and full of life, and it seems to me that I am the medium of all that; it seems that I exercise some involuntary control over them. . . . I imagine people losing their teeth; babies are dwarfed; people have nervous breakdowns, etc.,—all on my account. . . . I can't see how I could be such a freak of nature as to have these powers.[15]

Plots Against Me • One man wrote a book about his psychosis in which he described his delusion of persecution. He believed that individuals in the mental hospital around him were in a vast plot against him.

None of my food had its usual flavor. This soon led to that common delusion that some of it contained poison—not a deadly poison, for I knew that my enemies hated me too much to allow me the boon of death, but a poison sufficient to aggravate my discomfort. . . . Although I was not entirely unaware that something was ailing with my mind, . . . all these horrors I took for the work of detectives, who sat up nights racking their brains in order to rack and utterly wreck my own with a cruel and unfair "Third Degree."[16]

Talk About Me • A woman had the delusion that she was rotting away, that she had an offensive body odor, and that everywhere she went people talked about her unfavorably. She had a delusion of reference.

Everything which occurred around me I imagined was related to me. I would sit in a classroom and overhear a fragment of conversation and my sick mind would fasten upon a word or two that I thought referred to me. . . . If I heard the word "smell" I suffered tortures, knowing that it referred to the odor of corruption which, I was convinced, still clung to me. My hair had become coarse and dead, having something the appearance of dried seaweed and whenever I heard the word "hair" I knew that mine was being discussed.[17]

Interim Summary   The various strange behaviors seen in psychotic individuals are the symptoms of psychosis.   Psychotic symptoms include disturbances in perception, in ideas, in emotions, and in the movement of the body.   Psychotic hallucinations are like waking dreams and may involve hearing voices or seeing people who are not present.   Psychotic delusions are bizarre and irrational ideas.   Common types of delusions are delusions of grandeur (*I am the King of France*), delusions of persecution (*They are out to get me*), and delusions of reference (*Everybody is talking about me*).

Psychotic Disorders

The varieties of psychotic reactions have traditionally been grouped into two broad classes: **organic psychoses** (those with known physical causes) and **functional psychoses** (those without known physical causes).   An example of a psychosis with a known physical cause (an organic psychosis) is **senile psychosis,** a gradual psychological deterioration that sometimes occurs in elderly persons.   An inadequate blood supply to the brain results in symptoms of depression, loss of memory, suspicion, restlessness, and general confusion.   Most psychotic reactions, however, are of the functional type with no known physical cause.   The two most common types of functional psychoses are affective disorders and schizophrenia.

Affective Disorders

Some psychotic persons have severely disturbed affective behavior.   The term *affective* refers to emotions or moods.   In **affective disorders,** the mood is extremely high, extremely low, or alternates between these two extremes.

The One-Hundred-Foot Letter •   **Mania** is an affective psychosis in which people seem joyous, deliriously happy, and wildly energetic; people in a manic state talk a great deal, jumping from one idea to another, and feel extremely confident, making grandiose plans that are never carried out.   They move about constantly, running back and forth, jumping up and down, doing exercises, and shouting and singing. One man who was hospitalized for mania wrote letters on long rolls of wrapping paper and later described his experience.

More than once letters twenty or thirty feet long were written, and on one occasion the accumulation of two or three days of excessive productivity, when spread upon the floor, reached from one end of the corridor to the other—a distance of about one hundred feet.   My hourly output was something like twelve feet. . . . Under the pressure of elation one takes pride in doing everything in record time.[16]

The Weeping Man •   A different type of affective psychosis is **psychotic depression.**   Psychotic depression resembles the way you feel when you are discouraged and depressed, but in psychosis the mood is tremendously exaggerated.   A person suffering from psychotic depression may sit motionless for days, brooding, refusing to see anyone, feeling utterly hopeless and worthless.   The following case is an example of this type of affective psychosis.

Mr. T. S. . . . would spend most of his time sitting on a chair by the side of his bed, moaning and wringing his hands.   His facial expression was one of the deepest dejection, and his eyes were reddened from weeping. . . .   As a rule, Mr. S. would not speak unless spoken to, but occasionally he would address another patient or a member of the ward staff.   At such times he would usually blame himself in the harshest terms for having "ruined his family," saying that he did not deserve to live.[18]

The Alternating Woman   •   Just as you experience changes of mood from joy to discouragement, some psychotic persons swing from one extreme (mania) to the other extreme (depression). The cycle from mania to depression, and back again to mania, may take place over a period of just a few days, or it may take years to complete.

One woman was brought to the hospital after she had already gone through two periods of mania and two periods of depression. During her depressed periods she seems full of sorrow, acts dejected, is inactive, and speaks almost entirely in monosyllables. When she is asked a question, she may take a minute or two to answer, and then replies in a dismal tone with a single word. She typically sits quite still, with her head bowed, her brow wrinkled, and her hands clasped in her lap. By contrast, in her manic phase it is impossible for her to remain still even for a moment. She runs about the hospital singing, dancing, slapping patients and nurses on the back, and throwing things about. She tears off her clothes and throws her arms around any man who happens to appear.[19]

Schizophrenia

Schizophrenia is the most common form of psychosis; about half of all the patients in the mental hospitals in this country are diagnosed as schizophrenic.[20] "Schizo" means *split,* and "phrenia" means *mind;* **schizophrenia** may be thought of as a disorder in which the mind is split off, or separated, from reality.

The term "schizophrenia" is often used incorrectly in magazines and on television to refer to people with split personalities, those who at one time seem to be one kind of person and at another time seem to be another kind of person. Such people are not schizophrenics.

Rather, schizophrenics escape from reality to their own private world. Their thoughts are often irrational, disorganized, and bizarre; their feelings may appear totally absent or entirely inappropriate to the circumstances in the world around them; their language may be illogical, disconnected, and twisted; and they may experience hallucinations and delusions. Schizophrenics often have difficulty communicating with others and sharing their experiences. They live inside shells that nobody can penetrate. There are several varieties of schizophrenia.

Barbara   •   One variety of the disorder is called **simple schizophrenia** and is characterized mainly by symptoms of apathy and withdrawal from social contact, as shown in the case of Barbara. Barbara, a girl of fifteen, came from an unhappy home; her alcoholic father and her cold, bitter mother paid little attention to her. Barbara developed severe conflicts with the onset of menstruation (for which she was not prepared) and with the increase in her sexual feelings and thoughts (which she regarded as sinful). Now, during the first year of high school, she dropped all social contacts and would not see her friends or talk to them on the telephone. She spent hours alone in her room and was very withdrawn at home, becoming increasingly apathetic, moody, and irritable. Finally she stopped going to school and spent all her time alone in her room, sitting quietly by her window.

L. Percy King   •   Another variety of schizophrenia is called **paranoid schizophrenia.** Persons with this disorder have delusions of grandeur and persecution; that is, they believe themselves to be some great person or historical figure, and they believe that others are against them or out to get them. L. Percy King was a patient in a state hospital who believed that he had made the greatest discoveries in the history of the world (delusion of grandeur) and that he was the object of a group of pursuers who had been after him for thirty years (delusion of persecution). King heard these evil pursuers talk to him by way of what he called "radio voices" (hallucination).

Among these pursuers, I was gradually to discover by deduction, were evidently some brothers and sisters who inherited from one of their parents some astounding, unheard of, utterly unbelievable occult powers. Believe it or not, some of them, besides being able to tell a person's thoughts, are also able to project their magnetic voices—commonly called "radio voices" around here—a distance of a few miles without talking loud and without apparent effort. . . . Thus, in connection with their mind-reading ability, they are able to carry on a conversation with a person over a mile away and out of sight, by ascertaining the person's unspoken thoughts, and then by means of their so-called "radio voices," answer these thoughts aloud audibly to the person. An uninitiated person would probably be very much startled by such phenomena. For example, what would you think if you were on a level desolate tract of land without any vegetation or places of concealment upon it, and without a human being within miles, when you heard a mysterious seemingly unearthly voice answer a question you were just thinking about.[21]

Psychosis and Neurosis

How can you tell whether a person with abnormal behavior is neurotic or psychotic? Neurotic people have extreme anxiety and are unable to cope with it. Neurotics typically lack self-confidence, are unhappy, and are painfully insecure; but they are able to care for themselves, to work, and to relate to people, although often only with considerable difficulty. A neurotic's ability to function in life is only mildly disturbed. A neurotic commonly experiences depression, anxiety, and numerous bodily complaints, but has no bizarre disturbances in perception and thinking. Neurotics typically have some understanding of their own problems; they may know what they are, but not know what to do about them.

The behavior of the psychotic is more disturbed and bizarre than the behavior of the neurotic. Psychotic individuals are out of contact with reality; they cannot effectively operate in the world and their ability to communicate with and relate to other people is severely disturbed. Sometimes psychotics are unable to care for themselves and may be hospitalized for their own protection. They may hear strange voices or see people when there is no one there. Other bizarre behavior may occur such as jumbled language, inappropriate weeping and giggling, and unusual postures. These severe problems seriously interfere with the person's ability to meet the demands of life. Psychotics, however, typically have no insight into their problems. They often do not know what their problems are and are out of contact with the reality of themselves and the environment around them. They are, in a sense, living in another world. It is an unreal world created by the psychotic mind, a place of confusion and terror.

Interim Summary   Psychotic reactions are called organic when they have a known physical cause and functional when they do not. Two major types of functional psychosis are the affective psychoses and schizophrenia. Mania is a form of affective psychosis in which the person is wildly energetic, confident, and talkative. Psychotic depression is an affective psychosis in which the person is extremely dejected and inactive. Schizophrenia is a form of functional psychosis characterized by hallucinations, delusions, social withdrawal, and emotional reactions that are either inappropriate or absent. Two types of schizophrenia are simple schizophrenia, characterized by apathy and withdrawal, and paranoid schizophrenia, characterized by delusions of grandeur and persecution.

Causes of Psychological Disorders

Each neurotic person shows a unique pattern of self-defeating behavior.   The variety of different neurotic patterns suggests that there is no unique, single cause of neurosis.   Research on the origins of affective disorders and schizophrenia suggests that there is not just one cause of these problems.   Different theories of the causes of psychological disorders reflect different points of view about which particular influence is most important in understanding these problems. Four of these theories are described below.

The Psychoanalytic Model

According to Freud's psychoanalytic theory, neurosis results from a distorted or exaggerated use of **defense mechanisms,** which are unconscious strategies for protecting ourselves against the experience of anxiety.   As unconscious conflicts, primarily originating in childhood, threaten to become conscious, intense anxiety is produced.   While most people are able to control anxiety by using ordinary defense mechanisms, the neurotic is not able to do so effectively.   In the neurotic, the pressure of unconscious conflicts distorts and exaggerates the defense mechanism.   These distortions result in the neurotic pattern of behavior.

The psychoanalytic theory of phobias emphasizes the distorted use of the defense mechanism of **displacement.**   Anxiety arises from the threat that unconscious impulses from the id may become conscious.   This anxiety is then displaced to an object, person, or place, resulting in the irrational fear associated with the phobia.   Obsessive-compulsive reactions also have their origins in the inadequate repression of id impulses, but the defense mechanism involved is **reaction formation.**   An impulse from the id threatens to become conscious and is so unacceptable that not only is it denied, but the opposite attitude or impulse is expressed.   For example, a man's obsessive

fears about the safety of his son may represent unconscious hostile and aggressive impulses directed against the child.   The psychoanalytic view of neurotic amnesia relies upon the excessive use of **repression** as a defense mechanism.   According to this theory, the sexual impulses from the id are massively repressed, but the repression is not specific and selective.   The repression is so pervasive that a whole portion of the personality is split off from awareness.

Freud argued that schizophrenia represented a **regression**—a return to childish ways of thinking and acting—as a result of a complete breakdown of psychological defenses.   According to psychoanalytic theory, a schizophrenic person has "regressed" to an ear-

The role of unconscious conflicts and impulses in psychoanalytic theory is suggested by Goya's etching, "The Sleep of Reason Produces Monsters." (Courtesy Museum of Fine Arts, Boston. Bequest of William P. Babcock)

lier stage of personality development, one that was appropriate in the oral stage of development. At this stage, the ego has not yet been fully developed and is incapable of effectively dealing with reality.

For the schizophrenic, life is full of fear, people are dangerous, and a retreat to infancy provides a measure of security. By regressing, the schizophrenic can reject reality. Schizophrenics, like infants, often cannot provide for their own physical needs and must be cared for.

The Behavioral Model

According to the *behavioral model,* psychological disorders are "bad habits" that have been learned. The principles of operant and classical conditioning are used to explain how a particular "bad habit" could have been learned.

According to the behavioral model of neurosis, phobias are learned emotional reactions. For example, a spider phobia could be explained by the principle of classical conditioning. An intense fear of spiders is regarded as a conditioned response, resulting from the repeated association of spiders (conditioned stimulus) and the pain of their bites (unconditioned response). Such fears can also be learned vicariously, through observing adult models who express panic when encountering spiders. The behavioral model views obsessive-compulsive reactions as learned through operant conditioning because they have the rewarding effect of reducing anxiety. Conversion reactions are also seen as learned behaviors that are reinforced because they reduce the level of anxiety. For example, becoming paralyzed just before being sent to the front lines in a war has a highly rewarding consequence: survival. Becoming blind through a conversion reaction is rewarded through the sympathy that other people express. Amnesia serves to help avoid anxiety-provoking situations and is thereby rewarded. A woman who was ambivalent about her forthcoming marriage suddenly lost her memory and thus, for a while, avoided the anxiety associated with

her plans. One author uses the principle of operant conditioning to explain a case of blindness that was a conversion reaction.[22] The man's life was so miserable that blindness was, from his point of view, an improvement. As a result of his blindness, he received a pension, did not have to work, and spent his time at home listening to music. In effect, there were rewarding consequences to his blindness.

The behavioral model views schizophrenia as learned maladaptive behavior. According to this view, the schizophrenic, unlike the rest of us, has not received much reinforcement from interactions with other people. Because of the inadequacy of social reinforcement, the schizophrenic has little incentive to pay attention to what other people say or what they do. A child growing up in an environment in which social interactions are unpredictable, ambiguous, or punishing may learn to ignore other people. Paying attention to internal events, such as private fantasies and memories may be more rewarding than paying attention to the real world on the outside. This withdrawal from social reality is accompanied by even less social reinforcement as other people regard the individual as weird or strange. In this fashion, an individual may learn to become schizophrenic.

The Genetic Model

A third point of view on the cause of psychological disorders is that they are inherited neurological diseases.[23] This view can be called the *genetic model* for the origin of psychological disorder. This model applies better to some disorders than to others. According to some researchers, schizophrenia is an inherited problem. There is substantial evidence that a tendency toward schizophrenia runs in families. When two individuals have identical genes (identical twins), the chances are very high that the second twin will be schizophrenic if the first one is. The evidence is virtually conclusive that a tendency toward schizophrenia is inherited.[24,25] This implies that there should be physical differences between schizophrenics and normals; and, indeed, there is evidence that the nervous systems of schizphrenics and normals are different.[26,27] While the tendency for schizophrenia may be inherited, it is clear that other factors are also very important; the amount of psychological stress in people's early lives, the pattern of interpersonal relationships in their families, and the quality of parental care and loving they have received, all contribute significantly to their behavior in the world.

The Interpersonal Model

According to the *interpersonal model,* psychological disorder results from a pattern of distorted interpersonal relations in the family. The relationships of mother to child, father to child, and mother to father are crucial learning experiences for the child. From these experiences the child learns how to relate to other people and how to cope with personal and interpersonal conflict. When these relationships are distorted, the child may learn distorted or neurotic patterns of behavior. Through these relationships neurotic parents may pass on neurotic patterns to their children. Studies show that neurotic children tend to come from families with great conflict between the parents.[28] Parents who are confused, frightened, and unstable cannot provide their children with healthy models for responding to the stresses of life.

According to this theory, the origins of schizophrenia can be found in disturbed interpersonal relationships within the family. The families of schizophrenics have been studied by psychologists, and the family members have been found to have more interpersonal conflict than do normal families.[29] The members of schizophrenics' families also tend not to listen to each other.[30] Communications between parents of schizophrenics and their children have been found to be wandering, disruptive, and illogical.[31]

A pattern of disturbed relationships within the family could be either a *cause* of schizophrenia in the children or a *response* to the problem of having a schizophrenic child in the family. Since many recent studies show that the family abnormality exists before the onset of schizophrenia in the child, there is good evidence that disturbed families are a cause of schizophrenia, not simply a response to it.[31] The whole pattern of relationships in such a family is often disturbed and may be directly responsible in producing schizophrenia.[32]

Interim Summary   There are several theories of the causes of psychological disorders. According to Freud's psychoanalytic theory, neurosis results from distorted or exaggerated use of defense mechanisms such as displacement, repression, and reaction formation. Freud argued that schizophrenia represented a regression to earlier stages of personality development in order to reject reality. Behavioral theory uses the principles of operant and classical conditioning to explain how psychological disorders are "learned." The genetic model offers the point of view that certain psychological disorders, such as schizophrenia, are inherited neurological diseases. According to the interpersonal model, psychological disorders result from a pattern of distorted interpersonal relations within the family.

A Caution Against Labeling Yourself

One of the most common reactions of psychology students to material about abnormal behavior is the feeling that they themselves may be abnormal. Beginning psychology students as well as experienced graduate students learning about the details of different types of psychological disorders often note how similar they are to some of the cases being described. They then may conclude, "I am neurotic" or "I am psychotic."

There are two different explanations for the feeling that you may be abnormal. (1) One possible explanation is that you are, in fact, abnormal and are clearly different from other people, such as those sitting near you in class, who are regarded as normal. (2) A second possible explanation of your feeling of being abnormal is that you are normal, but you are sensitive enough to note your resemblance to those who are abnormal. Which of these explanations is more reasonable?

There are problems with the first explanation. The majority of people who read for the first time about abnormal behavior feel that their behavior may be abnormal. If this feeling were based on fact, then the majority of people would actually be abnormal. But this is not a reasonable assumption. A further problem with the first explanation is its assumption that normal and abnormal behavior are distinct categories. In fact, there is no evidence to support this view. Behavior ranges from one extreme to another, along a continuum. At this moment, some people are elated, some are fairly happy, some are slightly depressed, and some are extremely depressed—the difference is a matter of degree. Abnormal behavior differs from normal behavior only in degree. As you drive down a freeway or highway, you may have occasional unwanted thoughts of having a terrible accident; such thoughts differ only in degree from the obsessions of the neurotic. You may have had periods in your life in which you lost interest in your work or school, felt apathetic, and became less socially involved; such reactions differ in intensity from those of the schizophrenic who loses contact with reality. Since your behavior differs only in degree from abnormal behavior, it would be surprising if you did *not* notice your resemblance to those with psychological disorders. But the fact that you (and everybody else) resemble individuals displaying abnormal behavior does not mean that you are abnormal or that you should label yourself as "neurotic" or "psychotic."

A person may be labeled and diagnosed as psychotic on the basis of such symptoms as hallucinations and delusions. **Diagnosis** involves identifying or classifying a problem on the basis of the symptoms. Psychological diagnosis is different from medical diagnosis. Diagnosing a person as having a cold is based on the symptoms of a sore throat, a cough, and a runny nose. Diagnosing a person as psychotic or as a particular type of psychotic is not, however, so simple. A person who is classified or diagnosed as psychotic is judged to be out of contact with reality. But what is reality?

People are enough alike, whatever the culture, so that the concept of "reality" is similar in different parts of the world. Most people labeled as psychotic in this country would also probably be considered psychotic in most other countries in the world. But there are cultural differences among countries in the definition of reality and, consequently, in the use of the concept of "psychosis."

Reality is to some degree socially or culturally defined, and it therefore depends on where you live. Reality in one culture may include ghosts; reality in another may exclude ghosts. A person who hears the voice of God may be "out of contact with reality" in Los Angeles, California, but in contact with reality in rural Brazil.

People labeled as psychotic behave in ways unacceptable to their society. They do not have a "disease" that they have "caught"; they behave strangely and their behavior does not conform to the rules and reality of their culture.[33,34] There is a sense in which the meaning of "reality" is defined by the general agreement of the population. From this point of view people are psychotic if they have lost contact with the views of their culture and are thereby unable to communicate with persons around them. Because the use of psychological labels is influenced by social and cultural factors, they can easily be used in a biased and prejudiced way, so you should use special caution in applying them to yourself or to others.

Labels have a lot of power. The names discussed in this chapter for different kinds of abnormal behavior carry with them the discomfort and disapproval of society. Some researchers believe that being labeled is enough in itself to cause or aggravate a psychological problem. For example, once people are called "retarded," they are treated differently by their parents, friends, and school. Once people are called "schizophrenic," they are also treated differently by those around them. Once labeled, people also think of themselves differently—as deficient, sick, freakish, or out of control. Labels are "sticky"—once applied, they tend to stick and are not easily removed. Thus, for a lot of good reasons, you should use caution in labeling yourself or others, because doing so can have profound negative effects on a person's life.

Summary

1. Abnormal behavior is defined as behavior that is inappropriate, unusual, and maladaptive and that is typically associated with distress and anxiety.
2. Neurosis is a psychological disorder characterized by the presence of anxiety, either experienced directly or controlled in ways producing abnormal symptoms.
3. Neurotic reactions appear in a variety of forms: intense anxiety (anxiety reaction); an unreasonable fear (phobia); recurring, unwanted ideas (obsessions); irrational repetitive actions (compulsions); a splitting apart of the personality (disassociation) resulting in loss of memory (amnesia) or alternating distinct personalities (multiple personality); sensory or muscular problems without physical cause (conversion reaction); and a neurotic reaction to a physical or psychological shock (traumatic reaction).
4. Psychosis is a psychological disorder characterized by a disorganization of the personality and a loss of contact with reality. Psychotic symptoms include disturbances in perception (hallucinations) and disturbances in thought (delusions).
5. Psychoses are either organic (with some physical cause) or functional (without a physical cause).
6. One major type of functional psychosis is the affective psychosis. Forms of affective psychosis include mania and psychotic depression.
7. Another major type of functional psychosis is schizophrenia, characterized by hallucinations, delusions, social withdrawal, and emotional reactions that are either inappropriate or absent.
8. Two types of schizophrenia are simple schizophrenia, characterized by apathy and withdrawal, and paranoid schizophrenia, characterized by delusions of grandeur and persecution.
9. According to Freud's psychoanalytic theory, neurosis results from distorted or exaggerated use of defense mechanisms such as displacement, repression, and reaction formation. Freud argued that schizophrenia represented a regression to earlier stages of personality development in order to reject reality.
10. According to the behavioral theory, psychological disorders are learned behaviors, acquired through the principles of operant and classical conditioning. They are essentially the same as any other behaviors, except that they are maladaptive in some way.

11. The genetic model offers the point of view that certain psychological disorders, such as schizophrenia, are inherited neurological diseases.

12. According to the interpersonal model, psychological disorders result from a pattern of distorted interpersonal relations within the family.

13. Caution should be used when labeling persons as having a psychological disorder; labels are very powerful influencers of behavior.

Key Concepts

demonic possession   The assumption that an evil spirit, witch, or god was somehow inhabiting the body and causing an individual's abnormal behavior.

abnormal behavior   Behavior that is inappropriate, unusual, maladaptive, and typically associated with anxiety and distress.

neurosis   Psychological disorder characterized by the presence of anxiety.

anxiety reaction   The experience of excessive and uncontrollable anxiety.

acute anxiety reaction   The feeling of intense anxiety that comes on suddenly and then disappears.

chronic anxiety reaction   A feeling of intense anxiety that is continuous.

phobia   An intense, unreasonable fear of an object or event.

obsession   A recurring unwanted idea or impulse.

compulsion   An irrational, repetitive, involuntary act.

depression   Feelings of despair, rejection, and worthlessness.

neurotic depression   Intense and lasting depression.

dissociative reaction   A splitting apart of the personality into two or more relatively dependent parts.

amnesia   A dissociative reaction involving a loss of memory for personal identity or past events.

multiple personality   A dissociative reaction in which two or more distinct identities appear to alternate within the same individual.

conversion reaction   Sensory or muscular problems that exist without a physical cause.

secondary gain   An incidental benefit of a neurotic reaction in which individuals receive attention or sympathy for their problems.

traumatic reaction   A neurotic reaction to overwhelming psychological or physical shock or injury.

psychosis   A severe mental disorder characterized by loss of contact with reality, accompanied by disturbances in emotions, ideas, or perceptions.

symptom   A sign or indication of disorder; for example, hallucinations are an indication of psychosis.

hallucination   A disturbance in perception in which something is seen, heard, or felt that does not exist.

delusion   A false belief that is bizarre and irrational and is held in spite of contrary evidence; for example, the belief that one is Napoleon.

delusion of grandeur   A false belief that one is a great or powerful person; for example, the belief that one controls the world.

delusion of persecution   A false belief that one is being victimized; for example, a man may believe that others are out to get him.

delusion of reference   A false belief that unrelated events are personally directed; for example, a man may have the belief that everybody is talking about him.

organic psychosis A psychosis with a known physical cause; for example, senile psychosis.

functional psychosis A psychosis with no known physical cause.

senile psychosis A psychosis resulting from an inadequate blood supply to the brain, typically in an elderly person.

affective disorder A disorder characterized by moods that are extremely high or low.

mania An affective psychosis in which people are wildly energetic, confident, and talkative.

psychotic depression An affective psychosis in which people are extremely inactive and dejected.

schizophrenia A functional psychosis characterized by social withdrawal and disturbances in perception and ideas.

simple schizophrenia A type of schizophrenia characterized by apathy and social withdrawal.

paranoid schizophrenia A type of schizophrenia characterized by delusions of grandeur and persecution.

defense mechanisms Unconscious strategies for protecting ourselves from the experience of anxiety.

displacement A defense mechanism in which a reaction is shifted from one person to a safer substitute; for example, your anger at your father is shifted to your younger brother.

reaction formation A defense mechanism involving the repression of a feeling and the insistence that its opposite is true.

repression A defense mechanism in which thoughts and impulses that threaten to produce anxiety are pushed from consciousness and forgotten.

regression A return or retreat to an earlier stage of personality development; for example, a return to infantile behavior.

diagnosis The classification or identification of a problem on the basis of its symptoms; for example, classification of a person as psychotic on the basis of the person's delusions.

Chapter 21

Therapy

Key Questions   1. What is the history of the treatment of psychological disorders?
                   2. What are some major types of psychotherapy?
                   3. What are some major types of biological therapies?
                   4. How widespread are psychological disorders?
                   5. Do you, or does someone you know, need psychotherapy?

In the following letter to her therapist, a woman describes the distress she felt for several months before deciding to begin psychotherapy:

It's hard to explain what has happened to me in the past months . . . very hard. One of my first, strongest, and most persistent feelings was pain—all through the months I was in pain; not just mental pain, but actual physical pain, nausea, rapid heartbeat, poor circulation, headaches, and so on. I remember saying once that I felt as if I was putting a knife into myself and turning it around and around so that my blood and all my insides would gush forth. The pain began when I realized that I had to decide whether or not to begin therapy.

My first reaction to you, I think, was one of surprise at your sensitivity and awareness of what and how I was feeling, even when I expressed it very inarticulately or not at all. I knew you were quick and sensitive, but I didn't think anyone could be that understanding. Then I began to get the feeling that not only were you sensitive to and understanding of my feelings, but you also cared and cared very much.[1]

The woman goes on in the letter to describe the close relationship that developed with her therapist, a rela-

tionship of empathy and trust. Within the context of that relationship, she was able to explore her previously hidden feelings and solve some of her problems. Toward the end of therapy, she reports that "I felt as if I had leaped a brink and was safely on the other side."

The process that this woman experienced is called therapy. The term **therapy** refers to a treatment designed to bring about an improvement in some condition. You receive therapy from a medical doctor when you go to a clinic for help with a physical disease. You also receive therapy when you go to a clinic or a counseling center for help with a psychological problem. The forms of therapy used to help people with psychological problems can be either psychological or biological in nature. Most often, the chosen therapy for psychological problems is a treatment based on psychological techniques. This kind of treatment is called **psychotherapy**. Psychotherapy is a special kind of help provided by a professionally trained person. The treatment is designed to help people overcome obstacles to their personal growth, to help modify disabling emotional reactions, to promote the development of better social adjustment, and to help people acquire more effective means of coping with future stresses and problems.

The History of the Treatment of Psychological Disorders

Abnormal behavior and its treatment have been a special concern of people for thousands of years. In Egypt, three thousand years before Christ, a psychia-

trist named Imhotep warded off the evil spirits believed to be causing mental disorders by using magical amulets, opium, and olive oil.[2] Later, physicians healed by using mystical words of an ancient language, such as Greek or Hebrew, together with charms and amulets. Still later, words and phrases were used by themselves to drive off evil and restore mental health.

In the early Middle Ages, between the tenth and thirteenth centuries, people with psychological disorders were generally treated humanely. Monasteries served as refuges providing assistance and protection to those who were mentally disturbed. Abnormal behavior was typically treated with prayers, relics, and lucky charms.

Hospitalization and Physical Treatment

During the Renaissance, from the fourteenth to seventeenth centuries, the treatment of abnormal behavior became more violent. Special prisons ("asylums") were established for those with psychological disorders. The belief in witchcraft and demons as the cause of mental problems became stronger and more popular. Cotton Mather, in the late seventeenth century, believed that witchcraft caused insanity. He helped identify "witches" in Salem, Massachusetts, who he thought were putting spells on people and making them insane. The victims of the "witches" were treated with exorcism and special rites to drive out the "devils"; those who were believed to be witches were killed. In Europe, the emotionally disturbed were placed in chains in prison and were beaten, starved, and tortured in an effort to drive out the demons who were believed to be possessing their bodies.

During the Age of Reason, in the eighteenth century, Benjamin Rush—the father of American psychiatry—advocated treating those with psychological disorders with bloodletting (opening a vein in the fingers or tongue and draining off "impure" blood) and purgatives (enemas to relieve constipation, which was believed to cause insanity). During this period, the mentally disturbed were still kept in chains in prisons. In England, going to the madhouse to view the mentally disturbed was a popular entertainment for a Sunday afternoon. An observer of the conditions of mental patients during the early 1800s described what he found:

I have seen them naked, or covered with rags, and protected only by straw from the cold damp pavement upon which they were lying. I have seen them coarsely fed, deprived of fresh air, or water to quench their thirst, and of most of the necessary things for life. I have seen them in squalid, stinking little hovels, without air or light, chained in caves where wild beasts would not have been confined. There they remain to waste away in their own filth under the weight of chains which lacerate their bodies.[3]

These appalling conditions were changed as a result of the work of two reformers, one in France and the other in the United States. Phillipe Pinel, a French physician, was made director of a major French hospital in 1793. He had a radical new theory about how the mentally disturbed should be treated—with kindness. He prohibited beatings, removed their

In the late 1700s, Phillipe Pinel ordered the chains removed from hospitalized mental patients. He began a new approach to the treatment of psychological disorders—the idea that kindness and consideration should be used. (The Bettman Archive)

chains, let them relax in the sunshine, and treated them with kindness and consideration. Although this new approach was met with doubts and skepticism, it proved to be quite successful and was soon adopted in other hospitals. In 1841 in the United States, Dorothea Dix, a Boston schoolteacher, started a crusade to improve conditions in mental hospitals and to build new, more humane facilities. Her crusade, too, was quite successful in bringing about widespread improvement in the treatment of the mentally disturbed.

During the first half of the twentieth century, there was a growth in the number and size of mental hospitals until, in the mid-1950s, well over half a million people were residents of these institutions. Very little actual treatment was given to those in mental hospitals, although the basic human needs of the patients were met. The last half of the twentieth century has seen a decline in mental hospitals. There are far fewer people in mental hospitals now than in the 1950s; the mental hospital population has dropped by two-thirds in spite of the fact that the population of the country has increased by about 50 percent. The decline in mental hospital residents is partly due to the utilization of effective drugs in the treatment of the mentally disturbed and partly due to the new philosophy of treatment that advocates returning mentally disturbed people to their communities whenever possible.

Psychological Forms of Treatment

In the late 1800s, Sigmund Freud began developing his theories of psychological disorders and the ways in which they should be treated. As a young doctor Freud observed a demonstration of the effect of hypnotism in treating psychological problems. Josef Breuer, a friend of Freud, was treating a young woman named Anna O. While she was under hypnosis, Anna described the circumstances that led to her condition and seemed to reexperience the emotional feelings that she felt at the time. Talking about her problem resulted in a marked improvement in her condition, a fact that Freud noted with great interest. Freud theorized that talking about a problem freely was an important step toward a cure but that hypnosis was not a necessary part of the therapy.

In 1900 Freud published the first of his numerous books explaining his theory of personality and treatment of disorders. At first, his ideas were ridiculed, but eventually his theories were taken seriously and his influence became worldwide. Freud's method of treatment—psychoanalysis—became widely popular after World War II and began to be taught in medical schools as part of accepted medical practice.

Many other forms of therapy have also been developed during the past half century. Some of these therapies are based on known psychological principles that have been investigated in scientific laboratories. Other therapies are modification of Freud's psychoanalytic treatment. Examples of these types of therapies will be discussed later in this chapter.

In the history of therapy, one of the newest developments is the rise of the community mental health movement. Instead of treating a problem in a one-to-one relationship between a client and a therapist, the **community mental health** approach is concerned with the psychological welfare of the whole community. While the traditional approach is to treat whatever clients happen to come to the therapist for treatment, the community mental health approach is concerned with preventive and outreach activities designed to create conditions to support mental health in the community. Throughout the country community mental health centers have been established to provide short-term emergency care, outpatient treatment, educational services, and consultation with agencies or schools to help other professionals cope with individuals who need emotional support. The availability of these supportive services in communities makes it possible for individuals with psychological disorders to remain at home instead of being placed in a mental hospital.

Interim Summary   Psychotherapy is a form of treatment for psychological problems. It is provided by specially trained professionals and involves applying psychological techniques to help bring about an improvement in functioning. For thousands of years people with psychological disorders have received some kind of special treatment. At one time, this treatment was brutal and violent, but Phillipe Pinel and Dorothea Dix helped bring about more humane conditions in the 1800s. Later, Sigmund Freud developed a form of intensive psychotherapy that he called psychoanalysis. One of the newest developments is the community mental health approach, involving attempts to prevent psychological disorders in a whole community.

Psychoanalysis

Psychoanalysis is the method of psychotherapy developed by Freud. The method is based on Freud's concepts of personality and personality development. Two concepts particularly important in psychoanalysis are the principles of unconscious motivation and early determinism.

Principles and Methods of Psychoanalysis

Freud believed that our own needs, motives, and impulses are often unknown to us; that is, we are not conscious of them. The principle of **unconscious motivation** states that we are often unaware of our needs and impulses. Certain impulses, particularly sexual and aggressive ones, are taboo in our society. Because our parents and the rules of this society prohibit us from expressing these impulses freely, we repress them; we banish them to our unconscious. But even though they are unconscious, they nevertheless continue to affect our behavior in various ways. The primary goal of psychoanalysis is to make these unconscious motivations fully conscious.

Freud believed that early childhood experience is responsible for shaping the adult personality. The principle of **early determinism** states that the characteristics of the adult personality are controlled or determined by early childhood experience. During these early years of life significant feelings, impulses, and memories were repressed. One of the goals of psychoanalysis is to give clients insight into the historical causes of their behavior; that is, to help them discover what aspects of their early experiences are responsible for their present attitudes, feelings, and actions.

Freud believed that we use up "psychic energy" in keeping impulses and conflicts out of awareness; when in the course of psychoanalysis unconscious material becomes conscious, psychic energy is freed, and the influence of these unconscious impulses and conflicts on the personality is reduced.

There are two major methods used in psychoanalysis to get at unconscious material. The first method is called **free association;** the client is told to lie down and relax and then to say anything that comes to mind. The idea is to reveal freely the contents of your mind, with no censorship, regardless of how shocking or insignificant the thought may seem. To do this without censoring your own thoughts and words is difficult, but if you can do it, according to Freud, you will reveal without meaning to do so unconscious impulses and conflicts.

The second method used in psychoanalysis to get at unconscious material is called **dream analysis.** The dream, Freud believed, is a kind of window into the unconscious; the contents of dreams express un-

Free association and dream analysis are two techniques commonly used in psychoanalytic therapy. In this form of therapy, the patient lies on a couch with the therapist sitting behind. (Judy Sedwick/The Picture Cube)

conscious impulses and conflicts in a symbolic or disguised fashion. The content of the dream that you remember and report is called the **manifest content;** the true meaning of the dream—the unconscious meaning—is called the **latent content.** The goal of the psychoanalyst is to interpret the symbols in the manifest content of the dream in order to reveal the unconscious material in the latent dream content.

An Analysis of a Dream

In the following example from a psychoanalytic session, a man who has suffered from impotence in his sexual relationships with women describes a dream he had.[4] The therapist focuses his attention on specific details of the *manifest content* of the dream and interprets the meaning of some of the dream symbols.

Through this process, the patient gains insight into his problem.

Therapist: What about dreams; have you had any since our last visit?

Patient: Yes, quite a few. On Tuesday night I dreamed I was in some sort of revolutionary turmoil, and some dictator had his arm torn off. Then I became the dictator, and my arm is attached. As I proceed somewhere, each time someone touches my arm, I feel it's going to be torn off. This is followed by a dream in which I and a girl are going somewhere, and running to catch a bus, and my hand begins to bleed. I'm becoming covered with blood, and she says, "Look what's happening." I say, "It doesn't matter; let's get there in a hurry." Then I exclude from an appointment I had arranged with people, this girl.

Therapist: Exclude her?

Patient: Yes, she was excluded in some way.

Therapist: By whom?

Patient: By me.

Therapist: Mm hmm. Is that all?

Patient: Yes.

Therapist: What do you make of it, the dreams, I mean?

Patient: I suppose I am upset and afraid. I must be the dictator whose arm is hurt.

Therapist: Yes, as if you are in jeopardy of being attacked as a dictator and physically hurt.

Patient: Yes.

Therapist: But perhaps this dream tells us why it's difficult to get things done in a hurry. After all, your arm is mutilated. Could it be that in rushing into sex you feel you might be mutilated in some way?

Patient: (emotionally) There must be something that scares me. I feel anxious as I talk now.

Therapist: In what way could you be mutilated? Who would mutilate you and why?

Patient: I don't know.

Therapist: But what about the part of the dream where you exclude her? Is it possible that you exclude her because of feelings, indicated by the dream, of fear of bloody mutilation?

Patient: If I were to expect attack from this source, I can see that.

Therapist: One way to escape attack is to give up the sex object, remove yourself from her, become impotent and apathetic. (interpretation)

Patient: Yes, I can see something now; it occurs to me that the arm in the dreams is a symbol of my genitals.

Therapist: Mm hmm.

Patient: And the dictator, being in the position of dominance like a male, can have his genitals hurt and not be a man. If I try to be a man, I may be hurt— my superiority and power torn off so to speak.

Therapist: And sexually mutilated.

Patient: Yes, undoubtedly.

Therapist: And in a sexual role with a woman?

Patient: I'll be sexually hurt, hurt.

Therapist: It would explain your coldness with women, the impotence. If you expect to be castrated, that's no fun.

In this example from psychoanalytic psychotherapy, the therapist analyzes the patient's dream, interprets the "true" meaning of the dream, and regards the dream as revealing the content of the patient's unconscious mind.

Psychoanalysis is a very time-consuming therapy; an individual may spend one hour a day, five days a week, for several years in the process of psychoanalysis. Because there are relatively few trained psychoanalysts and a lengthy period is required for its completion, it is an opportunity for growth available to very few individuals. It is also extremely expensive, limiting it to those who are relatively wealthy. One survey of persons who completed psychoanalysis found that only 60 percent could be considered as cured or greatly improved. In this survey, for each person who was rated as markedly improved, more than 600 hours of psychoanalysis were required.[5] This finding implies that psychoanalysis may be an appropriate form of therapy for only a limited number of people—those who can afford the time and money it requires.

Although classical psychoanalysis is not very commonly practiced, the influence of psychoanalysis is quite strong. Many different therapies share some of the assumptions and approaches of psychoanalysis, but over time have evolved and developed other methods. For example, many modern therapists continue to believe, as Freud did, that adult psychological disorders have their origins in childhood and that unconscious conflicts lie at the root of many problems. Yet the approach that many therapists now take in treating problems draws on a variety of newer techniques and is not so lengthy as psychoanalysis.

Interim Summary   Psychoanalysis, the form of psychotherapy created by Freud assumes that the source of psychological problems lies in difficulties in early childhood and that unconscious impulses and conflicts affect everyday behavior. The goal of psychoanalysis is to make unconscious impulses and memories fully conscious so that they can be dealt with. Free association and dream analysis are two ways to get at unconscious material and bring it to light.

Behavior Therapy

Behavior therapy is a form of psychotherapy based on the principles of experimental psychology and designed to change behavior in the most direct way.

Unlike psychoanalysis, behavior therapy focuses on the symptoms, not on the supposed underlying causes, of a psychological problem. The behavior therapist assumes that what has to be treated is what the client actually *does;* no consideration is given to such ideas as unconscious impulses, underlying conflicts, insight, or dream analysis. "If a person has a fear of cats, eliminate the fear rather than look for subconscious conflicts which produce the fear. If a person is an alcoholic, stop the drinking behavior rather than look for underlying causes."[6] What a person does is primarily what that person has learned to do. Many persons learn bad habits, just as a cat in the laboratory can be taught to be neurotic.

An explicit assumption of the behavior therapist is that human behavior is subject to causal determination no less than that of billiard balls or ocean currents. . . . The general attitude of the behavior therapist to his patients is in accord with this deterministic outlook. He regards the patient as a joint product of his physical endowment and of the molding influence of the succession of environments through which he—an organism—has passed. Each environment, each exposure to stimulation, has modified, through learning, the character of the organism to a greater or lesser extent.

Since the patient has had no choice in becoming what he is, it is incongruous to blame him for having gone awry, or to disparage him for maintaining his unhappy state. . . . The behavior therapist schools the patient to realize that his unpleasant reactions are due to emotional habits that he cannot help; that they have nothing to do with moral fibre or an unwillingness to get well; that similar reactions are easily induced in animals, who remain neurotic for just as long as the experimenter chooses. . . . So the overcoming of a human neurosis is within the control of the therapist through techniques quite similar to those used in the laboratory.[7]

The goal of the behavior therapist, then, is to modify the behavior of the client; that is, the goal is to change what the client does. The methods of behavior therapy were developed in the laboratory by experimental psychologists and are based on simple principles of learning. With these methods the therapist helps the client unlearn old habits that are maladaptive and learn new habits that work better.

Desensitization

One technique of behavior therapy is called **desensitization.** The fear of snakes can be desensitized by repeatedly exposing clients to snakes in a special set of circumstances. Clients are first taught how to relax; they then relax as they are exposed to snakes in a mild and nonthreatening way. For example, clients may relax as they *imagine* a small garter snake enclosed in a glass jar across the room. According to the theory on which desensitization is based, these repetitive exposures cause the *fear* response to snakes to be replaced by a *relaxation* response to snakes. Thus, an old emotional habit is unlearned and a new emotional habit is learned.

The desensitization technique requires the construction of an **anxiety hierarchy**—a list of anxiety-provoking situations, ranging from some that are only mildly fearful to those that are extremely fearful. The client tries to imagine the scenes on the list. A person with a strong fear of snakes, for example, might be asked to imagine looking at a child's drawing of a snake on the wall across the room. If the individual is able to imagine this scene while remaining relaxed, another scene would be suggested, this one somewhat more anxiety-provoking. Remaining deeply relaxed while imagining a graded series of such situations, the individual is able to imagine more and more frightening scenes, without panic. After considerable practice with the imagined scenes, the individual is typically able to encounter real-life situations involving the feared object and remain calm. A desensitization hierarchy for persons with a fear of snakes might resemble this one:

1. You are looking at a child's drawing of a snake, pinned up on the wall across the room.
2. You are looking at a picture of a snake in a magazine.
3. You are looking at a dead garden snake in a jar.
4. You are looking at a live garden snake in a jar across the room.
5. You are looking at a live garden snake in a jar on

the table in front of you.

6. You are looking at a garden snake on the lawn twenty feet away.

7. You are looking at a garden snake on the lawn ten feet away.

8. You are watching me touch the tail of a small garden snake.

9. You are watching me pick up a small garden snake.

10. You are looking at a small garden snake near your feet.

11. You touch the tail of a small garden snake.

12. You pick up a small garden snake.

13. You pick up a large, but harmless, king snake.

Cognitive Restructuring

A second technique of behavior therapy is cognitive restructuring. **Cognitive restructuring** involves attempts to modify the thoughts that people have in different situations, the assumptions that underlie these thoughts, and the way in which people "talk to themselves." These thoughts and self-statements are regarded as behaviors just as other things that people may do. What distinguishes these behaviors from others is that they are cognitive (mental) behaviors. Some of your cognitive behaviors interfere with your ability to reach your goals and to do what you want to do. The aim of cognitive restructuring is to modify these cognitive behaviors.

What you say or think to yourself affects your performance. For example, students who are highly anxious about tests and students who are more relaxed about tests say different things to themselves during examinations. Students who are anxious about tests tend to make statements to themselves that are negative, depressing, or irrelevant to the task. Students who are more relaxed about exams tend to make more positive statements to themselves during tests.

Consider the situation in which other students hand in their exams early. For the high test-anxious individual this event elicits worrying-type self-statements, namely, "I

can't get this problem. I'll never finish—how can that guy be done?" etc. The result is an increase in anxiety and further task-irrelevant and self-defeating thoughts. In comparison, the low test-anxious student readily dismisses the other student's performance by saying to himself, "That guy who handed in his paper early must know nothing. I hope they score this exam on a curve."[8]

The method used to modify negative self-statements and replace them with positive self-statements involves five steps. The first step is to increase the client's awareness of the negative self-statements that he or she is making. The second step requires the client to monitor negative self-statements whenever they occur. The third step involves showing the client how these negative thoughts and self-statements interfere with performance. The fourth step is to develop more positive self-statements that are appropriate in different situations. And the final step is to rehearse these positive self-statements so that they will be more likely to occur than the negative self-statements.

A recent study compared desensitization and cognitive restructuring as treatments for test anxiety among college students.[9] Cognitive restructuring proved to be the more effective treatment method.

What are your thoughts or self-statements when you have to take an important exam? Do these statements tend to be task-oriented and positive or task-irrelevant and negative? The checklist on page 436 presents some common thoughts other students have reported. Check the ones that resemble thoughts you commonly have during exams.

The procedures of behavior therapy seem to be highly effective for certain kinds of psychological problems. Behavior therapy is often very brief and is therefore available to more people than is psychoanalysis. Many psychologists, however, believe that the course of psychological growth consists not in the acquisition of better habits (a change in doing), but rather in an evolution of consciousness (a change in being). This point of view is reflected in the third type of therapy presented here.

	Negative Thoughts	Positive Thoughts
Before the Big Exam	☐ I will never pass.	☐ I don't have to be perfect.
	☐ I'm going to panic as usual.	☐ Worrying won't help anything.
	☐ If only I could get out of it.	☐ Try not to take this too seriously.
	☐ There's far too much to learn before the test.	☐ I can manage the situation.
	☐ Why didn't I study more?	☐ Easy does it—it's only a test.
During the Big Exam	☐ Everyone else is working faster than I am.	☐ Don't think about the others—focus on the test.
	☐ I am just plain stupid.	☐ I don't need to prove myself.
	☐ People will notice my hands trembling.	☐ Just take one step at a time.
	☐ My mind is a total blank.	☐ I'm feeling tense—time to relax.
	☐ I can't think straight.	☐ Relax—you're in control—take a deep breath.
	☐ I might as well give up—what's the use?	☐ Getting upset won't help.
	☐ Other students are turning in their tests already.	☐ Use the time that's left—focus on the test.
After the Big Exam	☐ I knew I would blow it.	☐ I knew I could get through it.
	☐ I'm going to flunk out.	☐ It could have been a lot worse.
	☐ There's something wrong with my mind.	☐ I handled it pretty well.
	☐ I don't belong in college.	☐ Good—I did it.
	☐ What will my parents say?	☐ I may not be the best, but I'm not the worst either.

Interim Summary   Behavior therapy focuses on the symptoms of problems, not on possible underlying causes. The goal of the behavior therapist is to modify the unwanted behavior and emotional reactions of the client, to replace maladaptive habits and reactions with new habits and reactions that work better. Two methods used by behavior therapists are desensitization, a technique for reducing excessive fears, and cognitive restructuring, a technique for modifying negative and interfering thoughts.

Client-Centered Therapy

Carl Rogers, an American psychologist born in 1902, developed a theory of psychotherapy that has been quite influential in shaping the direction of modern psychotherapy. Unlike Freud, who began his career as a medical doctor, Rogers began as a psychology teacher and director of a college counseling center. This difference in the backgrounds of Freud and Rogers helps to explain the differences in their theories.

Nondirective Therapy

Rogers's approach to therapy is called **client-centered therapy**. The psychoanalysts refer to the people who come to them for help as "patients," while the client-centered therapists refer to those who come to them for help as "clients." This difference is more than just a difference in words. The term "patient" is consistent with the idea of someone who is *ill* coming to an *expert* for a *cure*. This idea reflects the attitudes of psychoanalysis, but not of client-centered therapy. The term "client" is consistent with the idea of someone who is *healthy* coming to a person who is an *equal* in order to obtain a professional service. This idea reflects the attitudes of client-centered therapy. The method is called *client-centered* because the client determines the whole course of the treatment. The method is described as **nondirective therapy** because the therapist does not tell the client what to do, does

In most forms of psychotherapy, the therapist and the client sit down together and explore the nature of the problem in a direct way. (Jean-Claude Lejeune)

not offer advice, and does not explain or interpret the reasons for the client's feelings.

According to client-centered therapy, the person in therapy (the client) has a drive toward health, has an innate tendency to grow and to actualize his or her own potential, and is innately good. The client will grow in a positive direction if the right circumstances are available. The goal of the therapist is to create the conditions necessary for growth, but the therapist is not responsible for making the client change or improve. The therapist may facilitate positive change, but clients are responsible for changing themselves. The therapist attempts to release the forces for growth by creating a special kind of therapeutic relationship with the client. This relationship is the key to the conditions necessary for growth.

The Special Relationship

Carl Rogers believed that positive growth spontaneously occurred within the context of a warm and accepting relationship. This special relationship is defined by the following conditions, each of which is necessary for positive changes in the personality:

1. **Unconditional positive regard** The client-centered therapist should convey uncritical acceptance, warmth, respect, and liking. The idea of unconditional acceptance means that the therapist accepts the client as a person and as a valuable human being regardless of what the client has done or says or feels. The therapist does not reject or judge the client but displays warmth and acceptance.
2. **Empathy** The client-centered therapist has a sensitive understanding of how the client feels. Empathy is the ability to understand how another person feels, from the "inside" as if you *were* the other person. The desire and the ability to understand accurately how someone else sees the world and feels about it are important characteristics of the client-centered therapist.
3. **Congruence** The client-centered therapist is *gen-*

uine—there is no contradiction between feelings, language, and action. You are congruent if you are aware of and accept your own feelings and can express these feelings appropriately in words and behavior. A person who is congruent is regarded as honest, open, and trustworthy.

In addition to creating a special relationship with the client, the client-centered therapist uses certain techniques for facilitating the client's growth. These techniques involve ways of communicating warmth and acceptance, and ways of clarifying the experiences and feelings of the client. One of the ways that the therapist attempts to clarify how the client feels is with the technique called **reflection.** Reflection involves restating what the client has just said—not with a parrot-like echo, but with a summary that expresses the emotional significance of what the client has said. The following case shows the use of reflection in an exchange that occurred during a course of therapy.

Mrs. Teral was a twenty-three-year-old married woman who came to the counseling center for help.[10] She described a number of problems, including excessive sleeping, feelings of worthlessness, and concern about her personal identity. At one point in therapy, she suddenly had a pained and stricken look.

Therapist: What . . . what's hitting you now?
Client: I don't know.
Therapist: Something upsetting, something that makes you feel like crying?
Client: (Pause; crying softly) I could use a little more self-control, too.
Therapist: You don't like to have to cry.
Client: No, I don't. (Pause). And I don't know why, either. I just got very upset (still crying).

Therapist: Um-hm. Something just came over you and you really don't know what started it.
Client: (long pause; still crying) I must have been getting a little too close to something—I didn't want to talk about, or something. . . . Something hit me.
Therapist: Hm?
Client: Something hit me.
Therapist: Something hurts.
Client: (Long pause). I'm not very. . . . I'm upset, 'cause I said something about being dependent on [my husband]. Maybe I just didn't want to start talking about that. That could be it.
Therapist: Maybe that's kind of a tender spot.

Within a therapeutic relationship marked by congruence, empathy, and unconditional positive regard, clients gradually become more aware of how they feel and become better able to accept their own feelings and experiences. Clients become aware of feelings which they had previously denied and rejected. They come to accept those parts of themselves and their experiences that they had previously disowned. In this way, the conflict between experience and self is reduced, and the processes of natural growth are restored.

Client-centered therapy is different from psychoanalysis in a number of ways. Client-centered therapy focuses on health and is oriented toward positive growth, while psychoanalysis is focused on illness and is concerned with curing "sickness." Client-centered therapy focuses on the present feelings of clients, while psychoanalysis focuses on early childhood experiences. Client-centered therapy assumes that our natural impulses are constructive and positive, while psychoanalysis assumes that our natural impulses are destructive and must be controlled.

Interim Summary   Client-centered therapy strives to establish, through the client-therapist relationship, a set of conditions viewed as necessary for the client's positive growth. These conditions are unconditional positive regard, empathy, and congruence. The therapist is supportive of the client and attempts to clarify how the client feels by using a technique called reflection. A major goal of client-centered therapy is for clients to become more aware of how they feel and more accepting of their own feelings and experiences.

Group Therapies

Psychoanalysis, behavior therapy, and client-centered therapy typically involve only two people—a therapist and a client. In contrast, **group therapy** is a form of psychotherapy involving a therapist and eight to twelve clients meeting together. Many personal problems stem from difficulties in communicating and relating to other people; individuals in group therapy have the opportunity to work with these problems by relating to each other.

One form of group therapy is the **encounter group** (sometimes called a sensitivity group or a T-group). The general purpose of encounter groups is to increase sensitivity to yourself and to others. The specific goals of these groups include increasing your awareness of your own feelings and the feelings of others, increasing your ability to understand other people and to communicate with them, becoming more authentic in the presentation of yourself to others, and developing openness and trust in interpersonal relations.[11]

The methods used by encounter groups are based on the assumption that openness in emotional expression broadens and deepens your experience of yourself. Attention is focused continually on current experiences. The discussion of feelings and memories of the past and the possible historical roots of present difficulties is discouraged. Dialogue is maintained at a level of feeling, not fact. Constant feedback is provided. This feedback is most often accepting and warm, so that a feeling of trust and togetherness develops in which masks and pretense can be dropped.[12] The openness that is achieved during the group session may not carry over into everyday life. The impersonal atmosphere of the school, factory, or office often does not support openness and trust.

The experience of the encounter group session is often deep and intense. Members may be profoundly moved and occasionally wind up weeping or hugging each other, or both at once. The effect can also be harmful to unstable participants when it is not guided by someone who is experienced.[13] Most often, how-

ever, participants leave the group with a feeling of joy.

A second type of group psychotherapy is **Gestalt therapy.** Founded by the late Fritz Perls, Gestalt therapy focuses on the "here and now" of experience. Awareness of body and behavior is often blocked by distortion and insensitivity; the Gestalt therapist strives to remove these blocks in the group sessions. One technique is to ask the group members to focus their attention on different parts of their bodies. The Gestalt approach emphasizes the value of spontaneity, sensory awareness, emotional responsiveness, and closeness and flexibility in relating to others.

According to one author, Gestalt therapy recommends that people follow a number of rules in living their lives.[14] These general principles of healthy behavior are:

1. Live now. Be concerned with the present rather than with past or future.
2. Live here. Deal with what is present rather than with what is absent.
3. Stop imagining. Experience the real.
4. Stop unnecessary thinking. Rather, taste and see.
5. Express rather than manipulate, explain, justify, or judge.
6. Give in to unpleasantness and pain just as to pleasure. Do not restrict your awareness.
7. Accept no *should* or *ought* other than your own.
8. Take full responsibility for your actions, feelings, and thoughts.
9. Surrender to being as you are.

One of the ways that Gestalt therapists help their clients "live in the here and now" is to focus their attention on what they are doing, at the present time, that they might be unaware of. In the following example a therapist acts as a kind of mirror, allowing the client to become more aware of his automatic patterns of behavior:

Client: I don't know what to say now. . .
Therapist: I notice that you are looking away from me.
Client: (Giggle)

Therapist: And now you cover up your face.

Client: You make me feel so awful!

Therapist: And now you cover up your face with both hands.

Client: Stop! This is unbearable!

Therapist: What do you feel now?

Client: I feel so embarrassed! Don't look at me!

Therapist: Please stay with that embarrassment.

Client: I have been living with it all my life! I am ashamed of everything I do! It is as if I don't even feel that I have the right to exist![14]

A third type of group psychotherapy is **transactional analysis,** or **TA.** According to transactional analysis, the personality has three parts, or "ego states"; these parts are called "Parent," "Adult," and "Child." Your "Parent" represents your perception of how your parents acted when you were a child. You can get in touch with your inner "Parent" by thinking now of something your parents told you when you were young that you still obey or fight against. Your "Adult" represents your capacity for objectively and realistically dealing with the world; you are at this moment (I hope) in your "Adult" state. Your "Child" is that part of your personality that thinks, feels, and acts as you did when you were a child.

According to transactional analysis, interpersonal relationships involve transactions between one part of your personality and one part of someone else's. For example, sometimes your relationships involve "Adult-Adult" transactions and sometimes "Child-Parent" transactions. By getting to know the parts of your personality and by analyzing your transactions with other people, you can become more aware of how you relate to people and can explore new ways of relating.

Interim Summary   Three types of group therapies are encounter groups, aimed at increasing sensitivity to yourself and others; Gestalt therapy, aimed at focusing attention on "here-and-now" experiences; and transactional analysis, aimed at analyzing and clarifying interpersonal relationships. One of the benefits of group therapy is that clients have the opportunity to work on difficulties in relating to and communicating with other people.

Biological Therapies

Not all methods of treating psychological disorders have a psychological basis. Some have a biological basis and are concerned with altering the chemistry or structure of the body in order to effect a cure. One of the oldest biological methods of treating mental problems is **psychosurgery,** or surgery done on the brain in order to cause an improvement in psychological condition.

The Greeks and Romans used a method of psychosurgery called **trephination,** an operation that makes an opening in the skull in order to permit "poisons" to run out. The Greeks believed that mental problems were caused by certain vapors in the brain, which trephining the skull would allow to escape. There is no reason to believe that this operation had any effect whatsoever on psychological problems.

A more modern form of psychosurgery is the operation called **prefrontal lobotomy.** The operation involves cutting the neural connections between the frontal lobes of the brain and a certain lower brain structure called the thalamus. Although used fairly commonly before the 1950s, the operation is used only rarely at the present time. It is still used occasionally as a treatment of last resort for severe depression. Two more common biological treatments of psychological disorders today are electroconvulsive therapy and chemotherapy.

Electroconvulsive Therapy

One form of biological treatment involves passing an electric current through the brain. **Electroconvulsive therapy (ECT)** was developed in the late 1930s as a method of artificially inducing convulsions in mental patients. It was believed that convulsions would somehow bring about an improvement in their psychological disorders.

In the ECT treatment, a patient is first given an injection of Pentothal or some other muscle relaxant. Then a brief (one-tenth of a second to one second) burst of current of 70 to 130 volts is passed through the patient's brain. The electric shock produces unconsciousness and convulsions.

ECT is used primarily in cases of severe, psychotic depression. A standard treatment involving six to ten shock sessions over two to three weeks typically brings about a significant improvement in the depressive symptoms. A side effect of ECT is memory loss, but this usually disappears within a month. Since ECT works so quickly in relieving depression, it is one of the treatments used in treating severely depressed individuals who have threatened suicide.

One man who was treated with electroconvulsive therapy wrote an article describing what it was like:

The next morning at six o'clock I was told to stay in bed. There would be no breakfast this morning, because I was getting shock treatment. I already knew quite a bit about shock treatment. I had helped them give it to other patients many times. . . . Now it was my turn. I climbed up on the high wagon and stretched out. Three sand bags in the form of a pyramid stuck into the small of my back to expand my chest. . . . I was mighty scared and there was no use kidding about it. Mac held my right arm and pressed hard with the elbow just inside my shoulder muscle. Sarge had the other arm. Another attendant climbed up on the wagon and lay across my knees gripping the side of the wagon with hands and toes. The three attendants would hold me down during my convulsion. The theory was: The more severe the convulsion, the better the results.

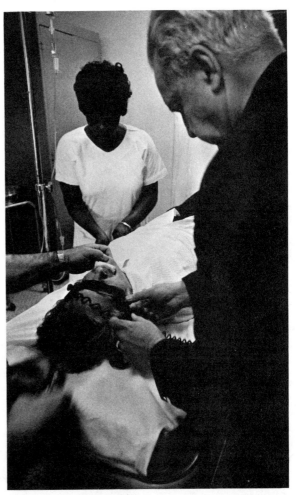

Electroconvulsive therapy (ECT) involves passing an electric current through the brain in order to produce convulsions. ECT, used in treating severe depression, has certain unpleasant side effects, such as the loss of memory. (Paul Fusco/Magnum Photos, Inc.)

I heard the doctor give the pretty blonde nurse a set of numbers, and I knew that she was setting dials. "God, don't let her give me an overdose." . . . Very deliberately, very slowly a black shade came up over my eyes. I woke up sometime later feeling completely refreshed, not tired or logy, or drugged with sleep, just ready for a big day.[15]

Why is ECT effective in treating severe depression? Although there is evidence that ECT works,[16] no one has yet established why it works. One theory argues that ECT alters brain chemistry, and there is evidence that electric shock causes the brain to increase its production of neurotransmitter chemicals, the chemicals used for communication within the brain.[17] At this point, however, there is no convincing evidence showing why ECT has the effect it does.

Chemotherapy

A second form of biological treatment for psychological disorders is **chemotherapy,** or drug treatment. Chemotherapy is the most commonly used form of biological treatment, far more commonly used than ECT.

The most common symptom of neurosis is a high level of anxiety. One means of treating anxiety is with chemotherapy, by administering a drug called a **minor tranquilizer.** Examples of minor tranquilizers are Valium, Miltown, and Librium. These drugs, taken in the form of pills, have the effect of relieving tension, producing muscular relaxation, and reducing fear and anxiety. A side effect of these drugs is drowsiness, which can sometimes be a problem during the daytime. If minor tranquilizers are used for a long time, suddenly stopping their use may produce withdrawal symptoms. So they are not a permanent solution to the problems of anxiety.

The most common form of psychosis is schizophrenia, a disorder in which the mind is withdrawn from reality. The most effective treatment of schizophrenia is chemotherapy—administering a drug called a **major tranquilizer.** One type of major tranquilizer is chlorpromazine, or Thorazine. First developed in the 1950s, the major tranquilizers have dramatically changed the rate of improvement in schizophrenia. These drugs have made a significant contribution to reducing the number of people who must stay in mental hospitals. The major tranquilizers enable many individuals who are diagnosed as schizophrenic to return to their families and school or work, and to lead reasonably normal lives.

Depression is also commonly treated by chemotherapy. A number of different drugs have proved to be effective in treating depression. The drug group that is most effective, with the least harmful side effects, appears to be the **tricyclic antidepressants.** Examples of these drugs are Elavil and Tofranil. These drugs apparently work by increasing the activity level of the brain by making more neurotransmitter chemical available for communication among brain cells.

Interim Summary   Three forms of biological treatments are psychosurgery, electroconvulsive therapy, and chemotherapy. An example of psychosurgery is a technique called prefrontal lobotomy, an operation in which the frontal lobes of the brain are cut. Electroconvulsive therapy (ECT) is a "shock treatment" used primarily in cases of severe, psychotic depression. Chemotherapy, or drug treatment, is the most commonly used biological treatment. Minor tranquilizers (for anxiety), major tranquilizers (for schizophrenia), and the tricyclic antidepressants (for depression) are examples of drugs used in chemotherapy.

The Prevalence of Psychological Disorders

Are psychological disorders, like the common cold, to be found nearly everywhere, or are they rare problems displayed by only a few unfortunate individuals? The **prevalence** of these problems (how widespread they are) is difficult to determine for several reasons. One reason is that many people with psychological disorders never seek assistance and therefore may never be identified. A second reason is that there is no clear line separating the normal from the abnormal, so the observed prevalence of a psychological disorder depends upon where the line is drawn. Since the definition of what constitutes abnormal behavior is somewhat hazy, different people come to different conclusions about how common mental disorders are.

Prevalence in the General Population

According to a recent estimate by the National Institute of Mental Health, about 7 million people each year are treated in mental health facilities in this country. Some of these people are treated at the facilities, but do not stay at them; just as you might go to a clinic as an outpatient to be treated for a physical injury or disease, you could also visit a mental health clinic for psychological treatment. Other people may spend time in a mental health facility as a resident, or inpatient—for example, in a psychiatric ward in a hospital.

The number of people who are treated each year for psychological disorders is far fewer than the number believed to suffer from them. Estimates of how many people need some kind of mental health care vary. According to one estimate, about 2 million people are seriously depressed, about 2 million people are or have been schizophrenic, and overall, 20 to 30 million need some kind of psychological treatment.[18]

Some psychological disorders are relatively common, while others are rare. Mild to moderate depression and anxiety are probably among the most widespread problems. Phobias and mild obsessive-compulsive reactions are less common but still fairly widespread. Multiple personality and conversion reactions are rare. Amnesia with a psychological origin is also quite rare.

Prevalence Among College Students

Because of the demands they place on students, colleges and universities are highly stressful environments. Because of the opportunities they offer students, colleges also stimulate growth and personal changes—but these changes often come at the cost of considerable anxiety. It is not surprising, then, that college students experience many psychological problems.

Common problems of students attending the University of Connecticut's Mental Health Service involve interpersonal difficulties (with family, spouse, or opposite-sex friend) and difficulties handling emotions (depression, anxiety, or anger).[19] Problems typical of students attending the University of Chicago's Mental Health Clinic are anxiety, depression, interpersonal difficulties, and feelings of self-doubt and self-blame; in addition, academic concerns are very common.[20] Of course, many students having psychological problems do not take them to a campus mental health clinic or counseling center.

A recent survey of the student population at a large university showed that most student problems are related to study habits and grades, disturbing thoughts, depression, sleep disturbances, and vocational choices.[21] Students also expressed high levels of concern about their feelings of frustration, test anxiety, irrational fears, and thoughts of suicide. However, only 22 percent of students with these serious problems brought them to one of the campus agencies concerned with providing psychological services. In this study, 38 percent of the student body indicated that they had three or more psychological problems and 29 percent indicated that their problems interfered with their functioning.

Choosing a Source of Help

The odds are that either you or someone you know within the next year, will experience a period of severe distress and could benefit from psychological help. But many people are uncomfortable with the idea of asking for help.

Although you might not hesitate to go to a medical doctor to seek relief for a physical problem, you may feel hesitant about going to a psychologist to seek relief for a psychological problem. You may feel that asking for such help is a sign of weakness or would prove that you were "mentally ill." Neither is the case. To ask for help is a sign of strength, not weakness. It takes some level of insight and awareness to recognize that you may need help, and it takes some courage to ask for it. Seeking psychological help is not a sign that you are "mentally ill." By far the majority of people who go to psychologists for help are normal people who are encountering problems of living and are having difficulty coping with these problems.

Do You, or Does Someone You Know, Need Professional Help?

The question of whether someone needs psychotherapy cannot adequately be answered by a book, but part of that answer can be given here. Like people who go to a medical doctor with a physical complaint, people who go to a psychotherapist typically have complaints that make them uncomfortable and that interfere with their ability to function fully in life. Only rarely (as in the case of a potential suicide) are these complaints life-threatening. A psychotherapist is typically consulted not to cure a "mental disease" but to help normal people, who may be experiencing a crisis, grow toward better psychological health. Someone who is experiencing such a crisis could benefit from consulting a psychotherapist.

One measure of the seriousness of a psychologi-cal problem is how much it interferes with a person's ability to live a normal life, relate to people, and work or go to school. Sometimes feelings of depression or anxiety are so intense that just getting through a day is difficult. People who experience such problems may not be able to work effectively or may not be able to make acceptable grades in school. Some of the serious problems for which professional help is desirable are listed below.

- Intense depression, with feelings of worthlessness and suicidal thoughts
- Unwanted intrusive thoughts and frightening, irresistable impulses
- Auditory or visual hallucinations in the absence of drugs
- Recurrent periods of blanking out
- Fears of objects, people, or situations so severe that you alter your life to avoid them
- Prolonged intense anxiety for no apparent reason, accompanied by such physical symptoms as chronic headaches, stomach upsets, or muscular tremors
- Sexual problems that are recurrent, severe, and distressing[22]

Someone experiencing such serious problems should seek the assistance of a psychotherapist.

If you feel that you might benefit fom consulting a psychotherapist but are uncertain about proceeding, you should talk it over with a teacher, a member of the clergy, or your parents. Often other people can help you clarify your feelings and can support you in times of crisis. Because you are so close to your problem, you may not be able to see it objectively; someone else, who is a good listener, may be able to help.

Types of Mental Health Professionals

If you decide that you want psychotherapy, whom should you see? There are several types of psychotherapists. A **clinical psychologist** has a postgraduate academic degree, an MA or a Ph.D. in psychology, plus specialized training in personality theory, mental testing, psychological research, and therapeutic techniques. A clinical psychologist does not have a medical degree and cannot administer drugs.

A **psychiatrist** is a licensed physician who in addition to regular medical training took a residency in psychiatry. Besides being qualified in verbal psychotherapy, the psychiatrist can administer drugs and other medical therapy.

A **counselor** is a person who has a graduate degree in counseling from a department of education or psychology. Like the clinical psychologist, the counselor is trained in testing and therapy. In addition, a counselor may have special training in vocational and career counseling, in the special problems of school children, or in rehabilitation. A counselor does not have a medical degree and cannot administer drugs.

A **clinical social worker** is a person with a degree in social work who has additional training in abnormal psychology and therapy. Some clinical social workers provide psychotherapy, while others work in hospital settings helping those who are admitted for psychological problems to adjust to the hospital and, upon release, to the home and community.

A **psychoanalyst** is a psychotherapist, usually a medical doctor, who has had extensive psychoanalytic training. Psychoanalysis is a particular theory of therapy that assumes that personality problems arise from unconscious conflicts.

College Counseling and Mental Health Services

Many colleges provide sources of psychological assistance on campus, in the form of a "student mental health service," a "psychiatric clinic," "counseling center," or a "student development center." Those colleges that do not provide such student services typically have established contacts with sources of help off campus to which students can be referred.

Student counseling centers are typically staffed by clinical psychologists, counseling psychologists, and graduate students in psychology and education. Many counseling services offer individual psychotherapy as well as groups dealing with relationship problems, eating management, and other issues of concern to college students. Student mental health services or psychiatric clinics are typically staffed by psychiatrists, clinical psychologists, and clinical social workers. Most mental health services offer psychotherapy as well as, when appropriate, chemotherapy in the form of tranquilizers or antidepressant drugs.

Who uses such campus services, and what happens to them? A large proportion of students go to

Meeting with a counselor one on one or with a group that has a particular problem in common, as these people are doing, has enabled many students to resolve their problem and return to concentrating on completing their education. (© *Alex Webb/Magnum Photos, Inc.*)

these services for assistance. The average usage rate of college counseling centers has recently been estimated at 10 to 15 percent of the student body per year.[23] In one university, 25 percent of the student body is seen one or more times during their four years on campus.[24] Studies suggest that students who use such campus services do not differ in scholastic ability from those who do not use such services.[25,26] However, students who use these services are less likely to leave school due to a low grade point average and are more likely to graduate in four years.[26] Thus, college students receiving psychological help seem to perform better academically; the problems that were interfering with their ability to study and take exams have been reduced.

Campus counseling and mental health services are staffed by professionals whose training and experience prepare them for understanding the special problems of college students and for offering effective assistance and treatment. Therefore, for students experiencing psychological problems, these services can be especially helpful.

Interim Summary   Estimates of the prevalence of psychological disorders vary, but up to 20 or 30 million people may need some kind of psychological treatment. Because colleges and universities are highly stressful environments, college students commonly experience many psychological problems. Often a friend, teacher, or parents can be helpful at times of stress. Anyone who experiences severe problems (such as intense depression with suicidal thoughts) should seek professional help without delay. Many colleges have counseling centers or student mental health centers, which provide assistance to students who have psychological problems.

Summary

1. Psychotherapy involves the treatment of psychological problems by specially trained professionals using psychological techniques. It is aimed at helping people overcome obstacles to their personal growth and helping them acquire more effective means of coping with stresses and problems.

2. At one time people with psychological disorders were regarded as possessed by demons or devils and were tortured and beaten to drive off the "evil spirits." Phillipe Pinel and Dorothea Dix, however, helped establish more humane treatment conditions in the 1800s.

3. One of the newest developments in the treatment of psychological disorders is the community mental health movement, which is concerned with preventive and outreach activities aimed at improving the condition of the whole community.

4. Psychoanalysis, an intensive method of psychotherapy developed by Freud, assumes that psychological disorders result from unconscious conflicts arising from early childhood experiences. The primary goal of psychoanalysis is to make unconscious material conscious so that such conflicts can be dealt with.

5. Free association, in which the client is told to say anything that comes to mind, and dream analysis, in which the psychoanalyst interprets the hidden meaning of dreams, are two methods used in psychoanalysis to get at unconscious material.

6. Behavior therapy is a form of psychotherapy that focuses on the symptoms, not the

possible underlying causes, of psychological problems.   The goal of the behavior therapist is to modify the behavior of the client by changing the client's habitual ways of reacting.

7. Desensitization, a method of progressively reducing fear, and cognitive restructuring, a method of changing negative thoughts, are two techniques used by behavior therapists to modify behavior.

8. Client-centered therapy, a nondirective therapy developed by Carl Rogers, assumes that personality growth will occur best within the context of a relationship marked by unconditional positive regard, empathy, and congruence.   A goal of client-centered therapy is to help clients become more aware of how they feel and more accepting of their own feelings and experiences.

9. Encounter groups, Gestalt therapy, and transactional analysis are three common types of group therapy.

10. Psychosurgery, involving a brain operation, is a treatment method that is not commonly used today but was relatively common a few decades ago.   Electroconvulsive therapy (ECT) is a shock treatment used for certain patients with severe psychotic depression.   Chemotherapy, the most commonly used biological treatment, involves administering drugs to treat psychological disorders.

11. Millions of people experience psychological problems severe enough to benefit from psychotherapy.   Mild to moderate depression and anxiety are probably the most common problems, especially among college students.

12. Clinical psychologists, counselors, clinical social workers, psychoanalysts, and psychiatrists are different types of professionals who provide mental health care.   Only the psychiatrist is licensed to prescribe drugs.   College counseling centers and mental health centers are staffed by professionals especially trained to understand the problems of college students.

Key Concepts

therapy   A treatment designed to bring about an improvement in some condition.

psychotherapy   A special kind of treatment provided by a trained professional and based in psychological techniques; aimed at assisting people to overcome their problems and to grow.

community mental health   An approach to psychological treatment that is concerned with preventive and outreach activities aimed at improving the psychological welfare of the entire community.

psychoanalysis   The method of psychotherapy developed by Freud; its major aim is to make unconscious material conscious.

unconscious motivation   Needs and impulses that have been repressed so that a person is unaware of them.

early determinism   The view that adult personality is determined by early childhood experiences.

free association   The procedure of saying anything that comes to mind, without censorship.

dream analysis   The technique of analyzing and interpreting dreams in order to reveal unconscious material.

manifest content   The events of dreams as they are experienced.

latent content   The "true" meaning of a

dream, as revealed by dream analysis.

behavior therapy   A form of psychotherapy, based on principles of learning, that focuses on the symptoms of a psychological problem, not the underlying causes.

desensitization   A technique for reducing fear by pairing relaxation with the feared situations.

anxiety hierarchy   An arrangement of feared situations, ranked from the least to the most threatening.

cognitive restructuring   The technique for modifying the negative thoughts that people have in different situations, the way in which people "talk to themselves."

client-centered therapy   The method of therapy developed by Rogers; its goal is to help clients become more aware of how they feel and more accepting of their own feelings and experience.

nondirective therapy   A method of therapy in which the client, and not the therapist, determines the course of the treatment.

unconditional positive regard   Uncritical acceptance of another person as a valuable human being, regardless of what that person has done or says or feels.

empathy   The ability to understand how another person feels; the ability to place yourself "in someone else's shoes."

congruence   The condition of agreement between one's feelings and expressed behavior; the quality of genuineness, honesty, openness.

reflection   A technique for clarifying the client's feelings; restatement of what the client has just said in summary form.

group therapy   Psychotherapy conducted with a group of eight to twelve people at once.

encounter group   A group psychotherapy that focuses on sensitivity and awareness of feelings, authentic communication, and interpersonal trust.

Gestalt therapy   The method of psychotherapy developed by Fritz Perls; a group psychotherapy that focuses on sensory awareness, body awareness, and "here-and-now" experience.

transactional analysis (TA)   A group psychotherapy that assumes the personality to have three parts—"Parent," "Adult," and "Child"; transactions with other people are analyzed in terms of these three parts of the personality.

psychosurgery   A biological treatment of mental problems that involves surgery on the brain.

trephination   A method of psychosurgery used by the Greeks and Romans that involved opening the skull to let "poisons" escape.

prefrontal lobotomy   A more modern form of psychosurgery that involves severing the neural connections between the frontal lobes of the brain and the thalamus.

electroconvulsive therapy (ECT)   A biological treatment of mental problems that involves passing an electric current through the brain; used primarily in cases of severe, psychotic depression.

chemotherapy   A biological treatment of mental problems that involves drugs such as tranquilizers and antidepressants.

minor tranquilizer   A drug, such as Valium, that is prescribed in the treatment of anxiety.

major tranquilizer   A drug, such as Thorazine, that is prescribed in the treatment of schizophrenia.

tricyclic antidepressants   Drugs, such as Elavil, that are prescribed in the treatment of depression.

prevalence   Frequency of occurrence.

clinical psychologist   A psychologist who specializes in treating personality disorders and providing therapy; typically has a Ph.D. degree with training in testing and research.

psychiatrist   A medical doctor trained in the treatment of personality disorder and licensed to prescribe drugs; has MD degree.

counselor   A psychologist who specializes in giving advice and guidance; usually has a graduate degree in psychology or education.

clinical social worker   A person with a degree in social work who has additional training in abnormal psychology and therapy.

psychoanalyst   A psychotherapist with extensive training in psychoanalysis.

Part VIII

Social Psychology

Chapter 22

Social Behavior

The following is from an interview with a twelve-year-old girl:

A. I like Superman better than the others because they can't do everything Superman can do. Batman can't fly and this is very important.
Q. Would you like to be able to fly?
A. I would like to be able to fly if everybody else did, but otherwise it would be kind of conspicuous.[1]

Being conspicuous used to be a lot easier. "Rugged individualism" (being self-sufficient) was at one time an important social value, but it has now been somewhat replaced by "togetherness." David Riesman has argued that Americans of past generations were more **inner-directed**—making decisions on the basis of their own personal, internalized values—whereas present-day Americans are more **other-directed**—depending upon the opinion of others to tell them what is right and wrong.[2] According to Riesman, the children of an earlier era were trained for independence, whereas modern children are trained for conformity.

Whether we tend to be relatively conforming or relatively independent, other people are extremely important. Nothing could be so reinforcing—or so punishing—as another person and what that person says and does. We are social creatures who grow up and live within a social environment. The field of psychology that is especially concerned with this fact is **social psychology**, the study of how individual behavior is affected by the presence of others.

Social psychologists are concerned with the effects of being isolated or being crowded, with the way people in groups behave, with the effects of group pressure, and with the way we see and judge other people. Social psychologists are also concerned with social problems like prejudice, crime, and aggression.

Social Perception and Attribution

The influence that other people have on our behavior depends to a degree on our perception of them. What do we notice first? Hair color, skin color, height, sex, dress style, or what? We make judgments and assumptions about the actions of others. We notice certain things and we fail to notice others. What is there about other people that first impresses us?

Impression Formation

Whenever we see other people, we form impressions of them. We make judgments about their character, intelligence, and honesty on the basis of very limited information. These impressions govern the way we behave toward other people. We tend to make snap judgments and then act accordingly. Have you ever made a snap judgment about someone and then later changed your mind?

Social judgments are often affected by our tendency to generalize from some limited piece of information to an impression of the personality as a whole. The tendency to see a person as desirable in all ways because that person has one desirable trait is called the **halo effect.** The halo effect distorts our judgments of others. When we judge a physically attractive person to be also witty, creative, and intelligent (before even hearing the person talk), we are displaying the halo effect.

Social judgments are also affected by the order in which we discover information about others. Do our first impressions dominate later impressions, or are the most recent impressions the most influential in shaping our perception of people? Judgments controlled by first impressions are said to conform to the **primacy effect.** Judgments controlled by the last or most recent impressions are said to conform to the **recency effect.** Which effect best describes the way in which we form impressions of other people? In general, research on impression formation supports the validity of the primacy effect.

In an experiment by Asch,[3] two groups of students were presented with lists of adjectives describing an imaginary person and were then asked to report their overall impressions of the person. One group was given a list of adjectives beginning with positive ones and ending with negative ones: "intelligent," "industrious," "impulsive," "critical," "stubborn," and "envious." The second group was given the same traits, but in a reverse order, from the more negative to the more positive. When the overall impressions of the two groups were compared, it was found that the primacy effect had predominated—the group's impressions tended to be based on whichever adjectives came first in the list.

Attribution Theory

As we perceive other people, we are concerned not only with forming impressions of their personalities but also with deciding why they act the way they do. The process of deciding what causes some behavior or what motivates people to act the way they do is called *attribution,* and the theory concerned with this process is called **attribution theory.** Attribution theory explains the rules we use in drawing conclusions about the causes of behavior.

You observe the behavior of your friends, and you wonder why they act the way they do. Someone was supposed to call but did not. Was it because he or she forgot, or was it a deliberate snub? One day while you are in the hall outside of class, John bumps into you rather roughly. Was it on purpose, or was it an accident?

In our concern with why people act the way they do, we typically attribute behavior to either internal causes or external causes. To attribute behavior to an internal cause is to explain it in terms of some personal disposition or characteristic. For example, why did John bump into you? You may attribute John's roughness to his meanness or hostility, thus explaining his behavior by referring to internal causes. To attribute behavior to an external cause is to explain it in terms of some aspect of the circumstances or situation. For example, you may attribute John's behavior to the rush and general confusion in the hall, an external cause. How you act toward John depends on whether you attribute his behavior to internal or external causes. If you believe that he intended to bump you (the act had an internal cause), then you may respond in kind—by bumping him back.

How are such attributions made? The evidence suggests that we follow three rules in deciding whether behavior had an internal or an external cause. The **consensus rule** states that we tend to attribute a behavior to external causes if other people in the same situation tend to act the same way. (The term *consensus* means that everybody believes or acts the same way.) For example, according to the consensus rule, you would be more likely to attribute John's bumping to external causes (situational forces) if many other people were also bumping into each other in that situation. The **inconsistency rule** states that we tend to attribute a behavior to external causes if the individual only occasionally shows that behavior in that situation. In other words, if John always bumps into you in the hall, you are likely to think he is doing it on purpose, while if he only occasionally does so, you are more likely to think that it was an accident resulting from the circumstances. The **distinctiveness rule** states that we tend to attribute a behavior to external causes if the individual performs the behavior only in one situation and not in others. If the behavior is unique to a specific situation, then you will be more likely to believe that it was a result of situational forces, instead of being a result of the person's character. If John bumps into you in the crowded hall but not in the dining room or yard or anywhere else, then you will probably attribute his behavior to external, situational forces, rather than to conscious intent on his part.

We perceive other people, form impressions of them, make judgments about their behavior, and on the basis of these judgments, respond to them. Understanding these interactions is important to understanding the behavior of people in groups.

Interim Summary   Social psychology is the study of how individual behavior is affected by the presence of others. One process of interest to social psychologists is how we see and judge others—social perception and attribution. In perceiving and judging others, we seem to be primarily affected by first impressions, or what is called the primacy effect. Attribution theory is concerned with how we decide the causes of behavior. The consensus rule, the inconsistency rule, and the distinctiveness rule describe how we attribute behavior to external causes (such as the circumstances or the situation).

Groups

All of us belong to groups. Your family is a group, your friends are a group, your classmates are a group, and you are a member of other groups as well. Groups offer many rewards but also present numerous difficulties.

How can we live together? The nineteenth-century philosopher Arthur Schopenhauer answered this question with a parable:

A company of porcupines crowded themselves very close together one cold winter's day so to profit by one another's warmth and so save themselves from being frozen to death. But soon they felt one another's quills, which induced them to separate again. And now, when the need for warmth brought them nearer together again, the second evil arose once more. So that they were driven backward and forward from one trouble to the other, until they had discovered a mean distance at which they could most tolerably exist.

The Need for Others

You may not always think so, but other people are more important than anything else in your environment. Sometimes the problem is: How can you live with them? Other times the problem is: How can you live without them? Actually, you haven't much choice. You live in a small world, and the world is full of people. You have to live with them. In fact, studies of human behavior indicate that you *need* to live with them; being able to interact with at least a few people is necessary for your well-being.

Because we are "social animals," we seek companionship. What happens when a person is alone for a prolonged period of time? To study this problem, researchers experimented with monkeys. They found that monkeys raised in social isolation become psychologically abnormal. Compared to their group-raised peers, the socially deprived monkeys do not play and explore their environments; they do not develop normal grooming habits; they do not form social relationships with other monkeys when they have the opportunity; and they do not mate.[4]

Small groups, isolated from other people in remote Antarctic stations, or confined together in prisons or on long sea voyages, report that boredom, apathy, and irritation are common results of the experience.[5,6] Socially isolated groups cannot solve their problems by escaping from each other or by changing from one group to another; they must stay together and live with the tensions that arise. One result is that members of such groups tend to keep a tight lid on their emotions, and they tend to develop more rigid rules for relating. One experimental study of socially isolated pairs of men found that during isolation signs of stress, emotional symptoms, and interpersonal conflicts increased, and task performance decreased.[7]

Group Dynamics

The study of the social interaction within groups is called **group dynamics.** In studying groups, one question that social psychologists have examined is what factors affect group performance. Suppose you had to organize a task force to study a problem, such as drug abuse, and to write a report making specific recommendations for combating the problem. What size and type of group organization would be most efficient and productive?

People have different ideas about the ideal size of a working group. If you were to rely on everyday wisdom, you might apply the old saying, "Too many cooks spoil the broth." But if you were to take this idea too seriously, you might wind up having to do all of the work yourself. Another old saying is that "Two heads are better than one." This suggests that there is something to be gained by joining together in a group.

In fact, the optimum size of the group—the size that would be maximally efficient and productive—depends upon certain characteristics of the task at hand. Certain tasks, those called **parallel coaction tasks,** involve completely separate functions. (The

For tasks requiring cooperation (group interaction tasks), adding group members does not always increase group productivity. (Alan Carey)

term "coaction" means "acting together".) In a parallel coaction task, each person works independently, in parallel. An example of a parallel coaction task is shoveling coal. If each person has a shovel, two people can shovel twice as much as one, and four people can shovel twice as much as two, and so forth. With parallel coaction tasks, the more people in the group, the more work gets done (so long as you don't run out of shovels). Other types of tasks, those called **group interaction tasks,** involve group members interacting, cooperating, and working together. One person does part of the job, and another person does another part. An example of a group interaction task is cleaning house. One person dusts, another sweeps the floor, and a third washes the windows. As long as the group members interact and work cooperatively, larger groups will accomplish more than smaller groups—but there is a diminishing return with adding group members. It is unlikely that twenty people could complete the task in half the time required by ten people. With group interaction tasks, after a point, adding additional group members does not increase group productivity.

The type of group leadership also affects group effectiveness and productivity. Some leaders tend to be all business—they are **task-oriented leaders.**[8] They are concerned with getting the job done as quickly and efficiently as possible. Other leaders are concerned with the emotional climate in the group— they are **social-emotional leaders.** They care about getting the job done but are more concerned with maintaining an atmosphere of good feeling and warmth within the group. If the life of the group is going to be short, as in a task force organized to solve a problem, a task-oriented leader would probably be more effective. However, if the group is going to have to work together for a long time, attention must be given to the social and emotional climate within the group.

The Experiment at Robber's Cave

The formation of groups and the interaction between groups was studied in a classic social psychology experiment by Sherif.[9] Sherif took a number of twelve-year-old boys to an isolated summer camp at Robber's Cave. The boys were divided into two groups and put into two different bunkhouses. Each group was treated separately and given separate group projects to

work on. After a short period of time, the groups named themselves and acquired a sense of belonging and cohesiveness. At this point, the researchers created conflict between the two groups by stimulating competition through games such as tug-of-war. The competition produced considerable hostility between the groups. The boys in one group hated the boys in the other. Each group began to raid the other's bunkhouse and to fight.

At this point the researchers decided to try to reduce the intergroup hostility. Their first attempt involved simply bringing the two groups together by having them eat at the same time and letting them shoot off firecrackers together. But the close contact between the groups did not reduce the bad feelings. It simply provided more opportunities for expressing hostility. The researchers' second attempt to reduce the hostility involved providing them with a third group of boys who served as a common enemy. But that did not work either. Finally, the researchers contrived some tasks that required the two groups to work together in order to achieve common goals. For example, on an overnight trip, the truck that was bringing their food stalled (apparently an accident, but actually on purpose). The boys had to work together to move the truck and get the food. This joint effort and other cooperative tasks dramatically reduced intergroup hostility. The experiment at the Robber's Cave summer camp showed that intergroup conflict, hostility, and fighting can result from competition between groups with separate group identities, and that these attitudes can be reduced by fostering cooperation between groups.

Interim Summary   The study of social interaction within groups is called group dynamics. A question of interest concerning group dynamics is what size and type of group organization are most effective. With parallel coaction tasks (tasks with completely independent functions), the more people in a group, the more work gets done. With group interaction tasks (tasks requiring cooperation) there is a diminishing return in adding new members to a group. If the life of a group is going to be short, task-oriented leaders are better; if not, social-emotional leaders are better. Sherif's experiment at Robber's Cave manipulated group structure to produce either intergroup hostility or cooperation.

Crowding

The population of the world is growing at an alarming rate. By 1850 there were about 1 billion people on earth; eighty years later, in 1930, the population had doubled to 2 billion. At the present rate of increase, the world's population will double about every thirty-seven years. If this rate of increase were to continue for the next nine hundred years, there would be one hundred persons for every square yard of the earth's surface, land or sea.[10] The problem of crowding in the modern world has not approached that degree of severity, but in certain parts of the world today crowding is a serious problem.

What does it mean to be crowded? Crowding can limit your freedom of choice: when the number of people you are in contact with is so great that you are unable to do things you would like to do, then you are experiencing crowding.[11] A few annoying and intrusive people may make you feel more crowded than a greater number of close friends. However, for the purposes of studying the psychological effects of crowding, **crowding** is defined simply in terms of an excessive number of people around you.

In cities there are two ways to think about crowding: (1) a high density of persons in a neighborhood, and (2) a high density of persons in a dwelling.[12] Although an urban ghetto is crowded by either definition, small rural farm dwellings are crowded on the inside while neighborhoods full of luxury apartments are only crowded on the outside—that is, in terms of the density of population in the neighborhood. In either case, the psychological effects of crowding come from human interaction and the consequences of that interaction on behavior and experience.

Crowding and Arousal

As the world becomes more crowded, you encounter more people. You have learned to attend to people:

they are your major sources of pleasure and pain. Encounters with people are personally meaningful and are a powerful source of stimulation.

Every encounter you have with another person tends to increase your level of arousal.[13] Your **arousal level** is your degree of activation. At low levels of arousal you feel drowsy; at very high levels of arousal you feel overstimulated and anxious.

The brain mechanisms involved in this arousal process become highly active under crowded conditions.[14] In animals these parts of the brain show abnormalities as a consequence of high population density.[15] Animals or humans exposed to high arousal levels for extended periods of time show physical and emotional signs of severe stress. You might expect persons living in crowded conditions to attempt to cope with crowding by reducing their arousal level. Alcohol and barbiturates reduce arousal; their use may be one way that people cope with the excessive stimulation and crowding so common in our cities.

Amphetamines excite the brain, increasing arousal levels. If crowding has its psychological effect through increasing arousal, amphetamines plus crowding should have a double effect. The combination of amphetamines and crowding has been studied with animals. The dosage of amphetamine required to produce death from overstimulation in mice is lower for crowded mice; the more the mice are crowded, the less the dosage of amphetamine needed to produce death.[16] Even mild stimulants like caffeine (found in coffee) can overstimulate crowded mice and produce death.[16]

Crowding and Health

Crowding increases arousal level, sometimes to the point of stress. Prolonged stress from overstimulation creates physiological changes in the brain and the body, particularly in the glands in the endocrine system. The endocrine glands (pituitary, adrenal, and thyroid) help regulate metabolism, growth, and sexual development. In animal populations that are crowded over an extended period of time, growth is stunted and the death rate increases. There is some evidence that the rate of heart attack in animals is increased as a result of crowding.[17] These deaths are believed to result from the stress resulting from unavoidable and excessive social interactions.

In any social system individuals develop different amounts of power and status. In a crowded social system individuals high on the social hierarchy have more social space (luxury apartment versus crowded tenement) and are less threatened by social interaction because they have power. In animal populations that are crowded, it is the low-ranking individuals who tend to die off; they are much more affected by the stresses of crowding than are high-ranking individuals.[18]

Crowding stresses have harmful effects on human health and social organization. There is reason to believe that some of the unfortunate effects of concentration camps on human health may have resulted from the crowded conditions that prevailed.

There is indirect evidence that inmates of concentration camps experienced acute forms of the stress syndrome that may have accounted for many deaths. Concentration camps are more appropriately compared with highly congested animal populations than are city slums, since even in very crowded cities, the poor do have some mobility. They can escape from their immediate congestion on streets and associate with other segments of the population. The incidence of street gangs and juvenile delinquency is especially characteristic of overcrowded city areas and constitutes a form of social pathology. Several studies have also indicated a higher incidence of schizophrenia and other psychotic and neurotic behavior in congested urban areas than in more spacious environments, but other factors may be involved here.[19]

In general, the rate of mental disturbance is higher in crowded areas and lower in more sparsely populated areas.[12] There is a decreasing incidence of diagnosed psychosis as you move from the center of a city outward to the suburbs. There is a similar relation between crowding and the rate of suicide; the rate is higher in more densely populated areas. Crowding stresses in the inner city may be responsible for the increase in psychological problems that are observed. There is considerable evidence that some forms of schizophrenia resemble reactions to excessively high arousal; there is some similarity between schizophrenics and normal individuals under excessive stimulation.[20]

Of course, just because the rate of psychosis is high where crowding is intense does not necessarily mean that crowding causes psychosis. It is possible that both crowding and psychosis result from the same social problems and that neither causes the other. For example, the likelihood of both crowding and psychosis may be increased by inadequate economic opportunity. It is also possible that people who are less prone to develop psychosis move away from the central city. Additionally, people in the suburbs may be less likely to be labeled psychotic—regardless of their mental condition—than people in the central city.

The Rat Sink

Crowding occurs when the population increases and the living space does not. The effects of crowding have been difficult to study because human population density cannot be manipulated for the purpose of scientific investigation, but animal populations can and have been controlled for this purpose.

In a series of important experiments, John Calhoun[21,22,23] created an experimental rat universe—an enclosed and separate world for rats, with abundant food, water, and nesting material. The idea was to create an originally ideal environment for rats, and then study their behavior as the rat population increased.

Calhoun soon found that as crowded conditions developed, the stress accompanying unavoidable social interaction caused severe behavioral problems. Calhoun describes his first rat universe:

I confined a population of wild Norway rats in a quarter-acre enclosure. With an abundance of food and places to live and with predation and disease eliminated or minimized, only the animals' behavior with respect to one another remained as a factor that might affect the increase in their number. There could be no escape from the behavioral consequences of rising population density. By the end of 27 months the population had become stabilized at 150 adults. Yet adult mortality was so low that 5,000 adults might have been expected from the observed reproductive rate. The reason this larger population did not materialize was that infant mortality was extremely high. Even with only 150 adults in the enclosure, stress from social

interaction led to such disruption of maternal behavior that few young survived.[22]

Crowding and Cannibalism • Calhoun next observed rats under controlled indoor conditions. They were confined to rooms that were provided with everything needed to maintain life and were studied as their population density increased. Calhoun found that crowded conditions caused rats to behave strangely. Females became progressively poorer at maternal functions such as nest building and caring for the young; eventually females stopped building nests altogether. Crowded females began to abandon their litters and to allow the young to starve to death. Cannibalism became increasingly common. Courtship and mating became rare. Some males seemed to go berserk, attacking females viciously and biting juvenile and infant rats. Other males became very passive and withdrawn, ignoring other rats of both sexes and not participating at all in the social structure of the rat colony. A third type of crowded male became hyperactive and hypersexual, but did not seem to be able to tell the difference between male and female partners. As crowding increasingly disrupted their normal social behavior, the rat population stopped growing and even began to decline. Thus, rat populations seem to have a built-in population control that prevents them from becoming permanently crowded and overpopulated.

Togetherness • A peculiar condition developed within the crowded rat universes that Calhoun called the "rat sink."[21] Although food was continuously available to the rats, they would eat only at certain times—when other rats were also eating—so that the feeding area became extremely crowded at certain periods of the day. Eating became a social habit; rats would eat only in the presence of other rats. Furthermore, only certain of the several feeding stations were used. Calhoun concluded that, as crowding increased, it became more likely that other rats would be present during eating. The accidental presence of other rats during eating had a conditioning effect. Eating food

In Calhoun's experiments with mice and rats, crowding has been shown to affect physical and mental health and to produce special areas of extreme congestion called "rat sinks." (National Institute of Mental Health)

became associated with the presence of other rats. Because of this association, the presence of other rats eventually became rewarding or reinforcing, and then rats began to seek the company of others. This created an extremely crowded area within the rat colony that Calhoun referred to as the **rat sink.** In colonies in which rat sinks developed, the disruptive effects of crowding were particularly severe.

Although humans have a lot of space in which to live in this world, we tend to congregate in extremely crowded cities, cities in which the effects of crowding seem to be particularly severe. The presence of other people, because of past associations, apparently has become rewarding, and we pursue those rewards. The problems of our cities resemble the problems of the rat sink.

Coping with Crowding

When an animal's space, or territory, is invaded, it may either attack the intruder (fight) or withdraw so as to preserve some distance (flight). This response to crowding is called the **fight-or-flight reaction.** Either strategy has the effect of reducing the experience of crowding by lowering the level of social stimulation. People also tend to react to crowding with either an aggressive or withdrawal response. People have a fight-or-flight reaction.

Fight • An effective means of blocking intrusions into your space is to become more aggressive and fight back. Evidence shows that aggressive reactions increase under crowded conditions. One study related the average number of persons per room to various behavior patterns observed among occupants. It was found that arousal levels, withdrawal reactions, and eruptions of violence all increased as crowding increased.[24] An experimental study of the effects of crowding varied the number of young children in a room and observed their aggressive tendencies and their social interactions.[25] As the number of children in the room was increased from six to twelve, individuals tended to become more aggressive (fighting, snatching toys) and more withdrawn from social interactions. These results are consistent with the point of view that crowding increases arousal and that two strategies for coping with crowding stress are "fight" and "flight," both of which tend to keep people away.

Flight • There seem to be signs of increasing withdrawal ("flight") in our society, some of which may be a consequence of our increasingly crowded landscape. An American visitor to England was told, "Forgive us our seemingly cold indifference. This is a small and crowded island. We can exist only by ignoring each other."[26]

Studies of the relationship of organizational size to behavior show that as size increases, absence rates and lateness increase and worker morale decreases.[27] Apparently one reaction to being a member of a large group or company is to withdraw. A study of 218 high schools showed that there is a relationship between population density and withdrawal from participation in school activities; the larger the school, the fewer activities an individual student was likely to become involved in.[28] The excessive use of drugs in our society may also be a type of withdrawal or "flight."

Our cities, organizations, and schools are increasing in size each year. There are probably optimal sizes for our groups, in terms not only of productivity but also of human health and happiness. These optimal sizes have been surpassed, but a recognition of the effect of crowding on human behavior may help reverse the trend toward bigness.

Interim Summary   One of the psychological effects of prolonged crowding is an increase in the arousal level. Crowded people become overstimulated and anxious, as crowding activates the brain's arousal system. Continued exposure to crowding results in physical and emotional signs of severe stress, increased rates of mental disturbance, and in harmful effects on human physical health. Calhoun's studies of crowding in rat colonies showed that crowding tended to produce cannibalism and a kind of maternal indifference in which mothers would abandon their litters. "Fight" and "flight" are two strategies for coping with stress by keeping people away.

Social Influence

Members of a group tend to be alike in some ways. The members of one club tend to be different from the members of another club; persons from the same country tend to have more in common than persons from different countries. Most groups have a shared belief system, a set of similar ideas and attitudes about the world. Groups have sets of common beliefs for several reasons; individuals tend to join only those groups with which they generally agree; the group often has shared experiences that give rise to similarity in attitudes among the members; and groups reward members who agree and punish members who disagree with group beliefs. Fads, fashions, and social norms are all different aspects of these shared beliefs among group members.

Fads and Fashions

Fads are short-lived practices or customs that sweep the country periodically. For a brief time practically everybody is disco dancing—and then it fades from popularity. "Pet rocks" and "mood rings" are seen everywhere for a while—then they disappear.

Fashions are more enduring social customs. When you do not behave according to the current fashion, you may be ridiculed or ostracized. There are fashions of dress (remember bell-bottom jeans?) that change every year or so; there are fashions in architecture (Victorian), painting (pop art), and books (sex manuals). There are fashions in raising and teaching children (progressive education).

When a fashion has been introduced and has become common, our eye is formed to it, and no one looks right or stylish who does not conform. We also know that after the fashion has changed, things in the discarded fashion look dowdy and rustic. No one can resist these temptations, try as he may.[29]

Hair style, cosmetics, and clothes seem to be particularly influenced by fashions that change every few years. The consequences for not being "in fashion" can often be quite severe. Lack of conformity to cur-

It's hard to resist participating in the latest fad. Whether it's a new dance step or roller skating, it feels good to be following the crowd. (© Bruce Kliewe/Jeroboam Inc.)

rent fashions can result in reduced opportunity for social relationships, in dismissal from school (because of hair style or clothes), or in being fired from a job. Have you ever been out of style because of your hair or clothes? How did other people respond to you? How do you feel about conformity to fashion?

Social Norms

A more permanent fad or fashion is called a **social norm**. Social norms are rules for behavior; they specify what is socially proper and what is improper. Each society develops its own set of social norms, so that social norms differ from one culture to another. In this country it is the norm to eat three meals a day; in other countries two or four meals a day may be eaten. Social norms govern appropriate forms of greeting, social interactions, manners while eating, attitudes toward the sick and disadvantaged, and codes of conduct at significant times in human life such as birth and death. It is not clear why social norms arise in the first place. Uniformity of belief and behavior may come from the need of individuals to have their behavior approved or validated by their peers. People validate others who are like themselves.

It is rare to have the opportunity to observe the origins of a social norm. One researcher had that chance with a group of Japanese monkeys. In order to control their movements and thus be able to observe this particular troop of monkeys, a Japanese scientist began placing sweet potatoes on the beach for the monkeys to eat. The monkeys stayed around the beach to eat the sweet potatoes. For some time the monkeys ate the potatoes without incident. Then one monkey did something different:

In 1953 a young female in the Ko-shima troop began to wash in the sea the potatoes that we set out on the beach. Little by little the habit spread to other monkeys in the troop, until today a full two-thirds of all the individuals in the group invariably wash their potatoes before eating them,

and the practice is more or less completely established as an element in the troop's cultural life. The washing of the sweet potatoes spread gradually, to the first young female's playmates, to her brothers and sister, then to their particular intimate associates.[30]

A new social norm had been started. Sweet potatoes were to be washed. The sweet potatoes must be carried to the sea in order to wash them, and this occupied both hands. In order to get to the water with the potatoes, the monkeys must walk on their hind legs. Thus the potato-washing custom required the monkeys to begin walking upright. The new social norm produced entirely new behavior. Various human behaviors may have had similar beginnings.

The Conformist

You belong to several social groups: your family, neighborhood, school, club, or country. Each of these groups has developed rules for behavior—that is, social norms. Sometimes in order to conform to the beliefs and behavior of those around you you must say or do things in which you do not believe. Thus there is often a conflict between your personal beliefs and the pressures to conform to the beliefs of others. Do you yield to those pressures easily?

The word **conformity** means to go along with the group, to change your beliefs or behavior so that they are consistent with the expectations of others. A *conformist* is a person who conforms by yielding to group pressure. Not all uniformity in behavior among members of a group is the result of group pressure. For example, the fact that you sneeze when you smell pepper is not an example of conformity; it is not a cause of your yielding to group pressure.

The character Stepan Arkadyevitch in Tolstoy's *Anna Karenina* provides a case study in conformity:

Stepan Arkadyevitch took in and read a liberal newspapaer, not an extreme one, but one advocating the views held by the majority.   And in spite of the fact that science, art, and politics had no special interest for him, he firmly held those views on all subjects which were held by the majority and by his paper, and he only changed them when the majority changed them—or, more strictly speaking, he did not change them, but they imperceptively changed of themselves within him.

Stepan Arkadyevitch had not chosen his political opinions or his views; these political opinions and views had come to him of themselves, just as he did not choose the shapes of his hats or coats, but simply took those that were being worn. And for him, living in a certain society—owing to the need, ordinarily developed at years of discretion, for some degree of mental activity—to have views was just as indispensable as to have a hat.   If there was a reason for his preferring liberal to conservative views, which were held also by many of his circle, it arose not from his considering liberalism more rational, but from its being in closer accord with his manner of life. . . .   And so liberalism had become a habit of Stepan Arkadyevitch's, and he liked his newspaper, as he did his cigar after dinner, for the slight fog it diffused in his brain.

The Nonconformist

There are two types of nonconformity, and these are called independence and anticonformity.[31]   **Anticonformity** is behavior that goes directly against the social norm.   One of the ways you can choose what to do is simply to choose what others say is the right thing to do; a second way you can choose what to do is always to do the opposite of what others say is right.   The first is the way of conformity.; the second is the way of anticonformity.   If you decide to wear long hair just because your parents want you to wear short hair, you are an anticonformist.   An anticonformist is just as dependent upon the crowd as a conformist is; neither is independent.

Independence is the expression of private belief in the face of group pressure to conform.   Independent people are able to resist group pressure to conform; in choosing what to do, independent people do not use the social norm as a guide.   Independent people maintain their private opinions and beliefs in spite of pressure to go along with the crowd.   Conformists go along with the social norm; anticonformists go against the social norm; and independents go their own ways.   Most people are a combination of each. How do you respond to group pressure?   Are you a conformist, an anticonformist, or an independent?

John F. Kennedy's book *Profiles in Courage*[32] provides numerous examples of independent people who had the courage to resist pressure to conform.   One of these people, Senator Edmund Ross, was pressured by members of his political party in 1868 to vote with them in favor of the impeachment of President Andrew Johnson.   The Republicans needed exactly thirty-six votes, and they had thirty-five.   Ross's vote would be decisive.   The senator's political career was at stake; he was pressured by his colleagues, by the voters, and by the newspapers to go against his beliefs and vote "guilty."   But his answer was "not guilty."

Interim Summary   Each society develops its own set of standards of behavior, or social norms; individual members of society are pressured to accept these standards and to conform to them.   A person who is a conformist yields to this pressure by giving up private beliefs or values. A person who is an anticonformist chooses to go directly against the social norm by doing the opposite.   A person who is independent is able to maintain private beliefs in spite of pressure to go along with the crowd.

Social Pressure

Each of us experiences pressure to conform. There are rewards for conforming and punishments for not conforming. If you conform, you feel that you belong and you are accepted by the other members of the group; if you do not conform, you are rejected or ostracized, and you may even lose your membership in the group.

Who sets the standards that you conform to? When you are young, you conform more to your parents' beliefs and behavior; when you are older you begin to conform more to the standards set by your peers—those individuals closer to your own age. In a study that showed this, children were asked to make choices between the advice given by parents and the advice given by children.[33] The children who participated in the study ranged in age from three to eleven. The results showed that as the children got older, the relative influence of their peers increased and the influence of their parents diminished. We all experience continual group pressure to conform; the identity of the group to which we conform, however, changes as we grow older.

Sherif's Experiment

You can easily imagine that choices related to aesthetics and values might be highly influenced by group pressure; your attitudes toward lipstick, beards, bras, or hair are affected by social norms. But what about your perception? Can you believe your eyes, or is what you see also influenced by the expectations of others?

In the 1930s Muzafer Sherif[34] recruited a number of participants for a psychology experiment and seated them in a completely dark room. At the end of the room there was a small stationary point of light. Although the light remains completely still, it looks as if it is moving. Without a reference or context, a small point of light in a dark room appears to move; this is called the **autokinetic illusion.** The illusion is

influenced by what other people say they see. Sherif's participants were asked to indicate the distance that they saw the light move in the dark. If these judgments were made privately, the amount of movement specified by each subject varied greatly, from a few inches to several feet. But when the group members made public judgments, the guesses tended to converge toward a common range of numbers; in other words, a group norm emerged.

In a similar experiment a male participant was put into a room with three persons who were secretly working for the experimenter and who had been told what to say. These individuals are called "confederates." The participant assumed that the confederates of the experimenter were other participants like himself.[35] While the participant's private estimates of the movement of the light averaged a little less than four inches, he radically changed his estimates when exposed to the judgments of the other "participants." The confederates of the experimenter stated that they thought the light was moving about fifteen inches; the participant then changed his estimate from four to fourteen inches. He had given up his own judgment in order to conform to the group.

Asch's Experiment

In the 1950s Solomon Asch conducted an experiment to find out what people would do when there was a conflict between the opinion of the group and the evidence of their own eyes.[36] Would people believe their own eyes, even though their perceptions went against the unanimous judgment of others?

The experimental task required participants to match line lengths. They were shown a straight line of a certain length, say ten inches, and three additional comparison lines, say eight, ten, and twelve inches. The participants had to choose the one of the three comparison lines that was the same length as the first line. With no group pressure operating, participants almost never made a mistake in this task; the task was very easy. With groups of eight male participants, when the first seven (all secret confederates of the experimenter) named the wrong line, then the last participant had the choice of going along with the error of the group or of believing the evidence of his own eyes. About one-third of the participants conformed fairly consistently to the incorrect majority opionion, while about one-fourth consistently followed their own independent judgment and always chose the correct line. The remaining participants sometimes conformed and sometimes did not.

These experiments show the power that others hold over you. It is not surprising that you conform to the fads and fashions of the day in order to be accepted by the groups to which you belong. These experiments show that a substantial proportion of people find the opinion of others so compelling that they are willing to base their judgments on the group's judgment rather than to believe the evidence of their own eyes.

Enforcing Conformity

How do groups exert pressure on individuals to conform to their social norms? Group pressure works because groups have great powers of reward and pun-ishment. Some groups have formal arrangements for rewarding members who conform: schools have honor rolls, industries have bonus payments, and cities have good citizenship awards. These awards are given to those group members who are judged to be "ideal" group members, because they comply with the group's set of rules for proper behavior. All groups have informal rewards for members who conform. Conformers receive the group's approval and acceptance.

Members who deviate from the social norms of their groups suffer **negative sanctions** (punishments) for not conforming. Some of these negative sanctions are formalized in jail sentences or fines. Most often a group applies informal pressure at first in order to get deviant members to "mend their ways" and begin conforming to the group's standards. If members refuse to comply, then the group may reject them so that they are no longer members.

A group has a potent punishment for a member who persists in his deviancy despite pressures on him to shift: it may redefine its boundaries so as to exclude the deviant, thereby protecting uniformity among members. Rejection of a deviant can be accomplished in various ways. He may be set apart so that no one talks or listens to him, he may be dropped from activities of the group, or he may be expelled.[37]

Interim Summary	Groups apply pressure to members in order to get them to conform, and members who deviate from the group norms are punished (suffer negative sanctions). The perceptual experiments by Sherif and Asch showed that a substantial proportion of people find the opinion of others so compelling that they are willing to ignore the evidence before their own eyes.

Blind Obedience

When you were a child, you did what you were told—most of the time. Adults also are often asked to obey. You are asked to obey teachers, policemen, the president, or an army sergeant. A soldier is ordered to kill and must obey or suffer punishment. During World War II German soldiers were ordered to murder thousands of Jews. Many obeyed.

What would you be willing to do under orders?

Following Orders

Psychologists have searched for tasks that persons would be unwilling to do under orders but have had difficulty finding one. One psychologist asked college students to sort garbage; they did, with little objection.[38] Other students were asked to pick up a poisonous snake; they obeyed (and were stopped just in time).[39] Students obeyed when they were asked to put their hands into a container of nitric acid (they were not permitted to do so), and they even obeyed when they were asked to throw acid into someone's face (but the experimenter did not allow them to do it).[39]

Why do people obey? What leads them to accept authority? Studies show that authority is accepted as legitimate and is obeyed when one of three conditions is met: (1) the authority is seen as beneficial to groups or values to which the individual is committed; (2) the authority is seen as trustworthy; and (3) the authority is seen as having the support of the majority of the people.[40] Psychology experimenters are often seen as having these three characteristics and so are obeyed by most people, even when they ask them to do absurd or dangerous tasks.

Milgram's Study of Obedience

Suppose you were told to electrocute someone. What would your reaction be? Would you obey and follow the orders? Stanley Milgram designed an elaborate experiment to find out the answer to that question.[41] People who volunteered for the experiment were told that they were participating in an experiment on the effects of punishment on learning. Their job was to administer a painful electric shock to a man—the "learner"—whenever he made a mistake and forgot one of the words he was supposed to memorize. Those who were to administer the electric shocks were actually the only ones studied, because the "learner" was a male actor who was working for the experimenter. The machinery was rigged so that no electric shock was actually given, although the participants believed that they were shocking people.

The participants observed the "learner" being strapped down in a chair and electrodes being attached to his arm. At this point the "learner" expressed some concern about the experiment and revealed that he had a heart condition. The "teachers" then went into another room, and the learning task proceeded. The "learner," of course, made many mistakes (as he had been instructed to do); at each mistake the "teachers" were supposed to press a switch that they believed would deliver an electric shock to the "learner." Every time the "learner" made a mistake, the "teachers" were supposed to increase the voltage of the shock. Participants faced a board with a row of switches on it, labeled from 15 to 450 volts, and had to pick one switch each time. Milgram wanted to find out how strong a shock people would be willing to administer.

He was surprised and dismayed by what he found. Over 60 percent of the participants were willing to give the highest level of shock to the "learner," even though the "learner" at lower levels screamed in pain and begged for mercy (all part of the actor's script).

The victim indicates no discomfort until the 75-volt shock is administered, at which time there is a slight grunt in response to the punishment. Similar reactions follow the 90- and 100-volt shocks, and at 120 volts the victim shouts to the experimenter that the shocks are becoming painful. Painful groans are heard on administration of the 135-volt shock, and at 150 volts the victim cries out, "Experimenter, get me out of here! I won't be in the experiment any more! I refuse to go on!" Cries of this type continue with generally rising intensity, so that at 180 volts the victim cries out, "I can't stand the pain," and by 270 volts his response to the shock is definitely an agonized scream. Throughout, he insists that he be let out of the experiment. At 300 volts the victim shouts in desperation that he will no longer provide answers to the memory test; and at 315 volts, after a violent scream, he reaffirms with vehemence that he is no longer a participant. From this point on, he provides no answers, but shrieks in agony whenever a shock is administered; this continues through 450 volts.[41]

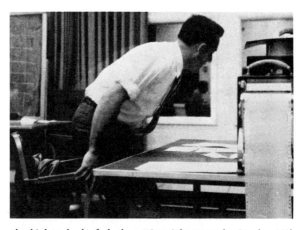

In Milgram's study of obedience, volunteers were instructed to shock a man with a weak heart by pressing buttons labeled from 15 to 450 volts. Over 60 percent of the participants obeyed by giving *the highest level of shock. (Copyright 1965 by Stanley Milgram. From the film* Obedience, *distributed by the New York University Film Library.)*

Milgram showed that, under some circumstances, people are willing to commit dangerous acts just because they are ordered to do so. Why did they obey such orders? An important reason is that they were able to yield all responsibility for their actions to an "authority"—in this case a researcher in a white coat. The participants in Milgram's study did not feel completely responsible for the "electrocution"; the responsibility was spread, or diffused, among two or more people. Thus, one condition that makes this kind of mindless obedience possible is **diffusion of responsibility**—a sharing or spreading of the responsibility for actions.

A second reason for the obedience shown in Milgram's study is that the participants were not treated in a personal manner, as individuals. There was a degree of anonymity—the participants knew that their names would not be disclosed publicly. The "teachers" and their "victim" were located in two different rooms during the study and had no personal contact. The participants could punish the victim by pulling a switch and did not have to face him directly. These conditions lead to what is called **deindividuation**—feeling anonymous, one of the crowd, without a unique identity.

Blind obedience, resulting from diffusion of responsibility and deindividuation, occurs other places than the psychology laboratory. For example, members of any large organization—an army or a corporation—may experience these conditions.

Milgram also found, in his study of obedience, that if there is a group of subjects in the room all at once, a single dissenter gives the others the courage to disobey and to use their own judgment.[42]   This shows that it is easier to think for yourself when you have social support for doing so.   It also shows that, by refusing to obey, you can have a strong effect on others.

Interim Summary

Individuals under some circumstances are willing to yield responsibility to an "authority" and obey orders without question.   Milgram showed that people will even obey an order to deliver a dangerous electric shock to another person.   A single dissenter from blind obedience, however, gives others the courage to disobey orders contrary to their own values.   Deindividuation and diffusion of responsibility are conditions that promote blind obedience.

Summary

1. Social psychology is the study of how individual behavior is affected by the presence of others.
2. In perceiving and judging others, we seem to be primarily affected by first impressions, or what is called the primacy effect.
3. Attribution theory is concerned with how we decide the causes of behavior.   Evidence suggests that we follow three rules in deciding whether behavior had an internal or external cause: the consensus rule, the inconsistency rule, and the distinctiveness rule.
4. Group dynamics is the study of social interaction within groups.
5. The optimal size of a group depends upon whether the task at hand is a parallel coaction task or a group interaction task.   In parallel coaction tasks, the larger the group, the better.   For group interaction tasks, adding group members beyond a certain point does not improve performance.
6. Task-oriented leaders are best for short-lived groups, and social-emotional leaders work better for groups that must work together for long periods of time.
7. Sherif's experiment at Robber's Cave manipulated group structure to produce either intergroup hostility or cooperation.   Hostility was reduced when the groups were made interdependent.
8. One of the psychological effects of prolonged crowding is an increase in the level of arousal.   Continued exposure to crowding results in physical and emotional signs of severe stress and increased rates of mental disturbance.
9. Calhoun's studies with rats showed that crowding can produce cannibalism and maternal indifference.
10. Two strategies for coping with the stress of crowding are "fight" and "flight."
11. Each society develops its own set of social norms, or standards of behavior; individual members of the society are pressured to accept these standards.   Individuals respond to this pressure with conformity, anticonformity, or independence.
12. The perceptual experiments by Sherif and Asch studied the effect that other people's opinions have on an individual.
13. Milgram's studies showed that under some circumstances individuals are willing to

yield responsibility to an "authority" and obey orders without question, even orders to "electrocute" a stranger.

14. Deindividuation and diffusion of responsibility are conditions that promote blind obedience.

Key Concepts

inner-directed Making decisions on the basis of personal values.

other-directed Depending upon the opinions of others to make choices.

social psychology The study of how individual behavior is affected by the presence of others.

halo effect The tendency to see a person as desirable in all ways because of one desirable trait.

primacy effect The tendency for judgments to be controlled by first impressions.

recency effect The tendency for judgments to be controlled by the last or most recent impressions.

attribution theory A theory that explains the rules we use in inferring the causes of behavior; for example, a particular action may be attributed to external circumstances ("he stumbled and accidentally fell against me") or to internal causes ("he intended to bump me").

consensus rule The tendency to attribute a behavior to external causes if other people in the same situation act the same way.

inconsistency rule The tendency to attribute a behavior to external causes if the individual only occasionally shows that behavior in that situation.

distinctiveness rule The tendency to attribute a behavior to external causes if the individual performs the behavior in one situation but not in others.

group dynamics The study of social interaction in groups.

parallel coaction tasks Group tasks that involve completely separate functions, with each person working independently.

group interaction tasks Group tasks that involve members interacting and working together.

task-oriented leaders Leaders focused on getting the job done quickly and efficiently.

social-emotional leaders Leaders focused on maintaining good feelings among group members.

crowding An excessive number of people.

arousal level Level of activation or stimulation.

rat sink In a rat colony, an extremely crowded area resulting from the social reinforcement provided by other animals.

fight-or-flight reaction The tendency to attack or withdraw from an intruder when personal space has been violated.

fads Short-lived practices that sweep the country periodically as social customs.

fashions Enduring social customs; for example, styles of dress.

social norm A behavior standard of a particular group or society; a rule for behavior that specifies what is proper.

conformity Going along with group standards or expectations and going against private beliefs.

anticonformity Doing the opposite of what the social norm dictates.

independence The expression of private beliefs in the face of group pressure to conform.

autokinetic illusion An illusion in which a stationary point of light in a dark room appears to move.

negative sanctions Punishment or threat of punishment for not conforming.

diffusion of responsibility A sharing or spreading of the responsibility for actions.

deindividuation Feeling anonymous, one of the crowd, without a unique personal identity.

Chapter 23

Social Attitudes and Prejudice

Key Questions
1. How are attitudes formed and changed?
2. What causes prejudice?
3. What are some important types of prejudice, and what are their effects?
4. How can prejudice be reduced?

Think of the perfect person.

Try to imagine an ideal human being standing before you. What is your ideal person like? What is your image of human perfection? For many Americans, the image is young, blond, blue-eyed, able-bodied, pink-skinned, and male. Yet few of us look like that. We cannot live up to that image. Because we are not young, blue-eyed males, we are judged inferior and are the victims of prejudice. Psychologists refer to such a prejudice as an attitude.

Attitudes

An **attitude** is a tendency to act in a consistently positive or negative way toward an object, a person, or a group of people. You have attitudes toward all sorts of things—the latest fashions, disco music, purple houses, ice cream, short people, children, and many other types of objects and people. Attitudes tend to be relatively long-lasting. While it is certainly possible to change your attitudes, you do not change your basic attitudes very often. In addition to involving positive or negative judgments, attitudes also involve tendencies to act in particular ways. For example, your attitude toward ice cream may dispose you to buy it and eat it, and your attitude toward purple houses may dispose you to avoid them.

Components of Attitudes

What is your attitude toward disco music?

As you think about it, you will notice that your attitude is somewhat complicated. It involves a way of feeling (liking or disliking), an opinion ("It's the greatest" or "It rots the mind"), and a tendency to act (to turn it off or to begin to dance). These different

An attitude is a tendency to act in a consistently positive or negative way toward an object or person. We have attitudes toward all sorts of things, and we express our attitudes in a variety of ways, including buttons that we wear, bumper stickers that we buy, and signs that we carry. (Hank Lebo/Jeroboam Inc.)

aspects of your attitude toward disco music characterize the three components of all attitudes: the affective, cognitive, and conative components.

The **affective component of attitudes** is the either positive or negative *feeling* that you have about the object or person toward whom the attitude is directed. The term "affective" refers to emotions, or feeling. All attitudes have some affective part—a liking, hating, fearing, respecting, loving, or other feeling. Are there types of people for whom you have attitudes that include very positive or very negative feelings?

The **cognitive component of attitudes** is the *belief* or *opinion* that you hold about the object or person toward whom the attitude is directed. The term "cognitive" refers to mental activities such as thinking. Your attitude toward children may include the opinion that they should be "seen but not heard." Often the beliefs that accompany attitudes are not very logical or rational and may have no basis in fact. What are your beliefs about different types of people?

The **conative component of attitudes** is the *tendency to respond* to a particular way or to act toward the object or person. The term *conative* refers to voluntary action or behavioral tendencies. Your attitude toward large dogs may include the conative component of avoiding them; this behavioral tendency is part of your attitude. Your attitude toward a particular political party may include the affective component of liking it, the cognitive component of agreeing with its positions, and the conative component of voting for it.

Measuring Attitudes

Psychologists who study social attitudes have devised numerous ways to measure them. These methods are concerned with objectively identifying what attitudes you hold, whether they are relatively strong or weak, and whether they are positive or negative.

The most common method used in measuring attitudes involves asking people to report how they feel about other people or things, a method called the **self-report measure.** Rather than ask how you feel about, say, handicapped people and then let you answer any way you pleased, the psychologist would be more likely to provide you with a list of possible answers and ask you to mark the one closest to your view. This approach provides the researcher with an index of how you feel and how strongly you feel. Such a measure is called an **attitude scale.**

The Likert Scale • One type of attitude scale is the **Likert scale,** a self-report measure consisting of a series of statements to which you respond by marking the extent of your agreement. The extent to which you agree with each statement is indicated on a five- or six-point scale. The following is an example of a Likert scale measuring attitudes toward handicapped people:

Instructions: Mark each statement with a number from $+3$ to -3 to indicate how strongly you agree or disagree with it.

$+3$ I agree very much
$+2$ I agree somewhat
$+1$ I agree a little
-1 I disagree a little
-2 I disagree somewhat
-3 I disagree very much

_____ 1. Handicapped people make me uncomfortable.
_____ 2. Normal children should not have to go to school with handicapped children.
_____ 3. I would be happier if handicapped people kept to themselves.
_____ 4. I tend to avoid looking directly at handicapped people.

By adding up your answers on this scale, you obtain a score which reflects the extent of your negative attitudes toward handicapped people.

The Guttman Scale • Another method used in measuring attitudes is the self-report measure called the **Guttman scale.** In a Guttman scale, you are asked to indicate where your view falls on a series of increasingly strong statements. On the following Guttman scale, what is the strongest statement you are willing to endorse as reflecting your feelings?

_____ 1. I would marry a handicapped person.
_____ 2. I would have a handicapped person as a friend.
_____ 3. I would work beside a handicapped person in an office.
_____ 4. I would live in a neighborhood with several handicapped persons.
_____ 5. I wouldn't mind living in the same town with a handicapped person.
_____ 6. I wouldn't mind living in the same country with a handicapped person.

Your answer on the Guttman scale reflects the strength of your positive or negative attitude toward handicapped persons. To assess your attitudes toward other groups of people, you might try substituting other words for the word *handicapped* (*short, tall, overweight, thin, black, white,* or other group names).

The Semantic Differential Scale • A third self-report measure of attitudes is the **semantic differential scale,** which presents a series of adjective pairs separated by a scale of numbers and asks that you check off the number corresponding to your attitude. The following is an example of a semantic differential scale:

Instructions: Mark the following scales to indicate your feeling about the handicapped.

Good	1	2	3	4	5	6	7	Bad
Clean	1	2	3	4	5	6	7	Dirty
Sweet	1	2	3	4	5	6	7	Sour
Pleasant	1	2	3	4	5	6	7	Unpleasant
Beautiful	1	2	3	4	5	6	7	Ugly

For comparison purposes, you might try responding on the semantic differential scales presented above to other group names, such as *children, men, old people,* or *thin people.*

Theories of Attitude Formation and Change

Obviously many things influence our attitudes toward people. Our experiences interacting with a particular individual shape positive or negative attitudes toward that person. Other people influence us when they attempt to persuade us by using different kinds of arguments or appeals to adopt attitudes that they want. Advertisers spend millions of dollars trying to persuade us to buy a particular product or to vote for a specific political candidate.

The way is which we form and change our attitudes has been of great interest to psychologists. Several theories of attitude formation and change have been developed and tested by numerous researchers. Two such theories that enjoy current credibility are the learning theory of attitudes and the cognitive dissonance theory of attitudes.

Attitudes toward products can be shaped through classical conditioning. Advertisers hope that the positive response that we have to an attractive woman will become associated with the brand of automobile that she stands next to. (© Copyright Joel Gordon 1979)

The Learning Theory • According to the **learning theory of attitudes,** our attitudes were acquired through processes of learning. Certain attitudes can be accounted for in terms of **operant conditioning** (conditioning by consequences). When we are reinforced for holding certain attitudes, these attitudes should become stronger. Parents shape the attitudes of their children by rewarding the expression of certain attitudes and punishing the expression of others. Attitudes can also be shaped through **classical conditioning** (conditioning by association). Advertisers attempt to exploit this principle when they present ads with attractive women shown next to the product they are trying to sell; the advertisers hope that the positive feelings stimulated by viewing the women will become associated with their product.

The Cognitive Dissonance Theory • According to the **cognitive dissonance theory,** we strive to establish and to maintain consistency among our attitudes and behaviors. From this point of view, we are made uncomfortable by inconsistency (**dissonance**) among the things that we know, the beliefs that we have, and our behaviors, and we are motivated to eliminate the inconsistency.

Suppose you had the belief that older people—men and women past seventy—were mentally slow, forgetful, and inactive. Then you meet Joanne who is seventy-five, mentally quick, and actively involved in her career and a social life. These two ideas (your prior beliefs and your present experiences) would be dissonant (inconsistent). You could reduce the dissonance either by changing your attitude toward older people or by discounting the facts about Joanne.

We are constantly learning new facts about ourselves, other people, and the world. We acquire experiences by interacting with other people, and we find ourselves involved with them as we participate in different tasks. Some of these experiences are inconsistent with previously held attitudes. For example, we may find ourselves enjoying an interaction with a per-

son who is a member of a group that we have highly negative attitudes about—say, teachers. In that event, we would be confronted with the following inconsistent ideas:

1. I believe that teachers are dull, forgetful, and useless.

2. I am enjoying a stimulating conversation with a teacher.

One of the ways in which this inconsistency could be resolved would be to change the attitude toward teachers so that it is more positive. By persuading ourselves that we actually believe that teachers are stimulating, we reduce the conflict between what we are doing and what we believe.

The discrepancy between belief and action results in a change in belief when we have no alternative in explaining our action other than by referring to our attitudes or beliefs. When our action could be accounted for in other ways, however, no change in belief will occur. If you contribute to a charity after only minimal inducement, you will probably explain your action in terms of your positive attitudes toward the charity—and if they were not very positive before the contribution, they will likely be more positive afterwards, due to your need to reduce dissonance. However, if you contribute to a charity only after extreme pressure, you will probably explain your action in terms of the sales pressure you experienced. In this event, if your attitudes toward the charity were not very positive before the contribution, they will likely remain relatively negative.

The cognitive dissonance theory assumes that we cannot tolerate much inconsistency between our attitudes and behaviors toward groups of people. If we act toward certain groups in a discriminatory, negative way, then—to be consistent—our attitudes toward these groups will also be negative. These negative attitudes are a major divisive force in our society and have been of great concern to psychologists.

Interim Summary   Attitudes are tendencies to act consistently in a positive or negative way toward people or objects. Attitudes are relatively long-lasting, and have affective, cognitive, and conative components. The most common method of measuring attitudes is with self-report measures such as the Likert scale, Guttman scale, and semantic differential scale. Two theories of attitude formation and change are the learning theory and cognitive dissonance theory.

Prejudiced Attitudes

Some of the most harmful social attitudes are prejudices. We live in a world that supports prejudice. In the home, in school, in magazines and books, and on radio and television, the images we have of members of different groups are shaped. These images are often negative. Do you have prejudiced attitudes toward members of different groups? Check your prejudices on the list below:

☐ men   ☐ blacks
☐ women   ☐ Hispanics
☐ children   ☐ Asians
☐ short people   ☐ Catholics
☐ tall people   ☐ Jews
☐ handicapped people   ☐ Protestants
☐ old people
☐ whites

What Is Prejudice?

"A woman's place is in the home."

"All Jews care about is money."

"Children should be seen and not heard."

"Some of my best friends are blacks, but I wouldn't want my sister to marry one."

You have heard remarks like these before. What is similar about them? First, each statement groups people of a particular type together; it regards them all as the same even though each individual is unique. This tendency to see all members of a group as the same is called **overgeneralization**. Second, each statement reflects a negative attitude toward the people who have been grouped together: women are seen as incapable of acting productively in the world; Jews are seen as having selfish motives; children are seen as stupid; and blacks are seen as undesirable mates. Regarding members of groups as having such negative characteristics is called **devaluation**. When you deny the value or worth of people, you devalue them.

Prejudice is a preconceived and unfavorable attitude toward an entire group; it consists of a combination of overgeneralization and devaluation. For example, a person who is prejudiced against women sees all women as similar in having certain traits.

You are an individual, but sometimes people see you as a category instead of a person. When people respond only to your group category of black, white, male, or female, you lose your individuality. You have become stereotyped. A **stereotype** is a set of fixed ideas about a person that is based on group membership. It is the consequence of categorizing first and observing second. It is the product of prejudice.

About fifty years ago one hundred white college students were asked to describe the personalities of persons from various national and ethnic groups.[1] These students showed definite stereotypes about the typical personalities of each of ten groups. "Americans" were most commonly rated as hard-working, intelligent, materialistic, ambitious, and progressive. "Italians" were rated as artistic, impulsive, passionate, quick-tempered, and musical. "Jews" were rated as shrewd, greedy, hard-working, and intelligent. "Negroes" were rated as superstitious, lazy, happy-go-lucky, ignorant, and musical. These students had fixed ideas about what black Americans were like, ideas that contrasted sharply with their view of themselves as "Americans."

Stereotypes of blacks have changed somewhat in the past fifty years since this study was completed. The evidence of several studies shows that the stereotype of blacks is less negative than it was, although it is still negative.[2,3] Fixed ideas about racial and ethnic groups are remarkably resistant to change; they tend to be learned early in life and to last over the years.

What are your stereotypes? Do you have fixed ideas about the personality of another person you have not met? Do you tend to categorize first and observe later?

People can be divided into many different groups, and each group has its subgroups. Prejudice is commonly reflected in our attitudes toward these subgroups. Recently attention has been drawn to prejudice against blacks, Hispanics, Jews, and women. Prejudice against Irish, Catholics, Asians, Iranians, and American Indians has also been a serious problem. The prejudice shown against children and men has been, for the most part, entirely ignored. Yet children have no equality before the law, are often treated as property, and are clearly "second-class citizens." Prejudice against men takes the form of a prejudgment that any particular man will show his "masculinity" by being insensitive, vulgar, unexpressive, materialistic, and violent.

Learning How to Hate

Some people are extremely prejudiced and others are not. What causes these differences? Studies show that some parents and schools distort the minds of children and teach them prejudice.

Children learn what attitudes and beliefs they are expected to hold. For the most part, children learn their prejudices from other people with whom they interact: parents, friends, and teachers. Studies show that there is a strong relationship between the extent of a child's prejudice and the extent of the parents' prejudice.[4] If parents are prejudiced, their child tends to be prejudiced also. In one study a psychologist invented a group of persons called the "Piraneans." Slides of people supposedly of this group were shown to 180 elementary school children; then their attitudes toward these people were measured and compared with their parents' attitudes toward blacks, Jews, and other subgroups. It was found that the attitudes of the children toward the imaginary group resembled the attitudes of their parents toward real groups; when the parents were prejudiced, the children were, too. These children had learned to be prejudiced not toward a particular group but in general.[5]

The learning of prejudice by children most likely takes place through the processes of modeling and identification. Children tend to imitate the behavior and beliefs of their parents and other significant adults. Furthermore, as children grow up, they typically identify with the parent of the same sex and adopt the attitudes and mannerisms of that parent. In this way, children can learn to hate from their parents.

Parents are not the only teachers of hate. Children adopt the attitudes of society that they experience around them. Until very recently, magazines, movies, and television consistently portrayed all persons except white Americans as inferior. The characters displayed to children conformed more to stereotypes than to reality. All blacks were shown in menial jobs; all Hispanics were shown as lazy. Recently, the representation of minorities in the media has improved, but it is still true that the hero of most stories is white and male and most servants on television are black and female.

Schools have taught a biased history. It has been, and to some degree still is, a history from the white person's point of view; it neglects important contributions made by nonwhites. Some school counselors still advise blacks and Hispanics to pursue careers as laborers and to take courses in school to prepare for menial jobs.

Schoolteachers speak for their culture; their attitudes and values reflect the attitudes and values of the rest of society.   But the attitudes held by teachers and taught by teachers are sometimes prejudiced.   One New York City school teacher classified a number of her Puerto Rican students as mutes, unable to speak. When questioned about this, she reported that they had not spoken a word to her in six months.   When asked if they talked to one another, she replied, "Sure, they cackle to each other in Spanish all day!"[6]   The school system, for the most part, is staffed by white English-speaking persons and reflects the values and beliefs of white English-speaking persons.   In a speech before the U.S. Senate, Dr. David Sanchez reported:

Equal education has been a fraud.   How can there be equal education if some of the students are looked on as defective?   The injuries of the Latin American child have been inflicted by those who claim to teach and motivate him, who have in reality alienated him and destroyed his identity through subtle rejection of his language which nobody speaks, his culture which nobody understands and ultimately him whom nobody values.[7]

Prejudiced Personalities

How can a person be prejudiced against a group that does not exist?   It cannot come from the experience of interacting with the people involved, since they are imaginary; such a prejudice cannot be learned, since no opportunity for learning was possible.   Yet studies have shown that many people are prejudiced against groups that do not exist, and these are the same people who are prejudiced against real groups.[5]   People who are prejudiced against one minority group tend to be prejudiced against other minority groups as well.[8] Findings such as these have led to the idea that prejudice has more to do with the personality of the person who is prejudiced than with present social conditions.   Prejudiced people may simply be different psychologically from other people.   From this point of view, the personality of the person who is prejudiced should differ from the personalities of others.

The personality pattern characterizing highly prejudiced people has been called the **authoritarian personality.** An individual with this type of personality keeps feelings under great control, is extremely conventional and resistant to change, and shows a dependence on and admiration of authority figures.

A massive study of the personalities of prejudiced people was undertaken during and immediately following World War II, and a report of this study was later published in a book entitled *The Authoritarian Personality.*[8]   For this study, about two thousand people took tests designed to measure prejudice, political beliefs, and personality.   One of the most important parts of the test was a set of questions called the **F scale,** designed to measure basic personality traits that were assumed to support prejudice.   High agreement with the items of this scale was supposed to reflect fascistic, authoritarian, or antidemocratic tendencies. Some of the items from the F scale appear below; check the ones that you agree with.

☐ Obedience and respect for authority are the most important virtues children should learn.

☐ Sex crimes, such as rape and attacks on children, deserve more than mere imprisonment; such criminals ought to be publicly whipped, or worse.

☐ When a person has a problem or worry, it is best for him not to think about it, but to keep busy with more cheerful things.

☐ People can be divided into two distinct classes: the weak and the strong.

☐ Nowadays when so many different kinds of people move around and mix together so much, a person has to protect himself especially carefully against catching an infection or disease from them.

☐ A person who has bad manners, habits, and breeding can hardly expect to get along with decent people.

☐ Young people sometimes get rebellious ideas, but as they grow up, they ought to get over them and settle down.

Prejudiced people tend to agree more with these items than nonprejudiced people.[9]   The results of this test and more intensive studies of prejudiced persons supported the idea that highly prejudiced people tend to have a particular personality pattern.   They tend to have unquestioning admiration for authorities and to hold in contempt persons they believe to have a status position lower than themselves. Interpersonal relationships for these people tend to be based on power and status. Highly prejudiced people show rigidity in their personality and thinking; they have little tolerance for unclear situations and prefer definite pat solutions to problems.[8]

What causes the prejudiced personality? One approach to this problem is to assume that prejudice is a form of displaced aggression and that the person who is prejudiced is scapegoating. According to the scapegoating theory, the prejudiced person has been frustrated or threatened by someone against whom retaliation was not safe; the impulse to fight back was inhibited because such action would be dangerous; and the aggression was therefore displaced or redirected to a relatively safe target, a minority group. The highly prejudiced person, then, should be someone who has been severely threatened or frustrated by someone against whom retaliation was dangerous or impossible.

Studies have shown that highly prejudiced persons tend to have aggressive and punishing parents.[8] The punishment they experienced as children was often arbitrary and violent. Whippings and beatings were commonly used punishments. One prejudiced person described her parents' disciplinary methods as follows:

. . . mother had a way of punishing me—lock me in a closet—or threaten to give me to a neighborhood woman who she said was a witch. . . .   I think that's why I was afraid of the dark. . . .

Father picked upon things and threatened to put me in an orphanage.[8]

It is easy to believe that such punishment might provide a source of frustration that would later cause a prejudiced personality. The reactions of anger, hostility, and aggression that are inhibited in the child emerge later in the authoritarian adult as prejudice.

Interim Summary   Prejudice is a preconceived and unfavorable attitude toward an entire group of people; it consists of a combination of overgeneralization (seeing all members of a group as the same) and devaluation (regarding them as inferior). One product of prejudice is a stereotype, a set of fixed ideas about members of a group. Stereotypes come from categorizing first and observing second. Research has shown that prejudice is learned and that certain personalities are more likely to be prejudiced than others. Some children learn prejudiced attitudes from their parents, peers, or teachers. In addition, children with aggressive and punishing parents tend to develop prejudiced personalities. People with authoritarian personalities are highly prejudiced and tend to have unquestioning admiration for authorities. The F scale is a test measuring the authoritarian personality.

Attitudes Toward the Elderly and the Handicapped

What determines which groups will be the victims of prejudice? According to the **competition theory of prejudice,** when two groups are in competition, they tend to develop negative attitudes toward each other. Two groups that were competing for scarce resources might be expected to develop hostility and prejudice toward each other. But this theory fails to explain why young people are prejudiced against old people. A second theory to explain prejudice is the **belief-difference theory of prejudice.** According to this theory, prejudice results from perceived differences in belief systems. From this point of view, people are prejudiced against blacks not because of racial differences but because they see blacks as having different beliefs, and they are suspicious of those with different beliefs. But this theory fails to explain why people are prejudiced against handicapped people, who may be different only as the result of a recent accident. A third theory is the **scapegoating theory of prejudice.** According to this theory, prejudice is a form of **displaced aggression** (aggression that is directed against someone or some object other than its original target). If you punish your dog, the dog may react with aggression against the cat. The dog's hostile reaction was displaced from you to a safer target—the cat. The cat serves as a **scapegoat,** a safe target for displaced aggression.

The old and the handicapped may be viewed as relatively safe targets for displaced aggression. They are physically marked with signs of their difference, making them relatively easy to identify. When certain sorts of people are frustrated or threatened, they apparently displace their anger toward a target group by expressing prejudice and even violence against their scapegoat.

Prejudice and the Handicapped

During the past few years there has been an increasing recognition of the rights of the handicapped. People who are blind or deaf, who are disfigured or missing limbs, who have arthritis or cerebral palsy, who are paralyzed or otherwise disabled have been the victims of discrimination in education and employment and have endured great prejudice and misunderstanding. What makes the handicapped different from others is as irrelevant to their personality, intelligence, and basic competence as is a difference in skin color. Yet they

are regarded as different not only physically, but also mentally. Understanding the similarity of the handicapped and the nonhandicapped is important. As one professional noted,

What the handicapped want, you and I want: a friend—someone to talk to, to share important things with; some warmth—someone to touch, put their hands on my shoulder in a way that says, "I like you"; approval—a message from others that tells me, "I'm O.K."; affection—demonstrated love, feeling and knowing you are loved, not necessarily in a sexual way; dignity—some communication from others that you are of worth; social outlets—avoiding loneliness and experiencing the above; identity as a sexual being—lustful, biological need for sex and sexual stimulation.[10]

Too often our attitudes toward the handicapped deny them the opportunity to fulfill these basic needs. Attitudes toward the handicapped to some degree depend upon the nature of the handicap. In general, a sensory handicap, such as blindness or deafness, results in less negative attitudes from others than a facial or body deformity or a loss of coordination through cerebral palsy. In these latter cases, the handicap results in extreme social and personal rejection.

Prejudice toward the handicapped takes the form of a belief that all people with a particular disability are alike and that they are to be pitied, treated as children, not permitted to act or speak for themselves, not looked at when present, and avoided when possible.

Ageism and the Old

We classify people on the basis of chronological age and respond to them accordingly. People of the same chronological age, however, are very different physically and psychologically. Yet we tend to lump them all together. In particular, the old are stereotyped and discriminated against. Prejudice against the old is called **ageism.**

Ageism is prejudice against people on the basis of their age.   We overgeneralize by assuming that all older people are alike, and we devalue them by mistakenly assuming that they are all feeble, forgetful, inactive, and inflexible.   The Gray Panthers attempt to combat ageism.   (© Bettye Lane/Photo Researchers, Inc.)

We tend to value the young more than the old. According to some authors, this tendency is so extreme that it involves the worship of youth and the neglect of the old.   Growing old in America can be a painful and lonely experience.   As one researcher explained,

The general tragedy of old age in America is that we have shaped a society which is extremely harsh to live in when one is old.   The tragedy of old age is not the fact that each of us must grow old and die, but that the process of doing so has been made unnecessarily and at times excruciatingly painful, humiliating, debilitating and isolating through insensitivity, ignorance and poverty.[11]

The condition of the old in America is a result of our attitudes toward them.

A person who is old is assumed to have certain characteristics simply because of age.   The stereotype of older people includes many myths.   All old people are assumed to be inflexible, conservative, irritable, feeble, and forgetful.   In fact, there are great differences among older people and they do not conform to the stereotype of them.

Many people over seventy are not inactive, gravely ill, institutionalized, mentally slow, incapable of learning, or lacking sexual interest.   Robert Butler, a psychiatrist and **gerontologist** (scientist specializing in the study of older people), wrote:

Those who think of old people as boobies, crones, witches, old biddies, old fogies, pains-in-the-neck, out-to-pasture, boring, garrulous, unproductive and worthless, have accepted the stereotypes of aging, including the extreme mistake of believing that substantial numbers of old people are in or belong in institutions.   On the contrary, most old people need not be and are not in institutions and, given a fighting chance in a society that has devalued them, can maintain a viable place in society. . . .   There is a deep and profound prejudice against the elderly which is found to some degree in all of us. . . .   Ageism allows the younger generations to see older people as different from themselves.   Thus they subtly cease to identify with their elders as human beings.[12]

A person who is prejudiced against one group is often prejudiced against other groups.   Research has shown that strong prejudice against the elderly, the handicapped, and ethnic minorities tends to be found in the same individuals, a pattern of hostility and hatred directed toward all people who are "different."[13,14,15]

Interim Summary   Three theories of prejudice are the competition theory, the belief-difference theory, and the scapegoating theory.   Of these, only the scapegoating theory provides a useful explanation of prejudice toward the elderly and the handicapped.   Handicapped persons with facial or body deformities experience extreme prejudice and rejection.   Ageism is expressed in a variety of negative attitudes toward older adults.

Racism

Racism is prejudice against a person primarily because of skin color.   Since racial prejudice has not yet been eliminated from the American scene, you probably have either directly experienced racism or at least witnessed examples of it.   Racism can affect blacks, Hispanics, Puerto Ricans, Asians, Indians—anyone who seems "different" from the white Anglo majority in this country.

Racism involves overgeneralization—all persons of a particular skin color are regarded as the same, in spite of clear individual differences.   Racism also involves devaluation—members of the other race are all seen as possessing undesirable traits.   Studies show that whites tend to have anti-black attitudes, although this is *less* true for younger white people.[16]   Blacks tend to have anti-white attitudes, and this is *more* true for younger black people.[17]   Racism appears at its worst in prejudice against black Americans and has too often been expressed violently.

Violence

Violence and prejudice seem to go together.   Violence against blacks is an ugly but significant part of the history of this country and is all too common even now.   Racial prejudice that leads to murder can be viewed as an expression of complete devaluation.

For the crime of killing a white man's cow, William Carr, a Negro, was killed at Planquemies, Louisiana.   The lynch-ing was conducted in a most orderly manner, Carr being taken from the sheriff without resistance by a mob of thirty masked men, hurried to the nearest railroad bridge and hanged without ceremony.[18]

When this lynching took place, around the turn of the century, an average of two black persons were lynched each week in this country.   In the 1960s there was violence against black Americans during the period of school desegregation in the South.   More recently, racial violence has resulted from the mandatory busing of school children to achieve integration.

Other groups, such as religious minorities, have also felt the violence in prejudice.   It is difficult, however, for the person who has never experienced prejudice to understand its cruelty fully.   This may contribute to the persistence of unexamined stereotypes in our culture.

The Effects of Racism

The consequences of racial prejudice affect both whites and blacks in this country.   Have you felt it, or can you imagine what it would be like to suffer from discrimination all of your life; to be denied the promise of society; to be seen as mentally crippled or dirty because of your color; to be feared as something unknown; to be labeled as "culturally disadvantaged"?   How would you react?

A common reaction is anger:

All blacks are angry.   White Americans seem not to recognize it.   They seem to think that all the trouble is caused by only a few "extremists.". . .   *The emerging rage now threatens to shatter this nation.*[19]

These remarks, from the book *Black Rage,* convey one response to racial prejudice—anger. When you are aggressed against, the natural reaction is to hit back, and this is how many blacks are now feeling. They have suffered from white aggression for several generations and they now feel like hitting back.

Another possible reaction to racism is for the victim to identify with the aggressor. "If you can't beat them, join them," the saying goes, and some blacks follow this saying by identifying with whites. The term "passing" refers to the attempt by light-skinned black people to "pass" for white and be accepted by white society without prejudice. While this practice is not as common today as it used to be, minor versions of passing are still common. One variety of passing is seen among blacks who try to look "white" by using skin bleaches. Preference for light skin among black people has been common since plantation days. Parents still tend to favor a light-skinned child. Among black college students, there is still a tendency for light-skinned persons to be preferred as dates.[20]

A third reaction to racial prejudice is to accept the negative judgment of society as true. To accept the racist view is to agree that you are inferior, dirty, and lazy. There is evidence that some black children by the age of four have been so influenced by their prejudiced society that they believe the racial stereotype about themselves. Black children in these studies tended to look down on blacks.

In one classic older study, 253 black children between the ages of two and seven were shown two dolls, one black and one white. The psychologists asked the children, "Which doll looks nice?", "Which doll looks bad?", and "Which doll is a nice color?" Most of the black children picked the white doll as the one that looked nice and had a nice color, and picked the black doll as the one that looked bad.[21] Another study found that 60 percent of black children, but only 10 percent of white children, preferred to play with children of the other race.[22]

Black Is Beautiful

But the times have changed. Feelings of black pride and racial identity are stronger now than ever before. In the 1960s, "Black Is Beautiful" was a slogan that gained wider acceptance among blacks. Black leaders emerged who called for "black power" and black control of black communities. The emergence of African nations has led to a rediscovery of "black culture" and "black heritage." Blacks rejected the prejudiced attitudes of white society and developed a higher sense of self-esteem.

Two black psychiatrists, William Grier and Price Cobbs, explain that blacks who embrace blackness and feel pride in their racial identity feel a sudden lifting of the spirit. Blacks who prize their blackness are freed from feelings of fear and inferiority that are the result of white racism.

The psychological realities of black life took shape under the pressure of white hatred. Black men were moved by the passions that move all men and faced life with the mixtures of courage and cowardice that all men have mustered— except with the difference that the complete range of life was lived under the press of American bigotry.

[Pride in] blackness has the effect of penetrating and shattering the pressure bearing down on and distorting black lives. It allows blacks to cleanse themselves of fear, and, in one act, remove not only the intimidation of immediate hostility, but also all ceilings, permitting freedom to move as far and as fast as one's wits will allow.

Freedom from fear is strong wine![23]

Interim Summary   Racism is prejudice against a person on the basis of skin color. It involves overgeneralization and devaluation, and has all too often been expressed in violence. Three reactions to racism are anger, "passing," and acceptance. Those who can take pride in their racial identity can be free of the feelings of fear and inferiority caused by racism.

Sexism

What's wrong with this story?

A father and his son were driving home when they had a terrible accident. The father was killed instantly and his son was severely injured. The son was taken to the hospital and rushed into the Emergency Room. The surgeon came in and said, "I can't treat this patient. He's my son!" Another doctor was called and the boy eventually recovered.

Since the child did not have two fathers, how can this story be explained? If this story sounds impossible to you, your thinking has been prejudiced by your sexist culture. You have been trained to think of women as housewives, secretaries, and maids and not as professionals. In the case of the story above, the doctor was the boy's mother; the story seems impossible only because you failed to see this possibility. Prejudice against a person on the basis of sex is called **sexism.** Attitudes toward and assumptions about women commonly reflect this kind of prejudice.

Overgeneralization is one part of sexual prejudice: all women are seen as alike, possessing certain standard personality characteristics. Categorization (by sex) comes first; observation comes second. The tremendous differences among women are ignored in the process of overgeneralization. Devaluation is another part of sexual prejudice. Women are regarded as inferior beings who are acceptable only so long as they "stay in their place."

Conflicting Roles

In 1792 a writer described the role of woman as follows:

She was created to be the toy of man, his rattle, and it must jingle in his ears whenever, dismissing reason, he chooses to be amused.[24]

The stereotype of the "ideal woman" is not much different today. Germaine Greer in her book *The Female Eunuch* described the female stereotype as follows:

The stereotype is the Eternal Feminine. She is the Sexual Object sought by all men, and by all women. . . . She need achieve nothing, for she is the reward of achievement. . . . Her glossy lips and mat complexion, her unfocused eyes and flawless fingers, her extraordinary hair all floating and shining, curling and gleaming, reveal the inhuman triumph of cosmetics. . . . She sleeps unruffled, her lips red and juicy and closed, her eyes as crisp and black as if new painted, and her false eyelashes immaculately curled. Even when she washes her face with a new and creamier toilet soap her expression is as tranquil and vacant and her paint as flawless as ever. . . . For she is a doll: weeping, pouting or smiling, running or reclining, she is a doll.[24]

Few women can live up to this stereotype, but many try. The image of the beautiful and desirable woman is held out before them continuously as they grow up. Magazine advertisements and movies manufacture the unreal but ideal woman. In the struggle to be the stereotype, a woman must give up herself.

Thoroughly opposed to the stereotype of the "Eternal Feminine" is individual achievement, self-reliance, intelligence, and competitive spirit. Yet these qualities are also held out before women as desirable. Women in schools and colleges particularly are encouraged to strive to develop their intellectual potential to the fullest, but this would conflict with the stereotyped sex roles. Thus, women are expected to move in two directions at once. They are pressured to fulfill the feminine role and be passive, dependent, and ignorant; and they are pressured to fulfill the achievement role and be active, independent, and intelligent. Women in this society have a **role conflict;** they are asked to live up to opposing sets of expectations. A successful woman is tolerated only if she also satisfies the feminine stereotype, but the roles are conflicting. One author expressed it this way:

Nobody objects to a woman's being a good writer or sculptor or geneticist if, at the same time, she manages to be a good wife, a good mother, good-looking, good-tempered, well-dressed, well-groomed, and un*aggressive.*[25]

Sex Discrimination

After struggling through four years of college, a twenty-four-year-old female secretary wrote:

I have a bachelor's degree in French literature. The smartest thing I ever did, however, was to take a typing course my junior year in high school; without it I would never be able to find a job.[26]

Her experience is not unusual. Nearly one out of every five employed women with a college degree is working as a clerical worker, sales worker, or service worker of some type.[27] These women are clearly working below their potential. The most common occupations for women are secretary, saleswoman, private household worker, teacher in elementary school, bookkeeper, waitress, and professional nurse.[28] Most of these jobs are poorly paid. Furthermore, the proportion of women working in less skilled and lower paid service occupations is increasing, while the proportion working in the leading professions is declining.[27] Only about 9 percent of the scientists, 7 percent of the physicians, and 3 percent of the lawyers are women.

A major investigation of sex discrimination in employment sampled 539 women and 993 men nationwide.[29] Only full-time regular workers were included in the final analysis. The results showed that the average woman earned $3,458 less than the average man with the same type of job and similar background. The annual incomes of about 95 percent of the women were less than comparable men. The average woman's annual income was less than 60 percent of a comparable man's income. The study concluded that about 95 percent of women workers suffer from sex discrimination in employment. A more recent study shows that the gap between the pay rates for men and women is growing larger each year.[30]

Putting Women in Their Place

There is a striking parallel between the roles of women and blacks in America. Women are regarded as irrational and incompetent just as blacks used to be. Women are expected to be submissive and nonaggressive, otherwise they will be seen as "pushy" or "uppity" just as blacks used to be. The "place" of women (and they should know their place) is in the home as unpaid servants or in poorly paid service jobs elsewhere; blacks compete with women for these positions. From early infancy women are trained to know their "place" and to be satisfied with it; blacks used to be similarly trained. The black woman suffers two kinds of discrimination: one because she is black and one because she is a woman.

But blacks in some ways have made greater progress toward freedom than have women.   Attention has been so focused on racist attitudes that you tend to be aware of them when they exist.   But prejudice against women is often a **nonconscious ideology**— an **ideology** (set of assumptions and beliefs) that you are not conscious of having.   This is made clear in the following example:

Consider an analogy.   Suppose that a white male college student decided to room or set up a bachelor apartment with a black male friend.   Surely the typical white student would not blithely assume that his black roommate was to handle all the domestic chores.   Nor would his conscience allow him to do so even in the unlikely event that his roommate would say: "No, that's okay.   I like doing housework.   I'd be happy to do it."   We suspect that the typical white student would still not be comfortable if he took advantage of this offer, if he took advantage of the fact that his roommate had been socialized to be "happy" with such an arrangement.   But change this hypothetical black roommate to a female marriage partner, and somehow the student's conscience goes to sleep.   At most it is quickly tranquilized by the thought that "she is happiest when she is ironing for her loved one."   Such is the power of a nonconscious ideology.

Of course, it may well be that she is happiest when she is ironing for her loved one.

Such, indeed, is the power of a nonconscious ideology![31]

The ideology, or set of assumptions and beliefs, underlying the oppression of blacks has recently been made conscious by focusing the attention of society on it, and it has been rejected.   Or, at least, it is in the process of being rejected.   But the ideology underlying the oppression of women has not been made conscious yet.   One of the purposes of the women's liberation movement is to make that ideology conscious, just as the civil rights movement made conscious the ideology supporting racial discrimination.

The attitudes toward women, including the attitudes women have toward themselves, are learned.   Women are socialized into the roles they fill in society.   Parents teach their little girls to be passive and nonassertive, that is, to be "feminine."   Parents actively discourage girls from being interested in science or mathematics and provide them with sewing lessons instead.   Girls also learn their place from advertising on television and in magazines, and from the roles they see women playing.

Prejudice against a person on the basis of sex is called sexism. In the past, girl children were trained to accept the traditional female role, but modern girls are playing Little League baseball and preparing for professional careers. (Read D. Brugger/The Picture Cube)

Blacks at one time were consistently portrayed in films and on television as stupid and lazy. Fortunately, this has changed, but the representation of women in the media has not improved very much. What is the effect of girls being exposed to ads such as this one from Parker Pens:

You might as well give her a gorgeous pen to keep her checkbook unbalanced with. A sleek and shining pen will make her feel prettier, which is more important to any girl than solving mathematical mysteries.[32]

The image of women on television teaches little girls to know their place. Women in television ads are shown as anxiously concerned about the adequacy of their laundry, cleaning, and cooking efforts. They are shown as endlessly devoted to the task of modifying their appearance so as to please men. They are rarely shown as independent and intellectual persons working in one of the professions.

Advertising did not create these images about women, but it is a powerful force for their reinforcement. It legitimizes the idealized, stereotyped roles of woman as temptress, wife, mother, and sex object, and portrays women as less intelligent and more dependent than men. It makes women believe that their chief role is to please men and that their fulfillment will be as wives, mothers, and homemakers. It makes women feel unfeminine if they are not pretty enough. . . . It creates false, unreal images of women that reflect male fantasies rather than flesh and blood human beings.[31]

Men's Liberation

Women are not the only victims of sexual prejudice. Men, too, must live up to impossible images of the ideal; they must be tall, strong, aggressive, decisive, and unemotional. When they are growing up, boys are taught over and over again that they must "act like a man." They are told that expressing emotions is not "manly." There is, however, a growing resistance to this sexist stereotype. One man said, "The overriding characteristic of men in this society is emotional constipation."[33] Another said, "We don't cry. We are machines. And we have been made that way by society because machines are better for production."[34] Some psychologists now believe that the price men pay for struggling to conform to society's image of masculinity is the high rate shown by men of ulcers and heart attacks. The men's liberation movement is an attempt to liberate men from the male stereotype.

The issue, for both men and women, is the right of individuality and choice. Sexist attitudes narrow the range of acceptable choices; for example, women are judged badly if they are aggressive and men if they are passive. Yet some men are by nature less aggressive than some women. Men and women alike are pressured to conform to preconceived models of "masculine" and "feminine." These models may fit some people, but they do not fit everyone. Thus, these models restrict choices and individuality. The problem of sexism is that it denies people the right to be different, to be individual.

Interim Summary   Sexism is prejudice against a person on the basis of sex. Sexist attitudes in society cause role conflicts in women; women experience opposing pressures to be both feminine and independent. A consequence of sexism is sex discrimination in employment; women are denied equal pay and equal opportunity. Men are also victims of sexual prejudice; men are expected to feel and behave in particular ways that correspond to the male stereotype. Combating sexual prejudice is particularly difficult because sexist attitudes involve a nonconscious ideology, a set of beliefs that you are not aware of having.

Reducing Prejudice

The world is becoming crowded. We must learn to live together, to work together to solve our common problems, and this requires the reduction of prejudice. Not so long ago some people thought we were on the verge of eliminating prejudice, but we have since learned, to our disappointment, that prejudice is deeply rooted and not so easily changed. There have been hundreds of studies examining the effect of different strategies for reducing prejudice; some have shown success and many have shown failure. What have we learned about how prejudice can be reduced? One approach is to attack the causes of prejudice.

Interdependence

Three of the possible causes of prejudice are economic competition, the perceived differences of beliefs, and scapegoating. Prejudice from competition might be reduced if everyone could have a satisfactory job so that fears of unemployment could be eliminated. During periods of high inflation and high unemployment, there is a special danger that economic problems could aggravate prejudiced feelings. If economic fears could be reduced through appropriate social legislation, prejudice might be reduced.

Prejudice stemming from competition might also be reduced by fostering cooperation between members of different groups. When two individuals or two groups must work together toward some mutually desired goal, their attitudes toward each other change. In Sherif's Robber's Cave study,[35] discussed in the preceding chapter, the hostility and conflict between two groups of campers were dramatically reduced when they had to work together to accomplish mutual goals. Being interdependent changed their attitudes.

One social psychologist devised a special program for increasing cooperation within the schoolroom.[36] His assumption was that if a situation could be created where students would have to cooperate and depend upon one another, the conflict between racial groups might be reduced. The children were divided into small racially mixed groups, and each child was given a different part of the total material. The children must fit the parts together to make the whole. Instead of individuals competing against one another, the performance of the groups was evaluated. The students within a group had to cooperate in order to succeed. The results of applying this method were to increase the extent to which Anglo, Hispanic, and black students liked each other.

Equal-Status Contact

Other methods of reducing prejudice attack the perception of belief differences, a second possible contributory cause of prejudice. Prejudice arising from the perceived differences of beliefs might be reduced by education about other cultures or by experience in interacting with members of other cultures and groups. Although contact between ethnic groups sometimes fails to reduce deeply rooted prejudice,[37] contact more often results in reduced prejudice.[38] In one study of children at a summer camp, attitudes were assessed both before and after a one-week experience in an integrated setting.[39] In each residential unit, half of the campers were black and half were white. After a week of living closely together and playing together, the attitudes of both the black and the white children changed to reflect less prejudice.

Several studies have shown that interracial contact by itself is often not very helpful in reducing prejudice; instead, it is the kind and quality of contact that is important. The best kind of contact—the contact most useful in reducing prejudice—seems to be between people of equal status.[40,41] Interactions between people of different status are typically status-oriented interactions. For example, in some parts of the South, whites are in close contact with blacks, but generally only with blacks of lower status (gardener or maid).   This kind of contact does not promote treating each other as equals and therefore is not very useful in reducing prejudice.

Improved Psychological Health

A final possible cause of prejudice is scapegoating, and this, too, might be attacked to reduce prejudice.   Prejudice from scapegoating, since it involves fundamental aspects of the personality, might be reduced through some form of psychotherapy.   Several studies have shown that therapy does reduce racial prejudice.[42,43]   Attempts to alter personality problems and improve psychological health should serve to reduce prejudice.   In one study, prejudiced attitudes were measured both before and after prison inmates experienced an integrated prison unit.[44]   Some inmates became more prejudiced and some became less prejudiced.   Those who became less prejudiced tended to be inmates with higher self-esteem and better attitudes toward people in general.   The results of this study suggest that efforts to improve the self-esteem of children might have the effect of reducing prejudice.   In addition, since scapegoating is considered to be caused by harsh child-rearing practices, changing our child-rearing practices might be helpful.   A change to more permissive discipline or to less physically abusive discipline should reduce scapegoating and thereby reduce prejudice.

Finally, for those men and women who have been socialized into accepting the racist or sexist views of themselves, some form of reeducation is necessary.   The ideology that supports racism and sexism must be revealed, made conscious, and rejected by both its adherents and its victims.

Summary

1. Attitudes are tendencies to act in a consistently positive or negative way toward people or objects.   They are relatively long-lasting and have affective (feeling), cognitive (belief), and conative (behavioral) components.
2. The most common method of measuring attitudes is self-report measures such as the Likert scale, Guttman scale, and semantic differential scale.
3. The learning theory of attitudes assumes that our attitudes are learned through the processes of operant and classical conditioning.
4. The cognitive dissonance theory proposes that we are motivated to eliminate any inconsistencies between our attitudes and behaviors.   Changes in attitude occur when we have no alternative for explaining our actions; if we act toward a group in a negative way, then our attitudes regarding that group will also be negative.
5. Prejudice is a preconceived and unfavorable attitude toward an entire group of people.   One product of prejudice is a stereotype, a set of fixed ideas about members of a group.
6. Research has shown that prejudice is learned from parents, peers, or teachers.
7. Children with aggressive and punishing parents tend to develop prejudiced personalities.   The authoritarian personality characterizes the highly prejudiced personality and can be measured by the F scale.
8. The competition theory of prejudice assumes that groups in competition tend to develop prejudice toward one another.
9. The belief-difference theory of prejudice assumes that prejudice results from the perceived differences in belief systems between different groups.

10. The scapegoating theory of prejudice assumes that prejudice is a form of displaced aggression. It provides a useful explanation of prejudice against the handicapped and the elderly.

11. Racism is prejudice against a person on the basis of skin color. Ageism is prejudice against the elderly. Sexism is prejudice based on a person's sex.

12. Studies have shown that fostering cooperation between groups reduces prejudice that stems primarily from competition.

13. Prejudice arising out of perceived differences in beliefs can be reduced by education and contact with other groups. Interaction between people of equal status is the most helpful in reducing prejudice.

14. Prejudice might also be reduced through changes in our child-rearing practices and through implementation of methods to improve psychological health.

Key Concepts

attitude A tendency to act in a consistently positive or negative way toward an object, a person, or a group of people.

affective component of attitudes The positive or negative feeling that you have about the object or person toward whom the attitude is directed.

cognitive component of attitudes The belief or opinion that you hold about the object or person toward whom the attitude is directed.

conative component of attitudes The tendency to behave in a particular way toward the object or person toward whom the attitude is directed.

self-report measure A method used to measure attitudes that involves asking people to report how they feel about other people or things.

attitude scale A measure of type and strength of various attitudes.

Likert scale A type of attitude scale that consists of statements answered by selecting a response indicating the extent of agreement (ranging from "disagree very much" to "agree very much").

Guttman scale A type of attitude scale that consists of a graded series of statements varying in strength of attitude.

semantic differential scale A type of attitude scale that consists of pairs of opposing adjectives.

learning theory of attitudes The theory that attitudes are learned; they are acquired through processes of operant and classical conditioning.

operant conditioning Conditioning by consequences; instrumental conditioning.

classical conditioning Conditioning by association; Pavlovian conditioning.

cognitive dissonance theory The theory that attitudes are formed and maintained so that they are consistent with our behavior; if you act toward a certain group in a negative, discriminatory way, then to be consistent, your attitudes toward that group will also be negative.

dissonance Inconsistency or lack of agreement.

overgeneralization The tendency to see all members of a group as the same; for example, to see all men as aggressive.

devaluation The tendency to regard some people as inferior or worthless.

prejudice   A preconceived and unfavorable attitude toward an entire group.

stereotype   A set of fixed ideas about a person based on categorizing the person as a member of a group.

authoritarian personality   A personality type characterized by resistance to change, admiration for authority figures, contempt for persons of lower status, and extreme prejudice.

F scale   A test measuring the authoritarian personality.

competition theory of prejudice   According to this theory, negative attitudes tend to develop between competing groups.

belief-difference theory of prejudice   According to this theory, prejudice results from perceived differences of belief systems.

scapegoating theory of prejudice   According to this theory, prejudice is a form of displaced aggression.

displaced aggression   Aggression that is directed against someone other than its original target.

scapegoat   A "safe" target for displaced aggression.

ageism   Prejudice against the old.

gerontologist   A scientist specializing in the study of older people.

racism   Prejudice against a person on the basis of skin color.

sexism   Prejudice against a person on the basis of sex.

role conflict   A problem resulting from having two opposing sets of expectations for how to behave; for example, college women are expected to be "feminine" (passive and dependent) but also are expected to be independent, successful, and intelligent.

nonconscious ideology   A set of assumptions and beliefs that one has but is not aware of.

ideology   A set of assumptions and beliefs.

Chapter 24

Crime and Aggression

Key Questions   1. What are the causes of aggression?
2. How can the criminal mind be understood?
3. What causes people to become criminals?
4. How can crime be prevented?

Americans have been called an aggressive and violent people. Crimes such as murder, rape, child abuse, assault, and assassination have been occurring in this country with increasing frequency. In the 1960s the news was full of massacres in Vietnam and murder cults in California. Now we hear of bombings, beatings, and riots.

A survey showed that 12 percent of American adults have punched or beaten another person and 17 percent have slapped or kicked someone. About 32 percent report that they were spanked frequently as children. Almost 70 percent of those surveyed agreed with this statement: "When a boy is growing up, it is very important for him to have a few fistfights."[1] Do you agree?

The term **aggression** refers to fighting or attacking behavior. It is a form of interaction, since it occurs between people, and it has the purpose or intent of hurt and injury. **Anger** is the feeling, or emotion, that accompanies aggression. Physical aggression, resulting in physical injury, is only one type of aggression; verbal aggression, where words are weapons, is another form of attack. Often, verbal aggression leads directly to physical aggression.

How Aggressive Are You?

People vary in the extent of their aggressiveness. Some react with aggression to the slightest irritation; others almost never react aggressively. To find out how aggressive you are, take the following aggression test.[2] Think about each of the statements carefully, and then check the statements that are true for you.

☐ 1. Once in a while I cannot control my urge to harm others.

☐ 2. I can think of no good reason for ever hitting anyone.

☐ 3. If somebody hits me first, I let the person have it.

☐ 4. Whoever insults me or my family is asking for a fight.

☐ 5. People who continually pester you are asking for a punch in the nose.

☐ 6. I seldom strike back, even if someone hits me first.

☐ 7. When I really lose my temper, I am capable of slapping someone.

☐ 8. I get into fights about as often as the next person does.

☐ 9. If I have to resort to physical violence to defend my rights, I will.

☐ 10. I have known people who pushed me so far that we came to blows.

☐ 11. When I disapprove of my friends' behavior, I let them know it.

☐ 12. I often find myself disagreeing with people.

☐ 13. I can't help getting into arguments when people disagree with me.

☐ 14. I demand that people respect my rights.

☐ 15. Even when my anger is aroused, I don't use "strong language."

☐ 16. If people annoy me, I am apt to tell them what I think of them.

☐ 17. When people yell at me, I yell back.

☐ 18. When I get mad, I say nasty things.

☐ 19. I could not put other people in their place, even if they needed it.

☐ 20. I often make threats I don't really mean to carry out.

Is it possible to measure aggressiveness with a true-false test? Your score on this brief test undoubtedly is influenced by many things, including how aware you are of your own behavior. Your score, therefore, is only a crude indication of your level of relative aggressiveness. Your score is a number that has meaning only when it is compared to the scores made on the test by many other people.

Your aggression score consists of points added up for certain items that you checked and for other items that you did not check. To score the aggression test, give yourself one point for each of the following items that you *did not* check: 2, 6, 15, 19. Give yourself one point for each of the remaining items that you *did* check. The sum of your points is your "aggression score."

Men and women score differently on this test. The average for men is about 10 points and the average for women is 8 points. A score of 1 to 4 could be interpreted as showing low aggression, a score of 5 to 16 moderate aggression, and a score of 17 to 20 high aggression. You might compare your score on the first 10 questions to your score on the remaining 10 questions. The first 10 items were designed to measure physical aggression and the remaining 10 items were designed to measure verbal aggression. Are you more aggressive physically or verbally?

The Instinct Theory of Aggression

If we can understand our violence, perhaps we can control it. Why do people strike one another? Are we born killers? Psychologists studying aggression have identified three factors associated with aggression: heredity, environmental events, and learning.

Suppose a wife kills her husband. To understand this killing, we can ask (1) Is the woman a killer by instinct—was she born a killer? (2) Was the killing a reaction to frustration or to some other environmental event? (3) Was the woman rewarded in the past for her aggression—did she learn to kill?

Two great minds of this century, Einstein and Freud, believed people were born killers. Einstein wrote that human beings had an inborn lust for hatred and destruction. Freud believed that "the tendency to aggression is an innate, independent instinctual disposition in man."[3] Freud proposed that people have a universal death instinct, **Thanatos,** which turns into aggression when directed toward others. According to the **instinct theory of aggression,** aggression is an inborn tendency and people have "killer instincts."

A major statement of the idea of aggression as an instinct appears in the book *On Aggression* by Konrad Lorenz.[4] Lorenz is an **ethologist,** a scientist who studies the behavior of animals in natural settings. Lorenz's study of animals has led him to believe that both animals and human beings have inborn compulsions to be aggressive, and that this biological need, like sex, requires periodic outlets.

What is an **instinct?** The term refers to complex behavior that is inherited; a genetically determined, not learned, pattern of behaving. It is a specific response pattern that is triggered by particular stimuli. Nestbuilding in birds has been called an instinct; there is a unique type of nest for each different species of birds, and no learning seems to be required for successful nest building. Fighting behavior in rats is also an instinct. For example, in the Norway rat, the sequence of fighting behavior is highly determined; when two rats fight, they follow the same rigid pattern, even if they were raised in the laboratory and had no opportunity to learn how to fight.[5]

Aggression exists in people as well as animals. The question is, Is that aggression instinctual or learned? If it is instinctual, it should be universally present and should have a distinct biological basis.

Murder, Murder Everywhere

Aggression seems to be universally present in animal and human life. Most animals display aggression in the competition over food, mates, and territory. Some animals, such as caribou, elephants, and sea otters do not stake out territories; they have no space that they will fight to protect.[6] Even animals that do fight over mates or territory rarely cause each other injury.[5] The combatants follow very strict "rules of the game" that prevent the death of the loser. An example is the male oryx antelope; he has rapier-shaped horns, but he does not gore his rival in battle. The "rules" provide that the only acceptable moves are pushing and clashing of forehead against forehead. Although threats are common among animals, violent aggressive acts are rare.[7] Human aggression is not like that. We don't follow the rules.[8]

To generalize from animals to people may not be valid. What is true for one may not be true for both. The case of human aggression will have to be considered separately from that of the animals. Some believe that people are killers by nature, and that the beast in us peers out whenever civilization fails to control our aggressiveness.

The situation relative to human aggression can be briefly stated under three headings. First, man has been a predator for a long time and his nature is such that he easily learns to enjoy killing other animals. Hunting is still considered a sport, and millions of dollars are spent annually to provide birds, mammals, and fish to be killed for the amusement of sportsmen. In many cultures animals are killed for the amusement of human observers (in bullfighting, cockfighting, bear baiting, and so forth). Second, man easily learns to enjoy torturing and killing other human beings. Whether one considers the Roman arena, public tortures and executions, or the sport of boxing, it is clear that humans have developed means to enjoy the sight of others being subjected to punishment. Third, war has

been regarded as glorious and, whether one considers recent data from tribes in New Guinea or the behavior of the most civilized nations, until very recently war was a normal instrument of national policy and there was no revulsion from the events of victorious warfare, no matter how destructive. . . . Man's nature evolved under these conditions. . . . The consequence of this evolutionary history is that large-scale human destruction may appear at any time social controls break down; recent examples are Nazi Germany, Algeria, the Congo, Vietnam.[9]

Other scientists believe that human aggressiveness is not due to the beasts from which human beings evolved, but is the result of our unique culture and technology. Human aggression is different from animal aggression. Animals rarely harm others of the same species; they threaten but do not kill. If the animals from which we evolved are less violent than we are, then it seems unlikely that aggression is a biological necessity in humans. It is more likely that the culture and technology that sets humans apart from the lower animals is responsible for aggression and war.

Your Violent Brain

Your brain plays a key role in the aggressive response. Thought, movement, and feeling originate in the human brain as tiny electrical impulses. Some scientists, in an attempt to control epileptic seizures, have tried to influence behavior by stimulating the brain with electrical impulses from wires. One patient, normally a mild-mannered woman, became extremely aggressive, verbally hostile, and threatened to strike the experimenter when electric current was provided to a particular region of her brain. When the current was turned off, she immediately returned to her peaceful and quiet condition.[10] Can you imagine what it would be like for someone else to turn your violence on and off by pressing a switch?

The outer wrinkled surface of the brain—the **cortex**—is the area most responsible for thought, problem solving, and other intellectual activities.

The brain centers for aggression are deep beneath this surface but are kept in control (usually) by the action of the cortex. What would happen if the cortex did not restrain the aggression centers? Scientists have surgically removed the cortex from certain animals, thus releasing the aggression centers from cortical control. They found that the animals responded aggressively to almost anything, even gentle petting. Because the aggressive reaction was so intense, yet seemed to lack all emotional involvement, it was called **sham rage.**

Numerous studies demonstrate that the brain system responsible for aggressive reactions to irritation or annoyance is separate from the brain system responsible for aggressive reactions to fear.[11] One study showed that a friendly cat will either attack a nearby rat or will attack the experimenter, depending upon which region of the brain is electrically stimulated. The cat could be controlled by turning a switch.[12]

A few persons, confined to mental hospitals, have uncontrollable rages, making them a threat to themselves and to those around them. Constant physical restraint is sometimes necessary for such persons. This form of superaggression has been found to be caused in many cases by brain tumors in a particular area of the brain. Following corrective brain surgery, these violent individuals typically become calm and passive.[13] It is clear that the brain has innate organized systems for the control of aggressive behavior and that these systems sometimes do not function properly.

Aggression involves the whole body, not just the brain. The heart rate and blood pressure increase; sugar is released into the muscles; breathing is faster; blood is diverted from the internal organs to the muscles (suddenly digestion is not as important as hitting or running). In both animals and people, the teeth are bared when rage is intense, and gutteral noises are made. The similarity of the rage reactions of animals and people suggests that the rage reaction is inborn and not learned.

There is no doubt that people have an inborn aggressive response system, involving the brain and the body. An aggressive response, however, is not automatically elicited or triggered by a specific external stimulus. There is great variability among people in what makes them angry and aggressive. The stimulus that elicits the aggressive response also changes with age and education. Although the aggressive response is innate, its relation to events in the environment is learned. Insults did not produce an aggressive reaction in you at birth; you could not even comprehend the language. You first learned the language and then learned to respond aggressively to certain words. Thus, the stimuli that produce aggression in human beings are not inborn, but learned.

The manner in which the aggressive response is expressed is also learned. There is a standard pattern to certain aspects of bodily reaction in aggression (blood pressure, heart rate, and so forth), but how we aggress against one another depends upon history and learning. People have invented wonderous machines for aggression, and their children learn from them how to use these machines.

Just as you have innate bodily structures that make it possible for you to talk, you have innate bodily structures in the brain and body that make it possible for you to express aggression. But what you say when you talk and what makes you aggressive and how you express your anger—these must be learned. Are people born killers? People are born with the capacity to kill, but there is no evidence that they have an inborn compulsion to use that capacity. Killing is something that is learned.

Interim Summary   The instinct theory of aggression proposes that people have inborn aggressive tendencies. In support of this theory, it is argued that aggression is universally present in human and animal life and that there is a distinct biological basis for aggression in certain brain structures. Animals, however, rarely kill members of their own species; unlike human beings, animals follow strict rules that prevent them from harming each other.   If we are basically beasts, born killers, it is surprising that animals from which we evolved are less aggressive than we are.   Furthermore, although we have innate biological structures that make aggression possible, these structures do not determine the direction or the form of the aggressive acts.   It is clear that learning must be involved.

The Reaction Theory of Aggression

According to the **reaction theory of aggression,** aggression occurs in response to external stimulation; it is a reaction to, and a way of coping with, events in the environment.

Reflexive Fighting

Attack is often followed by counterattack, in both animals and humans.   If someone hit you, you might hit back.   Several studies have shown that animals respond similarly.   Aggression seems to be an automatic reaction to pain, so long as there is something nearby to attack.   Reflexive fighting in response to pain has been demonstrated in mice, hamsters, cats, rats, and monkeys.[14]   In these studies researchers used electric shock to cause animals pain.   The animals themselves were not responsible for the occurrence of the shock, but when in pain they would attack each other anyway.

The scientists who perform such experiments are not sadistic or unfeeling; they believe that they are making important contributions to the body of knowledge about aggression and that understanding aggression is important for human survival.   There is no doubt that these studies have contributed to our understanding of pain and aggression.   By causing animals pain and studying animal aggression, scientists are able to learn more about how to control human pain and aggression.   But the price of that knowledge must be carefully weighed.   Some people believe that the price is too high and that the potential value of the knowledge gained from such studies does not warrant the methods used.

The Frustration-Aggression Hypothesis

Aggressive human behavior occurs in certain specific situations and not in others.   An early attempt to characterize what situations might lead to aggression is the **frustration-aggression hypothesis.**[15]   This proposal states simply that aggression is always a consequence of frustration; that is, the stimulus for aggressive responses is frustration.   One psychologist decided to study this hypothesis with pigeons.   But how do you frustrate a pigeon?   He reasoned that if a pigeon became used to being rewarded every time it made the correct response, it would be frustrated when the reward suddenly stopped.   This would be like failing to receive your paycheck on time.   The experiment was done using two pigeons in the same box.   When the reward suddenly stopped, one pigeon became enraged and viciously attacked the other pigeon in the box.[16]   The human analogy might be that after a man misses his paycheck, he goes home and yells at his wife.

It is clear from these studies that aggression often follows frustration, but this is not always the case.[2]   Aggression seems to occur at times when no frustrating event precedes it, and some things that appear frustrating are not followed by aggression.   The frustration-aggression hypothesis will work for those cases only if "frustration" is *defined* as any event that precedes aggression and "aggression" is defined to include unobservable internal processes.   In this way, whenever a clearly frustrating event is observed that is not followed by an observable aggressive response, it is possible to claim that there was an aggressive reaction but it was internal and therefore not observable.   Furthermore, whenever a clearly aggressive act occurs that is not preceded by an observable frustrating event, it is possible to claim that since aggression occurred, frustration must have occurred but was invisible. This kind of reasoning is circular and tends to go nowhere. Although the frustration-aggression hypothesis stimulated a lot of research, the circularity that developed from the vagueness of the definitions limited the usefulness of the idea.[17]

The reaction theory of aggression has consequently been more useful in accounting for aggressive behavior in animals than for human behavior.

Interim Summary The reaction theory of aggression assumes that aggression is a response to external stimuli. For example, pain seems to elicit automatic attack reactions in many animals. In human beings, the frustration-aggression hypothesis proposes that aggression is always a reaction to frustrating events. This hypothesis, however, has not been very well supported. Human aggression appears not to be a simple reaction to outside stimuli; it is far more complex than a reflex.

The Social-Learning Theory of Aggression

Certain forms of aggression are explicitly taught. The army trains its recruits to kill. High schools and colleges teach young people to be aggressive in football, boxing, and other sports. Parents expect male children to be physically aggressive and reward their sons with praise when they conform to these expectations. For the most part, however, aggression is not taught in the same way as arithmetic; instead the child learns violence by imitating violent individuals, by observing our violent society, and by being rewarded for aggressive acts. According to the **social-learning theory of aggression,** aggression results from imitation and reinforcement.

Imitating Models

Children learn through imitating adults. The adults serve as models for the child to copy. In one experiment Albert Bandura compared the behavior of three groups of children: one group witnessed an adult behaving aggressively; a second group witnessed an adult behaving nonaggressively; and the third group saw no adult model.[18] The aggressive adult model was observed attacking a large inflated doll with a

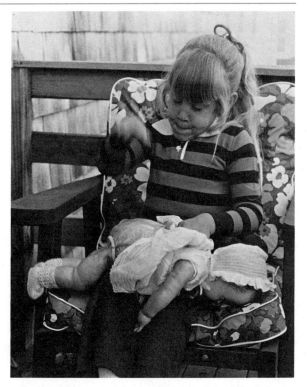

Why do children respond aggressively to their dolls and pets? According to the frustration-aggression hypothesis, children become aggressive when they are frustrated. According to the learning theory, aggression is acquired through imitation and reinforcement. (John Young)

mallet, then kicking the doll around the room. The nonaggressive adult model was observed quietly playing with Tinker Toys. Following their exposure to the adult models, the children were given some attractive toys to play with, and then the toys were taken away. The removal of the toys was an attempt on the part of the experimenter to make the children angry and frustrated. Finally, the children were allowed to play by themselves in the room with the large doll, the Tinker Toys, and other toys while they were secretly observed through a one-way mirror.

The children who had been exposed to the aggressive adult model played much more aggressively with the large doll than either the children exposed to the nonaggressive model or the children exposed to no model. The children tended to imitate the adult model they had witnessed, either by sitting quietly and playing or by attacking and beating the large doll, depending upon which adult model they had seen.

Children imitate their parents, and parents are often aggressive. Parents aggress against children when they use physical punishment. Physically punishing a child for being aggressive seems to be contradictory: the parent aggresses against the child in the attempt to teach the child not to be aggressive. The effect of parental aggression is that children copy it.[19] The best predictor of aggressiveness in children is aggressiveness in their parents; the child who has a history of severe physical punishment at home, including punishment for aggression, tends to be the child who will behave most aggressively.[20]

Observing Film and Television Violence

We are exposed to more violence today than ever before—on films, television, and in books and magazines. Should the "impressionable minds" of children be protected from this violence? Are the minds of children "impressionable"? A study by Bandura showed that children are influenced by violence portrayed on film. After watching either a realistic film or a cartoon film showing aggressive acts, children engaged in more aggressive behavior themselves.

Watching aggressive films made the children act more aggressively.[21] Several studies show that young adults are similarly affected by witnessing violence in films. A typical finding is that after watching a violent film, college students are more willing to administer painful electric shocks to another person in a psychology experiment. Apparently viewing the film increased their aggressiveness.[22,23]

However, experimental studies of the effects of film violence can be criticized. The laboratory situation in which these studies occurred, for example, is not at all like real life. The film strips children watch in these experiments are short and out of context. The question of what effect the observation of violence has remains without a definite answer; there is, however, enough evidence to warrant a strong suspicion that watching film and televison violence increases aggressiveness in viewers under some circumstances. Apparently people imitate not only "real-life" models, but also models shown in films or on television.

Reinforcement

Children learn that aggression "pays"; it is often rewarded, or reinforced. Male children may be punished for being a "sissy" and praised for fighting. When people are in conflict, often the more aggressive individual wins. Observations of nursery-school children show that aggressive acts are usually rewarded— the victim runs away or gives up a toy or candy to the aggressor; children who begin nursery school relatively unaggressive learn rather quickly to become more aggressive.[24] In a laboratory study, children were provided the opportunity to attack a large doll; each time they struck the doll they were rewarded with a marble. Later they were observed while playing games with other children. It was found that the children who were rewarded previously for attacking the doll were consistently more aggressive toward the other children.[25] We not only learn aggression by observing and imitating others but we also learn it because it has rewarding consequences.

Interim Summary   The social-learning theory of aggression proposed that aggression is learned through imitation and reinforcement. Children learn by imitating adults, whether the adults appear in "real life" or in films or television. Children exposed to aggressive adult models will themselves act more aggressively. In addition, children learn aggression because aggresssive acts are rewarded; reinforcement for aggression is provided both by parents and by peers.

Criminals

Life today is dangerous. Although your chances of dying from a disease have declined, your chances of being murdered have increased. Murder, mugging, beatings, rape, and other violent crimes are everyday occurrences in a big city. In many areas of big cities, grocery stores post armed guards by the cash registers to prevent robbery. Many people today are afraid to walk down the street at night.

Crime is becoming common even among the very young. Elementary and junior high schools are reporting crime waves on their campuses. A recent survey of boys and girls from thirteen to sixteen years of age found that more than 50 percent of the boys and more than 30 percent of the girls admitted to recent thefts, 39 percent of the boys and 15 percent of the girls admitted to recent physical assaults against others, and 34 percent of the boys and 14 percent of the girls admitted to involvement in gang fights.[26]

Who are the criminals and why do they commit crimes? How do they differ from you and me? As our society becomes more and more violent, the answer to these questions becomes increasingly important. The better we understand criminals, the better we will be able to prevent crime.

Some criminals are not really very different from us. For the most part, attempts to predict who will and who will not become a criminal have not been successful. Most murderers, for example, are related to or acquainted with their victims and have no criminal history or history of mental disturbance. As one author wrote,

Murderers are not a homogeneous group of "bad guys." Murderers are rarely colorful, careful, or ingenious. Most kill on the spur of the moment, often during a heated quarrel. A victim's own relative, friend or acquaintance usually kills him. These killers rarely try to escape; they are easily caught and readily confess.[27]

Certain people, however, establish a long pattern of criminal activity and appear to make a career of crime.

The Criminal Mind

Professional criminals have learned their trade, just as lawyers or plumbers learn their trades. Crime, for them, is a way of life. In some neighborhoods, crime is the norm, and children are, in effect, raised and trained to become criminals. John Allen was a mugger, pimp, dope pusher, and armed robber who grew up among criminals and later, from the perspective of prison, talked about his experiences:

There was a lot of people in my neighborhood, in the southwest part of Washington, D. C., that didn't do much work and there was a lot of people who did, but the majority didn't. Hustling was their thing: number running, bootlegging, selling narcotics, selling stolen goods, prostitution. There's so many things that go on—it's a whole system that operates inside itself. . . . I was sticking up; one of my brothers was stealing; one of my sisters was bootlegging; one of my uncles wrote numbers; one of my grandmothers occasionally wrote numbers; and my grandfather bootlegged.

In my neighborhood, the kids ran wild, and the adults were wild. . . . It's just a way of survival.[28]

Allen was first placed in juvenile detention when he was eight years old. When he was twelve, he shot a fellow gang member; when he was seventeen, he shot someone else; and when he was twenty-four, he was convicted of armed robbery. His criminal career ended at twenty-eight when he was shot in the spinal cord by a policeman and was paralyzed.

How do criminals differ from other people? Significant differences have been identified in the personalities of delinquent and nondelinquent juveniles. One study found delinquents to be different in several ways long before they committed their first offense.[29] They showed less regard for the rights and feelings of others, less respect for authority, more emotional problems, and more difficulties in maintaining attention on tasks. According to a review of several studies examining the criminal personality, delinquents tend to be unable to postpone gratification, are easily frustrated, are aggressive, feel apart from other people, and view them with resentment.[30]

A recent intensive study of criminals by Samuel Yochelson and Stanton Samenow[31] concluded that habitual criminals think differently from other people. Their deviant patterns of thought are present from an early age and may lead to criminal behavior. According to these researchers, the professional criminals have the following characteristics:

- Extreme fearfulnesss. From an early age, the criminals are consumed by fears, large and small. Fears of heights, fears of closed spaces, fears of injury and death dominate consciousness.
- Extreme and persistent anger. The habitual criminals are chronically angry—they boil inside all the time, even when they don't show it.
- Criminal pride. The criminal has an extremely and inflexibly high evaluation of self. The male criminal has a conception of "manhood" that involves being independent of others and better than others and able to conquer all obstacles.

- "Superoptimism." The criminal convinces himself that the crime will succeed and that he will not be caught. This unrealistic optimism can temporarily replace fear.

Yochelson and Samenow argue that, for the professional criminal, crime is the "oxygen" of life. Thinking about crime, planning crime, committing crime, getting caught—all are intensely exciting, and it is this excitement that draws the criminal into the criminal life.

Crime and Psychological Disorder

What are criminals like? Psychologists studying criminals have found that a significant proportion of them have psychological disorders. In one study of 500 prisoners, only 15 percent were found to be free of psychological disorder. A second study of 1,720 North Carolina felons found less than 5 percent free of psychological disorder. A more recent study of 32,511 military prisoners found 21 percent free of psychological disorder.[32] The different estimates are due to the different groups of criminals studied and to different methods of diagnosing potential psychological disorder. In any case, a significant proportion of criminals have serious psychological problems.

Certain types of habitual criminals are called **psychopaths**. (Other terms that mean the same thing and that are used interchangeably are "sociopath" and "antisocial personality.") The psychological disorder characterizing such individuals is called **psychopathy** and is used to describe those who are chronically antisocial, aggressive, manipulative, and in constant conflict with society. The psychopath is a person who is antisocial and impulsive and feels little or no attachment to other people. Psychopaths also feel little or no guilt or anxiety about the crimes they have committed and feel no remorse or shame for the harm they have done others. They are unreliable, insincere, and habitual liars who may at times be charming and completely convincing.   One psychopath, Don F., described himself as follows:

I can remember the first time in my life when I began to suspect I was a little different from most people.   When I was in high school my best friend got leukemia and died and I went to his funeral.   Everybody else was crying and feeling sorry for themselves and as they were praying to get him to heaven I suddenly realized that I wasn't feeling anything at all.   He was a nice guy but what the hell. That night I thought about it some more and found out that I wouldn't miss my mother and father if they died and that I wasn't too nuts about my brothers and sisters, for that matter.   I figured there wasn't anybody I really cared for but, then, I didn't need any of them anyway so I rolled over and went to sleep.[33]

During his teenage years Don was involved in many criminal activities and was caught by the police again and again.   But he was always able to manipulate them:

I could con the [the police] the same as I fooled my own folks.   When I got caught by the cops I always blamed the other guy.   I would admit to just enough to make me

appear to be a slightly imperfect but honest guy who deserved another chance.   They went for it time and time again. . . .[33]

Don's pattern of insincerity, lack of remorse, absence of emotional attachments, maneuvering and manipulation, and antisocial behavior is typical of the psychopathic disorder.   Other types of criminals may show other psychological disorders.

While most murderers are wives, husbands, and lovers who lose control in the heat of an argument, a small percentage of murderers are mentally disturbed. The rare, highly publicized mass murder is typically the work of a psychotic mind, a white male who is either a paranoid schizophrenic or a sexual sadist.[27] **Paranoid schizophrenia** is a psychosis characterized by hostility, delusions of persecution, and auditory hallucinations.   The paranoid schizophrenic may hear voices telling him to kill.   **Sexual sadists** torture and kill their victims in order to achieve a sexual climax. It is important to remember that most mentally disturbed individuals are in fact quite harmless; only a very small percentage are dangerous, but these individuals often receive an enormous amount of publicity because of their violent crimes.

Interim Summary   Most murderers are not very different from other people, but habitual or professional criminals have a number of distinguishing characteristics, such as fearfulness, anger, criminal pride, and "superoptimism."   Also, a significant proportion of criminals have psychological disorders.   Three psychological disorders associated with crime are psychopathy, paranoid schizophrenia, and sexual sadism.

Theories of Crime

What is the cause of crime?

A theory of crime would provide a general explanation of why crime occurs, or what causes criminals to engage in the various types of criminal activity.

But obviously no single explanation could account for the different types of crimes and the great differences among criminals.   For example, certainly the petty thief is not motivated by the same forces that motivate the paranoid schizophrenic mass murderer.   Nevertheless, attempts have been made to explain, in a very general way, why crime occurs. Three theories of crime are the biological theory, the psychoanalytic theory, and the social-psychological theory.

The Biological Theory

One type of theory is a **biological theory of crime,** which explains crime by assuming that criminals are physically different from noncriminals and that this difference accounts for their involvement in criminal activity. For example, one early explanation of this sort was the **atavistic theory** of Cesare Lombroso (1836–1909). The term *atavism* means a genetic "throwback," a biological reversion to an earlier stage in evolution. Lombroso believed that criminals were born to act the way they do, and he believed that by measuring the skulls of criminals, their genetic differences could be proved. Receding chins, low foreheads, and deformations of the teeth and ears were regarded as signs of atavism. In fact, his theory has been completely discredited. Modern researchers find no evidence to support the notion that criminals are evolutionary throwbacks, nor can they find evidence of a physical "criminal type."

While criminals are not genetically more primitive, certain criminals may be physically different from noncriminals. There is evidence that criminals who are psychopaths may have nervous systems that are different from the normal nervous system. Brain wave abnormalities have been found in 30 to 50 percent of psychopaths examined in different studies.[34] This kind of difference in the electrical activity of the brain may help to explain why the behavior of psychopaths is so antisocial and different from that of the normal individual.

The Psychoanalytic Theory

A second type of theory of crime is the **psychoanalytic theory of crime.** From this point of view,

crime is not a hereditary condition but is instead a disease. As one author expressed it, "The criminal is a sick person; crime is a disease, a symptom of mental aberration."[35]

The psychoanalytic theory of crime assumes that crime is a symptom of a mental disorder resulting from unresolved conflicts arising in early childhood. According to one researcher, the aggressive acts of criminals result from patterns established most often in the oral stage of psychosexual development,[35] the stage occurring during the first year of life, when the infant gains satisfaction from sucking and biting. During the oral stage of development, aggressive impulses from the id are expressed in biting and chewing behavior directed toward the mother; these impulses are eventually repressed and made unconscious. Later in life, unconscious aggressive impulses arising from the id must continue to be repressed. If they are not repressed or channeled constructively, they may "break through" into consciousness and result in an aggressive criminal act. Thus, the psychoanalytic theory assumes that one cause of crime is the inadequate repression of aggressive impulses.

The force which compels a person to commit homicide is a conscious or unconscious feeling of sexual, intellectual, social, or financial inadequacy, often caused by frequent frustrations. Even when there is an apparent conscious motive for a crime such as a desire to obtain money or a wish to get rid of a person, unconscious motivations can rarely if ever, be ruled out. A murderer is so completely dominated by his inner forces that apparently no means is too foul for achieving his goal.[36]

The psychoanalytic view of crime holds that the criminal's superego (or conscience) is unable to control the primitive drives of the id, and so these drives are expressed in the form of criminal acts. As one psychiatrist explained it,

The only difference between the criminal and the normal individual is that the normal man partially controls his

criminal drives and finds outlets for them in socially harm-less activities.   This power of controlling, and the domesti-cation of the primitive, unsocial tendencies is acquired by the process of education.   In other words, criminality, gen-erally speaking, is not a congenital defect but a defect in the bringing up.[37]

An uncontrolled id, according to this viewpoint, is expressed in ways resembling the behavior of the new-born baby.   A noted British psychiatrist says that ba-bies are greedy, dirty, violent in temper, without con-science or moral attitude, inconsiderate and sadistic. "In fact," he writes, "judged by adult social standards, the normal baby is for all practical purposes a born criminal."[38]   How are these "criminal tendencies" controlled?   In the normal individual, identification with a parent results in the internalization of parental values and standards and the development of a strong superego that can control the drives of the id.

The Social-Psychological Theory

A third theory of crime is the **social-psychological theory.**   According to this approach, criminals learn to become criminals through association with other criminals.   One example of a social-psychological the-ory is Sutherland's **differential association theory** of crime.[39]   Sutherland argues that crime is learned from exposure to criminal and antisocial patterns of life; an individual who is exposed to relatively more criminal patterns of behavior than to noncriminal patterns is highly likely to become a criminal.   This theory of crime is consistent with the social-learning theory of personality, which assumes that people learn by ob-serving and imitating models around them.   If your adult models are criminals, it is likely that you will learn from them and grow up to engage in some de-gree of antisocial behavior yourself.

   Neither the biological, psychoanalytic, nor so-cial-psychological view of crime seems to offer a satis-factory explanation of crime in general.   The great

According to the social-psychological theory of crime, people learn to become criminals through association with other criminals.   By observing and imitating criminal models around them, young peo-ple acquire criminal habits.   These habits thus become established patterns of living which are difficult to break away from.   (Wide World Photos, Inc.)

differences among types of criminals and types of crimes argue against the possibility of any one expla-nation.   Rather, these three types of theories, by offer-ing three different perspectives on crime, may in com-bination provide some understanding of the range of criminal behavior.

Interim Summary   A theory of crime is a general explanation of why crime occurs. The biological theory explains crime by assuming that criminals are physically different from noncriminals. Lombroso's atavistic theory, which assumed that criminals were genetic throwbacks, is a discredited biological theory. The psychoanalytic theory of crime assumes that crime is a symptom of a mental disorder (a "disease") resulting from the inadequate repression of aggressive impulses arising from the id. The social-psychological theory explains crime by assuming that criminals learn antisocial patterns of behavior through associating with other criminals.

Crime Control

Two common approaches to crime control involve rehabilitation and punishment. Society has invested tremendous energy and resources into each of these methods of controlling crime, but neither has proved very effective.

Rehabilitation

If crime is a disease, as assumed by psychoanalytic theory, then it should be possible to treat it effectively and eventually to cure it. Beginning in the 1930s, the view that psychotherapy should be given to criminals became popular. A wide range of different types of counseling and therapies has been provided to juvenile delinquents and adult criminals in the hope of achieving a personality change resulting in a return to normal society. The results of systematic studies of the effect of psychotherapy, however, have been mixed. At this time, there appears to be little evidence that psychotherapy is effective in reducing crime or preventing further crime.[40]

Numerous innovative programs have been developed aimed at preventing delinquency or rehabilitating criminals and thus reducing crime. A recent study of several innovative programs designed to rehabilitate delinquents concluded that little evidence could be found that the treatment programs succeeded in reducing further delinquency.[41] Programs based on guided group interaction, intensive supervision, and placement in foster homes had little impact on tendencies to return to crime. Although probation and parole are widely regarded as effective aids in rehabilitating criminals and reducing further crime, little evidence can be found that they are effective. In one experimental program developed by the California Youth Authority, two groups of delinquents were compared, one with regular detention and a second with a supervised community-based probation period with an intensive treatment program.[42] The results showed that the special treatment group committed more offenses later than the control group, which had received no special treatment. Thus, attempts to develop effective rehabilitative programs have been discouraging.

One approach to crime control that has received considerable publicity recently involves briefly exposing juvenile delinquents to the brutality of prison life in the hope that they will be "scared straight." In this approach, developed at Rahway State Prison in New Jersey, the delinquents are taken into the prison for a two-hour meeting with convicts serving twenty-five or more years in maximum security. The convicts intimidate and harrass the young offenders and make vividly clear the dangers of physical assault and homosexual rape that are ever present in prison life. Although a nationally syndicated television documentary about this program claimed that it was extraordinarily successful in keeping delinquents out of trouble, recent studies show that the program has little effect.

One study, in fact, showed that the program had an effect opposite to that which was intended.   In a six-month follow-up of delinquents who went through the "scared straight" treatment, it was found that 41 percent got into trouble again; of a matched control group of delinquents, who were not sent through this special program, only 11 percent got into trouble during the same six-month period.[43]

Psychotherapy is not consistently effective.   Scaring delinquents does not appear to help.   What about punishment or the threat of punishment?

Punishment

Punishing criminals by sending them to prison does not appear to reduce their tendency to continue criminal activity.   In fact, if anything, prisons have the opposite effect—they increase criminal tendencies.   From the perspective of the social-psychological theory of crime, crime is taught through association with other criminals.   If this is true, prisons are schools for crime.

It has been said that prison is a sort of graduate school of crime.   In American prisons inmates learn more than new criminal techniques.   They acquire, through association with diverse criminal types, additional socialization into criminal activity. . . .   When the first offender steps through the prison gates, he finds support for almost any form of criminal activity.   Those inmates who have had the most successful careers, generally the meanest and most ruthless, receive deference, privileges, and respect. . . .   The question that needs to be asked is how many one-time offenders become irrevocably submerged in criminal reality through their prison experience?[44]

Since various studies show that 50 to 80 percent of criminals who are sent to prison become involved again in criminal activity and return again to prison, prisons do not seem to reduce criminal behavior.   Of course, they do isolate the antisocial individual from

Prisons tend to increase criminal tendencies; they are schools of crime where new criminal techniques are taught.   Over half of those sent to prison return to a life of crime; for them, crime has become a way of life.   (Paul Conklin)

society for a period of time, and this in itself may help to reduce crime.

A question of long-standing interest is the relation of murder and capital punishment.   The issue is the degree, if any, to which the the threat of the death penalty prevents or deters people from murdering.   On the face of it, it certainly seems reasonable that an individual would be less likely to murder another if he or she were facing the prospect of a death penalty.

Although the death penalty may reduce the number of murders by removing potential murderers from society, research indicates that it has no effect in deterring others from committing murder or in reducing the murder rate. (*United Press International Photo*)

On the other hand, this argument assumes that the murderer is capable—at a moment of decision—of weighing the possible consequences of the act. But most murders are impulsive and not carefully considered.

Research on the effect of capital punishment, with few exceptions, shows that the death penalty has no deterrent effect on murder. One approach in investigating this question is to compare murder rates in states with capital punishment and in states without it. Such comparisons show that the murder rate in states with the death penalty is two or three times greater than in states without the death penalty.[45] However, since there are many other differences among these groups of states, such comparisons may not be fair. Attempts to make fairer comparisons by comparing matched states lead, however, to the same conclusion: states with the death penalty have higher murder rates than states without it. Another approach in investigating this issue is to compare the murder rates in a state before and after a change in the death penalty law, such as abolishing the death penalty. Such comparisons show essentially no change in murder rates when the death penalty has been abol-

ished.[45] In conclusion, while the death penalty may be effective in removing certain people from society and from the possibility of doing further harm to innocent citizens, the evidence shows that it has no deterrent effect on murder rates.

Problems and Opportunities

Evidence on the effectiveness of rehabilitation and punishment in controlling crime is disappointing. Most people continue to believe that neither approach should be abandoned; yet there is at present little reason to expect that either approach works very well. This does not mean that rehabilitation and punishment in principle are ineffectve but rather that our present methods of implementing these approaches have not worked. A problem in our present approach to rehabilitation has been the failure to separate different kinds of criminals and to develop particular treatment approaches for different types of problems; in addition, no systematic theory of rehabilitation has emerged with strong empirical support. A problem with our present approach to punishment is that the deterrent effect of punishment depends upon both how certain and how fast the punishment is. But punishment for crime today is neither certain nor fast; many criminals are not punished at all, and for those who are there are delays of months or years between the offense and the punishment. "Deals" involving greatly reduced sentences are made to speed things up. The criminal justice system in this country is overloaded and in deep trouble.

Perhaps more resources should be devoted to crime prevention. The best way to control and reduce crime may be to work to prevent its occurrence in the first place. There are basically two ways in which this can be accomplished. First, crime can be prevented by controlling the opportunity for crime. Our homes, stores, neighborhoods and even cities can be designed to reduce criminal opportunities. This includes improved physical security and surveillance, but also includes changing the architectural design of cities to create safer streets. According to one author, this requires creating neighborhoods used and watched by people with "eyes on the streets," instead of the deserted streets common in our cities today.[46] Crime prevention will also require greater effort to identify and remove the social conditions fostering crime. Unemployment, poverty, lack of education and skills, and a degree of cultural disintegration all lead to increased criminality.

Interim Summary   Two approaches to the problem of crime control are to rehabilitate criminals and to punish them. Probation and parole, special treatment programs, and psychotherapy have been tried and tested as methods to rehabilitate criminals, but there is little evidence that any of these methods are effective in reducing crime. Although prisons remove criminals from society for a while, they serve to teach crime to inmates and have no rehabilitative effect. Most research shows that capital punishment has no deterrent effect on murder rates. In sum, the available evidence supports the conclusion that neither rehabilitation, punishment, nor the threat of punishment, as presently applied, is effective in reducing crime. Although our present methods are ineffective, this does not mean that improved methods will not work.

Summary   1. Aggression refers to fighting or attacking behavior, while anger is the feeling or emotion that accompanies aggression.
2. The instinct theory of aggression proposes that people have inborn aggressive tendencies and that there is a distinct biological basis for aggression in certain brain structures. However, it appears that although the aggressive response system itself is inborn, the stimuli that trigger the response must be learned.
3. The reaction theory of aggression assumes that aggression is a response to external stimuli, such as pain and frustration. However, it appears that aggression is far more complex than this theory suggests.
4. The social-learning theory of aggression proposes that aggression is learned through imitation and reinforcement. Children learn by imitating adults, whether the adults appear in real life or in films or television. Children exposed to aggressive adult

models will themselves act more aggressively. In addition, reinforcement for aggresssion is provided both by parents and by peers.

5. Habitual, or professional, criminals share a number of distinguishing characteristics: fearfulness, anger, criminal pride, and "superoptimism." A significant proportion of habitual criminals have psychological disorders. Psychopathy, paranoid schizophrenia, and sexual sadism are severe disorders associated with crime.

6. The biological theory of crime assumes that criminals are physically different from noncriminals. Lombroso's atavistic theory, which assumed that criminals were genetic throwbacks, is a discredited biological theory.

7. The psychoanalytic theory of crime assumes that crime is a "disease" resulting from the inadequate repression of aggressive impulses arising from the id.

8. The social-psychological theory of crime assumes that criminals learn antisocial patterns of behavior through associating with other criminals. Sutherland's differential association theory is an example of a social-psychological theory.

9. The available evidence supports the conclusion that neither rehabilitation, punishment, nor the threat of punishment, as recently applied, is effective in reducing crime.

Key Concepts

aggression Fighting or attacking behavior; actions having the intent of hurting others.

anger The feeling of emotion that accompanies aggression.

Thanatos Freud's term for a universal death instinct.

ethology The study of animals in their natural settings.

instinct A complex behavior that is inherited; for example, nestbuilding in certain birds.

cortex The outer wrinkled surface of the brain; an area especially important for human perception and intelligence.

sham rage Intense aggressive behavior observed in animals lacking a cortex.

frustration-aggression hypothesis The proposal that aggression is always a consequence of frustration.

instinct theory of aggression The theory that aggression is an inborn tendency; that we are born with "killer instincts."

reaction theory of aggression The theory that aggression occurs in response to external stimulation.

social-learning theory of aggression The theory that aggression results from learning through imitation and reinforcement.

psychopath An antisocial, impulsive, and aggressive person who feels little or no attachment to others.

psychopathy A psychological disorder characterized by chronic antisocial, aggressive, manipulative behavior.

paranoid schizophrenia A psychological disorder characterized by hostility, delusions of persecution, and auditory hallucinations.

sexual sadism A psychological disorder in which a sexual climax can be achieved only through torture or murder.

biological theory of crime The theory that criminals are physically different from noncriminals, and this difference accounts for crime.

atavistic theory The theory that criminals

are genetic throwbacks and are born to act the way they do.

psychoanalytic theory of crime   The theory that crime is a symptom of a mental disorder resulting from unresolved conflicts in early childhood.

social-psychological theory of crime   The theory that criminal behavior is learned by observing and imitating people with criminal tendencies.

differential association theory of crime   The theory that people are likely to become criminals if they are exposed to relatively more criminal patterns of behavior than noncriminal patterns.

Part IX

Applied Psychology

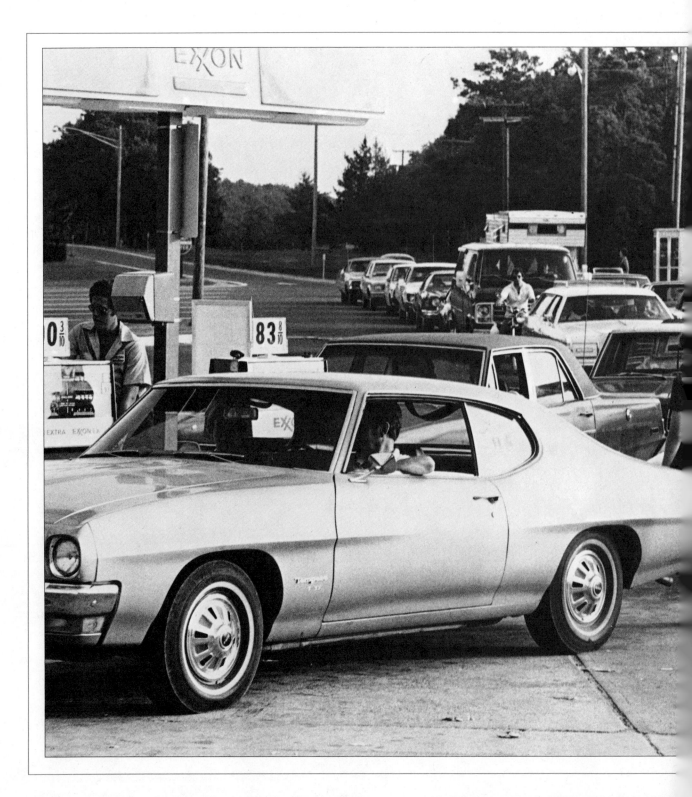

Chapter 25

The Psychology of Consumers
and Energy Conservation

Key Questions   1. What is consumer psychology, and how is consumer behavior studied?
                  2. What are the basic principles of consumer behavior?
                  3. What is the psychology of advertising?
                  4. What is the psychology of energy conservation?
                  5. How can a behavioral approach help solve the energy crisis?

What's the difference between these two advertising claims?

Aren't you tired of the sniffles and runny noses all winter? Tired of always feeling less than your best? Taking ERADICOLD PILLS as directed will get you through a whole winter without colds.

Aren't you tired of the sniffles and runny noses all winter? Tired of always feeling less than your best? Get through a whole winter without colds. Take ERADICOLD PILLS as directed.

You may have noticed that the first claim directly asserts that the pills will "get you through a whole winter without colds," while the second claim only suggests, or *implies,* that the pills will have this effect. Recent research has shown that most consumers remember the implied claim as *fact* and are not able to distinguish between what is only implied and what is directly asserted in a commercial.[1]   The regulations concerning "false advertising," however, are only rarely applied to commercials making implied false claims.   Perhaps this policy should be modified in light of the tendency of human memory to equate implications and facts.

Research on the effects of advertising is part of the domain of consumer psychology. **Consumer psychology** is the study of the dynamics underlying and determining consumer behavior.[2,3]   Consumer behavior involves acquiring, consuming, and disposing of goods and services.   One important aspect of consumer behavior today is the behavior associated with consuming and conserving energy resources. Consumer psychologists are interested in understanding why consumers behave as they do, in predicting consumer behavior, and in learning how to modify consumer behavior.   In studying consumer behavior, researchers employ a number of basic psychological methods.

Methods of Studying Consumer Behavior

The methods applied by psychology to the study of consumer behavior are the same as those used in the study of human behavior generally.   Consumer research ranges in formality from carefully controlled laboratory experimentation to field studies in stores or other natural settings.   The measures taken by consumer researchers range from physiological measures of changes in brain waves when a proposed new advertisement is seen to measures of the number of products sold.   In any case, the element linking together these diverse studies is a focus on the human being as consumer.

Field Studies

One type of consumer research is the **field study,** so called because it is conducted in the "field" (outside

Consumer psychology is concerned with understanding why consumers behave as they do, in predicting consumer behavior, and in learning to modify consumer behavior. Taste testing is one approach used to evaluate new products. (Carl Frank/Photo Researchers, Inc.)

A school age boy and his parents enter the aisle. The parents hurry down the aisle, looking straight ahead and not even glancing at the cereals. "Can't I have some cereal?" askes the boy winningly. "No," answers the father very sternly, and quickly continues up the aisle. "You dirty crumb," is the boy's reply as he walks up the aisle with his head lowered.

In this episode, a child attempted to influence a purchase but failed. Overall, the results of the field study showed that, when children were present with adults, they attempted to influence cereal purchases 59 percent of the time, and they succeeded on about 60 percent of their attempts.

The study also showed that only 13 percent of the shoppers displayed any interest or concern for the price of the cereal they purchased. As far as the observers could determine, 87 percent of those buying cereal did not even look at the price. Of the adult females, however, 17 percent looked at prices, while only 10 percent of the children shopping alone looked at prices. Thus, it is possible to learn a great deal about consumer behavior simply by carefully observing what people do at the point of purchase.

Case Studies

A second type of consumer research is the **case study,** based on an in-depth examination of a single consumer. An advantage of a case study is that it is possible to examine in great detail and at great length an individual's behavior. The data that result provide a rich source of hypotheses for further research. A disadvantage of the case study in consumer research is that the individual studied may not be representative of consumers generally, and therefore conclusions based on that person's behavior may not apply to others. In a recent case study, a series of intensive, unstructured interviews was conducted with two consumers in the hope of understanding their reasons for their choice of brands.[5] Questionnaires were also administered in the study. One of the individuals

the laboratory, in a store or other setting). An advantage of the field study is that it involves directly observing consumer behavior where it naturally occurs. This approach avoids some of the pitfalls of studies based on asking consumers to report what they have done; since memory is imperfect, such reports may be distorted. A disadvantage of the field study is that while it may be easy to describe *what* happened, it is typically not possible to determine *why* some behavior occurred.

One field study involved directly observing the behavior of shoppers in a supermarket.[4] The researchers observed more than 1,500 episodes of consumer behavior during 600 hours of systematic observation. The following episode was recorded as occurring at 7:30 on a Thursday evening:

studied was Roger, a forty-one-year-old man with a BS in mechanical engineering who operates an automobile-body repair service. At the time of the study, Roger had a yearly family income of $25,000. The study showed that when Roger purchased beer, he based his brand choice on the requirement that the beer be well-known, low-priced, and liked by his friends. When the researchers gave him six different beers to sample in a blind taste test, he could not identify any of them. When he was asked to recall any beer advertising he might have seen, he was able to recall only one theme from a television advertisement. Although Roger tended to buy two favorite brands of beer, he was not strongly loyal to either, could not remember their advertising themes, and could not identify them by taste.

Surveys

A third type of consumer research is the **survey,** which is a poll, or questionnaire, consisting of questions aimed at obtaining information about some aspect of attitudes or behavior of a large number of people. Surveys of consumers may ask about brand preferences, shopping habits, attitudes toward advertising, rates of consumption, or many other factors relevant to consumer behavior.

To be valid, surveys must carefully sample a population of people and must use questions that are not biased toward one particular answer. A problem with surveys is that people do not always tell the truth about themselves, sometimes because of a faulty memory, and other times because of deliberate distortion. An advantage of surveys, however, is that they obtain information about a large number of people relatively quickly with minimal expense.

One recent survey was concerned with assessing attitudes toward what is called "social marketing."[6] Most marketing or advertising is focused on persuading people to buy some specific item like a car or loaf of bread. By contrast, **social marketing** focuses on

persuading people to accept some socially relevant idea like conserving energy, stopping smoking, controlling pollution, practicing family planning, or voting. In the study of social marketing, four groups of individuals were surveyed: professors of ethics, psychologists, economists, and marketing professionals. Not surprisingly, their views of social marketing turned out to be rather different. In general, the economists and professors of ethics were less favorable about the concept than the psychologists and marketing professionals. For example, the professors of ethics were more likely to agree with the following statement on the survey:

The application of marketing techniques to social issues and ideas is a step toward a society wherein the opinions held by the population can be manipulated.

The researchers concluded that there are serious ethical issues raised by the practice of social marketing and that these issues must be faced squarely if the potential benefits of such marketing are to be realized.

Experiments

A fourth type of consumer research is the experiment. Unlike field studies, case studies and surveys, **experiments** involve examining cause-and-effect relationships. Experiments studying consumer behavior manipulate and control certain conditions while observing the effect on other conditions. As a result, theories about what influences consumers can be tested. A disadvantage of experiments is that in order to control the variables properly, the context may become so unnatural that the results may be meaningless. For example, the results of a laboratory experiment testing the effect of a new advertisement may not apply to consumer reactions outside the laboratory, in the "real world." Nevertheless, controlled experiments often can provide excellent tests of the effect of advertising or other promotional campaigns.

Sometimes an experiment need not be conducted in the laboratory. In one experiment conducted outside the laboratory (a "field experiment"), the effect of different antilittering appeals was studied.[7] The authors noted that previous research had not provided much encouragement for the idea that antilittering signs or other printed messages about littering could significantly reduce the problem. One reason for this may be what the social psychologists call reactance.[8] **Reactance** is a form of resistance to the threat of diminished freedom. According to this view, a sign saying "Don't Walk on the Grass," by telling you what not to do, threatens to reduce your freedom of choice. As a result, your response to the sign may very well be to walk on the grass, to do exactly what you were warned not to do (thus establishing your freedom of choice).

The antilittering experiment was conducted at a public swimming pool on a summer afternoon. Each teenager or adult buyng food at a concession stand was given a piece of paper with one of three messages printed on it: (1) "Don't Litter," (2) "Help Keep Your Pool Clean," or (3) "Obey Safety Rules." The researchers expected that the "Don't Litter" message would not be very effective because reactance would create a counterreaction. The second type of message was expected to work, and the third type was a control. After closing time, the papers on the ground were collected and counted. It was found that, of the three types of messages, most of the litter had the "Don't Litter" message, and paper with the other two

People are motivated to maintain their freedom of choice. When they encounter signs or advertisements telling them what to do, they sometimes do the opposite. This tendency is called reactance. (Michael Weisbrot and Family)

messages had not been thrown on the ground as much. The authors concluded that the "Don't Litter" message, as expected, increased littering, while the other message was ineffective, neither increasing nor reducing littering. By showing how littering behavior can be influenced, this experiment provides useful information to those designing signs and advertisements.

Interim Summary   Consumer psychology is the study of the dynamics underlying and determining consumer behavior. Research on consumer behavior uses a variety of methods. A field study is conducted outside the laboratory, in a store or other natural setting where relevant behavior occurs. A case study is an in-depth study of a single individual. A survey is a poll or questionnaire obtaining information about attitudes or behavior. An experiment examines cause-and-effect relationships by manipulating certain conditions while observing the effect on other conditions. One of the conditions studied by consumer experiments is reactance, resistance to the threat of diminished freedom.

Consumer-Psychology Principles and Research

An understanding of consumer behavior must be based on an understanding of the psychology of human behavior in general. The principles of consumer behavior are the principles of psychology. Important areas of consumer research are no different from important areas of psychological research in general. Some of these areas of research examine the relation of perception, learning and memory, personality, and social influences to consumer behavior.

Perception and Consumption

Principles of the psychology of perception have been of great interest to scientists studying consumer behavior. Advertising can be effective only when it is perceived, and many studies have been conducted to examine how, for example, the size or color of an ad influences the degree to which it is noticed.[9] Generally the decisions that consumers make about their purchases depend upon the information they have acquired about the products, and this information comes from the senses. In addition, consumer satisfaction with many products depends upon the sensory satisfaction. Thus, it is not surprising that much consumer research consists of perceptual research.

One type of perceptual research is aimed at understanding the effects of advertising. The visibility and legibility of ads or posters cannot be taken for granted, and so are frequently pretested.

In a laboratory in Chicago, a man is staring intently at a small dark box. Little by little, the illumination in the box increases, and he begins to see the outlines of an outdoor poster. As the poster brightens, the man begins to make out the largest letters. As soon as he can make out any of the wording or can make sense out of the illustration, he gives a signal and writes a quick description of what he sees.[10]

In studies such as this one, psychologists studying consumers attempt to determine how to make advertisements that are easily noticed and highly readable.

Taste perception plays an important role in consumer behavior because of the great amount of money spent on food and beverages. A number of studies have shown we are less able to discriminate among different brands than we would like to believe. In one study, 326 beer drinkers were each given a six-pack of beer.[11] Each pack contained three different brands, but all identifying labels and marks had been removed. For each participant, one of the three brands given was his or her favorite. The consumers rated each bottle of beer on an overall scale of "excellent" to "very poor" and also on each of several scales concerned with taste qualities (such as bitterness, body, lightness, and so on). Asking consumers to taste and evaluate unknown products is called a **blind taste test**. The results showed no overall difference among the brands of beer and also showed that beer drinkers could not tell the difference between their favorite beer and other brands in a blind taste test. Later, each participant was given a second six-pack of beer, identical to the first except that this time the brand labels were attached. The consumer ratings of the beer with the labels was quite different from the blind ratings. When they knew which bottle was which brand, they rated their usual brand significantly higher than the other brands. Thus, consumer knowledge of brands strongly influences perceptual judgment and preference.

Learning and Memory

Consumers change their attitudes and behavior toward various products as their information and experiences change. A man stops buying one brand and begins to buy another. After hearing a commercial dozens of times, a child knows it by heart. A woman recognizes her favorite brands of various products from just a brief glance at the container. These examples all show the importance of learning and memory to an understanding of consumer behavior.

Research on human learning and memory provides important implications for those concerned with effectively marketing new products.[12] Numerous studies show, for example, that both recall and recognition increase as commercials are repeated, but that as ads are repeated, later exposures contribute less to memory than earlier ones. This suggests that there is a degree of decreasing return in repeating commercials on television.[13]

What do people remember after watching commercials on television? After an evening watching television, perhaps you feel that you have seen so many different commercials that none of them could affect you. The number of commercials and announcements that clutter television programming has been the subject of a number of studies. One study varied the amount of clutter and examined the effect on viewers' memory.[14] Participants viewed two half-hour television programs in a homelike atmosphere. Different groups experienced a different amount of "cluttering." For one group, there were three commercial breaks within each program, containing a total of seven commercials and announcements, and four commercials or announcements between programs; this was called the "standard," or typical, amount of programming clutter. Another group viewed the same program but with thirteen commercials and announcements within the program; this was called "very heavy" clutter. After watching the programs, the participants were asked to complete questionnaires indicating what their attitudes toward the products advertised were and how much they recalled from the commercials. The results showed that attention and memory declined as cluttering increased. Viewers were able to recall four to five ads regardless of the total number presented. The very first ad shown had a significant advantage and was recalled more frequently. These results show the limitations of human memory and have clear implications for television advertisers.

Social Influences

Consumer behavior, like all human behavior, occurs within a social context. We are influenced by the attitudes, perceptions, and behavior of those around us. Advertisements exploit this tendency by claiming that many other people have already bought a product, by offering testimonials from actors pretending to be neighbors, and by dramatizing the suggestion that a particular product will make us more popular with our friends or family.

Consumer researchers have studied how our preference for products is socially influenced. One study of social influence was patterned closely after Asch's classic experiment on conformity. In Asch's study,[15] participants were asked to match lines of different lengths to a comparison line. Asch used confederates who, on specified trials, gave unanimous but incorrect responses; participants announcing their choice after a unanimous false choice were frequently influenced to make false choices themselves. In the consumer study based on Asch's design, 144 college juniors and seniors were asked to evaluate three identical suits and select the "best" one.[16] The students were told, incorrectly, that the suits were from different manufacturers and of different quality. When a control group of students made their selections independently, the suits were chosen equally; but when students were told to announce their selections after they had heard three other students choose suit "B," many of them conformed to the majority judgment and "went along with the crowd." Of course, unknown to the subjects of the experiment, the three students choosing suit "B" were confederates working for the experimenter. Thus, group pressure affects product choice as well as many other kinds of behavior.

The Social Psychology of Advertising

Advertising is a form of persuasion, aimed at changing your attitudes and behavior. Millions of dollars are spent in an effort to modify your attitudes toward certain products and to alter your purchasing behavior. While you may not be an advertiser in the literal sense of the word, you, too, spend a great deal of effort trying to modify the attitudes of other people and to alter the way they behave. They, in turn, work hard to persuade you of their own views and to get you to act in ways that please them. Psychologists have studied the processes of attitude change and have learned a great deal about the principles and techniques that apply.

Source Credibility

In the process of attitude change, the source of the message is very important. When someone tries to persuade you of something, in addition to listening to the logic of the argument, you evaluate the person who is making the argument. As a result of this evaluation, you either believe the person or you do not. If you regard the person as an authority, you quite naturally will be more likely to believe what is said. How believable the person is, or **source credibility,** makes a great deal of difference in how persuasive the message will be. Advertisers strive to associate their products with credible people—people who are authorities (an actor dressed in a doctor's white gown), people who are admired (a famous athlete or sports hero), or people who are attractive (movie stars). Another way advertisers try to increase the credibility of their claims is to have them come from an actor who looks like a neighbor, a person who would "spontaneously" offer a testimonial instead of doing it for money. Many television advertisements are carefully staged to appear as unrehearsed interviews with average consumers.

In one experiment, college students were presented with a message about the effects of smoking on health.[17] For each of three groups of students, the message was identical, but the apparent source varied. For one group, the source was represented as the United States surgeon general; for a second group, the source was said to be a *Life* magazine article; and for the third group, the source was supposed to be the American Tobacco Company. The credibility of the sources varied from fairly high (surgeon general), to

moderate (*Life* magazine), to low (tobacco company, which might have a biased view). After the students read the smoking message, they indicated how much they agreed with it. The results showed that the more credible the source, the more persuasive the message.

The Persuasive Message

Aside from source credibility, the persuasiveness of an advertisement depends upon the advertising message itself—the type of claim that is made and how it is organized. One question of interest is how strong a claim should be. It would be possible for an advertisement to provide television viewers with certain arguments or evidence concerning a product and then to encourage people to draw their own conclusions.

The universality and constant presence of advertising have become so well accepted that advertising has become part of our life style, the decoration of our homes and offices, and even our clothes. (© *1980 William Thompson/Limited Horizons*)

Or alternatively, the advertisement could draw the conclusion itself. Some research on attitude change supports the idea that drawing explicit conclusions is more effective than letting people make up their own minds.[18] This technique, however, seems to work best for an audience with low intelligence. Furthermore, a danger in telling people explicitly what to do ("Buy Brand X without delay!!") is the **boomerang effect,** or what is called *reactance.* When people feel that their freedom is being limited or when they feel that someone is pushing too hard to get them to do something, they react by doing the opposite in order to reestablish their freedom of choice. Thus, advertisers should be wary of using commercials that appear to threaten the consumers' freedom of choice.

A second issue concerning the nature of the advertising message is whether it makes only a one-sided argument, or whether it covers arguments both in favor of and against the product. Presenting only one side of an argument may stimulate the audience to think up counterarguments against the product; on the other hand, being objective and presenting both sides of the case may persuade some people not to buy the product. In an experiment using radio commercials, half of a group of students were presented with one-sided commercials and half with two-sided commercials.[19] The two-sided commercials were significantly more effective in producing attitude change, both immediately and after a six-week delay.

A compromise solution to this issue is a strategy called **inoculation,** in which the advertiser makes strong arguments in favor of the product but also discusses some weak arguments against it. These weak arguments are then rebutted. Just as you can be immunized against a disease by receiving an inoculation containing a weakened form of the germ (which stimulates your body's defense against the disease), you can be immunized against an argument by hearing someone present a weakened form of the argument and then vigorously destroy it. The strategy of inoculation is used to strengthen your resistance to counterarguments that may be made to get you to change your mind.

Cognitive Dissonance

One of the ways that advertising gains its power is that we are induced to listen to it or watch it. There are two basic ways in which we are changed by this experience. First, and most obviously, we gain new information about the product or acquire new attitudes about it directly from the advertisement. Second, we are changed by a more subtle kind of aftereffect of the experience. How this change comes about will require several steps of explanation.

According to the theory of **cognitive dissonance,** developed initially by Leon Festinger,[20] people are strongly motivated to be consistent. Having two inconsistent (dissonant) ideas or beliefs (cognitions) makes us uncomfortable, so we strive to reduce the inconsistency to achieve greater comfort. Suppose that you believe that smoking is hazardous to your health, but then, for various reasons, you become a heavy smoker. You would then have two inconsistent cognitions: (1) your realization that you were a heavy smoker, and (2) your belief that smoking was dangerous. According to cognitive dissonance theory, you would be motivated to reduce the discomfort resulting from this inconsistency. The easiest way to reduce the inconsistency would be to change your attitude about smoking and become skeptical about the danger involved. This, in fact, is apparently what happens to heavy smokers.[21]

Now suppose that you are watching television in the evening and you have just sat through three rather annoying commercials for some brand of mouthwash. You might have the following two inconsistent cognitions: (1) your attitude that you did not want to watch the unpleasant mouthwash commercial, and (2) your realization that you have, in fact, been watching three such commercials. According to cognitive dissonance theory, you would be motivated to reduce this inconsistency. The easiest way to do so would be to change your unfavorable attitude about the commercial and the product to a favorable attitude of liking and agreement. Research supports the conclusion that this kind of attitude change occurs.[22]

Advertisements affect consumers not only before a purchase but also afterwards. After you have bought a particular brand of car, stereo, or refrigerator, you continue to be exposed to commercials about these products. After you have bought a Ford, watching a Chevrolet commercial may cause some dissonance—you may realize (1) that the Chevrolet has many attractive features, and (2) that your car lacks some of these features. How can such dissonance and the accompanying discomfort be avoided? Apparently what happens after a purchase is that people tend to read advertisements for the brand they just bought, and they tend to avoid reading advertisements for competitive brands.[23] By avoiding ideas and information inconsistent with their recent purchase decision, consumers are able to maintain a degree of internal consistency—as predicted by cognitive dissonance theory.

Interim Summary   Perception, learning and memory, personality, and social influences have been studied as important areas of consumer research. Consumer psychologists studying perception are interested in how to make advertisements that are easily noticed and highly readable and in the perceptual conditions affecting consumer preference. Consumer psychologists studying learning and memory are concerned with such issues as how people acquire brand preferences and what they remember from television ads. Consumer psychologists studying social influences are concerned with the effects of social pressure, source credibility, and the type of argument that is most persuasive; they also study how attitudes toward products are changed.

Energy Consumers and the Energy Crisis

The world has an energy shortage as a result of diminishing supplies and increasing consumption. One approach to this problem is to seek new supplies of energy, by investing in the search for new oil fields, by improving retrieval of oil from existing fields, or by developing sources of solar or geothermal energy. An alternative approach is to conserve energy.

Until about ten years ago, the price of energy was relatively low and consumed a decreasing part of everyone's budget. Because it was so cheap, people were not much concerned about saving energy. A number of events occurred in the 1970s, however, that dramatically changed our consciousness of energy efficiency. One of these events was the oil embargo in 1973, which made us realize how vulnerable we were to external control. In the 1970s it also became ap-

parent that nuclear power would be developed more slowly and much more expensively than previously believed, requiring us to continue to rely on fossil fuels such as oil and gas. President Carter called our energy problems the "moral equivalent of war" and began an effort to increase energy conservation. Polls taken in the late 1970s indicated that more than 80 percent of Americans were convinced that the energy shortage was a serious problem.[24] Conserving energy became a realistic possibility.

Conservation and the Energy Shortage

What is conservation? It is sometimes defined as the necessity for *other people* to give up their energy-consuming luxuries and conveniences so that we can keep ours. Although this may be a happy fantasy, if everybody thinks this way, obviously there will not be very much energy conservation.

Kenneth Boulding remarked, "Conservation is just thinking before using energy."[25] Indeed, we do tend to consume energy mindlessly, but we are beginning to change. **Conservation** means preserving our resources by changing consumer behavior. It means insulating our homes, using less heat in the winter and less air conditioning in the summer; it means buying more fuel-efficient automobiles; and it means driving less often and more efficiently.

We have begun to conserve energy, but we need to do more. We have become more efficient, but we need to improve. But our efforts have already had a significant effect on the energy crisis. As one author wrote,

Welcome to the efficient society.
Almost unnoticed, Americans have begun to save energy by wasting less. In the process, they have almost halted the growth in oil imports, lessened the drain on the dollar, deflected some inflationary forces, avoided a lot of pollution and eased the tension over such issues as nuclear power and strip mining.[26]

Understanding the psychology of consumer behavior is an important step in solving the energy crisis. Conservation requires changing human behavior, behavior that is highly reinforced and deeply ingrained. Conservation requires a behavioral solution to the energy crisis.

The Psychology of Energy Conservation

A behavioral solution to the crisis would depend upon changing the behavior of masses of people in order to reduce their rates of energy consumption. According to one estimate, about half of all the energy that people consume for their homes and apartments could be saved.[27] Political leaders, utility companies, and large corporations involved in energy production have recently attempted to persuade people to conserve energy. A primary element in the government's energy policy is energy conservation. Regulations concerning speed limits, thermostat settings, automotive fuel efficiency, and industrial fuel consumption have been passed to force some degree of energy savings, but in the final analysis the success of conservation efforts will depend upon changing the behavior of people to increase voluntary conservation.

Along with reducing the total energy consumption the pattern of energy use also needs to be changed. The present pattern of energy usage results in an extremely inefficient system of energy production. It is not possible for plants producing electricity to operate at full capacity and maximum efficiency. The reason is the daily **peaking** in energy use, with one or two periods of extremely heavy demand and other periods of much lighter demand. This peaking results from the fact that people tend to turn on air conditioners, clothes dryers, electric stoves, and other appliances at about the same times. Since electricity cannot be stored, it must be produced when it is used. The result is that plants with production capacities adequate for the peak periods operate at much less than full capacity at other periods. If a solution to the peaking problem could be found, a huge savings in electricity (and fossil fuels) would result. But such a solution would require a significant change in the behavior of consumers.

How can the behavior of energy consumers be changed to promote energy conservation? If conservation resulted in some immediate, positive consequence, or **reinforcement,** then people quite naturally would be motivated to conserve. But conservation is not reinforced; instead, most acts of conservation have greater immediate costs than immediate benefits, and are therefore punishing. For example, the fifty-five-mile-per-hour speed limit was intended to save gasoline, but it is routinely violated by gasoline consumers. There appears to be little incentive for drivers to comply with the rule. As one author put it,

Even an "energy crisis" and several years of government messages have left many people apathetic regarding a behavior change in these areas [of fuel consumption and speed of driving]. . . .   The 55-mile-per-hour speed limit case . . . highlights the difficulty of marketing to an entire society. . . . The behavior of those who comply with the limit is not reinforced when they see the energy conserved at the expense of their time wasted by fellow citizens.   It is difficult to accomplish meaningful change when the majority has no incentive to comply.[28]

Of course, as the cost of gasoline soars, the monetary benefits of driving fifty-five miles per hour will begin to outweigh the time costs of slower driving, and consumers may begin to have the needed incentive to assure compliance with the speed limit.

The Conflicts of the Energy Diet

Conservation involves a conflict between the short-term good of individuals and the long-term good of the group.   In the short-term, an individual gains maximum profit from exploiting resources and using as much energy as needed for luxury and comfort. This short-term rationality, however, leads to long-term collective ruin.

Hoarding and panic buying develop when supplies are threatened and people do not trust each other.   Such irrational behavior may be in the short-term interest of the individual, but it is damaging in the long term to the community.   One author explained,

Whether one thinks of the gasoline as coming from foreign suppliers or the local service station, the resource is available in limited quantities over time, and many consumers draw from each supply point.   Conflict between the short-term interest of the individual consumer and the long-term interest of everyone who uses a supply point becomes quite evident

when supplies dwindle, sometimes resulting in frayed tempers and arguments at the pumps.

If supplies are limited, and the consumer thinks only of his or her own immediate needs—harvesting as much gas as possible each trip—gas pools are likely to be threatened. The results can be seen in premature sell-outs at the station.   The problem is, in part, one of group dynamics and involves a lack of communication and some lack of trust within the consumer society.[29]

Another way of viewing the conflict is to express it in terms of operant conditioning.   From this perspective, the conflict for the individual is between two courses of action:

1. Consuming energy resources, which leads to short-term reinforcement but to long-term punishment; and
2. Conserving energy resources, which leads to short-term punishment but to long-term reinforcement.

Thus, the challenge in designing a behavioral solution to the energy shortage is to motivate people to choose course 2, involving short-term punishment (deprivation) in order to ensure the long-term survival of our society.

In a way, people must be persuaded to go on an "energy diet."   Overweight people who diet give up the short-term reinforcement of the chocolate cake in order to achieve the long-term reinforcement of personal health.   The person on the energy diet may have to give up the short-term reinforcement of the gas guzzler or the air conditioner in order to achieve the long-term reinforcement of social and environmental health.   But, as everyone knows, it's difficult to stay on a diet when there are so many temptations around.   Three approaches to dieting are changing attitudes toward consumption, acquiring feedback about consumption, and receiving reinforcement for reduced consumption.   Each of these approaches has been applied to the energy crisis.

Promoting Energy Conservation

There is no doubt that energy needs are increasing rapidly and that energy supplies are limited and endangered. There is a worldwide energy crisis, and the development of new sources of energy will not have a significant impact on the problem for a number of years. While this problem involves natural resources, it is also a human problem. People are clearly part of the problem—wasting energy and hoarding fuels—and they must be involved in the solution to the problem. Research on the psychology of energy conservation offers some hope for a solution to the human problem in the energy crisis.

Changing Consumer Attitudes

Attempts to change attitudes and behavior concerning energy use have been made in many appeals from politicians, utility companies, and oil companies. Political leaders appeal to our sense of patriotism and our love of country; utility companies appeal to our economic interests and emphasize monetary savings; other appeals are made emphasizing our fear of cold winters or of economic ruin. In all cases, the assumption is made that if our attitudes toward energy and conservation can be changed, our behavior will also change.

One study examined the relationship between homeowners' attitudes toward energy use and their actual summer electricity consumption.[30] The researchers assessed attitudes and energy use in two separate surveys. They found strong correlations between certain attitudes and energy consumption. The best predictor of how much electricity would be consumed were attitudes toward personal comfort and health. For example, the respondents were asked to agree or disagree with the following statements:

- It's not worth it at all to sweat a little in the summer to try to save a little energy.

- It's essential to my family's health for the house to be air conditioned in the summer.

Since air conditioning uses more electricity during the summer than anything else, attitudes toward the need for air conditioning are important determinants of total energy consumption.

The authors of the survey also tested the relationship between energy use and attitudes toward the legitimacy of the energy crisis. It might be expected that individuals who believed more strongly in the reality of the crisis would attempt to use less energy in their homes. However, in this survey there appeared to be little relationship between energy use and such attitudes. For example, those who agreed with each of the following statements used no more or less electricity than those who disagreed with them:

- The energy crisis is a hoax.
- The energy crisis is largely due to supply and price manipulations by the major oil companies.

The attitudes of people toward the energy crisis did not affect the amount of energy they used. The results of the survey of attitudes suggest that energy conservation campaigns should not be aimed at convincing people of the legitimacy of the energy crisis but instead at the issue of personal health and comfort. Perhaps advising people how to achieve some measure of comfort in the heat of the summer or in the cold of the winter with less electricity use would be an effective approach to changing relevant attitudes and behavior.

The form of the appeal to save energy is also important. For example, psychologists have shown that messages are more persuasive when they come from a credible source—that is, from a person or organization whom we trust and respect. Other aspects of persuasive messages are also important. For example, the terrible consequences of failing to conserve energy have been described in numerous corporate and political appeals to consumers. This type of persuasive

Studies of attempts to change consumer attitudes toward energy consumption have had mixed results. The problem is that changed attitudes do not necessarily lead to changed behavior. (© Tom McHugh, 1978/Photo Researchers, Inc.)

message is called the **fear appeal.** You have been exposed to many fear appeals, concerning the need for dental hygiene, the advantages of exercise, and the dangers of cigarette smoking. One study examined the effect of fear appeals on attitudes toward energy conservation.[31] The researchers asked subjects to read essays concerning the energy crisis, then to indicate their intentions to use or save energy. The essays varied in describing how unpleasant and how likely the consequences of the energy shortage would be. The researchers found that the degree of threat in the essay using the fear appeal influenced the intention to use less energy, but that differences in the perceived likelihood of the unpleasant consequences had no effect. The implication of the study is that attempts to persuade consumers to decide to use less energy might effectively be based on a description of the unpleasant consequences of the energy shortage.

Approaching the energy shortage by trying to change consumer attitudes toward energy consumption has, however, certain problems. There is no necessary link between consumer attitudes and consumer behavior. People may decide to use less energy but not follow through. For example, consumers overwhelmingly support the fifty-five-mile-per-hour speed limit, but they also generally violate it. For this reason, attempts to change behavior directly may be more successful than attempts to change behavior by changing attitudes.

Feedback for Energy Consumption

One of the most widely used techniques in dieting is to monitor calorie consumption—to keep track of the calorie value of everything you eat. Monitoring the calorie value of what you eat provides important feedback that enables you to assess how successful your attempts to diet are. Monitoring your calories also has the effect of providing you with immediate consequences of your eating behavior—you don't have to wait to see whether you will gain or lose weight. Immediate consequences for behavior are much more effective in producing change than delayed consequences. In dieting, the immediate feedback about calories consumed is very effective in reducing consumption.

In the same way, providing feedback to energy consumers has proved to be effective in promoting energy conservation. Without feedback, your attempt to master a new skill would be nearly impossible—you wouldn't know when you were doing well and when you were doing poorly. In the same way, energy consumers without feedback have little idea of the success or failure of their attempts to conserve. With good feedback, energy consumers can tell when they are consuming too much gasoline or electricity and can try to cut back.

One study systematically varied the feedback given to energy consumers and examined the effect on the rate of energy consumption.[32] Twenty-nine identical three-bedroom homes were used in the study. Half (fifteen) were randomly assigned to the experimental condition (to be given feedback) and half to the control condition (to be given no feedback). Four times a week for about a month the experimental group was given feedback of their energy use showing their energy consumption each day. A comparison of the actual energy use of the two groups showed that the group given feedback used about 10 percent less electricity than the control group. Thus, this study supports the idea that feedback could reduce energy consumption.

Two other recent studies have confirmed that energy consumption can be reduced by providing people with daily feedback about their use of electricity.[33,34] One of these studies[34] showed that temporary reduction in energy use follows the knowledge that your energy use is being monitored daily, but that this has little long-term effect. However, providing families with daily feedback indicating how much electricity they have used and how much it costs does have a lasting effect in reducing consumption. Immediate feedback is the key.

Reinforcing Conservation

Conserving energy means driving smaller cars, driving more slowly, using fewer electrical appliances, and tolerating greater heat in the summer and cold in the winter. It's not very reinforcing.

Attempts to make conservation more reinforcing have been tried, with some success. One researcher examined the effect of commendation as a type of reinforcement for reducing energy use.[35] One hundred eighty homes using fuel oil for heating were randomly divided into three groups: one group was given feedback about fuel-oil consumption (once only, accompanying a fuel-oil delivery); a second group was given feedback plus a "commendation" (a decal saying "We Are Saving Oil"); and a third group was given neither (this was the control group). Comparing the results of the three groups, the authors found that only the group that was reinforced for saving fuel oil reduced their consumption. While this study indicates the value of a kind of reinforcement, it also shows that infrequent feedback is probably of little value.

Another way to reinforce conservation is to pay consumers to save energy. One study compared the effect of monetary payments, energy information, and daily feedback on electricity consumption.[34] Providing consumers with information about ways to conserve energy and about the energy cost of various appliances had little effect. Daily feedback helped to reduce consumption, but monetary payments for reducing consumption had the largest effect. Cash payments were made at the end of several weeks, according to the percentage reduction in energy use. The results of the study imply that a rebate system of cash payments for energy conservation may be effective in lessening the energy crisis.

Monetary payments have also been used to reinforce consumers for changing the pattern of their energy use to reduce peaking.[36] The demand for electricity over a twenty-four-hour period is not even but shows peaks when consumers use especially large amounts of electricity. This peaking makes energy production quite inefficient and requires investment in new generating facilities to meet the peak demand. In one study, a combination of information feedback about peaking and monetary payments reduced peaking about 50 percent.[36] When the feedback and monetary incentives were eliminated, the families returned to their old pattern of energy use.

These studies suggest that providing incentives for conserving resources through monetary reinforcement may be effective in changing consumers' behavior. Unfortunately, many utility companies provide no incentives for consumers to save energy. In fact, the typical pattern is that the less energy you use, the more it costs per kilowatt. This system punishes people who use less energy. A few years ago, during a water shortage in Los Angeles, an appeal was made to reduce water consumption. The citizens rallied and conserved water. The water company, however, responded by raising their rates—the conservation reduced their income. This, in effect, punished people for conserving.

The present evidence suggests that there are ways to change the behavior of people and encourage them to save energy. A behavioral solution to the energy crisis, as part of a large national policy which includes the development of new sources of energy, can help in reducing the energy shortage. Informational campaigns aimed at changing consumer attitudes, daily feedback about energy use, and reinforcement for conserving all could be combined to create an effective behavioral solution.

Interim Summary   Conservation means preserving resources by changing consumer behavior. A behavioral solution to the energy crisis would involve changing the behavior of people in order to reduce their energy consumption. A problem with this effort is that conservation is generally not very reinforcing. Conservation presents a conflict between the short-term good of the individual and the long-term good of the community as a whole. Three approaches to promoting conservation are (1) changing consumer attitudes, (2) providing feedback for energy consumption, and (3) reinforcing conservation. A problem with the first approach is that there is no necessary link between changed attitudes and changed behavior. Providing immediate feedback for reducing energy use has been shown to be effective in reducing consumption. Several studies show that monetary reinforcement for energy conservation is effective in reducing consumption. Thus, a behavioral approach—as part of a broader solution—can contribute to the solution to the energy crisis.

Test Yourself: What Do You Know About Saving Energy?

Even if they wanted to save energy, many people would not know where to start. When you think of trying to conserve energy, what do you think of first? You may have heard that it is possible to buy specially designed homes that are extremely energy efficient. They use solar heating as much as possible, and they are built to minimize energy waste. But many people cannot afford to buy new, high-technology homes and must find other ways of saving energy. There are many other ways to save energy at home and on the road. In the sections that follow, you can check how much you know about saving energy.

Saving Energy at Home

Mark each of the following true (T) or false (F); then check your answers in the discussion that follows.[37,38]

Home Energy Quiz

T F   1. Incandescent lighting uses less energy and creates less heat than fluorescent lighting.

T F   2. A shower uses more hot water than a bath.

T F   3. If your hot water heater is in an unheated area, you should buy an insulating cover for it.

T F   4. Lack of adequate weather stripping can cause heat loss that could raise your heating bill more than 10 percent.

T F   5. You can save about 5 percent of the energy used for air conditioning by setting your thermostat five degrees warmer in the summer.

T F   6. One-third of all gas used for cooking is wasted by pilot lights.

T F   7. If you set your thermostat down in winter when you retire at night, reheating the house in the morning will use as much fuel as you saved at night.

T F   8. Storm windows can cut heat loss in your house by as much as 50 percent.

T F   9. You can save energy in the winter by using your wood-burning fireplace.

T F   10. To feel warmer in the winter, you should wear two light sweaters instead of one heavy one.

Your answers to the home energy quiz should be compared to the correct answers which follow: (1) F. Fluorescent lights are cooler, and they burn less energy. (2) T. Actually, the correct answer to this one depends upon how long your showers are. A three-minute shower uses less hot water than an average bath; if you take long showers, you should consider speeding them up. (3) T. If your hot water heater is located in a cold area, you can save 8 to 10 percent by covering it with an insulating blanket. (4) T. More than half of the energy costs of an average home are consumed by heating, and heat loss due to lack of caulking and weatherstripping can be a significant factor. (5) F. The best estimate of how much you can save by setting your summer thermostat five degrees warmer is not 5 percent but 20 percent. (6) T. Pilot lights waste a huge amount of energy. (7) F. By lowering your thermostat at night ten to fifteen degrees, you can save 10 to 15 percent of your heating costs. (8) T. A great deal of energy is wasted because of heat loss through windows. (9) F. In general, more heat is lost through a fireplace than is added by

it; a fireplace is a very inefficient source of heat and actually draws warm air up the chimney and out of the house. (10) T. The principle of staying warm in the winter is to dress in several layers, each of which can trap warm body air.

Saving Energy While Driving

As you did in the previous quiz, mark each item true or false, then check your answers against the discussion following.[39,40]

Driving Economy Quiz

T F   1. You should warm up your car for a couple of minutes before starting to drive it.

T F   2. Sudden "jack rabbit" starts burn large amounts of extra gas.

T F   3. If you have to wait for a few minutes, it's more efficient to idle your engine than to stop it—turning the engine off and restarting it burns extra gas.

T F   4. Driving fairly close behind another car ("drafting") saves gas because of reduced wind drag.

T F   5. A constant speed is most efficient—varying your highway speed by as little as five miles per hour can reduce gas economy.

T F   6. Driving fifty-five miles per hour is more gas-efficient than either seventy miles per hour or forty-five miles per hour.

T F   7. Drive with the windows open, when possible, to reduce drag and thereby save gas.

T F   8. When possible, park in the sun on sunny days, since a warm motor is most efficient.

T F   9. Avoid stopping whenever possible, even if you have to reduce your speed greatly as you approach a red light.

T F   10. Use radial tires, since they are most gas-efficient.

T F   11. Regular tune-ups can save a great deal of gas.

T F   12. Avoid using your car's air conditioner whenever possible, since it reduces gas mileage.

Your answers to the driving economy quiz should be compared with the following correct answers: (1) F. Warming your car up is unnecessary and wastes gas; instead, drive slowly for the first mile or two. (2) T. Sudden starts are very inefficient; slow starts are best. (3) F. If you have to wait more than a minute, it is more gas-efficient to turn your car off, then restart it later. (4) F. This works only on the race track; on the highway, tailgating is not only illegal, but is also inefficient because it causes more braking and acceleration. (5) T. Varying highway speed by as little as five miles per hour can reduce gas mileage by more than one mile per gallon. (6) F. Forty-five miles per hour is significantly more efficient than fifty-five or seventy miles per hour; you will get about one-third better gas mileage at forty-five than at seventy. (7) F. Driving with the windows open creates more turbulence, and it reduces gas economy.

(8) F. The heat of the sun warms the gasoline and speeds up evaporation; this can be a significant loss on a hot day. The sun also expands gasoline, resulting in further loss if your tank was completely full, since it will cause the gas to run out. (9) T. It takes much more gas to move a car from a dead stop than to increase its speed once it is moving. (10) T. Radial tires are more gas-efficient; you can also save gas by making sure that your tires are properly inflated. (11) T. If your car needs a tune-up, you are using 10 to 20 percent more fuel than necessary. A misfiring sparkplug can cost you two miles per gallon; a sticky carburetor can cost three miles per gallon. (12) T. All accessories—air conditioner, electric windows, heater, radio, power steering—consume extra gas and reduce mileage.

Summary

1. Consumer psychology is the study of the dynamics underlying and determining consumer behavior.

2. Methods used to research consumer behavior include (1) field studies (conducted outside of the laboratory), (2) case studies (in-depth studies of a single individual), (3) surveys (polls or questionnaires), and (4) experiments (studies involving the manipulation of certain conditions while observing the effect on other conditions).

3. One of the conditions studied by consumer experiments is reactance, the resistance to the threat of diminished freedom.

4. Consumer research examines the relation of perception, learning and memory, personality, and social influences to consumer behavior.

5. An area of great interest to the advertising business is the psychology of attitude change. In the process of attitude change the source of the message is very important. Sources of high credibility are more persuasive.

6. The nature of the advertising message itself is also important. The principle of reactance (the "boomerang effect") suggests that telling people explicitly what to do may not be very effective. The strategy of inoculation is used to strengthen people's resistance to counterarguments.

7. According to the theory of cognitive dissonance, when people have two inconsistent ideas or beliefs, they strive to reduce the inconsistency in order to achieve greater comfort. The cognitive dissonance theory explains why people who are exposed to unpleasant advertisements adopt more favorable attitudes toward the advertised products.

8. A behavioral solution to the energy crisis would involve changing the behavior of

people in order to reduce their energy consumption. A problem with this effort is that conservation is generally not very reinforcing.

9. One approach to promoting conservation has been to attempt to change consumer attitudes toward energy use. An effective way to change consumer attitudes is the fear appeal, a description of the unpleasant consequences of wasting energy. A problem with changing attitudes, however, is that changed attitudes do not necessarily lead to changed behavior.

10. A second approach to promoting conservation has been to provide feedback for energy consumption. When people are provided feedback about their use of energy, they tend to reduce their energy consumption.

11. A third approach to promoting conservation is to reinforce conservation. Consumers who are paid to do so, reduce their level of consumption.

Key Concepts

consumer psychology   The study of the dynamics underlying and determining consumer behavior.

field study   A research project conducted in a natural setting, such as in a store, as opposed to a study in a laboratory.

case study   An in-depth examination of a single individual.

survey   A poll or questionnaire aimed at obtaining information about some aspect of attitudes or behavior.

social marketing   Advertising concerned with persuading people to accept some socially relevant idea.

experiment   A controlled study of cause-and-effect relationships.

reactance   A form of resistance to the threat of diminished freedom that involves doing the opposite in order to reestablish freedom of choice.

boomerang effect   Reactance.

blind taste test   A comparison of different products involving testing them with labels hidden or removed.

source credibility   The believability of the source of a message.

inoculation   A persuasive technique that involves presenting weak arguments against your position, then vigorously rebutting them.

cognitive dissonance   A theory that states that we are motivated to be consistent and that we form and maintain attitudes that are consistent with our behavior.

peaking   A pattern of energy use resulting in periods of extremely high demand.

reinforcement   Giving a favorable consequence following a behavior.

fear appeal   A type of persuasive message stressing the dangers of not buying the product or complying with the request presented in the message.

conservation   Preservation of our resources by changing consumer behavior.

Chapter 26

The Psychology of Career Choice and Development

Key Questions

1. What accounts for career choice?
2. What factors lead to job satisfaction and success?
3. What are the psychological effects of job loss and unemployment?
4. What special problems do working women face?

Jerry is a nineteen-year-old college sophomore who works part-time in his father's store and makes only average grades. He remembers that in the eighth grade he wanted to be an airline pilot. In high school, encouraged by his biology teacher, he decided to be a doctor or a veterinarian. Now, in college, he's not at all sure what he wants to be. He's been thinking about going into business like his father, but he worries about whether he would have to compromise his values. He spends a lot of time wondering what he should do with his life. The question seems to be tied up with the problem of figuring out what kind of a person he is. Jerry feels that he has to solve this problem before he can do anything else.

For some people, the choice of occupation is easy—their parents make the choice for them. For other people, the choice is more difficult, but their circumstances narrow their choices considerably. For example, those who have dropped out of high school have very limited options. But other people find the choice of occupation painfully difficult.

Psychology has important applications to problems of career choice, to the understanding of work behavior, and to the variety of professions that many college students enter. Many psychologists work as **vocational counselors** whose job it is to meet with students and assist them in making that very important choice of a career.

Career Choice

Your choice of job will determine much of your adult life-style. Because you spend so much of your time on the job, the conditions in which you work will have a strong influence on your life and health. Your job will determine your income, your friends, your mode of dress, your daily activities, your social status, and where you will live.

How do people make such an important decision? The *Dictionary of Occupational Titles* lists more than twenty thousand different jobs, far more than any individual could possibly explore. Typically, people decide what they want to do after exploring only a few alternatives. Many people never seriously consider more than one or two career options.

Measures of Vocational Interest

Psychologists have developed **interest tests** to help people choose careers best suited to them. These tests involve questions about preferences for a wide variety of activities and objects. The pattern of the resulting answers is compared to the pattern of preferences of people in different occupational categories.

The Strong Vocational Interest Blank • One of the best-known interest tests is the **Strong Vocational Interest Blank**. This test asks about your likes and dislikes concerning hobbies, people, sports, plays, books, and school subjects. Your answers are compared to the answers of workers from a variety of occupational groups, and the similarity of your interests to those of the different groups can be assessed. For example, if the pattern of your interests matches the pattern exhibited by lawyers, you will be counseled to consider the possibility of becoming a lawyer.

The Kuder Vocational Preference Record • A second common interest test used in counseling people concerning career choice is the **Kuder Vocational Preference Record.** This test, too, requires you to indicate your likes and dislikes of a variety of activities. Your answers are scored to yield your degree of interest in ten general areas of work: outdoor, mechanical, computational, scientific, persuasive, artistic, literary, musical, social service, and clerical activities. On the basis of your scores on these ten scales of interest, a counselor will be able to direct you to a number of possible occupations.

　　While interest tests can be helpful by pointing to occupations for you to consider, no test can tell you what job is best for you. The pattern of your preferences measured by interest tests is not based on much real information about what different occupations would be like. The guidance gained from such tests can never replace knowledge gained from direct experience by trying out several types of jobs.

Personality and Career

Members of different occupational groups have, on the average, different personalities. Personality differences are found both among workers and professionals in different fields and among students preparing for different occupations. Some of the typical findings are listed in Table 26-1:[1]

　　Personality comparisons among occupational groups should be regarded with some caution. There are several different possible explanations for such differences. While it is possible that people with different personality patterns are attracted to different occupations, it is equally possible that people's personalities are shaped by their occupations, so that differences to

Table 26-1 Personality and Occupation

Occupation	Personality Characteristics
Engineers	Independent, self-sufficient; a preference to work with impersonal objects, not people
Artists	Creative, unaggressive, independent, unconcerned with approval and status
Actors	Impulsive, emotionally unstable, exhibitionistic
Theological students	Serious, introspective, sensitive, dependent
Teachers	Socially oriented, preference for stable and predictable lives, low achievement motivation

some degree come after the fact. Another reason for caution in thinking about these results is that there is a great amount of overlap in the personality scores of members of different occupations. Not all teachers are alike nor do all actors share a number of personality qualities. Many individuals are quite different from the personality pattern that characterizes their occupational group as a whole.

Theories of Career Choice and Development

How do people sort themselves into the thousands of different jobs? People differ in terms of their interests, personalities, talents, and goals, and jobs differ in terms of their activities, demands, constraints, and opportunities. Somehow people wind up in jobs for which they are more or less suited.

　　The conventional way of viewing career choice is as a rational, logical process that occurs at some point in time. Choosing a career, from this perspective, is a matter of obtaining the right information and reaching a logical conclusion. It is a matter of reasoning and is a single event—namely, a career "decision."

　　But this conventional view has recently been questioned. There is now good reason to believe that the selection of a career involves a process that continues over a period of years and is influenced by "irrational" emotional and motivational forces. Two theories attempting to account for career selection are John Holland's Theory of Personality and Career Types and Donald Super's Theory of Vocational Development.

Holland's Theory of Personality and Career Types • Research on career selection has showed a variety of relationships between personality characteristics and occupational group. According to John Holland's **Theory of Personality and Career Types,** these relationships exist because career choice is an extension of personality. People express their personalities through the different ways they perceive their occupations and select their career.

According to this theory, there are six types of occupations and, corresponding to these, there are six personality orientations that best fit these occupational types.[2] The six occupational types and sample occupations are listed in Table 26-2.

In addition to characterizing six occupational types, Holland's theory describes six personal orientations. Each individual, Holland argues, has a personality pattern in which one of the six orientations is dominant. People whose personality pattern has a strong "artistic" orientation will be motivated to select occupations from the "artistic" type. People who are "enterprising" would be more likely to pick a job from the "enterprising" group. The six personality types are described as follows:[1]

- *"Realistic" Personality Type:* Interested in activities requiring physical skill and strength; avoidance of interpersonal and verbal tasks; preference for concrete rather than abstract problems.
- *"Intellectual" Personality Type:* Prefers activities involving thinking and understanding rather than dominating or persuading; avoidance of close interpersonal contact; introverted.
- *"Social" Personality Type:* Prefers close interpersonal situations; avoidance of intellectual problem solving; skilled in interpersonal relations; preference for teaching or therapeutic service.
- *"Artistic" Personality Type:* Emotionally expressive and impulsive; dislike of structure; feminine; introverted.

According to Holland's theory of personality and career types, career choice is an extension of personality. "Intellectual" occupations, like veterinarians, tend to be selected by "intellectual" personality types, whose preferred activities involve thinking and understanding. (Kent Reno/Jeroboam Inc.)

Table 26-2 Personalities and Occupations

"Realistic" Occupation Type	"Social" Occupation Type
Architect	Dental Technologist
Construction Worker	Minister
Engineer	Nurse
Farmer	Physical Education Coach
Forester	Psychologist/Counselor
Metal/Machine Worker	Social Worker
Printer	Teacher

"Intellectual" Occupation Type	"Enterprising" Occupation Type
Anthropologist	Economist
Biologist	Lawyer
Home Economist	Manager/Administrator
Medical Technologist	Political Scientist
Military Officer	Public Relations/Advertising
Physical Therapist	Real Estate Agent
Physician	Secretary
Veterinarian	

"Artistic" Occupation Type	"Conventional" Occupation Type
Artist	Accountant
Cosmetologist	Business Teacher
Drama Coach	Clerk
English Teacher	Data Processing Worker
Musician	Finance Expert
Photographer	
Writer/Journalist	

- *"Enterprising" Personality Type:* Concerned about power and status; verbally skilled; interested in manipulating and dominating others.
- *"Conventional" Personality Type:* Concern for rules and regulations; great self-control; identification with power and status; preference for structure and order.

Research supports the assumption of Holland's theory that people of the different personality types choose careers matching their type.[2,3]   There is evi-

dence that the more closely people match the occupational type they have selected, the more satisfied they tend to be with their work[4] and the more likely they are to remain in that field of work.[5]

Super's Theory of Vocational Development • The choice of career is not a single event but is part of a lifelong process of vocational development. According to Donald Super's **Theory of Vocational Development,** vocational development is a continuous process that begins in middle childhood and ends with

"Artistic" occupations, according to Holland's theory, tend to be selected by people who have an "artistic" personality type—that is, by people who are emotionally expressive, introverted, and impulsive. (© F. B. Grunzweig, 1975/Photo Researchers, Inc.)

retirement. The process of your vocational development is closely linked to the development of your **self-concept**—the set of ideas you have about your needs, abilities, interests, and personality. Super assumes that people make occupational choices that fit their self-concepts.

The self-concepts of children are based largely around their needs—for example, the needs for power and independence—and their vocational preferences reflect these needs. In their fantasies and play, children can be seen exploring such vocational roles as police officer, airline pilot, and rock star. These fantasies reflect the children's need for power and independence. As they grow older, their self-concept includes

their unique set of interests, and their preferred vocational roles reflect this change. Still later, as a result of much self-testing in school and the world, children's self-concepts begin to reflect an understanding of their special abilities (as well as their areas of weakness). Vocational preferences during this period are narrowed to take account of this more realistic self-concept.

The Theory of Vocational Development assumes that individuals pass through a series of stages during the life cycle. These stages are:

1. *The Growth Stage.* Between birth and about the age of fourteen, children explore possible occupational roles through play and fantasy. They gather information about the variety of adult roles by observing their parents and other nearby adults, watching television and movies, and reading books.

2. *The Exploration Stage.* During adolescence and early adulthood individuals develop a more mature self-concept and seriously examine a number of possible careers. Part-time and temporary jobs are used to gather concrete information about career options. Toward the end of this stage, one career may be tentatively selected.

3. *The Establishment Stage.* The period from early adulthood to middle age is marked by increasing commitment to a particular occupation, an identification with the chosen field of work, and a concern for achievement and advancement.

4. *The Maintenance Stage.* During middle age individuals are concerned with maintaining their positions and enjoying the benefits of their work. For some, this is a period of resignation and the acceptance of the limitations and frustrations of their work.

5. *The Decline Stage.* Toward the end of the work life, the phase of occupational decline is marked by a reduction in job activity, a preparation for retirement, and eventual retirement.[6]

Research testing Super's Theory of Vocational Development generally supports the assumption that occupational preference is an expression of self-concept and that commitment to a career emerges in the sequence assumed by the theory.[1,7]   It should be noted, however, that the five stages of vocational development that are outlined in the theory do not apply to everyone and that the rate at which individuals progress through the stages of development varies considerably.

<table>
<tr><td>Interim Summary</td><td>Two interest tests that help people choose careers are the Strong Vocational Interest Blank and the Kuder Vocational Preference Record. Both tests ask about your preferences for different kinds of activities; on the basis of your answers, vocational counselors are able to help you select a possible career. Two theories accounting for career selection are Holland's theory of personality and career types and Super's theory of vocational development. Holland assumes that there are six types of people, that there are six types of occupations, and that each type of person has a best-fitting type of occupation. Super's theory assumes that career development is a lifelong process that involves a sequence of five stages, ranging from the growth stage to the decline stage.</td></tr>
</table>

Job Satisfaction

Some people find their jobs are so fulfilling that they cannot imagine doing anything else. They look forward to going to work and miss a day only when they are sick. Other people find their jobs boring, frustrating, and unpleasant. They hate going to work and miss a day whenever they feel they can get away with it. How can such differences be explained?

Measuring Job Satisfaction

Several methods are used to assess levels of job satisfaction. The most common method is to use an **attitude scale,** consisting of a series of job statements that employees rate. A job satisfaction attitude scale is designed to measure how satisfied you are with your job. For example, such an attitude scale might ask questions like the following:

How satisfied are you with the company you work for?

____ 1. Not satisfied

____ 2. Only slightly satisfied

____ 3. Satisfied

____ 4. Very satisfied

____ 5. Extremely satisfied

How satisfied are you with your present supervisor?

____ 1. Not satisfied

____ 2. Only slightly satisfied

____ 3. Satisfied

____ 4. Very satisfied

____ 5. Extremely satisfied

In an attitude scale of ten to twenty items, the answers would be scored and summed to yield an overall index of job satisfaction.

The *Minnesota Satisfaction Questionnaire (MSQ)*[8] is an attitude scale designed to measure job satisfaction. The scale measures employee attitudes toward working conditions, advancement, supervisors, salary, and a variety of other job-related items. For each item mentioned employee attitude is indicated on a five-part scale, ranging from "Not satisfied" to "Extremely satisfied." A sample of the MSQ is shown below:

Answer scale: 1—Not satisfied
                 2—Only slightly satisfied
                 3—Satisfied
                 4—Very satisfied
                 5—Extremely satisfied

On my present job, this is   1 2 3 4 5
how I feel about:

    my job security   — — — — —

    the amount of pay for the   — — — — —
       work I do

    the way I get full credit   — — — — —
       for the work I do

    the physical working   — — — — —
       conditions of the job

    the friendliness of my   — — — — —
       co-workers

    the variety in my work   — — — — —

Satisfying and Unsatisfying Jobs

A great deal of research has been conducted to examine how satisfying different jobs are. It has been found that a number of factors contribute to overall job satisfaction.[9] Three factors are especially important. The first factor is occupational level (authority and status). The higher the level of the job, the greater the average level of job satisfaction. For example, professionals and managers report higher levels of job satisfaction than clerical workers, sales workers, or unskilled workers. A second factor contributing to job satisfaction is variety in job activity. A study of workers in an automobile assembly plant found that those with jobs involving several distinct operations liked their jobs much more than those with jobs involving only one operation.[10] A third factor contributing to job satisfaction is level of pay and the oppor-

tunity for promotion. Not surprisingly, workers with higher pay are happier.

In a recent survey of more than twenty thousand workers, the importance of different features of jobs was assessed.[11] The workers were asked to indicate how important each of several listed features was to them. Some of these job features appear in the list below—but in a scrambled order. What aspect of a job is most important to you? Check the ones that are most important to you, then turn to the footnote following the Key Concepts at the end of the chapter to find the way the workers in the survey ranked these items.

_____ Physical surroundings of your job
_____ Chances for getting a promotion
_____ The amount of fringe benefits you get
_____ Amount of praise you get for job well done
_____ The friendliness of people you work with
_____ The way you are treated by the people you work with
_____ Amount of pay you get
_____ The amount of job security you have
_____ Your chances for taking part in making decisions
_____ Amount of information you get about your job performance
_____ The respect you receive from people you work with
_____ The resources you have to do your job
_____ Chances you have to do things you do best
_____ The amount of freedom you have on your job
_____ Opportunity to develop your skills and abilities
_____ Chances to learn new things
_____ Chances to accomplish something worthwhile
_____ Chances to do something that makes you feel good about yourself

What kind of job has the features that are most important to you? If you are aware of what you like and don't like about different jobs, it may be possible for you to find the job that best fits your needs.

If you are presently working, would you choose the same work if you could start all over again? In one study a cross section of workers was asked this question.[12] Widespread dissatisfaction was found among the workers surveyed. The results of the survey are shown in Table 26-3.

Table 26-3 Percentage Who Would Choose Similar Work Again

Occupation	Percentage
University Professors	93
Mathematician	91
Physicists	89
Biologists	89
Lawyers	83
Journalists	82
White-collar workers (cross section)	43
Skilled auto workers	41
Skilled steelworkers	41
Textile workers	31
Blue-collar workers (cross section)	24
Unskilled steelworkers	21
Unskilled auto workers	16

Theories of Job Satisfaction

A theory of job satisfaction is an attempt to account for the relationships among job features, worker characteristics, and level of job satisfaction. The level of job satisfaction depends upon certain aspects of the job—for example, the pay rate—and the nature of the employee—for example, the needs and expectations of the worker. There are three common theories of job satisfaction.

The **need-fulfillment theory** assumes that a job will be found satisfying to the degree that it meets the needs of the workers.[13,14] The more a job provides in pay, variety of work, independence, and so on, the more it meets the needs of the workers, and therefore the more satisfying it should be. In applying the need-fulfillment theory to assess how satisfying a particular job might be for you, you would determine what you would receive from the job and then compare that to your needs.

The **discrepancy theory** of job satisfaction takes a slightly more complicated approach.[15] It assumes that satisfaction results from having your expectations met. For some jobs, there is a large difference (or discrepancy) between what you receive and what you think you *should* receive. A salary of six dollars an hour may be about what Susan expects, but may be much less than Joan expects; Susan would be satisfied and Joan would be unsatisfied with the same job. In applying discrepancy theory to assess how satisfying a particular job would be for you, you would first review your job expectations and then determine how well the job in question matched your expectations.

The **equity theory** of job satisfaction emphasizes the importance of the balance between what you give to a job and what you get from it.[16] In this context, the word *equity* refers to justice, or fairness. Satisfaction, from this point of view, results from perceived fairness. Workers are assumed to determine how equitable their jobs are by comparing themselves to others; when they find that they are giving more to the job but receiving less from it, they are unsatisfied with the job. In applying equity theory to assess how satisfying a particular job might be for you, you would examine the balance between what you would be giving to the job and what you would be getting from it, then reach a judgment about how fair that balance would be.

Interim Summary   The most common method used to assess job satisfaction is the attitude scale, such as the Minnesota Satisfaction Questionnaire. Three important factors contributing to overall job satisfaction are (1) occupational level, (2) variety in job activity, and (3) level of pay and opportunity for promotion. Three theories of job satisfaction are the need-fulfillment theory (a satisfying job is one that meets your needs), the discrepancy theory (a satisfying job is one that meets your expectations), and the equity theory (a satisfying job is a job that balances what you give to it and what you get from it).

Getting Ahead

As you look around you, it seems that some people are winners and some are losers. You read in the paper about young people who achieve almost instant success in life. Is it luck, intelligence, hard work, the right "connections," or something else that makes the difference? In many cases, all of these factors seem to be involved. But one factor that is primary is motivation.

Achievement Motivation

Some people work hard, striving for success, and others take it easy. There are differences in the forces, or drives, that motivate people. The desire to succeed and do things well is called **achievement motivation.** Students with low achievement motivation tend to be **underachievers**—they do not perform up to their level of ability. Students with high achievement motivation try harder and strive for success. On the job, workers with high achievement motivation seek higher positions with more responsibility and greater pay. Workers with low achievement motivation are content just to do their daily work and keep their jobs. How great is your achievement motivation?

Studies have shown that parents influence their children's level of achievement motivation. Children with high achievement motivation typically have parents who expected them to be independent at an early age and who rewarded them for their successes. For example, their parents may have expected them, at an early age, to take care of themselves, to choose their own clothes, and to earn their own money.[17] In one study, children with high achievement motivation were found to have parents who also had high achievement motivation.[18] The study concluded that children learn to value achievement from their parents.

Job Prestige

One measure of success is the level of your job in your chosen field of work—whether you are a clerk, a supervisor, or a manager, for example. A second measure of success is the status of the field of work. Jobs differ in how prestigious they are viewed to be. Those with high incomes and many years of educational preparation are seen as relatively more prestigious than jobs with low income and low educational requirements. Researchers who study work behavior use as their yardstick of status and success the **Duncan Scale** (see Table 26-4),[19] which provides a ranking of occupa-

Table 26-4 The Duncan Scale

Occupation	Scale Value	Occupation	Scale Value
Dentists	96	Manufacturing foremen	53
Lawyers and judges	93	Clergymen	52
Physicians (including interns)	92	Sales clerks	47
Architects	90	Nurses	46
Social scientists	81	Plumbers	34
Natural scientists	80	Bus drivers	24
Salaried managers in manufacturing	79	Automobile mechanics	19
Authors	76	Waiters and waitresses	16
Teachers	72	Farmers	14
Insurance agents and brokers	66	Manufacturing laborers	8
Actors	60	Farm laborers	6
Retail-trade managers	56	Coal miners	2

tions according to their relative status. (In the Duncan Scale, the ranking of physicians is lower than the ranking of dentists because low-paid interns were included in the physician group but not in the dentist group. If interns were excluded, physicians would be the highest occupational category.)

Career Strategies

Some of the reasons for success are beyond your ability to control. For example, it makes a great deal of difference whether or not you come from the "right" family—a father in a high-status and high-income position, both parents with good educations, not many brothers and sisters.[20] But not all success is due to luck or family connections.

Finishing college, for example, has been shown to make a substantial difference in future earning power. Other things being equal (family background, test scores, and other factors), college graduates earn 50 percent more than college dropouts.[20] College is part of the basic preparation necessary for most high-paying occupations. *Being prepared* is one of the most important career strategies.

A study of eighty-one managers examined the strategies they used to develop and advance their careers.[21] The most commonly used strategy was to improve their qualifications. Other commonly used methods were to do the job particularly well, to develop and improve social relationships within the firm, and to choose jobs that are stepping-stones to better positions. A second study of top executives showed the importance of the "stepping-stone" strategy in career development.[22] This study showed that a second effective strategy was to form alliances with individuals in management who were on their way up—to "hitch your wagon to a star."

Being Unemployed

The severe economic problems in the world result in high unemployment rates. Not only do people lose their jobs as factories close down, government programs shrink, and small businesses go bankrupt, but fewer new jobs become available. College students attempting to enter the job market for the first time find it increasingly difficult to obtain work.

Being unemployed is psychologically stressful. For many people, work is central to their self-esteem, and losing a job is a severe blow to their sense of self-worth. The loss of a job involves a loss of social role and to some degree a loss of identity. Your identity may be tied up in your work, so that you cannot conceive of yourself apart from the kind of work you do. Because of your job, you are able to think of yourself as a competent, productive, and useful person. If you lose your job, your view of yourself may drastically change.

The Physical and Psychological Effects of Losing a Job

People who lose their jobs typically pass through three phases: (1) a period of anticipation, during which they suspect or know that they are going to be laid off; (2) the loss of the job itself; and (3) a period of adjustment following the loss. In a large study of workers laid off when two plants closed, the period of anticipation was found to be the most stressful.[23,24] The period of readjustment for the unemployed workers lasted four to five months; during that time significant difficulties were experienced. Unemployed workers had more physical illness and greater emotional problems during the period of anticipation and the period of readjustment.

Unemployment rates are associated with the rates of first admissions to mental hospitals.[25] During periods of high unemployment, more people are admitted to mental hospitals than during periods of low

Unemployment is highly stressful and is associated with high rates of suicide, alcoholism, and psychosomatic illness. Losing a job can be a devastating blow to the ego, but can also be viewed as an opportunity to explore new options. (© 1978 Ed Lettau/Photo Researchers, Inc.)

unemployment. This result is consistent with the idea that unemployment is a powerful psychological stress factor. For some people, losing their jobs seems to contribute to losing their minds. Unemployment is also associated with high rates of suicide and alcoholism.[26] **Psychosomatic illnesses** (medical problems having a psychological cause), such as high blood pressure, may also accompany unemployment.

In one study, men with working wives were particularly affected by unemployment.[26] The adjustment problems for such men were apparently more severe because of the role conflicts that they experienced. These men not only stopped providing for their families, but were also forced to assume additional duties of child care and other traditionally feminine roles. Some men experienced this sudden change in role function as a crisis in their conception of themselves and their place in the world.

In a description of joblessness during the Great Depression before World War II, one author reported:

Bewilderment, hesitation, apathy, loss of self-confidence, were the commonest marks of protracted unemployment. A man no longer cared how he looked. Unkempt hair and swarthy stubble, shoulders a-droop, a slow dragging walk, were external signs of defeat, often aggravated by malnutrition. Joblessness proved a wasting disease.[27]

Long-term unemployment produces confusion, apathy, loss of self-esteem, and eventually bitterness and cynicism. The psychological impact may be more devastating than the financial impact.

Surviving the Loss of a Job

How can the impact of losing a job be minimized? To view the loss realistically, to explore your full range of options, and to develop a social support system are all important steps that can be taken to help you survive being suddenly laid off.

The loss of a job can be viewed in many different ways. It is easy to see it as proof of the fact that you are a worthless and incompetent person. Viewed in this light, losing a job is a terrible and devastating blow to the ego and will result in loss of confidence and self-esteem and feelings of depression. A different, more realistic way of viewing a job loss is as a relatively impersonal business decision. Such decisions are often influenced more by general business conditions than by an individual's level of performance.

The loss of a job is often experienced as the end of one's productive life, but in fact it is typically just a step in series of career stages that will continue until retirement. Viewed in this way, losing a job is an opportunity, a chance to change to a better job, to move to another place, or to try doing something else. Most people have more options than they realize, and exploring these options can be a rewarding consequence of losing a job.

Exploring new jobs can be exciting, especially for young adults starting out. There are so many different occupations available in this country that it is impossible for people to become fully acquainted with all of them. How, then, can young adults make informed choices that will lead to the best possible fit between themselves and their jobs? The fact is that they cannot. Most people choose their life's work from a limited number of options. Young adults often explore their options by trying out several different jobs before settling on the one they will keep. Moving from job to job—whether voluntarily or involuntarily—provides young adults the essential information needed to select appropriate occupations.

An individual's discovery of a compatible occupation is a result of his shifting from one line of work to another until he finds work that he likes. Often the individual leaves jobs which he does not like until he stumbles upon something better. It is during this period that he acquires the knowledge and skills suitable for his more mature occupational choice.[28]

The negative impact of unemployment—as well as other types of stress—is much less for those people who benefit from a strong **social support system.** An individual has social support when there are close and supportive relationships with family, neighbors, or friends. When you can share your problems with other caring people, you can survive unemployment with less psychological and physical stress. Studies show that good friends, families, and other social support systems are effective in reducing stress reactions in workers.[26]

Interim Summary   One factor in getting ahead on the job is achievement motivation. Workers with high achievement motivation seek higher positions with more responsibility and greater pay. The Duncan Scale is a measure of how prestigious different jobs are. Coming from the "right" family, finishing college, and improving your qualifications are three paths toward achieving success on the job. For many people, work is central to their self-esteem, and losing a job can be a devastating blow. Unemployment results in severe stress and may cause psychosomatic illness. The negative impact of unemployment can be reduced by strong social support systems.

Women and Work

Over half of American women between the ages of sixteen and sixty-four are in the work force, and half of the mothers of children aged six to seventeen are working.[29] While there are not yet as many women working as men, over 40 percent of the total work force consists of women, and more women are going to work than ever before.

One of the reasons for the increase in the number of women in the work force is that they need the money. The standard of living desired by many families requires that both the husband and wife work. But work means more than money. It is a means of meeting people, learning, acquiring new experiences, and feeling competent and useful. For many women, work provides a necessary sense of accomplishment and self-fulfillment. But there are special problems faced by the increasing number of women who want to work or who find it necessary to work.

Career and Sex Role

The traditional conception of the role of women is that of homemaker and mother. Even now, girls are brought up to be wives and mothers first, workers second. They are often taught that if they must work, their work should be only supplemental, not primary, and that their basic responsibility lies in the home. By contrast, boys are taught to be workers first, fathers and husbands second. These teachings form the accepted **sex roles** of men and women, the set of behaviors that society considers appropriate to individuals of different sexes.

Is it possible for women to break from the stereotyped sex role and decide to devote themselves to a career? An increasing number of women are doing so, but there are conflicts and costs involved. Working women experience pressure from parents, family, and peers to devote themselves to the roles of wife and homemaker. Often they find themselves trying to do two full-time jobs, one at work and the other at home.

When women do choose a career, the occupation that they select is often one that is perceived as "sex-appropriate." Many people believe that only men have the qualities necessary to perform certain jobs, and only women have the qualities necessary to perform other jobs. While these prejudices are not generally supported by any facts, they influence the career choices of men and women. And it is no accident that those occupations viewed as more appropriate for women pay significantly less than the occupations seen as appropriate for men.

Which of the following occupations do you see as more appropriate for women, and which do you see as more appropriate for men? Do your choices reflect sexual prejudice?

M	F	
☐	☐	Secretary
☐	☐	Pilot
☐	☐	Bartender
☐	☐	Social worker
☐	☐	School superintendent

Women who work typically face conflicts between the demands of their careers and their sex roles. Parents, family, and peers pressure them to fulfill their sex roles by being good homemakers while economic pressures keep them at work. (Roger Malloch/© 1970 Magnum Photos)

M	F	
☐	☐	Elementary school teacher
☐	☐	Construction supervisor
☐	☐	Librarian
☐	☐	Nurse
☐	☐	Surgeon
☐	☐	Engineer
☐	☐	Telephone operator

Working Mothers

The traditional view is that mothers should stay home and take care of their children, particularly if their children are of preschool age. Yet, millions of mothers are currently working, either from preference or necessity. Many women are heads of households and must work to support themselves and their children.

Other women work to provide the necessary family income to buy items beyond the reach of the husbands' wages. But many working mothers join the work force because they find staying home boring and working, fulfilling.

Working mothers often find themselves attempting three full-time jobs: (1) worker, (2) mother, and (3) wife and homemaker. Because they cannot satisfy all of the demands of each job, they may feel they are doing none of the three jobs very well. Because of the time required by the mother and wife roles, the woman may be unable to invest the energy and dedication expected in her career. At the same time, she may feel guilty because she feels that she is neglecting her children and housework. Although there is evidence that indicates that the children of working mothers do not suffer from the mother's absence,[30,31] many working mothers continue to feel guilty and conflicted.

The children of working mothers have certain advantages. Women who want to work are much happier and more satisfied with life when they are working. Women who are satisfied are better mothers than women who are frustrated with their roles. The *quality* of the mother-child interaction appears to be more important for the welfare of the child than the *quantity* of the mother-child interaction. A second advantage that children of working mothers have is that they benefit from observing a competent role model. A **role model** is a person who displays the behaviors and traits associated with a particular role, or place in society. Children learn about their future options by observing adult role models, and they acquire particular attitudes and behaviors by imitating adult role models. Mothers serve as models for their children, and working mothers model qualities of achievement, competence, drive, and self-sufficiency. The aspirations of children are influenced by the qualities of their adult models. The children of working mothers are more likely to strive for independence and competence.

This is not to say that all mothers should work. Rather, the point of this discussion is that working is an acceptable alternative for women, including women with children. There appear to be no adverse psychological effects on the children of working mothers, and there are certain advantages that children of working mothers have. Thus, the choice to work or not to work can be made on the basis of values and preference for different kinds of life-styles, rather than on the basis of concerns about possible harm to children.

College Women and Career Commitment

For women in college, the conflict between traditional sex-role expectations and career aspirations is more severe. Many college women wonder why they should spend so much money, time, and energy preparing for a career if their roles of wife, mother, and homemaker will prevent them from pursuing a career seriously. Some women resolve this conflict by deciding not to apply their college education to a career, while others decide that dedication to a career does not necessarily rule out getting married and having a family.

Sandy decided that college had taught her a lot that would be useful in her life, but that while she was interested in work, her first commitment would be to her husband and children:

Whether I will ever work or not, I don't know. I imagine I'll be married in the next year or two. If the situation warranted my working, then I definitely would. If I were bored with housework, I would probably work. I would not work if I had enough to do. I'm not a typical career person. I'm not that dedicated.

When you take the responsibility of a family, it is your duty to do it as well as you can and devote as much time to it as possible. Home and family are probably the most important things a woman ever has to do. I don't know what to do about children. A career really interferes with children and children interfere with a career. I would not want my children to be taken care of by anyone else and feel they are unloved by me.[32]

According to Sandy's values, home and family have greater importance than a career. If she decides to work, she will do so only if it will not interfere with the responsibilities of home and children. Other women, such as Carol, have other values and resolve their role conflicts differently.

Carol did not do particularly well in her freshman year of college, but she improved her grades and eventually earned a B average. Her parents encouraged her to think of pursuing a career. She eventually decided to make a career of writing and teaching English. Carol plans to marry, but wants a marriage that involves a full partnership. She expects her husband to participate fully in the household tasks of cooking and cleaning:

My mother has a fantastic influence on me. When she got out of high school, she had to support her family. Yet every year she's taking a new course or reading piles of books or sculpting. This is very nice but if that intellect could have been directed, she'd be more satisfied as a person and be of greater use to society.

I wouldn't ever consider stopping work to have children. I think that it is a crime in our society to slave all these years and become a productive writer and then say I'll see you in 15 years after my children grow up. If I want children, they're just going to have to be worked in. I can't say for sure because I've no desire to have children right now. The thought of being a housewife makes me say "never" because woman's intellect should be used to capacity. It shouldn't be used in the kitchen.[32]

According to Carol's values, having a productive career and making a professional contribution to society are more important than being a housewife and mother. What are your values about the proper role of women? Do you agree more with Sandy or with Carol?

Interim Summary   Women who work face a number of special problems. One is the conflict between career and sex role. Working women experience pressure from parents, family, and peers to devote themselves to the roles of wife, mother, and homemaker. Sometimes they find themselves trying to do three full-time jobs and then feeling guilty because they are unable to do them all well. Studies show that, contrary to popular opinion, the children of working mothers do not suffer. In fact, such children have the advantage of observing competent and independent female role models.

Summary   1. The Strong Vocational Interest Blank and the Kuder Vocational Preference Record are examples of interest tests used to help select possible career choices.
2. Two theories accounting for career selection are Holland's Theory of Personality and Career Types and Super's Theory of Vocational Development.
3. Holland's Theory of Personality and Career Types assumes that there are six types of people, that there are six types of occupations, and that each type of person has a best-fitting type of occupation.
4. Super's Theory of Vocational Development assumes that career development is a lifelong process that involves a sequence of five stages, ranging from the growth stage to the decline stage.

5. The Minnesota Satisfaction Questionnaire is an example of an attitude scale, the most common method used to assess job satisfaction.

6. Three important factors contributing to overall job satisfaction are (1) occupational level, (2) variety in job activity, and (3) level of pay and opportunity for promotion.

7. The need-fulfillment theory of job satisfaction assumes that a job will be found satisfying to the degree that it meets the needs of the workers.

8. The discrepancy theory of job satisfaction assumes that job satisfaction results from having one's expectations met.

9. The equity theory of job satisfaction assumes that job satisfaction results from a balance between what the worker puts into the job and how much that worker perceives that he gets out of it; a satisfying job is one that strikes a fair balance.

10. One factor in getting ahead on the job is achievement motivation, the desire to succeed and do things well. Studies have shown that parents influence their children's level of achievement motivation.

11. The Duncan Scale is a measure of how prestigious different jobs are.

12. Coming from the "right" family, finishing college, and improving one's qualifications are three ways of achieving success on the job.

13. Loss of one's job, and the resulting unemployment, can produce psychological problems such as loss of self-esteem, confusion, apathy, and even psychosomatic illness. The negative impact of unemployment can be reduced by strong social support systems such as family and friends.

14. Women who work must often deal with the conflict between career and the traditional female sex role. They must also face the limitations imposed by society's traditional definition of the "sex appropriateness" of various occupations.

15. Studies show that children of working mothers do not suffer from their mothers' absence and may in fact benefit from certain advantages.

Key Concepts

vocational counselors   Counselors, often psychologists, who assist people in making career choices.

interest test   A test involving questions about preferences for a wide variety of activities or objects.

Strong Vocational Interest Blank   An interest test used in vocational counseling.

Kuder Vocational Preference Record   An interest test used in vocational counseling.

Theory of personality and career types   John Holland's theory of career choice, which assumes that there is a relationship between six personality types and six career types and that people tend to select careers that best fit their personality orientations.

Theory of vocational development   Donald Super's theory of career choice, which assumes that vocational development is a continuous process that begins in middle childhood and ends with retirement (from the growth stage through the decline stage) and is an expression of an individual's self-concept.

self-concept   The set of ideas you have about your needs, abilities, interests, and personality.

attitude scale   A test consisting of a series

of statements designed to measure the strength of the attitudes of the person being tested.

Minnesota Satisfaction Questionnaire (MSQ)   An attitude scale designed to measure job satisfaction.

need-fulfillment theory   A theory of job satisfaction that assumes that a job will be found satisfying to the degree that it meets the needs of the workers.

discrepancy theory   A theory of job satisfaction that assumes that a job will be found satisfying to the degree that it meets the expectations of the workers.

equity theory   A theory of job satisfaction that assumes that a job will be found satisfying to the degree that the worker perceives it to be "fair" (what the worker puts into the job and what the worker gets out of it are balanced).

achievement motivation   The desire to succeed and do things well.

underachievers   Individuals with low levels of achievement motivation whose level of performance is lower than would be expected from knowledge of their ability.

Duncan Scale   A ranking of occupations by their relative status, or prestige.

psychosomatic illness   A medical disorder of psychological origin.

social support system   The family, neighbors, or friends with whom you have close and supportive relationships.

sex roles   The set of behaviors that society considers appropriate to individuals of different sexes.

role model   A person who displays the behaviors and traits associated with a particular role, or place, in society; for example, parents or teachers.

Answer to the question of the ranking of job features on page 544: The order listed is the reverse of the ranking of the features by the workers in the survey. The most important feature for them was "Chances to do something that makes you feel good about yourself" and the least important feature was "Physical surroundings of your job."

Appendix
Research Methods and Statistics

Barbara was a bright student but was having trouble with exams during her freshman year of college. It was not that she failed to study or that she was confused by the material. She studied efficiently and hard, and she understood the material very clearly. Her problem was that she fell apart on exams. She became so nervous before and during midterms and finals that she couldn't think straight. Her mind would seem to go blank, and the material she knew the night before was totally lost to her. She was a severe case of test anxiety.

Many psychologists have studied test anxiety in college students. They have found that the higher the levels of anxiety, the poorer the performance on exams. A number of different methods have been proposed to help students like Barbara who have severe test anxiety. How could you determine which of these methods works best?

In order to determine which method for treating test anxiety was most effective, you would first have to find a way of measuring test anxiety. Without a measure of test anxiety, you would not know whether a particular method of treatment reduced the anxiety or increased it. In fact, several such measures have been devised and used in studies comparing different methods of treatment.

Measuring Behavior

You **measure** something when, on the basis of some rule, you assign a number to it. One measure of a crowd is a number determined by counting the people; one measure of temperature is a number determined by the reading on a thermometer; one measure of intelligence is the score achieved on an IQ test. Measurement is used extensively in all sciences, including the science of psychology.

Measurement is a tool scientists use when they want to be precise in describing an individual's behavior, when they want to summarize the characteristics of a large group of people, and when they want to generalize from the few to the many.

Numbers and Individuals

Psychologists use numbers when they want to describe an individual's behavior precisely. Rather than describe Barbara's intelligence as "a little smarter than average," they will say that her IQ is 110. Rather than describe her reflexes as unusually fast, they might say that her reaction time to a sound is one-eighth of a second. Rather than describe her hearing ability as slightly worse than average, they might say that 60 percent of the people her age can hear better than she can. Barbara's eyesight, her personality, her reading rate, her achievement level in mathematics, her eye-hand coordination, her level of test anxiety, and numerous other traits and behaviors can be measured. The resulting numbers or measures describe Barbara more precisely than can be achieved with a general verbal description. The numbers, of course, do not tell the whole story of Barbara.

Numbers and Groups

Psychologists use numbers when they want to summarize the traits or characteristics of a group of people. How are women different from men? How are children of age two different from children of three? What are schizophrenics like, and how do they differ from other people? The answers to these types of questions typically involve numbers—numbers representing such characteristics as size of vocabulary, aggressiveness, intelligence, age, strength, and many other factors. The example that follows shows how numbers are used in research.

A group of psychology students were asked to report their ages and also the number of dreams they were able to recall from the past four nights of sleep. Their responses are listed in Table A-1.

A list of different numbers, such as the ones in Table A-1, can sometimes be confusing. It may be difficult to see from a simple list the pattern or the general tendency of what is true for the group as a whole. Instead of a list of numbers, psychologists may use a **frequency distribution,** a table showing the number of cases falling within different intervals of scores. Instead of listing the score for each person, a frequency distribution lists the number of people having a score of one, the number having a score of two, and so on. Table A-2 shows the frequency distribution for the number of dreams recalled. It shows that two different people reported having three dreams each, and one person reported having six dreams. This figure also shows that the highest number of dreams recalled was six and the lowest number was zero.

The responses of the students could also be represented visually, on a graph. A **histogram** is a bar graph showing the frequency of different responses with bars of different heights. Figure A-1 shows a histogram summarizing the results of the question about dream recall.

Describing Central Tendency

How could you summarize the responses of the students to the question about dream recall? One way would be to show the histogram drawn in Figure A-1. A shorter way would be to summarize the re-

Table A-2 Frequency Distribution Showing Number of Dreams Recalled from Four Nights of Sleep

Number of Dreams	Frequency
0	2
1	1
2	1
3	2
4	4
5	1
6	1

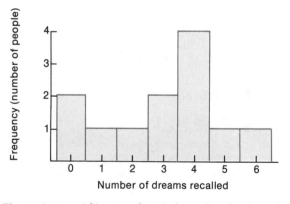

Figure A-1. *A histogram showing the number of students who recalled different numbers of dreams during four nights. The mode (most common number of dreams reported) was four.*

Table A-1 Dream Recall

Name	Age	Number of Dreams Recalled
Juan	21	5
Ted	18	4
Linda	19	4
LeRoy	19	3
Sue	18	0
Felicia	17	1
Don	18	2
Lisa	31	6
Vernon	24	4
Ellie	18	0
Cheryl	18	4
Sheila	19	3

sponses with a single representative number—the **average.** An average is a single number that represents a group of scores. It is a central, or typical, value (a **central tendency**) that reflects the group as a whole.

There are three kinds of averages: the mean, the mode, and the median. The **mean** is the most commonly used measure of central tendency. It is computed by adding up the scores from a group and dividing by the number of scores. If you have two dogs, one weighing twenty pounds and one weighing thirty pounds, their mean weight is twenty-five pounds [mean weight = (20 + 30)/2 = 25 pounds]. A second measure of central tendency is the mode. The **mode** is the score that occurs most often in the group. Some scores may occur only once, while others occur several times. The particular score that occurs most often (the score that more people make than any other) is the mode. A third measure of central tendency is the median. The **median** is the middle score, the score above which and below which an equal number of other scores fall. To calculate the median, you have to rank the scores from lowest to highest, then determine which score is in the middle of the distribution.

The three measures of central tendency—the mean, mode, and median—are summarized in Table A-3. Remember that each of these is a kind of average, a typical, or central, value. Sometimes the mean, mode, and median of a group of scores are the same, and sometimes they are different. Thus, the same group of scores can have different averages, depending upon which measure of central tendency you use.

What is the average number of dreams recalled by the students in the survey reported previously? There are, in fact, three different averages. The *mean* number of dreams recalled by the students in the group is three. (Add up the number of dreams reported by the twelve students, then divide by the number of students. Mean dreams = 36/12 = 3). The *modal* number of dreams is four. (Examine the frequency distribution in Table A-2 and note the most commonly recalled number of dreams.) The *median* number of dreams recalled is 3.5. (Six students reported fewer dreams and six reported more dreams than this). Can you determine the mean, mode, and median of the distribution of ages of the students in the group?

Describing Variability

Sometimes letting a single number represent the scores of a group of people can be deceptive. Although the mean reflects the central value of the distribution of scores, many scores will differ from the mean. These differences reflect the **variability** among the scores of the group.

Two common measures of the variability of a distribution of scores are the range and the standard deviation. The **range** of a distribution is the difference between the upper and lower bounds of the distribution. In general, highly variable scores have a large range, and less variable scores have a small range. If the students reporting their dreams all reported the same number of dreams—say, three dreams—then the range of the distribution would be one—the entire range would consist of one number. If half the students reported having three dreams and half reported having four, the range would be two—the distribution would extend over two numbers. In fact, the number of dreams reported by the twelve students ranged from zero to six, a range of seven (0, 1, 2, 3, 4, 5, 6).

Table A-3 Three Measures of Central Tendency

Measure	Method of Calculation
Mean	Add up all the scores, then divide by the number of scores
Mode	Count the number of people making different scores; the score made by more people than any other is the mode.
Median	Rank the scores from lowest to highest, then count the number of scores; the point dividing the scores in half is the median.

In order to calculate the range of a distribution of scores, you must first determine the values of the highest and lowest scores. Then subtract the highest from the lowest and *add one to the result.* This will be the range of the distribution. If "H" stands for the highest score and "L" stands for the lowest score, than the range can be determined from the following formula:

$$Range = H - L + 1$$

In the case of the number of dreams reported, the highest was six and the lowest was zero, so the range equals $6 - 0 + 1$, or 7. Can you determine the range of ages in the group of students? (See Table A-1 for a list of ages.)

But the range is not always an adequate way to describe the variability of the scores. Two groups of scores can have the same range, but greatly different degrees of variability. In one distribution, the scores may be mostly clustered in the center, while in the second distribution the scores may be widely spread. Figure A-2 shows histograms of two different distributions of scores, one with relatively little variability and one with greater variability, but both with exactly the same range.

In Figure A-2, the left histogram shows a distribution with a range of 10, but with most of the scores clustered in the middle. The right-hand histogram shows a second distribution, also with a range of 10, but with the scores more dispersed, or spread, across the range. A measure of variability that reflects the degree of dispersion or spread in a distribution is the **standard deviation.** In Figure A-2, the left graph has a smaller standard deviation than the right one.

Making Inferences

Psychologists use numbers when they want to relate their findings on a small group to a larger population of people. Consider the question, Are women smarter than men? You cannot measure the intelligence of all women and all men to answer this question; there are too many in the population. You must obtain measures from a limited number—a **sample**—and then estimate what is true for all women and men on the basis of what holds true for your sample. **Inference** is the process of generalizing from the characteristics of a few to the characteristics of many, from characteristics of the sample to characteristics of the population. What is the average IQ of college graduates? You can infer that the average IQ for all graduates is around 120 after you have measured the IQ's of a sample of one hundred representative college graduates and found that their IQ's average 120.

In their research on human behavior, psychologists typically measure some aspect of behavior in a limited number of people—a sample—in the expectation that from this they will learn about people in general—the human population. Errors can easily be made in drawing inferences from a sample to come to a conclusion about a population. The methods of psychology have been carefully developed to reduce the likelihood of such errors of inference.

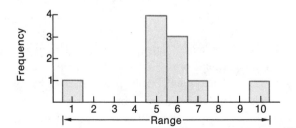

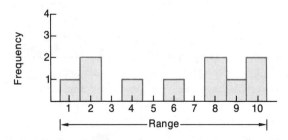

Figure A-2. *Histograms of two different distributions of scores. They have the same number of scores (10) and the same range (10), but because the right distribution is more spread out, it has a larger standard deviation.*

Correlational Studies

In earlier chapters it was pointed out that schizophrenics tend to come from families with disturbed relationships, that men tend to act more aggressively than women, that adults spend less time dreaming than children, and that highly prejudiced persons tend to come from families in which severe discipline is used. These are observations of relationships, of things in the world that are associated. The term **correlation** describes such relationships or associations.

Variables and Variation

Psychologists are interested in finding relationships between particular behaviors and other conditions. A condition or characteristic having different values is called a **variable**. "Intelligence" is a variable, having many different values such as very low, average, or high; "height" is a variable, having different values such as five feet, six feet, and seven feet; "sex" is a variable, having the two values, male and female; "age" is a variable, having many different values such as sixteen years, seventeen years, or ninety-six years; "frequency of dreaming" is a variable, having values ranging from never to, say, thirty times a day.

Sometimes the values of two variables tend to go together. For example, people who are young in age tend also to be short in height. When variables are related in the way that age and height are related, the variables are said to be *correlated*. The values of one variable tend to get together with the values of a second variable. Variation in one variable is somewhat predictable from variation in the second variable; for example, knowing age helps you to predict height.

Consider the example of aggression. "Aggressiveness" is a variable, since people differ in the level of their aggressiveness. If the variable "aggressiveness" were correlated with the variable "sex," then their relationship would enable you to predict values of one if you knew the values of the other (although you might

make some mistakes); knowledge of a person's aggressiveness would help you to guess the person's sex. For example, if you knew that a person was highly aggressive, you would guess that the person was a male, and you would be right more often than wrong. Knowing the level of aggressiveness helps you to predict sex.

Correlation Coefficient

Variables can be highly related or only slightly related. A measure of the degree of relationship between two variables is the **correlation coefficient**. The correlation coefficient is a number that ranges from minus one to plus one (all values between -1 and $+1$ are possible).

If two variables are not correlated, their correlation coefficient is zero. If two variables are perfectly correlated (one is perfectly predictable from the other), their correlation coefficient is either plus one or minus one. A positive (plus) correlation coefficient indicates that the relation is such that high values of one variable tend to go together with high values of the second variable, and low values of one to go together with low values of the other. For example, there is a positive correlation between height and age in children: the higher your age is, the higher your height is. A negative (minus) correlation coefficient indicates a relation in which high values of one variable tend to go together with low values of the second variable, and vice versa. For example, there tends to be a negative correlation between education and prejudice: the more education you get, the less prejudiced you tend to be.

An example of a perfect *positive* correlation (correlation coefficient of $+1.00$) can be seen in the following (imaginary) data. Each person in my psychology class has two scores, one for each of two variables. The first variable is the amount of time spent studying for the midterm (measured in hours); the second variable is the performance on the midterm (measured as the number of questions answered correctly out of thirty).

	# Hours of Study	# Questions Correct
Mary	40	28
Rafael	35	26
Pat	30	23
Caryn	25	22
Le Roy	20	20
Earl	10	19
Kathy	1	5

Notice that the variables co-vary; that is, they vary together. The higher the number of hours of study, the higher the number of questions correct. The lower the number of hours of study, the lower the number of questions correct. Because the two variables are related in this way, they are *correlated*. Notice also that they vary together perfectly; that is, the person with the highest score on one variable is also the person with the highest score on the second variable. In fact, each person is ranked the same on each variable. Therefore, the correlation coefficient for these data is +1.00.

Suppose that the measure of performance on the psychology midterm was the number of questions missed, instead of the number correct. Then the results would look like this:

	# Hours of Study	# Questions Missed
Mary	40	2
Rafael	35	4
Pat	30	7
Caryn	25	8
Le Roy	20	10
Earl	10	11
Kathy	1	25

Notice that the two variables still co-vary, but now they vary inversely; that is, the higher one score is, the lower the other score is. The higher the hours of study, the lower the number of questions missed. Variables related in this inverse way are *negatively* correlated. The correlation coefficient describing the relationship would be −1.00.

Causation

Certain variables are said to show **causation,** to be causally related; one variable is believed to cause the other. Consider the two variables "amount of alcohol drunk in the past thirty minutes" and "degree of intoxication." Observation at parties and elsewhere would indicate that the two variables are correlated; further, we have reason to believe that one causes, or produces, the other. Science attempts to discover such causal relationships, but the discovery of causes is often very difficult.

The idea of causation implies not only that two variables are correlated, but also that (1) changes in one precede changes in the other, and that (2) other possible causes have been ruled out of consideration. First, if two variables are causally related, one of them (the cause) must come before the other (the effect). The effect cannot precede the cause. Second, in order to claim that two variables are causally related, you must be able to demonstrate that the correlation between them is not a result of some other factor. To claim that alcohol causes intoxication, you must show that the intoxication was not a result of some other factor, such as the olives in the martini.

Correlation Is Not Always Causation

A common mistake people make is to regard evidence for correlation as sufficient evidence of causation. As we have just seen, in order to claim that a causal relationship exists between two variables, you need to have not only evidence of correlation but also additional evidence concerning such questions as the order of the variables (the cause must precede the effect).

A psychologist interested in the relationship between *religious attitudes* and *criminal tendencies* might visit fifty cities and obtain from each a measure of religious belief and a measure of criminal tendencies. The measure of religious attitudes might be the number of churches that the city supports, and the measure of criminal tendencies, the average daily number of serious crimes committed. When the data are examined, a correlation coefficient is computed and the psychologist is surprised to discover that there is a high positive correlation between the two variables: the greater the number of churches, the greater the average number of crimes per day.

Does this mean that religion causes crime?

There are two important reasons why this evidence for correlation cannot be regarded as evidence for causation. The psychologist is not justified in concluding that religion causes crime because (1) there is no evidence that changes in religious belief preceded changes in the crime rate—perhaps the heavy crime rate caused an upsurge in religious interest; and (2) there is no reason to exclude other possible causes— perhaps the high population in some cities leads to both a high number of churches and a high number of crimes, compared to cities of low population. Since the third variable, population, could be responsible for the variations in the number of churches in a city *and* for the variations in the number of crimes in a city, the relation between the number of churches and the number of crimes cannot be regarded as causal.

Controlled Experiments

What is the effect of motivation on learning? Do you learn more when you are highly motivated? Correlational studies have shown that people with high motivation score higher on learning tests than people with lower motivation; that is, there is a positive correlation between motivation and learning. But this correlation does not prove that motivation influences or causes learning. There are several possibilities: (1) making high scores on learning tests may cause you to be highly motivated; (2) being highly motivated may cause you to make high scores on learning tests; and (3) some third factor, such as genetic endowment, may cause both, but motivation and learning have no effect on each other. Combinations of these alternatives are also possible. How can you decide among the alternatives?

To discover which alternative is the best requires an **experiment**—a method of observing behavior systematically under carefully controlled conditions. In the experimental method, as opposed to the correlational method, researchers partially control what happens. Because they control the conditions of the study, the experimenters are able to investigate the causes of behavior. They produce changes in one variable, keeping other variables constant, and observe the effects on behavior.

A Sample Experiment

To discover experimentally the effect of motivation on learning, an experimenter would have to manipulate levels of motivation and then observe the consequences in behavior. One way to do this would be to attempt to produce different levels of motivation in different groups of students. For example, a large psychology class might be divided in half by randomly assigning students to one of two groups. One group, called the **experimental group,** is given some kind of special treatment in an attempt to increase their motivation to learn; the second group, called the **control group,** is treated as usual, with no special treatment. The second group is a kind of comparison group.

Because the class is large and is divided randomly, it is extremely unlikely that the two groups differ systematically before the experiment is conducted. For example, it is unlikely that one group would be all male and the other all female; it is unlikely that one group would be significantly more intelligent than the other group. With a large number of participants and with random assignment to groups, it turns out that differences between groups average out. At the beginning of the experiment, then, the experimental and control groups can be regarded as equivalent.

Students in both groups are asked to learn the same list of twenty psychology terms. Before the lists are presented, students in the experimental group are offered $.50 for every term learned correctly, while students in the control group are offered no reward. At the end of the experiment, if the two groups are significantly different in the number of terms they learn, the difference can be attributed to the difference in monetary reward (and, by assumption, in motivation), since in all other respects the two groups are believed to be equivalent.

In order to claim that changes in motivation *cause* changes in learning, you must demonstrate that (1) changes in motivation are correlated with changes in learning; (2) changes in motivation precede changes in learning; and (3) possible alternative explanations, such as differences in genetic endowment, can be ruled out.

Correlation would be shown if the "high motivation" group (experimental group) learned more than the "low motivation" group (control group); the variables of motivation and learning would be positively correlated.

Precedence of motivational changes can be assumed; the changes in motivation would have preceded the changes in learning, since motivational differences were produced by the experimenter before the learning task was presented (the experimenter offered to pay one group but not the other).

Alternative explanations of differences in learning between the two groups can be ruled out because the students were randomly assigned to one of the two groups and because the experimenter produced the motivational differences. Thus, it could not be claimed that the difference in learning between the two groups was due to a genetic difference, since it is extremely unlikely that two large, randomly selected groups would be systematically different in genetic structure. It is therefore possible in an experiment of this sort to come to a conclusion about the effect of motivation on learning.

Independent and Dependent Variables

In the experiment just described, the experimenter is interested in examining the possible relationship between two variables: (1) motivation level, and (2) the amount learned. If the two variables are found to be correlated—for example, if people learn more if motivated, then the experimenter will assume that there is probably a causal relation between the two variables; namely, that high motivation *causes* increased learning.

The variable that the experimenter manipulates or varies (in this case level of motivation) is called the **independent variable.** The independent variable is often considered as a cause of behavior. The variable that the experimenter does not manipulate directly is called the **dependent variable;** the dependent variable (amount learned) is affected by (depends upon) the independent variable. The values of the independent variable are called the "conditions" or the "treatments" of the experiment. The learning experiment just described had two conditions (two values of the independent variable): (1) high motivation, and (2) normal motivation.

Experimental Design

The **experimental design** is a plan for research. Different experimental designs describe different ways of manipulating the independent variable and different ways of assigning participants to the conditions of the experiment. A common design involves the assignment of one group of people to one experimental condition and a second group to another condition. After the conditions of the experiment are experienced by the groups, the behavior of the groups is measured and compared.

In one experimental study of observational learning, eighty-four children were randomly divided into three groups.[1] One group observed an adult model express opinions contrary to the children's beliefs and observed the adult receive rewards for doing so. Children in a second group were themselves induced to express opinions contrary to their true beliefs and were rewarded directly for doing so. A third group experienced both of the above conditions of "direct" and "vicarious" reward. Which group of children would be more likely to change their beliefs? The results showed that both groups observing adult models reversed a large number of their beliefs, but that children in the group without the opportunity for observational learning did not change many of their beliefs. You can conclude from these results that adult "modeling" behavior *causes* changes in children's expressions of their beliefs.

Sources of Problems

Experiments, as methods of discovering causal relations in the world, are open to many errors of inference and design. Some of the more common problems that experimenters face in designing experiments include order effects, placebo effects, and selection errors.

Order Effects • Sometimes behavior is measured both before and after an experimental manipulation; the assumption is that a difference between the first and the second measurements will be due to the experimental condition. A researcher might, for example, give you one creativity test, then give you a cup of coffee (the experimental treatment), and then measure your creativity again with a second test. An increase

in your creativity score could not be attributed exclusively to the effect of the coffee; the increase might be due to an **order effect**. That is, you might have done better on the second test because it was second—you had learned something from the first test that helped you the second time around.

Placebo Effects • Psychologists studying the effects of a particular drug on behavior must be concerned with the manner of administering the drug. Pills have effects beyond the effects of the chemical they contain. For example, pills containing only inactive substances, such as sugar pills, are known to produce improvement in feelings of well-being. Medically inactive pills ("placebos") are given by many doctors to patients whom they cannot help in other ways. If a person is given a pill containing a drug and subsequently feels better or performs better, you do not know whether the improvement in mood or performance is due to the drug or to the **placebo effect**—the psychological effect of a treatment such as taking a pill.

The true effects of a drug can be determined by giving one group of people pills containing the drug and giving a second group of people identical-looking pills that do not contain the drug. Differences between the two groups can be then attributed to the effects of the drug alone.

Selection Errors • If an experimenter uses two groups of participants, each experiencing a different experimental condition, the two groups must be equivalent in all ways except for the differences in experimental treatment. Thus, if the results show that behavior of the two groups is different, the experimenter would like to be able to attribute the difference in behavior to the difference in experimental conditions, not to other differences. A **selection error** occurs if the participants selected for groups are unequal to start with.

In order to test the effects of sleep on memory, you might have a group of fourth-graders learn a list of words just before going to sleep, then test them in the morning; then have a group of high school seniors learn a list of words in the morning, and test them after eight hours. If the two groups showed a difference in the amount of material remembered, you would not be able to attribute that difference to the experimental condition of sleep or wakefulness, since there were other significant differences between the two groups (age) that could have caused the differences in memory.

In order to avoid selection errors of this sort, the experimenter is careful to assign participants randomly to the experimental conditions, or to match the people in one group with the people in the other group. The aim is to make the groups equal in all ways except for the effects of the experimental condition.

What's Wrong with This Experiment?

Professor Z. believed that vitamin C had the capacity to prop up tired minds and that aspirin also had a mysterious power to make students more clever. To test this idea, he decided to give vitamin C pills to his psychology class and to give aspirin tablets to his ad-vanced calculus class. All students were given a standard IQ test, then they took a pill, and then they took the IQ test over again. Professor Z.'s hypothesis was that both classes would show a significant increase in IQ between the first and second tests as a consequence of the magic chemicals.

The results of the experiment were as follows: the average IQ for the thirty students in his psychology class was 115 on the first test; after the vitamin C pills, their average IQ increased to 135. The average IQ for the thirty students in the advanced calculus class was 117 on the first test; after the aspirin tablets, their IQ increased to 122. Thus, average IQ in the psychology class increased 20 points after taking vitamin C and the average IQ in the calculus class increased 5 points after taking aspirin.

Professor Z. called a press conference and triumphantly announced his conclusion: vitamin C and aspirin both increase IQ, but vitamin C increases it more. Other scientists severely criticized this conclusion, saying that his experiment had at least three serious defects. What are they? (Check your answers against those given in the footnote following the Key Concepts at the end of this chapter.)

Key Concepts

measurement Assigning a number to behavior on the basis of a rule (for example, by using an IQ test).

frequency distribution A table showing the number of cases having each particular score; for example, the number of cases with a score of one, the number of cases with a score of two, and so on.

histogram A graph that uses bars of different heights to represent the frequency of different responses.

average A single number that represents a group of scores.

central tendency An average or typical value that reflects a group of scores as a whole.

mean The most commonly used measure of central tendency; computed by dividing the sum of the scores by the number of scores.

mode Another measure of central tendency; the score that occurs most often in the group of scores.

median A third measure of central tendency; the middle score, the score above which and below which an equal number of other scores fall.

variability The differences among a group of scores; the distribution of the scores.

range A measure of variability that reflects the difference between the upper and lower boundaries of the distribution.

standard deviation   A measure of variability that reflects the spread of a distribution.

sample   A subset or selection from a larger group or population.

inference   The process of reaching a general conclusion on the basis of observing only a sample.

correlation   The correspondence or relationship between two things; the degree to which things vary together; for example, up to a point, age and height vary together and are therefore correlated.

variable   A concept having different values; "intelligence" is a variable, having many different values.

correlation coefficient   A measure of the degree of correlation that ranges in value from −1.00 to +1.00; both extremes (−1.00 and +1.00) reflect perfect correlation.

causation   The degree to which one variable produces, influences, or modifies the other; a cause-and-effect relationship.

experiment   A form of controlled observation in which the researcher manipulates one factor and then observes the consequences.

experimental group   In an experiment, the group receiving special treatment.

control group   In an experiment, the group receiving no special treatment; the comparison group.

independent variable   In an experiment, the variable manipulated by the experimenter; for example, in an experiment to test the effect of alcohol on reaction time, the independent variable is alcohol dosage.

dependent variable   In an experiment, the variable influenced by the independent variable; for example, in an experiment to test the effect of alcohol on reaction time, the dependent variable is reaction time.

experimental design   A plan for conducting an experiment, consisting of a method for manipulating the independent variable and observing the dependent variable, and a method of assigning participants to conditions.

order effect   A change in behavior that may be due to repeating the conditions of measurement; for example, the second time that a test is given you may do better merely because you are more familiar with the test.

placebo effect   A change in behavior due to taking a pill or other treatment, independent of the content of the pill; for example, some people may feel better after taking a medically inactive sugar pill.

selection error   A difference in behavior between groups that results from the groups being unequal to start with; an error resulting from bias in assigning participants to experimental conditions.

Answers to "What's Wrong with This Experiment?"

1. For both classes, the improvement in IQ may have resulted from having the opportunity to take the IQ test a second time; that is, the *order effect* may have operated.

2. For both classes, the improvement in IQ may have resulted from the psychological effect of taking a pill—any pill; that is, the *placebo effect* may have influenced the results.

3. There were at least two differences between the two classes: (a) one group got aspirin, the other vitamin C; and (b) one group elected to take psychology, the other, advanced calculus. Differences in IQ gain between the two classes could be due to (a) or to (b) or to both. Since the two classes were not initially equivalent, a *selection error* was made.

Glossary

ablation   The removal of brain tissue.

abnormal behavior   Behavior that is inappropriate, unusual, maladaptive, and typically associated with anxiety and distress.

absolute threshold   The lower limit of sensitivity; the minimum level of energy necessary for sensation.

abstinence before marriage   A standard of sexual behavior stating that intercourse is acceptable only after marriage.

achievement motivation   The desire to succeed and do things well.

acute anxiety   The feeling of intense anxiety that comes on suddenly but does not last for long.

adaptation   Sensitivity changes with repeated stimulation.

adolescence   The period of growth between childhood and adulthood, or from about twelve to seventeen years of age.

adrenal glands   Endocrine glands located just above the kidneys; play role in growth and metabolism, response to stress and strong emotion.

affective component of attitudes   The positive or negative feeling that you have about the object or person toward whom the attitude is directed.

affective disorder   A disorder characterized by moods that are extremely high or extremely low.

afferent neurons   Nerve cells that carry messages to the brain.

agape   The Greek word for spiritual love; love as giving and caring.

ageism   Prejudice against the old.

agoraphobia   Fear of open spaces.

aggression   Fighting or attacking behavior; actions having the intent of hurting others.

aggressiveness   Violation of the rights of others, hurting others by putting them down, demanding that your own needs be met at the expense of others.

alarm reaction   First stage of the general adaptation syndrome, in which heart rate increases to prepare for a "fight-or-flight" response.

alcohol   A sedative drug found in beer, wine, and whiskey; physically addictive.

alcoholism   A disorder involving repeated and uncontrolled use of alcohol that results in interference with social and occupational behavior and with health.

all-or-none law   The principle that the size or intensity of a neuron's nerve impulse is always the same; the neuron is either stimulated enough to fire or it is not.

alpha wave   A type of brain wave associated with relaxed awareness; voltage fluctuations from eight to twelve cycles per second.

altered states of consciousness   A level of awareness that is higher or lower than normal; a state of mind different from normal waking consciousness.

amnesia   A loss of memory for past events or personal identity as a result of brain injury or psychological stress; also, a dissociative reaction involving a loss of memory for personal identity or past events.

amphetamines   Stimulant drugs (sometimes also called "speed" or "uppers"); heavy use may produce a psychotic reaction.

anal character   A personality pattern of stinginess, stubbornness, compulsive cleanliness and punctuality, and extreme orderliness.

anal stage   The second psychosexual stage during which the infant gains sexual pleasure from urinary and bowel activities.

analysis   The act of separating something into its component parts.

androgynous   Possessing both masculine and feminine traits.

anger   The feeling of emotion that accompanies aggression.

antecedents   The prior context; the events that precede behavior; for example, studying is an antecedent for success on a final exam.

anticonformity   Doing the opposite of what the social norm dictates.

anxiety   The vague worry or apprehension that has no specific known cause; a person may feel anxiety in crowds but not know the reason for this feeling.

anxiety hierarchy   An arrangement of feared situations, ranked from the least to the most threatening.

anxiety reaction   The experience of excessive and uncontrollable anxiety.

apnea   The inability to breathe when asleep.

approach-approach conflict   A conflict involving a choice between two desirable alternatives.

approach-avoidance conflict   A conflict involving a choice that is both desirable and undesirable.

arousal level   Level of activation or stimulation.

assertiveness   The honest expression of how you feel and the standing up for your own rights without violating the rights of others.

atavistic theory   The theory that criminals are genetic throwbacks and are born to act the way they do.

attitude   A tendency to act in a consistently positive or negative way toward an object, a person, or a group of people.

attitude scale   A test consisting of a series of statements designed to measure the strength of the attitudes of the person being tested.

attribution theory   A theory that explains the rules we use in inferring the causes of behavior; for example, a particular action may be attributed to external circumstances ("he stumbled and accidentally fell against me") or to internal causes ("he intended to bump me").

authentic communication   A true exchange of information and feelings involving openness and self-disclosure.

authoritarian personality   A personality type characterized by resistance to change, admiration for authority figures, contempt for persons of lower status, and extreme prejudice.

autokinetic illusion   An illusion in which a stationary point of light in a dark room appears to move.

autonomic nervous system   The network of nerves connecting the brain to the glands and organs of the body; responsible for regulating automatic functions such as blood pressure.

average   A single number that represents a group of scores.

aversive   Unpleasant or punishing; for example, pain and nausea are aversive.

avoidance-avoidance conflict   A conflict involving a choice between two undesirable alternatives.

axon   A long, thin fiber that extends from the cell body.

barbiturates   Sedative drugs (sometimes called "reds" or "downers"); physically addictive.

baseline   The normal level or pattern of a response that occurs before an experiment is conducted; the baseline rate of behavior is the frequency of occurrence of the behavior before any attempt is made to change it.

basilar membrane   A structure within the cochlea that contains the special cells that transform sound energy into nerve impulses.

behavior   Activities; things that are done; includes actions, thoughts, attitudes, memories, perceptions, language, feelings, etc.

behavior therapy   A form of psychotherapy, based on principles of learning, that focuses on the symptoms of a psychological problem, not the underlying causes.

behavioral genetics   The study of the inheritance of behavior.

behaviorism   A system of psychology started by John Watson; according to this system, psychology is limited to the study of publicly observable behavior.

being-love (B-love)   Maslow's term for an unselfish love; the person does not require the satisfaction of his or her own needs.

belief-difference theory of prejudice   According to this theory, prejudice results from perceived differences of belief systems.

beta waves   Brain waves produced when you are awake, with your eyes open; voltage fluctuations from thirteen to twenty-eight cycles per second.

biased sample   An unrepresentative sample; a sample with characteristics systematically different from its population.

biofeedback   A technique for measuring subtle changes in the body and revealing them; this technique can be used to provide people with knowledge of their heart rate, blood pressure, and brain waves.

biological theory of crime   The theory that criminals

are physically different from noncriminals, and this difference accounts for crime.

biological theory of homosexuality The theory that homosexuals are biologically different from heterosexuals.

bisexual An individual who can achieve sexual gratification equally from both sexes.

blind spot The blind area in the field of vision resulting from the absence of receptor cells on the retina where the optic nerve leaves the eye.

blind taste test A comparison of different products involving testing them with labels hidden or removed.

block design test Tests ability to construct a particular design with blocks.

body messages Nonverbal communications, such as hand gestures or emotional expressions, that convey actual information.

boomerang effect Reactance.

brain waves Rhythmic changes in the electrical activity of the brain.

broken-record technique A technique for increasing assertiveness that involves calmly repeating your main point over and over until the other person understands it.

caffeine A stimulant drug found in coffee and tea.

Cannon-Bard theory of emotion According to this theory, bodily changes are independent from emotional experience and follow these experiences rather than cause them.

case study An in-depth examination of a single individual.

cataracts A visual disorder resulting from a loss of transparency in the lens.

causation The degree to which one variable produces, influences, or modifies the other; a cause-and-effect relationship.

cell body The part of a cell that contains the cell's nucleus.

central deafness Deafness resulting from problems with the auditory centers of the brain or from certain psychological disorders such as conversion reactions.

central nervous system (CNS) That part of the nervous system consisting of the brain and spinal cord.

central tendency An average or typical value that reflects a group of scores as a whole.

cerebellum A structure at the back and bottom of the brain that regulates muscle tone and muscle coordination.

cerebral cortex The outer covering of the brain.

cerebral hemispheres The right and left halves of the brain.

cerebrum The outer brain, which, along with its cerebral cortex, is the seat of our higher mental processes, such as learning, memory, intelligence, and thinking.

chemotherapy A biological treatment of mental problems that involves drugs such as tranquilizers and antidepressants.

chromosome A rodlike structure within the nucleus of each cell in the body that carries hereditary information.

chronic anxiety Anxiety that is continual.

chronic phase The fourth and final stage in the development of alcoholism in which the drinker's entire life is organized around the problem of obtaining alcohol.

chunking Grouping items to be remembered into units or clusters.

circadian rhythms Daily cycles of certain biological processes such as sleep and body temperature.

classical conditioning Conditioning by association; a form of conditioning in which a neutral stimulus acquires the power to produce a response by being paired with another stimulus that already consistently elicits the response.

client-centered therapy The method of therapy developed by Rogers; its goal is to help clients become more aware of how they feel and more accepting of their own feelings and experiences.

clinical psychologist A psychologist who specializes in treating personality disorders and providing therapy; typically has a Ph.D. degree with training in testing and research.

clinical psychology The study of the causes of personality disorders and the effectiveness of different types of treatment.

clinical social worker A person with a degree in social work who has additional training in abnormal psychology and therapy.

cocaine A stimulant drug (sometimes called "coke" or "snow"); extended use may produce episodes of drug psychosis.

cochlea   The inner ear structure that contains the receptors sensitive to sound vibrations.

cocktail-party phenomenon   The ability to switch your attention to tune in one message and tune out others.

codeine   A narcotic drug similar to morphine but less potent; physically addictive.

cofigurative culture   A culture in which children and adults learn from their peers.

cognition   Mental activities such as thinking, perceiving, knowing, or understanding.

cognitive component of attitudes   The belief or opinion that you hold about the object or person toward whom the attitude is directed.

cognitive development   The changes that occur with age in cognitive activities.

cognitive dissonance theory   The theory that attitudes are formed and maintained so that they are consistent with our behavior; if you act toward a certain group in a negative, discriminatory way, then to be consistent, your attitudes toward that group will also be negative.

cognitive psychology   The study of mental activities such as thinking, knowing, perceiving, and remembering.

cognitive restructuring   The technique for modifying the negative thoughts that people have in different situations, the way in which people "talk to themselves."

cognitive theory of dreams   The theory that dreams consist of fragments of thoughts and memories that have been associated with emotions.

cognitive theory of emotion   According to this theory, emotional experience results from an interpretation of perceived bodily arousal.

cognitive theory of moral development   Kohlberg's theory that describes moral development in terms of a succession of stages that are believed to be universal.

color blindness   An inherited condition that results in varying degrees of difficulty in discriminating different colors.

community mental health   An approach to psychological treatment that is concerned with preventive and outreach activities aimed at improving the psychological welfare of the entire community.

compensation theory   The theory that orgasms in sex dreams make up for a lack of sexual activity while awake.

competition theory of prejudice   According to this theory, negative attitudes tend to develop between competing groups.

compulsion   An irrational, repetitive, involuntary act.

conative component of attitudes   The tendency to behave in a particular way toward the object or person toward whom the attitude is directed.

concentrated reading   A type of reading that involves looking for relationships, making up questions, highlighting, and restating main ideas.

concrete operations stage   The third of Piaget's cognitive stages, lasting from about seven to eleven.

conditioned reflexes   Involuntary reactions acquired through an elementary form of learning; for example, when your mouth waters in reaction to a picture of food.

conditioned reinforcer   A secondary reinforcer.

conditioned response   The learned reaction to the conditioned stimulus; for example, the reaction of salivating to a bell.

conditioned stimulus   The initially neutral stimulus that is paired with the unconditioned stimulus; for example, a bell.

conditioning   A form of simple learning: learning by association or learning by consequences.

conductive deafness   Deafness resulting from problems in the outer or middle ear that block the passage of sound energy to the inner ear; for example, a perforated eardrum.

cones   Specialized cells in the retina that respond to differences in wavelength as well as to differences in light intensity; responsible for our "color vision."

conflict   A struggle between opposing wishes, needs, or forces.

conformity   Going along with group standards or expectations and going against private beliefs.

congruence   A condition in which inner feelings, awareness of feelings, and outward expression of feelings all correspond.

conscious level   That level of consciousness consisting of immediate thoughts and feelings; one's current awareness.

consciousness   Mental life; the private awareness of thoughts, feelings, and perceptions.

consensus rule   The tendency to attribute a behavior to external causes if other people in the same situation act the same way.

consequence   An event occurring after a response that occurs only when the response occurs.

conservation   The idea that things retain their properties of weight, number, and volume, even though their surface appearance may change; also, the preservation of our resources by changing consumer behavior.

consumer psychology The study of the dynamics underlying and determining consumer behavior.

continuous schedule of reinforcement Delivery of a reinforcer for every correct response.

control group In an experiment, the group receiving no special treatment; the comparison group.

conversion reaction Sensory or muscular problems that exist without a physical cause.

corpus callosum The broad band of nerves that connects the two hemispheres of the brain.

correlation The correspondence or relationship between two things; the degree to which things vary together; for example, up to a point, age and height vary together and are therefore correlated.

correlation coefficient A measure of the degree of correlation that ranges in value from -1.00 to $+1.00$; both extremes (-1.00 and $+1.00$) reflect perfect correlation.

cortex The outer wrinkled surface of the brain; an area especially important for human perception and intelligence.

counselor A psychologist who specializes in offering advice and guidance; usually has a graduate degree in psychology or education.

creativity The ability to respond uniquely and appropriately.

cross-sectional method A method of studying developmental changes by comparing different groups of people who are of different ages.

crowding An excessive number of people.

crucial phase The third stage in the development of alcoholism, marked by the inability to stop drinking once it is started. In this stage the drinker will experience withdrawal symptoms if alcohol is not taken every day.

dark adaptation Adjustment to reduced light; this results in increased sensitivity to low levels of light.

death instincts According to Freud, those inborn needs that serve destructive purposes; for example, aggression.

decay theory A theory of forgetting that states that memories fade with time.

defense mechanism An unconscious strategy for protecting ourselves against the experience of anxiety.

deficiency-love (D-love) Maslow's term for a selfish possessive love; the person's love is conditional upon the satisfaction of his or her own needs.

deindividuation Feeling anonymous, one of the crowd, without a unique personal identity.

delta waves Brain waves produced in stages three and four of sleep; voltage fluctuations are from one-half to two cycles per second.

delusion A false belief that is bizarre and irrational and is held in spite of contrary evidence; for example, the belief that one is Napoleon.

delusion of grandeur A false belief that one is a great or powerful person; for example, the belief that one controls the world.

delusion of persecution A false belief that one is being victimized; for example, a man may believe that others are out to get him.

delusion of reference A false belief that unrelated events are personally directed; for example, a man may have the belief that everybody is talking about him.

dementia A progressive deterioration of mental functioning that sometimes occurs in older persons.

demonic possession The assumption that an evil spirit, witch, or god was somehow inhabiting the body and causing an individual's abnormal behavior.

dendrite A relatively short, branching fiber that extends from the cell body of a neuron.

dependent variable In an experiment, the variable influenced by the independent variable; for example, in an experiment to test the effect of alcohol on reaction time, the dependent variable is reaction time.

depression Feelings of despair, dejection, and worthlessness.

depth perception The ability to see in three dimensions; the awareness of the distance between yourself and objects.

desensitization A technique for reducing fear by pairing relaxation with the feared situation.

devaluation The tendency to regard some people as inferior or worthless.

developmental psychology The study of the changes in behavior and ability that occur as people age.

deviation IQ A measure of intelligence that reflects how far a particular score deviates from the average score made by people of similar age.

diagnosis The classification or identification of a problem on the basis of its symptoms; for example, classification of a person as psychotic on the basis of the person's delusions.

dichotic listening   A procedure in which research subjects are given earphones playing two competing messages, one in the left ear and another in the right ear.

difference threshold   Lower limit of sensitivity to a change in the stimulus; the minimal change in a stimulus that can be detected.

differential association theory of crime   The theory that people are likely to become criminals if they are exposed to relatively more criminal patterns of behavior than noncriminal patterns.

diffusion of responsibility   A sharing or spreading of the responsibility for actions.

digit-span test   Test of the ability to repeat, both forward and backwards, a series of numbers that are read aloud.

direct learning   Learning by doing.

discovery method   A method of teaching that encourages students to discover important principles on their own.

discrepancy theory   A theory of job satisfaction that assumes that a job will be found satisfying to the degree that it meets the expectations of the workers.

discrimination   Responding to certain stimuli but not to others as a result of learning.

displaced aggression   Aggression that is directed against someone other than its original target.

displacement   A defense mechanism in which a reaction is shifted from one person to a safer substitute; for example, your anger at your father is shifted to your younger brother.

dissociative reaction   A splitting apart of the personality into two or more relatively independent parts.

dissonance   Inconsistency or lack of agreement.

distinctiveness rule   The tendency to attribute a behavior to external causes if the individual performs the behavior in one situation but not in others.

distributed practice   Studying or practicing a little bit at a time.

DNA   The complex molecule that makes up the genes.

dominance   A personality trait describing the tendency to be confident, independent, and controlling.

dominance hierarchy   A group that can be ordered from most dominant to most submissive; an individual in this group dominates those below and is dominated by those above; a "pecking order."

double-bind   A condition in which two opposing atti-

tudes have been communicated; a double message, such as, "I love you" and also "I hate you."

double standard   A standard of sexual behavior stating that premarital intercourse is acceptable for men but not for women.

dream analysis   The technique of analyzing and interpreting dreams in order to reveal unconscious material.

dream deprivation   A condition caused by waking people each time REM begins, in order to prevent dreaming.

drive   A need (or motive) that arouses behavior and "pushes" a person into action; for example, the hunger drive pushes you to obtain food.

drive stimulus   According to Hull, certain bodily changes (associated with different drive conditions), which serve as cues for directing behavior toward the desired goal.

Duncan Scale   A ranking of occupations according to their relative status, or prestige.

duplex theory of memory   A theory that there are two memory systems for storing information—one for remembering something for a short time and a second for remembering something for a long time.

duplicative theory of memory   A theory that remembering involves retrieving copies of past experience.

duplicity principle of vision   The principle that the eye has two types of light-sensitive cells, each specializing in a different type of visual task.

dyadic effect   The tendency for self-disclosure to be reciprocated; when one person is open and honest in a relationship, the other person is encouraged to be open and honest in return.

early determinism   The view that adult personality is determined by early childhood experiences.

ectomorph   A body type which is tall and thin, with a flat chest, long limbs, and a narrow face.

educable mentally retarded (EMR)   Another term for the mildly retarded, as they are able to learn reading and math skills up to a sixth-grade level.

educational psychology   The study of teaching and school learning.

EEG (electroencephalograph)   A machine that measures the electrical activity of the brain (brain waves).

efferent neurons   Nerve cells that carry messages from the brain to muscles or glands.

egalitarian marriage model   In this type of marriage the roles and responsibilities are shared.

ego According to Freud, that part of the personality that deals with reality and is responsible for voluntary processes of thinking, perceiving, and remembering.

egocentrism The tendency to see things only from one's own point of view.

eidetic imagery A kind of photographic memory in which whole pictures or scenes can be remembered in detail.

elaborative rehearsal A form of rehearsal involving thinking of meaningful relationships and placing the material to be remembered in different meaningful contexts.

electroconvulsive therapy (ECT) A biological treatment of mental problems that involves passing an electric current through the brain; used primarily in cases of severe, psychotic depression.

electroencephalogram (EEG) A record of the electrical activity of the brain.

electromyogram (EMG) A record of the electrical activity of muscles, such as in the face or shoulders.

electrooculogram (EOG) A record of the electrical activity of the eye muscles.

eliciting effect A type of observational learning which results in the increased tendency to perform some behavior.

emotion A subjective feeling accompanied by changes in behavior and in the physiology of the body.

empathy The ability to participate in the feelings and perceptions of others.

empirical question A question that can be answered by observation.

encoding Putting information into memory by changing the physical energy in the environment into memory codes.

encoding-specificity principle The rule that memory is best when the information encoded at the time of learning is the same as the information presented at the time of testing.

encounter group A group psychotherapy that focuses on sensitivity and awareness of feelings, authentic communication, and interpersonal trust.

endocrine glands Glands in the body that secrete chemicals (hormones) into the bloodstream.

endomorph A body type which is short and plump, with a short neck and broad hands.

endorphin A group of chemicals produced by the brain that have the ability to suppress pain.

engram The physical basis of memory in the brain.

environment The physical and psychological context of behavior; trees, storms, your mother, school, and this book all form part of the context of your behavior.

equity theory A theory of job satisfaction that assumes that a job will be found satisfying to the degree that the worker perceives it to be "fair" (what the worker puts into the job and what the worker gets out of it are balanced).

erogenous zones Sexually sensitive areas of the body, such as lips, breasts, or genitals.

eros The Greek word for erotic or passionate love.

erotic love A feeling that combines adoration and tenderness with sexual desire.

ESB (electrical stimulation of the brain) A technique in which a weak electrical current is sent through a part of the brain.

estrogen A female sex hormone; produced by the ovaries.

ethology The study of animals in their natural settings.

evoked potential The electrical response of the brain to a stimulus.

exchange theory of friendship The theory that you form friendships by estimating your "market value," then forming relationships with those with equal or higher value.

exhaustion Third stage of the general adaptation syndrome, in which the body is unable to continue resisting the stress.

exhibitionism A compulsion for bodily exposure, usually exposure of the sexual organs.

experiment A form of controlled observation in which the researcher manipulates one factor and then observes the consequences.

experimental design A plan for conducting an experiment, consisting of a method for manipulating the independent variable and observing the dependent variable, and a method of assigning participants to conditions.

experimental group In an experiment, the group receiving special treatment.

experimental neurosis A mental disorder in laboratory animals caused by an approach-avoidance conflict.

experimental psychology The study of behavior through the use of experiments.

extended family A social grouping consisting of a married couple with their children living with the parents of either the husband or the wife.

extinction   The procedure and result of eliminating a conditioned response; in classical conditioning, brought about by presenting the conditioned stimulus without the unconditioned stimulus; in operant conditioning, brought about by withholding reinforcement.

extrasensory perception (ESP)   The sensing of information about the world, other people, or the future in ways other than through the normal human senses of seeing, hearing, touching, tasting, smelling, and the body senses.

extrinsic motivation   Forces outside the person that motivate behavior, for example, money, applause, or punishment.

extrovert   A personality type that turns outward, seeks social contacts, is friendly, outspoken, and tolerant.

F scale   A test measuring the authoritarian personality.

facilitate   To make easier.

fact   Information based on observation; a statement based on careful observation or experience.

fads   Short-lived practices that sweep the country periodically as social customs.

family history studies   A research method consisting of examining the resemblance on particular traits among family members.

family of orientation   The family consisting of you, your parents, and your siblings.

family of procreation   The family consisting of you, your spouse, and your children.

fashions   Enduring social customs; for example, styles of dress.

fear   The reaction of dread or apprehension to a specific threatening object; a person may feel fear when confronted with a loaded gun.

fear appeal   A type of persuasive message stressing the dangers of not buying the product or complying with the request.

feedback   Knowledge of results; knowing whether an action was or was not successful.

femininity   The degree to which an individual conforms to behavior typical of women in a culture.

fetish   An object that a person associates with sexual activity and requires for sexual gratification; for example, a shoe.

field study   A research project conducted in a natural setting, such as in a store, as opposed to a study in a laboratory.

fight-or-flight reaction   The tendency to attack or withdraw from an intruder when personal space has been violated.

figure-ground principle   The rule that perceptual experiences are organized into two parts: objects and their background.

filter theory of attention   A theory of attention that assumes that we somehow set different thresholds for detecting different sounds, depending upon the significance of the sounds to us.

fixation   A pause between eye movements.

fixed interval schedule (FI schedule)   Delivery of a reinforcer for the first correct response to occur after a set period of time has elapsed; for example, asking for your paycheck at the end of the week.

fixed ratio schedule (FR schedule)   Delivery of a reinforcer after a certain number of correct responses have occurred; for example, factory piecework.

flashback   A spontaneous recurrence of the drug effect at a time when the drug has not been taken.

fogging technique   A technique for increasing assertiveness that involves expressing understanding and agreeing in principle with some portion of the other person's criticism but still maintaining your rights.

formal-operations stage   The fourth and last of Piaget's cognitive stages, beginning at about age eleven and continuing through adulthood, in which a person develops abstract reasoning ability.

fovea   The center of the retina; a small area densely packed with light-sensitive cells.

fraternal twins   Twins resulting from two eggs being fertilized by two sperm cells at about the same time; their genetic structure is no more similar than that of other siblings.

free association   The procedure of saying anything that comes to mind, without censorship.

frequency distribution   A table showing the number of cases having each particular score; for example, the number of cases with a score of one, the number of cases with a score of two, and so on.

frequency theory   A theory of pitch discrimination that hypothesizes that sounds of different frequencies stimulate the basilar membrane to transmit different frequencies of nerve impulses to the brain.

Freudian theory of dreams   The theory that dreams reveal unconscious wishes that are expressed symbolically in dream images.

frontal lobe   A region at the front of each side of the brain that specializes in planning, abstract thinking, and problem solving.

frustration-aggression hypothesis   The proposal that aggression is always a consequence of frustration.

fully functioning person   Rogers's term for the psychologically healthy person; one who is happy, creative, and socially effective.

functional psychosis   A psychosis with no known physical cause.

games   Stereotyped interactions in which the hidden motive is to win, not to exchange information or feelings.

general adaptation syndrome   A patterned response to prolonged extreme stress in the environment.

generalization   Reasoning from evidence obtained from a sample to a conclusion about a population.

generalized drive   According to Hull, the idea that there is only one kind of drive and that it is increased similarly by any kind of deprivation.

generation gap   The difference between parents and their children in values, opinions, and beliefs.

generativity versus stagnation   Erikson's psychosocial crisis of middle age in which the individual becomes concerned with others outside the immediate family—with society and future generations.

genes   The basic units of genetic information found on chromosomes.

genetics   The study of inherited characteristics.

genital stage   The fifth and final psychosexual stage during which sexual pleasure is gained from masturbation and intercourse.

genius   The term sometimes applied to individuals with IQ's over 140, but is more accurately used to refer to those with exceptional creativity.

gerontologist   A scientist specializing in the study of older people.

Gestalt movement   A school of psychology that stressed the significance of pattern and organization in perception; founded by Max Wertheimer.

Gestalt therapy   The method of psychotherapy developed by Fritz Perls; a group psychotherapy that focuses on sensory awareness, body awareness, and "here-and-now" experience.

grammar   The rules that people follow when they construct sentences.

group dynamics   The study of social interaction in groups.

group interaction tasks   Group tasks that involve members interacting and working together.

group therapy   Psychotherapy conducted with a group of eight to twelve people at once.

Guttman scale   A type of attitude scale that consists of a graded series of statements varying in strength of attitude.

hallucination   A disturbance in perception in which something is seen, heard, or felt that does not exist; for example, hearing voices when no one is near.

halo effect   The tendency to see a person as desirable in all ways because of one desirable trait.

hashish ("hash")   A more concentrated form of marijuana.

hedonism   The desire to achieve the greatest possible pleasure.

hedonistic standard   A standard of sexual behavior stating that no limitations should be placed on intercourse between consenting adults.

heroin   A narcotic drug made from morphine; physically addictive.

heterosexual   A man or woman who seeks sexual satisfaction primarily from members of the opposite sex.

histogram   A graph that uses bars of different heights to represent the frequency of different responses.

homosexual   A man or woman who seeks sexual satisfaction exclusively—or almost exclusively—from members of the same sex.

hormone   A chemical produced by a gland and deposited into the bloodstream.

humanistic psychology   The "third force" in psychology; emphasizes personal growth and creativity.

humanistic theory   A theory that views personality as a process of growth or becoming, rather than as something determined by the past.

humanistic theory of motivation   Maslow's theory that all people are born with a desire to achieve their maximum potential.

hyperopia   A condition in which the eye can focus on objects far away but not on those nearby.

hypersexuality   An extremely high level of sexual drive resulting in almost continuous sexual activity.

hypnosis   A state of heightened suggestibility in which a person is under the influence of someone else.

hyposexuality   An extremely low level of sex drive resulting in little or no sexual activity.

hypothalamus   A small brain structure immediately below the thalamus that acts as the master control organ for the autonomic nervous system; regulates sex, hunger, and thirst.

id   According to Freud, the storehouse of unconscious memories and impulses; a part of the mind that remains infantile, rejecting reason and morality and demanding instant gratification.

idealized model   A standard of masculinity and femininity based on what is considered perfect or ideal.

identical twins   Twins resulting from a single fertilized egg, each having exactly the same genes; they are therefore always of the same sex and of very similar physical appearance.

identification   The process by which children observe and imitate adults, and incorporate their values and beliefs.

identity   A sense of who you are, often in terms of social roles, relationships, goals, activities, interests.

identity crisis   According to Erikson, a period in adolescence marked by great uncertainty about one's identity.

identity versus role diffusion   Erikson's psychosocial crisis of adolescence in which the individual strives to achieve a firm sense of self.

ideology   A set of assumptions and beliefs.

I-E Scale   A personality test designed to measure how much control you feel you have over your life.

I-it relationship   A relationship in which one person is treated as an object, a thing to be manipulated, instead of as a unique being.

illusions   Distorted or incorrect perceptions.

immature love   Fromm's term for a selfish love that lasts only as long as needs are satisfied.

impair   To interfere with or reduce in effectiveness; for example, "The damage to his eye impaired his vision."

incentive   A goal or condition that you strive to obtain; something that "pulls" a person into action.

incompatible behavior   Behavior that interferes with the desired behavior.

incongruity   A lack of consistency between your awareness and reality; for example, a lack of consistency between your awareness of how you feel and your actual feelings.

inconsistency rule   The tendency to attribute a behavior to external causes if the individual only occasionally shows that behavior in that situation.

independence   The expression of private beliefs in the face of group pressure to conform.

independent variable   In an experiment, the variable manipulated by the experimenter; for example, in an experiment to test the effect of alcohol on reaction time, the independent variable is alcohol dosage.

inference   The process of reaching a general conclusion on the basis of observing only a sample.

inhibitory effect   A type of observational learning which results in a reduced tendency to perform some behavior.

innate ideas   Ideas, concepts, or ways of perceiving the world that are inborn or present at birth.

inner-directed   Making decisions on the basis of personal values.

inoculation   A persuasive technique that involves presenting weak arguments against your position, then vigorously rebutting them.

insecurity   The opposite of security; refers to the tendency to feel threatened by living, unloved, pessimistic, and discontented.

insomnia   Chronic difficulty in getting to sleep or staying asleep.

instinct   A complex, unlearned behavior sequence, such as nest building in some birds.

instinct theory of aggression   The theory that aggression is an inborn tendency; that we are born with "killer instincts."

instrumental conditioning   Another term for operant conditioning.

integrity versus despair   Erikson's final psychosocial crisis of old age in which the individual reflects on life and the coming of death.

intelligence   The ability to learn and to solve problems.

intelligence quotient (IQ)   A score on an intelligence test that reflects a person's level of intelligence compared to others of the same age.

interest test   A test involving questions about preferences for a wide variety of activities or objects.

interference theory   A theory of forgetting that states that memories are disrupted by newer and older memories.

internal conflict   A struggle between two opposing wishes or needs within an individual.

interneurons   Nerve cells that carry messages between afferent and efferent neurons and are primarily involved in the "mental" processes of thought, memory, feeling, and problem solving.

intimacy versus isolation Erikson's psychosocial crisis of young adulthood in which the individual seeks to establish deep relationships with friends or with a mate.

intrinsic motivation Factors that make an activity enjoyable or rewarding in and of itself; for example, participation in some tasks such as games, puzzles, or artwork is enjoyable and interesting.

introvert A personality type that turns inward, withdraws from social engagements, is introspective, self-controlled, and reflective.

intuition The ability to come to a conclusion without having direct evidence.

iris The muscle surrounding the pupil that gives color to the eye.

irresistible impulse A sudden strong compulsion to do something socially unacceptable or unlawful.

I-Thou relationship A relationship in which each person confirms the other by recognizing, validating, and accepting the other's nature.

James-Lange theory of emotion According to this theory, the experience of emotion results from the perception of bodily changes.

kinesthetic sense The sense that responds to body movement and the positions of muscles and joints.

kleptomania A compulsion to steal.

Kuder Vocational Preference Record An interest test used in vocational counseling.

latency stage The fourth psychosexual stage during which sexual interests are repressed.

latent content The "true" meaning of a dream, as revealed by dream analysis.

Law of Contiguity Under certain circumstances, a stimulus that occurs about the same time as a response will acquire the power to elicit that response.

Law of Effect The principle that actions with favorable consequences tend to be repeated, while actions with unfavorable consequences tend to be abandoned; for example, an action followed by reward is more likely to recur than an action followed by punishment.

learning A change in behavior or behavior potential as a result of experience.

learning set A learned ability to learn, making later

learning easier; for example, after learning one foreign language, it may be easier to learn others.

learning theory of attitudes The theory that attitudes are learned; they are acquired through processes of operant and classical conditioning.

lens The structure in the eye that focuses light on the retina.

lesbian A female homosexual.

lesion An injury to brain tissue; for example, a cut.

levels-of-processing theory of memory The theory that how well information is remembered depends on how deeply it is processed.

libido A form of psychic energy constituted by the life instincts; sexual energy.

life instincts According to Freud, those inborn needs that serve the purpose of the survival of the individual and the human species, for example, hunger, thirst, and sex.

Likert scale A type of attitude scale that consists of statements answered by selecting a response indicating the extent of agreement (ranging from "disagree very much" to "agree very much").

limbic system A group of interconnected brain structures that are involved in emotional expression and experience.

longitudinal method A method of studying developmental changes by examining individuals as they grow older—for example, studying a group of women when they are twenty and again when they are forty.

long-term memory (LTM) The memory system for storing information for long periods of time.

love deprivation For children, the condition of experiencing inadequate love.

LSD A psychedelic drug producing hallucinations; sometimes called "acid."

maintenance rehearsal A shallow level of processing information for memory; the information is rehearsed over and over (rote repetition) without being placed within a context of meaning.

major tranquilizer A drug, such as Thorazine, that is prescribed in the treatment of schizophrenia.

mania An affective psychosis in which people are wildly energetic, confident, and talkative.

manifest content The events of dreams as they are experienced.

marasmus A condition of extreme weakness, loss of appetite, and apathy found in infants experiencing prolonged love deprivation.

marijuana   A psychedelic drug that is smoked or eaten; marked tolerance develops with high doses.

masculinity   The degree to which an individual conforms to behavior typical of men in a culture.

massed practice   Studying or practicing all at once.

massed-spaced issue   The question of whether it is preferable to practice in one long session or in several shorter sessions.

maturation   Developmental changes that are relatively independent of experience, but result instead from genetically programmed growth processes.

mature love   Fromm's term for love based primarily on giving; an unselfish love that allows people in relationship to maintain their independent identities.

maturity   Allport's state of psychological health characterized by such things as self-awareness, involvement, and a unifying philosophy of life.

mean   The most commonly used measure of central tendency; computed by dividing the sum of the scores by the number of scores.

measurement   Assigning a number to behavior on the basis of a rule (for example, by using an IQ test).

median   A measure of central tendency; the middle score, the score above which and below which an equal number of other scores fall.

meditation   An ancient procedure for controlling attention and making the mind more aware, relaxed, and receptive.

medulla   A structure at the top of the spinal cord that controls heart rate, blood pressure, and other reflex movements.

menarche   A girl's first menstrual period.

menopause   That stage in a woman's life when menstruation stops due to a decrease in the production of estrogen. This "change of life" results in both physical and psychological changes.

mental age   Equal to the chronological age of an average child with similar intelligence. A ten-year-old child with the intelligence of a fifteen-year-old has a mental age of fifteen.

mentally gifted   Individuals with IQs above 130.

mentally retarded   Individuals with IQ below 70 who are below average in adaptive behavior and have a dullness of childhood origin.

mesomorph   A body type which has a muscular build, with a narrow pelvis and broad shoulders.

mid-life crisis   According to Levinson and Gould, a period in middle age when individuals may experience doubt, reassessment, and depression regarding their lives, directions, and goals.

mild retardation   The least severe level of retardation; the mildly retarded have IQs of 50 to 70 and are typically able to care for themselves.

Minnesota Multiphasic Personality Inventory (MMPI)   A general personality inventory consisting of hundreds of true-false questions; it is designed to test for a variety of abnormal personality traits.

Minnesota Satisfaction Questionnaire (MSQ)   An attitude scale designed to measure job satisfaction.

minor tranquilizer   A drug, such as Valium, that is prescribed in the treatment of anxiety.

mode   A measure of central tendency; the score that occurs most often in the group of scores.

model   A person who is observed and imitated.

modeling effect   The way in which novel responses are acquired through observation.

moderate retardation   A more severe level of retardation; the moderately retarded have IQs from 35 to 50 and can perform simple manual jobs. Although able to speak, they usually cannot learn to read. Only minimal supervision required.

monochromatism   Total color blindness in which only blacks, whites, and grays can be seen.

morphine   A narcotic drug made from the opium poppy; physically addictive.

motivation   The forces that determine the arousal and direction of purposeful behavior.

motive   Something that arouses behavior and directs it toward a specific goal; for example, hunger results in behavior directed toward obtaining food.

multiple personality   A dissociative reaction in which two or more distinct identities appear to alternate within the same individual.

myelin sheath   A special tissue encasing and insulating the axon from the electrical activity of neighboring cells.

myopia   A condition in which the eye can focus on nearby objects but not on those at a distance.

mystification   A form of miscommunication in which the participants are hiding their real feelings or intentions.

narcolepsy   The inability to stay awake in the daytime.

nature-nurture issue   The debate about the relative effects of heredity and learning in determining human behavior.

need for achievement   The motivation to succeed or win.

need-fulfillment theory   A theory of job satisfaction that assumes that a job will be found satisfying to the degree that it meets the needs of the workers.

negative afterimages   After viewing a stimulus, then looking at a neutral background, the persisting image of the stimulus can sometimes be seen in complementary colors.

negative assertion technique   A technique for increasing assertiveness that involves acknowledging a mistake or agreeing with criticism without agreeing that you are a bad or worthless person.

negative practice   A technique of deliberately practicing a bad habit in order to gain increased voluntary control over it; for example, by practicing knuckle cracking at regular intervals each day, the habit may be controlled.

negative sanctions   Punishment or threat of punishment for not conforming.

nerve   A group of neurons strung together to form a cord.

nerve impulses   Pulses of electrical current carried by neurons.

neural deafness   Deafness resulting from problems in the inner ear or with the auditory nerve.

neuron   The nerve cell; the fundamental unit of the nervous system.

neurosis   Psychological disorder characterized by the presence of anxiety.

neurotic depression   Intense and lasting depression.

neurotransmitter   A chemical secreted into the synapse by the terminal buttons of a neuron, which then stimulates the dendrites of other neurons to generate electrical nerve impulses.

nicotine   A stimulant drug found in tobacco; physically addictive.

noise pollution   An excess of unwanted sound.

nonconscious ideology   A set of assumptions and beliefs that one has but is not aware of.

nondirective therapy   A method of therapy in which the client, and not the therapist, determines the course of the treatment.

nonsense syllables   Meaningless groups of letters used in studies to measure memory.

nonverbal communication   Communication through facial expression, posture, speech inflection, and body movements; that is, communication that does not depend upon the meaning of words.

normal   Refers to behavior that either is good or typical for a culture.

normative model   A standard of masculinity and femininity based on the norm.

norms   Standards based on the way people typically behave in a particular society.

nuclear family   A social grouping consisting of two adults of opposite sex, living in some socially approved relationship with their children; usually a married couple and their children.

object permanency   The concept that objects continue to exist even when they cannot be perceived.

observational learning   Learning by watching and imitating others.

obsession   A recurring unwanted idea or impulse.

obsessive-compulsive neurosis   A type of psychological disorder involving uncontrollable thoughts and actions.

occipital lobe   A region at the back of each side of the brain that specializes in vision.

Oedipus complex   A crisis occurring at the end of the phallic stage resulting from a conflict between the child's desire for the parent of the opposite sex and fear of the parent of the same sex.

one-parent family   Children living with a single parent.

operant conditioning   Conditioning by consequences; instrumental conditioning.

operational definition   A definition of a concept based on a description of the method of measuring it.

opponent-process theory   A theory of color vision that proposes that there are three pairs of color processes in the brain: a black-white pair, a red-green pair, and a blue-yellow pair.

optimal interpersonal distance   The physical distance between two people at which they feel most comfortable; close enough for comfort, but far enough away so that personal spaces are not violated.

optimal level of arousal   The best or ideal level of arousal or stimulation for human beings, neither too high nor too low.

oral character   A personality pattern of excessive dependency, passivity, sarcasm, and pessimism.

oral stage   The first psychosexual stage during which the infant gains sexual pleasure from sucking and biting.

order effect   A change in behavior that may be due to repeating the conditions of measurement; for example, the second time that a test is given you may do better merely because you are more familiar with the test.

organic psychosis   A psychosis with a known physical cause; for example, senile psychosis.

orgasm   The climax of sexual feeling, associated with high levels of muscle tension and contraction.

other-directed   Depending upon the opinions of others to make choices.

ovaries   Endocrine glands in females that produce sex hormones as well as egg cells.

overgeneralization   The tendency to see all members of a group as the same; for example, to see all men as aggressive.

overlearning   Continuing to study the material after you feel you have mastered it.

parallaction   A pseudo-interaction, without real involvement, in which each participant acts independently and does not exchange information.

parallel coaction tasks   Group tasks that involve completely separate functions, with each person working independently.

paranoid delusions   False beliefs that one is being victimized—for example, believing that others are "out to get you."

paranoid schizophrenia   A psychological disorder characterized by hostility, delusions of persecution, and auditory hallucinations.

parapsychology   The scientific study of ESP, or extrasensory perception; at the present time, there is a lack of strong and reliable scientific evidence for the existence of extrasensory perception.

parasympathetic nervous system   The part of the autonomic nervous system that is active when the body is at rest.

parenting   Taking care of children; serving as a caretaker.

parietal lobe   A region at the top of each side of the brain that specializes in skin and body sensations.

partial schedule of reinforcement   Delivery of a reinforcer after some correct responses but not after others.

peak experiences   Moments of great joy, wonder, or awe; moments of self-actualization.

peaking   A pattern of energy use resulting in periods of extremely high demand.

peripheral nervous system   All the nerves that lie outside of the central nervous system; for example, the nerves connecting muscles and internal organs with the CNS.

permissiveness with love   A standard of sexual behavior stating that intercourse is acceptable before marriage only for those who are deeply in love or engaged to be married.

personal face   A private image; an individual's self-concept.

personal space   The immediate area surrounding the body that a person defends from invasion; the person's portable territory.

personality   An individual's typical way of relating to people and reacting to the world.

personality inventory   A personality test consisting of a large number of personal questions concerning what you like or dislike, what you feel, or what you typically do in various situations.

personality trait   A characteristic or dimension of personality that each person possesses in varying degrees, such as aggressiveness, dominance, or insecurity.

personality type   A set of personality characteristics that one group of people has in common that makes them different from other groups.

phallic stage   The third psychosexual stage during which the child gains sexual pleasure from manipulating his penis or her clitoris.

phallic symbol   A dream image—such as a pencil or snake—that symbolically represents the penis.

phi phenomenon   An illusion of movement created by flashing still pictures; the basis of apparent movement in "movies."

phobia   An intense, unreasonable fear of an object or event.

physical addiction   An effect produced by some drugs in which—if the drug is not taken—there are physical withdrawal symptoms, such as nausea and sweating.

physiological psychology   The study of how bodily processes, such as the activity of the brain, relate to behavior.

physiology   The functions and processes of the body.

pituitary gland   Endocrine gland located at the base of the brain; "master gland" which controls functions of all other endocrine glands.

place theory   A theory of pitch discrimination that hypothesizes that sounds of different frequencies stimulate different areas of the basilar membrane and that our experience of a sound depends on which areas are stimulated by that sound.

placebo effect   A change in behavior due to taking a pill or other treatment, independent of the content of the pill; for example, some people may feel better after taking a medically inactive sugar pill.

pleasure center   A brain area that, when stimulated with electricity, produces satisfaction or pleasure.

pleasure principle   The principle that governs the operation of the id, namely, the seeking of pleasure and the avoiding of pain.

polygraph   A machine that detects, amplifies, and records the electrical activity of the body.

population   An entire group; the set being sampled.

pornography   Sexually stimulating books, pictures, or films.

postfigurative culture   A culture in which children learn primarily from their parents.

prealcoholic symptomatic phase   The first stage in the development of alcoholism in which regular drinking is used as a means of avoiding problems and dealing with stress.

precision   Accuracy; being exact and specific.

preconscious level   That level of consciousness consisting of thoughts and images not now in the conscious level but accessible to it; those things we are not now thinking about, but could recall.

prefigurative culture   A culture in which parents learn from their children.

prefrontal lobotomy   A modern form of psychosurgery that involves severing the neural connections between the frontal lobes of the brain and the thalamus.

prejudice   A preconceived and unfavorable attitude toward an entire group.

preoperational stage   The second of Piaget's cognitive stages, lasting from two to seven.

prereading   The process of examining the text you are about to read in order to get a general idea of its structure.

prevalence   Frequency of occurrence.

primacy effect   The tendency for judgments to be controlled by first impressions.

primary process thinking   A way of thinking whose sole aim is the immediate gratification of pleasure and the avoidance of pain; utilized by the id.

primary reinforcer   An event having a reinforcing effect without the need of prior learning; for example, food.

primary sex characteristics   The sex organs themselves (penis, vagina).

principle of complementarity   The idea that people like others who are unlike themselves, and that one looks for someone to supply what the other lacks; in other words, that "opposites attract."

principle of empirical verification   The rule of science that a scientific claim should be regarded as true only if it agrees with experience or observation.

principle of infantile sexuality   Freud's idea that sexual gratification is obtained throughout childhood.

principle of orderly association   A rule for improving memory that suggests associating material to be remembered with an organized set of images.

principle of public evidence   The rule of science that no claim should be accepted as true without evidence that is accessible to many people and thus can be checked by more than one person.

principle of reliable evidence   The rule of science that no claim should be accepted as true without consistent evidence, evidence that is repeatable.

principle of similarity   The idea that people like others who are similar to themselves in values, beliefs, and background; in other words, that "birds of a feather flock together."

proactive interference   Older items in memory interfere with the memory for more recent items.

procrastination   The tendency to delay working.

prodromal phase   The second stage in the development of alcoholism marked by periods of amnesia or "blackouts."

profound mental retardation   The most severe level of retardation; they have IQs below 20 and require total care.

progressive relaxation   A method of producing deep muscular relaxation by alternately tightening and relaxing sets of muscles.

projection   Attributing to others certain thoughts or impulses an individual may have but cannot admit.

projective personality test   A test to assess personality that consists of a set of ambiguous stimuli, often pictures, which the individual is encouraged to interpret according to his or her own private meanings.

psychedelic drugs   Drugs that change perceptions and consciousness.

psychiatrist   A medical doctor trained in the treatment of personality disorders and licensed to prescribe drugs; has an MD degree.

psychic energy   According to Freud, the total amount of energy available to the human system.

psychoanalysis   The method of psychotherapy developed by Freud; its major aim is to make unconscious material conscious.

psychoanalyst   A psychotherapist with extensive training in psychoanalysis.

psychoanalytic theory   Freud's theory of personality; according to this theory, personality is determined at an early age.

psychoanalytic theory of crime   The theory that crime is a symptom of a mental disorder resulting from unresolved conflicts in early childhood.

psychoanalytic theory of homosexuality   The theory that homosexuality results from the failure to resolve the Oedipus complex; this failure comes about from disturbed parent-child relationships.

psychoanalytic theory of moral development   Freud's theory that moral development results from the development of the superego, or conscience, through identification with the parents.

psychoanalytic theory of motivation   Freud's theory that behavior is motivated by the tension created from unsatisfied inborn needs.

psychology   The science of behavior.

psychopath   An antisocial, impulsive, and aggressive person who feels little or no attachment to others.

psychopathy   A psychological disorder characterized by chronic antisocial, aggressive, manipulative behavior.

psychosexual stages   According to Freud, periods of development in childhood defined by the different sources of sexual pleasure that dominate.

psychosis   A severe mental disorder characterized by loss of contact with reality, accompanied by disturbances in emotions, ideas, or perceptions.

psychosocial crisis   According to Erikson, the stress produced by a set of demands that the social world places on individuals at different ages.

psychosocial stages   Erikson's description of the eight stages of personality development, beginning with birth and ending with death.

psychosocial theory   Erikson's theory of personality development that assumes that personality is shaped by the demands of the social world and continues to develop throughout life.

psychosomatic illness   A medical disorder of psychological origin.

psychosurgery   A biological treatment of mental problems that involves surgery on the brain.

psychotherapy   A special kind of treatment provided by a trained professional and based on psychological techniques; aimed at assisting people to overcome their problems and to grow.

psychotic depression   An affective psychosis in which people are extremely inactive and dejected.

psychological dependence   An effect produced by some drugs in which—if the drug is not available—there is a strong craving for it and a feeling of anxiety.

puberty   That age at which the body becomes sexually mature, typically around the age of eleven or twelve.

punisher   An unfavorable consequence; for example, a shock.

punishment   The procedure of providing a punisher or other unfavorable consequence following a response.

pupil   The hole in front of the lens through which light enters the eye.

pursuit movements   Smooth tracking movements that occur when the eyes follow a moving target.

pyromania   A compulsion to set fires.

racism   Prejudice against a person on the basis of skin color.

range   A measure of variability that reflects the difference between the upper and lower boundaries of the distribution.

rat sink   In a rat colony, an extremely crowded area resulting from the social reinforcement provided by other animals.

rationalization   The attempt to explain away failure so as to protect self-esteem.

reactance   A form of resistance to the threat of diminished freedom that involves doing the opposite in order to reestablish freedom of choice.

reaction formation A defense mechanism involving the repression of a feeling and the insistence that its opposite is true.

reaction theory of aggression The theory that aggression occurs in response to external stimulation.

real face The true self; what an individual is in reality.

reality principle The principle that governs the operation of the ego, namely, the delaying of instant gratification for the maximum gain of the long run.

recall method A method of measuring memory in which you are asked to reproduce exactly what you have read or seen.

recency effect The tendency for judgments to be controlled by the last or most recent impressions.

recognition method A method of measuring memory in which you are shown an item and asked whether you have seen it before.

reconstructive theory of memory A theory that remembering involves an imaginative reconstruction of the past.

reflection A psychotherapeutic technique for clarifying the client's feelings; restatement of what the client has just said in summary form.

reflex A simple, involuntary reaction occurring to a specific stimulus; for example, a sneeze.

regression A return or retreat to an earlier stage of personality development; for example, a return to infantile behavior.

regression movements Saccadic eye movements that jump backwards to reexamine words previously seen.

regulators Body signals sent between two people that indicate whether comprehension is occurring and that control the flow of the conversation.

reinforcement The procedure of providing a reward or other favorable consequence following a response.

reinforcer A favorable consequence; for example, a reward.

reinforcement theory of friendship The theory that you like those people who reward you.

relearning method A method of measuring memory in which the length of time you spend learning some new material is compared to the length of time required to relearn that same material at a later time.

reliability Consistency or dependability.

REM sleep A period of sleep marked by periodic rapid eye movements and dreaming.

repression A defense mechanism in which thoughts and impulses that threaten to produce anxiety are pushed from consciousness and forgotten.

resistance Second stage of the general adaptation syndrome, in which bodily resources are consumed adapting to the stress.

response Any kind of behavior or reaction that results from a stimulus.

retina The light sensitive part of the eye; a layer of light-sensitive cells on the back of the eye.

retrieval The process of getting out of memory the stored information so that it can be used.

retrieval cue Something that helps you remember; a stimulus that helps you find information in memory.

retroactive interference More recent items in memory interfere with the memory for older items.

reversed-roles marriage model In this type of marriage the traditional roles and responsibilities of husband and wife are reversed, with wives supporting the family and husbands caring for the house and children.

RNA Ribonucleic acid; a substance that guides the manufacture of protein molecules.

rods Specialized cells in the retina that respond only to differences in light intensity and not to differences in wavelength.

role conflict A problem resulting from having two opposing sets of expectations for how to behave; for example, college women are expected to be "feminine" (passive and dependent) but also are expected to be independent, successful, and intelligent.

role diffusion A state in which the sense of self is confused and the diverse roles that a person plays are not integrated.

role model A person who displays the behaviors and traits associated with a particular role, or place, in society; for example, parents or teachers.

rooting reflex An automatic response of infants to being touched on the cheek; they turn toward the source of stimulation and try to take it into their mouths.

Rorschach A test of personality using "inkblots" on cards.

Rule of Closure The principle that areas of figures tend to appear as whole or closed, even if they are incomplete or broken.

Rule of Proximity   The principle that things that are close together appear to belong together; close things are grouped in perception.

Rule of Similarity   The principle that things that resemble each other appear to belong together; similar things are grouped in perception.

saccade   A single saccadic movement.

saccadic movements   Jerky movements that occur when your eyes jump from spot to spot.

sample   A subset or selection from a larger group or population.

saturation   The physical growth and development of the body.

scapegoat   A "safe" target for displaced aggression.

scapegoating   A displacement of negative feelings in which a person or group of people is unfairly blamed for a problem.

scapegoating theory of prejudice   According to this theory, prejudice is a form of displaced aggression.

schedule of reinforcement   The frequency with which reinforcers accompany responses; how often a reinforcer is given for a correct response.

schema (*plural,* **schemata**)   A mental structure consisting of interrelated facts, rules, and plans.

schema theory of knowledge   The theory that knowledge consists of sets of organized facts, rules, and plans.

schizophrenia   A functional psychosis characterized by social withdrawal and disturbances in perception and ideas.

school psychologist   A psychologist who works in the schools, counseling and testing students.

science   A method of acquiring knowledge; also, the body of knowledge acquired by that method.

scientific method   A method for acquiring knowledge based on the rules of science; questions are answered by seeking facts from observations.

secondary gain   An incidental benefit of a neurotic reaction in which individuals receive attention or sympathy for their problems.

secondary process thinking   A way of thinking that is in line with the reality principle; utilized by the ego.

secondary reinforcer   An event having a reinforcing effect as a consequence of prior learning; for example, money.

secondary sex characteristics   Those physical characteristics which classify a body as "male" or "female." Male secondary sex characteristics include facial hair, deepened voice, more developed musculature. Female secondary sex characteristics include breasts and rounded thighs.

security   A personality trait describing the tendency to relate easily to other people, to feel accepted, to be optimistic and self-confident; individuals with this trait have a firm sense of their own identities.

sedative drugs   Drugs that reduce the level of arousal.

seduction theory   A theory that assumes that homosexuality results from early homosexual experiences.

selection error   A difference in behavior between groups that results from the groups being unequal to start with.

selective attention   The ability to attend to and perceive only one thing at a time.

selective breeding   A procedure for strengthening a trait in a population by mating only those animals from each generation which show the trait in the extreme.

self-actualized person   Maslow's term for the ideally healthy person, one whose needs have been met and whose potential is fulfilled.

self-concept   A private image of oneself; the set of ideas a person has about his or her needs, abilities, interests, and personality.

self-fulfilling prophecy   The tendency for one's expectations to come true.

self-monitoring effect   The principle that behavior will change if it is systematically observed; problem behavior that is monitored tends to decline in strength and frequency.

self-report measure   A method used to measure attitudes that involves asking people to report how they feel about other people or things.

semantic differential scale   A type of attitude scale that consists of pairs of opposing adjectives.

semicircular canals   Area in the inner ear filled with liquid and lined with special hair receptors that provides us with information regarding the orientation of our bodies.

senile psychosis   A psychosis resulting from an inadequate blood supply to the brain, typically in an elderly person.

sensorimotor stage   The first of Piaget's cognitive stages, from birth until about age two.

sensory deprivation   An extreme reduction in stimulation.

sensory overload   An extreme excess of stimulation.

septal area   A brain area near the hypothalamus which contains a pleasure center.

serial-position effect   The tendency to have greater difficulty recalling items in the middle of a list than items at either the beginning or end of the list.

severe retardation   The severely retarded have IQs of from 20 to 35 and require special training to learn how to talk and perform simple tasks.   Continual supervision is required.

sex hormones   Chemicals released into the bloodstream by the male and female sex glands, the testes and the ovaries.

sex role   The style and mannerisms typical of members of one sex.

sex roles   The set of behaviors that society considers appropriate to individuals of different sexes.

sexism   Prejudice against a person on the basis of sex.

sexual sadism   A psychological disorder in which a sexual climax can be achieved only through torture or murder.

sham rage   Intense aggressive behavior observed in animals lacking a cortex.

shaping   A training procedure that involves reinforcing closer and closer approximations to the desired response.

short-term memory (STM)   The memory system for storing information for just a few seconds.

shyness   Discomfort in the presence of others; inability to express oneself openly and honestly.

simple schizophrenia   A type of schizophrenia characterized by apathy and social withdrawal.

Sixteen Personality Factor Questionnaire   A personality inventory designed to assess an individual in terms of Cattell's source traits.

skimming   The process of reading subheadings, summaries, picture captions, and so on, to get an overview of the material to be read.

Skinner box   A device developed by B. F. Skinner for studying animal behavior.   The box contains a lever which, when pressed, automatically delivers a small pellet of food.

sleep spindles   Brief bursts of voltage fluctuations ranging from twelve to sixteen cycles per second.

social conflict   A struggle between the needs of one person and the opposing needs of someone else or of society.

social-emotional leaders   Leaders focused on maintaining good feelings among group members.

social face   A public image; the false front that is presented to other people.

social-learning theory   The theory that a person's pattern of behavior is learned and results from experiences with other people and the environment.

social-learning theory of aggression   The theory that aggression results from learning through imitation and reinforcement.

social-learning theory of homosexuality   The theory that homosexuality results from observing adult models, from imitation, and from rewards and punishments.

social-learning theory of moral development   A theory that assumes that moral behavior results from rewards, punishments, and the imitation of parental models.

social-learning theory of personality   A theory that stresses the ways in which patterns of behavior are learned through interaction with other people and the environment; assumes that personality is always changing as new learning occurs.

social marketing   Advertising concerned with persuading people to accept some socially relevant idea.

social norm   A behavior standard of a particular group or society; a rule for behavior that specifies what is proper.

social-psychological theory of crime   The theory that criminal behavior is learned by observing and imitating people with criminal tendencies.

social psychology   The study of how individual behavior is affected by groups.

social support system   The family, neighbors, or friends with whom you have close and supportive relationships.

socialization   The process by which children are shaped to become members of their culture.

somatic nervous system   The part of the peripheral nervous system consisting of the nerves that connect the CNS, major muscles, and major sense organs.

somatotypes   Body types, such as mesomorph, endomorph, and ectomorph.

source credibility   The believability of the source of a message.

source traits   Cattell's term for basic personality traits.

species-specific behavior   A behavior pattern that is characteristic of a species and distinguishes it from other species; for example, in a bird species, the inborn tendency to build a particular type of nest; an instinct.

stage   A period of growth in which behavior can be distinguished from that of other periods.

standard deviation   A measure of variability that reflects the spread of a distribution.

Stanford-Binet Intelligence Test   One of the earliest tests of intelligence; assumes that (1) intelligence consists of many different kinds of abilities, and (2) intelligence grows with age.

state   A relatively temporary characteristic or way of behaving; for example, "Following her accident, she was in a highly anxious state."

stereotype   A set of fixed ideas about a person based on categorizing the person as a member of a group.

stimulant drugs   Drugs that increase the level of arousal and make people feel more energetic.

stimulus (*plural,* **stimuli**)   Anything that is sensed or that produces a reaction; at the simple level, these can be lights, tones, or odors; at a more complex level, they can be events, people, situations, words, or even books.

stimulus control   The principle that your behavior is controlled to a degree by the stimuli in the environment in which the behavior has occurred.

stimulus generalization   The tendency to respond to stimuli similar to the conditioned stimulus; in classical conditioning, the tendency to react to stimuli that have not been paired with the UCS; in operant conditioning, the tendency to respond to stimuli that have not been associated with reinforcement.

storage   The process of retaining information over time.

stress   The changes, demands, threats, and other conditions in life that produce tension.

Strong Vocational Interest Blank   An interest test used in vocational counseling.

submissiveness   The opposite of dominance; refers to the tendency to be timid, dependent, and conforming.

superego   According to Freud, that part of the personality that is the internalized moral code or conscience.

surrogate mother   A fake or artificial mother; for example, in Harlow's work, a "mother" made of wire and wood.

survey   A poll or questionnaire aimed at obtaining information about some aspect of attitudes or behavior.

sympathetic division   The part of the autonomic nervous system that prepares the body for action; the "accelerator."

sympathetic nervous system   The part of the autonomic nervous system that prepares the body for action; becomes active when the body is "threatened."

symptom   A sign or indication of disorder; for example, hallucinations are an indication of psychosis.

synapse   The gap separating the terminal buttons of one neuron from the dendrites of another.

tabula rasa   A "blank slate," or empty mind; according to Aristotle, the state of mind before any outside impressions.

tactile stimulation   Sensations resulting from touch or pressure.

task decomposition   The process of analyzing the task to be accomplished and breaking it down into smaller parts.

task-oriented leaders   Leaders focused on getting the job done quickly and efficiently.

taste buds   Groups of cells on the tongue that are sensitive to the chemical composition of food and liquids.

temporal lobe   A region along the side of each half of the brain that specializes in memory and hearing.

tendency   How people are inclined or prone to behave; an "aggressive tendency" refers to behavior that is, on the average, somewhat aggressive.

tension sensation   The feeling associated with a tightened muscle.

terminal branches   Branching fibers at the end of the axon of a nerve cell.

terminal buttons   The tips of the terminal branches, which contain and release neurotransmitters.

territory   Geographical area that a person or animal lives in and defends against invasions.

test anxiety   Anxiety concerning examinations.

testes   Endocrine glands in males that produce sex hormones as well as sperm cells.

testosterone   A male sex hormone; produced by the testes.

thalamus   A structure in the center of the brain that acts as a relay station for nerve messages going to and from the brain.

Thanatos Freud's term for a universal death instinct.

Thematic Apperception Test (TAT) A personality test that involves making up stories about pictures.

theory of cognitive stages Piaget's theory that intellectual development proceeds through a succession of qualitatively different stages.

Theory of personality and career types John Holland's theory of career choice, which assumes that there is a relationship between six personality types and six career types and that people tend to select careers that best fit their personality orientations.

Theory of vocational development Donald Super's theory of career choice, which assumes that vocational development is a continuous process that begins in middle childhood and ends with retirement (from the growth stage through the decline stage) and is an expression of an individual's self-concept.

therapy The treatment of psychological problems and disorders.

theta wave A type of brain wave that appears to be associated with learning and with stage one of sleep; voltage fluctuations from three to seven cycles per second.

thyroid gland Endocrine gland located in the neck; controls metabolism and is important in regulating growth.

tip of the tongue phenomenon Knowing that a memory is in storage but being unable to retrieve it.

tolerance An effect resulting from some drugs in which ever-increasing doses are needed to obtain the same impact.

toxicity level The amount of a drug that will kill.

traditional marriage model One of the most common views of sex roles in marriage; the roles and responsibilities of husbands and wives are distinct, with husbands supporting the family while wives take care of the house and children.

trainable mentally retarded (TMR) Another term for the moderately to severely retarded.

trained introspection A method of studying experience through self-observation under controlled conditions.

trait A relatively enduring characteristic; a way of reacting or feeling that is lasting; for example, "She displays the trait of dominance."

transactional analysis (TA) A group psychotherapy that assumes the personality to have three parts—"Parent," "Adult," and "Child"; transactions with other people are analyzed in terms of these three parts of the personality.

transsexualism A condition of cross-sex identity; an intense discomfort with one's biological sex. Sex-change operations are sometimes used to adjust the body so that it conforms to the inner sense of sexual identity.

transvestism The act of dressing in the clothes of the opposite sex in order to achieve sexual gratification.

traumatic reaction A neurotic reaction to overwhelming psychological or physical shock or injury.

trephination A method of psychosurgery used by the Greeks and Romans that involved opening the skull to let "poisons" escape.

trichromatic theory A theory of color vision that assumes that all color experiences result from different combinations of three types of cones, each sensitive to a different primary color: red, green, and blue-violet.

tricyclic antidepressants Drugs, such as Elavil, that are prescribed in the treatment of depression.

twin studies A research method consisting of comparing fraternal and identical twins on particular traits; greater resemblance among identical twins is viewed as evidence that the trait is hereditary.

tympanic membrane The eardrum; transmits the sound energy to the tiny bones of the middle ear.

unconditional positive regard Uncritical acceptance of another person as a valuable human being, regardless of what that person has done or says or feels.

unconditioned response A response to an unconditioned stimulus; for example, the response of salivating to food in the mouth.

unconditioned stimulus A stimulus that automatically elicits a response; for example, food in the mouth elicits salivation.

unconscious conflict An internal conflict of which a person is unaware; an example might be the conflict between moral standards and sexual desire.

unconscious level That level of consciousness consisting of those impulses, drives, and memories that we are not aware of and that we could not recall.

unconscious motivation Needs and impulses that have been repressed so that a person is unaware of them.

underachievers Individuals with low levels of achievement motivation whose level of performance is lower than would be expected from knowledge of their ability.

validity The degree to which an instrument actually measures what it is supposed to measure.

value judgment A conclusion based on values or beliefs.

value question A question that must be answered by preference, opinion, or belief; it cannot be answered by observation.

variability The differences among a group of scores; the distribution of the scores.

variable A concept having different values; "intelligence" is a variable, having many different values.

variable interval schedule (VI schedule) Delivery of a reinforcer for the first correct response after a variable period of time has elapsed; going to the mailbox is occasionally reinforced by a letter from a friend, but such letters arrive at variable intervals.

variable ratio schedule (VR schedule) Delivery of a reinforcer after a variable number of correct responses have occurred. For example, a door-to-door salesman is reinforced with a sale after making a variable number of approaches; sometimes only two houses must be visited, and other times twenty houses, before making a sale.

vestibular sense The sense, located in the inner ear, that responds to body orientation and rotation.

visual cliff An apparatus used for studying depth perception in infants; consists of a piece of heavy glass covering shallow and deep surfaces.

vocational counselors Counselors, often psychologists, who assist people in making career choices.

Wechsler Adult Intelligence Scale (WAIS) and Wechsler Intelligence Scale for Children (WISC) Tests of intelligence that assume that intelligence consists of a limited number of specific abilities; they yield deviation IQ scores.

whole-part issue The question of whether it is better to practice the whole act every time or to practice one part at a time until it is mastered.

wish fulfillment The idea that unconscious wishes are revealed and satisfied in dreams.

X and Y chromosomes Chromosomes determining sex; an XX pair is female and an XY pair is male.

Yerkes-Dodson law The principle that performance is best at an intermediate level of arousal and that the optimal level of arousal is higher for easy tasks than for difficult tasks.

Yoga meditation A type of meditation in which one's concentration is focused on a special word which is repeated silently over and over.

Zen meditation A type of meditation in which concentration is focused on one's breathing.

References

Chapter 1 The Nature of Psychology

1. *Los Angeles Times,* January 20, 1975.
2. *Los Angeles Times,* January 20, 1975.
3. *Los Angeles Times,* March 28, 1975.
4. DeKoninck, J. M., & Koulack, D. Dream content and adaptation to a stressful situation. *Journal of Abnormal Psychology,* 1975, *84,* 250–260.
5. Fromkin, V., *et al.* The development of language in Genie: A case of language acquisition beyond the "critical period." *Brain and Language,* 1974, *1,* 81–107.
6. Laughlin, H. P. *The neuroses.* Washington, D.C.: Butterworth, 1967.
7. Russell, R. K., & Sipich, J. F. Treatment of test anxiety by cue-controlled relaxation. *Behavior Therapy,* 1974, *5,* 673–676.
8. Miller, G. A. *Psychology: The science of mental life.* New York: Harper & Row, 1962.
9. Jones, E. *The life and work of Sigmund Freud.* New York: Basic Books, 1961.
10. McKeachie, W. P. A tale of a teacher. In T. S. Krawiec (Ed.), *The psychologists.* New York: Oxford University Press, 1972.
11. Boneau, C. A., Golann, S. E., & Johnson, M. M. *A career in psychology.* Washington, D.C.: American Psychological Association, 1970.

Chapter 2 The Art and Science of Psychology

1. Miller, A. G. Role of physical attractiveness in impression formation. *Psychonomic Science,* 1970, *19,* 241–243.
2. Lawson, E. Hair color, personality and the observer. *Psychological Reports,* 1971, *28,* 311–322.
3. Roll, S., & Verinis, J. S. Stereotypes of scalp and facial hair as measured by the semantic differential. *Psychological Reports,* 1971, *28, 975–980.*
4. Pellegrini, R. J. Impressions of the male personality as a function of beardedness. *Psychology,* 1973, *10,* 29–33.
5. Strongman, K. T., & Hart, C. J. Stereotyped reactions to body build. *Psychological Reports,* 1968, *23,* 1175–1178.
6. Rosenthal, R., & Jacobson, L. *Pygmalion in the classroom.* New York: Holt, Rinehart and Winston, 1968.
7. Muensterberg, H. *On the witness stand: Essays on psychology and crime.* New York: Clark Boardman, 1908.
8. Thigpen, C. H., & Cleckley, H. A. *The three faces of Eve.* New York: McGraw-Hill, 1957.
9. Leon, G. R. *Case histories of deviant behavior: An Interactional Perspective.* Boston: Holbrook Press, 1974. Copyright ©1977 by Allyn and Bacon, Inc., Boston. Reprinted with permission.
10. Reik, T. *Listening with the third ear.* New York: Farrar, Straus, 1948.
11. Kagan, J. A psychologist's account at mid-career. In T. S. Krawiec (Ed.), *The psychologists.* New York: Oxford University Press, 1972.
12. Rogers, C. R. *On becoming a person.* Boston: Houghton Mifflin, 1961.

Chapter 3 Conditioning and Learning

1. Frankenburg, W. K., & Dodds, J. B. The Denver developmental screening test. *Journal of Pediatrics,* 1967, *71,* 181–191.
2. Aldrich, C. A., & Norval, M. A. A developmental graph for the first year of life. *Journal of Pediatrics,* 1946, *29,* 304–308.
3. Orlansky, H. Infant care and personality. *Psychological Bulletin,* 1949, *46,* 1–48.
4. Dennis, W., & Dennis, M. G. The effect of cradling practices upon the onset of walking in Hopi children. *Journal of Genetic Psychology,* 1940, *56,* 77–86.
5. Gardner, R. A., & Gardner, B. T. Teaching sign language to a chimpanzee. *Science,* 1969, *165,* 664–672.
6. Bandura, A., & Walters, R. H. *Social learning and personality*

development. New York: Holt, Rinehart and Winston, 1963.

7. Holland, M. K., & Swiryn, M. Improvement following the imaginary practice of a perceptual-motor skill. Unpublished manuscript, 1973.

8. Harlow, H. F. The information of learning sets. *Psychological Review,* 1949, *56,* 51–65.

9. Bruner, J. S. *The process of education.* New York: Vintage Books, 1960, p. 16.

10. Levinson, B., & Reese, H. W. Patterns of discrimination learning set in pre-school children, fifth graders, college freshmen, and the aged. *Monographs of the Society for Research in Child Development, 32,* 1967 (Whole No. 115).

11. Warren, J. M., & Baron, A. The formation of learning sets by cats. *Journal of Comparative and Physiological Psychology,* 1956, *49,* 227–231.

12. Koronakos, C., & Arnold, W. J. The formation of learning sets in rats. *Journal of Comparative and Physiological Psychology,* 1957, *50,* 11–14.

13. Miller, G. A. *Psychology: The science of mental life.* New York: Harper & Row, 1962.

14. Pavlov, I. P. *Conditioned reflexes.* New York: Oxford University Press, 1927.

15. Watson, J. B., & Rayner, R. Conditioned emotional reactions. *Journal of Experimental Psychology,* 1920, *3,* 1–12.

16. Skinner, B. F. "Superstition" in the pigeon. *Journal of Experimental Psychology,* 1948, *38,* 168–172.

17. Rogers, C. R., & Skinner, B. F. Some issues concerning the control of human behavior: A symposium. *Science,* 1956, *124,* 1057–1066.

18. Skinner, B. F. *Beyond freedom and dignity.* New York: Alfred A. Knopf, 1971.

19. Williams, C. D. The elimination of tantrum behavior by extinction procedures. *Journal of Abnormal and Social Psychology,* 1954, *59,* 269.

20. Breland, K., & Breland, M. A field of applied animal psychology. *American Psychologist,* 1951, *6,* 202–204.

21. Watson, D., & Tharp, R. *Self-directed behavior: Self-modification for personal adjustment.* Belmont, Calif.: Brooks/Cole, 1972.

22. Wooden, H. E. The use of negative practice to eliminate nocturnal headbanging. *Journal of Behavior Therapy and Experimental Psychiatry,* 1974, *5,* 81–82.

23. Azrin, N. H., & Powell, J. R. Behavioral engineering: The reduction of smoking behavior by a conditioning apparatus and procedure. *Journal of Applied Behavior Analysis,* 1968, *1,* 193–200.

24. Keutzer, C. S., Lichenstein, E., & Mees, H. L. Modification of smoking behavior: A review. *Psychological Bulletin,* 1968, *70,* 520–533.

25. Stuart, R. B. Situational versus self control of problematic behaviors. In R. D. Rubin (Ed.), *Advances in behavior therapy, 1970.* New York: Academic Press, 1970.

Chapter 4   The Psychology of Memory

1. Halacy, D. S. *Man and memory.* New York: Harper & Row, 1970, p. 88.

2. Sperling, G. The information available in brief visual presentations. *Psychological Monographs,* 1960, *74,* Whole No. 498.

3. Conrad, R. Acoustic confusions in immediate memory. *British Journal of Psychology,* 1964, *55,* 75–83.

4. Conrad, R., & Hull, A. J. Information, acoustic confusion and memory span. *British Journal of Psychology,* 1964, *55,* 429–432.

5. Baddeley, A. D., & Dale, H. C. A. The effect of semantic similarity on retroactive interference in long- and short-term memory. *Journal of Verbal Learning and Verbal Behavior,* 1966, *5,* 417–420.

6. Bousfield, W. A. The occurrence of clustering in the recall of randomly arranged associates. *Journal of General Psychology,* 1953, *49,* 229–240.

7. Wickelgren, W. A. Size of rehearsal groups and short-term memory. *Journal of Experimental Psychology,* 1964, *68,* 413–419.

8. Miller, G. A. The magical number seven, plus or minus two: Some limits on our capacity for processing information. *Psychological Review,* 1956, *63,* 81–97.

9. Mandler, G. Organization and memory. In K. W. Spence & J. T. Spence (Eds.), *The psychology of learning and motivation, Vol. II.* New York: Academic Press, 1968.

10. Brown, R., & McNeill, D. The "tip of the tongue" phenomenon. *Journal of Verbal Learning and Verbal Behavior,* 1966, *5,* 325–337.

11. Earhard, M. The facilitation of memorization by alphabetic instructions. *Canadian Journal of Psychology,* 1967, *21,* 15–24.

12. Haber, R. N., & Haber, R. B. Eidetic imagery: I. Frequency. *Perceptual and Motor Skills,* 1964, *19,* 131–138.

13. Holt, R. R. Imagery: The return of the ostracized. *American Psychologist,* 1964, *19,* 254–264.

14. Stromeyer, C. F., III. Eidetikers. *Psychology Today,* 1970, *4,* 76–80.

15. Luria, A. R. *The mind of a mnemonist.* New York: Basic Books, 1968.

16. Lashley, K. S. *Brain mechanisms and intelligence.* Chicago: University of Chicago Press, 1929.

17. Brierley, J. B. The neuropathology of amnesic states. In C. W. M. Whitty & O. L. Zangwill (Eds.), *Amnesia.* Washington: Butterworth, 1966.

18. Smith, A., & Burklund, C. W. Dominant hemispherectomy: Preliminary report on neuropsychological sequelae. *Science,* 1966, *153,* 1280–1282.

19. Deutsch, J. A. The physiological basis of memory. *Annual Review of Psychology,* 1969, *20,* 85–104.

20. Davis, R. E., Bright, P. J., & Agranoff, B. W. Effect of ECS and puromycin on memory in fish. *Journal of Comparative and Physiological Psychology,* 1965, *60,* 162–166.

21. Zemp, J. W., Wilson, J. E., Schlesinger, K., Boggan, W. O., & Glassman, E. Brain function and macro-molecules, I. Incorporation of uridine into RNA of mouse brain during short-term training experience. *Proceedings of the National Academy of Science,* 1966, *55,* 1423–1431.

22. Penfield, W. The interpretive cortex. *Science,* 1959, *129,* 1719–1725.

23. Jenkins, J. J. Remember that old theory of memory? Well forget it! *American Psychologist,* 1974, *29,* 785–795.

24. Bransford, J. D., & Franks, J. J. The abstraction of linguistic ideas. *Cognitive Psychology,* 1971, *2,* 331–350.

25. Shepard, R. N. Recognition memory for words, sentences, and pictures. *Journal of Verbal Learning and Verbal Behavior,* 1967, *6,* 156–163.

26. Gomulicki, B. R. The development and present status of the trace theory of memory. *British Journal of Psychology, Monograph Supplement,* 1953, No. 29.

27. Guttman, N., & Julesz, B. Lower limits of auditory periodicity analysis. *Journal of the Acoustical Society of America,* 1963, *35,* 610.

28. Underwood, B. J. Interference and forgetting. *Psychological Review,* 1957, *64,* 49–60.

29. Anon. *I lost my memory: The case as the patient saw it.* London: Faber & Faber Ltd, 1932.

30. Williams, M. *Brain damage and the mind.* Baltimore, Md.: Penguin Books, 1970.

31. Williams, M., & Zangwill, O. L. Retrograde memory disturbances. *Journal of Neurology, Neurosurgery, and Psychiatry,* 1952, *15,* 54.

32. Milner, B. Amnesia following operation on the temporal lobe. In C. W. M. Whitty & O. L. Zangwill (Eds.), *Amnesia.* Washington: Butterworth, 1966.

33. Laughlin, H. P. *The neuroses.* Washington: Butterworth, 1967.

34. Yates, F. A. *The art of memory.* London: Routledge & Kegan Paul, 1966.

35. Hunter, I. M. L. *Memory.* Baltimore, Md.: Penguin Books, 1957.

Chapter 5 Academic Learning and Retention

1. Brandsford, J. D. *Human cognition: Learning, understanding, and remembering.* Belmont, Calif.: Wadsworth Publishing Co., 1979.

2. Dooling, D. J., & Lachman, R. Effects of comprehension on retention of prose. *Journal of Experimental Psychology,* 1971, *88,* 216–222.

3. Brandsford, J. D., & Johnson, M. K. Contextual prerequisites for understanding: Some investigations of comprehension and recall. *Journal of Verbal Learning and Verbal Behavior,* 1972, *11,* 717–726.

4. Bjork, R. A. Information processing analysis of college teaching. *Educational Psychologist,* 1979, *14,* 15–23.

5. Tulving, E. Relation between encoding specificity and levels of processing. In L. S. Cermak & F. I. M. Craik (Eds.), *Levels of processing and human memory.* Hillsdale, N.J.: Lawrence Erlbaum Associates, 1978.

6. Moray, N. Attention in dichotic listening: Affective cues and the influence of instructions. *Quarterly Journal of Experimental Psychology,* 1959, *11,* 56–60.

7. Mowbray, G. H. Simultaneous vision and audition. *Journal of Experimental Psychology,* 1953, *46,* 365–372.

8. Fisher, J. L., & Harris, M. B. Effect of note taking and review on recall. *Journal of Educational Psychology,* 1973, *65,* 321–325.

9. Thomas, G. S. Use of student notes and lecture summaries as study guides for recall. *Journal of Educational Research,* 1978, *71,* 316–319.

10. Carmen, R. A., & Adams, W. R. *Study skills.* New York: John Wiley, 1972.

11. Huey, E. B. *The psychology and pedagogy of reading.* 1908; reprint ed., Cambridge, Mass.: M. I. T. Press, 1968.

12. Gibson, E. J., & Levin, H. *The psychology of reading.* Cambridge, Mass.: M. I. T. Press, 1975.

13. Foss, D. J., & Hakes, D. T. *Psycholinguistics: An introduction to the psychology of language.* Englewood Cliffs, N.J.: Prentice-Hall, 1978.

14. Langan, J. *Reading and study skills.* New York: McGraw-Hill, 1978.

15. Wood, N. V. *College reading and study skills.* New York: Holt, Rinehart and Winston, 1978.

16. Fowler, R. L., & Barker, A. S. Effectiveness of highlighting for retention of text materials. *Journal*

of Applied Psychology, 1974, *59*, 358–364.

17. Fass, W., & Schumacher, G. M. Effects of motivation, subject activity, and readability on the retention of prose materials. *Journal of Educational Psychology*, 1978, *70*, 803–807.

18. Beneke, W. M., & Harris, M. B. Teaching self-control of study behavior. *Behavior Research and Therapy*, 1972, *10*, 35–41.

19. Lakein, A. *How to get control of your time and your life.* New York: New American Library, 1973.

20. Locke, E. Q. *A guide to effective study.* New York: Springer, 1975.

21. Richards, C. S., McReynolds, W. T., Holt, S., & Sexton, T. Effects of information feedback and self-administered consequences on self-monitoring study behavior. *Journal of Counseling Psychology*, 1976, *23*, 316–321.

22. Underwood, B. J. Ten years of massed practice on distributed practice. *Psychological Review*, 1961, *68*, 229–247.

Chapter 6   Brain and Behavior

1. Milner, B. Memory and the medial temporal regions of the brain. In E. H. Pribram & D. E. Broadbent (Eds.), *Biology of memory.* New York: Academic Press, 1970.

2. Lebrum, Y. Neurolinguistic models of language and speech. In H. Whitaker & H. A. Whitaker (Eds.), *Studies in neurolinguistics.* New York: Academic Press, 1976.

3. Landfield, P. W., & McGaugh, J. L. Effects of electroconvulsive shock and brain stimulation on EEG cortical theta rhythms in rats. *Behavioral Biology*, 1972, *7*, 271–278.

4. London, P. *Behavior control.* New York: Harper & Row, 1969.

5. Delgado, J. M. R. *Physical control of the mind: Toward a psychocivilized society.* New York: Harper & Row, 1969.

6. Heath, R. G. Electrical self-stimulation of the brain in man. *American Journal of Psychiatry*, 1963, *120*, 571–577.

7. Hubel, D. H. The brain. *Scientific American*, 1979, *241*, 45–53.

8. Cotman, C. W., & McGaugh, J. L. *Behavioral neuroscience.* New York: Academic Press, 1980.

9. Treisman, M. Mind, body, and behavior: Control systems and their disturbance. In P. London & D. Rosenhan (Eds.), *Foundations of abnormal psychology.* New York: Holt, Rinehart and Winston, 1968.

10. Gazzaniga, M. S. *The bisected brain.* New York: Appleton-Century-Crofts, 1970.

11. Sperry, R. W. Brain bisection and mechanisms of consciousness. In J. C. Eccles (Ed.), *Brain and conscious experience.* New York: Springer, 1966.

12. Ornstein, R. E. *The psychology of consciousness.* San Francisco: W. H. Freeman, 1972.

13. Milner, B. Amnesia following operation on the temporal lobes. In C. W. Whitty & O. L. Zangwill (Eds.), *Amnesia.* London: Butterworth, 1966.

14. Stevens, C. F. The neuron. *Scientific American*, 1979, *241*, 54–65.

15. Iversen, L. L. The chemistry of the brain. *Scientific American*, 1979, *241*, 134–149.

16. Schidkraut, J. J. The catecholamine hypothesis of affective disorders: A review of supporting evidence. *American Journal of Psychiatry*, 1965, *122*, 509–522.

17. Coppen, A. Indoleamines and affective disorders. *Journal of Psychiatric Research*, 1972, *9*, 163–171.

18. Snyder, S. H. Opiate receptors and internal opiates. *Scientific American*, 1977, *236*, 44–56.

19. Tseng, L. *et al.* Human beta endorphin: Development of tolerance and behavioral activity in rats. *Biochemistry and Biophysics Research Communication*, 1977, *74*, 390–396.

20. Liebskind, J. C., Mayer, D. J., & Akil, H. Central mechanisms of pain inhibition: Studies of analgesia from focal brain stimulation. *Advances in Neurology*, 1974, *4*, 261–268.

Chapter 7   Sensation and Perception

1. Zubek, J. P., Sansom, W., & Prysiazniuk, A. Intellectual changes during prolonged perceptual isolation (darkness and silence). *Canadian Journal of Psychology*, 1960, *14*, 233–243.

2. Freedman, S. J., Grunebaum, H. U., & Greenblatt, M. Perceptual and cognitive changes in sensory deprivation. In P. Solomon, P. E. Kubzansky, P. H. Leiderman, J. H. Mendelson, R. Trumbull, & D. Wexler (Eds.), *Sensory deprivation.* Cambridge, Mass.: Harvard University Press, 1961.

3. Rosenzweig, N. Sensory deprivation and schizophrenia: Clinical and theoretical similarities. *American Journal of Psychiatry*, 1959, *116*, 326–329. Copyright 1959, the American Psychiatric Association. Reprinted by permission.

4. Targ, R., & Puthoff, H. Information transmission under conditions of sensory shielding. *Nature*, 1974, *251*, 602–607.

5. Hanlon, J. Uri Geller and science. *New Scientist*, 1974, *64*, 170–185.

6. Randi, J. The psychology of conjuring. *Technology Review*, 1978, *80*, 56–63.

7. Gardner, M. Dermo-optical perception: A peek down the nose. *Science*, 1966, *151*, 654–657.

8. Makous, W. L. Cutaneous color

sensitivity: Explanation and demonstration. *Psychological Review,* 1966, *73,* 280–294.

9. McBurney, D., & Collings, V. *Introduction to sensation/perception.* Englewood Cliffs, N.J.: Prentice-Hall, 1977.

10. Marks, W. D., Dobelle, W. H., & MacNichol, E. F., Jr. Visual pigments of single primate cones. *Science,* 1964, *143,* 1181–1183.

11. DeValois, R. L. Behavioral and electrophysiological studies of primate vision. In W. D. Neff (Ed.), *Contributions to sensory physiology,* Vol. I. New York: Academic Press, 1965.

12. Kilbride, P. L. Factors affecting the magnitude of the Ponzo perspective illusion among the Baganda. *Perception and Psychophysics,* 1975, *17,* 543–548.

13. Segall, M. H., Campbell, D. T., & Herskovitz, M. J. Cultural differences in the perception of geometrical illusions. *Science,* 1963, *139,* 769–770.

14. Haber, R. N. Nature of the effect of set on perception. *Psychological Review,* 1966, *73,* 335–351.

15. Bruner, J. S., & Postmas, L. On the perception of incongruity. *Journal of Personality,* 1949, *18,* 206–223.

16. Kohler, I. The formation and transformation of the visual world. *Psychological Issues,* 1964, *3,* 28–46.

Chapter 8 Drugs and Consciousness

1. Williams, M. *Brain damage and the mind.* Middlesex, England: Penguin Books, 1970.

2. Schwartz, G. E. Cardiac responses to self-induced thoughts. *Psychotherapy,* 1971, *8,* 462–466.

3. Schaefer, H. Psychosomatic problems of vegetative regulatory functions. In J. C. Eccles (Ed.),

Brain and conscious experience. New York: Springer, 1966.

4. Bakal, D. A. Headache: A biopsychological perspective. *Psychological Bulletin,* 1975, *82,* 369–382.

5. Sawrey, W. L., Conger, J. J., & Turrell, E. S. An experimental investigation of the role of psychological factors in the production of gastric ulcers in rats. *Journal of Comparative and Physiological Psychology,* 1956, *49,* 457–461.

6. Brady, J. V. Behavioral stress and physiological change: A comparative approach to the experimental analysis of some psychosomatic problems. *Transactions of the New York Academy of Science,* 1964, *26,* 483–496.

7. Triesman, M. Mind, body, and behavior: Control systems and their disturbance. In P. London & D. Rosenhan (Eds.), *Foundations of abnormal psychology.* New York: Holt, Rinehart and Winston, 1968.

8. James, W. *The varieties of religious experience.* New York: New American Library, 1958.

9. Wallace, R. K. Physiological effects of transcendental meditation. *Science,* 1970, *167,* 1751–1754.

10. Glueck, B. C., & Stroebel, C. F. Biofeedback and meditation in the treatment of psychiatric illnesses. *Comprehensive Psychiatry,* 1975, *16,* 303–321.

11. Anand, B. K., Chhina, G. S., & Singh, B. B. Some aspects of EEG studies in Yogis. *Electroencephalography and Clinical Neurophysiology,* 1961, *13,* 452–456.

12. Smith, J. C. Meditation as psychotherapy: A review of the literature. *Psychological Bulletin,* 1975, *82,* 558–564.

13. Hoover, E. L. Alpha: The first step to a new level of reality. *Human Behavior,* 1972, May–June.

14. Weitzenhoffer, A. M. *General techniques of hypnotism.* New York: Grune and Stratton, 1957.

15. Barber, T. X. *Hypnosis: A scientific approach.* New York: Van Nostrand Reinhold, 1969.

16. Orne, M. T., & Evans, F. J. Social control in the psychological experiment: Antisocial behavior and hypnosis. *Journal of Personality and Social Psychology,* 1965, *1,* 189–200.

17. Evans, F. J. Hypnosis and sleep: Techniques for exploring cognitive activity during sleep. In E. Fromm & R. E. Shor (Eds.), *Hypnosis: Research developments and perspectives.* Chicago: Aldine Publishing, 1972.

18. Zimbardo, P., Maslach, C., & Marshall, G. Hypnosis and the psychology of cognitive and behavioral control. In E. Fromm & R. E. Shor (Eds.), *Hypnosis: Research developments and perspectives.* Chicago: Aldine Publishing, 1972.

19. Taugher, V. J. Hypno-anesthesia. *Wisconsin Medical Journal,* 1958, *57,* 95–96.

20. Blum, R. H., & Funkhouser-Balbaky, M. L. Mind-altering drugs and dangerous behavior: Dangerous drugs. Annotations and Consultants' Papers, Task Force on Narcotics and Drug Abuse, President's Commission on Law Enforcement and Administration of Justice, 1967.

21. Corder, B. W., *et al.* An analysis of trends in drug use behavior at five American universities. *Journal of School Health,* 1974, *44,* 386–389.

22. Single, E., Kandel, D., & Faust, R. Patterns of multiple drug use in high school. *Journal of Health and Social Behavior,* 1974, *15,* 344–357.

23. Wogan, M. Illicit drug use among college students. *College Student Journal,* 1974, *8,* 56–62.

24. Goldstein, J. W., Gleason, T. C., & Korn, J. H. Whither the epidemic? Psychoactive drug use

career patterns of college students. *Journal of Applied Social Psychology,* 1975, *5,* 16–33.

25. Becker, H. Becoming a marijuana user. *American Journal of Sociology,* 1953, *59,* 235–242.

26. Blum, R. H., *et al. Students and drugs.* San Francisco: Jossey-Bass, 1969.

27. Tassinari, C. A., Peraita-Adrados, M. R., Ambrosetto, G., & Gastaut, H. Effects of marijuana and delta-9-THC at high doses in man: A polygraphic study. *Electroencephalography and Clinical Neurophysiology,* 1974, *36,* 94.

28. Klonoff, H., & Low, M. D. Psychological and neurophysiological effects of marijuana in man: An interaction model. In L. Miller (Ed.), *Marijuana: Effects on human behavior.* New York: Academic Press, 1974.

29. Winters, W. D., & Wallach, M. B. Drug-induced states of CNS excitation: A theory of hallucinosis. In D. H. Efron (Ed.), *Psychotomometic drugs.* New York: Raven Press, 1970.

30. Ray, O. S. *Drugs, society, and human behavior.* St. Louis: C. V. Mosby, 1972.

31. Perez-Reyes, M., Timmons, M. C., & Wall, M. E. Long-term use of marijuana and the development of tolerance or sensitivity to delta-9-tetrahydrocannabinol. *Archives of General Psychiatry,* 1974, *31,* 89–91.

32. Jones, R. T., & Benowitz, N. The 30-day trip: Clinical studies of cannabis tolerance and dependence. In S. Szara & M. Braude (Eds.), *Pharmacology of marijuana.* New York: Raven Press, 1975.

33. Canadian Government's Commission of Inquiry, *The non-medical use of drugs.* Middlesex, England: Penguin, 1971.

34. DeRopp, R. S. *Drugs and the mind.* New York: Grove Press, 1964.

35. Fehr, K. O., *et al.* Cannabis: Adverse effects on health. *The Journal* (Addiction Research Foundation), *9,* 1980, 6–7.

36. Cohen, S., & Ditman, K. S. Complications associated with lysergic acid diethylamide (LSD-25). *Journal of the American Medical Association,* 1962, *189,* 181–182.

37. Cohen, S. Lysergic acid diethylamide: Side effects and complications. *Journal of Nervous and Mental Disease,* 1960, *130,* 30–40.

38. National Commission on Marihuana and Drug Abuse, *Marihuana: A signal of misunderstanding.* New York: New American Library, 1972.

39. Unwin, J. R. Non-medical use of drugs with particular reference to youth. *Canadian Medical Association Journal,* 1969, *101,* 72–88.

40. Smith, D. E. Acute and chronic toxicity of marijuana. *Journal of Psychedelic Drugs,* 1968, *2,* 37–47.

41. Hekimian, L. J., & Gershon, S. Characteristics of drug abusers admitted to a psychiatric hospital. *Journal of the American Medical Association,* 1968, *205,* 124–130.

42. Rosenthal, S. H. Persistent hallucinosis following repeated administration of hallucinogenic drugs. *American Journal of Psychiatry,* 1964, *121,* 238–244.

43. Horowitz, M. J. Flashbacks: Recurrent intrusive images after the use of LSD. *American Journal of Psychiatry,* 1969, *126,* 147–151.

44. McGlothlin, W. H., & Arnold, D. O. LSD revisited: A ten-year follow-up of medical LSD use. *Archives of General Psychiatry,* 1971, *24,* 35–49.

45. Keeler, M. H. Adverse reactions to marijuana. *American Journal of Psychiatry,* 1967, *124,* 128–131.

46. Keeler, M. H., Rifler, C. B., & Liptzin, M. B. Spontaneous recurrence of marijuana effect.

American Journal of Psychiatry, 1968, *125,* 384–386.

47. Ray, O. S. *Drugs, society and human behavior.* St. Louis, Mo.: C. V. Mosby Co., 1972.

48. Jellinek, E. M. *The disease concept of alcoholism.* Highland Park, N.J.: Hillhouse Press, 1960.

49. Weil, A. T., Zinberg, N. E., & Nelson, J. M. Clinical and psychological effects of marijuana in man. *Science,* 1968, 1234–1242.

50. McGlothlin, W. H. Cannabis: A reference. In D. Solomon (Ed.), *The marijuana papers.* New York: New American Library, 1966.

51. DeLong, F. L., & Levy, B. I. A model of attention describing the cognitive effects of marijuana. In L. L. Miller (Ed.), *Marijuana: Effects on human behavior.* New York: Academic Press, 1974.

52. Dornbush, R. L., Fink, M. & Freedman, A. M. Marijuana, memory and perception. *American Journal of Psychiatry,* 1971, *128,* 194–197.

53. Finkleberg, J. R., Melges, F. T., Hollister, L. E., & Gillespie, H. K. Marijuana and immediate memory. *Nature,* 1970, *20,* 226.

54. Kolodny, R. C. Research issues in the study of marijuana and male reproductive physiology in humans. In J. R. Tinklenberg (Ed.), *Marijuana and health hazards: Methodological issues in current research.* New York: Academic Press, 1975.

Chapter 9   Sleep and Dreaming

1. Bromberg, W. *The mind of man: A history of psychotherapy and psychoanalysis.* New York: Harper & Row, 1959.

2. Von Grunebaum, G. E., & Caillois, R. *The dream and human societies.* Berkeley: University of California Press, 1966.

3. Dement, W. C. *Some must watch*

while some must sleep. San Francisco: W. H. Freeman, 1974.

4. Webb, W. B., Agnew, J. W., & Williams, R. L. Effect on sleep of a sleep period time displacement. *Aerospace Medicine,* 1971, *42,* 152–155.

5. Sokolove, P. G. Localization of the cockroach optic lobe circadian pacemaker with microlesions. *Brain Research,* 1975, *87,* 13–21.

6. Menaker, M. Aspects of the physiology of circadian rhythmicity in the vertebrate central nervous system. In F. O. Schmitt & F. G. Worden (Eds.), *The neurosciences.* Cambridge, Mass.: M.I.T. Press, 1974.

7. Broadbent, D. E. *Perception and communication.* London: Pergamon Press, 1958.

8. Treisman, A. M. Selective attention in man. *British Medical Bulletin,* 1964, *20,* 12–16.

9. Treisman, A. M. Contextual cues in selective listening. *Quarterly Journal of Experimental Psychology,* 1960, *12,* 242–248.

10. Aarons, L. Sleep-associated instruction, *Psychological Bulletin,* 1976, *83,* 1–40.

11. Simon, C. W., & Emmons, W. H. Responses to material presented during various stages of sleep. *Journal of Experimental Psychology,* 1965, *51,* 89–97.

12. Dement, W. C. An essay on dreams: The role of physiology in understanding their nature. In T. M. Newcomb (Ed.), *New directions in psychology II.* New York: Holt, Rinehart and Winston, 1965.

13. Dement, W. C. *Some must watch while some must sleep.* San Francisco: W. H. Freeman, 1972.

14. Hartman, E. *The biology of dreaming.* Springfield, Ill.: Charles C. Thomas, 1967.

15. Snyder, F. The physiology of dreaming. In M. Kramer (Ed.), *Dream psychology and the new biology of dreaming.* Springfield, Ill.: Charles C. Thomas, 1969.

16. Evarts, E. Activity of neurosis in visual cortex of cat during sleep with low voltage fast EEG activity. *Journal of Neurophysiology,* 1962, *25,* 812–816.

17. Vaughn, C. J. Behavioral evidence for dreaming in rhesus monkeys. *Physiologist,* 1964, *1,* 275.

18. Goodenough, D., Shapiro, A., Holden, M., & Steinschriber, L. A comparison of "dreamers" and "nondreamers": Eye movements, electroencephalograms, and the recall of dreams. *Journal of Abnormal and Social Psychology,* 1959, *59,* 295–302.

19. Antrobus, J., Dement, W., & Fisher, C. Patterns of dreaming and dream recall: An EEG study. *Journal of Abnormal and Social Psychology,* 1964, *69,* 341–344.

20. Cohen, D. B. Current research on the frequency of dream recall. *Psychological Bulletin,* 1970, *73,* 433–440.

21. Hill, A. B. Personality correlates of dream recall. *Journal of Consulting and Clinical Psychology,* 1974, *42,* 766–773.

22. Hall, C. S. The significance of the dream of being attacked. *Journal of Personality,* 1955, *24,* 168–180.

23. Hall, C. S. What people dream about. *Scientific American,* 1951, *184,* 60–63.

24. Snyder, F. The phenomenology of dreaming. In L. Madow & L. H. Snow (Eds.), *The psychodynamic implications of the physiological studies on dreams.* Springfield, Ill.: Charles C. Thomas, 1970.

25. Kahn, E., Dement, W., Fisher, C., & Barmack, J. Incidence of color in immediately recalled dreams. *Science,* 1962, *137,* 1054–1055.

26. Feldman, M. J., & Hyman, E. Content analysis of nightmare reports. *Psychophysiology,* 1968, *5,* 221.

27. Bonime, W. *The clinical use of dreams.* New York: Basic Books, 1962.

28. Jacobson, A., & Kales, A. Somnambulism: All-night EEG and related studies. In S. S. Kety, E. V. Evarts, & H. L. Williams (Eds.), *Sleep and altered states of consciousness.* Baltimore, Md.: William & Wilkins, 1967.

29. Laughlin, H. P. *The neuroses.* Washington D.C.: Butterworth, 1967.

30. Dement, W. The effect of dream deprivation. *Science,* 1960, *131,* 1705–1707.

31. Jouvet, M. Paradoxical sleep—A study of its nature and mechanisms. In K. Akert, C. Bally, & J. Schade (Eds.), *Sleep mechanisms.* Amsterdam, New York: Elsevier Publishing Company, 1965.

32. Kleitman, N. Patterns of dreaming. *Scientific American,* November 1960.

33. Freud, S. *The interpretation of dreams.* London: Hogarth Press, 1953.

34. Dement, W., & Wolpert, E. The relation of eye movements, body mobility, and external stimuli to dream content. *Journal of Experimental Psychology,* 1958, *55,* 543–553.

35. Dement, W., & Wolpert, E. Relationships in the manifest content of dreams occurring on the same night. *Journal of Nervous and Mental Disease,* 1958, *126,* 568–578. © The Williams and Williams Co. Reproduced by permission.

36. Garma, A. *The psychoanalysis of dreams.* London: Pall Mall Press, 1966.

37. Boss, M. *The analysis of dreams.* New York: Philosophical Library, 1958.

38. Breger, L., Hunter, I., & Lane, R. W. The effect of stress on dreams. *Psychological Issues,* 1971, 7, Monograph 27.

39. Hall, C. S. A cognitive theory of dreams. *Journal of General Psychology,* 1953, *49,* 273–282.

40. Stewart, K. Dream theory in Malaya. In C. T. Tart (Ed.), *Altered states of consciousness.* New York: John Wiley, 1969.

Chapter 10 The Family

1. Marshall, A. J. *Bower birds.* London: Oxford University Press, 1954.

2. Beach, F. A. The descent of instinct. *Psychological Review,* 1955, *62,* 401–410.

3. McNemar, Q. Twin resemblance in motor skills, and the effect of practice thereon. *Journal of Genetic Psychology,* 1933, *42,* 70–97.

4. Lennox, W. G., Gibbs, E. L., & Gibbs, F. A. The brain wave pattern, an heredity trait: Evidence from 74 "normal" pairs of twins. *Journal of Heredity,* 1945, *36,* 223–243.

5. Conrad, H. S., & Jones, H. E. A second study of familial resemblance in intelligence. *39th Yearbook, Part II, National Society for the Study of Education.* Chicago: University of Chicago Press, 1940.

6. Leahy, A. M. Nature-nurture and intelligence. *Genetic Psychology Monographs,* 1935, *17,* 235–308.

7. Thompson, W. R. The inheritance and development of intelligence. *Proceedings of the Association for Research in Nervous and Mental Disease,* 1954, *33,* 209–231.

8. Newman, H. H., Freeman, F. N., & Holzinger, K. J. *Twins: A study of heredity and environment.* Chicago: University of Chicago Press, 1937.

9. Freedman, D. An etiological approach to the genetical study of human behavior. In S. G. Vandenberg (Ed.), *Methods and goals in human behavior genetics.* New York: Academic Press, 1965.

10. Mead, M. The impact of cultural changes on the family. In M. Mead (Ed.), *The family in the urban community.* Detroit: The Merril-Palmer School, 1953.

11. Frank, L. K. *On the importance of infancy.* New York: Random House, 1966.

12. Aberle, D. The psycho-social analysis of a Hopi life history. In Y. A. Cohen (Ed.), *Social structure and personality.* New York: Holt, Rinehart and Winston, 1951.

13. Aldrich, C. K. Thief! *Psychology Today,* 1971, *4,* 67.

14. Douvan, E., & Adelson, J. *The adolescent experience.* New York: John Wiley, 1966.

15. Winterbottom, M. R. The relation of need for achievement to learning experience in independence and mastery. In J. W. Atkinson (Ed.), *Motives in fantasy, action, and society.* Princeton, N.J.: D. Van Nostrand, 1958.

16. Adorno, T. W., Frenkel-Brunswik, E., Levinson D. J., & Sanford, N. R. *The authoritarian personality.* New York: Harper & Row, 1950.

17. Sears, R. R., Maccoby, E. E., & Levin, H. *Patterns of child rearing.* Evanston, Ill.: Row, Peterson, 1957.

18. Glueck, S., & Glueck, E. *Unraveling juvenile delinquency.* New York: Commonwealth Fund, 1950.

19. Harper, L. V. The scope of offspring effects: From caregiver to culture. *Psychological Bulletin,* 1975, *82,* 784–801.

20. Gruenberg, E. M. On the psychosomatics of the not-so-perfect fetal parasite. In S. A. Richardson & A. F. Guttmacher (Eds.), *Childbearing: Its social and psychological aspects.* Baltimore, Md.: Williams & Wilkins, 1967.

21. Chess, S. Temperament in the normal infant. In J. Hellmuth (Ed.), *The exceptional infant (Volume I: The Normal Infant).* New York: Brunner/Mazel, 1967.

22. Davis, K. Final note on a case of extreme isolation. *American Journal of Sociology,* 1947, *52,* 554–565.

23. Koluchová J. Severe deprivation in twins: A case study. *Journal of Child Psychology and Psychiatry,* 1972, *13,* 107–144.

24. Fromkin, V., *et al.* The development of language in Genie: A case of language acquisition beyond the "critical period." *Brain and Language,* 1974, *1,* 81–107.

25. Spitz, R. A. Motherless infants. *Child Development,* 1949, *20,* 145–155.

26. Spitz, R. A. Hospitalism: A follow-up report. In A. Freud, W. Hoffer, & E. Glover (Eds.), *The psychoanalytic study of the child.* Vol. II. New York: International Universities Press, 1946.

27. Bettelheim, B. *Truants from life.* New York: The Free Press, 1955.

28. Harlow, H. F., & Zimmerman, R. R. Affectional responses in the infant monkey. *Science,* 1959, *130,* 421–432.

29. Harlow, H. F. The nature of love. *The American Psychologist,* 1958, *13,* 673–685.

30. Harlow, H. F., & Harlow, M. K. Learning to love. *American Scientist,* 1966, *54,* 244–272.

31. Flint, B. M. *The child and the institution: A study of deprivation and recovery.* Toronto: University of Toronto Press, 1966.

32. Taylor, A. Deprived infants: Potential for affective adjustment. *American Journal of Orthopsychiatry,* 1968, *38,* 835–845.

33. Stendler-Lavatelli, C. B. Environmental intervention in infancy and early childhood. In M. Deutsch, I. Katz, & A. R. Jensen (Eds.), *Social class, race and psychological development.* New York: Holt, Rinehart and Winston, 1968.

34. Skeels, H. M. & Dye, H. B. A

study of the effects of differential stimulation on mentally retarded children. *Proceedings of the American Association of Mental Deficiency,* 1939, *44,* 114–136.

35. Rheingold, H. L. The modification of social responsiveness in institutional babies. *Monograph of the Society for Research in Child Development,* 1956, *21,* (2), Series No. 63.

36. Hetherington, G. M., Cox, M., & Cox, R. The aftermath of divorce. In J. H. Stevens, Jr., & M. Mathews (Eds.), *Mother-child, father-child relations.* Washington, D.C.: National Association for the Education of Young Children, 1977.

37. Raschke, H. J. & Raschke, V. J. Family conflict and children's self-concepts: A comparison of intact and single-parent families. *Journal of Marriage and the Family,* 1979, *41,* 367–374.

38. Burchinal, L. G. Characteristics of adolescents from unbroken, broken, and reconstituted families. *Journal of Marriage and the Family,* 1964, *26,* 44–51.

39. Frank, L. K. *On the importance of infancy.* New York: Random House, 1966.

40. McCurdy, H. G. The childhood pattern of genius. *Journal of the Elisha Mitchell Scientific Society,* 1957, *73,* 448–462.

41. Baldwin, A. L., Kalhorn, J., & Breese, F. H. Patterns of parent behavior. *Psychological Monographs,* 1945, *58,* No. 268.

42. Rosenberg, M. *Society and the adolescent self-image.* Princeton, N.J.: Princeton University Press, 1965.

43. Coopersmith, S. Studies in self-esteem. *Scientific American,* 1968, *218,* 96–107.

44. Bacon, M. K., Child, I. L., & Barry, H. A cross-cultural study of correlates of crime. *Journal of Abnormal and Social Psychology,* 1963, *66,* 291–300.

45. Lane, R. C., & Singer, J. L. Familial attitudes in paranoid schizophrenics and the normals from two socioeconomic classes. *Journal of Abnormal and Social Psychology,* 1959, *59,* 328–339.

46. Lidz, T., Fleck, S., & Cornelison, A. R. *Schizophrenia and the family.* New York: International Universities Press, 1965.

47. Fleck, S. Family dynamics and origin of schizophrenia. *Psychosomatic Medicine,* 1960, *22,* 333–343.

48. Mead, M. Future family. *Transaction,* 1970, *8,* 50–53.

Chapter 11   Childhood

1. Dennis, W. *The Hopi Child.* New York: Appleton-Century-Crofts, 1940.

2. Hilgard, E. R. Learning and maturation in preschool children. *Journal of Genetic Psychology,* 1932, *41,* 35–56.

3. Gibson, E. J., & Walk, R. D. The "visual cliff." *Scientific American,* 1960, *202,* 67–71.

4. Campos, T. J., Langer, A., & Krowitz, A. Cardiac responses on the visual cliff in prelocomotor infants. *Science,* 1970, *170,* 196.

5. Kaplan, E. L., & Kaplan, G. A. Is there such a thing as a prelinguistic child? In J. Eliot (Ed.), *Human development and cognitive processes.* New York: Holt, Rinehart and Winston, 1970.

6. Chomsky, N. Language and the mind. *Readings in psychology today.* Del Mar Calif.: CRM Books, 1969.

7. Milne, A. A. "The End" from *Now We Are Six.* Copyright 1927 by E. P. Dutton and Co., Inc. Copyright renewal 1955 by A. A. Milne. Reprinted by permission of the publisher, E. P. Dutton.

8. Bloom, B. S. *Stability and change in human characteristics.* New York: John Wiley, 1964.

9. Sears, R. R., Maccoby, E. E., & Levin, H. *Patterns of child rearing.* Evanston, Ill.: Row, Peterson, 1957.

10. Wittenborn, J. R. A study of adoptive children. *Psychological Monographs,* 1956, *70,* 1–115.

11. Macfarlane, J. W., Allen, L., & Honzik, M. P. A developmental study of the behavior problems of normal children between twenty-one months and fourteen years. *University of California Publications in Child Development,* Vol. II. Berkeley: University of California Press, 1954.

12. Despert, J. L. Urinary control and enuresis. *Psychosomatic Medicine,* 1944, *6,* 294–307.

13. Huschka, M. The child's response to coercive bowel training. *Psychosomatic Medicine,* 1942, *4,* 301–308.

14. Beloff, H. The structure and origin of the anal character. *Genetic Psychology Monographs,* 1957, *55,* 141–172.

15. Erikson, E. H. *Childhood and society.* New York: Norton, 1963.

16. Mischel, W. *Introduction to personality.* New York: Holt, Rinehart and Winston, 1971.

17. Brown, D. G. Masculinity-femininity development in children. *Journal of Consulting Psychology,* 1957, *21,* 197–202.

18. Whiting, J. W. M. Resource mediation and learning by identification. In I. Iscoe & H. W. Stevenson (Eds.), *Personality development in children.* Austin: University of Texas Press, 1960.

19. Chwast, J. Sociopathic behavior in children. In B. Wolman (Ed.), *Manual of child psychopathology.* New York: McGraw-Hill, 1972.

20. Fischer, W. F. Sharing in preschool children as a function of amount and type of reinforcement. *Genetic*

Psychology Monographs, 1963, *68,* 215–245.

21. Grusec, J. W., & Skubiski, S. L. Model nurturance, demand characteristics of the modeling experiment and altruism. *Journal of Personality and Social Psychology,* 1970, *14,* 352–359.

22. Kohlberg, L. Stage and sequence: The cognitive-development approach to socialization. In Goslin, D. A. (Ed.), *Handbook of socialization theory and research.* Chicago: Rand McNally, 1969.

Chapter 12   Adolescence and Adulthood

1. Erikson, E. H. *Childhood and society.* New York: Norton, 1963.

2. Sheehy, G. *Passages: Predictable crises of adult life.* New York: Dutton, 1976.

3. Levinson, D. J. The mid-life transition: A period in adult psychosocial development. *Psychiatry,* 1977, *40,* 99–112.

4. Levinson, D. J., *et al. The seasons of a man's life.* New York: Knopf, 1978.

5. Gould, R. L. The phases of adult life: A study in developmental psychology. *American Journal of Psychiatry,* 1972, *129,* 521–531.

6. Gould, R. L. Adult life stages: Growth toward self-tolerance. *Psychology Today,* 1975, *8.*

7. Rogers, D. *The adult years.* Englewood Cliffs, N.J.: Prentice-Hall, 1979.

8. Armour, R. *Through darkest adolescence: With tongue in cheek and pen in checkbook.* New York: McGraw-Hill, 1963.

9. Adelson, J. Adolescence and the generalization gap. *Psychology Today,* 1979, *12,* 33–37.

10. Rosenberg, M. *Society and the adolescent self-image.* Princeton, N.J.: Princeton University Press, 1965.

11. Coopersmith, S. *Antecedents of self-esteem.* San Francisco: W. H. Freeman, 1967.

12. Gornick, V. Consciousness. *The New York Times Magazine,* January 10, 1971.

13. Heilbrun, A. B., & Fromme, D. C. Parental identification of late adolescents and level of adjustment: The importance of parent-model attributes, ordinal position, and sex of the child. *Journal of Genetic Psychology,* 1965, *107,* 49–59.

14. Elder, G. H. Parental power legitimation and its effect on the adolescent. *Sociometry,* 1963, *26,* 50–65.

15. Mead, M. *Culture and commitment: A study of the generation gap.* New York: Doubleday, 1970.

16. Neugarten, B. L. *The psychology of aging.* Master lectures on developmental psychology. Washington, D.C.: Americn Psychological Association, 1976.

17. Schaie, K. W., Labouvie, G. V., & Buech, B. U. Generational and cohort-specific differences in adult cognitive functioning. *Developmental Psychology,* 1973, *9,* 151–166.

18. Rollins, B. C., & Feldman, H. Marital satisfaction over the family life cycle. *Journal of Marriage and the Family,* 1970, *32,* 20–28.

19. Puner, M. *To the good long life: What we know about growing old.* New York: Universe Books, 1974.

20. Rubin, I. The "sexless older years"—a socially harmful stereotype. *Annals of the American Academy of Political and Social Science,* 1968, *376,* 86–95.

21. Schaie, K. W., Labouvie, F., & Buesch, B. Intellectual changes with age, cross-sectional and within-cohort. *Developmental Psychology,* 1973, *9,* 151–166.

22. Troll, L. E. *Early and middle adulthood.* Monterey, Calif.: Brooks/Cole, 1975.

23. Schaie, K. W., & Labouvie-Vief, G. Generational versus ontogenetic components of change in adult cognitive behavior: A fourteen-year cross-sequential study. *Developmental Psychology,* 1974, *4,* 305–320.

24. Bischof, L. J. *Adult psychology.* New York: Harper & Row, 1969.

25. Schneidman, E. S. *Deaths of man.* New York: The New York Times Book Co., 1973.

26. Parkes, C. M. *Bereavement.* New York: International Universities Press, 1972.

27. Kübler-Ross, E. *On death and dying.* New York: Macmillan, 1969.

28. Shultz, R. *The psychology of death, dying, and bereavement.* Reading, Mass.: Addison-Wesley, 1978.

Chapter 13   Relationships

1. Rubin, Z. *Liking and loving.* New York: Holt, Rinehart and Winston, 1973.

2. Luft, J. *Of human interaction.* Palo Alto, Calif.: National Press Books, 1969.

3. Berne, E. *Games people play: The psychology of human relationships.* New York: Grove Press, 1964.

4. Johnson, D. W. *Reaching out: Interpersonal effectiveness and self-actualization.* Englewood Cliffs, N.J.: Prentice-Hall, 1972.

5. McCroskey, J. C., Larson, C. E., & Knapp, M. L. *Introduction to interpersonal communication.* Englewood Cliffs, N.J.: Prentice-Hall, 1971.

6. Scheflen, A. E. Communication and regulation in psychotherapy. *Psychiatry,* 1964, *27,* 126–136.

7. Wiener, M., Devoe, S., Rubinow, S., & Geller, J. Nonverbal behavior and nonverbal communication. *Psychological Review,* 1972, *79,* 185–214.

8. Ekman, P., Sorenson, E. R., & Friesen, W. V. Pan-cultural

elements in facial displays of emotion. *Science,* 1969, *164,* 86–88.

9. Family Circle, February 1976.

10. Zimbardo, P. G., Pilkonis, P. A., & Norwood, R. M. The social disease called shyness. *Psychology Today,* 1975, *8,* 68–72.

11. Zimbardo, P. G. *Shyness: What is it, what to do about it.* Reading, Mass.: Addison-Wesley, 1977.

12. Smith, M. J. *When I say no, I feel guilty.* New York: Dial Press, 1975.

13. Burgess, E. W. & Wallin, P. Homogamy in social characteristics. *American Journal of Sociology,* 1943, *49,* 109–124.

14. Reed, E. W., & Reed, S. C. *Mental retardation: A family study.* Philadelphia: W. B. Saunders, 1965.

15. Garrison, R. J., Anderson, V. E., & Reed, S. C. Assortative marriage. *Eugenics Quarterly,* 1968, *15,* 113–127.

16. Byrne, D., & Nelson, D. Attraction as a linear function of proportion of positive reinforcements. *Journal of Personality and Social Psychology,* 1965, *1,* 659–663.

17. Byrne, D., & Griffitt, W. A developmental investigation of the law of attraction. *Journal of Personality and Social Psychology,* 1966, *4,* 699–703.

18. Winch, R. F., Ktsanes, T., & Ktsanes, V. The theory of complementary needs in mate selection: An analytic and descriptive study. *American Sociologists Review,* 1954, *19,* 241–249.

19. Izard, C. E. Personality similarity and friendship. *Journal of Abnormal and Social Psychology,* 1960, *61,* 47–51.

20. Miller, N., Campbell, D. T., Twedt, H., & O'Connell, E. J. Similarity, contrast and complementarity in friendship choice. *Journal of Personality and Social Psychology,* 1966, *3,* 3–12.

21. Becker, G. The complementary-need hypothesis: Authoritarianism, dominance and other Edwards Personality Preference Schedule scores. *Journal of Personality and Social Psychology,* 1964, *32,* 45–56.

22. Banta, T. J., & Hetherington, M. Relations between needs of friends and fiancées. *Journal of Abnormal and Social Psychology,* 1963, *66,* 401–404.

23. Byrne, D., & Clore, G. L. A reinforcement model of evaluative responses. *Personality: An International Journal,* 1970, *1,* 103–128.

24. Carnegie, D. *How to win friends and influence people.* New York: Simon & Schuster, 1936.

25. Aronson, E., & Worchel, P. Similarity vs. liking as determinants of interpersonal attractiveness. *Psychonomic Science,* 1966, *5,* 157–158.

26. Shraugher, J. S., & Jones, S. C. Social validation and interpersonal evaluations. *Journal of Experimental Social Psychology,* 1968, *4,* 315–323.

27. Jacobs, L., Berscheid, E., & Walster, E. Self esteem and attraction. *Journal of Personality and Social Psychology,* 1971, *17,* 84–91.

28. Homans, G. *Social behavior.* New York: Harcourt, Brace and World, 1961.

29. Kiesler, S. B., & Barol, R. L. The search for a romantic partner: The effects of self-esteem and physical attractiveness on romantic behavior. In K. J. Gerger & D. Marlowe (Eds.), *Personality and social behavior.* Reading, Mass.: Addison-Wesley, 1970.

30. Buber, M. *I and thou.* New York: Scribner's, 1970.

31. Coleman, J. C. *Personality dynamics and effective behavior.* Chicago: Scott, Foresman, 1960.

32. Bachman, J. G., & Johnston, L. D. The freshman, 1979. *Psychology Today,* 1979, *13,* 79–87.

33. Pietropinto, A., & Simenauer, J. *Husbands and wives.* New York: Times Books, 1979.

34. Rosner, S., & Hobe, L. *The marriage gap.* New York: McGraw-Hill, 1974.

35. Derlega, V. J., & Janda, L. H. *Personal adjustment.* Morristown, N.J.: General Learning Press, 1978.

36. Ables, B. S., & Brandsma, J. M. *Therapy for couples.* San Francisco: Jossey-Bass, 1977.

37. Albrecht, S. L., Bahr, H. M., & Chadwick, B. A. Changing family and sex roles: An assessment of age differences. *Journal of Marriage and the Family,* 1979, *41,* 41–50.

Chapter 14 Male and Female

1. Bem, S. L. The measurement of psychological androgyny. *Journal of Consulting and Clinical Psychology,* 1974, *42,* 155–162.

2. Mead, M. *Sex and temperament in three primitive societies.* New York: William Morrow, 1935.

3. Brown, D. G. Sex-role development in a changing culture. *Psychological Bulletin,* 1958, *55,* 232–242.

4. Freud, S. *A general introduction to psychoanalysis.* New York: Washington Square Press, 1952.

5. Kagan, J. The concept of identification. *Psychological Review,* 1958, *65,* 296–305.

6. Mussen, P. H., & Distler, L. Masculinity, identification, and father-son relationships. *Journal of Abnormal and Social Psychology,* 1959, *59,* 350–356.

7. Payne, D. E., & Mussen, P. H. Parent-child relations and father-identification among adolescent boys. *Journal of Abnormal and Social Psychology,* 1956, *52,* 358–362.

8. Green, R. Children's quest for sexual identity. *Psychology Today,* 1974, *7,* 45–51.

9. Money, J., & Tucker, P. *Sexual signatures: On being a man or a woman.* Boston: Little, Brown, 1975.

10. Bentler, P. M. A typology of transsexualism: Gender identity theory and data. *Archives of Sexual Behavior,* 1976, *5,* 567–584.

11. Kinsey, A. C., Pomeroy, W. B., Martin, C. E., & Gebhard, P. H. *Sexual behavior in the human female.* Philadelphia: W. B. Saunders, 1953.

12. Kinsey, A. C., Pomeroy, W. B., & Martin, C. E. *Sexual behavior in the human male.* Philadelphia: W. B. Saunders, 1948.

13. Rosen, D. H. *Lesbianism: A study of female homosexuality.* Springfield, Ill.: Charles C. Thomas, 1974.

14. Acosta, F. X. Etiology and treatment of homosexuality: A review. *Archives of Sexual Behavior,* 1975, *4,* 9–29.

15. Raybin, J. B. Homosexual incest. *Journal of Nervous and Mental Disease,* 1969, *148,* 104–110.

16. Kallman, F. J. Comparative twin study on the genetic aspects of male homosexuality. *Journal of Nervous and Mental Disease,* 1952, *115,* 283–298.

17. West, D. J. *Homosexuality.* London: Gerald Duckworth, 1955.

18. Myerson, A., & Neustadt, R. Bisexuality and male homosexuality. *Clinics,* 1942, *1,* 932–957.

19. Moore, T. V. The pathogenesis and treatment of homosexual disorders: A digest of some pertinent evidence. *Journal of Personality,* 1945, *14,* 47–83.

20. Kolodny, R. C., Masters, W. H., Hendryx, J., & Toro, G. Plasma testosterone and semen analysis in male homosexuals. *New England Journal of Medicine,* 1971, *285,* 1170–1174.

21. Snortum, J. R., Gillespie, J. F., Marshall, J. E., McLaughlin, J. P., &

Mosberg, L. Family dynamics and homosexuality. *Psychological Reports,* 1969, *24,* 763–770.

22. Hooker, E. Parental relations and male homosexuality in patient and nonpatient samples. *Journal of Consulting and Clinical Psychology,* 1969, *33,* 140–142.

23. Bieber, I. (Ed.), *Homosexuality: A psychoanalytic study.* New York: Basic Books, 1962.

24. Kenyon, F. E. Studies in female homosexuality. *British Journal of Psychiatry,* 1968, *114,* 1337–1350.

25. Bene, E. On the genesis of female homosexuality. *British Journal of Psychiatry,* 1965, *111,* 815–821.

26. Feldman, M. P., & MacCulloch, M. J. *Homosexual behavior: Therapy and assessment.* Oxford, England: Pergamon Press, 1971.

27. Litin, E. M., Giffin, M. E., & Johnson, A. M. Parental influences in unusual sexual behavior in children. *Psychoanalytic Quarterly,* 1956, *25,* 37–55.

28. Salter, A. *Conditioned reflex therapy.* New York: Capricorn Books, 1961.

Chapter 15 Love and Sex

1. Montagu, A. *The practice of love.* Englewood Cliffs, N.J.: Prentice-Hall, 1975.

2. Pam, A., Plutchik, R., & Conte, H. R. Love: A psychometric approach. *Psychological Reports,* 1975, *37,* 83–88.

3. Fromm, E. *The art of loving.* New York: Harper & Brothers, 1956.

4. Maslow, A. H. *Toward a psychology of being.* Princeton, N.J.: D. Van Nostrand, 1962.

5. Maslow, A. H. *Motivation and personality.* New York: Harper & Brothers, 1954.

6. Ehrmann, W. *Premarital dating behavior,* New York: Holt, Rinehart and Winston, 1959.

7. Reiss, I. L. How and why America's sex standards are changing. *Trans-action,* 1960, *5,* 26–32.

8. Kaats, G. R., & Davis, K. E. The dynamics of sexual behavior of college students. *Journal of Marriage and the Family.* 1970, *32,* 390–399.

9. Kinsey, A. C., Pomeroy, W. B., Martin, C. E., & Gebhard, P. H. *Sexual behavior in the human female.* Philadelphia: W. B. Saunders, 1953.

10. Scoville, W. B. The limbic lobe in man. *Journal of Neurosurgery,* 1954, *11,* 64–66.

11. Blumer, D., & Walker, E. Sexual behavior in temporal lobe epilepsy. *Archives of Neurology,* 1967, *16,* 37–43.

12. Delgado, J. M. R. *Physical control of the mind.* New York: Harper & Row, 1969.

13. Sawyer, C. H. Reproductive behavior. In J. Field (Ed.), *Handbook of physiology.* Vol. II. Washington: American Physiology Society, 1960, 1225–1240.

14. Caggiula, A. R., & Hoebel, B. G. "Copulation-reward site" in the posterior hypothalamus. *Science,* 1966, *153,* 1284–1285.

15. Olds, J. Hypothalamic substrates of reward. *Physiology Review,* 1962, *42,* 554–604.

16. Heath, R. G. Electrical self-stimulation of the brain in man. *American Journal of Psychiatry,* 1963, *120,* 571–577.

17. Vaughan, E., & Fisher, A. E. Male sexual behavior induced by intracranial electrical stimulation. *Science,* 1962, *137,* 758–760.

18. Bandura, A. A social learning interpretation of psychological dysfunctions. In P. London & D. Rosenhan (Eds.), *Foundations of abnormal psychology.* New York: Holt, Rinehart and Winston, 1968.

19. Stekel, W. *Sexual aberrations: The*

phenomena of fetishism in relation to sex. Vol. II. New York: Liveright, 1930.

20. Mosher, D. L. Sex differences, sex experiences, sex guilt, and explicitly sexual films. *Journal of Social Issues,* 1973, *29,* 95–112.

21. Goldstein, M. J. Exposure to erotic stimuli and sexual deviance. *Journal of Social Issues,* 1973, *29,* 197–220.

22. Kinsey, A. C., Pomeroy, W. B., & Martin, C. E. *Sexual behavior in the human male.* Philadelphia: W. B. Saunders, 1948.

23. Ford, C. S., & Beach, F. A. *Patterns of sexual behavior.* New York: Harper & Row, 1951.

24. Group for the Advancement of Psychiatry. *Sex and the college student.* New York: Atheneum, 1966.

25. Ellis, A. Masturbation. In M. F. De Martino (Ed.), *Sexual behavior and personality characteristics.* New York: Grove Press, 1963.

26. Masters, W. H., & Johnson, V. E. *Human sexual response.* Boston: Little Brown, 1966.

27. Packard, V. *The sexual wilderness.* New York: McKay, 1968.

28. Luckey, E., & Nass, G. D. A comparison of sexual attitudes and behavior in an international sample. *Journal of Marriage and the Family,* 1969, *31,* 364–379.

29. Groves, W. E., Rossi, P. H., & Grafstein, D. Study of life styles and campus communities. A preliminary report to students who participated. Department of Social Relations, John Hopkins University, 1970.

30. Luria, Z., & Rose, M. D. *Psychology of Human Sexuality.* New York: John Wiley, 1979.

31. Pilpel, H. F. Sex vs. the law: A study in hypocrisy. In A. Shiloh (Ed.), *Studies in human sexual behavior: The American scene.* Springfield, Ill.: Charles C. Thomas, 1970.

32. Athanasiou, R., Shaver, P., & Tavris, C. Sex. *Psychology Today,* 1970, *4,* 37.

33. Reiss, I. *The social context of premarital sexual permissiveness.* New York: Holt, Rinehart and Winston, 1967.

34. Freeman, H. A., & Freeman, R. S. Senior college women: Their sexual standards and activity. *Journal of the National Association of Women Deans and Counselors,* 1966, *29,* 136–143.

Chapter 16   Personality

1. Jourard, S. M. *The transparent self: Self-disclosure and well-being.* Princeton, N.J.: D. Van Nostrand, 1964.

2. Dymond, R. F. Adjustment changes over therapy from self-sorts. In C. R. Rogers & R. F. Dymond (Eds.), *Psychotherapy and personality change.* Chicago: University of Chicago Press, 1954.

3. In De Laszlo, V. (Ed.) *The basic writings of C. G. Jung.* New York: The Modern Library, 1959.

4. Schjelderup-Ebbe, T. Social behavior of birds. In C. Murchison (Ed.), *Handbook of social psychology.* Worcester, Mass.: Clark University Press, 1935.

5. Mischel, W. *Personality and assessment.* New York: John Wiley, 1968.

6. Rotter, J. B. External control and internal control. *Psychology Today,* 1971, *5,* 37–42, 58–59.

7. Ulrich, R. E., Stachnik, T. J., & Stainton, N. R. Student acceptance of generalized personality interpretations. *Psychological Reports,* 1963, *13,* 831–834.

8. Offer, D. Studies of normal adolescents. *Adolescence,* 1966, *1,* 305–320.

9. Golden, J., Mandel, N., Glueck, B. C., & Feder, Z. A summary description of fifty "normal" white males. *American Journal of Psychiatry,* 1962, *119,* 48–56.

10. Bond, E. D. The student council study. *American Journal of Psychiatry,* 1952, *109,* 11–16.

11. Benedict, R. Anthropology and the abnormal. *Journal of General Psychology,* 1943, *10,* 59–80.

12. Slotkin, J. S. Culture and psychopathology. *Journal of Abnormal and Social Psychology,* 1955, *51,* 269–275.

Chapter 17   Motivation and Emotion

1. Beck, R. C. *Motivation: Theories and principles.* Englewood Cliffs, N.J.: Prentice-Hall, 1978.

2. Lepper, M. R., & Greene, D. *The hidden costs of reward: New perspectives on the psychology of human motivation.* New York: John Wiley, 1978.

3. Deci, E. L., & Pornac, J. Cognitive evaluation theory and the study of human motivation. In M. R. Lepper & D. Greene (Eds.), *The hidden costs of reward: New perspectives on the psychology of human motivation.* New York: John Wiley, 1978.

4. Leiderman, P. H., Mendelson, J. H., Wexler, D., & Solomon, P. Sensory deprivation: Clinical aspects. *Archives of Internal Medicine,* 1958, *101,* 389–396.

5. Butler, R. A. The effect of deprivation of visual incentives on visual exploration motivation in monkeys. *Journal of Comparative and Physiological Psychology,* 1957, *50,* 177–179.

6. Berlyne, D. E., & Slater, J. Perceptual curiosity, exploratory behavior, and maze learning. *Journal of Comparative and Physiological Psychology,* 1957, *50,* 228–232.

7. Krech, D., Rosenzweig, M. R., &

Bennett, E. L.   Relations between brain chemistry and problem-solving among rats raised in enriched and impoverished environments. *Journal of Comparative and Physiological Psychology*, 1962, *55*, 801–807.

8. Rosenzweig, M. R.   Environmental complexity, cerebral change, and behavior. *American Psychologist*, 1966, *21*, 321–342.

9. Scott, T. H., Bexton, W. H., Heron, W., & Doane, B. K. Cognitive effects of perceptual isolation. *Canadian Journal of Psychology*, 1959, *13*, 200–209.

10. Goldberger, L., & Holt, R. R. Experimental interference with reality contact: Individual differences.   In P. Solomon, P. E. Kubzansky, P. H. Leiderman, J. H. Mendelson, R. Trumbull, & D. Wexler (Eds.), *Sensory deprivation*.   Cambridge, Mass.: Harvard University Press, 1961.

11. Zubek, J. P., Sansom, W., & Prysiaznniuk, A.   Intellectual changes during prolonged perceptual isolation (darkness and silence). *Canadian Journal of Psychology*, 1960, *14*, 233–243.

12. Zubek, J. P., Pushkar, D., Sansom, W., & Gowing, J. Perceptual changes after prolonged sensory isolation (darkness and silence). *Canadian Journal of Psychology*, 1961, *15*, 83–100.

13. Bexton, W. H., Heron, W., & Scott, T. H.   Effects of decreased variation in the sensory environment. *Canadian Journal of Psychology*, 1954, *8*, 70–76.

14. Hebb, D. O.   The motivating effects of exteroceptive stimulation. *American Psychologist*, 1958, *13*, 109.

15. Zuckerman, M., Albright, R. J., Marks, C. S., & Miller, G. L. Stress and hallucinatory effects of perceptual isolation and confinement. *Psychology Monograph*, 1962, *76*, 30.

16. Heron, W., Doane, B. K., & Scott, T. H.   Visual disturbances after prolonged perceptual isolation. *Canadian Journal of Psychology*, 1956, *10*, 13–18.

17. Freedman, S. J., Grunebaum, H. U., & Greenblatt, M.   Perceptual and cognitive changes in sensory deprivation.   In P. Solomon, P. E. Kubzansky, P. H. Leiderman, J. H. Mendelson, R. Trumbull, & D. Wexler (Eds.), *Sensory deprivation*.   Cambridge, Mass.: Harvard University Press, 1961.

18. Lipowski, Z. J.   The conflict of Buridan's ass or some dilemmas of affluence: The theory of attractive stimulus overload. *American Journal of Psychiatry*, 1970, *127*, 273–279.

19. Holland, M. K., & Tarlow, G. Blinking and mental load. *Psychological Reports*, 1972, *31*, 119–127.

20. Ettemo, J. H.   Blood pressure change during mental load experiments in man. *Psychotherapy and Psychosomatics*, 1969, *17*, 191–195.

21. Zuckerman, M., Persky, H., Miller, L., & Levin, B.   Contrasting effects of understimulation (sensory deprivation) and overstimulation (high stimulus variety.) *Proceedings*, 77th Annual Convention, American Psychological Association, 1969, 319–320.

22. Usdansky, G., & Chapman, L. J. Schizophrenic-like responses in normal subjects under time pressure. *Journal of Abnormal and Social Psychology*, 1960, *60*, 143–146.

23. Wohlwill, J.   The concept of sensory overload.   In C. Eastman (Ed.), *EDRA: Environmental Design Research Association Proceedings*, 1970.

24. Cameron, P., Robertson, D., & Zaks, J.   Sound pollution, noise pollution, and health: Community parameters. *Journal of Applied Psychology*, 1972, *56*, 67–74.

25. Kryter, K. D.   *The effects of noise on man*.   New York: Academic Press, 1970.

26. Newell, M.   The effects of acoustic disruption on short term memory. *Psychonomic Science*, 1968, *12*, 61.

27. Sloboda, W.   The disturbance effect of white noise on human short term memory. *Psychonomic Science*, 1969, *14*, 82–83.

28. Jerison, H. J.   Effects of noise on human performance. *Journal of Applied Psychology*, 1959, *43*, 96–101.

29. Laird, D. A.   The effects of noise. *Journal of the Accoustical Society of America*, 1930, *1*, 256–261.

30. Finkle, L. L., & Poppen, J. R. Clinical effects of noise and mechanical vibrations of a turbojet engine. *Journal of Applied Psychology*, 1948, *1*, 183–204.

31. Berrien, F. K., & Young, C. W. The effects of acoustical treatment in industrial areas. *Journal of the Acoustical Society of America*, 1946, *18*, 453–457.

32. Glass, D., Singer, J. E., & Friedman, L.   Psychic cost of adaptation to an environmental stressor. *Journal of Personality and Social Psychology*, 1969, *12*, 200–210.

33. Farr, L.   Medical consequences of environmental home noises. *Journal of the American Medical Association*, 1967, *202*, 171–174.

34. Abey-Wickrama, I., A'brook, M. F., Gattoni, F. E. G., & Herridge, C. F.   Mental hospital admissions and aircraft noise. *Lancet*, 1969, *2*, 1275–1277.

35. Schultz, D. P.   *Sensory restriction: Effects on behavior*.   New York: Academic Press, 1965.

36. Schultz, D. P.   Evidence suggesting a sensory variation drive in humans. *Journal of General Psychology*, 1967, *77*, 87–99.

37. Vitz, P. C.   Affect as a function of stimulus variation. *Journal of Experimental Psychology*, 1966, *71*, 74–79.

38. Wohlwill, J. Amount of stimulus exploration and preference of differential functions of stimulus complexity. *Perception and Psychophysics,* 1968, *4,* 307–312.

39. Fiske, D. W., & Maddi, S. R. *The functions of varied experience.* Homewood, Ill.: Dorsey, 1961.

40. Zuckerman, M., Kolin, E. A., Price, L., & Zoob, I. Development of a sensation-seeking scale. *Journal of Consulting Psychology,* 1964, *28,* 477–482.

41. Zuckerman, M. *Manual and research report for the Sensation-Seeking Scale (SSS).* Mimeograph, University of Delaware, Newark, Delaware, April 1972.

42. Izard, C. E. *The face of emotions.* New York: Appleton-Century-Crofts, 1971.

43. Ekman, P., Friesen, W. V., & Ellsworth, P. *Emotion in the human face: Guidelines for research and an integration of findings.* New York: Pergamon, 1972.

44. Schachter, S. The interaction of cognitive and physiological determinants of emotional state. *Advances in Experimental Social Psychology,* 1964, *1,* 49–80.

45. Schachter, S., & Singer, J. Cognitive, social, and physiological determinants of emotional state. *Psychological Review,* 1962, *69,* 378–399.

Chapter 18   Potential

1. Otto, H. A. *Human potentialities: The challenge and the promise.* St. Louis, Mo.: Warren H. Green, 1968.

2. Cox, C. M. The early mental traits of three hundred geniuses: II. In L. M. Terman (Ed.), *Genetic studies of genius.* Stanford, Calif.: Stanford University Press, 1926.

3. Ashby, W. R., & Walker, C. C. Genius. In P. London &

D. Rosenhan (Eds.), *Foundations of abnormal psychology.* New York: Holt, Rinehart and Winston, 1968.

4. Erlenmeyer-Kimling, L., & Jarvik, L. F. Genetics and intelligence: A review. *Science,* 1963, *142,* 1477–1479.

5. Wolf, R. M. The identification and measurement of environmental process variables related to intelligence. Unpublished Ph.D dissertation, University of Chicago, 1963.

6. Rosenthal, R., & Jacobson, L. *Pygmalion in the classroom: Teacher expectation and pupils' intellectual development.* New York: Holt, Rinehart and Winston, 1968.

7. Honzik, M. P., Macfarlane, J. W., & Allen, L. The stability of mental test performance between two and eighteen years. *Journal of Experimental Education,* 1948, *17,* 309–324.

8. Albee, G. W., *et al.* Statement by SPSSI on current IQ controversy: Heredity versus environment. *American Psychologist,* 1969, *24,* 1039–1040.

9. McNemar, Q. Lost: Our intelligence? Why? *American Psychologist,* 1964, *19,* 871–882.

10. McClelland, D. C. Testing for competence rather than for "intelligence." *American Psychologist,* 1973, *28,* 1–14.

11. Elton, C. F., & Shevel, L. R. *Who is talented? An analysis of achievement.* Iowa City, Ia.: American College Testing Program, 1969.

12. Berg, I. *Education and jobs: The great training robbery.* New York: Praeger, 1970.

13. Barron, F. The psychology of creativity. In T. Newcomb (Ed.), *New directions in Psychology II,* New York: Holt, Rinehart and Winston, 1965.

14. Getzels, J. W., & Jackson, P. W.

Creativity and intelligence. New York: John Wiley, 1962.

15. Wallach, M. A., & Kogan, N. *Modes of thinking in young children: A study of the creativity-intelligence distinction.* New York: Holt, Rinehart and Winston, 1965.

16. MacKinnon, D. W. The study of creative persons: A method and some results. In J. Kagan (Ed.), *Creativity and learning.* Boston: Beacon Press, 1967.

17. Barron, F. *Creativity and psychological health.* Princeton, N.J.: D. Van Nostrand, 1963.

18. Gough, H. G. Techniques for identifying the creative research scientist. In *Conference on the creative person.* Berkeley: University of California, Institute of Personality Assessment and Research, 1961.

19. Dellas, M., & Gaier, E. L. Identification of creativity: The individual. *Psychological Bulletin,* 1970, *73,* 55–73.

20. Anderson, H. H. Creativity in perspective. In H. H. Anderson (Ed.), *Creativity and its cultivation.* New York: Harper & Brothers, 1959.

21. Reid, J. B., King, F. J., & Wickwire, P. Cognitive and other personality characteristics of creative children. *Psychological Reports,* 1959, *5,* 729–737.

22. Moustakas, C. *Creativity and conformity.* Princeton, N.J.: D. Van Nostrand, 1967.

23. Rogers, C. R. *On becoming a person: A therapist's view of psychotherapy.* Boston: Houghton Mifflin, 1961.

24. Wilson, C. Existential psychology: A novelist's approach. In J. F. T. Bugental (Ed.), *Challenges of humanistic psychology.* New York: McGraw-Hill, 1967.

25. Jourard, S. M. *The transparent self: Self-disclosure and well-being.* Princeton, N.J.: D. Van Nostrand, 1964.

26. Maslow, A. H. *Toward a psychology of being.* Princeton, N.J.: D. Van Nostrand, 1962.

27. Maslow, A. H. A theory of metamotivation: The biological rooting of the value-life. *Journal of Humanistic Psychology,* 1967, *7,* 93–127.

28. Maslow, A. H. Self-actualization and beyond. In J. F. T. Bugental (Ed.), *Challenges of humanistic psychology.* New York: McGraw-Hill, 1967.

29. Shostrum, E. L. An inventory for the measurement of self-actualization. *Educational and Psychological Measurement,* 1964, *24,* 207–218.

30. McClain, E. W. Further validation of the personal orientation inventory. *Journal of Consulting and Clinical Psychology,* 1970, *35,* 20–22.

31. Allport, G. W. *Pattern and growth in personality.* New York: Holt, Rinehart and Winston, 1961.

32. Okun, B. F. *Effective helping: Interviewing and counseling techniques.* North Scituate, Mass.: Duxbury Press, 1976.

33. Brammer, L. M. *The helping relationship: Process and skills.* Englewood Cliffs, N.J.: Prentice-Hall, 1973.

Chapter 19   Anxiety and Stress

1. Selye, H. *The stress of life.* New York: McGraw-Hill, 1956.

2. Mims, C. Stress in relation to the processes of civilization. In S. V. Boyden (Ed.), *The impact of civilization on the biology of man.* Toronto: University of Toronto Press, 1970.

3. Rahe, R. H., & Holmes, T. H. Life crisis and major health change. *Psychosomatic Medicine,* 1966, *28,* 774.

4. Rahe, R. J., Gunderson, E. K. E., & Arthur, R. J. Demographic and psychosocial factors in acute illness

reporting. *Navy Medical Neuropsychiatric Research Unit Report No. 69-35.* San Diego, Calif., 1969.

5. Horowitz, M., Wilner, N., & Alvarez, W. Impact of event scale: A measure of subjective stress. *Psychosomatic Medicine,* 1979, *41,* 209–218.

6. Rahe, R. H. Life change events and mental illness: An overview. *Journal of Human Stress,* 1979, *5,* 2–10.

7. Sarason, I. G., Johnson, J. H., & Siegel, J. M. Assessing the impact of life changes: Development of the life experiences survey. *Journal of Consulting and Clinical Psychology,* 1978, *46,* 932–946.

8. Holmes, T. H., & Rahe, R. H. The social readjustment rating scale. *Journal of Psychosomatic Research,* 1967, *11,* 213–218. Copyright 1967, Pergamon Press, Ltd. Reprinted with permission from *Journal of Psychosomatic Research.*

9. Basowitz, H., Persky, H., Korchin, S. J., & Grinker, R. R. *Anxiety and stress.* New York: McGraw-Hill, 1955.

10. Rathus, S. A., & Nevid, J. S. *B. T. behavior therapy.* New York: New American Library, 1977.

11. Maier, N. R. F. *Studies of abnormal behavior in the rat.* New York: Harper & Row, 1939.

12. Pavlov, I. P. *Conditioned reflexes.* London: Oxford University Press, 1927.

13. Masserman, J. *Behavior and neurosis: An experimental psychoanalytic approach to psychobiologic principles.* Chicago: University of Chicago Press, 1943.

14. Miller, N. E. Studies of fear as an acquirable drive. I. Fear as motivation and fear reduction as reinforcement in the learning of new responses. *Journal of Experimental Psychology,* 1948, *38,* 89–101.

15. Shapiro, D. H., & Zifferblatt, S. M.

Zen meditation and behavioral self-control: Similarities, differences, and clinical applications. *American Psychologist,* 1976, *31,* 519–532.

16. Boudreau. L. Transcendental meditation and yoga as reciprocal inhibitors. *Journal of Behavior Therapy and Experimental Psychiatry,* 1972, *3,* 97–98.

17. Girodo, M. Yoga meditation and flooding in the treatment of anxiety neurosis. *Journal of Behavior Therapy and Experimental Psychiatry,* 1974, *5,* 157–160.

18. Mead, M. One vote for this age of anxiety. *New York Times Magazine,* May 20, 1956, p. 13.

Chapter 20   Psychological Disorders

1. Rokeach, M., *The three Christs of Ypsilanti.* New York: Vintage Books, 1964.

2. President's Commission on Mental Health. *Report to the President from the President's Commission on Mental Health.* Washington, D.C.: U.S. Government Printing Office, 1978.

3. Schreber, D. P., in *Memoirs of my nervous illness,* ed. and trans. by I. Macalpine & R. A. Hunter. London: Dawson, 1955.

4. Laughlin, H. P. *The neuroses.* Washington, D.C.: Butterworth, 1967.

5. Leon, G. R. *Case histories of deviant behavior.* Boston: Holbrook Press, 1974.

6. Thorpe, L. P., Katz, B., & Lewis, R. T. *The psychology of abnormal behavior: A dynamic approach.* New York: The Ronald Press, 1961.

7. Thigpen, C. H., & Cleckley, H. A. *The three faces of Eve.* New York: McGraw-Hill, 1957.

8. White, R. W. *The abnormal personality.* New York: The Ronald Press, 1956.

9. Bloch, H. S. Army clinical psychiatry in the combat zone,

1967-1968. *American Journal of Psychiatry,* 1969, *126,* 289-298. Copyright 1969, the American Psychiatric Association. Reprinted by permission.

10. Moore, H. E. Some emotional concomitants of disaster. *Mental Hygiene,* 1958, *42,* 45.

11. Tichener, J. L., & Kapp, F. T. Family and character change at Buffalo Creek. *American Journal of Psychiatry,* 1976, *133,* 295-299.

12. Stern, G. M. From chaos to responsibility. *American Journal of Psychiatry,* 1976, *133,* 300-301.

13. Courtney, J. E. Dangerous paranoiacs: With autobiography of one. *Alienist & Neurologist,* 1901, *22,* 139-149.

14. Davidson, D. *Remembrances of a religio-maniac.* Stratford-on-Avon, England: Shakespeare Press, 1912.

15. Karpman, B. Dream life in a case of hebephrenia. *Psychiatric Quarterly,* 1953, *27,* 262-316.

16. Beers, C. W. *A mind that found itself.* New York: Longmans, Green, 1908.

17. McCall, L. *Between us and the dark.* Philadelphia: J. B. Lippincott, 1947.

18. Hofling, C. K. *Textbook of psychiatry for medical practice,* 2nd ed. Philadelphia: J. B. Lippincott, 1968.

19. Thorpe, L. P., Katz, B., & Lewis, R. T. *The psychology of abnormal behavior: A dynamic approach.* New York: The Ronald Press, 1961.

20. Mosher, L. R., & Feinsilver, D. *Special report on schizophrenia.* National Institute of Mental Health, April 1970.

21. White, R. W. *The abnormal personality.* New York: The Ronald Press, 1956.

22. Brady, J. P., & Lind, D. L. Experimental analysis of hysterical blindness: Operant conditioning techniques. *Archives of General Psychiatry,* 1961, *4,* 331-339.

23. Meehl, P. E. Schizotaxia, schizotypy, schizophrenia. *American Psychologist.* 1962, *17,* 827-838.

24. Murray, H. G., & Hirsch, J. Heredity, individual differences, and psychopathology. In S. C. Plog & R. B. Edgerton (Eds.), *Changing perspectives in mental illness.* New York: Holt, Rinehart and Winston, 1969.

25. Matthysse, S. W., & Kidd, K. K. Estimating the genetic contribution to schizophrenia. *American Journal of Psychiatry,* 1976, *133,* 185-191.

26. Lynn, R. Russian theory and research on schizophrenia. *Psychological Bulletin,* 1963, *60,* 486-498.

27. Matthysse, S., & Lipinski, J. Biochemical aspects of schizophrenia. *Annual Review of Medicine,* 1975, *26,* 551-565.

28. Gassner, S., & Murray, E. J. Dissonance and conflict in the interactions between parents and normal and neurotic children. *Journal of Abnormal Psychology,* 1969, *74,* 33-41.

29. Lidz, T., Fleck, S., & Cornelison, A. R. *Schizophrenia and the family.* New York: International Universities Press, 1965.

30. Ferriera, A. J., & Winter, W. W. Information exchange and silence in normal and abnormal families. In W. W. Winter & A. J. Ferriera (Eds.), *Research in family interaction.* Palo Alto, Calif.: Science & Behavior Books, 1964.

31. Reiss, D. The family and schizophrenia. *American Journal of Psychiatry,* 1976, *133,* 181-185.

32. Laing, R. D. *The divided self: An existential study in sanity and madness.* Baltimore: Penguin Books, 1965.

33. Szasz, T. S. *The myth of mental illness.* New York: Hoeber, 1961.

34. Scheff, T. J. *Labeling madness.* Englewood Cliffs, N.J.: Prentice-Hall, 1975.

Chapter 21   Therapy

1. Rogers, C. R. *Client-centered therapy: Its current practice, implications, and theory.* New York: Houghton Mifflin, 1965.

2. Bromberg, W. *The mind of man: A history of psychotherapy and psychoanalysis.* New York: Harper Colophon Books, 1963.

3. Kisker, G. W. *The disorganized personality,* 2nd Ed. New York: McGraw-Hill, 1972.

4. Wolberg, L. R., M. D. *The technique of psychotherapy.* New York: Grune & Stratton, 1977. Copyright 1977 by L. R. Wolberg.

5. Masserman, J. H. Ethology, comparative biodynamics, and psychoanalytic research. In J. Scher (Ed.), *Theories of the mind.* New York: The Free Press, 1963.

6. Mikulas, W. L. *Behavior modification: An overview.* New York: Harper & Row, 1972.

7. Wolpe, J., & Lazarus, A. A. *Behavior therapy techniques: A guide to the treatment of neuroses.* New York: Pergamon Press, 1966.

8. Meichenbaum, D. Clinical implications of modifying what clients say to themselves. *University of Waterloo Research Reports in Psychology no. 42,* December 19, 1972.

9. Kaplan, R. M., McCordick, S. M., & Twitchell, M. Is it the cognitive or the behavioral component which makes cognitive-behavior modification effective in test anxiety? *Journal of Counseling Psychology,* 1979, *26,* 371-377.

10. Lewis, M. K., Rogers, C. R., & Shlien, J. M. Time-limited, client-centered psychotherapy: Two cases. In A. Burton (Ed.), *Case studies in counseling and psychotherapy.* Englewood Cliffs, N.J.: Prentice-Hall, 1959.

11. Bradford, L. P., Gibb, J. R., &

Benne, K. D.   T-group theory and laboratory method.   New York: John Wiley, 1964.

12. Rogers, C. R.   Process of the basic encounter group.   In J. F. T. Bugental (Ed.), Challenges of humanistic psychology.   New York: McGraw-Hill, 1967.

13. Yalom, I., & Lieberman, M.   A study of encounter group casualties.   Archives of General Psychiatry, 1971, 25, 16–30.

14. Naranjo, C.   Present-centeredness: Technique, prescription, and ideal. In J. Fagan & I. L. Shephard, What Is Gestalt therapy?   New York: Harper & Row, 1970.

15. Alper, T.   An electric shock patient tells his story.   Journal of Abnormal and Social Psychology, 1948, 43, 201.

16. Scovern, A. W., & Kilmann, P. R. Status of electroconvulsive therapy: Review of the outcome literature. Psychological Bulletin, 1980, 87, 260–303.

17. Kety, S. S., et al.   A sustained effect of electroconvulsive shock on the turnover of norepinephrine in the central nervous system of the rat. Proceedings of the National Academy of Sciences, 1967, 58, 1249–1254.

18. President's Commission on Mental Health.   Preliminary report to the President, September 1, 1977.

19. Wogan, M., & Amdar, M. J. Changing patterns of student mental health, 1964 to 1972.   Journal of American College Health Association, 1974, 22, 202–208.

20. Winer, J. A., & Dorus, L. W. Complaints patients bring to a student mental health clinic. Journal of American College Health Association, 1972, 21, 134–139.

21. Indrisano, V. E., & Auerbach, S. M.   Mental health needs assessment of a major urban university.   Journal of American College Health Association, 1979, 27, 205–209.

22. Holland, M., & Tarlow, G.   Using psychology: Principles of behavior and your life, 2nd ed.   Boston: Little, Brown, 1980.

23. Schoenberg, B. M. (Ed.)   A handbook and guide for the college and university counseling center.   Westport, Conn.: Greenwood Press, 1978.

24. Kirk, B. A.   Characteristics of users of counseling centers and psychiatric services on a college campus. Journal of Counseling Psychology, 1973, 20, 463–470.

25. Snyder, B. R., & Kahne, M. J. Stress in higher education and student use of university psychiatrists.   American Journal of Orthopsychiatry, 1969, 39, 23–35.

26. Frank, A. C., & Kirk, B. A. Differences in outcomes for users and nonusers of university counseling and psychiatric services: A 5-year accountability study. Journal of Counseling Psychology, 1975, 22, 252–258.

Chapter 22   Social Behavior

1. Wolfe, K. M., & Fiske, M.   The children talk about the comics.   In P. F. Lazarsfeld & F. Stanton (Eds.), Communications research 1948–1949. New York: Harper, 1949.

2. Riesman, D.   The lonely crowd. Garden City, N.Y.: Doubleday, 1953.

3. Asch, S. E.   Forming impressions on personality.   Journal of Abnormal and Social Psychology, 1946, 41, 258–290.

4. Harlow, H. F., & Harlow, M. K. Social deprivation in monkeys. Scientific American, November 1962.

5. Ellenberger, H. F.   Behavior under involuntary confinement.   In A. H. Esser (Ed.), Behavior and environment: The use of space by animals and men. New York: Plenum Press, 1971.

6. Haythorn, W. W., & Altman, I.

Together in isolation.   Trans-action, 1967, 4, 18–22.

7. Altman, I.   Ecological aspects of interpersonal functioning.   In A. H. Esser (Ed.), Behavior and environment: The use of space by animals and men. New York: Plenum Press, 1971.

8. Bales, R. F.   Personality and interpersonal behavior.   New York: Holt, Rinehart and Winston, 1970.

9. Sherif, M., & Sherif, C. W.   An outline of social psychology.   New York: Harper & Row, 1956.

10. Ehrlich, P. R.   The population bomb. New York: Ballantine, 1968.

11. Proshansky, H. M., Ittelson, W. H., & Rivlin, L. G.   Freedom of choice and behavior in a physical setting. In J. F. Wohlwill & D. H. Carson (Eds.), Environment and the social sciences.   Washington, D.C.: American Psychological Association, 1972.

12. Zlutnick, S., & Altman, I. Crowding and human behavior.   In J. F. Wohlwill & D. H. Carson (Eds.), Environment and the social sciences.   Washington, D.C.: American Psychological Association, 1972.

13. Welch, B. L.   Psychophysiological response to the mean level of environmental stimulation.   In D. M. Rioch (Ed.), Medical aspects of stress in the military climate. Washington, D.C.: United States Government Printing Office, 1965.

14. Christian, J. J.   Endocrine adaptive mechanisms and the physiological regulation of population growth. In W. Mayer & R. Van Gelder (Eds.), Physiological mammalogy, Vol. I.   New York: Academic Press, 1963.

15. Myers, L., Hale, C. S., Mykytowycz, R., & Hughes, R. L.   The effects of varying density and space on sociability and health in mammals. In A. H. Esser (Ed.), Behavior and environment: The use of space by

animals and men. New York: Plenum Press, 1971.

16. Thiessen, D. D. Amphetamine toxicity, population density, and behavior: A review. *Psychological Bulletin,* 1964, *62,* 401–410.

17. Dubos, R. *Man adapting.* New Haven: Yale University Press, 1965.

18. Christian, J. J. The potential role of the adrenal cortex as affected by social rank and population density on experimental epidemics. *American Journal of Epidemiology,* 1968, *87,* 255–266.

19. Hoagland, H. Cybernetics of population control. *Bulletin of the Atomic Scientists,* February 1964, 1–6.

20. Esser, A. H. A biosocial perspective on crowding. In J. F. Wohlwill & D. H. Carson (Eds.), *Environment and the social sciences.* Washington, D.C.: American Psychological Association, 1972.

21. Calhoun, J. B. A behavioral sink. In E. Bliss (Ed.), *Roots of behavior.* New York: Hoeber, 1962.

22. Calhoun, J. B. Population density and social pathology. *Scientific American,* 1962, *206,* 139–148.

23. Calhoun, J. B. Space and the strategy of life. In A. H. Esser (Ed.), *Behavior and environment: The use of space by animals and men.* New York: Plenum Press, 1971.

24. Marsella, A. J., Escudero, M., & Gordon, S. The effects of dwelling density on mental disorder in Filipino men. *Journal of Health and Social Behavior,* 1970, *11,* 288–294.

25. Hutt, C., & Vaizey, M. J. Differential effects of group density on social behavior. *Nature,* 1966, *209,* 1371–1372.

26. Sommer, R. *Personal space: The behavioral basis for design.* Englewood Cliffs, N.J.: Prentice-Hall, 1969.

27. Indik, B. P. Some effects of organization size on member attitudes and behavior. *Human Relations,* 1963, *16,* 369–384.

28. Barker, R. G., & Hall, E. R. Participation in interschool events and extracurricular activities. In R. G. Barker & P. V. Gump, *Big school, small school.* Stanford, Calif.: Stanford University Press, 1964.

29. Sumner, W. S. *Folkways: A study of the sociological importance of usages, manners, customs, mores, and morals.* New York: Dover, 1959.

30. Itani, J. The society of Japanese monkeys. *Japan Quarterly,* 1961, *8,* 4.

31. Willis, R. H. Conformity, independence, and anticonformity. *Human Relations,* 1965, *18,* 373–388.

32. Kennedy, J. F. *Profiles in courage.* New York: Harper, 1955.

33. Utech, D. A., & Hoving, K. L. Parents and peers as competing influences in the decisions of children of differing ages. *Journal of Social Psychology,* 1969, *78,* 267–274.

34. Sherif, M. *The psychology of social norms.* New York: Harper, 1936.

35. Jacobs, R. C., & Campbell, D. T. The perpetuation of an arbitrary tradition through several generations of a laboratory micro culture. *Journal of Abnormal and Social Psychology,* 1961, *62,* 649–658.

36. Asch, S. E. Effects of group pressure upon the modification and distortion of judgment. In H. Guetzkow (Ed.), *Groups, leadership and men.* Pittsburgh, Pa.: Carnegie Press, 1951.

37. Cartwright, D., & Zander, A. *Group dynamics: Research and theory.* New York: Harper & Row, 1968.

38. Gamson, W. *Power and discontent.* Homewood, Ill.: Dorsey Press, 1968.

39. Orne, M. T., & Evans, F. J. Social control in the psychological experiment. *Journal of Personality and Social Psychology,* 1965, *1,* 189–200.

40. Flacks, R. Protest or conform: Some social psychological perspectives on legitimacy. *Journal of Applied Behavioral Science,* 1969, *5,* 127–150.

41. Milgram, S. Some conditions of obedience and disobedience to authority. *Human Relations,* 1965, *18,* 57–75.

42. Milgram, S. Liberating effects of group pressure. *Journal of Personality and Social Psychology,* 1965, *1,* 127–134.

Chapter 23 Social Attitudes and Prejudice

1. Katz, D., & Braly, K. W. Racial stereotypes in one hundred college students. *Journal of Abnormal and Social Psychology,* 1933, *28,* 280–290.

2. Karlins, M., Coffman, T. L., & Walters, G. On the fading of social stereotypes: Studies in three generations of college students. *Journal of Personality and Social Psychology,* 1969, *13,* 1–16.

3. Brigham, J. C. Ethnic stereotypes. *Psychological Bulletin,* 1971, *76,* 15–38.

4. Mosher, D. L., & Scodel, A. A study of the relationship between ethnocentrism in children and the ethnocentrism and authoritarian rearing practices of their mothers. *Child Development,* 1960, *31,* 369–376.

5. Epstein, R., & Komorita, S. S. Childhood prejudice as a function of parental ethnocentrism, punitiveness, and outgroup characteristics. *Journal of Personality and Social Psychology,* 1966, *3,* 259–264.

6. Stein, A. Strategies for failure. *Harvard Educational Review,* 1971, *41,* 186.

7. Sanchez, D. Testimony before the U.S. Senate Committee on Education. *New York Times,* August 19, 1970.

8. Adorno, T. W., Frankel-Brunswik, E., Levinson, D. J., & Sanford,

R. N. *The authoritarian personality.* New York: Harper, 1950.

9. Christie, R., & Cook, P. A guide to published literature relating to the authoritarian personality through 1956. *Journal of Psychology,* 1958, *45,* 171–199.

10. Dunham, J. R., & Dunham, C. S. Psychosocial aspects of disability. In M. Goldenson (Ed.), *Disability and rehabilitation handbook.* New York: McGraw-Hill, 1978.

11. Butler, R. N. *Why survive? Being old in America.* New York: Harper & Row, 1975.

12. Butler, R. N. Successful aging and the role of the life review. In S. H. Zarit (Ed.), *Readings in aging and death: Contemporary perspectives.* New York: Harper & Row, 1977.

13. Kogan, N. Attitudes toward old people: The development of a scale and examination of correlates. *Journal of Abnormal and Social Psychology,* 1959, *59,* 44–55.

14. Chesler, M. A. Ethnocentrism and attitudes toward the physically disabled. *Journal of Personality and Social Psychology,* 1965, *2,* 877–882.

15. English, R. W. Correlates of stigma towards physically disabled persons. *Rehabilitation Research and Practice Review,* 1971, *2,* 1–17.

16. Selznick, G. J., & Steinberg, S. *The tenacity of prejudice.* New York: Harper & Row, 1969.

17. Marx, G. T. *Protest and prejudice: A study of belief in the black community.* New York: Harper & Row, 1969.

18. Delany, L. T. The other bodies in the river. In J. V. McConnell (Ed.), *Readings in social psychology today.* Del Mar, Calif.: CRM Books, 1967.

19. Grier, W. H., & Cobbs, P. M. *Black rage.* New York: Basic Books, 1968.

20. Dansby, P. G. Black pride in the seventies: Fact or fantasy? In R. L. Jones (Ed.), *Black psychology.* New York: Harper & Row, 1972.

21. Clark, K. B., & Clark, M. P. Racial identification and preference in Negro children. In T. M. Newcomb & E. L. Hartley (Eds.), *Readings in social psychology.* New York: Holt, Rinehart and Winston, 1947.

22. Morland, J. K. Racial acceptance and preference of nursery school children in a southern city. *Merrill Palmer Quarterly,* 1962, *8,* 271–280.

23. Grier, W. H., & Cobbs, P. M. *The Jesus bag.* New York: McGraw-Hill, 1971.

24. Greer, G. *The female eunuch.* New York: Bantam Books, 1971.

25. Mannes, M. The problems of creative women. In S. M. Farber & R. H. L. Wilson (Eds.), *The potential of woman.* New York: McGraw-Hill, 1963.

26. Salzman-Webb, M. Woman as secretary, sexpot, spender, sow, civic actor, sickie. In M. H. Garskof (Ed.), *Roles women play: Readings toward women's liberation.* Belmont, Calif.: Brooks/Cole, 1971.

27. Koontz, E. D. *Underutilization of women workers.* Washington, D.C.: U.S. Government Printing Office, 1971.

28. Suelzle, M. Women in labor. *Trans-action,* 1970, *8,* 50–58.

29. Levitin, T., Quinn, R. P., & Staines, G. L. Sex discrimination against the American working woman. *American Behavioral Scientist,* 1971, (Nov.-Dec.), 237–254.

30. *1975 Handbook on women workers.* U.S. Department of Labor, Employment Standards Administration Bulletin 297, 1975.

31. Bem, D. J. *Beliefs, attitudes, and human affairs.* Belmont, Calif.: Brooks/Cole, 1970.

32. Komisar, L. The image of woman in advertising. In V. Gornick & B. K. Moran (Eds.), *Woman in sexist society.* New York: Signet Books, 1972.

33. Farrell, B. You've come a long way, buddy. *Life,* 1971, *97,* 52–59.

34. *Time,* 1971, *97,* 54.

35. Sherif, M., Harvey, O. J., White, J., Hood, W., & Sherif, C. *Intergroup conflict and cooperation: The Robber's Cave Experiment.* Norman, Okla.: University of Oklahoma Institute of Intergroup Relations, 1961.

36. Aronson, E. *The jigsaw classroom.* Beverly Hills, Calif.: Sage, 1978.

37. Newcomb, T. M., Turner, R. H., & Converse, P. E. *Social psychology: The study of human interaction.* New York: Holt, Rinehart and Winston, 1965.

38. Amir, Y. Contact hypothesis in ethnic relations. *Psychological Bulletin,* 1969, *71,* 319–342.

39. Clore, G. L., Bray, R. M., Itkin, S. M., & Murphy, P. Interracial attitudes and behavior at a summer camp. *Journal of Personality and Social Psychology,* 1978, *36,* 107–116.

40. Deutsch, M., & Collins, M. E. *Interracial housing: A psychological evaluation of a social experiment.* Minneapolis: University of Minnesota Press, 1951.

41. Cook, S. W. Interpersonal and attitudinal outcomes in cooperating interracial groups. *Joural of Research and Development in Education,* 1978, *12,* 97–113.

42. Pearl, D. Psychotherapy and ethnocentrism. *Journal of Abnormal and Social Psychology,* 1955, *50,* 227–230.

43. Rubin, I. M. Increased self-acceptance: A means of reducing prejudice. *Journal of Personality and Social Psychology,* 1967, *5,* 233–238.

44. Foley, L. A. Personality and situational influences on changes in prejudice: A replication of Cook's railroad game in a prison setting. *Journal of Personality and Social Psychology,* 1976, *34,* 846–856.

Chapter 24 Crime and Aggression

1. Stark, R., & McEvoy, J. Middle-class violence. *Psychology Today,* 1970, *4,* 52.

2. Buss, A. H. *The psychology of aggression.* New York: John Wiley, 1961.

3. Freud, S. *Civilization and its discontents.* New York: Jonathan Cape and Harrison Smith, 1930.

4. Lorenz, K. *On aggression.* New York: Bantam Books, 1966.

5. Eibl-Eibesfeldt, I. The fighting behavior of animals. In R. C. Atkinson (Ed.), *Contemporary psychology.* San Francisco: W. H. Freeman, 1971.

6. Carrighar, S. War is not in our genes. In M. F. A. Montagu (Ed.), *Man and aggression.* New York: Oxford University Press, 1968.

7. Holloway, R. L. Human aggression: The need for a species-specific framework. In M. Fried, M. Harris, & R. Murphy (Eds.), *War: The anthropology of armed conflict and aggression.* Garden City, N.Y.: The Natural History Press, 1968.

8. Morris, D. *The naked ape.* New York: Dell, 1967.

9. Washburn, S. L., & Hamburg, D. A. Aggressive behavior in Old World monkeys and apes. In P. C. Jay (Ed.), *Primates: Studies in adaptation and variability.* New York: Holt, Rinehart and Winston, 1968.

10. King, H. E. Psychological effects of excitation in the limbic system. In D. E. Sheer (Ed.), *Electrical stimulation of the brain.* Austin: University of Texas Press, 1961.

11. Kaada, B. Brain mechanisms related to aggressive behavior. In C. D. Clemente & D. B. Lindsley (Eds.), *Aggression and defense.* Berkeley: University of California Press, 1967.

12. Egger, M. D., & Flynn, J. P. Effect of electrical stimulation of the amygdala on hypothalamically elicited attack behavior in cats. *Journal of Neurophysiology,* 1963, *26,* 705–720.

13. Sano, K. Sedative neurosurgery: With special reference to posteromedial hypothalamotomy. *Neurologia medico chirrwigica,* 1962, *4,* 112–142.

14. Arzin, N. H., Hutchinson, R. R., & Hake, D. F. Pain-induced fighting in the squirrel monkey. *Journal of Experimental Analysis of Behavior,* 1963, *6,* 620.

15. Dollard, J., Doob, L., Miller, N., Mowrer, O., & Sears, R. *Frustration and aggression.* New Haven: Yale University Press, 1939.

16. Arzin, N. H., Hutchinson, R. R., & Hake, D. F. Extinction-induced aggression. *Journal of Experimental Analysis of Behavior,* 1966, *9,* 191–204.

17. Kaufman, H. Definitions and methodology in the study of aggression. *Psychological Bulletin,* 1965, *64,* 351–364.

18. Bandura, A., Ross, D., & Ross, S. A. Transmission of aggression through imitation of aggressive models. *Journal of Abnormal and Social Psychology,* 1961, *63,* 575–582.

19. Sears, R. R., Maccoby, E. E., & Levin, H. *Patterns of child rearing.* Evanston, Ill.: Row, Peterson, 1957.

20. Feshbach, S. Aggression. In P. H. Mussen (Ed.), *Carmichael's manual of child psychology* (rev. ed.). New York: John Wiley, 1970.

21. Bandura, A., Ross, D., & Ross, S. A. Imitation of film-mediated aggressive models. *Journal of Abnormal and Social Psychology,* 1963, *66,* 3–11.

22. Berkowitz, L. Impulse, aggression and the gun. *Psychology Today,* 1968, *2,* 18–23.

23. Walters, R. H., Thomas, E. L., & Acker, C. W. Enhancement of punitive behavior by audio-visual displays. *Science,* 1962, *136,* 872–873.

24. Patterson, G., Littman, R., & Bricker, W. Assertive behavior in children: A step toward a theory of aggression. *Monographs of the Society for Research in Child Development,* 1967, *32.*

25. Walters, R., & Brown, M. Studies of reinforcement of aggression: III. *Child Development,* 1963, *34,* 563–571.

26. Haney, B., & Gold, M. The juvenile delinquent nobody knows. *Psychology Today,* 1973, *7,* 49–55.

27. Lunde, D. T. Our murder boom. *Psychology Today,* 1975, *9,* 35–42.

28. Allen, J. *Assault with a deadly weapon: The autobiography of a street criminal.* New York: Pantheon Books, 1977.

29. Conger, J. J., Miller, W. C., & Walsmith, C. R. Antecedents of delinquency: Personality, social class, and intelligence. In P. H. Mussen, J. J. Conger, & J. Kagan (Eds.), *Basic and contemporary issues in developmental psychology.* New York: Harper & Row, 1975.

30. Berkowitz, L. *Aggression: A social psychological analysis.* New York: McGraw-Hill, 1962.

31. Yochelson, S., & Samenow, S. *The criminal personality.* New York: J. Aronson, 1976.

32. Brodsky, S. L. *Psychologists in the criminal justice system.* Marysville, Ohio: American Association of Correctional Psychologists, 1972.

33. McNeil, E. B. *The quiet furies.* Englewood Cliffs, N.J.: Prentice-Hall, 1967.

34. Hare, R. D. *Psychopathy: Theory and research.* New York: John Wiley, 1970.

35. Karpman, B. *The sexual offender and his offenses: Etiology, pathology, psychodynamics and treatment.* New York: Julian Press, 1954.

36. Abrahamsen, David. *The psychology of crime.* New York: Columbia University Press, 1960.

37. Alexander, F., & Staub, H. *The criminal, the judge, and the public.* New York: Macmillan, 1931.

38. Glover, E. *The roots of crime.* New York: International Universities Press, 1960.

39. Sutherland, E. H., & Cressey, D. R. *Criminology,* 8th ed. Philadelphia: J. B. Lippincott, 1970.

40. Wood, A. L. *Deviant behavior and control strategies.* Lexington, Mass.: Lexington Books, 1974.

41. Clarke, S. H. Juvenile offender programs and delinquency prevention. In S. L. Halleck, *et al.* (Eds.), *The Aldine crime and justice annual 1974.* Chicago: Aldine Publishers, 1975.

42. Martinson, R. What works—questions and answers about prison reform. In S. L. Halleck *et al.* (Eds.), *The Aldine crime and justice annual 1974.* Chicago: Aldine Publishers, 1975.

43. Finckenauer, J. O. Scared crooked. *Psychology Today,* 1979, *13,* 6–11.

44. Schmalleger, F. World of the career criminal. *Human Nature,* 1979, *2,* 50–56.

45. Bailey, W. C. Murder and capital punishment: Some further evidence. *American Journal of Orthopsychiatry,* 1975, *45,* 669–688.

46. Jacobs, J. *The death and life of great American cities.* New York: Random House, 1961.

Chapter 25   The Psychology of Consumers and Energy Conservation

1. Harris, R. J. Comprehension of pragmatic implications in advertising. *Journal of Applied Psychology,* 1977, *62,* 603–608.

2. Katona, G. What is consumer psychology? *American Psychologist,* 1967, *22,* 219–226.

3. Jacoby, J. Consumer psychology as a social psychological sphere of action. *American Psychologist,* 1975, *30,* 977–987.

4. Wells, W. D., & LoSciuto, L. A. Direct observation of purchasing behavior. *Journal of Marketing Research,* 1966, *3,* 227–233.

5. Woodside, A. G., & Fleck, R. A., Jr. The case approach to understanding brand choice. *Journal of Advertising Research,* 1979, *19,* 23–30.

6. Laczniak, G. R., Lusch, R. F., & Murphy, P. E. Social marketing: Its ethical dimensions. *Journal of Marketing,* 1979, *43,* 29–36.

7. Reich, J. W., & Robertson, J. L. Reactance and norm appeal in anti-littering messages. *Journal of Applied Social Psychology,* 1979, *9,* 91–101.

8. Brehm, J. *Responses to loss of freedom: A theory of psychological reactance.* New York: General Learning Press, 1972.

9. Anastasi, A. *Fields of applied psychology,* New York: McGraw-Hill, 1979.

10. Brown, J. M., Berrien, F. K., & Russell, D. L. *Applied psychology.* New York: Macmillan, 1966.

11. Allison, R. I., & Uhl, K. P. Influence of beer brand identification on taste perception. *Journal of Marketing Research,* 1964, *1,* 36–39.

12. Bettman, J. R. Memory factors in consumer choice: A review. *Journal of Marketing,* 1979, *43,* 37–53.

13. Sawyer, A. G. The effects of repetition: Conclusions and suggestions about experimental laboratory research. In G. D. Hughes & M. L. Ray (Eds.), *Buyer consumer information processing.* Chapel Hill, N. C.: University of North Carolina Press, 1974.

14. Webb, P. H., & Ray, M. L. Effects of clutter. *Journal of Advertising Research,* 1979, *19,* 7–12.

15. Asch, S. E. Studies of independence and submission to group pressure. *Psychology Monographs,* 1956, *70,* No. 9.

16. Venkatesan, M. Experimental study of consumer behavior conformity and independence. *Journal of Marketing Research,* 1966, *3,* 384–386.

17. Zagora, S., & Harter, M. Credibility of source and recipient's attitude: Factors in the perception and retention of information on smoking behavior. *Perceptual and Motor Skills,* 1966, *23,* 155–168.

18. Hovland, C. I., & Mandell, W. An experimental comparison of conclusion-drawing by the communicator and by the audience. *Journal of Abnormal and Social Psychology,* 1952, *47,* 581–588.

19. Faison, E. W. J. Effectiveness of one-sided and two-sided mass communications in advertising. *Public Opinion Quarterly,* 1961, *25,* 468–469.

20. Festinger, L. *A theory of cognitive dissonance.* Stanford, Calif.: Stanford University Press, 1957.

21. Pervin, L. A., & Yatko, R. J. Cigarette smoking and alternative methods of reducing dissonance. *Journal of Experimental Social Psychology,* 1965, *1,* 30–36.

22. Jones, R. A., & Brehm, J. W. Attitudinal effects of communicator attractiveness when one chooses to listen. *Journal of Personality and Social Psychology,* 1967, *6,* 64–70.

23. Ehrlich, D., Guttman, I., Schonbach, P., & Mills, J. Post-decision exposure to relevant information. *Journal of Abnormal and Social Psychology,* 1957, *54,* 98–102.

24. Fusso, T. E. The polls: The energy crisis in perspective. *Public Opinion Quarterly,* 1978, *42,* 127–137.

25. Schipper, L. Another look at energy conservation. *American Economic Review,* 1979, *69,* 362–368.

26. Parisi, A. J. Creating the energy efficient society. *New York Times*

Magazine, September 23, 1979, pp. 46–50.

27. Ross, M. H., & Williams, R. H. Energy efficiency: Our most underrated energy resource. *The Bulletin of the Atomic Scientists,* Nov. 1976, pp. 30–38.

28. Rothschild, M. L. Marketing communications in nonbusiness situations, or why it's so hard to sell brotherhood like soap. *Journal of Marketing,* 1969, *43,* 11–20.

29. Edney, J. Free riders en route to disaster. *Psychology Today,* 1979, *13,* 80–87.

30. Seligman, C., Kriss, M., Darley, J. M., Fazio, R. H., Becker, L. J., & Pryor, J. B. Predicting summer energy consumption from homeowners' attitudes. *Journal of Applied Social Psychology,* 1979, *9,* 70–90.

31. Hass, J. W., Bagley, G. S., & Rogers, R. W. Coping with the energy crisis: Effects of fear appeals upon attitudes toward energy consumption. *Journal of Applied Psychology,* 1975, *60,* 754–756.

32. Seligman, C., & Darley, J. M. Feedback as a means of decreasing residential energy consumption. *Journal of Applied Psychology,* 1977, *62,* 363–368.

33. Palmer, M. H., Lloyd, M. E., & Lloyd, K. E. An experimental analysis of electricity conservation procedures. *Journal of Applied Behavior Analysis,* 1977, *10,* 665–671.

34. Hayes, S. C., & Cone, J. D. Reducing residential electrical energy use: Payments, information, and feedback. *Journal of Applied Behavior Analysis,* 1977, *10,* 425–435.

35. Seaver, W. B., & Patterson, A. H. Decreasing fuel oil consumption through feedback and social commendation. *Journal of Applied Behavior Analysis,* 1976, *9,* 147–152.

36. Kohlenberg, R., Phillips, T., & Proctor, W. A behavioral analysis of peaking in residential electrical-

energy consumers. *Journal of Applied Behavior Analysis,* 1976, *9,* 13–18.

37. *Business Week,* August 6, 1979, p. 83.

38. Energy Answers. *House and Garden,* January 1980, *152,* 98–100.

39. Sikorsky, R. *How to get more miles per gallon.* New York: St. Martin's Press, 1978.

40. How to figure "fuelishness." *Better Homes and Gardens,* June 1979, *57,* 17.

Chapter 26 The Psychology of Career Choice and Development

1. Holland, J. L. *Making Vocational Choices.* © 1973. Adapted by permission of Prentice-Hall, Inc., Englewood Cliffs, New Jersey.

2. Holland, J. L. The present status of a theory of vocational choice. In J. M. Whiteley & A. Resnikoff (Eds.), *Perspectives on vocational development.* Copyright 1972, American Personnel and Guidance Association. Reprinted with permission.

3. Holland, J. L. Some explorations of a theory of vocational choice: I. One- and two-year longitudinal studies. *Psychological Monographs,* 1962, *76,* No. 26.

4. Holland, J. L. Explorations of a theory of vocational choice: VI. A longitudinal study using a sample of typical college students. *Journal of Applied Psychology, Monograph Supplement,* 1968, *52.*

5. Cole, N. S., Whitney, D. R., & Holland, J. L. A spatial configuration of occupations. *Journal of Vocational Behavior,* 1971, *1,* 1–9.

6. Super, D. E. *The psychology of careers: An introduction to vocational development.* New York: Harper & Row, 1957.

7. Super, D. E. Vocational development theory: Persons,

positions, and processes. In J. M. Whiteley & A. Resnikoff (Eds.), *Perspective on vocational development.* Washington, D.C.: American Personnel and Guidance Association, 1972.

8. Weiss, D. J., Dawis, R. V., England, G. W., & Lofquist, L. H. *Manual for the Minnesota Satisfaction Questionnaire.* Minneapolis: University of Minnesota, Work Adjustment Project, 1967.

9. Korman, A. *Industrial and organizational psychology.* Englewood Cliffs, N. J.: Prentice-Hall, 1971.

10. Walker, C., & Guest, R. *Man on the assembly line.* Cambridge, Mass.: Harvard University Press, 1952.

11. Renwick, P. A., & Lawler, E. E. What you really want from your jobs. *Psychology Today,* 1978, *11,* 53–65.

12. Special Task Force, Department of Health, Education and Welfare. *Work in America.* Cambridge, Mass.: M.I.T. Press, 1973.

13. Schaffer, R. H. Job satisfaction as related to need satisfaction in work. *Psychological Monographs,* 1953, *67,* No. 364.

14. Vroom, V. H. *Work and motivation.* New York: John Wiley, 1964.

15. Katzell, R. A. Personal values, job satisfaction, and job behavior. In H. Borow (Ed.), *Man in a world of work.* Boston: Houghton Mifflin, 1964.

16. Adams, J. S. Injustice in social exchange. In L. Berkowitz (Ed.), *Advances in experimental social psychology.* Vol. 2. New York: Academic Press, 1965.

17. Winterbottom, M. R. The relation of childhood training in independence to achievement motivation. In D. McClelland, et al. (Eds.), *The achievement motive.* New York: Appleton-Century-Crofts, 1953.

18. Singer, R. D., & Singer, A.

Psychological development in children. Philadelphia: W. B. Saunders, 1969.

19. Duncan, Otis. Socioeconomic index for all occupations, properties, and characteristics of the socioeconomic index. In J. A. Reiss (Ed.), *Occupations and Social Status.* New York: Free Press, 1961.

20. Jencks, C., *et al. Who gets ahead?— The determinants of economic succession in America.* New York: Basic Books, 1979.

21. Sofer, C. *Men in mid-career: A study of British managers and technical specialists.* Cambridge: Cambridge University Press, 1970.

22. Glickman, A. S., *et al. Top management development and succession.* New York: Macmillan, 1968.

23. Kasl, S. V., Gore, S., & Cobb, S. Reports of illness and illness behavior among men undergoing job loss. *Psychosomatic Medicine,* 1972, *34,* 475.

24. Kasl, S. V., Gore, S., & Cobb, S. The experience of losing a job: Reported changes in health, symptoms and illness behavior. *Psychosomatic Medicine,* 1975, *37,* 106–122.

25. Brenner, H. M. *Mental illness and the economy.* Cambridge, Mass.: Harvard University Press, 1973.

26. McLean, A. A. *Work stress.* Reading, Mass.: Addison-Wesley, 1979.

27. Wechter, D. *The age of the Great Depression: 1929–1941.* New York: Macmillan, 1948.

28. Brim, O. Adult socialization. In J. Clausen (Ed.), *Socialization and society.* Boston: Little, Brown, 1968.

29. Rogers, D. *The adult years.* Englewood Cliffs, N.J.: Prentice-Hall, 1979.

30. Hoffman, L. W., & Lye, F. I. *Working mothers.* San Francisco: Jossey-Bass, 1974.

31. Bee, H. *Social issues in developmental psychology.* New York: Harper & Row, 1974.

32. Angrist, S. S., & Almquist, E. M. *Careers and contingencies: How college women juggle with gender.* New York: Kennikat Press Corp., 1975. By permission of Kennihat Press Corp.

Appendix: Research Methods and Statistics

1. Bandura, A., and McDonald, F. J. Influence of social reinforcement and the behavior of models in shaping children's moral judgments. *Journal of Abnormal and Social Psychology,* 1963, *67,* 274–281.

Index